TRANSPORTATION

IN

AMERICA

Users, Carriers, Government

TRANSPORTATION

IN

AMERICA

Users, Carriers, Government

DONALD V. HARPER, Ph.D.

Professor of Transportation and Logistics
College and Graduate School of Business Administration
University of Minnesota

PRENTICE-HALL, INC., Englewood Cliffs, New Jersey 07632

Library of Congress Cataloging in Publication Data

Harper, Donald Victor, (date)
    Transportation in America.

    Includes bibliographical references and index.
    1. Transportation—United States. 2. Transportation
and state—United States. I. Title.
Title.
HE203.H26-1978   380.5'0973   77-12222
ISBN 0-13-930214-X

Printed in the United States of America

10 9 8 7 6 5 4 3 2

Prentice-Hall International, Inc., *London*
Prentice-Hall of Australia Pty. Limited, *Sydney*
Prentice-Hall of Canada, Ltd., *Toronto*
Prentice-Hall of India Private Limited, *New Delhi*
Prentice-Hall of Japan, Inc., *Tokyo*
Prentice-Hall of Southeast Asia Pte. Ltd., *Singapore*
Whitehall Books Limited, *Wellington, New Zealand*

To Christine

Diane

David

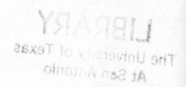

Contents

15

Decision-Making in
Transportation Companies   *317*

PART THREE
Government

16

Rationale of
Government Promotion of Transportation;
Government Promotion
of Railroad and Highway Transportation   *347*

17

Government Promotion of Water, Oil Pipeline, and Air Transportation   *379*

18

The Decision-Making Process in and Evaluation of Government Promotion of Transportation   *402*

19

Rationale of Government Economic Regulation of Transportation   *419*

20

The Decision-Making Process
in Government Economic Regulation
of Transportation   *440*

21

Government Economic Regulation
of Railroad Transportation   *458*

List of Illustrations

List of Tables

Preface

This book is about transportation in the United States. The significance of transportation in our every day lives is clear. We are dependent upon transportation for economic, social, recreational, educational, cultural, political, and other purposes. Nevertheless, because transportation is a means to an end and not an end in itself, it is often taken for granted. Most Americans, including many business executives, know very little about the system and how decisions are made. This is particularly true of freight transportation.

The transportation system in this country, although probably the best in the world, is beset by financial, operating, technological, and other problems that threaten to cause serious transportation breakdowns and eventual nationalization of important parts of the system. Among the difficulties are environmental and energy problems that increasingly affect the nature of the transportation system and how it is managed.

The purpose of this book is to acquaint the reader with the domestic freight and passenger transportation system in the United States and the role played in it by users of transportation service (shippers, receivers, and passengers), providers of transportation service (carriers), and government (federal, state, and local). The book examines the make up of the system and its economic and service characteristics; trends and problems in traffic, revenue, and other areas; and how decisions are made and by whom. The role of each of the three groups in our transportation system, and decision-making by them, is discussed. Although the book is primarily focussed on the user of transportation, particularly the business firm, readers interested in any of the three segments—users, carriers, or government—will benefit from reading the book. Domestic intercity transportation of property (freight) and passengers is emphasized.

The author extends his thanks to his colleague, Frederick J. Beier, for writing Chapter 15, and to Susan J. Boonstra for typing the manuscript.

A special vote of thanks for their many invaluable suggestions to Professor

Thomas M. Corsi of the University of Maryland; Professor John J. Coyle of Pennsylvania State University; Professor Gary N. Dicer of the University of Tennessee, and Professor Randall W. Kirk of the University of Texas at Austin.

DONALD V. HARPER

Minneapolis, Minnesota

PART ONE

Users of

Transportation Service

1

Introduction

Former United States Secretary of Transportation, Alan S. Boyd, once defined transportation as follows:

> To the carrier and the shipper, transportation is a knot of government red tape that can be untied only by lawyers, tax consultants, and lobbyists. To the poor commuter, it is a road to hell paved with good intentions. To the cities which need better transit systems, it is a desire named streetcar. To the air traveler, transportation is the friendly skies full of fast planes, slow ticket counters, and hundreds of suitcases that look exactly like his. To the social scientists, of course, transportation is an intermodal, multi-purpose capability inherently responsive to the parametrical methodologies of interfacing disciplines.[1]

Regardless of one's definition of transportation and whether it be satirical or serious, transportation has always been a vital factor in the cultural and economic development of the human race and the effort to improve transportation has occupied much of man's time and effort through the centuries. Nations, regions, cities, industries, and business firms have grown or failed to grow because of the presence or absence of adequate transportation facilities. Those areas of the world that have developed culturally and economically the earliest and fastest have been those that had adequate transportation. Hence the great old cities of the world were all located where adequate and long-distance water transportation was available. Those areas without adequate water transportation had to await the coming of other modes of transportation before their development could really begin. In modern times we find that the interior of the continent of Africa is still to a great extent underdeveloped culturally and economically partly because it has been in the past, and still is to some degree, inaccessible.

[1] Speech to the National Association of Railroad and Utilities Commissioners. Reported in *Traffic and Distribution Management,* January, 1968, p. 41.

In the short history of the United States the cultural and economic development of the nation has paralleled the developments in transportation that have taken place. The early turnpikes, the steamboat, the Erie and other canals, the early railroads, and the highway programs of the 1920's are examples of significant transportation improvements that have had an important impact on the country. The United States has been very fortunate in that its transportation system has developed into perhaps the finest system in the world while transport over much of the earth and for most of its people is still primitive.[2]

IMPORTANCE OF TRANSPORTATION TO THE ECONOMY

An obvious benefit that society derives from good property or freight transportation is that it enables consumers to enjoy the benefits of goods which are not to be had in their immediate neighborhood because of climate or soil conditions, the lack of raw materials, power, or skill, or because the cost of production is too great.[3] Good passenger transportation makes possible mobility of our population for economic, educational, social, or other purposes and, in addition, reduces or eliminates isolation, while promoting economic, social, and political development and economic and political unity in the country. But, other than making goods available and fostering mobility of the people, why is it that transportation is said to be essential to the economy? What is there about it that makes it of "public importance" or "affected with the public interest?" Why is it that our federal government goes to extreme lengths to prevent labor strikes in transportation?

Geographic Specialization

There are many ways in which the economic importance of transportation can be categorized and described. For society or the economy as a whole, transportation makes possible geographic specialization or territorial division of labor. Geographic specialization takes place when a nation or region or state or city produces those products and services that it is best suited for in terms of its capital, labor, raw materials, and other resources and talents. Thus, California and Florida specialize in the production of citrus fruits, the Great Lakes region produces much of the nation's steel, cotton is grown in the South and Southwest, and furniture is manufactured in North Carolina because those areas are highly suited for such production. In this way the most efficient utilization of those areas' resources and talents is made. If such geographic specialization does not occur, then a nation, region, state, or city will be forced to devote some of its resources and energies to production of goods and/or services that it is *not* well suited for. Then some economic inefficiency and a lower standard of living for all concerned are the result.

---

[2]Wilfred Owen, "Transportation and Economic Development," *American Economic Review*, May, 1959, p. 179.

[3]Stuart Daggett, *Principles of Inland Transportation*, 4th ed. (New York: Harper and Brothers, 1955), pp. 15–16.

Transportation's role in all this is clear. In a simple example, if area A is to specialize in producing product (1), then area A must rely on imports from other areas for the things other than (1) that it wants to consume. Area A must also depend on other areas to import from A the surplus of (1) that A will produce if it concentrates on (1). If, however, there is no adequate transportation between A and the areas it wishes to export to and/or import from, or if the transportation charges are so high as to make the landed costs for the various products involved too high, then trade between A and the other areas will not take place and geographic specialization by A will be impossible. Thus, for international or interregional or interstate or intercity trade to take place, and hence geographic specialization, adequate transportation at a reasonable cost must be available.

In the real world things are more complex than we have indicated in our example. Thus, a given geographic area may be better suited than other geographic areas to produce several products, not just one. In such a case, the principle of "comparative advantage" states that such an area will specialize in the production of goods for which it has the *greatest* advantage, even if this means that it must import from other areas products which it is able to produce itself at less cost. In this way the area can concentrate on the production of the products in which its advantages are the greatest and the result will be the most efficient use of resources and talents.

Adam Smith referred to the importance of transportation in geographic division of labor,[4] and the principle involved in geographic specialization has been summarized by G. Lloyd Wilson as follows:

> The principle may be stated that the most efficient use of land, labor, capital, and management is effected if each geographic subdivision engages in the production of goods which it can produce more cheaply than any other district, and each area produces the goods in which it has the greatest comparative advantage or lowest comparative costs, exchanging the goods so produced through marketing channels and transportation facilities and services operated at costs which do not offset the gains derived from economic specialization.[5]

Large-Scale Production

An effect of transportation similar to that discussed in connection with geographic specialization is that the availability of adequate transportation is a requirement for the existence of large-scale production. The benefits of large-scale production in terms of economies of scale, production efficiencies, lower prices, and so on, are well-known. The United States is probably the leading exponent of the principle of large-scale production. But large-scale production by a firm in one or a few production locations usually requires that raw materials, parts, and supplies be collected from distant sources and/or that a large geographic market for the product(s) produced be accessible at reasonable cost. Therefore, adequate transportation service at reasonable cost is indispensable to large-scale production.

[4] Adam Smith, *An Inquiry into the Nature and Causes of the Wealth of Nations,* 1776, Book I, Chapter 3 and Book II, Chapter 5.

[5] G. Lloyd Wilson, *Transportation and Communications* (New York: Appleton-Century-Crofts, Inc., 1954), p. 12.

In the economy of the United States the growth of large-scale production in the nineteenth century was accompanied by the rapid development of the railroad system plus some development of water transportation. In more recent times, especially since 1920, other forms of transportation have become available and the trend toward large-scale production has continued. Large-scale production in the United States certainly could not have reached its present advanced stage if it were not for the presence of an adequate transportation system at reasonable cost to bring in raw materials, parts, and supplies and to carry the mass-produced products to distant buyers. If large-scale production truly does offer to our society the benefits claimed for it, then our transportation system has helped to make those benefits possible. It also, of course, has helped make possible any negative aspects of large-scale production that may have resulted.

Land Values

Improvements in transportation usually are credited with having some effect on the value of the land that is adjacent to or served by the improvements. "Improvement" means faster and/or cheaper transportation service. The principal factor involved here is one of accessibility. If land previously unserved by any transportation is suddenly served by a new transportation facility, for example, a road or an airport, the value of the land will ordinarily increase because the land is now accessible and hence useful. The same can be said if land is already served by some form of transportation, but the transportation is improved, for example, when an interstate freeway is added to or replaces a conventional 2-lane highway. The accessibility of the land has now been increased primarily because the time, effort, and, perhaps, the cost involved in getting to and from the land have been reduced. This greater accessibility should result in an increase in the value of the land.

The history of transportation in the United States contains many examples of increases in land values that occurred as a result of improvements in transportation. Some of these improvements have been very dramatic in their effect, such as the opening of the Erie Canal in 1825, the building of railroads in the West after the Civil War, and the current Interstate highway program. Many others have been less dramatic, but nonetheless they also have been important. Such repercussions on the value of land are still taking place today as we continuously improve our highway system, expand the system of oil pipelines, engage in various waterway improvements and extensions, improve our airports and build new ones, and make rather modest adjustments in the railroad plant.

However, the effect of a transportation improvement is not always a positive one. Sometimes a transportation improvement will decrease land values as well as increase them. This was true in the past and is true today. For example, when a new Interstate freeway is built, it may increase certain land values along its route, particularly land used for commercial purposes and located near interchange or access points. However, farmers and homeowners located adjacent to the freeway, and especially if they are some distance from access points, may find that the freeway is a nuisance in terms of noise, air pollution, and visual effect and their property values may fall. Fortunately, airport, highway, and other transportation planners are more aware today then ever in the past of the possible negative effects on land values and other economic and social costs involved in transportation improvements. A further point is that if certain land becomes more accessible and, therefore, more valuable because of a transportation improvement, it may become a substitute for land that was previously used for that purpose (such as growing wheat) and the result may well be that the previously used land will decline in value.

Competition Among Sellers

By helping to make possible geographic specialization and large-scale production and by making land accessible, transportation also encourages competition among different sellers of the same product by permitting several sellers, perhaps many sellers, to compete in a given geographic area. Because goods can be brought in from a distance, local monopolies are discouraged or made impossible. The total effect of this can be to keep prices lower than they would be if fewer sellers, perhaps only one, served a given market area.

The effects of transportation availability on competition vary with the circumstances surrounding the sellers and the product(s) in question, such as the degree of product differentiation involved, the transportability of the product(s), the number of sellers in the industry, and so on.

Economic Development

From the foregoing, it should be clear that transportation can play a very important role in the economic development of any geographic area, whether it be a nation, region, state, or city. A geographic area's type and level of economic activity actually depend to a great extent on the quantity, quality, and cost of transportation service available to it. Evidence of this is found in the fact that the underdeveloped or developing countries of the world have, among other deficiencies, inadequate transportation systems. Studies have shown that the amount of money spent for transportation investment in relation to population or land area and the quantity of transportation facilities per square mile of area or per capita is small in most underdeveloped countries as compared with the more developed countries.[6]

It seems that no economy has developed to a high level of productivity without heavy investment in transportation facilities.[7] The result is that programs designed to spur economic development of the less developed countries often stress investment in transportation improvements. Such investment has been a significant economic development instrument in the post-World War II period.[8] According to one author, in underdeveloped countries between 20 and 40 per cent of total public expenditures is devoted to transportation.[9] In many under-

---

[6] See Wilfred Owen, "Transportation and Technology," *American Economic Review*, May, 1962, p. 406 and Owen, "Transportation and Economic Development," p. 180.

[7] John B. Lansing, *Transportation and Economic Policy* (New York: The Free Press, 1966), p. 73.

[8] See Gary Fromm, ed., *Transport Investment and Economic Development* (Washington, D.C.: The Brookings Institution, 1965) and Owen, "Transportation and Economic Development."

[9] George W. Wilson, "Transportation Investment and Economic Development in Underdeveloped Countries," *Proceedings of Transportation Research Forum, 1965,* p. 425.

developed countries transportation absorbs one-third or more of the total economic development plan.[10]

It appears that economic progress is inevitably tied to transportation. This is basically because trade or commerce cannot flourish without an adequate transportation system at reasonable cost, and without trade there can be little in the way of industrial activity and the employment and income that this brings about.

The paradox here is that usually no transportation will be provided unless there is trade, i.e., traffic to be carried. Unless there is transportation, however, trade cannot develop. An outstanding exception to the rule that transportation will not be provided unless there is traffic available took place after the Civil War in the area west of the Mississippi River where transportation in the form of railroads was introduced (with considerable government assistance) *before* there was much in the way of population or trade. In this example, transportation was used as a tool to encourage economic development because those railroads, which were an attempt to meet future needs, became a stimulus to settlement, population growth, and trade.

Thus, transportation's role in economic development need not be merely a passive one of meeting the current and immediately forseeable demands of the economy. It can also be a dynamic role by facilitating the exploitation of unutilized resources through the construction of transportation facilities for future industrial and agricultural development or, in other words, taking the initiative in economic growth.[11]

National Defense

The adequacy of transportation of military personnel and supplies can make or break a military operation, as Napoleon learned in his invasion of Russia and the Confederacy learned after much of its railroad system was destroyed during the Civil War. And in modern times military logistics is truly the life blood of military operations. Sir Winston S. Churchill wrote: "Victory is the beautiful, bright-coloured flower. Transport is the stem without which it could never have blossomed."[12]

With the great emphasis on military and defense activity in the United States since World War II, it is not surprising that the connection between transportation and national defense should currently be stressed. It is, in fact, well recognized that an adequate domestic transportation system is vital to national defense. The result has been that some governmental expenditures designed to improve our transportation system have been partly justified on the ground that

[10] Owen, "Transportation and Technology," p. 407. That the importance of transportation in the development of underdeveloped countries can be exaggerated is argued in Thomas C. Campbell, "Transport and Its Impact in Developing Countries," *Transportation Journal*, Fall, 1972.

[11] This point is discussed by John H. Kaufmann in "Planning for Transport Investment in the Development of Iran," *American Economic Review*, May, 1962, p. 399 and by Owen in "Transportation and Economic Development," p. 182. The desirability of a program in East Africa that will recognize the need to use transportation as an agent of development opening up the country to trade and industry is discussed in P. J. Habenga, "The Relation Between Education and Transportation in East Africa," *Transportation Journal*, Summer, 1965.

[12] Winston S. Churchill, *The River War* (London: Thomas Nelson and Sons, 1899), p. 202.

they will contribute to the nation's ability to defend itself. Thus, federal expenditures to improve our waterways are partly justified this way and the official title of the Interstate highway system is "National System of Interstate and *Defense* Highways." Without delving into the wisdom of such expenditures at this point, it is enough to say here that national defense and transportation are closely interrelated and, consequently, this fact helps to make transportation "important" to the economy and to society in general.

Some Statistical Measures of the Importance of Transportation

Statistics indicating the importance of transportation as a factor in our economic life are readily available in abundance. In Table 1-1, for example, we see that in 1975 the people of the United States spent 141 billion dollars on the movement of freight. In Table 1-2 we see that the nation spent 177 billion dollars on the movement of passengers in that year. As is shown in the tables, the total transportation bill represented 21 per cent of the nation's gross national product (GNP) in 1975 (9.3 per cent on freight transportation and 11.7 per cent on passenger transportation). This percentage relationship has been fairly consistent for a number of years.

Shown in Table 1-3 is the growth in total intercity ton–miles carried and total intercity passenger–miles carried in the United States compared with the growth in the GNP since 1947. This table clearly indicates how closely related are the volume of transportation demand and the condition of the economy. Although passenger traffic growth has exceeded the growth in the country's GNP since 1947, freight transportation traffic has grown more slowly than the GNP, as a

TABLE 1-1 *Expenditures for the Movement of Property in the United States, 1975**

Mode of Transportation	Amount Spent (000,000)	Per cent
Railroad	$ 16,573	11.8
Highway	109,710	78.0
Water (including international)	8,057	5.7
Oil Pipeline	2,229	1.6
Air (including international)	1,838	1.3
Freight Forwarders and REA Express	419	.3
Other Shipper Costs	1,800	1.3
Total	140,626	100.0
Gross National Product[†]	$1,516,300,000,000	
Freight Bill as a Percentage of Gross National Product	9.3	

*Includes mail and express; includes payments made to for-hire carriers and expenditures on private transportation.

[†]Total output of goods and services in 1976 dollars.

Source: Transportation Association of America, *Transportation Facts and Trends,* 13th ed. (Washington, D.C.: Transportation Association of America, July, 1977), p. 4.

TABLE 1–2 *Expenditures for the Movement of Passengers in the United States, 1975*

	Amount Spent (000,000)	Per cent
PRIVATE		
Automobile Transportation		
New and used cars and other expenditures	$149,627	84.5
Air Transportation		
Aircraft and other expenditures	4,734	2.7
Total Private	154,361	87.2
FOR-HIRE		
Local Transportation (including railroad)	5,957	3.4
Intercity		
Railroad Transportation	340	.2
Highway Transportation	1,009	.6
Water Transportation	16	.0
Air Transportation	11,581	6.5
Total Intercity	12,946	7.3
International Air and Water	3,726	2.1
Total For-Hire	22,629	12.8
TOTAL PRIVATE AND FOR-HIRE	176,990	100.0
Gross National Product*	$1,516,300,000,000	
Passenger Bill as a Percentage of Gross National Product	11.7	

*Total output of goods and services in 1976 dollars.

Source: Transportation Association of America, *Transportation Facts and Trends,* 13th ed. (Washington, D.C.: Transportation Association of America, July, 1977), p. 5.

result of lighter weight metals used in products, decentralization of production sites, and improved transport and distribution systems.[13] Another contributing factor has probably been the trend toward consumer purchases of more services relative to physical goods. Services usually generate less need for transportation than do physical goods. The correlation of passenger and freight traffic growth with the growth in the GNP has, of course, varied by mode of transportation, with the growth in traffic of some modes exceeding the growth rate of the GNP and the growth in the traffic of other modes falling behind the growth rate of the GNP.[14]

[13] United States Railway Association, *Preliminary System Plan,* Volume I (Washington, D.C.: U.S. Government Printing Office, 1975), p. 5.

[14] The effects of changes in national economic activity on the freight traffic volume of the 5 modes of transportation are analyzed in Charles R. Snow, "The Effects of Economic Fluctuations on U.S. Freight Traffic," *Transportation Journal,* Spring, 1973.

TABLE 1-3 *Transportation Volume as Compared with Gross National Product, 1947-1976*

YEAR	Gross National Product Amount* (billions)	Index‡	Domestic Intercity Ton–Miles Amount† (billions)	Index‡	Domestic Intercity Passenger–Miles Amount† (billions)	Index‡
1947	$ 626	100	1,019	100	429	100
1950	714	114	1,063	104	505	118
1955	876	140	1,274	125	713	166
1960	986	157	1,314	129	784	183
1965	1,238	198	1,638	161	920	214
1970	1,438	230	1,936	190	1,185	276
1975	1,594	254	2,070	203	1,311	306
1976	1,692	270	2,216	217	1,390	324

*Total output of goods and services in 1976 dollars.
†Includes all transportation, both private and for-hire.
‡Index with 1947 = 100.

Source: Transportation Association of America, *Transportation Facts and Trends,* 13th ed. (Washington, D.C.: Transportation Association of America, July, 1977), p. 2.

Other statistics that help to establish the importance of transportation to our economy show that transportation and related activities (such as transportation equipment manufacturing) amounted to 11 per cent of the employment in the United States in 1976; transportation and related industries contributed approximately 15 per cent of the federal taxes collected and 26 per cent of the state taxes collected in 1975;[15] and the federal and state governments together spent over 34 billion dollars to provide domestic transportation facilities (such as airports and highways) in 1976.[16]

Trying to quantify the importance of transportation to the economy is difficult, not because of a lack of statistics, but because the statistics really cannot tell the story—they at best understate the case.[17] Perhaps this quotation from Dudley F. Pegrum will serve to indicate the very broad impact of transportation on our society:

> The unique position which transportation occupies in economic activity arises from the reduction by it of the resistances of time and space to the production of economic goods and services. The significance of this in terms of the allocation of economic resources is indicated by the fact that probably at least one-third of our national wealth is directly devoted to transportation. So important is it that without it organized human activity would be impossible; complete stoppage of a community's transport services is the quickest way to

[15] These figures are reported by the Transportation Association of America. See *Transportation Facts and Trends,* 13th ed. (Washington, D.C.: Transportation Association of America, July, 1977), pp. 23 and 27.

[16] Association of American Railroads, *Government Expenditures for Highway, Waterway, and Air Facilities and Private Expenditures for Railroad Facilities* (Washington, D.C.: Association of American Railroads, September, 1977), Table 1 (unpublished).

[17] The problems of measuring the benefits derived by the economy from transportation are discussed in Daggett, *Principles of Inland Transportation,* pp. 19-22.

assure complete paralysis of cooperative effort, economic, political, and social.[18]

And, from an article in the *Harvard Business Review:*

Without doubt, transportation is one of our most important services. Transportation of passengers and goods accounts for approximately one-fifth of our gross national product, and it is a powerful force in shaping our society. Transportation has been a factor in urban sprawl and downtown congestion; it has linked distant cities to form megalopolises; it has shrunk transcontinental and transoceanic travel time to a few hours. Most of our modern family life is unthinkable without the automobile, and without the airplane business would be very different. At the same time, improvements in freight service have changed industrial logistics into a very dynamic activity.[19]

IMPORTANCE OF TRANSPORTATION TO THE USER

Users of transportation include freight shippers and receivers and passengers. Among the more important users of transportation are business firms. Some of the reasons why transportation is important to the economy as a whole have been discussed in the preceding sections of this chapter. But what about the individual user of transportation, in particular, the individual business firm? Of what significance is transportation to the manufacturer, the wholesaler, the retailer, the mining firm, or other business enterprise? Certainly the effects accruing from transportation to the economy as a whole also accrue to business firms as well. Thus, good transportation helps make possible geographic specialization and large-scale production and can foster competition among sellers in a given market. The individual business firm is also involved in transportation's effect on land values, economic development, and national defense. In addition, there are other factors peculiar to the firm rather than to the economy as a whole. These are discussed in the following paragraphs. Some of these also apply to users other than business firms.

Although transportation of passengers is of some consequence to the business firm as it is to all citizens and other organizations in the economy, it is transportation of property (freight) that is of more concern to business management as an area for decision making. Every business firm, regardless of what it produces or distributes, is somehow or other involved in the movement of goods from one point to another and, therefore, is involved in transportation. Transportation essentially has to do with the spatial dimension of the business firm. "The spatial dimension refers to geographical relationships and reflects the juxtaposition of firms with respect to their materials sources, markets, and competitors, *plus* the spatial relations of the latter to *their* sources and markets."[20] The purpose or

[18] Dudley F. Pegrum, *Transportation Economics and Public Policy,* 3rd ed. (Homewood, Illinois: Richard D. Irwin, Inc., 1973), p. 19.

[19] William W. Seifert, Siegfried M. Bruening, and Anthony Kettanek, "Investing in the Future of Transportation," *Harvard Business Review,* July–August, 1968, p. 4. Copyright © 1968 by the President and Fellows of Harvard College; all rights reserved.

[20] Merrill J. Roberts and Wilbur A. Steger, "Transportation in a Graduate School of Business Curriculum," *Proceedings of Transportation Research Forum, 1964,* p. 111.

function of transportation is to serve as a connecting link between the spatially separated units within a firm's own organization (such as between plants and warehouses) and between units of the firm and units of other firms and individuals (such as suppliers and customers). Good transportation has the effect of holding to a minimum the time and cost involved in the spatial relationships of the firm.

Time and Place Utility

In economic theory terms, transportation's function in the spatial relations of a firm is to create place utility for the goods produced or distributed by the firm (this is, of course, a contribution also to the economy as a whole and many writers have discussed it as such). The word "utility" means usefulness or ability to give satisfaction. Place utility exists when goods are in the place where they can be consumed. Goods that are not in the place where they are to be used up have no value and so transportation creates value by creating place utility. Along with the necessity to have goods in the right place, the goods must be there at the right time (time utility) and in the right form (form utility) and in the posession or ownership of the person(s) who wants to consume them (possession utility). Time utility is created basically by the storage or warehousing function in business, but it is also related to transportation because transit time certainly affects time utility. Form and possession utility are the result of the production process and of marketing, respectively.

Without place, time, form, and possession utility, goods have no value and, in a broad sense, the production process is really not complete until all 4 utilities have been created because until then goods are not capable of giving satisfaction. Therefore, transportation, which creates place utility and contributes to time utility, is an essential part of the total production process that cannot be omitted or done away with.

The above discussion about place utility is not intended to imply that all business firms do or should regard transportation and the creation of place utility as extremely important. The degree of importance attached depends on several factors including the cost and difficulty involved in creating place utility.

Transportation and User Decision Making

Because transportation creates place utility and contributes to time utility, both of which are necessary for a business firm, its availability, adequacy, and cost have an effect on several kinds of decisions made by a business firm other than decisions related to managing the transportation function itself.

Product Decisions. For those firms that deal in tangible products, one such decision is the product decision or the decision as to what product or products to produce or to distribute. The transportability of a product in terms of its physical attributes and the cost, availability, and adequacy of transportation should enter into any product decision.

Market Area Decisions. Closely related to the product decision for firms dealing in tangible products is the decision relative to where the product(s) should be sold. This can be affected by transportation availability, adequacy, and cost plus the physical characteristics of the product(s) itself.

Purchasing Decisions. What to purchase and where to purchase can be affected greatly by transportation considerations, regardless of the nature of the firm, whether it be a manufacturer, wholesaler, retailer, service organization, mining company, or whatever. The goods involved may be parts, raw materials, supplies, or finished goods for resale. The availability, adequacy, and cost of transportation plus the transportation characteristics of the goods involved have a bearing on the "what and where" decision.

Location Decisions. Although decisions relative to where plants, warehouses, offices, stores, and other business units should be located are influenced by many factors, transportation availability, adequacy, and cost can be extremely important in such decision making. The significance of the transportation factor varies widely from industry to industry and from firm to firm, but transportation usually is worthy of some consideration in making location decisions.

Pricing Decisions. Since transportation is a cost factor in business operations, it can have a bearing on the pricing decisions made by business firms, especially those firms that have a cost-oriented pricing policy. In fact, because transportation is one of the nation's "basic" economic activities, price changes in transportation can have a serious effect on the prices of industry in general. This does not mean that in any individual firm there is an automatic cause-and-effect relationship between transportation cost changes and the firm's prices, but transportation cost is one of the factors that usually should be considered in pricing decisions.

Transportation as a Cost Factor

Every business firm of every size must in some way deal with transportation and, therefore, usually has a cost of transportation. In Tables 1-1 and 1-2 the total freight and passenger bills for the United States are indicated. For any individual firm, however, the freight transportation bill varies as a percentage of its total costs or of its total sales dollar depending on a number of factors, such as the kind of firm it is (wholesaler, manufacturer, etc.), kinds of products transported, the distances involved, the number and size of individual shipments, the peculiarities of the transportation rate structure, and so on. For example, the coal mining industry might have a freight bill that amounts to 40 per cent or more of its sales dollar. This is primarily caused by the very low value of the commodity relative to its weight. In the computer manufacturing industry, however, the freight bill is less than 1 per cent of the sales dollar mainly because of the extremely high value of the product relative to its weight.

For some firms, then, transportation is a major cost factor; for others, it is a minor cost factor. Unfortunately, the attitude of top management toward transportation as a business function often depends on how significant transportation is as a cost factor when, in fact, a better approach in evaluating the importance of transportation would be to consider, in addition to the size of the freight bill, the contribution transportation can make to such things as customer satisfaction and minimizing inventory costs.

Transportation as an Element in a User's Logistics System

The previous discussion of the importance of transportation to the business firm amounts to this: Transportation of freight is a vital factor in the logistics system of the firm. The logistics system includes all those activities, such as transportation, warehousing, inventory management, materials handling, and others, that have to do with the physical movement of goods, both inbound and outbound. As a factor in its logistics system, transportation has much to do with how well a firm serves its various units and its customers and how high are its total logistics costs. Collectively, the logistics systems of our business firms add up to the logistics system of the private sector of our nation where total customer service and total logistics costs are affected by transportation's availability, adequacy, and cost. In other words, the importance of freight transportation to the business firm and to the economy must be measured not only in terms of the total transportation bill of the firm or of the economy or by other statistics and factors mentioned earlier in this chapter, but also by the contribution it makes to consumer satisfaction and to business efficiency.

Because of the importance of transportation to the economy and to the business firm and other users, knowledge of the transportation system's basic characteristics, its strengths and weaknesses, its decision-making process, and the problems that beset the system and its decision makers is important to anyone who is a student or practitioner of business administration or is otherwise interested in transportation as a user or citizen.

The Passenger as a User

The previous discussion of the importance of transportation to the user has focused on the user of property or freight transportation service. In the transportation of persons there is a greater variety of users than is true in the transportation of freight in which business firms predominate. Users of passenger service include, of course, not only business firms, but also government and other nonprofit organizations. The predominant users are, however, individual citizens who purchase passenger service from "for-hire" carriers and/or provide their own passenger service in the form of the private automobile.

The importance of transportation to users of passenger service is obvious in that it enables our population to be mobile for economic, social, educational, cultural, recreational, political, or other purposes. Americans are probably the most mobile people in history. They rely heavily both on the for-hire transportation system and the private automobile for their mobility and they spend a great deal of money on passenger service. The American way of life is, in fact, so entwined with the automobile that a major reduction in the availability of that form of transportation, caused by an energy shortage or some other crisis, would alter our life styles dramatically.

OVERALL VIEW OF THE TRANSPORTATION SYSTEM

The transportation system we have has developed into its present state because of the direction given to it by the numerous individuals and organizations who are responsible for making decisions concerning transportation. The administration of transportation in the United States is in the hands of literally millions of these decision makers who decide how much money is invested to provide transportation facilities and service, the character of the facilities and service, how the transportation system is operated, what kind of traffic is carried by which facilities, the prices charged for transportation service, what industries and business firms use what part of the system, how the system is regulated by government, to what extent private carriage is used, the rate of technological development in transportation, etc. These decision makers may be viewed as falling into three major decision-making groups or segments: (1) users of transportation service (shippers, receivers, and passengers), (2) providers of transportation service (carriers), and (3) government.

Users of Transportation Service

The first segment includes the users of transportation service or, in other words, the shippers, receivers, and passengers. This segment includes virtually every business firm or other organization and every adult individual in the country.

We have already noted that transportation can to a large extent affect the decision-making process of business firms and other users and that it can be of extreme importance to users in terms of costs. At the same time, shippers and other users of transportation help to direct the development and growth of the transportation system through the decisions they make when using transportation since the individual decisions made by users add up to the sum total of transportation demand to which both carriers and government respond in their decision making. Transportation decisions made by users are also of importance to the growth of the economy in that they help determine the efficiency of utilization of the resources devoted to the movement of goods and persons. In fact, users may be considered to be the most important group of transportation decision makers:

> Therefore, while transportation is of great importance to our economy and our economic growth for many reasons, the final decisions with respect to the effects of transportation on the economy are made by individuals (users) based on a consideration of the alternative choices available to them. It is assumed that for the most part these choices are made on the basis of rational economic considerations. Probably this whole area of decision making can be summed up by consideration of two basic factors—cost and service. These two factors are, in essence, the expression at the marketplace of the relative advantages of the various carriers or the various media of transportation that are alternatively available to the individual.[21]

The problem of managing the transportation function and making decisions about property and passenger transportation is approached in various ways by users in terms of time, effort, and kind of organization devoted to it. It is sufficient to say at this point that the management of freight transportation by the

[21] Charles A. Kelly, "Transportation—Government—and Economic Growth," *Proceedings of Transportation Research Forum, 1964*, p. 141.

user organization, whether it be a business firm, government agency, or other organization, is ordinarily referred to as *industrial traffic management.* A new business science called *business logistics,* which involves the coordination of the management of the transportation function with inventory management, warehousing, and other activities related to physical supply (inbound) and physical distribution (outbound) of goods, has recently evolved and adds a new dimension to the problem of the user in dealing with transportation.

The role of the user, then, is to make decisions relative to transportation that will maximize whatever transportation and/or logistics goals the user has. The number of decision makers in this segment is obviously very large because every adult individual, business firm, or other organization is a decision maker relative to transportation and, therefore, the quality of decision making varies widely.

Providers of Transportation Service

The second major decision-making segment consists of the various business firms and other organizations and individuals who provide transportation service. These "carriers" provide service either to the public on a for-hire basis or to themselves in what is usually called *private carriage.* The for-hire carriers include the transportation companies such as railroads, motor trucking and motor bus companies, water carriers, pipelines, and airlines that provide transportation service for others. Private carriers include the many business firms and other organizations and individuals who provide their own freight and/or passenger service by operating their own trucks, airplanes, automobiles, or other transportation equipment. The business firm is usually a user of for-hire transportation service and may also be an operator of private freight and/or passenger service. Hence the business firm is sometimes both a user and a carrier.

The carrier segment consists of 5 major modes of transportation: railroad, highway, water, pipeline, and air. In all five modes there is some private carriage along with for-hire carriage. The importance of private transportation varies by mode, being the least important in terms of proportion of freight traffic carried in railroad transportation and the most important in water and highway transportation. Private transportation of passengers is, of course, most important in highway transportation where the private automobile predominates.

The for-hire part of our nation's transportation system, with a few minor exceptions (such as the Alaska Railroad which is owned and operated by the federal government), has been and is owned by individuals, partnerships, and corporations as part of the private sector of the economy and under free enterprise. This is unlike other countries of the world where the usual practice is for national government ownership of at least part of the for-hire transportation system. This, however, does not mean that government in the United States is completely detached from the for-hire transportation system, as is seen in the next section of this chapter.

These various carriers, both for-hire and private, along with other transportation agencies such as freight forwarders and transportation brokers, constitute that segment of transportation which provides transportation service. The decisions made by these carriers are obviously very important in determining the character of the transportation system and service and the growth of the economy. The decisions of for-hire carriers are made in response to the actions of competitors, governmental promotional and regulatory decisions, and the demand for transportation on the part of users. From the point of view of society, the role of the for-hire carriers is to provide the public with the best possible transportation at reasonable cost. Perhaps it may be assumed that if this is done, the carriers' objectives relative to profits, etc., will also be reached. The private carriers are expected to perform a level of service consistent with the objectives of the operating organization or individual.

The total number of for-hire and private transportation ownership units is very large in the United States, particularly if private automobile owners are included. The for-hire carriers, who are usually considered to be the backbone of the transportation system, primarily because they have an obligation to serve the public, are fairly large in number and exhibit different degrees of management ability both within and between modes. Any deficiency in management in the for-hire sector contributes heavily to waste in the system and makes it difficult for that sector to perform its role properly.

We often refer to the "transportation industry" when, in fact, it can be seen that transportation is made up of many different kinds of operators or carriers whose common denominator is the provision of transportation service and each of whom has his own particular characteristics. Thus, we have private carriers, common carriers, contract carriers, local carriers, intercity carriers, as well as the traditional classification of 5 modes of transportation—railroad, highway, water, pipeline, and air. Each of the operators and modes has its own peculiarities, but each is also able to provide some service that is substitutable for that offered by the others.[22]

In 1976 domestic intercity ton-miles of freight traffic and intercity passenger-miles were distributed among the 5 modes of transportation as indicated in Tables 1-4 and 1-5. In the freight traffic market, railroads still are the nation's most important mode of intercity transportation when ton-miles are the measure, accounting for 36.7 per cent of the traffic.[23] Highway carriers and oil pipe-

TABLE 1-4 *Domestic Intercity Private and For-Hire Freight Traffic by Modes, 1976**

Mode of Transportation	Ton–Miles (billions)	Per cent
Railroad	796	36.7
Highway	490	22.6
Water—Great Lakes	102	4.7
Water—Rivers and Canals	250	11.6
Oil Pipeline	525	24.2
Air	4	.2
Total	2,167	100.0

*Does not include deep-sea domestic water traffic. Includes mail and express traffic.

Source: Estimated by Association of American Railroads in *Railroad Facts,* 1977 ed. (Washington, D.C.: Association of American Railroads, 1977), p. 36.

[22] See Pegrum, *Transportation Economics and Public Policy,* p. 24 and G. Lloyd Wilson, *Transportation and Communications,* pp. 52-54.

[23] The distribution of freight traffic among modes would be significantly different if tons instead of ton–miles were being measured or if local as well as intercity traffic were included.

TABLE 1-5 *Domestic Intercity For-Hire Passenger Traffic by Modes, 1976*

Mode of Trans-portation	Passenger-Miles (billions)	Per cent
Railroad	10.2	5.3
Highway	25.1	13.1
Water	4.0	2.1
Air	152.3	79.5
Total	191.6	100.0

Source: Transportation Association of America, *Transportation Facts and Trends,* 13th ed. (Washington, D.C.: Transportation Association of America, July, 1977), p. 18.

lines accounted for 22.6 per cent and 24.2 per cent, respectively, while water carriers (not including deep-sea water traffic) accounted for 16.3 per cent. Air transportation, although it carries a considerable number of intercity ton–miles, still represented less than 1 per cent of the total intercity traffic.

In the domestic passenger market the for-hire segment represented only 13.9 per cent of the intercity passenger–miles in 1976, the remaining 86.1 per cent being accounted for by the private automobile (85.3 per cent) and the private airplane (.8 per cent).[24] Table 1-5 contains data for the for-hire carriers for 1976. It can be seen in the table that airlines dominate the for-hire passenger market with 79.5 per cent of the intercity passenger–miles, followed by highway carriers with 13.1 per cent, railroads with 5.3 per cent, and water carriers with 2.1 per cent.

A more detailed discussion of the distribution of traffic among the several modes of transportation is found in Chapters 10 through 14, along with material dealing with the changes that have taken place over time. At this point, it is only necessary to comment that in the past several decades the railroad industry has experienced a decline in its share of both total intercity ton–miles and passenger–miles. At the same time highway carriers, water carriers, oil pipelines, and air carriers have increased their shares of the total freight traffic, while in the passenger market only the airlines have enjoyed an increase in share of intercity for-hire passenger–miles. All other modes have suffered some decrease.

Before drawing any conclusions from Tables 1-4 and 1-5, it is well to keep in mind that the welfare or condition of the several modes of transportation, the importance of each one to the economy and to the user, the quality of service performed, and the caliber of decision making in each mode cannot be measured or determined by a traffic distribution analysis alone. Much more information and analysis are required before any such conclusions are possible.

Government

The third major decision-making segment in transportation is government. Government has considerable interest in transportation because transportation is an important economic resource, it is a source of employment, it has environmental and energy implications, it is important to national defense, and it has various social effects. However, we are interested mainly in government's role as

[24] Transportation Association of America, *Transportation Facts and Trends,* p. 18.

a promoter and regulator of transportation. Government at various levels, from federal to local, is relied upon to promote transportation by providing various facilities, such as streets, highways, and airports, which the carriers then make use of. Occasionally, cash, loans, and guarantees of loans have also been given to the for-hire carriers who perform transportation service.

In addition to the promotional role of government, there is the very important regulatory role, again found at almost all levels of government, but which is most important at the federal and state levels. Such regulation involves certain requirements having to do with safety of operations and also includes "economic" regulation, which is regulation of the business of for-hire transportation. It includes government control of entry into the transportation industry, regulation of rates and fares charged, and regulation of carrier service and other matters.

As noted earlier, the United States is unusual because it has avoided nationalization of any important part of its for-hire transportation system. Instead the approach in this country has been for government to assist and regulate for-hire transportation but to leave its operation to private enterprise. Nevertheless, the decisions made by government relative to promotion and regulation of transportation are of extreme consequence to both users of transportation and carriers. The policies and attitudes of government have a lot to do with the decisions made by both users and carriers. In other words, the quantity and quality of transportation service and the prices charged for it are, in part, the result of governmental decision making, and the transportation system reflects the soundness and efficiency of governmental decision making relative to transportation.

The ideal situation would be that government would play its role in such a way as to promote the system and to regulate it so that the most efficient utilization of transportation (and nontransportation) resources would be achieved and the public would receive good for-hire transportation service at reasonable cost. Whether or not this role of government has been properly played will be discussed in later chapters.

Government is big business in the United States today and the number of individuals and agencies who make governmental decisions concerning transportation is very large. In the executive branch of the federal government, for example, the departments of Interior, Commerce, Transportation, State, Housing and Urban Development, Defense, and Post Office all make critical decisions that directly affect the carriers who perform transportation service. In addition to decisions made in the executive branch, there are decisions made by Congress and by the federal regulatory agencies, for example, the Interstate Commerce Commission (ICC), the Civil Aeronautics Board (CAB), and the Federal Maritime Commission (FMC). Also, of course, there are thousands of other individuals and agencies making governmental decisions affecting transportation at the state and local governmental levels. Although these decisions have to do with several aspects of transportation, we shall deal only with government promotion and economic regulation in this book.

The decisions made within each of these 3 transportation decision-making segments—users, carriers, and government—are made in response to the internal and external environments the decision makers find themselves in. Their decisions interact with each other in an intrasegment relationship, which means that the decisions made by one unit (such as one carrier) affect other units (other carriers) within that segment and hence the decisions made by them. There is also an intersegment relationship, that is, the decisions made in one segment affect the other two segments and hence the decision making in those segments. The decisions made by individual units within each of the 3 segments add up in total to the "decision-making process" in transportation or "transportation administration" and determine the character and efficiency of the system.

PLAN OF THE BOOK

The subject of transportation may be treated from several different points of view and the material organized in several different ways. From one point of view, transportation is an engineering problem because it involves design, construction, operation, and maintenance of highways, airplanes, locomotives, railroad roadbeds, and so on. Transportation can also be viewed as a social issue because it has considerable impact on social mobility, housing requirements, population location and concentration, urban congestion, employment opportunities, and other such matters. In addition, transportation is an environmental problem because of its effects on air and water quality and other aspects of the environment. Transportation is also an economic problem because adequate transportation at reasonable cost is recognized, as we have seen, as being essential to economic development and a modern economy. Transportation is also of interest to the political scientist, since it is promoted and regulated by government.

In this book we present the broad subject of transportation in the context of being a decision-making problem and mainly from the point of view of the user of transportation. We recognize that there are the previously mentioned 3 major decision-making groups or segments involved in transportation. These are users of transportation service (shippers, receivers, and passengers), providers of transportation service (carriers), and government. As to users, we shall examine how transportation affects users and the user's decision making. We shall also examine decision making by the user relative to transportation itself and business logistics management. In addition, we shall deal with transportation decision making by carriers and by government and the role of the user in that decision making. The examination of transportation decision making or administration in the 3 segments will include discussion of what decisions are made, what the process of decision making is, and, where appropriate, an evaluation of the decision-making process. In other words, this book is concerned with transportation decision making or transportation administration as it is found in the 3 major segments of transportation, primarily as it affects the user of transportation, although it is hoped that readers interested in any of the 3 major segments—users, carriers, or government—may also benefit from reading this book.

Accordingly, the book is organized around the 3 major decision-making segments. The remainder of Part 1 is devoted to a discussion of the implications of transportation for the user and the user's transportation decision-making process (Chapters 2–6). Part 2 deals with the providers of transportation service and their decision making (Chapters 7–15). In Part 3 the important role of government in transportation administration is examined (Chapters 16–25).

Throughout the book the emphasis is on domestic intercity transportation. Both the movement of property (freight) and the movement of passengers is dealt with, although there is more emphasis on the former because of the book's orientation toward the business firm as a user and the fact that for-hire passenger service is negligible or nonexistent in 2 of the modes of transportation—water and oil pipeline transportation.

SELECTED REFERENCES

The importance of transportation to the economy and society is discussed in most books on principles, fundamentals, or economics of transportation. See, for example, Truman C. Bigham and Merrill J. Roberts, *Transportation,* 2nd ed. (New York: McGraw-Hill Book Company, Inc., 1952), Chapters 1, 2, and 3; Michael R. Bonavia, *The Economics of Transport,* rev. ed. (Cambridge: Cambridge University Press, 1946), Chapter 1; Stuart Daggett, *Principles of Inland Transportation,* 4th ed. (New York: Harper and Brothers, 1955), Chapter 2; Marvin L. Fair and Ernest W. Williams, Jr., *Economics of Transportation and Logistics* (Dallas, Texas: Business Publications, Inc., 1975), Chapters 1, 2, and 3; Kent T. Healy, *The Economics of Transportation in America* (New York: The Ronald Press, 1940), Chapter 2; Charles E. Landon, *Transportation: Principles, Practices, Problems* (New York: William Sloane Associates, 1951), Chapter 1; D. Philip Locklin, *Economics of Transportation,* 7th ed. (Homewood, Illinois: Richard D. Irwin, Inc., 1972), Chapter 1; Hugh S. Norton, *Modern Transportation Economics,* 2nd ed. (Columbus, Ohio: Charles E. Merrill Publishing Company, 1971), Chapter 1; Dudley F. Pegrum, *Transportation Economics and Public Policy,* 3rd ed. (Homewood, Illinois: Richard D. Irwin, Inc., 1973), Chapter 1; Roy J. Sampson and Martin T. Farris, *Domestic Transportation: Practice, Theory and Policy,* 3rd ed. (Boston: Houghton-Mifflin Company, 1975), Chapter 1; Russell E. Westmeyer, *Economics of Transportation* (Englewood Cliffs, N.J.: Prentice-Hall, Inc., 1952), Chapter 1; and G. Lloyd Wilson, *Transportation and Communications* (New York: Appleton-Century-Crofts, Inc., 1954), Chapter 1.

Very early publications dealing with the general importance of transportation are Dionysius Lardner, *Railway Economy* (New York: Harper and Brothers, 1850), Chapter 1 and Harry T. Newcomb, *Railway Economics* (Philadelphia: Railway World Publishing Company, 1898), Chapter 1.

Discussions of geographic specialization can be found in texts on the principles of economics.

The role of transportation in economic development is treated in many writings. Books include Gary Fromm, ed., *Transport Investment and Economic Development* (Washington, D.C.: The Brookings Institution, 1965); John B. Lansing, *Transportation and Economic Policy* (New York: The Free Press, 1966), Chapters 6–11; Wilfred Owen, *Strategy for Mobility* (Washington, D.C.: The Brookings Institution, 1964); and A. R. Prest, *Transport Economics in Developing Countries* (New York: Frederick A. Praeger, Inc., 1969). See also Fair and Williams, *Economics of Transportation and Logistics,* Chapter 2; Robert T. Brown, *Transport and The Economic Integration of South America* (Washington, D.C.: The Brookings Institution, 1966); Wilfred Owen, *Distance and Development:*

Transport and Communications in India (Washington, D.C.: The Brookings Institution, 1968); and George W. Wilson, et al., *The Impact of Highway Investment on Development* (Washington, D.C.: The Brookings Institution, 1966). Articles on the subject are Raymond A. Austrotas, "Low Density Air Transportation in Developing Countries," *Proceedings of Transportation Research Forum, 1974;* Thomas G. Campbell, "Transport and Its Impact in Developing Countries," *Transportation Journal,* Fall, 1972; Edwin T. Haefele, "Transport Planning for Underdeveloped Areas," *Proceedings of Transportation Research Forum, 1963;* Hans Heymann, Jr., "Air Transport and Economic Development: Some Comments on Foreign Aid Programs," John F. Kaufmann, "Planning for Transport Investment in the Development of Iran," and Wilfred Owen, "Transportation and Technology," all in *American Economic Review,* May, 1962; Mahlon R. Straszheim, "Air Passenger Technology and Public Policy in the Developing Countries," *Proceedings of Transportation Research Forum, 1968;* Wilfred Owen, "Transportation and Economic Development," *American Economic Review,* May, 1959; and George W. Wilson, "Transportation Investment and Economic Development in Underdeveloped Countries," *Proceedings of Transportation Research Forum, 1965.*

The relationship between transportation and sociopolitical development is discussed in Fair and Williams, *Economics of Transportation and Logistics,* Chapter 3.

Selected references relevant to other subjects discussed in this chapter are listed at the end of succeeding chapters where these topics are treated in more detail.

2

Transportation Considerations in Product, Purchasing, Market Area, and Location Decisions

In this chapter we begin our discussion of the user's role in transportation and the implications of transportation for the user. Users may be passengers or shippers or receivers of property or freight. In the following discussion we examine the transportation considerations that are important to the user of freight transportation relative to product, purchasing, market area, and location decisions the user must make. The discussion is appropriate mainly for business firms, although some elements are also of interest to government agencies and other nonprofit organizations.

All business firms must make product, purchasing, market area, and location decisions and the nature of these problems varies with the nature of the business, depending on whether it is manufacturing, distribution, or extraction (such as agriculture, mining, or lumbering). For purposes of brevity, however, the discussion in this chapter is in terms of manufacturers and distributors only, although much of the discussion also applies to extractive industries.

PRODUCT DECISIONS

Nature of the Product Decision

One of the basic decisions that must be made by a business firm is what product(s) [or service(s)] the firm is to deal in. Thus, the manufacturer must decide what product(s) to manufacture. The distributor, i.e., the wholesaler and retailer, must decide what product(s) he wants to purchase for resale.

Among the several factors that might be weighed in a manufacturer's product selection decision are a product's potential sales volume, willingness of middlemen to handle the product, expected costs associated with the product, degree of product differentiation enjoyed by the product, the number and size of potential competitors, patent protection, raw materials and/or parts required to produce the product, the effect on products currently in the firm's "line," consistency of the product with the firm's established image, and technical ability required to produce the product.

The principal function of wholesalers is to obtain the products of many manufacturers and distribute them in smaller quantities to other wholesalers and to retailers. The retailer's main function is to obtain the products of many manufacturers and distributors and distribute them to individual consumers.

Most distributors consider themselves as purchasing agents for their customers and, hence, the product decision (what to carry) is vitally important to the distributor's success or failure. The distributor should try to provide a product assortment that is attractive to the customers he is seeking to attract. The particular assortment carried varies with the kind of customers served. However, certain specific factors, such as potential sales volume, costs associated with the product, degree of product differentiation, and the effect on other products carried by the firm, should be considered by the distributor.

Transportation as a Factor in the Product Decision

Although the transportation aspects of the product decision of manufacturers and distributors are sometimes of secondary importance, in some cases they are of major consequence and can outweigh other factors in the product decision. Transportation factors may dictate whether or not a product can be made and sold at a profit by a manufacturer or carried at a profit by a distributor, where it can be sold, as well as playing a part in determining prices of the product. A principal transportation aspect that must be considered is the cost of transportation associated with a product. Another is the transportability of the proposed product in a physical sense, i.e., can it be carried the required distances without deterioration, does it need special temperature control while being transported, how does it "load" into a vehicle in terms of using the vehicle's capacity efficiently, is it subject to a great deal of loss and damage while being transported, does it require special loading and unloading equipment, does it require special transportation equipment, and, lastly, does it require special protective packaging?

Packaging deserves elaboration. *Packaging* refers to any kind of protective covering or container, for example, a barrel, wood crate, cardboard carton, bag, and so on. From a transportation point of view, the function of the container is to protect the product while being transported, and, depending on the characteristics of the product in question, the necessary packaging may be expensive. In addition, because common carriers are generally liable for what they carry if the product is damaged, carriers have the right to refuse to carry a product that, in their judgment, is improperly packaged.

The combination of transportation factors mentioned in the two preceding paragraphs can affect the decision on the kind of product(s) a manufacturer should produce or a distributor should deal in. Unless these various factors are taken into account while the product decision is being made, the firm may find that it has made a less than optimum decision on product selection.

PURCHASING DECISIONS

Nature of the Purchasing Decision

The purchasing decision of the manufacturer basically involves deciding on what raw materials, parts, and supplies to buy and where to buy them. For the distributor, it is a question of where to buy the products he has decided to purchase for resale.

Among the many factors that might be considered in a purchasing decision by a manufacturer are various product characteristics including economy in purchase price and in use, productivity, uniformity of the product, purity of the product, and ability to make the buyer's product more suitable. In addition to product characteristics, industrial buyers consider the reliability of the seller, the cooperativeness of the seller, repair service offered by the seller, previous experience with the seller, and ability to provide continuous supply.[1]

The purchasing decision of the distributor is, of course, closely tied to the product decision since he purchases for resale rather than for manufacturing or processing. Therefore, what to purchase is determined by the decision on what to carry for resale to potential customers. However, the distributor must decide where to obtain the products to be carried. The factors to be considered in that decision include price, uniformity and purity of the product, reliability of the seller, cooperativeness of the seller, and ability to obtain a continuous supply.

Transportation as a Factor in the
Purchasing Decision

In some cases, transportation is very important in the purchasing decision. In other cases, it is not. The transportation considerations of the manufacturer in deciding on what to buy in the way of raw materials, parts, and supplies are similar to those related to the product decision and have to do with transportation cost and the transportability of the purchased item.

For both manufacturers and distributors, once the decision on *what* to buy has been made, transportation as a factor can affect which *suppliers* to buy from. The manufacturer or distributor is interested in dependable and fast delivery of the purchased items and the cost of transportation. These factors are affected by distance from the suppliers, because distance is related to time in transit and to transportation cost, and by the kinds of transportation serving the suppliers in terms of quantity and quality of transportation service available. The combination of these transportation considerations can have an important influence on the decision on where purchases should be made. Once purchasing decisions are made, a firm should keep up with information on transportation costs and services for the things it buys in order that it may make changes, if necessary, so that it may secure the most favorable service available.

A recent survey among purchasing managers indicated that physical supply service (including transportation and related activities associated with the movement of goods) rated second only to quality of the product in importance in

---

[1]E. Jerome McCarthy, *Basic Marketing: A Mangerial Approach,* 5th ed. (Homewood, Illinois: Richard D. Irwin, Inc., 1975), pp. 174–175.

their decisions on which suppliers to buy from, ranking ahead of price and 5 other factors included in the study. The survey also showed that there was less satisfaction with the transportation aspects of physical supply service, such as delivery time variability and average delivery time, than with aspects of physical supply dealing with matters such as billing procedures, order methods, and accuracy in filling orders.[2]

MARKET AREA DECISIONS

Nature of the Market Area Decision

Market area decisions must be made by manufacturers and wholesalers and have to do with the determination of which geographic area(s) and size of the area(s) the firm is to sell in. For most manufacturers, the market area decision is a crucial one. For some wholesalers, the geographic market areas served by them are so small, perhaps limited to a single city or a metropolitan area, that differences in the cost of shipping goods to customers are negligible. Many wholesalers, however, serve fairly large geographic markets and the transportation element is important to them. Retailers must decide on which areas they want to sell in and they do this in their retail store location decision. Since, in most cases, retailers draw customers from the immediate surrounding area rather than from large geographic areas, the market area problem relative to transportation does not exist in the same sense that it does for most manufacturers and many wholesalers.

Obviously, there are many nontransportation factors that must be considered in a manufacturer's or wholesaler's decision on the choice of a market area(s) and the size of a market area(s). These factors include the character of demand for the product sold in the area(s) under consideration, the sales and promotion effort required, the sales force available, the availability of appropriate distributors in the area(s) being considered, and the ability to produce or acquire the quantity to be sold in the area(s) being studied.

Transportation as a Factor in the Market Area Decision

General Considerations. The transportation element is often of great importance in decisions on the choice of and size of a market area. Certainly, the firm must take into account the availability, adequacy, and cost of transportation in determining which market area(s) to sell in and the size of the area(s). Also, the transportability of the product(s) involved, particularly in terms of being able to be carried the required distances without deterioration, is an important factor to consider.

Most business firms, whether large or small, should gather and analyze information on transportation costs and services available for new or existing products when deciding upon which geographic markets to serve or whether or not to

---

[2]William D. Perreault, Jr. and Frederick A. Russ, "Physical Distribution Service in Industrial Purchase Decisions," *Journal of Marketing*, April, 1976, pp. 5–7.

expand markets for existing products and also to keep up with current developments in current markets. This is true even when shipments to customers are
made collect or when all transportation costs are recovered from customers. The
importance of such gathering and analysis of information varies, of course, with
the importance of transportation costs and delivery service. Only when transportation costs are very small and delivery service is unimportant or when the firm
finds itself without competition can these factors be ignored.

When introducing a new product to a geographic market or trying to expand
markets for existing products, it is obvious that transportation costs that must
be incurred to reach the new points involved can determine whether or not a
firm can profitably serve such points at competitive prices. Similarly, the transportation services available to these points determine whether or not a firm can
give delivery service comparable to that given by competitors.

The same things are true of changes that take place in transportation costs
and services in markets already being served. Since transportation costs and
services offered by the various modes of transportation can change very often,
a firm should attempt to keep up with these changes in order that it might take
the greatest possible advantage of them, on the one hand, and remain competitive with other sellers, on the other.

Competition with Other Sellers. In addition, depending on the nature of the
product(s) being sold, competition with other sellers located at other points is
a transportation-related factor to consider. Thus, if there is little or no product
differentiation between the offerings of competing sellers located at different
points, and if the sellers have similar costs and pricing policies, and if there is
equal transport availability, the cost of transportation to the market area(s) can
have substantial influence on the sellers' sales volume because it affects the total
landed cost (total cost including transportation cost) to the buyers. When there is
little or no product differentiation, the buyer is usually very sensitive to landed
cost and often makes his decision to purchase on that basis. Therefore, there can
be a "natural" market area for each seller. This natural market is determined by
the landed costs because buyers will buy from the seller who provides the lowest
landed cost. That seller tends to be the one who is closest to the buyer because
transportation costs tend to be related to distance.[3] Thus, in Figure 2-1 the
seller at A has a natural market which lies to the left of the line C-D (the line of
indifference to the buyer) and seller B has a natural market to the right of the
line C-D. The line C-D is equidistant from A and B.

These relationships can be affected by the pricing policies of the competing
sellers, i.e., one seller may decide to lower his price in order to offset his transportation cost disadvantage in a distant area, or freight rate changes may take
place on some routes but not on others, thereby causing a greater or lesser
market area size for a given seller. Suppose, for example, that the seller at A in
Figure 2-1 decides to lower his price while the transportation cost and the price

---

[3] A summary of theory related to the question of fixed production and variable markets
can be found in Roy J. Sampson and Martin T. Farris, *Domestic Transportation: Practice,
Theory, and Policy,* 3rd. ed. (Boston: Houghton-Mifflin Company, 1975), pp. 243-247.
See also D. Philip Locklin, *Economics of Transportation,* 7th ed. (Homewood, Illinois:
Richard D. Irwin, Inc., 1972), pp. 78-83.

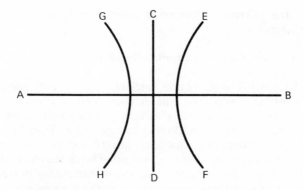

FIGURE 2-1 *Market Areas and Landed Costs.*

of the seller at B remain the same. A's market area will be expanded because the landed cost of his product will be less than before. The line dividing the market areas of the two sellers then becomes E-F. The line of indifference E-F tends to curve about the point that has the smaller market. The same result would occur if, instead of a price adjustment by A, the transportation charge from B to the market were increased but the rate from A was not changed. This would mean that the landed cost from B would increase while that from A would stay the same and B's market area would become smaller while A's would become larger, as indicated by the line of indifference E-F. If, because of a seller's price change or a change in transportation cost, the landed cost from the producer at B were reduced, the opposite result would occur and the line of indifference could change to G-H.

When several sellers at several different points are competing against one another, the same relationships apply, with each seller's market area limited by the landed cost of his product relative to the landed cost of his competitors' products.

When there is considerable differentiation between the products of different sellers (usually manufacturers, not distributors) located at different points, then the landed cost factor is somewhat diminished in importance in the buyer's purchasing decision because he may be willing to incur a higher landed cost in order to gain the differentiation in the product of a given seller. Consequently, unlike the case in which there is little or no product differentiation, there is no "natural" market area for a given seller determined by transportation cost, although transportation cost does have an influence on the size of the market area and there are often strong tendencies for the landed cost factor to heavily influence the buyer's choice of supplier and hence the seller's market area size.

LOCATION DECISIONS

One of the more difficult and complex business decisions is where to locate a firm's physical facilities. All manufacturers and distributors must deal with this problem. Transportation as a factor in a location decision is usually not significant in the choice of where to locate a retail store, but it is sometimes extremely important in deciding where to locate a manufacturer's plant or warehouse or a wholesaler's warehouse, particularly when the wholesaler serves a fairly large

market area. The following discussion is devoted to this problem of manufacturers and wholesalers.

Nontransportation Factors in Location Decisions

Because the location of plants and warehouses, particularly plants, has great
ramifications for the organization, the location decision is often a very time-
consuming one and one in which a wide variety of factors are considered. Many
of these have little, if anything, to do with transportation. These factors include,
among others, such things as the quantity, quality, and cost of available labor;
real estate, corporate income, inventory, and other taxes; the climate (for reasons
having to do with the effect of climate on the manufacturing or storage operation or on the ability to attract employees, or both); the local political environment; the availability and cost of power; construction and real estate costs; local
inducements such as low-cost leasing of facilities, tax benefits, etc.; educational
opportunities for employees; the cultural environment; the location of competitors; environmental control requirements; licensing requirements; the cooperativeness of local government; public services available; the cost of living; the local
urban transportation adequacy; the size of the urban community; and the
financing available.[4]

The above list indicates that there are many facets to the location problem
and that some location factors are intangible and not quantifiable and not easily
analyzed with the usual methods of economic analysis. Therefore, considerable
judgment is usually involved in a location decision, despite the various available
theories and models that deal with the location problem and despite the availability of computers that has enabled a greater amount of data to be considered.
The above list of location factors also indicates that a variety of people in the
firm should ordinarily be involved in the decision. Which of the factors listed
above are the most critical in the decision will, of course, vary with the situation.

Transportation as a Location Factor

In addition to the many factors discussed briefly above, transportation availability, adequacy, and cost are usually worthy of consideration in a manufacturer's or wholesaler's location decision. How much weight should be given to
the transportation factor varies with the circumstances because the importance
of transportation varies considerably from situation to situation. It is highly
important in some, relatively unimportant in others, but usually deserving of
some consideration. The transportation cost element, rather than availability
and adequacy of service, has received the most attention in the literature on the
subject and, because transportation costs have traditionally been considered
major determinants of total costs, transportation costs, in combination with the
volume of goods in movement, have typically provided the heart of location
models.[5] Transportation tends to receive more attention as a location factor

[4] For a discussion of plant location factors, see Maurice Fulton, "New Factors in Plant
Location Decisions," *Harvard Business Review*, May–June, 1971.

[5] See Herbert Milgrim, "The Temporal Factor in Spatial Monopoly," *Transportation
Journal*, Winter, 1972, pp. 33–34 and J. L. Heskett, "A Missing Link in Physical Distribution System Design," *Journal of Marketing*, October, 1966, p. 39.

when the transportation costs are large (either in total dollar terms or as a percentage of total costs or total revenue) than when they are small.

Objectives of a Location Decision Relative to Transportation

In considering transportation as a factor in a location problem, there are several different objectives relative to transportation that the decision maker could have in mind.

The first is that he may wish to minimize aggregate transportation costs, meaning both inbound and outbound transportation costs. In other words, he may seek to locate the plant or warehouse where the lowest possible total transportation costs are incurred.

A second objective could be to minimize total logistics costs, meaning all costs associated with the physical movement of goods, including warehousing, inventory management, materials handling, packaging, and order processing costs, as well as transportation costs. Both the inbound and outbound, or aggregate, logistics costs would be considered. The objective would be to locate the plant or warehouse so that these costs are the least possible.

A third objective could be to try to attain the customer service levels the firm desires. This primarily has to do with availability and adequacy of transportation service and such things as minimizing loss and damage and getting the desired delivery time after an order is placed with the seller. Delivery time depends heavily on where the plant or warehouse is located relative to the customer.

The 3 objectives listed above can be considered mutually exclusive or the firm can try to combine objectives. This would not be possible with the first 2 objectives, but it could be possible with combinations of objectives 1 and 3 or 2 and 3.

Location Theory and Transportation

The older theories of location often assume that minimizing aggregate transportation costs (objective 1, above) is the goal of the firm. They also assume that there is equal availability and adequacy of transportation at all possible locations and that the cost of transportation always is in direct relationship to the mileage or tonmileage purchased by the user. These theories also assume that all nontransportation factors in the location decision are equal for all possible locations. Two of the more well-known theories are those of J. H. von Thünen[6] and Alfred Weber.[7]

These and other theories indicate what some of the basic transportation factors are that should be considered in a location decision. These factors are discussed briefly in the following paragraphs.

Market Location. Obviously, where the market is has a bearing on where a plant

[6] J. H. von Thünen, *Der Isolierte Staat in Beziehung Auf Landwirthschaft und Nationalökonomie* (Berlin: Wiegandt, Hempel and Parey, 1875).

[7] Alfred Weber, *Über den Standort der Industrien* (Tübingen: 1909), translated by C. J. Friedrich as *Alfred Weber's Theory of the Location of Industries* (Chicago: University of Chicago Press, 1929).

or warehouse should be located because of the cost of transportation to the market. Many firms are "market oriented" in that they locate as close as possible to the market(s) they serve. Among other reasons for locating at or near the market(s), in addition to transportation cost, is high perishability of the finished product, making long-distance transportation difficult or impossible.

Location of Inbound Materials. The location of the major inbound raw materials, parts, or finished goods that are purchased by the firm will have an influence on the location decision, because the location of the inbound materials relative to the plant or warehouse affects the cost of transportation. Some manufacturing industries are "raw materials oriented" in that their firms tend to locate their plants at or near the source of their principal raw materials. A reason for this, other than cost of transportation, can be high perishability of the major inbound material, thus making long-distance transportation difficult or impossible.

Weight Loss in Manufacturing. A transportation factor that applies to manufacturing and processing firms, but usually not to wholesalers, is the weight loss that occurs in the manufacturing or processing operation. Weight loss means that for a given amount of weight of the major inbound material(s), there is a lesser weight in the form of the finished product. Thus, if for every 1,000 pounds of raw material there is produced 800 pounds of finished product, the weight loss is 200 pounds, or 20 per cent. When weight loss is substantial, there is a tendency, if transportation cost minimization is the goal, to locate the plant near the source of the weight-losing raw material to avoid paying to transport weight that does not turn up in the finished product. Fuel consumed in a manufacturing operation can be considered a complete weight-losing material.

Ubiquitous Materials. Ubiquitous inbound materials are those that are found, at the same cost, everywhere or, at least, over large geographic areas. When a manufacturing firm's principal inbound raw material is ubiquitous, the firm can locate its plant for reasons other than the location of the principal raw material, since it is found everywhere or nearly everywhere and does not require transportation. The tendency is for these firms to locate at or near the market, as far as transportation costs are concerned.

Usefulness of Location Theory

The factors referred to above—market location, location of inbound materials, weight loss, and ubiquitous materials—are traditional transportation factors discussed in the theories of location. The reader will recall that the theories of location often assume that minimization of aggregate transportation costs is the goal of the firm, that there is equal availability and adequacy of transportation at all possible locations, that the cost of transportation is always in direct relationship to distance, and that the transportation factor is being looked at in isolation, assuming that all other factors, such as labor costs, taxation, etc., are equal at all possible locations.

Obviously, these assumptions remove the discussion of the location problem far from reality. Location theory is not usually intended to be used to locate a particular plant or warehouse in a specific location situation. Instead, it is usually intended to indicate the major transportation factors that should be considered, such as market location and weight loss, in a location problem and to that extent the theories are useful.

Transportation Rate Structure and Location Decisions

One of the crucial assumptions often made in location theory is that transportation costs are always in direct relation to distance so that if the user increased the number of miles of transportation service purchased, he would also increase his transportation cost in the same proportion as the increase in miles purchased, regardless of what mode of transportation was being used, the commodity carried, or other circumstances. Figure 2-2 shows the relationship in which when 100 miles of transportation service are purchased, the transportation cost is $20. When 200 miles are purchased with the weight involved not changed, the transportation cost is $40. The distance was doubled and so was the freight bill. This, in effect, means that to minimize aggregate transportation costs, one should minimize total miles purchased.

Tapering Rates. Although it was convenient for von Thünen, Weber, and others to make the assumption about the relationship between freight rates and distance, it is far from what is the case in the real transportation world in the United States. The actual freight rate structure is such that transportation charges can vary with the mode of transportation being used, the particular carrier within a mode being used, the length of the haul, the direction of the haul, the particular route being used, and the commodity being shipped.

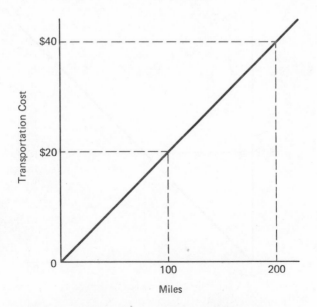

FIGURE 2-2 *Transportation Costs and Distance.*

It is well at this point to explain what a transportation freight rate is. A rate is a charge in dollars and/or cents levied by the for-hire carrier, usually per unit of weight (usually per 100 pounds), to carry something from some specific origin point to some specific destination point or, in other words, over some specific distance. The total transportation charge, or the total amount charged by the carrier on the freight bill (invoice), is determined by multiplying the rate times the weight. Thus, if the rate is $.18 per 100 pounds and the weight of the shipment is 20,000 pounds, the charge is determined by multiplying $.18 × 200 = $36.

When von Thünen and Weber assumed that transportation costs varied directly with distance, regardless of the mode, the carrier, the length of haul, and so on, they were really saying that the rate (as defined above) is the same in all situations and varies only with distance. Thus, Figure 2-2 can be relabeled as in Figure 2-3 in which the rate is on the vertical axis and the distance is on the horizontal axis. If we double the distance from 100 to 200 miles, the rate per 100 pounds will double from $.18 to $.36. The total transportation charge will, of course, also double.

The above is generally *not* the case in transportation in the United States. Distance is not the only variable in the determination of freight rates. For one thing, rates may vary with the mode of transportation, the particular carrier, the direction of the haul, the route used, and the commodity being shipped. In addition, rates are not usually in direct proportion with distance. Instead, freight rates in the United States are said to "taper" with distance, meaning that they usually increase with increases in distance but not in proportion to the increase is distance. Figure 2-4 is representative of the general freight rate structure. In this case, when the distance is doubled from 100 to 200 miles, the rate

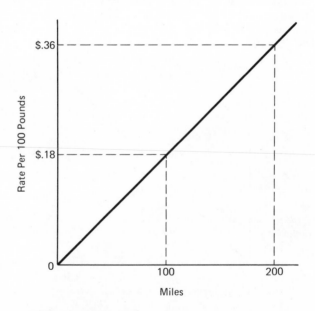

FIGURE 2-3 *Freight Rates and Distance.*

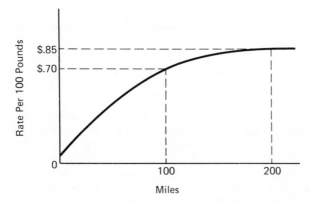

FIGURE 2-4 *Tapering Freight Rates.*

also increases, but it does not double. The curve begins above the origin (O) on the diagram because it is assumed that a minimum charge is made regardless of the distance to be covered. The reason for the tapering is principally that the terminal costs of picking up and delivering shipments and the associated paper work are the same, regardless of the length of the haul, so that the carriers spread their terminal costs over more miles on a longer haul, thereby incurring a lower cost per mile. In turn, the tapering rate provides a lower rate *per mile* to the longer-distance user. Other reasons for the tapering of rates are that (1) carriers tend to be more efficient over longer hauls than shorter hauls and (2) rates are sometimes tapered to prevent rates from restricting the movement of long-distance traffic. If rates increased in direct proportion to increases in distance, they would become so high that they would prevent the movement of some long-distance traffic,[8] i.e., the value of the service to the long-distance users may not be such that they are willing to pay the rates based on a direct relationship to distance.

The fact that most rates taper with distance means that if the objective in a location decision is to minimize aggregate transportation costs, the firm is better off to buy transportation in long hauls than in a number of short hauls, i.e. the length of haul affects total transportation costs. This, in turn, tends to lead firms to locate at the source of supplies or at the market, not at some point in between the two extreme points. In Figure 2-5 a manufacturer would be better off to locate at either A, the source of raw materials, or at B, the market, than at some intermediate point, such as C, if his objective is to minimize transportation costs. If located at A or C, his rate would be $.80 as against a combination rate of $.50 plus $.50, or $1, if he located at C.

Relation Between Rates on Inbound and Outbound Materials. Because freight rates vary depending on the commodity being carried, it is often the case that the rate on a principal raw material for a given distance is not the same as the rate on the finished product made from that raw material for the same distance. If, for example, the rate on the raw material is lower, a manufacturer would tend to locate at or near the market because that would minimize his transportation

[8]Locklin, *Economics of Transportation*, p. 189.

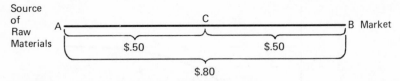

FIGURE 2-5 *Effect of Tapering Rates on Location.*

costs, assuming there is no significant weight loss in manufacturing (a significant weight loss could cancel out the difference in rates). Since the usual situation is that the rate on the finished product is higher for a given distance than the rate on the raw material from which it is made, there is a general tendency for manufacturers to locate near the market. If, however, the rate on the raw material is higher for a given distance, then the firm would tend to locate at or near the source of the raw material. A significant weight loss would accentuate that tendency.

Other Peculiarities in the Rate Structure. There are many other examples of peculiarities in the rate structure wherein rates are not the same in all situations and are not in direct relation to distance. These include group rate systems in which all points in a geographic area are given the same rate on a given commodity that is shipped from (if an origin group) or shipped to (if a destination group) that geographic area; transit privileges, where the user, in effect, pays the through rate plus a transit charge, if any, even though his shipment is stopped for processing or storage at some intermediate point; higher rates in one direction than in the opposite direction on the same commodity on the same route and the same carrier; different rates on the same commodity on different routes on the same carrier when distances are identical; different rates on different shipments of the same commodity, depending on the size of the shipment; and various "incentive" rates designed to encourage traffic that apply at some points but not others on the routes of the same carrier.[9]

The point of this discussion on the rate structure is that, when making a location decision, there is really little that one can assume about the rates to or from a given point or points. We have seen that rates may vary depending on the mode of transportation, the particular carrier involved, the length of the haul, the direction of the haul, the route used, the commodity being carried, and whether or not some peculiarity such as a group rate or a transit privilege exists. In order to deal with transportation as a location factor, then, one must thoroughly investigate the rate structure that applies to the points under consideration. Nothing can be assumed in advance about transportation costs.

A further thought is that the rate structure and its peculiarities should not be considered fixed and unchangeable. Changes can be made and are made, even when the carriers are regulated by government, and a specific location can be improved as a result.

Transportation Availability and Adequacy

A difficulty with location theories and models is that they often assume that transportation is equally available in terms of both quantity and quality at all points under consideration. This is, of course, hardly the case in the real world.

[9]These and other aspects of the transportation rate structure are discussed in Chapter 9.

Different locations often have different transportation availability in terms of what modes serve the point and the number and quality of individual carriers. There is, for example, no rail service at some points in the United States and there is no water carrier service in much of the country. The interstate highway system, however, which is nearing completion, provides excellent motor truck transportation service to many points that were relatively inaccessible previously.

As with the rate structure, however, the availability and adequacy of transportation service should not be considered a fixed element. Changes can be made although, admittedly, sometimes it is difficult and time-consuming, particularly when the carriers involved are under government regulation. If a location is a sound one for reasons other than transportation availability and adequacy, then the inbound and/or outbound traffic should be substantial enough to justify additional and/or improved for-hire transportation service or the institution of private carrier service.

SELECTED REFERENCES

Product, purchasing, and market area decisions are discussed in books on the principles of marketing as well as in managerial marketing books.

The relationship between purchasing and business logistics is discussed in James L. Heskett, Nicholas A. Glaskowsky, Jr., and Robert M. Ivie, *Business Logistics,* 2nd ed. (New York: The Ronald Press Company, 1974), Chapter 3 and in Grant M. Davis and Stephen W. Brown, *Logistics Management* (Lexington, Massachusetts: D. C. Heath and Company, 1974), Chapter 3. The results of a study of the importance of physical supply service, including transportation, in the purchasing decisions of purchasing managers are reported in William D. Perreault, Jr. and Frederick A. Russ, "Physical Distribution Service in Industrial Purchase Decisions," *Journal of Marketing,* April, 1976. See also Donald R. Lehmann and John O'Shaughnessy, "Difference in Attribute Importance for Different Industrial Products," *Journal of Marketing,* April, 1974, pp. 36–42.

The fixed production and variable markets question has been dealt with in John D. Black, *Introduction to Production Economics* (New York: H. Holt and Company, 1926), pp. 923–930; Frank A. Fetter, "The Economic Law of Market Areas," *Quarterly Journal of Economics,* May, 1924 and the *Masquerade of Monopoly* (New York: Harcourt, Brace and Company, 1931); Edgar M. Hoover, *The Location of Economic Activity* (New York: McGraw-Hill Book Company, Inc., 1948), Chapter 4; and August Losch, *Economics of Location* (New Haven, Connecticut: Yale University Press, 1954). See also D. Philip Locklin, *Economics of Transportation,* 7th ed. (Homewood, Illinois: Richard D. Irwin, Inc., 1972), pp. 78–83 and Roy J. Sampson and Martin T. Farris, *Domestic Transportation: Practice, Theory, and Policy,* 3rd ed. (Boston: Houghton-Mifflin Company, 1975), pp. 243–247.

A classic theoretical treatment of the location of industrial activity is Alfred Weber, *Über den Standort der Industrien* (Tübingen: 1909), translated by C. J. Friedrich as *Alfred Weber's Theory of Location of Industries* (Chicago: University of Chicago Press, 1929). A discussion and evaluation of Weber's theory may be found in Stuart A. Daggett, *Principles of Inland Transportation,* 4th ed. (New York: Harper and Brothers, 1955), pp. 434–443. Modern discussions of the location of industry are found in Melvin A. Greenhut, *Plant Location in*

Theory and Practice (Chapel Hill, North Carolina: Univeristy of North Carolina Press, 1956) and Hoover, *The Location of Economic Activity*. The location of industry is also discussed in John B. Lansing, *Transportation and Economic Policy* (New York: The Free Press, 1966), pp. 19–26; Locklin, *Economics of Transportation*, pp. 67–77; and Sampson and Farris, *Domestic Transportation*, pp. 237–241. See also Maurice Fulton, "New Factors in Plant Location," *Harvard Business Review*, May–June, 1971 and Linzy D. Albert and James H. Kellow, "Decision-Makers Reactions to Plant Location Factors: An Appraisal," *Land Economics*, August, 1969.

The theoretical relationship between transportation costs and agricultural location was set forth in J. H. von Thünen, *Der Isolierte Staat in Beziehung Auf Landwirthschaft und Nationalökonomie* (Berlin: Wiegandt, Hempel, and Parey, 1875). Von Thünen's theory is discussed and evaluated in Daggett, *Principles of Inland Transportation*, pp. 430–434. Agricultural location and transportation costs are also discussed in Łocklin, *Economics of Transportation*, pp. 86–89 and Sampson and Farris, *Domestic Transportation* pp. 235–237.

3

Transportation Considerations in
Pricing Decisions *

Among the more important and difficult decisions made by business firms and other organizations are those having to do with what price policy(s) to follow and the procedures to carry out the policy(s). In this chapter the discussion is devoted to the implications of transportation cost for the user of transportation in making pricing decisions. Again, the discussion is primarily in terms of manufacturers and distributors, although many of the things discussed are applicable to other kinds of organizations also.

NATURE OF THE PRICING DECISION

Price System

Prices determine how resources are to be used. Prices are also the means by which products and services that are in limited supply are rationed among buyers. The price system of the United States is a complex network comprised of all the prices of all the products bought and sold in the economy as well as those of myriad services, including transportation, labor, professional, and public utility services, and others ranging from dry cleaning to lawn mower repair. The interrelationships of all these prices make up the "system" of prices. The price of any particular product or service is not an isolated thing. Each price is linked to a broad, complicated system of prices in which everything seems to depend more or less on everything else.

*Major parts of this chapter are adapted from Donald V. Harper, *Price Policy and Procedure* (New York: Harcourt, Brace, Jovanovich, Inc., 1966).

Kinds of Pricing and Price Making

There are several kinds of price making practiced in the United States. These kinds of price making have been described by Jules Backman as market pricing, administered or business-controlled pricing, and government-controlled pricing.[1]

Market Pricing. Market pricing exists whenever the seller has no control over the price he receives in the marketplace. In such a situation, price is determined solely by the free play of the forces of supply and demand. The seller either accepts the price determined by this mechanism or he refuses to sell. He cannot sell at a price higher than that established in the market. Clearly, when market pricing exists, the seller makes no price decisions and needs no price policy.

True market pricing is rare and is found mainly in the organized commodity exchanges (such as those where grain, cotton, and other products are traded), in some other agricultural markets, and the security exchanges. Manufacturers and distributors seldom are involved in true market pricing, although they sometimes find themselves in situations that approach market pricing. Such situations occur when the product involved is close to being homogeneous (little product differentiation between the offerings of competing sellers), entry into the industry is relatively easy, and there is a fairly large number of sellers.

When market pricing or its close approximation exists, transportation cost, as well as other factors, is not a part of the price-making decision process because no "decision" is being made by the seller; the price, instead, is determined by the forces in the marketplace. However, transportation cost does influence the level of market prices and transportation cost can influence the decision of the seller as to whether or not to sell at the price offered in the market and it will also affect, as indicated in Chapter 2, the market area(s) in which the firm operates.

Administered or Business-Controlled Pricing. Administered or business-controlled pricing[2] exists when prices are established by business firms or other sellers at their own discretion. The seller sets the price and buyers either buy or do not buy as they wish. Prices are not fixed automatically by the forces in the marketplace but are, instead, the result of policies and decisions made by sellers. Although the free play of the forces of supply and demand, along with other factors, have an influence on pricing decisions, they do not actually establish the price, as they do in market pricing.

Most prices in the American economy are administered prices as that term is used here and administered prices are found in all areas of economic activity, both profit-making and nonprofit activities. The amount of control that a seller has over the price of his product or service varies because of variations in the degree of product differentiation, the size of the seller, and the number of com-

---

[1] Jules Backman, *Price Practices and Price Policies* (New York: Ronald Press, 1953), pp. 3–4.

[2] Some confusion surrounds the term *administered pricing.* In this text the term is used to denote all situations in which prices are established by sellers at their own discretion. Some writers have used it to designate a kind of pricing behavior (usually undesirable) rather than a method of arriving at or determining a price. Other writers use the term to identify price making in heavily concentrated industries only.

petitors in the industry. Clearly, unlike the situation with market pricing, because sellers in administered pricing situations have some degree of control over price, the seller can consider transportation cost, as well as other factors, in determining prices.

Government-Controlled Pricing. Government-controlled pricing exists when the prices of goods and services produced by private organizations are set or regulated by government, for example, in the transportation and public utilities industries or when wartime or other emergency price controls are instituted. In such cases, public administration of prices replaces or works in conjunction with privately administered prices or market prices. When government-controlled pricing exists, the seller must work with or yield to government in dealing with transportation cost and other factors that affect the pricing decision.

Nature of Price Policies

The dominant form of price making in the American economy is administered, or business-controlled pricing, in which the seller has the right and the responsibility to set prices for his products and services. This means that most sellers have need of a price policy.

A price policy is an overall guide to action in pricing. It involves general principles or rules that a seller tries to follow in making everyday pricing decisions. There are many examples of price policies that a business firm could adopt, such as to "follow the market," that is, to copy competitors' prices; to follow the prices of a particular competitor; to price in order to provide the firm with a given percentage return on investment; never to sell any units of output at prices below fully distributed costs; and to price in such a way as to discourage competition from entering the market. A seller may need more than one price policy to fit the different kinds of products or services that he offers.

Routine daily pricing decisions and procedures should conform to these policies. Thus, if a firm has decided as a matter of policy that it will follow the prices of a certain competitor, its routine pricing procedure will simply be to change prices whenever the competitor's prices change. A more complicated routine pricing mechanism is required when a firm's policy is to try to obtain a given percentage rate of return on investment.

No matter what kind of activity an organization is engaged in, and regardless of whether the output is a physical product or service, certain basic factors should be considered in developing a price policy or price policies for the organization. Some of these factors are internal to the organization and some are external. Internal factors are more easily identified and controlled than are the external factors. An understanding of the various internal and external influences on pricing is required before intelligent decisions concerning pricing can be made.

Internal Considerations

The several internal considerations important in developing a price policy include:

1. The long-run and short-run objectives of the firm relative to such things as maximizing profits, increasing market share or rate of growth, avoidance of legal problems, or immediate survival.

2. Who is to have responsibility for determining price policy and the mechanism of pricing and the size of and kind of organization available and/or needed to handle the pricing function.

3. The importance of price in the marketing effort of the firm, i.e., is price considered an important sales producing tool or is price deemphasized in the sales process, and how price is to relate to other elements in the "marketing mix."

4. Characteristics of the product or service including whether it is an industrial or consumer good and the degree to which the firm's product or service is differentiated in a physical or psychological sense, or both, from competing products or services in the eyes of buyers. Generally, the more product differentiation a firm enjoys, the more independent it can be in its price-making activities.

5. The costs associated with producing and/or distributing the product or service. Costs are dealt with in more detail later in this chapter.

External Considerations

Unlike the controllable internal factors discussed above, the external factors that should be considered in developing a price policy are largely out of the seller's control. They represent the uncontrollable "environment" within which pricing decisions must be made and include:

1. The nature of demand for the product or service including the relationship between changes in prices and changes in demand (elasticity of demand).

2. The market structure or nature of competition. The market structure consists of the number of competitors, the size of each competitor, and the degree of product differentiation. The market structure is affected by the ease of entry into the industry by new competitors, their ability to provide effective competition, and the pricing program they adopt. Together, these elements determine the market structure or, in other words, the nature of competition the firm faces.

3. The organization's suppliers. Although their influence is usually somewhat indirect, suppliers of raw materials, parts, and other industrial goods and labor can have some effect on the pricing decisions of producers, in that the prices charged by suppliers can affect the prices charged by the producer, particularly when the raw material, part, or whatever is a large cost element for the producer. The prices of goods supplied, of course, play an extremely important role in pricing by wholesalers and retailers because the prices charged by suppliers represent a very large cost element for such distributors and, to a great extent, the prices charged by suppliers are a starting point for pricing over which the distributor has no control.

4. The organization's customers. The kind of people and firms that buy a product or service can affect the price policy of a seller. This consideration has to do with the number of buyers and their size. These factors determine the influence they have on the pricing decision.

5. Economic conditions in the market, whether prices are rising in an upward swing of the economy or prices are falling as the economy turns downward, must be considered in pricing decisions.

6. The legal framework within which pricing decisions are made. At the federal government level, there are several laws with implications for the price maker. These are the Sherman Antitrust Act of 1890, the Clayton Act of 1914, the Robinson–Patman amendment to the Clayton Act, enacted in 1936, and the Federal Trade Commission Act of 1914. In addition to the federal laws, the states have a number of similar laws, some of which apply to pricing. Closely associated with legal questions are various ethical and moral issues associated with pricing decisions.

TRANSPORTATION COST AS A FACTOR IN PRICING DECISIONS

Relationship Between Costs and Prices

Cost is often one of the most important factors considered in pricing, although the importance of cost is sometimes exaggerated. One of the problems in using cost as a price-making factor is the fact that costs are often very difficult to identify and measure. This problem is complicated by the fact that many sellers are multi-product or mult-service organizations and, under such circumstances, allocation of joint or common costs to specific products or services is often difficult. Furthermore, cost information that is appropriate for accounting purposes is often inappropriate for pricing purposes.

Future costs are the most important type of costs in pricing. Past costs have little relevance in a pricing decision unless costs tend to be stable over time. The same is true of current costs. In general, estimated future costs, when reliable, are more useful in pricing decisions than past or current costs.

The proper role of costs in pricing is to establish a "floor" below which a seller will not price his offerings. Many sellers make use of full-cost pricing in which the fully allocated costs, both fixed and variable, associated with the product or service in question, plus a fixed or variable profit margin, are covered by price. Other sellers, in individual pricing situations, use the extra or variable costs associated with producing or distributing additional amounts of a product or service or adding a new product or service as the floor in pricing and they are satisfied, under some circumstances, if they receive a price above that level and thus receive some contribution toward the fixed expenses of the organization.[3]

Role of Transportation Cost in Pricing Decisions

As seen in Chapter 1, transportation represents a significant percentage of the total cost of production and distribution in the United States and, therefore, it has an effect on the pricing decisions of business firms and other organizations.

It has been pointed out that there are numerous internal and external factors that should be considered in pricing decisions and that cost is one of these factors. One of the costs of the organization is, of course, transportation cost. For some business firms, the transportation of goods involves the expenditure of many millions of dollars. For other firms, the size of the freight bill is insignificant.

[3]Full-cost versus variable-cost pricing as applied to transportation companies is discussed in Chapter 8.

One measure of the importance of transportation cost to the firm, in addition to the absolute size of the freight bill, is the size of the transportation bill as a percentage of total costs or total revenues, or as a percentage of the value of the goods (selling price) being transported. This latter percentage varies greatly depending on the commodity being transported. Thus, freight charges may represent a high proportion of the value of commodities, for example, sand, gravel, coal, and some agricultural commodities, but a very small percentage of the value of products such as aircraft parts, computer parts, and cigarettes. The percentages could range from well over 50 per cent to less than 1 per cent of the value of the commodities. The principal reason for the difference is the difference in the value or selling price of the articles per unit of weight. A given freight rate per 100 pounds, applied equally on all commodities, would result in a transportation cost percentage that would vary widely for different commodities if their value per pound varies widely. Thus, a freight rate of $.20 per 100 pounds is a very large percentage of the value of a commodity like gravel, which is very low in value per pound, but a very small percentage of the value of an article such as a computer part, which has a very high value per pound.

Other reasons for the wide variation in transportation cost relative to the value or selling price of different commodities are that some commodities require longer distance transportation or more expensive kinds of transportation (such as air freight) than others, but the principal reason is differences in the value of what is being carried.

Obviously, the size of the freight bill, in both absolute and percentage terms, should ordinarily affect the role of transportation cost in the decision the firm makes relative to the prices of its products. Transportation will be a more important pricing factor when the freight bill is large than when it is small.

Transportation Cost Changes

When for-hire transportation companies increase or decrease freight rates or when the cost of private transportation changes, there is a possible effect on the prices charged by sellers for the commodities whose transportation cost has changed. Thus, an increase in freight rates on a given commodity may lead the sellers of that commodity to increase their prices to compensate for the increase in transportation cost. However, we have seen that there are other costs in addition to transportation costs and that there are other factors in addition to costs that a price maker should consider in making price decisions. Therefore, whether or not a change in transportation cost will be reflected in commodity prices and to what extent depends on how important transportation cost is relative to the other costs and to other price-making factors. For example, if transportation cost represents less than 1 per cent of all costs, a seller may, with little trouble, absorb a moderate freight rate increase and not pass it on to customers. Or, even if transportation cost is a fairly important cost item to the firm, a rate increase may be absorbed in total or in part if some other factor in the price-making process dictates that the increase not be passed on to buyers. Thus, if an objective of a business firm is to increase its market share or its rate of growth, even at the expense of immediate profits, the firm may decide to absorb a rate increase rather than pass it on to buyers because the latter step would be contrary to the objective.

Character of Demand. One of the most important pricing factors to take into account when a firm is considering whether or not to pass a transportation cost increase (or decrease) on to customers is the character of demand for the product being sold. Demand for a product is determined by a number of factors, including the price of the offering, the prices and availability of substitutes, the incomes of buyers, the tastes and preferences of buyers, the character of non-price competition, the characteristics of the product offered, the number and size of competitors in the industry, and the number and size of buyers. In short, demand for a product is shaped by many factors, all of which are interdependent. Price is only one of these factors. The effect of a change in any one of these factors depends to some extent on the behavior of the other factors. For example, if price is increased, its effect on demand depends in part on the behavior of the prices of substitute products. The firm must determine the precise relationship between changes in price and demand. This can be done only if the price maker appreciates the effects of simultaneous changes in other demand-influencing factors.

Thus, essentially, the problem is to estimate the price elasticity of demand for the product in question. Price elasticity is a measure of the responsiveness of the quantity sold to price changes (assuming all other variables are constant). Specifically, it is a measure of the ratio of the percentage response of the quantity sold to a percentage change in price. The demand for a product is *elastic* if the total revenue increases when the price is reduced. Demand is *inelastic* if the total revenue decreases when the price is reduced. If there is no change in total revenue when prices are changed, demand is said to display *unitary elasticity.* Thus, the more sensitive that the quantity demanded is to price changes, the more elastic is the demand for the offering.

The organization must really consider two kinds of demand. The first is the nature of demand for the generic product (industry demand) as it is affected by industry-wide price changes. The second is the nature of demand for the individual brand the seller is offering, or the output of the particular firm, sometimes referred to as "brand elasticity" or "market-share elasticity."

When an upward change in transportation cost occurs, and the industry and brand elasticity are both high, and assuming that all other pricing factors have no bearing, the seller would probably choose to not pass any or not pass part of the increase on to customers in the form of higher prices because the result would be to reduce demand to the extent that the organization would be worse off after the price increase than before. By definition, total revenue would decrease.

If there were a reduction in transportation cost, under the same conditions, the seller may decide to pass the savings on to buyers in the form of a lower price in order to take advantage of the elasticity of demand.

When industry and brand elasticity are highly inelastic, however, transportation cost increases, with other pricing factors assumed away, would tend to be passed on to buyers in the form of a higher price because buyers are not very sensitive to price changes, demand would not be significantly curtailed, and total revenue would increase. In the case of a transportation cost decrease, however, the seller would tend to not pass it on to buyers.

When industry and brand elasticity differ considerably, the problem is made more complex and is beyond our discussion here.

General Versus Selective Rate Changes. When the transportation cost change results from a rate change made by for-hire transportation companies rather than from changes in the cost of private transportation, a matter of importance in elasticity of demand is whether the rate change is general or selective in nature.

A general rate change occurs when carriers of a given mode change the rates on everything they carry, usually by a percentage amount. This means that all shippers or receivers of everything will pay a different amount for transportation than they did before the change.

A selective rate change occurs when the carriers of a given mode change the rates on only one or a limited number of commodities and/or only between selected points.

In the case of a general rate increase, it is easier for a seller to pass the increase on to customers without substantially affecting quantity demanded because buyers cannot easily avoid the price increase by buying substitute products— everything shipped via that mode is subject to a rate increase—assuming that most sellers of most commodities will try to pass it on. General rate increases are also likely to be passed on to buyers when they come at frequent intervals as in an inflationary economy.

In the case of a selective rate increase, there is more difficulty in passing it on successfully because buyers may switch to substitutes that are not subject to the freight rate increase and the corresponding price increase.

Another factor to consider is whether or not the rate change, general or selective, is being made by only one mode (the usual case) or all modes of transportation at about the same time. The reader can easily see that this would affect the decision of the price maker relative to whether or not his prices should be changed.

Flat Changes Versus Percentage Changes. The impact of freight rate changes on different shippers and receivers and commodity prices depends on whether the rate change on a commodity is a fixed or flat amount per 100 pounds, regardless of the length of the haul, or a percentage increase. In the case of a flat rate change, the increase or decrease is the same dollars and/or cents amount for all users. All users are treated equally and, in that sense, the impact is equal. However, as a proportion of transportation cost, the impact is greater on those users who had previously been paying low rates compared with users who had been paying high rates prior to the rate change. The users involved would consider the factors discussed previously, such as elasticity of demand for the products being carried, in deciding on whether or not to pass a rate increase or decrease on to customers.

The effects on users of a percentage change in rates are somewhat different from when a flat change occurs. A percentage increase results in a greater aggregate increase for the users who previously paid the highest rates than for the users who had been paying low rates. Because rates generally have a relationship to distance, the impact of a percentage rate increase is, therefore, greater on the long-distance user. In other words, the relative position of competing users is changed, with the long-distance user being the most adversely affected.[4] If the

---

[4]The types of rate increases and their effects are discussed by D. Philip Locklin, *Economics of Transportation,* 7th ed. (Homewood, Illinois: Richard D. Irwin, Inc., 1972), pp. 63–65.

long-distance users attempt to pass the rate increase on to their customers in the form of a price increase, they may, at least under certain circumstances, find that they are unable to sell in certain markets.

Rate Changes and the Carrier. The reaction of users relative to their own prices when rate adjustments are made by transportation companies is of extreme importance to the latter. The reason is that the demand for transportation service is dependent on the sales of the things carried by the carriers, i.e., the demand for transportation service is "derived" from, or based on, the demand for steel beams, refrigerators, grain, shoes, and all the other things carried by transportation companies. Hence, if a rate adjustment is reflected in the prices of the things carried, the price changes may affect the quantity sold and, therefore, the quantity of transportation service demanded. For these reasons, when carriers make rate adjustments, they should try to anticipate the reaction of users to rate changes and the ultimate effect on the quantity of goods sold and the demand for transportation service.

Rate Changes and Regulators. The same can be said for the various regulatory agencies that regulate transportation rates. Since their principal purpose in regulating transportation is to provide the public with adequate transportation service at a reasonable cost, they should be concerned with the eventual effect on the demand for transportation service when freight rates are changed. A serious decrease in the demand for transportation service could reduce carrier revenues and impair their ability to provide adequate service to the public.

Our discussion here has been mainly in terms of an individual user's reaction to a transportation cost change in a specific situation, and we have seen that he may or may not adjust prices to reflect transportation cost changes. We should keep in mind that, in the long run, there is a strong general tendency for changes in transportation costs to be reflected in prices since transportation cost is one of the costs of production and distribution and, in the long run, all costs must be covered by prices.

GEOGRAPHIC PRICING PRACTICES

Regardless of the amount of money involved in an organization's transportation bill, every seller incurs transportation costs in one way or another and must take them into account when setting prices on the product(s) sold.

As we have noted, in the long run (although in various individual situations it may not be true), transportation costs must be covered by prices. Thus, as a general rule, buyers ultimately bear the cost of transportation. The seller, however, has the option of deciding exactly how this is to be accomplished by deciding on what kind of geographic pricing policy he is to follow. The geographic pricing policy determines who is to pay the freight bill, who is to actually bear the cost of transportation, who owns the goods while they are in transit, and who is responsible for filing claims for loss and damage against the carrier and bears the loss if it is not recoverable from the carrier. It must be recognized, however, that sometimes a seller has little choice in deciding on a geographic pricing policy, particularly if the practice is regarded as customary in a given industry. To deviate from the accepted practice in such a case would be highly confusing to buyers, might damage a seller's competitive position, and might even lead to price warfare in the industry. The following discussion is primarily in terms of manufacturers, but much of what is set forth also applies to other kinds of business firms.

As far as manufacturers are concerned, the way in which this problem is handled can greatly influence the success of a firm's marketing program by helping to determine the scope of the geographic market area the firm is able to serve, the vulnerability of the firm to price competition in areas located near its production facilities, the net margins earned on individual sales of the product, the ability of the firm to control or influence resale prices of distributors, and how difficult it is for salespeople in the field to quote accurate prices and delivery terms to their potential customers.

Every manufacturer who ships his products to customers must decide whether or not he will try to account for these shipping costs in prices and, if so, how he will do this. This same decision must be made regardless of the mode of transportation involved, or whether the transportation facility is internal or external to the operations of the firm. Although there are no freight bills to pay when a manufacturer has his own transportation facilities (private transportation), he still must decide how the costs associated with transportation are to be accounted for in pricing. There are two general ways in which the manufacturer can attempt to account for transportation costs in pricing, the F.O.B. origin[5] method and the delivered-pricing method.[6]

F.O.B. Origin

Nature of F.O.B. Origin Pricing. Often prices are quoted "F.O.B. mill," "F.O.B. factory," or "F.O.B. origin." When this is done, the seller quotes to every buyer a price for the product that is ready for shipment at the plant or warehouse. Title passes at the point of shipment. The buyer selects the mode of transportation, chooses the specific carrier, handles any damage claims that might arise, and pays the freight bills associated with the shipment. This also permits the buyer to pick up the shipment with his own private transportation equipment if he wishes. The net return[7] received by the manufacturer under F.O.B. origin pricing is the same for all sales of the product that take place under the same circumstance,[8] regardless of where the buyer is located. However, the total landed cost to the buyer (price plus transportation cost) obviously varies

---

[5] F.O.B. is the abbreviation for "free on board."

[6] The terminology concerning geographic pricing varies somewhat from industry to industry and from firm to firm and, in some cases, may be different from that being used here. Also, there are various versions of both F.O.B. origin pricing and delivered pricing not gone into here. They include, among others, F.O.B. origin with freight prepaid, F.O.B. origin with freight prepaid and charged back, and F.O.B. destination with freight collect.

[7] Net return is sometimes referred to as *mill net.*

[8] The prices charged by a firm can be different for different buyers of the same product because of differences in quantities purchased, trade status of buyers, time of purchase, and uses to which the product is put. In this discussion of geographic pricing the phrase "under the same circumstances" is intended to mean that the quantities purchased, the trade status of buyers, the time of purchase, and the uses to which a product is put are the same.

under these circumstances depending on the transportation cost involved, which is largely a function of the distance of the buyer from the point of shipment.[9]

The responsibility for freight charges and claim filing and the point of transfer of title under F.O.B. origin pricing and other geographic pricing systems are shown diagrammatically in Figure 3-1.

It is sometimes claimed that the use of F.O.B. origin pricing by competing sellers imposes upon them a geographic market limitation because of differences in their prices and transportation charges. In other words, under these circumstances no one seller is able to invade the home territory of another seller because the total landed cost to the buyer would be higher than it would be if he purchased from the local seller. An increase or decrease in the F.O.B. origin price can thus contract or expand each seller's geographic market.

This effect is most evident when the product involved is highly standardized. Some industrial products, such as semifinished steel, cement blocks, and aluminum bars probably fall into this category. Producers of raw materials have the same geographic limitations. For many manufacturers, however, there is sufficient product differentiation, either "real" or psychological, so that F.O.B.

F.O.B. Origin Pricing

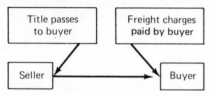

Buyer - - Pays freight charges
Buyer - - Owns goods in transit
Buyer - - Files claims, if any

Delivered Pricing - - Zone Systems and Basing Point Systems

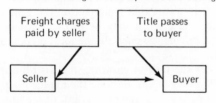

Seller - - Pays freight charges
Seller - - Owns goods in transit
Seller - - Files claims, if any

F.O.B. Origin Pricing with Freight Allowed

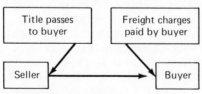

Buyer - - Pays freight charges
Buyer - - Owns goods in transit
Buyer - - Files claims, if any

FIGURE 3-1 *Geographic Pricing Systems.*

[9]As indicated in Chapter 2, although there are many exceptions, transportation rates charged by for-hire carriers generally increase with distance. Transportation costs involved in private carriage also increase as the length of haul increases.

origin pricing does not rigidly confine their markets to a geographic zone based on prices and transportation costs. This is particularly true in the consumer goods field. Product differentiation makes it possible to sell in distant markets even though the total landed cost to the buyer is higher than it is from some nearer manufacturer because the product involved is unique and cannot be obtained in its exact form from other manufacturers. Thus, although F.O.B. origin pricing definitely makes it difficult to sell in distant markets, unless all competing manufacturers are shipping from the same general area, it does not necessarily impose upon the seller a rigid restriction of the size of the geographic market unless there is practically no product differentiation in the industry in question.

Advantages of F.O.B. Origin Pricing. The chief advantage in using F.O.B. origin pricing is that the firm receives the same net return from every sale of the product under the same circumstances regardless of where the buyers happen to be. This enables the firm to more easily predict future revenues and to make decisions relative to adding new customers or new sales territories since there is no possibility that the firm will ever receive less than the expected net return. This is not true of delivered-pricing systems. Another advantage of F.O.B. origin pricing is that it relieves the manufacturer of the burden of handling the transportation problem; he need not worry about loss and damage claims or any other possible complications that are associated with using for-hire transportation.

Disadvantages of F.O.B. Origin Pricing. As we indicated earlier, the chief disadvantage of F.O.B. origin pricing is that it may make it difficult to sell a product in distant markets unless there is considerable product differentiation in the industry, or heavy demand for the product, or unless all competing manufacturers are located near one another. If plants that manufacture the generic product in question are geographically scattered, it may be difficult for one manufacturer who is using F.O.B. origin pricing to penetrate the local market of another because of transportation costs.

F.O.B. origin pricing also complicates the task of ensuring that distributors sell the product at the same or at similar resale prices. Because their landed costs vary depending on how distant they are from the shipping point, distributors will tend to set different resale prices on the product, assuming that they are all trying to earn about the same margin on the product. This, in turn, makes it difficult for a manufacturer to advertise a resale price to ultimate customers or to encourage the maintenance of a uniform resale price on his product.

Another possible disadvantage in F.O.B. origin pricing is that it may mislead the manufacturer into thinking that outbound transportation costs are of no concern to him, although, in fact, they are important to him to the extent that the buyer of a product is concerned with the total landed cost of the product, rather than just the price of the product alone. Consequently, although the manufacturer may avoid dealing with the transportation companies, the matter of transportation costs may affect the purchase decision. Furthermore, the manufacturer's salespeople are faced with the problem of trying to inform prospective buyers what the total landed cost will be on a particular order, which means that a salesperson must be able to determine what the specific

transportation charges are on a given shipment when for-hire carriers are
This, in turn, means that the salesperson must contact the manufacturer's tr
department for the information. The traffic department thus becomes involve
in checking freight rates much as it would if the manufacturer were paying the
freight bills himself. The outbound transportation problem simply cannot be
avoided by means of F.O.B. origin pricing.

Delivered Pricing: Zone Systems

Nature of Zone Systems. The price quoted by the manufacturer may include
both the price of the product itself and the transportation cost involved in
getting the product to the buyer. This is known as *delivered pricing.* Here again
transportation may be in the form of either for-hire or private carriage. In either
case, the customer is buying both the product and the transportation service
from the manufacturer. The invoice in these transactions carries the designation
"F.O.B. delivered," or "F.O.B. buyer's warehouse," or some similar phrase. In
this case, when for-hire transportation is used, the manufacturer selects the
mode of transportation and the particular carrier, handles the damage claims and
other paper work, and pays the freight bills. Title passes at the destination point.

Under what is known as a single-zone delivered-pricing system, the manufacturer sells the product under the same circumstances at a uniform delivered
price throughout the entire market area he serves, whether it be a local, regional,
or national market. In effect, the seller determines a price for the product and
then adds a uniform amount for transportation costs that is charged all buyers
who buy under the same circumstances. Clearly, the amount added for transportation costs should reflect the number of buyers the firm expects to serve, as
well as their locations, for it is the "average" transportation cost that should be
added to the price of the product in arriving at the delivered price.

Under single-zone pricing the manufacturer receives a different net return
(delivered price minus transportation cost) depending on the transportation cost
involved in each sale, which, in turn, is largely determined by distance. The
buyer pays the same price (under the same circumstances) as any other buyer,
regardless of how far he is from the shipping point. In effect, the nearby buyers
pay more for transportation than the actual cost of that transportation, and the
more distant buyers pay less for transportation than the actual cost involved.

A variant of single-zone pricing is a multiple-zone system of delivered pricing,
whereby delivered prices are uniform within each of two or more zones. Here,
the differences in delivered prices among the several zones are often based on
distance from the point of shipment, although other factors, such as competition, may dictate the differences.[10]

---

[10]When a seller uses a zone delivered pricing system some customers may choose to pick up
shipments at the place of business of the seller using their own private carrier trucks and
insist that an "allowance" be given to them (reduction in the delivered price) to account for
the fact that the seller need not incur any outbound transportation cost. After a series of
rather confusing "advisory opinions" dating back to 1967 relative to what kinds of allow-
ances could and could not be given, the Federal Trade Commission, in 1975, stated that
sellers using zone delivered pricing systems could offer to all their customers who picked up
their own purchases, in lieu of a delivered price, the option of purchasing at an F.O.B. origin
price that was uniform for all buyers and available to all customers on a nondiscriminatory

Advantages of Zone Systems. Single- and multiple-zone pricing clearly make it easier for the manufacturer to sell his product in distant markets, since distant buyers are not penalized by high transportation costs (particularly under a single-zone system). In fact, they pay less for transportation than the actual cost involved. This is particularly important to those manufacturers who have fixed costs or excess capacity and, therefore, find that they cannot rely on a small geographic market alone.

A second advantage of single- and multiple-zone pricing is that they help to ensure that distributors will resell the product at a uniform price and perhaps the price that the manufacturer suggests. Because all distributors within a zone who buy under the same circumstances are charged the same delivered prices, they have the same landed costs, which, in turn, means that it is possible for them to price uniformly and still earn adequate margins. In short, if a manufacturer wants to advertise a resale price to ultimate customers, affix a resale price to containers, or otherwise encourage the maintenance of a uniform resale price on his product, he is far better advised to make use of a zone delivered-pricing system so that he can be sure that his distributors have similar landed costs and can, therefore, price the product at the level he desires.

For the manufacturer, single- and multiple-zone pricing also offer the advantage that, once the transportation cost factor has been calculated for a zone, the salesperson can quote the delivered price to prospective buyers without having to consult the firm's traffic department. The full landed cost to the buyer is a known quantity. Also, when invoices are prepared, there is no need to determine which freight rates apply to a particular transaction. All that needs to be done is to add the previously determined transportation cost factor.

An advantage that is peculiar to multiple-zone pricing, and a reason why it is sometimes preferred to single-zone pricing, is that a manufacturer may find it impossible to arrive at a satisfactory delivered price if he is trying to use just 1 price for the entire market area served. For example, a manufacturer who is located on the East Coast may find it impossible to maintain 1 delivered price throughout the entire United States because the high transportation costs for shipments to points in the Far West may raise the average transportation cost factor used in pricing to such a level that the resultant delivered price is non-competitive. As an alternative, the manufacturer may choose to make use of 1 delivered price for buyers who are located, say, east of the Rocky Mountains and another, higher delivered price for buyers located west of the Rocky Mountains.

A related advantage in using multiple-zone pricing is that it may enable a manufacturer to segment his market geographically in terms of price, adjusting delivered prices according to the price elasticity of demand in the different geographic sectors.

Competitive reasons may also lead a manufacturer to use multiple zones. If the degree of competition faced by a manufacturer varies from one geographic area to another, the manufacturer may wish to price differently in the different areas. A multiple-zone system of pricing can help him accomplish this objective.

basis. See Advisory Opinion 147, Federal Trade Commission, 1967; Advisory Opinion 438, Federal Trade Commission, 1973; Ray O. Werner, ed., "Legal Developments in Marketing," *Journal of Marketing,* October, 1975, p. 82; and William A. Borghesani, "FTC Opinions on Backhauls Analyzed by PCC Counsel," *The Private Carrier,* October, 1975, p. 6.

Disadvantages of Zone Systems. Among the disadvantages for a manufacturer in using single- and multiple-zone pricing is the fact that the firm does not receive the same net return from each sale. As we pointed out earlier, the net return varies according to the distance of the buyer from the shipping point and the size of the transportation costs involved. If the transportation cost factor(s) has been determined in such a way that it incorporates the overall transportation costs, this difference in net return should present no particular problem. If however, the transportation factor(s) has been determined so that it does not incorporate the overall transportation costs, then the manufacturer discovers that he is paying out more for transportation than he gets back from customers. This is particularly likely to occur if transportation costs are high. Whether or not a firm can successfully absorb freight charges depends, of course, on the margin of profit it is getting on the product itself. Because of the threat of this hidden freight expense, single- and multiple-zone pricing are most likely to work out satisfactorily for firms that face transportation costs that are low relative to the value of the products involved.

Another difficulty with single- and multiple-zone pricing is that, although the transportation cost factor(s) used in pricing has been designed to provide an overall return to the firm that covers transportation costs, the factor(s) selected may become obsolete as the market for the firm's products shifts geographically. For example, if the firm sells more and more of its output to distant buyers, the transportation cost factor(s) originally selected may no longer yield enough to cover the total current transportation bill. Therefore, it is important that the manufacturer continually review the delivered-pricing system and the transportation cost factor(s) used lest it become out-of-date.

Another problem with single- and multiple-zone pricing is that buyers who are located near the manufacturer usually pay more for transportation than the actual costs involved, and this may create ill will; it may even cause buyers to switch to another manufacturer if this is possible. However, since manufacturers in a given industry tend to use the same systems when pricing geographically, it may be difficult for a buyer to find a manufacturer who could offer him a better price. In any event, one way to overcome possible resentment among nearby buyers is to price F.O.B. origin for customers in the immediate area and to use a delivered zone pricing system for buyers that are farther away.

Unlike F.O.B. origin pricing, single- and multiple-zone pricing also mean that when the manufacturer uses for-hire transportation, he must choose the mode of transportation, select the carrier, handle the damage claims, and pay the freight bills. These may be a burden on the firm.

One last problem that sometimes arises with multiple-zone pricing is that buyers who are located near the boundary lines of the zones sometimes complain of differences in delivered prices paid by themselves and by other buyers who are nearby but located in another zone.

Delivered Pricing: Freight Allowed

A manufacturer may quote his prices "F.O.B. origin with freight allowed." Under this arrangement, title passes at the origin point and the buyer arranges for and pays for the transportation, but the manufacturer then permits him to deduct the transportation costs from the amount on the invoice. This means that all buyers who buy under the same circumstances are charged the same price and that the seller receives a varying net return from each sale depending on the transportation costs involved. In this respect, it is really the same as a delivered-pricing system. The main difference is that the responsibility for arranging for transportation and paying for it is shifted to the buyer, thus permitting him to choose the mode and carrier he prefers. Indeed, in some situations it may enable the buyer to lower the net price he actually pays if the allowance permitted by the manufacturer is based on rates charged by some other, more expensive mode of transportation. For example, because it is traditional and because published rail rates are readily available, the freight allowance is often based on rail rates even though other forms of transportation are actually used.

Delivered Pricing: Basing-Point Pricing

Nature of Basing-Point Pricing. Another form of delivered pricing is called basing-point pricing. Under this approach, the delivered price on any shipment is calculated by adding together the price of the product at the basing point and the cost of transportation from that basing point to the customer. A basing point is some designated city where the product being priced is produced. It is a basing point if delivered prices are determined by adding together the price of the product at that city and the transportation costs required to move the product from that city to the buyer. This delivered price is used even though the product may, in fact, be shipped from some other producing point directly to the buyer. The actual location of the firm or plant from which the shipment is made in any given transaction has no effect on the delivered price. One or more basing points can be used, depending on whether the system used is a single basing-point system or a multiple basing-point system. The system may be a unilateral company-wide system used only by one firm, for example, a firm that has several plants located at different geographic points, or it may be an industry-wide system used by all or most firms in a given industry. In the latter case, a given manufacturer may or may not have production facilities at a given basing point. An industry-wide basing-point system can develop as the result of price leadership in which the firms in the industry follow the prices established by a leader(s) that uses a basing-point system. Industry-wide basing-point pricing can also be an accepted industry tradition in which traditional basing points are used. It can also be the result of collusion between the firms involved.

Under a single basing-point system, the firms or plants located at the basing point receive the same net return from each of their sales made under the same circumstances regardless of where the buyer is located, since the delivered price is the sum of the price at the basing point plus transportation charges from that point to the buyer. Firms or plants that are not located at the basing point receive different net returns from different sales, however. The net return received varies because there are differences between actual transportation costs and the transportation cost factor used in calculating the delivered price. If the transportation cost factor used is greater than the actual transportation charges incurred, the seller collects what is termed *phantom freight* or *fictitious freight*. If the actual transportation costs from the point of shipment are greater than the transportation cost factor used, the firm is said to be engaging in *freight absorption.*

Thus, in Figure 3-2, suppose that B is the basing point. Then, if a plant at B should sell and deliver to a buyer at y, the delivery would be made from B and transportation cost would be incurred accordingly. The delivered price would be the price at B plus the transportation cost from B to y. The net return to the plant at B would be the same as it would be if the plant sold and delivered to buyers at x or z or w since the transportation cost incurred (solid line) always equals the transportation cost collected (dotted line) from the buyer.

If a plant at A should sell and deliver to a buyer at x, however, then the transportation cost incurred would be less than the transportation cost collected from the buyer, assuming rates were related to distance, since the charge from B, the basing point, would be collected, and the distance from B is much greater than the distance from A. This is an example of collecting phantom freight.

If a plant at C should sell and deliver to a customer at z, then the freight cost would exceed the transportation cost collected from the buyer, and freight absorption would take place.

When several points are designated as basing points, the system is called a multiple basing-point system. The basing point used for calculations on a particular sale is usually determined by adding the prices at the various basing points to the transportation costs necessary to ship from those points to the particular buyer in question and then selecting the basing point that provides the lowest delivered price to the buyer. This is usually the basing point closest to the buyer, assuming that product prices are the same or similar at the several basing points. Under multiple basing-point pricing, both the firms or plants located at the basing points and the firms or plants not located at the basing points receive varying net returns from different sales. Since any given basing point is sometimes not the "applicable" basing point, plants or firms located at a basing point sometimes have to absorb freight charges on shipments for which some other basing point is applicable.

Suppose that in Figure 3-3 points B and D are both basing points. If a plant at B should sell and deliver to a buyer at y, the result would be the same as under the single basing-point system since B is closer to y than is D. B would be

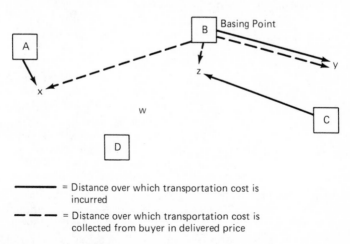

——— = Distance over which transportation cost is incurred

— — — = Distance over which transportation cost is collected from buyer in delivered price

FIGURE 3-2 *Single Basing Point Pricing.*

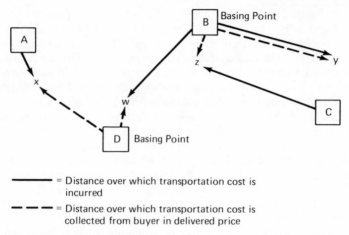

FIGURE 3-3 *Multiple Basing Point Pricing.*

the applicable basing point for that sale. No phantom freight or freight absorption would be involved.

If a plant at A should sell and deliver to a buyer at x, the applicable basing point would be D, because D is closer to x than is B. Phantom freight would be collected accordingly.

If a plant at C should sell and deliver to a buyer at z, the result would be the same as in Figure 3-2. B would be the applicable basing point and freight absorption would occur.

If a plant at B should sell to a buyer at w, the applicable basing point would be D, since it provides a lower transportation cost than does B, and the seller at B would be forced to absorb some of the freight charges. As can be seen, sellers located at basing points tend to avoid sales near other basing points because freight absorption becomes necessary when selling to those customers.

A variation of industry-wide basing-point pricing involves the quotation of prices F.O.B. origin but with the understanding that any prices of competitors that result in a total landed cost to a buyer that is less than the buyer would receive from that firm or plant under the F.O.B. origin method will be matched by the seller. In other words, the manufacturers are willing to absorb freight charges in order to be competitive and, in effect, every firm or plant in the industry becomes a potential basing point. This is because whenever the delivered price associated with a given firm or plant is matched by competitors, that firm or plant has become the basing point for that sale. Such a pricing arrangement is usually referred to as *freight equalization* and is designed to eliminate price as a factor in a buyer's purchasing decision. The practice is limited, of course, by the unwillingness or inability of the manufacturer to absorb freight charges in large amounts.

Advantages of Company-Wide Basing-Point Pricing. A unilateral company-wide basing-point system can effectively eliminate price competition between the various production facilities of the firm. Since all plants within the firm's production system quote prices according to the basing-point formula, the buyer, no matter where he might be located, pays the same price regardless of which plant the product is shipped from. This also enables the firm to make shipments from plants that otherwise might not receive enough orders to keep them operating at a satisfactory percentage of capacity.

A further advantage of a unilateral company-wide basing-point system is that it simplifies to some degree the task of price quotation in that a schedule of delivered prices to various points throughout the market area need be prepared only for the basing point(s) and not for every production point within the firm's production system.

Disadvantages of Company-Wide Basing-Point Pricing. The manufacturer who makes use of a unilateral company-wide system of basing-point pricing may find that he faces the familiar problem of creating ill will among certain customers who discover that they pay more for transportation than the actual cost involved while other customers pay less for transportation than the actual costs. Indeed, what might at first seem to be the locational advantages of some buyers are turned into disadvantages by the basing-point system. Another possible disadvantage of the unilateral company-wide system of basing-point pricing is the fact that it may result in a considerable amount of freight absorption. Also, as with other delivered-pricing systems, the return to the seller varies on each sale and, for this reason, may be unsatisfactory when compared to F.O.B. origin pricing. Finally, unilateral company-wide basing-point pricing may embroil the firm in legal complications.

Advantages of Industry-Wide Basing-Point Pricing. When an *industry* follows a basing-point system of pricing, price competition is eliminated among the competing firms, especially that based on transportation costs. This is a particularly important advantage in industries in which the product involved is highly standardized and when price warfare is a possible problem. Industry-wide basing-point pricing also tends to be advantageous to industries that face large transportation costs and high fixed costs or excess capacity and to industries in which the firms feel they must sell in distant markets in order to secure greater volume without being limited to a relatively small geographic market area by large transportation costs. By eliminating transportation costs as a factor for buyers to consider, any firm or plant in the industry can sell in a much larger geographic market than otherwise. This is especially true for firms or plants located at the basing point(s). In order for an industry-wide basing-point system to be effective, however, experience seems to indicate that the industry should consist of a relatively small number of firms; otherwise, the tendency to deviate from the basing-point formula is great enough to cause the system to break down.

For the reasons discussed above, the industries that have used industry-wide basing-point systems have generally been those that produce a relatively homogeneous product, attach great importance to transportation costs, face high fixed costs or overcapacity, and consist of a relatively small number of firms. The steel, cement, asphalt roofing, sugar, and wood pulp industries are good examples.

Disadvantages of Industry-Wide Basing-Point Pricing. The disadvantages in using an industry-wide system of basing-point pricing include the ill will it creates among buyers who find that they are paying transportation costs from production points that are not involved in the particular transaction in question. Since basing-point pricing inherently involves price discrimination, this reaction is to be expected. Buyers may also object that industry-wide basing-point pricing deprives them of a choice as far as price is concerned since they receive the same delivered price regardless of which firm is supplying the product or the location of the point of shipment.

Another objection to industry-wide basing-point pricing, and one that may or may not be generated by buyers, is the fact that basing-point pricing results in a good deal of waste in transportation. Since the delivered price is the same from all producing points, the customer does not care where the product comes from. As a result, there is unnecessary transportation of the product to the extent that a customer could be served by a nearby production point but instead purchases the product from a production point many miles distant. Although this criticism can also be directed to unilateral company-wide systems, it is more frequently directed to industry-wide systems.

Industry-wide basing-point pricing is also said to result in higher and more inflexible prices since there is practically no competitive pressure among the firms in the industry to keep them low or to cause them to change very often.

Finally, as with any kind of basing-point system, industry-wide basing-point pricing may lead to excessive freight absorption on the part of the manufacturer, unsatisfactory, varying returns to the seller, and legal problems.

Geographic Pricing Practices of Wholesalers

Although the cost of shipping goods to customers can be an important pricing consideration for wholesalers, the geographic market areas served by some of them are so small that differences in the cost of shipping goods to customers are negligible. For example, some wholesalers limit their trading area to a single city or to a single metropolitan area. In such situations, most wholesalers follow a policy of single-zone delivered pricing.[11] Wholesalers who serve large geographic markets, however, should consider using F.O.B. origin or multiple-zone delivered pricing and, perhaps, freight equalization pricing, instead of single-zone pricing. These approaches to geographic pricing may be used by wholesalers as well as by manufacturers.

Legal Problems Associated with Geographic Pricing Practices

The legality of geographic pricing practices has long been questioned, particularly by agencies of the federal government. The inquiries have dealt exclusively with the various forms of delivered pricing; F.O.B. origin pricing, by its very nature, is unquestionably legal.

Zone Systems. Single- and multiple-zone pricing are subject to the charge of price discrimination. Price discrimination may be considered to be inherent in zone pricing because the net return received by a seller from different sales made

---

[11]Richard M. Hill, *Wholesaling Management* (Homewood, Illinois: Richard D. Irwin, Inc., 1963), p. 164.

under the same circumstances within a zone actually varies depending on the distance of the buyer from the shipping point. The fact that some buyers pay for more transportation than is actually involved in a given transaction while others pay for less transportation than is involved is discriminatory on behalf of the latter. In effect, the nearby buyers pay part of the transportation bill for the more distant buyers. Or, to put it another way, nearby buyers are not allowed to exploit their locational advantage under a zone-pricing system. In addition, under a multiple-zone pricing system, buyers located in different zones pay different delivered prices and this, too, can be construed as price discrimination.

Despite the price discrimination inherent in single- and multiple-zone pricing, it has had relatively little legal difficulty. Neither the Federal Trade Commission (FTC) nor the federal courts have attempted to prevent an individual seller who practices single-zone pricing from maintaining a uniform delivered price as long as no concert of action among competing sellers exists. The reason there has been so little criticism of single-zone pricing systems by the Commission and the courts is apparently the fact that, in this instance, they view as discriminatory differences in prices that exist at the point of *destination*, and under single-zone pricing there are no price differences among buyers at the destination point, and hence there is no discrimination. As we have pointed out, there are price differences at the point of *origin* of the product; a seller in effect charges a different price on every sale that has a different freight cost. If the Commission and the courts viewed price differences at the point of origin as discriminatory, as they have with basing-point pricing, then single-zone pricing systems would be of doubtful legality.

Multiple-zone pricing systems have had little legal trouble except when several producers in an industry, or all the firms in the industry, have adopted similar or identical zone-pricing systems. The FTC has stated that a single firm is free to adopt any geographic pricing system as long as no monopolistic advantage is being maintained through unfair methods of competition.[12] If a multiple-zone pricing system is used by several or all firms in a given industry, then the firms are open to a charge of price fixing in violation of Section 5 of the Federal Trade Commission Act. In this regard, the Commission has said that when a group of competing firms establish an artificial zone system with identical boundaries and identical price differentials, it is difficult to believe that they could have been achieved and maintained without collusion.[13] The view has been upheld by the federal courts.[14]

Basing-Point Pricing. In sharp contrast to zone pricing, basing-point pricing has had considerable legal difficulty under the Robinson–Patman Act and Section 5 of the Federal Trade Commission Act. The Robinson–Patman amendment to the Clayton Act has been applied against unilateral company-wide systems of basing-point pricing and also against industry-wide basing-point systems on the grounds that they involve unjust price discrimination. In addition,

[12] *Federal Trade Commission, Notice to the Staff: In Re: Commission Policy Toward Geographic Pricing Practices* (Washington, D.C.: U.S. Government Printing Office, October 12, 1948), p. 4.

[13] *Ibid.*

[14] *Fort Howard Paper Company v. Federal Trade Commission,* 156 F. (2d) 899 (1946). See also *Federal Trade Commission v. National Lead Company et al.,* 352 U.S. 419 (1957).

the Federal Trade Commission Act has been applied to industry-wide basing-point systems on the ground that they are the result of price fixing among competitors.

When a single firm unilaterally adopts a basing-point system of pricing that it imposes upon its various shipping points, or when an entire industry adopts a basing-point system, price discrimination is said to occur much as it might be said to occur under a single-zone or multiple-zone system of pricing. This is because the various firms or plants or warehouses involved receive varying net returns from the different sales that are made under the same circumstances, depending on the distance the buyer happens to be from the applicable basing point, and because these varying returns have little or no cost justification. Also, some buyers pay for more transportation than they incur (phantom freight) while others pay for less (freight absorption), and this may be said to be discriminatory in favor of the latter. Finally, basing-point pricing may be said to be discriminatory on the grounds that buyers who are located close to the shipping point are not permitted to exploit their natural locational advantages if the applicable basing point is farther away from the buyer than is the actual point of shipment. In fact, they may be penalized for being close to the shipping point because they must pay more in transportation costs than do buyers who are much farther away from the very same point of shipment.

When several or all firms in an industry practice basing-point pricing, the suspicion that price fixing is present naturally arises. Indeed, any industry-wide practice is suspected of being the result of collusive action on the part of the sellers. This means that industry-wide basing-point pricing can be construed as a violation of the Federal Trade Commission Act, which prohibits unfair methods of competition.[15]

Because of these and other criticisms of basing-point pricing, the FTC attacked the practice for many years, but it had little success until the 1940's,[16] when in two cases that reached the United State Supreme Court the Commission was upheld in its attack on basing-point systems as used by two producers of glucose. These well-known decisions are referred to as the "Glucose" rulings. In *Corn Products Refining Company v. Federal Trade Commission*[17] the Supreme Court declared that the single basing-point system used by the Corn Products Refining Company resulted in unlawful price discrimination. The Court ruled that varying net returns received by the firm bore no relation to the differences in the actual costs of delivery. Such discrimination, the Court continued, is prohibited by the Robinson–Patman Act if it has the effect of reducing competition substantially or of tending to create a monopoly. In this instance, the Court held that the discrimination in the basing-point system of pricing had, in fact, injured competition among candy manufacturers who purchased glucose from the Corn Products Company by giving some candy manufacturers an unwarranted price advantage over others.

In *Federal Trade Commission v. Staley Manufacturing Company*[18] the same

---

[15] Industry-wide basing-point pricing can also be construed as a violation of the Sherman Antitrust Act.

[16] In 1924 the Commission forced the steel industry to give up the single basing-point system, but the industry then adopted a multiple basing-point system to replace it.

[17] 324 U.S. 726 (1945).

[18] 324 U.S. 746 (1945).

decision was reached, with the additional feature that both the Commission and the Court rejected Staley's defense that it had absorbed freight in order to meet the lower prices of a rival seller (the Corn Products Company). The Court ruled that Section 2b of the Robinson–Patman Act, which permits discrimination if it is practiced in good faith to meet a competitor's prices, does not apply to price systems but only to individual competitive situations.

The Glucose cases applied to single companies (not industry-wide basing-point pricing) and to single basing-point systems only. But in 1948 the United States Supreme Court extended the rule to apply to an industry-wide multiple basing-point system when it upheld the Commission by finding that the system of pricing used was unlawful. The case involved the 74 member companies of the Cement Institute.[19] Specifically, the Court held that the multiple basing-point system used by the cement industry involved unlawful discrimination and also unfair competition. The varying net returns received from different sales through the collection of freight differentials bearing no relation to the actual costs of delivery were held to amount to systematic price discrimination among the customers of each producer. The Court further found that such discrimination was practiced for the purpose of eliminating competition among the cement companies and was illegal under the Robinson–Patman Act. The Court rejected the claim of the cement companies that the discrimination was legal under the "good-faith clause" of the Robinson–Patman Act by saying that this clause can be used as a defense only in individual competitive situations and that it does not apply to a general system of pricing. Furthermore, the Court found that the discrimination was not accomplished in good faith to meet a competitor's low price since it was the result of cooperation.

The Court also ruled that the Cement Institute had violated Section 5 of the Federal Trade Commission Act by restraining competition in the sale of cement through combinations, understandings, and agreements to employ a multiple basing-point system of pricing. The system of pricing under consideration could be practiced only through concerted action on the part of the competing companies and therefore constituted a conspiracy to maintain identical prices.[20]

Another important case involving basing-point pricing was the 1948 Conduit decision of a United States Circuit Court of Appeals.[21] In this case the Court upheld the Commission and declared that the use of basing-point pricing by an individual company when there is knowledge that competitors also use the system amounts to unfair competition and unlawful price discrimination, even though no actual conspiracy can be shown. This decision was appealed and resulted in a 4-to-4 tie vote in the United States Supreme Court (one justice did not participate) and thus, in effect, was upheld by that Court.[22]

Immediately after the Cement decision, advocates of basing-point pricing succeeded in getting a bill passed by Congress that would have legalized basing-

---

[19] *Federal Trade Commission v. Cement Institute et al.,* 333 U.S. 683.

[20] The Commission had successfully applied Section 5 of the Federal Trade Commission Act to basing-point pricing in two other cases. See *U.S. Maltsters Association v. Federal Trade Commission,* 152 F. (2d) 161 (1945) and *Milk and Ice Cream Can Institute v. Federal Trade Commission,* 152 F. (2d) 478 (1946).

[21] *Triangle Conduit and Cable Company, Inc., v. Federal Trade Commission,* 168 F. (2d) 175.

[22] *Clayton Mark et al. v. Federal Trade Commission,* 336 U.S. 956 (1949).

point pricing by amending both the Federal Trade Commission and Robinson-Patman Acts. This bill was vetoed by President Harry S. Truman in 1950, however. The FTC thereupon modified its stand somewhat on the concurrent use of basing-point pricing by competing firms. In a case decided in 1951 the Commission stated that (1) it was not considering evidence of uniformity of prices, or any element thereof, between two or more sellers at any destination, or destinations, to be in and of itself a violation of law and that (2) it had no intention of prohibiting or interfering with the practices of delivered pricing or freight absorption as such when innocently and independently pursued, regularly or otherwise, in such a way as to promote competition.[23]

Subsequent to the rush of legal activity surrounding basing-point pricing in the late 1940's and early 1950's, there has been little legal action, and thus little to clarify the status of basing-point pricing. In general, it would seem that, at present, industry-wide systems of arriving at identical delivered prices (including basing-point systems) are suspect. However, the FTC appears to be unwilling to apply the decision in the 1948 Conduit case, which condemned the concurrent use of basing-point pricing when the practice could be shown to have the effect of restraining competition. In fact, the Commission has indicated that it will not initiate proceedings against the use of delivered-pricing systems except on clear-cut grounds of conspiracy, despite the fact that the Corn Products, Staley, and Conduit cases were not based upon conspiracy charges.[24] As a result, the Commission has limited its intervention to those practices that make it probable, rather than merely possible, that competition will be injured. Furthermore, the Commission seems to have adopted the view that conscious parallelism of action alone is insufficient evidence of conspiracy.

This suggests that sellers are free to absorb freight charges in order to get into a market, or to continue to serve a market, as long as they do not do this as part of a collusive scheme with competitors for the purpose of, or with the effect of, restraining competition.

It appears that basing-point pricing can still be used without interference by the federal government. The legal uncertainty surrounding basing-point pricing, however, has led to a decline in its use in the United States. In general, basing-point pricing is an objectionable practice and should be avoided by sellers for several reasons. First, any kind of basing-point pricing is highly unfair to at least some of a firm's customers because it is inherently discriminatory in its effects. Second, in industry-wide basing-point pricing all sellers who are using the system quote identical delivered prices, which has the same effect as price fixing. This prevents customers from being able to choose between differently priced products. Third, the unfairness of the system usually leads to dissatisfaction among customers of a firm and a desire to buy the product in question or a substitute either from other firms within the same industry (if this is possible) or from

---

[23] *Federal Trade Commission v. American Iron and Steel Institute et al.,* 48 FTC 123, 154. This case is cited in Vernon A. Mund, *Government and Business,* 3rd ed. (New York: Harper and Brothers, 1960), p. 348.

[24] Mund, *Government and Business,* p. 350. A recent FTC basing-point case that involved the plywood industry resulted in a consent order to cease and desist. See *Agreement Containing Consent Order to Cease and Desist,* File Number 721-0012, Federal Trade Commission, 1974.

another industry. Fourth, basing-point pricing may lead to excessive freight absorption. Lastly, the possibility of legal complications is always present.

Thus, although basing-point pricing offers some advantages to a seller, a firm is better advised as a practical matter to avoid the practice as much as possible. If the seller is eager to set up a delivered-pricing system, a single- or multiple-zone system is clearly preferable.

SELECTED REFERENCES

The nature of price making and the price system in the American economy are discussed in Jules Backman, *Price Practices and Price Policies* (New York: The Ronald Press Company, 1953) and *Pricing: Policies and Practices* (New York: National Industrial Conference Board, 1961); Donald V. Harper, *Price Policy and Procedure* (New York: Harcourt, Brace, Jovanovich, Inc., 1966); Robert A. Lynn, *Price Policies and Marketing Management* (Homewood, Illinois: Richard D. Irwin, Inc., 1967); and Alfred R. Oxenfeldt, *Pricing for Marketing Executives* (San Francisco: Wadsworth Publishing Company, Inc., 1961). An excellent article that describes the price-making process is Harvey W. Huegy, "Price Decisions and Marketing Policies," in Hugh G. Wales, ed., *Changing Perspectives in Marketing* (Urbana, Illinois: University of Illinois Press, 1951).

The price policies of 20 large corporations are reported on by A. D. H. Kaplan, Joel B. Dirlam, and Robert F. Lanzillotti in *Pricing in Big Business* (Washington, D.C.: The Brookings Institution, 1958). See especially Chapters 1 and 2. Price policies of small business are discussed in some detail by W. Warren Haynes in *Pricing Decisions in Small Business* (Lexington, Kentucky: University of Kentucky Press, 1962) and by Robert F. Lanzillotti and Gordon O. Parrish in *Pricing, Production, and Marketing Policies of Small Manufacturers* (Pullman, Washington: Washington State University Press, 1964).

The role of costs in pricing has been the subject of many publications. For example, see Oxenfeldt, *Pricing for Marketing Executives,* pp. 39-47 for a discussion of the fact that the only relevant costs in pricing are added costs. A critical discussion of full-cost pricing may be found in Theodore E. Wentz, "Realism in Pricing Analysis," *Journal of Marketing,* April, 1966. Various aspects of the relationship between costs and prices are described by Backman in *Price Practices and Price Policies,* Chapter 5 and in *Pricing: Policies and Practices,* pp. 28-40. The several books on managerial economics contain some discussion of the relationship between costs and prices.

The relationship between transportation costs and prices is discussed in D. Philip Locklin, *Economics of Transportation,* 7th ed. (Homewood, Illinois: Richard D. Irwin, Inc., 1972), Chapter 3.

Pricing as it relates to business logistics is discussed in James L. Heskett, Nicholas A. Glaskowsky, Jr., and Robert M. Ivie, *Business Logistics,* 2nd ed. (New York: The Ronald Press Company, 1973), Chapter 7 and in John F. Magee, *Industrial Logistics* (New York: McGraw-Hill Book Company, 1968), Chapter 11.

Geographic pricing practices are usually dealt with in general marketing texts such as Theodore M. Beckman, William R. Davidson, and W. Wayne Talarzyk,

Marketing, 9th ed. (New York: The Ronald Press Company, 1973), pp. 390–393; in texts dealing with government regulation of business such as Vernon L. Mund, *Government and Business,* 3rd ed. (New York: Harper and Brothers, 1960), Chapter 15; and in business logistics texts such as Heskett, Glaskowsky, and Ivie, *Business Logistics,* pp. 211–221. See also Fritz Machlup, *The Basing-Point System* (Philadelphia: The Blakiston Company, 1949); George W. Stocking, *Basing-Point Pricing and Regional Development* (Chapel Hill, North Carolina: University of North Carolina Press, 1954); and Backman, *Price Practices and Price Policies,* Chapter 7. Arguments in favor of F.O.B. origin pricing over delivered pricing for the firm and the public are presented in Martin J. Beckmann, "Spatial Price Policies Revisited," *Bell Journal of Economics,* Autumn, 1976. The effects of delivered pricing on competition and the public are discussed in James C. Johnson, "How Competitive Is Delivered Pricing?" *Journal of Purchasing and Materials Management,* Autumn, 1976.

4

Industrial Traffic Management

In this and the following chapter we continue our discussion of the implications of transportation for the user by examining the management of the transportation function by the user. This chapter is devoted to what is called industrial traffic management, or the management of transportation as such. Chapter 5 deals with the management of a broader activity, called business logistics, of which transportation and industrial traffic management are a very important part.

As pointed out in Chapter 1, in a sense, the user is the most important of the decision makers in transportation. The user views transportation, however, as a means to an end instead of a goal in itself, whether it be a user of passenger transportation or a user of freight transportation. In most cases, the passenger looks upon transportation as merely a method of getting from one place to another for economic, social, recreational, or other purposes, and he does not consider the journey an objective in itself. The user of freight transportation service sees transportation as a means to move goods from one point to another for purposes of sale to someone else, to transfer goods from one unit in an organization to another where they are needed, to acquire goods from someone else, and so on. The transportation of the goods, although necessary to accomplish the objective, is not, in itself, an objective. In other words, transportation is a facilitating activity that makes possible the attainment of some goal. It is also something that goes unnoticed for the most part by users and the general public until something goes wrong or it breaks down entirely.

Among the attributes of transportation that are of interest to all users are the cost of transportation, the time in transit, the reliability of the carrier in meeting schedules, and the frequency of service. In addition, users of passenger transportation are concerned about such things as comfort and safety and users of freight transportation are interested in many aspects of transportation, including availability of pickup and delivery service, frequency and extent of loss and damage to freight carried, vehicle sizes available, loading and unloading facilities and equipment needed, and protective packaging requirements.

DEFINITION OF INDUSTRIAL
TRAFFIC MANAGEMENT

Expenditures on freight transportation constitute an important part of the total expenses of many organizations. Inadequate mangement of these expenditures results in the organization's being unprepared to deal with the problem of providing for the transportation of the products it buys and/or sells. The result is that the organization may pay more for transportation than it should and, in addition, will perhaps not get the best possible service for itself, its customers, and its suppliers.

Industrial traffic management[1] is the term used to denote the management of the transportation function by the user of freight service. Charles A. Taff defines industrial traffic management as follows:

A traffic manager . . . is responsible for the planning, direction, selection, purchase, and use by his company or organization of all aspects of transportation or transportation service, with the objective of serving the organization . . . in the most efficient manner possible.[2]

The results of efficient industrial traffic management include the lowest possible transportation costs, the greatest possible customer satisfaction and, through assistance given to other departments and individuals in the organization, the smooth working, efficient operation of the organization. In contrast to activities such as production or marketing, industrial traffic management is a service activity in that its main purpose is to render some kind of service related to transportation to other departments and individuals in the organization.

The persons engaged in industrial traffic management carry various titles, such as general traffic manager, traffic manager, traffic supervisor, transportation manager, director of traffic, vice president of transportation, and transport control manager. Industrial traffic management exists in all organizations that deal with transportation, regardless of whether or not it is recognized and labeled as a special activity. This includes business firms, government agencies, and various nonprofit organizations in the private sector.

DEVELOPMENT OF INDUSTRIAL
TRAFFIC MANAGEMENT

As the railroads developed in the United States in the latter half of the nineteenth century, a specialized activity devoted to buying transportation service developed among shippers and receivers of freight, particularly those with large

---

[1] Industrial traffic management is to be carefully distinguished from *carrier traffic management* which denotes an activity in the management of transportation companies.

[2] Charles A. Taff, *Management of Traffic and Physical Distribution,* 4th ed. (Homewood, Illinois: Richard D. Irwin, Inc., 1968), p. 9.

transportation costs. This specialized activity eventually grew into what is now called industrial traffic management.

In the early days of industrial traffic management, the people involved were often formerly employed by railroads and the decision making involved in traffic management was limited. To a great extent this was because the options available to the user were usually few, for, in most cases, the railroads were the only form of transportation available. Actually, the sign of a good traffic manager apparently was his ability to negotiate secret rebates (secret freight rate reductions) from the railroads. He was a bargainer instead of a manager. When federal government economic regulation of railroads came into being in 1887, which attempted to prohibit rebates and other forms of discrimination, the stature of the industrial traffic manager declined during the next two decades.[3] The traffic manager became a specialist in rail rates and routes and his principal value to his organization was his ability to deal with the many complex rail rate tariffs. He was looked upon as a very narrow specialist, not a manager. The decision making involved in traffic management remained at a low level.

After the turn of the century, however, and particularly after 1920, as non-rail modes entered the transportation picture and as management began to attach more importance to transportation as an activity, industrial traffic management in some cases began to change for the better and became more involved with decision making and became more professional. The first national association of industrial traffic managers, the National Industrial Traffic League, was formed in 1907. Other organizations that included industrial traffic managers, at both the national and local level, followed.

For a long period, however, industrial traffic management remained in many cases a very narrow activity, concerned primarily with buying transportation service from for-hire carriers. It was very heavily oriented toward selecting modes and individual carriers and dealing with the complications of the transportation rate structure. The image projected by many traffic management people was a man wearing a green eyeshade on his head and elastic bands on his shirt sleeves, huddled in a corner surrounded by stacks of rate tariffs.

Since the end of World War II, however, a significant change has taken place in industrial traffic management. Many traffic managers and traffic departments today are highly progressive and very important parts of the user organization. They are concerned not just with rates and tariffs, but with many other activities involving transportation and with working with other areas and individuals in the organization. Although there are still some green eyeshade types in the field, industrial traffic management has changed dramatically for the better in recent years. According to one writer:

> The image of the traffic man whose *sole* concern is getting the shipment to Kalamazoo in the cheapest possible manner is quickly fading. He has come out from behind the heaps of tariffs and regulations, renewed his perspective, and is taking on a wider professional challenge.[4]

In some cases, the traffic department has expanded (by growing in the variety

[3] *Ibid.,* 3rd ed., 1964, p. 2.

[4] Linda Lufkin, "Developments and Trends in the Traffic–Physical Distribution Profession," *Traffic Management,* January, 1972, p. 54.

of functions, responsibilities, and personnel) into a physical distribution or logistics department. This matter is dealt with further in Chapter 5.

Despite the change in character of industrial traffic management, in some cases, higher management has continued to regard traffic management as a necessary evil requiring only the services of a narrow specialist whose effectiveness is judged by how well he minimizes direct transportation cost. The result is that traffic managers in these organizations continue to operate as did the narrow specialists of the past.

FUNCTIONS OF INDUSTRIAL TRAFFIC MANAGEMENT

A wide variety of activities may be included as functions performed in industrial traffic management, and these functions are broader than in the past. The actual functions performed in any one industrial traffic management unit, however, vary with the circumstances. The specific functions performed and the emphasis placed on each depend on such things as the kind of organization—manufacturer, mining company, wholesaler, retailer, government agency, and so on; the kinds of commodities being moved in terms of value and transportation characteristics; the volume of movement in ton-miles; the number of shipments; and the size of the freight bill. Certainly, one would not expect the emphasis in traffic management to be the same in a steel manufacturing company as it is in a computer manufacturing firm or the same in a coal mining company as in a department store.

Despite the variance in functions and emphasis from situation to situation, however, there are certain basic functions that can be expected to be found in most legitimate industrial traffic management operations. These functions, of course, mainly have to do with the movement of property or freight, although many traffic departments in large corporations today are also heavily involved in the movement of passengers, i.e., the handling of passenger reservations for traveling employees of the firm and, in some cases, management of company-operated automobiles and/or aircraft. The more important industrial traffic functions are discussed below.

Selection of Modes and Specific Carriers

Mode and carrier selection is probably *the* traffic management function. It is difficult to conceive of a traffic department that does not get involved in this activity.[5] This function involves the selection of transportation modes and specific carriers to use and the purchase of transportation service from those carriers. It is a purchasing activity subject to all the usual purchasing situation constraints and pressures. The factors to consider include such things as points served, economy (rates), transit time, reliability of service, frequency of service, claim record of the carrier, cooperativeness of the carrier, financial stability of

[5] Some surveys have shown, however, that some individuals and departments claiming to be engaged in industrial traffic management do not get involved in selection of modes and carriers. See, for example, Janet Bosworth, "What Does a Traffic Manager Do?" *Distribution Worldwide*, March, 1971.

the carrier, availability of pickup and delivery service, vehicle sizes available, maximum weight restrictions on shipments, minimum shipment weights required to qualify for certain promotional rates, who is to assume responsibility for loading and unloading vehicles, and previous experience with the carrier. Users are also interested in frequency and extent of loss and damage to freight carried, the loading and unloading facilities and equipment needed, protective packaging requirements, and special services, such as transit privileges or refrigerated service, that are available. In addition, there may be reciprocal issues involved when carriers are customers of the using firm, i.e., preference might be given in buying freight transportation service from for-hire carriers to those carriers who are also customers of the user.

Routing

The term *routing* is used here to describe the practice of some industrial traffic managers to indicate the route(s) they want the for-hire carriers to follow. This occurs when more than one route between origin and destination points may be followed by a carrier because he is interchanging or interlining with another carrier(s) (multiple carriers are involved in the haul). Imagine, for example, a shipment by rail from Minneapolis, Minnesota to Miami, Florida. Because railroads serving Minneapolis do not serve south of Chicago, the number of possible rail carriers involved and routings that could be followed is very large. The user has the right, under our regulatory system, to specify the routing to be followed when a rail carload shipment is involved. This means that the user may indicate which carriers are to participate in the haul, at which points the shipment will be transferred from one carrier to another, and the specific routes to be followed by each carrier.

In the case of highway, water, oil pipeline, and air carriers, or when using freight forwarders,[6] there is no legal requirement that the initial carrier or freight forwarder follow the routing instructions of the user. In fact, a great deal of controversy has arisen concerning this matter in connection with highway carriers. However, the general tenor of the cases that have been decided by the Interstate Commerce Commission (ICC) is that interstate highway carriers should follow a user's routing instructions, because to do otherwise would be an "unreasonable practice,"[7] but a highway common carrier may refuse a shipment because the user has specified designated highway carriers. In spite of this interpretation, most highway common-carrier shipments do not contain routing instructions beyond the originating carrier.

Rate Determination

As will be seen later, the rate structure in transportation in the United States is a highly complex matter and rate tariffs (price lists) and classifications (groupings of commodities for rate quotation purposes) used are difficult to deal with.

[6] A freight forwarder is a middleman in transportation who receives small shipments from shippers, consolidates them into larger lots, and buys large-lot transportation from for-hire carriers.

[7] Taff, *Management of Physical Distribution and Transportation,* 5th ed. (Homewood, Illinois: Richard D. Irwin, Inc., 1972), p. 406.

In addition, in some situations, although more than one rate is available to a user, only one rate is "applicable." The result is that, unlike most other pricing situations in other industries, determination of the rate that applies to a given shipment between two points is sometimes difficult and this function has become an important activity in industrial traffic management. The objective is to pay the applicable rate and not pay a rate other than that, particularly one that is higher than the applicable rate. The user should not rely solely on rate quotations received from carriers because the possibility for error is great. In order to accomplish the rate determination task effectively, knowledge of the rate structure and appropriate tariffs and classifications is necessary.

Negotiation with Carriers

It is sometimes assumed that, because parts of the transportation industry in the United States are heavily regulated by government as to rates, services, and so on, decisions about rates and services are made by government and handed down to the carriers and users and the latter do not have any voice in the matter. In practice, as we shall see later, this is not the case. In fact, users are free to negotiate or bargain with carriers on rates charged and services rendered, just as any buyer can negotiate with sellers in other nontransportation industries. Thus, a traffic manager may bargain for a reduced rate or a change in service provided by a for-hire carrier, but when the parties have arrived at a mutually satisfactory conclusion, and if the activity is regulated, the new rate or service must be submitted to the appropriate regulatory authority for approval. The point is that negotiation is possible and it is a function that should be handled by the industrial traffic people.

Participation in Regulatory Process

Because transportation is an activity heavily regulated by government, industrial traffic managers should, in fact may be forced to, participate in the regulatory process. This means keeping up with regulatory developments, preparing evidence, appearing at hearings of regulatory agencies and courts, and actually testifying in these hearings. It also includes assisting the legal representatives of the organization. In order that the interests of the organization are adequately represented, the industrial traffic manager should participate in the process as much as is appropriate.

Processing Claims

Claims for loss or damage may be filed against common carriers when freight arrives at the destination in damaged condition or does not arrive at all.[8] Claims may also be filed against a carrier for losses caused by delay if a carrier has established guaranteed or regular schedules and fails to meet the schedule, thus causing loss to the shipper or consignee. Claims may also be filed for overcharges if a carrier has collected an amount higher than legally appropriate.

The responsibility for gathering the evidence necessary, accumulating the

---

[8]The liability of for-hire carriers for loss and damage is discussed in Chapter 6.

supporting documents required, filing the claims against the carriers, following up on the claims, and appearing in court, if necessary, is appropriately an industrial traffic management function and one of extreme importance to the organization. The traffic manager may also be involved in claim prevention, that is, programs designed to reduce the incidence of loss and damage.

Auditing Freight Bills

Auditing freight bills (invoices received from carriers) is a highly important clerical function in industrial traffic management. The reason that auditing takes on special importance is that the possibility of error on a freight bill is greater than is the case with invoices in most other industries. This is because of the complexity of the rate structure mentioned earlier which means that an incorrect rate may inadvertently be applied to a shipment and thus appear on a freight bill. There is, in fact, evidence that top management in many organizations does not effectively control transportation costs, partly because of its inability to understand and deal with the complex rate structure.[9]

Another reason for the need for carefully auditing freight bills is the large number of freight bills issued daily by carriers of any size. This leads to a greater chance for an arithmetic error or an error to be made in the rate or weight applied to the shipment.

The possibility of error is so great in transportation billing that outside auditing companies offer to audit freight bills after they are paid by the user on the condition that they will be paid a percentage of overcharges they find (usually 50 per cent) and will be paid only if they find an error(s).

Thus, auditing freight bills can be a productive activity in saving money for the user. Auditing requires knowledge of the rate structure and rate tariffs, and it is normally a traffic management function.[10] Auditing may be accomplished either before or after payment of the bills and may include only those freight bills over a certain minimum amount. Because there are legal requirements that set time limits within which freight bills must be paid, many organizations audit freight bills after they are paid. In other cases, organizations have developed pre-payment auditing systems in order to avoid the costly process of recovering overpayments. The pre-payment auditing is sometimes done by an outside firm under a retainer fee arrangement. Many organizations make use of an external auditor in addition to an internal audit. Since the outside post-payment audit often costs nothing unless errors are found, many users of all sizes have their freight bills sent to an outside firm for auditing. Small users are the ones that can benefit the most from an outside audit since they often cannot afford to have any or all of the tariffs available against which to check rates charged and they do not often have experienced people to make an adequate audit. It is, however, misleading to think that an outside post-payment audit is "free" and may be relied on *exclusively* since, if an internal audit is done properly, outside auditors will find nothing and no charge at all will be made.

[9] George L. Stern, "Traffic: Clear Signals for Higher Profits," *Harvard Business Review,* May–June, 1972, p. 73.

[10] The need for improved methods of freight bill auditing is discussed in Mario E. Russo, "Paying Freight Bills Correctly," *Handling and Shipping,* December, 1972.

Operation of Private Transportation

Private transportation (the user operates his own freight or passenger-carrying vehicles) is an important and growing aspect of transportation in the United States. The management of private carriage is often assigned to industrial traffic management.[11]

Providing Information to Other Departments

As traffic management emerged from the green eyeshade era, traffic managers began to get involved in decisions outside the transportation area and to provide information on transportation to other departments and people. For example, industrial traffic managers may advise the marketing people on the transportation implications of a decision to expand the market area served, or they may advise top management when a decision is to be made on introducing a new product. Traffic management may also advise purchasing on quantities to buy and how purchases should be packaged in order to obtain the lowest possible freight rate. Traffic managers may also advise the organization's legal representatives on various transportation-related matters and advise on and participate in plant and warehouse location decisions. These and other examples indicate that perhaps the greatest importance of traffic management lies in these cooperative activities instead of in the more traditional basic functions of traffic management, for example, selection of carriers, rate determination, and so on.

Research

In order to perform effectively in the areas noted above, traffic managers should be involved in various kinds of research. For example, in order to effectively negotiate with carriers, a traffic manager must be prepared with the information necessary to support his case and he may have to do some research to get that information. To participate effectively in the regulatory process, research may be required in order to obtain the necessary information. Other kinds of research that might be done by traffic managers include investigating the pros and cons of using various modes of transportation or various specific carriers, studying the advantages and disadvantages of private transportation, doing research for the purpose of achieving loss and damage reduction, doing research on equipment improvements, and investigating packaging improvement possibilities.

Other Industrial Traffic Management Functions

In addition to the functions above, industrial traffic managers might also be involved in consolidating and pooling shipments (combining small shipments to gain large shipment rates), operating warehouses, packing and marking, loading and unloading vehicles, maintaining tariff files, dealing with demurrage and detention matters (charges made by carriers when a shipper or receiver holds a freight vehicle beyond a specified length of time), preparing shipping documents

---

[11]Private transportation is discussed further in a later section of this chapter.

(in particular, the bill of lading), expediting and tracing shipments, arranging for the movement of employees' household goods, diverting and reconsigning shipments, and arranging for insurance on shipments in transit.

Variance in Industrial Traffic Management Functions

We have noted previously that the functions performed by industrial traffic managers vary with the circumstances, depending on the kind of organization, the kinds of commodities being moved, and so on. In addition, what traffic managers do also depends on their own initiative and ability and what top management expects from them. Thus, of the 10 traffic management functions discussed previously, such as selection of modes and carriers, rate determination, etc., most traffic managers, regardless of their initiative and ability or the demands of top management, are involved in selecting modes and carriers, determining rates, processing claims, and auditing freight bills. Only the better and more progressive traffic people (often in larger organizations), however, attempt to route shipments, negotiate with carriers on rates and services, participate adequately in the regulatory process, provide useful information to other departments and people on a regular basis, and do any kind of meaningful research. In other words, the quality of industrial traffic management, in terms of what is being accomplished, varies considerably from organization to organization.

Computerization of Industrial Traffic Management Functions

Many industrial traffic management people and departments have made use of computers in carrying out the various traffic management functions. Computers have been used in analyzing traffic movements and transportation costs, routing of shipments, preparing bills of lading, processing carrier freight bills, studying possible fixed facility locations, controlling private carrier equipment, forecasting future traffic volumes, and determining applicable freight rates. Some traffic departments also have computer linkups with suppliers, with customers, and with for-hire carriers. Although some progress has been made toward computerizing traffic management activities, traffic management is a long way from complete reliance on computers, and no one has designed a complete system embracing all the areas of data flow bearing on the industrial traffic management function and correlating the necessary interfaces that are essential to a completely informed traffic management operation.[12]

PLACE OF INDUSTRIAL TRAFFIC MANAGEMENT IN THE ORGANIZATION

Organization for Industrial Traffic Management

In larger organizations industrial traffic management is usually the responsibility of a traffic manager and a staff and is usually regarded as a middle-manage-

---

[12]Kenneth U. Flood, *Traffic Management,* 3rd ed. (Dubuque, Iowa: William C. Brown Company Publishers, 1975), pp. 22–23.

ment activity. In some cases, however, the traffic department may be a large group headed by a vice president or a director of transportation who reports directly to the president of the organization. In other cases, the traffic department reports to the purchasing department or the sales manager or other non-transportation department or individual.

In small organizations the traffic management functions may be spread out among several nonspecialists, or not accomplished at all. In other small organizations one person may be in charge of the traffic functions but devote only part of his time to that activity. The employment of a full-time person to handle transportation matters is seldom found in small organizations. When a specific person is responsible for traffic functions, although he may hold the title of traffic manager, he is often without any formal training in traffic management.

It is also true that in small organizations all the usual traffic functions are not being performed. A particular problem in small organizations is the lack of an adequate rate tariff file, which means that the organizations rely on the carriers to tell them what the appropriate rates are and, because the organizations have no tariffs of their own, they cannot make reasonable comparisons among different kinds of transportation and they cannot effectively audit freight bills internally. In small organizations great reliance is made on the carriers for information and advice on routing, services available, and other matters, in addition to rates. Many smaller organizations handle carrier selection and routing in accordance with specific instructions furnished to them by their customers. They may also permit their inbound shipments to be routed by companies from whom they buy.

Regardless of the size of the organization, where there is a specialized industrial traffic management person or staff, industrial traffic management does not have a natural "home" in an organization since it is, in a sense, a service activity performed for many different other departments and individuals in the organization. Thus, it is related to sales, to purchasing, to production, to storage, and so on. Consequently, the traffic management function may be found almost anywhere on an organization chart. In some cases, it is attached to production or manufacturing. In other cases, it is part of the sales operation. In still other cases, it is found under purchasing. In others, it is independent of all other activities in terms of organization.

When industrial traffic management departments exist, they may be organized in several ways. In many cases, they are organized around the modes they deal with or by geographic area or by function. In large organizations with multiunit operations (multiple plants, warehouses, and/or stores) a traffic department can be either centralized or decentralized, depending on the circumstances. Under a decentralized structure, the traffic people at each plant or warehouse or store operate independently of the headquarters office. The traffic department at headquarters, however, may supply information whenever needed, in addition to providing policy guidance. In a centralized traffic management operation the major traffic management functions are performed and the important decisions are made at headquarters with the personnel at plants and warehouses and stores mainly concerned with shipping and receiving freight. Actually, the personnel responsible for shipping and receiving in a decentralized structure may or may not be part of the traffic department. Obviously, combinations and modifications of the decentralized and centralized versions of organization are also possible. The industrial traffic management function in smaller organizations does not ordinarily have to face the problem of decentralization versus centralization.

Industrial Traffic Management and Business Logistics

When an organization has adopted the business logistics concept, as will be defined in Chapter 5, then industrial traffic management becomes part of the logistics effort of the organization, and its organizational place is governed by the organizational structure adopted to accommodate the logistics idea.

Role of the Traffic Consultant

In those situations, usually in small organizations, in which there is too little transportation activity or too little management talent available to assign the management of the transportation function to one person or a few people, outside traffic management consulting firms may be used. These firms usually deal in the more basic traffic management functions, such as selecting carriers, determining rates, and auditing freight bills, but many firms also go beyond that and perform almost all of the usual traffic functions for their clients. For users who cannot justify a specialist within the organization to handle the traffic function, using an outside consultant can be an excellent idea and far superior to neglecting or assigning the function to someone who is not interested in it or qualified to deal with it. Trade associations and chambers of commerce may also provide assistance in dealing with the traffic management problem, for example, a shippers' association[13] may be of help if the organization belongs to such an association.

Status of Industrial Traffic Management in the Organization

The title "industrial traffic manager" is carried by a wide variety of individuals in terms of their ability, motivation, innovativeness, the responsibility given to them by management, and their status in the organization, and they range from people who have the title of vice president working for giant corporations to others who are actually shipping clerks in small businesses.

The status of industrial traffic management, like that of any other activity in an organization, depends on how top management perceives the activity in terms of its importance to the success or failure of the organization. This, in turn, depends in great part on the extent of and complexity of the organization's transportation problems. The greater the role of transportation and its complexity, the greater the status of the traffic management people is likely to be. Indications of the importance and complexity of traffic management in an organization, in

[13]A shippers' association is an organization of small users created for the purpose of consolidating their small shipments into large lots and buying large-lot transportation from for-hire carriers.

addition to the amount of money spent on it, include the F.O.B. points used for inbound and outbound shipments and, hence, whether or not the traffic manager has control over the movements; the amount of choice the organization has in making transportation decisions, given the kinds of commodities dealt with; the importance of reliability of inbound and outbound transportation service to the rest of the organization; the importance of time in transit to the rest of the organization; the seriousness of problems of packaging, loading, and unloading freight; the degree of difficulty in dealing with the rate structure for the commodities the organization is concerned about; the amount of private carriage, if any, the organization engages in; the difficulties associated with transportation of the commodities the organization buys or sells (high susceptibility to loss and damage, for example); and distances from sources of supply and to market areas.[14]

How top management perceives the importance of transportation also depends in part on the ability of the traffic management people to "sell" the importance of what they are doing. In many cases, traffic people have failed to convince top management of their importance. The traffic peoples' importance also depends on the capabilities of the people in traffic management to perform well.

Unfortunately, top management often tends to measure the importance of traffic management mainly by the amount of money spent to move goods, either in an absolute sense or as a percentage of sales, or both, thus ignoring the various contributions that good traffic management makes, some of which are not quantifiable. The latter include improving transportation service to customers, thereby increasing customer satisfaction with the organization, and providing various services to other departments or individuals in the organization itself, for example, providing information on transportation costs to salespeople, which makes for a smoother running, more efficient organization.

The emphasis on the size of the freight bill also means that the effectiveness of traffic management is often measured by top management in terms of the amount of money it saves. Thus, a telephone and mail survey conducted by a trade magazine reported on in 1973 asked traffic and distribution people which activities their top management considered most important. The first ranking answer was "money you save the company in transportation/distribution."[15] Actually, the amount of money saved by good traffic management is a poor measure of traffic's productivity. Dollars saved are used as a measure because of management's interest in the transportation bill, it is an easy measure to use, and other better measures often are not readily available.

In many organizations the traffic manager has not ranked high in the management hierarchy. Most traffic managers of the past and a large number today cannot be properly classified as high-level managers.[16] Thus, traffic management is rarely considered to be at the top in a list of functional areas when ranked on their importance to the organization. For example, in a large food processing firm in which the freight bill is fairly high, there is an elaborate system of evaluation of each job or position in the firm relative to its contribution to the success

[14] Flood, *Traffic Management*, pp. 7–9.

[15] Janet Bosworth Dower, "How Top Management Evaluates the Traffic/Distribution Function," *Distribution Worldwide*, May, 1973.

[16] Roy J. Sampson and Martin T. Farris, *Domestic Transportation: Practice, Theory, and Policy*, 3rd ed. (Boston: Houghton-Mifflin Company, 1975), p. 256.

of the firm. The traffic positions are consistently ranked as being less important than positions in other areas of the firm.

There has, however, been a general upgrading of the status of traffic management. Thus,

> The traditional concept of the transportation department as specialists in freight rates, routing, service, complex transportation laws, etc., has undergone a change. In more and more companies today the traffic man is respected as a full-fledged operating executive, at times on the vice-president level. Sharp increases in freight transportation costs and the realization that the transportation–distribution complex is a major cost element in almost every industry have had a great deal to do with this change. Beyond that is the realization that transportation is tied in closely with important phases of company profits.[17]

In any event, the status of industrial traffic management varies widely from organization to organization ranging from large, independent departments headed by directors of traffic or vice presidents of transportation to situations in which the traffic manager is subordinate to and reports to some other functional area such as production or purchasing. In some organizations traffic management is regarded as a highly specialized and technical activity not really involved in higher-level decision making. In other organizations, and increasingly so, traffic management is regarded as an important part of the management structure and is given appropriate status in the organization.

PRIVATE TRANSPORTATION

One of the alternatives that users have in managing freight transportation is to make use of private transportation. Private transportation (the user and the operator of the vehicle are one and the same) has been a growing phenomenon in American freight transportation for many years. It is today found in all modes of transportation and is of particular importance in highway and water transportation. The growth of private transportation has been such that some observers have warned that it will eventually destroy for-hire common carriage by taking away the most lucrative freight traffic and leaving the less profitable and less desirable traffic for the for-hire carriers. One writer has stated that it is practically inevitable that sooner or later the government must prohibit private carriage of general commodities above certain levels because of its adverse effects on common carriers.[18] It may be argued, however, that private carriage keeps pressure high on common carriers and keeps them technologically progressive and efficient and, thus, it is a benefit to society.

In addition to private carriage of freight, private transportation also exists in passenger transportation where it is dominated by the privately operated automobile.

---

[17]Charles H. Wager, Richard C. Colton, and Edmund S. Ward, *Industrial Traffic Management*, 5th ed. (Washington, D.C.: The Traffic Service Corporation, 1973), pp. 385–386.

[18]Warren Blanding, "The Shipper's Dilemma," *Transportation and Distribution Management*, October, 1973, p. 18.

Importance of Private Transportation

Because private carriage is not a regulated activity, reporting private carrier traffic to government agencies usually is not required. The result is that the total amount and kinds of freight traffic carried in private transportation are really unknown. It has been estimated that in 1975, 62.3 per cent of all intercity freight ton–miles were under federal economic regulation, with the balance accounted for by unregulated for-hire carriage, for-hire carriage regulated by the states, and by private carriage.[19] There is no way of knowing what share of the remaining 37.7 per cent was private carriage. The percentage under federal regulation was slightly higher (62.3 per cent versus 59.1 per cent) than it was in 1962, perhaps indicating that regulated common carriage has been doing well in its struggle against private and other nonregulated transportation.

Forms of Private Transportation

Private transportation of freight is found is all 5 modes of transportation, although its importance varies considerably from mode to mode.

Railroad. In the case of railroads, there are some "industrial" railroads in the country which are found in large industrial complexes, such as steel plants or mining companies, and which are, in a sense, a form of private carriage, although they are usually operated by separate companies (controlled by the user) and they interchange freight with for-hire railroads.

More important than industrial or private railroads are the thousands of private railroad freight cars—cars that are owned or leased by users but are hauled in freight trains operated by for-hire railroads and over the railroads' tracks. An allowance based on mileage is paid by the railroad to the car owner or lessee for the use of the car. In 1976 approximately 20 per cent (332,870) of the nation's fleet of approximately 1.7 million freight cars were owned by shippers or car companies.[20] Many of the cars owned by car companies are leased to users for use as private cars.

The principal reason for using private rail cars is that the user needs specialized cars, such as refrigerator or tank cars, that the railroads do not ordinarily provide. In addition, users sometimes enter into private car ownership or leasing in order to avoid demurrage charges caused by holding freight cars beyond time limits set by the railroads.

Oil Pipeline. As will be seen later, most of the slightly more than 100 oil pipeline companies in the United States are owned and operated by oil companies. However, most of these oil pipeline companies, plus those owned by non-oil company owners, serve as for-hire common carriers in that they carry the crude oil or products of crude oil of any oil company on a for-hire basis. A few confine their activities to carrying the shipments of their own oil company only and are

---

[19]Transportation Association of America, *Transportation Facts and Trends,* 13th ed. (Washington, D.C.: Transportation Association of America, July, 1977), p. 9.

[20]Association of American Railroads, *Railroad Facts,* 1977 ed. (Washington, D.C.: Association of American Railroads, 1977), p. 49.

classified as private carriers. In 1975 84 percent of the oil pipeline intercity ton-miles were regulated by the federal government.[21] The remainder was either regulated by the states or was private carriage.

Air. Private air transportation of freight is limited. In fact, the Transportation Association of America does not include any private transportation in its annual estimates of air freight traffic.[22] Although private (general) aviation aircraft in the United States numbered 182,000, as compared with only 2,260 scheduled airline aircraft in 1976,[23] very few of them were involved in the movement of freight. In most cases, shippers do not have enough air freight traffic to support a private aircraft operation.[24] Private air transportation is much more prevalent in the passenger side of transportation, including a fair amount of business-controlled aircraft used to transport business personnel.

Water. In domestic water transportation along and between ocean coasts and on the Great Lakes, and in river and canal transportation, private or "proprietary" or "industrial" transportation is fairly extensive. In the case of the Great Lakes, much of the private carriage is found in iron ore and taconite traffic in which ore boats owned by steel companies ply between the Lake Superior area and ports on Lake Michigan and Lake Erie. On the rivers, barge transportation is operated by chemical, coal, grain, and other shippers of bulk commodities. It is estimated that only approximately 0.3 of 1 per cent of Great Lakes traffic (intercity ton-miles), 15.5 per cent of river and canal traffic, and 4.1 per cent of domestic deep-sea traffic in 1975 were subject to federal economic regulation.[25] The remainder was for-hire carriage exempt from regulation, or was regulated by the states, or was private. In 1965 it was reported that there were 1,700 companies engaged in commercial domestic water transportation on the inland waterways of the United States, and 400 of these were private carriers.[26]

Highway. It is in highway transportation that private carriage has developed the most extensively. There were 24,607,708 trucks registered in the United States in 1975.[27] Approximately 96 per cent of these trucks were in private transportation.[28] Even very small organizations use private trucking if the circumstances

---

[21] Transportation Association of America, *Transportation Facts and Trends*, p. 9.

[22] *Ibid.*

[23] Air Transport Association of America, *Air Transport, 1977* (Washington, D.C.: Air Transport Association of America, 1977), p. 28.

[24] The possibilities of private air transportation of freight are discussed in Joseph S. Coyle, "Private Carriage in the Air?" *Traffic Management,* June, 1969 and in R. Stanley Chapman, "Air Cargo Marketers Ponder Threat Posed by Shipper Interest in Private Jet Fleets," *Traffic World,* March 15, 1969, p. 21. A successful private air freight operation is discussed in "Why Blue Bell Flies by the Seat of its Jeans," *Business Week,* November, 1973, p. 48.

[25] Transportation Association of America, *Transportation Facts and Trends*, p. 9.

[26] American Waterways Operators, Inc., *Big Load Afloat* (Washington, D.C.: American Waterways Operators, Inc., 1965), p. 3.

[27] American Trucking Associations, Inc., *American Trucking Trends, 1976 Statistical Supplement* (Washington, D.C.: American Trucking Associations, Inc., 1977), p. 17.

[28] *Ibid.,* p. 20.

are right. Although the great majority of private trucks are single-unit trucks used in local service, the vehicles range from small panel or pickup trucks to large fleets of large tractor-trailer combinations. Approximately 56 per cent of total intercity truck ton-miles were in nonfederal regulated service in 1975,[29] much of this in private transportation. According to one writer, fully 40 per cent of the intercity truck ton–miles are believed to be performed by private carriers.[30] Private transportation by highway is so extensive that two large organizations, the Private Carrier Conference of the American Trucking Associations and the Private Truck Council of America, represent private truck interests in Washington, D.C.

Reasons for Using Private Transportation

Shippers and receivers become involved in private transportation as an alternative to for-hire freight transportation or in addition to for-hire transportation for a variety of reasons. These reasons fall generally into two broad categories— cost savings and service improvements.

Cost Savings. Cost savings in private transportation compared with for-hire transportation may occur whenever private operations are efficient enough to generate costs that are lower than those incurred when using for-hire carriage and paying for-hire transportation rates. In fact, there is a correlation between for-hire carrier rate increases and the incidence of private carriage. It should be noted, however, that, in many cases, users have gone into private transportation when costs would not be lower than when using for-hire carriers, in fact, even when costs would be higher, because of the service advantages received from private carriage. A service consideration in deciding to use private transportation is that transportation is an element in an overall logistics system and the higher cost of private transportation may pay off in cost reductions elsewhere, particularly in inventory costs.[31]

Service Improvements. There are several kinds of service advantages that may be found in private carriage, some of which also might result in cost savings. Some of these service advantages are discussed in the following paragraphs.

Faster delivery time may be a reason for entering into private carriage. This is particularly likely to result if the for-hire carriers are involved in interlining or interchanging the freight with other carriers and especially when small shipments are involved. Faster delivery time, in turn, offers other benefits to the organization, for example, lower inventory levels.

Special transportation requirements of the user, such as the need to handle very small shipments, special requirements for delivery, or the need for very precise time schedules, may be met more easily with private than with for-hire transportation.

[29]Transportation Association of America, *Transportation Facts and Trends*, p. 9.

[30]Allen Van Cranebrook, "Private Carriage: Facts and Fallacies," *Traffic Management*, June, 1969, p. 45.

[31]The results of a survey among shippers dealing with their reasons for entering into private highway transportation are reported in "Survey: Private Carriage," *Transportation and Distribution Management*, July–August, 1974.

A leading reason for private carriage is that it enables the user to have better control of the transportation activity and the service provided to the organization and its customers. This control reveals itself in various ways, and it includes better control over pickup and delivery schedules, overall time elapsed between pickup and delivery, the kind of equipment used, personal dealings between transportation employees and customers, and so on. In addition, private carriage enables the user to avoid stoppages caused by for-hire carrier labor problems or equipment shortages.

Because of better control over the transportation function, private carriage can be better coordinated with other aspects of an organization's operation. Transportation can be made more readily available when it is needed rather than at the convenience of a for-hire carrier. Thus, a private carrier operation may be more satisfactorily tied in with production line schedules on both the inbound and the outbound sides than when using for-hire carriers.

Because private-carrier transportation is not subject to government economic regulation, there are few, if any, limitations on where it can operate geographically, unlike the case with many regulated for-hire carriers. Thus, a user can use private carriage to reach geographic points not served well or at all by regulated for-hire carriers.

Unlike regulated for-hire carriers, there are no restrictions on what a private carrier can carry, provided that what is being carried is legitimate private carriage and that state-imposed size and weight limits are observed.

A benefit that may accrue from private carriage is that, through more careful handling, and perhaps less handling, there may be less loss and damage to freight if the freight is under the complete control of the user than under the control of for-hire carriers. This, in turn, results in better relations with customers and suppliers and in lower cost because claim processing is eliminated and because less expensive protective packaging is needed. Less expensive packaging can also result because, with private carriage, the user does not have to adhere to the packing specifications of for-hire carriers.

Private carriage usually is much more flexible than for-hire carriage in adapting to the changing needs of the user in terms of where service can be performed, what can be carried, when pickups and deliveries can be made, what kind of vehicles can be used, and routes followed. In addition, it is more flexible because special services can be more easily obtained in emergencies.

In some cases, users enter into private transportation because they need specialized vehicles that common carriers do not ordinarily provide. In the highway carrier field, for example, there is a tremendous variety of vehicles that can be used. For-hire common carriers find it difficult to have a wide variety available to users. Private transportation also makes it possible for users to avail themselves of technological changes in vehicles whenever they occur.

A positive result of private highway carriage, particularly if it is used as a complete substitute for for-hire transportation, is that the user avoids the loading dock congestion that often results when several for-hire carriers are used and their vehicles arrive at the loading dock at approximately the same time because of lack of coordination among them. This congestion can be avoided when the user controls the vehicles via private carriage. The user can also avoid detention and demurrage charges when he operates his own vehicles.

Other Reasons for Private Transportation. In addition to the cost and service considerations noted above, there are other reasons for using private rather than, or in addition to, for-hire transportation.

Private carriage avoids problems associated with regulated for-hire transportation in addition to avoiding restrictions on points served and commodities carried. As will be seen later, there is usually considerable regulatory delay when a regulated for-hire carrier attempts to adjust rates and/or services to meet the needs of his customers, delays which are avoided when private carriage is used. The user is also relieved of the task of dealing with the regulatory mechanism, i.e., attending hearings, preparing evidence, etc., when using private carriage.

Sometimes the use of private transportation is intended as a threat to for-hire carriers. If the for-hire carriers' rates and services are not satisfactory to the user, the private carriage operation may be expanded and the for-hire carriers may eventually be eliminated from that user's transportation program.

Finally, a benefit that accrues from private transportation is that the vehicles can bear the advertising of the user at lower cost than if some other medium were used. This assumes, of course, that the vehicles are clean and have a generally good apperance and, thus, convey a positive image of the organization.

Reasons for Not Using Private Transportation

As indicated above, the benefits that might be derived by a user from private transportation can be significant. There are, however, important drawbacks associated with private transportation that lead users to limit their use of it or to avoid it altogether. The result is that the majority of intercity freight traffic in the United States is carried by for-hire carriers. The disadvantages associated with private carriage are discussed in the following paragraphs.

Cost. In some cases, private transportation is too expensive in relation to the cost of using for-hire carriage. This is particularly true when the organization has a traffic pattern not suited for private carriage (see below) or when the commodity involved is one whose for-hire carrier rates are relatively low, for example, some bulk commodities.

Wrong Traffic Pattern. A leading reason for avoiding private transportation is that the organization does not have a traffic pattern suitable for economical private carrier operation. Although this problem is more likely to occur with smaller users, it can occur with organizations of any size. The problem exists if the organization does not have enough total traffic to justify operating its own vehicle(s) (usually small users) or if its traffic, although substantial in total, is not concentrated heavily enough between any set of origin and destination points or on any route(s) to justify operating vehicles in private carriage. Thus, a firm making many small shipments to widely separated points may not be able to operate a private transportation system economically. The dispersed traffic means that the vehicle(s) would be operating at less than full capacity, thus incurring costs per ton–mile perhaps higher than would be incurred if for-hire carriers were used.

A traffic pattern problem also exists when the user, although having substantial traffic on a given route has traffic mainly or only in one direction, with little or no traffic in the opposite direction, although the vehicle(s) must be returned to the origin point. This unbalanced traffic problem occurs to some degree in all modes of transportation, except pipelines, both private and for-hire, and its significance in a decision to undertake private carriage varies with each situation.

This return haul or back haul problem is aggravated by regulatory restrictions that apply to what private carriers are allowed to carry. Generally speaking, private carriers are not permitted to carry regulated commodities on a for-hire basis for other parties on the back haul in order to utilize the otherwise empty or partially empty equipment. This matter has received considerable attention in the case of interstate private highway carrier operations. The result of the rulings handed down by the ICC is that the alternatives available to a private highway carrier on the return haul are to (1) buy something and carry it back to the origin point and use it in the business of the organization, (2) carry commodities exempt from regulation (mainly agricultural products) for-hire, (3) return empty or practically empty, or (4) carry for-hire on an illegal basis and hope not to be detected.[32]

Thus, because of these restrictions, if a user has a return haul problem with private carriage, he may decide to forego private carriage entirely.

Administrative Considerations. Some organizations decide to stay out of private carriage because they do not want to dilute their administrative resources in order to carry out an activity that is not really part of their main mission, or the organizations do not have the administrative talent available. It should be also noted that management of private transportation often requires management skills and accounting procedures and labor relations problems that may be difficult to deal with. Not entering private carriage avoids these management problems.

Capital Investment. Private transportation is avoided in some cases because the user either does not have the capital required to invest in vehicles or the user prefers to use his capital in the main business of the organization and not in transportation.

Union Considerations. When entering into private transportation, the organization should take into account the matter of labor force requirements. If the labor to be used in operating and maintaining vehicles is unionized, the organization may prefer to not enter private carriage if the organization has a non-union policy or if it does not want to get involved with another union or with the particular union involved.

Reciprocal Considerations. Sometimes the for-hire carriers are important customers of the user and the user wishes to avoid the ill will that would be created

---

[32] Leasing a truck along with the driver to someone else for a single trip on back hauls (trip leasing) is possible in some states, but in other states it is illegal. It is unlawful in interstate commerce unless the initial haul involves the carriage of agricultural commodities. The legal problems associated with private truck transportation are dealt with further in Chapter 22.

by entering private transportation. This is a matter of reciprocation, meaning that the organization will buy transportation service from those carriers who buy from the organization. In addition, traffic managers sometimes are reluctant to go into private carriage on a partial basis for fear of alienating the for-hire carriers they will continue to rely on to move the bulk of their freight.

Adequate For-Hire Service. Finally, when a user finds that the transportation service received from for-hire carriers is satisfactory, and at reasonable cost, he does not even consider private carriage.

Purchasing Versus Leasing Equipment

When a decision is made to enter into private transportation, the organization must also decide whether to purchase or to lease the vehicle(s) to be used. The pros and cons of purchasing versus leasing are similar to those found in any purchasing versus leasing situation and are beyond the scope of this book. It is well to note, however, that leasing equipment can help to avoid several of the problems associated with private carriage. In the case of highway transportation, for example, a "full-service" lease may be entered into in which the leasing company provides the vehicle(s) and all maintenance, service, record keeping, insurance, washing, fuel, and even garaging, and pays all the taxes involved. All the user provides is the driver (if leasing companies could legally provide drivers, they would probably do so). The lease is usually for 5 years and the vehicle is fully depreciated at the end of the lease period. When such an arrangement is entered into, the user avoids several of the problems associated with private transportation, including the need for extensive administration of the operation, the need for capital investment, and tying up capital. The user also has better control over expenses because he knows the cost of operating the vehicle(s) in advance. In addition, the equipment used is more flexible, the risks of ownership are avoided, and there is no possiblity of loss due to obsolescence. The cost of leasing, however, is relatively high, and after the lease expires the user has no equity in the vehicle(s).

Making the Private Transportation Decision

Deciding whether or not the organization should enter into private transportation should be made with traffic management considerations in mind. Although the traffic manager cannot in most cases be expected to be given the responsibility of making the decision (these decisions are ordinarily made at higher levels in the organization), traffic people should participate in the decision and, perhaps, manage the operation if the decision is made to enter private carriage.

As has been pointed out earlier, there are many possible advantages that may result from the use of private transportation. There are, of course, reasons why a particular organization should not engage in private transportation, as we have also seen. In any event, the decision to enter into private transportation and to what extent should not be made without some analysis of the transportation needs of the organization and the advantages and disadvantages associated with user-operated vehicles. Private transportation certainly should not be entered into just because it is the usual practice of the industry or because of other similar reasons.

One of the objects of study should be costs. Private transportation costs should be compared with costs incurred when using for-hire transportation. Costs, however, should not be the only consideration for, as we have seen, other things, for example, better service to customers, may outweigh the fact that costs are higher with private carriage. But costs may, in some cases, be the most important factor and, in any case, they should be studied so that they can be properly controlled, even though they are not the primary consideration in deciding on private transportation.

In analyzing costs, care should be taken to ensure that all costs are included in the analysis of private carrier costs, including wages, employee-related taxes, and employee fringe benefits; employee training and safety programs and employee expenses away from home; interest on investment, depreciation on equipment and buildings, and insurance on vehicles, buildings, and goods carried; license fees and other user taxes, toll charges, and road fines; accidents; personal property taxes; maintenance, emergency repair costs away from the organization's facilities, and repair parts; fuel; utilities; office, garaging, and repair space; accounting and bookkeeping costs; and clerical and supervisory costs and executive time.

Service considerations must also be accounted for in the analysis, including those discussed earlier. One service factor easily overlooked is that the user of private transportation is vulnerable to fluctuations in demand for transportation service. These fluctuations may result in equipment shortages some of the time and idle equipment at other times.

The decision to use private carriage need not be an either–or proposition because a combination of both private and for-hire service can be used. Thus, whenever appropriate, many organizations use both forms. Unfortunately for for-hire carriers, this often means that the higher-grade, larger shipments are carried by private vehicles while the low rate-paying traffic and smaller shipment traffic destined for out-of-the-way places is consigned to for-hire carriers. Since users withhold high-rated traffic from for-hire carriers, the private carrier is able to "make money" because he can lower his transportation costs, but the common carrier has to raise his charges in order to compensate for the loss of these revenues.[33] This is one of the reasons why some observers predict that private carriage may eventually destroy for-hire common carriage in the United States.

SELECTED REFERENCES

There are several books dealing with the general subject of industrial traffic management, including Charles A. Taff, *Management of Physical Distribution and Transportation,* 5th ed. (Homewood, Illinois: Richard D. Irwin, Inc., 1972) and Kenneth U. Flood, *Traffic Management,* 3rd ed. (Dubuque, Iowa: William C. Brown Company Publishers, 1975.)

[33] Paul H. Reistrip, "Private Carriage: Benefit, Problem, Threat," *Transportation and Distribution Management,* September, 1973, p. 1.

An excellent discussion of the development of industrial traffic management may be found in Roy J. Sampson and Martin T. Farris, *Domestic Transportation: Practice, Theory, and Policy,* 3rd ed. (Boston: Houghton-Mifflin Company, 1975), pp. 255–259.

The functions involved in industrial traffic management are discussed in Charles A. Taff, *Traffic Management Principles and Practices,* rev. ed. (Homewood, Illinois: Richard D. Irwin, Inc., 1959), Chapter 1. The functions performed by industrial traffic managers, as indicated by a survey among traffic executives, are discussed in Janet Bosworth, "What Does a Traffic Manger Do?" *Distribution Worldwide,* March, 1971.

The organization for traffic management is discussed in Charles H. Wager, Richard C. Colton, and Edmund S. Ward, *Industrial Traffic Management,* 5th ed. (Washington, D.C.: The Traffic Service Corporation, 1973), Chapter 14 and in Taff, *Management of Traffic and Physical Distribution,* 3rd ed., 1964, Chapter 2. See also John H. Frederick, *Traffic Department Organization* (Philadelphia: Chilton Company, 1956). The planning for and organization for industrial traffic management activities in small business firms is dealt with in Donald V. Harper, *Basic Planning and the Transportation Function in Small Manufacturing Firms* (Minneapolis: School of Business Administration, University of Minnesota, 1961). Traffic management as an element in a business logistics system is discussed in James L. Heskett, Nicholas A. Glaskowsky, Jr., and Robert M. Ivie, *Business Logistics,* 2nd ed. (New York: The Ronald Press Company, 1973), Chapter 19.

Most of the literature on private transportation deals with private highway transportation. The economics of private highway transportation are discussed in Walter Y. Oi and Arthur P. Hurter, Jr., *Economics of Private Truck Transportation* (Dubuque, Iowa: William C. Brown Company, Inc., 1965). The costs of private trucking are dealt with in William J. Morgan, "The Financial Aspects of Private Truck Fleets—Capital/Operating Cost Analysis," *Transportation Journal,* Summer, 1970 and Dwight Stuessy, "Cost Structure of Private and For-Hire Motor Carriage," *Transportation Journal,* Spring, 1976. The pros and cons of private trucking, and the decision process to follow in entering into private trucking, are discussed in Kenneth U. Flood, "Questions in Company-Operated Transport," *Harvard Business Review,* January–February, 1961 and *Traffic Management,* Chapter 2. The decision to use private carriage is discussed in Taff, *Management of Physical Distribution and Transportation,* 5th ed., pp. 178–194. See also William A. Tett, "Financial Considerations in Planning for Private Motor Transportation," *Transportation Journal,* Winter, 1972 and Thomas R. Henke, "Going Private? Simulate First," *Transportation and Distribution Management,* January–February, 1976. Colin Barrett, "The Elements of Private Carriage," *Transportation and Distribution Management,* July, August, and September, 1970 is a 3-part article dealing with the advantages and disadvantages, the regulatory requirements, and the managerial decision related to private truck transportation.

The characteristics of private trucking as indicated by Census of Transportation data are analyzed in James P. Rakowski, "Characteristics of Private Trucking in the United States," *ICC Practitioners' Journal,* July–August, 1974. For the results of a study of 9,950 current and prospective members of the Private Carrier Conference to determine the reasons for and characteristics of private trucking, see "Private Carriage—All We Want Are the Facts," *Handling and Shipping*, October–November, 1967. See also "Preliminary Data on Private Trucking Survey Show 77% Don't Haul Exempt Commodities," *Traffic World*, June 17, 1967, p. 50. The extent of private highway transportation as revealed by a survey among shippers is reported in Robert M. Butler, "Private Carriage Is Dominant Transport Factor—47.2% of Major Shippers Operate Own Trucks," *Traffic World*, February 11, 1974, p. 77. The use of private truck transportation by small manufacturers is discussed in Harper, *Basic Planning and the Transportation Function*, pp. 24–29 and 40–41.

Leasing equipment to use in private transportation is dealt with in William B. Wagner, "The Choice of Leasing," *Transportation and Distribution Management*, October, 1970. See also Tom Foster, "Leasing: Decisions, Decisions," *Distribution Worldwide*, May, 1977.

5

Business Logistics Management

In this chapter we continue our discussion of the implications of transportation for the user. The chapter is devoted to business logistics management, an activity broader than industrial traffic management, but of which industrial traffic management is a very important part. The discussion deals mainly with business logistics as it applies to business firms although the concept is applicable to other kinds of organizations as well.

PHYSICAL SUPPLY AND PHYSICAL DISTRIBUTION

As we shall see, business logistics management can be divided into two parts, management of physical supply and management of physical distribution.

Physical Supply and Physical Distribution Defined

Physical supply has to do with the inbound side of the problem of moving goods and includes all those activities required to move physical goods, such as raw materials, parts, or finished goods, from their source of supply to the place of processing, manufacture, or resale (the latter would be the case in wholesaling and retailing). Physical distribution includes all those activities necessary to move physical goods from the point of their processing, manufacture, or resale to customers.

For example, for a steel manufacturer, physical supply has to do with the movement of iron ore or taconite, coal, and other materials from their source of supply to the steel-making facility. Physical distribution has to do with the movement of the finished steel plates, bars, and so on, to the firm's customers who may be manufacturers in other industries, wholesalers, contractors, and others.

Increasing Interest in Physical Supply and Physical Distribution

Since the early 1950's there has been an increasing interest on the part of business firms in the problems of physical supply and physical distribution and how these activities may be made more efficient and carried out at a lower cost. The military logistics experience of World War II and the increasing uses of systems analysis and quantitative methods in management accelerated this interest. Specific reasons for the increased interest in these subjects are many and include those described in the following paragraphs.

Competition. Despite the general prosperity that has prevailed throughout most of the post-World War II period in the United States, competition has been very active in most industries and the firms in those industries have been pressed to find ways to be more effective competitors in order to succeed. Improvement in the service derived from and in the cost incurred in physical supply and physical distribution presented opportunities to be more effective competitors.

Narrow Profit Margins. Small profit margins in some industries, and declining profit margins in some cases, encouraged business firms to seek ways to reduce costs and to improve service to customers in the hopes of improving the profit picture.

Rising Physical Movement Costs. The costs of performing the various functions involved in moving goods have risen in the post-World War II period, particularly in certain industries. This has encouraged business managers to try to manage physical supply and physical distribution in such a way that they can keep these costs at the lowest level possible. Although freight rate increases were not a leading factor, increased costs associated with the other activities involved in physical supply and physical distribution were important. For example, the fact that wholesalers and retailers were curtailing their inventory levels, thus pushing the inventory problem and its costs back onto manufacturers, contributed to the greater costs of physical supply and physical distribution of many manufacturers.

Proliferation of Products. As a consequence of the intense competition in many industries, business firms since World War II have introduced many new products and new variations of old products to the market with the result that the number of different products and versions of products increased, thus proliferating product lines. When proliferation occurs, there are more products to be stored, transported, and kept under management control. The problems associated with physical supply and physical distribution become much more complex and difficult to deal with and inefficiency tends to increase. These facts have led firms that have wide product lines to become interested in improving their management of physical supply and physical distribution.

Increased Customer Orientation. It was in the 1950's and 1960's that many American business firms became more oriented toward the needs of their customers and adopted what became known as the *marketing concept.* This led these firms to be concerned about the kind and quality of service being performed for customers, many aspects of which involve physical distribution considerations.

Availability of Computers. Increasing interest in physical supply and physical distribution coincided with the introduction and general availability of computers. Before the computer age, the many variables and considerable data, and the many details involved in physical supply and physical distribution, could not readily be handled and analyzed manually, even in those cases in which there was interest in doing so. Consequently, it was not until computers were available that strides could be made toward analysis, planning, and improvement of physical supply and physical distribution systems. An important factor was that computers made simulation of such systems possible and, thereby, added to the ability to successfully plan and operate them. Most organizations that have adopted the business logistics idea rely heavily on the use of computers in business logistics management.

Lack of Attention in the Past. Finally, physical movement of goods had in many organizations been neglected in the past, in terms of any real analysis and planning. When competitive pressures and low profit margins emerged, physical supply and physical distribution appeared to be a good place to seek improvement.

CONCEPT OF BUSINESS LOGISTICS MANAGEMENT

As the interest in physical supply and physical distribution increased, and as some industrial traffic managers broadened their interests into areas beyond just transportation, a new management concept began to develop which we call business logistics management.

Business Logistics Management Defined

Business logistics management, as defined here, deals with the *coordination* of the physical movement aspects of an organization's operations so that a *flow* of raw materials, parts, and/or finished goods (both inbound and outbound) is achieved in such a way that *cost* in minimized for the levels of *service* desired. The key words in the definition are italicized—coordination, flow, cost, and service.[1]

---

[1] The terminology in the field of business logistics varies somewhat and there is no generally accepted title for or definition of the concept. The reader is cautioned that many writers and business firms use the term *physical distribution management* essentially to describe the entire logistics system, both inbound and outbound, but in this text *physical distribution* refers to the outbound side only. Other terms used are materials management, total distribution management, industrial logistics management, distribution logistics management, and marketing logistics management. In addition, different writers and practitioners include somewhat different activities under the concept.

A simple diagram of a business logistics system is shown in Figure 5-1.

FIGURE 5-1 *Business Logistics System.*

The objective in business logistics is for the organization to get the right thing in the right quantity to the right place at the right time at the right cost and in good condition. The system starts at the source of inbound materials and ends when goods are delivered to customers. Both the inbound side (physical supply) and the outbound side (physical distribution) are part of the system and the idea, as indicated in the definition given above, is to coordinate all the activities involved in physical supply and physical distribution in such a way that a flow of materials through the logistics system is developed. This is sometimes referred to as the *systems approach* in that the entire process of moving goods—both physical supply and physical distribution—is viewed as one continuous flow or system. This should all be done at the lowest possible cost while still achieving the desired service levels for the organization's customers.

Every organization that deals in physical products has a logistics system and the concept of business logistics management, as presented here, can be applied to any such organization, regardless of size and whether or not it is a profit-making or nonprofit organization. In some organizations, the entire flow or system is important. In others, either the problems of physical supply or those of physical distribution may dominate. Retailing is an activity in which the problems of physical supply are more important than the problems of physical distribution. A coal mining firm, however, is concerned primarily with physical distribution instead of physical supply.

Service Levels as a Constraint

The definition of business logistics management given above indicates that the logistics system is to be designed so that the desired service levels are achieved. Service levels are important in all stages of a logistics system, in both physical supply and in physical distribution. The service levels referred to in the definition of business logistics management are *customer* service levels and they are the culmination of the entire logistics effort, including both physical supply and physical distribution. Customer service levels have to do with the kind of and quality of logistics service to be given to customers and can be described in various ways. Since the service level factors are goals or objectives, they are also constraints on the designer of the system. They are the limits within which the designer must work.

It should be clear to the reader, then, that business logistics management is an important part of the relationship between seller and buyer and that it is an important aspect of the marketing effort of the seller and a key aspect of the channel of distribution being used by the seller. Some logistics customer service level factors are discussed in the following paragraphs.

Customer Delivery Requirements. A logistics system must take into account the physical delivery requirements of customers, meaning which modes of transportation they desire to make deliveries to them. This must be considered whether transportation is actually controlled by the buyer or by the seller. Some customers have rail sidings; an increasing number do not. Some prefer to use their own trucks and pick up shipments instead of having them delivered by for-hire carriers. Ideally, a logistics system will take these different preferences into account. The reliability and frequency of delivery are also important to customers and must be considered in setting up a business logistics system.

Size of order. A logistics system must also provide for handling the size of order customers prefer to place, whether it be carloads or very small shipments. This, in turn, greatly affects the modes of transportation to be used and the need for and location of warehouses. The assortment of different items that a customer can request in one order is also a factor to be taken into account.

Delivery Time. An extremely important customer service level factor is the delivery time that is acceptable to customers. Delivery time is ordinarily measured by counting the time elapsed between the placing of an order by a customer and the time the actual delivery to the customer is made (order cycle time). It could be a matter of minutes or hours or a matter of months. In any case, delivery time is usually a key element in logistics system design and has a lot to do with modal choice and warehouse need and location.

Out-of-Stock Levels. The out-of-stock ratio refers to the proportion of orders that the seller is unable to fill at a warehouse, plant, or store because the item requested is not in stock. The seller must decide what out-of-stock ratios are acceptable to customers. For example, a firm may decide that a ratio of 95 per cent is satisfactory on a certain item, meaning that it is acceptable if the item is available in stock in 95 out of 100 cases when an order for it is received. In most cases, the firm must weigh the desires of salespeople and customers for a situation where the firm is never out of stock and the associated high costs of carrying a high level of inventory against the economies associated with carrying a lower level of inventory. The out-of-stock levels established have a significant impact on inventory management and costs and modes of transportation used.

Condition of Goods. As we shall see in Chapter 6, lost or damaged goods are a serious problem in transportation in the United States. One of the important service level factors is the amount and frequency of loss and damage that customers will tolerate. This consideration affects decisions on transportation modes and specific carriers and can also influence warehouse location and design decisions as well as material handling practices.

A Total Cost Approach

The definition of business logistics management given earlier refers to minimizing costs. The costs to be minimized in a logistics system are the *total* costs of moving goods, not just the costs of individual logistics activities, such as transportation or warehousing. The idea is to minimize the aggregate logistics costs. This may mean increasing the costs of performing some of the activities and decreasing the costs of other activities.

Activities Involved in Business Logistics Management

Business logistics management involves elements of several major functional areas in a firm's operations, including purchasing, production management, finance, traffic, and marketing. The idea is to coordinate the various specific activities involved in moving goods. What are these activities? Although there has been some disagreement among logisticians and others on what should be included, the activities in the following paragraphs are representative. The relative importance of any specific activity varies with individual firms. The important thing is that these activities must be coordinated so that the overall logistics costs are minimized.

Transportation. Transportation is a component of any logistics system and, in many cases, it is the chief contributor to costs. This means that industrial traffic management, as discussed in Chapter 4, is a key element in the management of business logistics.

Warehouse Operation. Since storage is usually a vital part of a logistics system, warehouse operation is included as a logistics activity. The warehouse(s) may be used to store inbound or outbound goods and may be located in conjunction with or away from production facilities.

Inventory Management. There are various places where inventory may be kept, for example, at plants and/or warehouses or in retail stores. Management of inventory with the objective of not having more or less on hand than is needed, given the service level objectives that have been established, is an important part of the logistics system. Too high an inventory level causes high carrying costs. Too low an inventory results in high restocking and production costs, as well as the risk of lost sales and loss of customer good will. The costs of carrying inventory include warehousing, insurance, taxes, damage, obsolescence, and interest on investment. The control of inventory starts at the source of the inbound materials and ends at the point where goods are transferred to customers. Inventory costs can be increased or decreased as a result of inventory management decisions and also of decisions made on other activities in a logistics system.

Production Scheduling. In firms in which a production activity, such as manufacturing, exists, it is important that scheduling of when and how much of certain items are to be produced be coordinated with transportation, warehousing, inventory management, and so on, so that excess or short inventory does not occur and so that transportation and warehousing facilities are available when needed. This is not to say that logistics personnel should take over the production function. It merely means that there should be coordination between the scheduling of production and the other logistics activities.

Materials Handling. The movement of goods around plants and warehouses via forklift trucks, conveyor belts, and so on, is usually referred to as *materials handling* and is logically considered in the design of plants and warehouses and should be included as a logistics activity. Both the speed of movement and the prevention of loss and damage are important aspects of the materials handling function.

Packaging. Protective packaging was discussed briefly in Chapter 2. Since it is closely related to storage and transportation, as well as to loss and damage levels, it is appropriately included as a business logistics activity.

Order Processing. Order processing is the process of physically filling orders for customers. Although an internal activity, it affects the customer because the time involved in filling orders directly affects the order cycle or delivery time. Thus, a slow manual order-filling system may not be feasible in a situation that calls for an order cycle time of 24 hours. A more sophisticated, perhaps mechanized, system may be required. Therefore, order processing properly is a logistics activity.

Plant and Warehouse Location. Decisions on where plants and warehouses are to be located, as discussed in Chapter 2, have a direct bearing on both the cost of logistics and the customer service levels attained, particularly on the order cycle time, and should be considered a logistics activity.[2]

Logistics Decision Making

The traditional way in which the activities discussed above are handled is to have the various logistics activities be the responsibility of various autonomous individuals or departments within the organization. Thus, transportation is traditionally handled by an industrial traffic manager or department, outlying finished goods warehouses may be under the control of the sales department, production scheduling is handled by the manufacturing department, management of inventory is scattered among various individuals or departments, and so on. In other words, a compartmentalized approach is taken. The situation is reinforced by traditional accounting practices in which departments are held accountable for specific cost categories.[3] This fragmentation may result in duplication and waste and may hinder the logistics effort of the organization.

A fragmented approach to logistics management means that the objectives

---

[2] In some of the literature dealing with business logistics, purchasing and market forecasting are included as business logistics activities. Purchasing is not included here as a logistics activity because we view logistics as a supportive function to other activities such as sales, financing, production, and purchasing. It would appear no more logical to include purchasing as a logistics activity than it would to include sales. Market forecasting has an important relationship to business logistics because market forecasts (forecasts of demand) are used to design a logistics system. Thus, market forecasts are a basic factor in planning and coordinating business logistics operations. The forecasting itself, however, is not considered here to be a logistics activity.

[3] Robert J. Holloway and Robert S. Hancock, *Marketing in a Changing Environment,* 2nd. ed. (New York: John Wiley and Sons, Inc., 1973), p. 419 (the chapter was written by Federick J. Beier).

of the different decision-making areas may be in conflict with one another. Thus, salespeople want maximum finished product inventories carried while those concerned with finance want minimum inventories carried. Salespeople may also want frequent changes in production plans and short production runs in order to serve the demands of customers while production people may want long production runs for cost economy purposes. As one writer has put it "Only the President really seeks maximum total company returns on investment, and the individual executives . . . often conflict with the overall objective–and with each other."[4]

The compartmentalized approach leads, in turn, to decision making wherein each decision-making area tends to try to optimize the individual activity that it is responsible for. For example, the industrial traffic manager may seek to optimize the transportation function by securing the most transportation at the least possible cost. The sales manager in charge of a finished goods warehouse may tend to optimize customer satisfaction and carry excessive inventories–he never wants to be out of stock. The production manager may schedule production so that there will be long production runs, thereby achieving the greatest efficiency in production in terms of cost per unit produced.

This suboptimization may lead to efficiency in each area, but it may be at the cost of not optimizing the business logistics activity as a whole. Thus, the traffic manager's desire to have low transportation cost may mean choice of a mode of transportation that, in turn, increases the levels of inventory needed and the number of warehouses required beyond what they would be if a more expensive, but faster, form of transportation were used. By keeping transportation costs down, he raises costs in other logistics areas and the total logistics effort may not be optimized. In addition, service levels may be improved by using a different form of transportation.

Suppose, for example, that a manufacturer in St. Louis, Missouri has been using rail carload transportation to serve customers in New York City and that the customers purchase in relatively small quantities, say 500 pounds or less. In order to use the relatively low-cost rail carload service, the manufacturer must accumulate goods at the point of shipment in order to make the minimum weight required for carload shipments. This means that inventories and storage are necessary at the point of manufacture.

While the goods are in transit between St. Louis and New York, say 1 week, the manufacturer incurs the usual costs of holding goods, including the interest on the investment he has in the goods.

Since customers purchase in small quantities, the manufacturer must arrange for reception of the carloads at New York and for breaking them down into small shipments for local delivery. Suppose that he operates a warehouse in New York City or buys public warehouse space there for that purpose. Then the carloads from St. Louis are received at the warehouse, brought into storage, and shipped out to local customers in the form of small shipments as the orders are received. This necessitates warehouse operation expense and the cost of carrying inventory at New York.

The manufacturer's objective has been to keep the transportation cost down

[4] John F. Stoll, "How to Manage Physical Distribution," *Harvard Business Review*, July–August, 1967, p. 94. Copyright © 1967 by the President and Fellows of Harvard College; all rights reserved.

while performing satisfactory service to the customers in New York. The transportation function is being optimized in terms of cost.

Suppose further that the firm is convinced to shift from rail carload service to air freight transportation. This, of course, causes a substantial increase in the freight bill, perhaps as much as tenfold or twelvefold. The transportation activity in terms of cost incurred is no longer optimized. But by using a much faster and more frequent form of transportation and one which is conducive to small shipments and one in which the buildup of large shipments beforehand is not necessary, the firm may be able to (1) reduce the amount of inventory carried at the point of manufacture, (2) reduce the amount of storage space required at the point of manufacture, (3) reduce the length of time goods are in transit and the associated costs, (4) eliminate the need to carry inventory at New York by delivering directly from the airport to customers, (5) eliminate the need for warehousing at New York, and (6) may also reduce loss and damage and reduce packaging costs.

The cost savings from reduced inventories, elimination of the warehouse operations, less time in transit, and less cost of loss and damage and packaging may more than offset the increased transportation cost. The result would be a lower *total* logistics cost and the same or better service to the customer. The total logistics effort has been optimized, not transportation and not any other individual logistics activity.

What this amounts to is that the manufacturer has *traded off* the low freight bill for savings elsewhere in the logistics effort. Other examples could be cited, for example, managers of other activities in logistics, such as warehousing or production scheduling, can trade off for the benefit of the entire system. Thus, Frederick J. Beier has said,

All such interrelationships between logistics activities demand attention. Changes in order processing—say, shortening the time between when the customer submits an order and when he can expect it—has an effect on inventory levels and the location of warehouses. Production scheduling—that is, determining when and how many of each item will be produced—has obvious relationships with inventory control, warehousing, and materials handling. Added investments in branch warehouses or multiple production facilities often result in decreased order-processing time and lower transportation rates. However, such changes also encourage the storage of more inventory in the system and thus increase inventory holding costs. Changes in protective packaging may be offset by higher transportation costs or the need to redesign the materials-handling system. The point of these examples is that a logistics manager must be willing to incur higher costs in one area if he can thereby achieve savings from another activity. A manager must be able to think through proposed changes, identify all the significant trade offs, and evaluate their net impact on his firm.[5]

The trading-off idea and the optimization of the entire logistics effort mean that the various managers who make decisions involving logistics activities must think in terms of the big picture and less in terms of optimizing the particular activity they manage. The various components in a logistics system must be

[5] Holloway and Hancock, *Marketing in a Changing Environment*, p. 408.

linked and worked together into a system to minimize total logistics costs while providing the desired levels of service to customers. This amounts to a substantial change in thinking, philosophy, and attitude that is sometimes difficult to accomplish.

Complexity of a Business Logistics System

Every organization that deals in some way with physical goods, either inbound or outbound, or both, has a logistics system, although it may not be recognized as such. The need for improving the logistics operation varies from situation to situation and one of the principal factors that determines the need for better management of the logistics activities is the complexity of the system, i.e., the more complex a logistics system is, the more likely improvement is needed and can be of substantial benefit to the organization. The business firms that have shown the most interest in improving their logistical operations have been those that have the most complex systems, particularly those in highly competitive industries, and those that have narrow profit margins.

The complexity of a logistics system is determined by the several factors discussed in the following paragraphs.

Number of Sources of Supply. Firms that have numerous sources of supply of inbound materials find that their logistics problems are more complicated than those firms that have only one or a limited number of sources of supply. This has to do with the number of different *suppliers* that are involved as well as the number of different *places* from which inbound items are shipped.

Number of Processing, Manufacturing, or Resale Locations. A firm that has only one processing, manufacturing, or resale point ordinarily has a much more simple logistics system than a firm that has many such facilities at many different geographic locations.

Number of Products in the Line. A firm that has a wide product line has considerable interest in trying to improve its logistics operations because a wide product line means a highly complex system overall and one in which considerable inefficiency can develop. In contrast, a firm that has only one product in its line has a much more simple problem in getting the right thing to the right place in the right quantity at the right time at the right cost and in the right condition.

Number of Finished Product Storage Locations. If a firm has many finished goods warehouses scattered around the country, its overall logistics system is much more difficult to analyze, plan, and improve than when only one or two or no outlying storage locations are involved.

Number of Consumption Points (Geographic Markets). A firm that sells in many different geographic markets has a more complex logistics system than a firm that serves only one or a very small number of geographic locations. Again, as with the factors discussed above, the numbers involved are important in determining complexity.

Is Production to Stock or to Order? In most production situations, production is to stock, that is, the goods are produced before they are sold in the anticipation that they will be sold. In other situations, production is to order, that is, production does not begin until the firm has received an order.

In most cases when production is to stock, the logistics complexities are mainly on the physical distribution side because considerable estimating, and perhaps, guesswork, may be involved in predicting what will be in demand and where and when. The physical supply side of the problem is more routine in nature and with less uncertainty.

When production is to order, the reverse is true. The physical distribution side is relatively simple since there is no guesswork on what will be in demand and where and when since production does not begin until the sale has been made. On the physical supply side, however, the task is more difficult because it involves anticipating what should be in stock and available to use in production when an order is received.

Difficulty in Forecasting Demand. Because logistics decisions are based to a great extent on forecasts of demand—what will be in demand and in what quantities and where and when—that are made by the firm, perhaps by the marketing area, a determinant of how well logistics decisions are made is the accuracy of such forecasts. This accuracy, in turn, is a function of such things as the seasonality of demand, how demand is affected by cyclical forces, to what degree demand is tied in with population growth, and so on. The more difficult it is to forecast demand accurately, the more errors in forecasting will be made, and the more errors will be made in logistics decision making.

Further Comments on Complexity. Taking the foregoing factors into consideration, at one extreme a manufacturer might use only one raw material which is obtained from a single source and can move by only one means of transportation to the firm's only plant. All production is shipped to a single customer at a single location and only one means of transportation is feasible for these shipments. At the other extreme a manufacturer might obtain goods or materials from thousands of suppliers representing hundreds or thousands of shipping origins and have those goods shipped to any one of dozens of company plants at various locations. Upon completion of the production process, the many different finished goods might then be shipped to any one of dozens of the firm's distribution warehouses and then to hundreds or thousands of customers.

For firms that have many hundreds of outbound products and supply items and many production points, warehouses, and consuming points, the logistics problem is sometimes so complex that it is not feasible to attempt at one time to design a single overall system encompassing all phases of the firm's logistics problem. The process of improvement must be undertaken on something other than a total system basis. This means that the logistics problem may best be attacked on a subsystem basis.

The smallest subsystem that can be dealt with would include only one supply item or outbound product. One approach is to group the various supply items or outbound products into a number of subsystems on the basis of their "commonality" in terms of logistics factors such as transportation characteristics, warehousing characteristics, demand patterns, service requirements, sources of supply, etc. This process permits the buildup of larger subsystems and could eventually make it possible to develop a total logistics system.

From the foregoing discussion it can easily be seen that concern about the logistics activities of the organization will be in direct relationship to the factors discussed. Thus, the business firms that have shown the most interest in improving their logistics operations have been those that have a large number of sources of supply, production locations, products in the line, warehouses, and geographic markets to serve, where production is to stock, and where demand estimation is somewhat difficult.

ORGANIZATION FOR BUSINESS LOGISTICS MANAGEMENT

The possible benefits to be derived from a coordinated logistics system are obvious. Lower cost and, perhaps, improved service to customers are possible. However, implementing the concept is something else again. It is probably easier in most cases to analyze the logistics problem than it is to manage it.[6] It is clear that the implementation of the concept so that the various activities involved in logistics are handled in a coordinated manner can involve serious organizational problems. This is because crossing traditional department lines (marketing, purchasing, production, finance, traffic) is necessary in order to achieve the systems or flow idea. Traditional organizational structures are often inadequate for the implementation of the concept of business logistics. The drastic organizational changes that may be required make it essential that top management be convinced that improvement of the logistics operation is needed and that something must be done about it. Unless top management believes in the logistics idea and actively supports it, it is doubtful that much in the way of improvement can be accomplished.

Because organizational change is often an unpleasant experience in a business firm, there is often some hesitancy in carrying it out. If top management is serious about implementing the concept of business logistics, it must be prepared to endure as well as to inflict the discomforts of organizational change.[7]

Since there are as many different organizational structures as their are organizations, it is difficult to generalize on what is an appropriate organizational structure to deal with logistics. Among the various organizational approaches that have been suggested are those discussed in the following paragraphs.

Minimum Organizational Disruption

One approach is to attempt to implement the business logistics concept with minimum organizational change. It involves maintaining the traditional organizational pattern but providing more cooperation among the people and depart-

[6] John F. Stoll, "How to Manage Physical Distribution," p. 94.

[7] Alan F. Gepfert, "Business Logistics for Better Profit Performance," *Harvard Business Review,* November–December, 1968, p. 84.

ments involved in managing logistics activities. This might, for example, be accomplished by establishing a logistics committee in which the several logistics activities would be represented. The committee would meet frequently to ensure that conflicting decisions are avoided and that coordination is achieved.

Instead of the committee approach, certain individuals can be assigned the responsibility for coordinating logistics activities, perhaps by having them assigned to work in two or more of the logistics areas.

Coordination may also be sought through less formal procedures in which the various areas are merely expected to cooperate and coordinate their various decisions relating to logistics and in which there would be no coordinating agent.

Separate Logistics Unit

Another approach to implementing the business logistics concept is to reorganize the firm so that all or almost all of the logistics activities are under one person or department. Under this approach, transportation, warehousing, order processing, and the other logistics activities are the responsibility of a single person or department. This approach has great impact on the firm because it significantly disrupts the usual way of doing things and it is difficult to get those who are affected by it to accept it. This is particularly true of those who lose a measure of control over an activity, such as warehousing, when that activity is placed under the jurisdiction of the new entity. Other obstacles to setting up a separate logistics unit include lack of understanding by management, the expense of staffing the new unit, and the difficulty in finding qualified personnel. In many cases, these obstacles mean that progress toward establishing a separate and unified logistics unit must be gradual and evolutionary. There should not be a sudden change.

Organization in Practice

Both approaches described above have been used by business firms. The most appropriate organization depends on the nature of the firm and the products it is involved with as well as the industry of which it is a part. The need for a separate logistics unit is influenced by the size of logistics costs, the size of the firm, the importance of customer service standards, whether customer service standards are high or low, the nature of the inbound and outbound materials, the number of production points, and other factors that determine the complexity of the logistics problem. As indicated earlier, firms that have shown the most interest in business logistics are those that have the most difficult logistics problems, and they are the most likely to take the separate logistics unit approach to organizing for it.

Despite the difficulty of implementation, the separate logistics unit approach often appears to have more chance for real accomplishment than the minimum organizational disruption approach since the logistics problem receives greater organizational recognition and since more clear-cut decision-making responsibility is established.

The separate logistics units that have been established did not spring into being overnight. In some firms an existing department, often the traffic department, was given the additional responsibilities. In other firms, a small department, often with staff or advisory responsibility only, was created. Generally, the evolution to a full-fledged department with important line responsibilities did not begin until the late 1950's. The new departments met with considerable resistance from existing departments in the typical organizational structure.[8]

Titles given to logistics departments vary greatly from firm to firm and include the following: Distribution Department, Planning Department, Sales Service Department, Transportation and Distribution Department, Materials Handling Department, Supply and Distribution Department, Distribution Services Department, Materials Management Department, Traffic and Distribution Department, and Traffic Department. The heads of the departments hold various titles including manager, director, superintendent, and vice president and they report to a variety of executives. The latter include the president, the executive vice president, the vice president of sales or marketing or manufacturing or production or operations or purchasing or finance or merchandising, the director of purchasing, the treasurer, and the director of production. Surveys taken between 1962 and 1971 indicate that the number of firms in which the logistics function reported directly to top management increased substantially in that period, with 43.9 per cent of the reporting firms having this arrangement in 1971.[9] Thus, there appears to be a trend toward placing logistics units on an equal basis with the other major departments of the firm. In this way, the managers of logistics are expected to be able to better manage the trade offs required and other aspects of logistics management.

There is controversy on whether or not a unified separate logistics group is necessary or even desirable. Although a number of business firms have established separate logistics units, most firms prefer not to put all logistics activities under one organizational unit. Instead, the responsibility is divided among several units. Actually, most business firms probably do not need to reorganize the firm and centralize the physical movement activities in one place. Although they are interested in improving their logistics operations, they can successfully function organizationally very much as they have in the past but with greater coordination among the various individuals and departments. This is the minimum organizational disruption approach mentioned earlier.

Many firms have no logistics department and still do an excellent job of managing the logistics function. Other firms have formally established logistics departments and do an inadequate logistics management job. In the words of a leading educator in the field, it is not important that a firm have a formal logistics organization. It is important that all levels of management in a firm think and act in terms of logistics capabilities and economics.[10]

Centralization Versus Decentralization

Another aspect of the organizational problem is to decide when a separate logistics unit is established whether it is to be organized on a centralized or de-

---

[8]Herbert W. Davis, "Organization and Management of the Logistics Function in Industry," *Logistics Spectrum,* Fall, 1972, p. 3.

[9]*Ibid.,* p. 5.

[10]Donald J. Bowersox, "Physical Distribution in Semi-Maturity," *Air Transportation,* January, 1966. p. 10.

centralized basis. In a centralized organization the manager of the logistics function is given authority and control over all people engaged in planning and carrying out logistics activities in the organization, no matter where they are located. In a decentralized organization managers responsible for logistics activities required for the operation of an individual plant, warehouse, or store, or a company division at a level below the corporate organization have direct line responsibility to warehouse, plant, or store, or division operating management. Under these circumstances, logistics managers in the line organization call on a corporate logistics staff organization for planning assistance, information, and advice. Under this kind of staff organization, local managers may not be bound to follow the advice of the corporate staff and they are not held responsible for their subsequent actions by the staff.

Business Logistics Management and the Industrial Traffic Manager

We have said that every organization has a logistics system. This is true even if formal recognition of the need for a coordinated logistics system has not taken place. Where does industrial traffic management fit into the system?

Although some industrial traffic managers in the 1950's and 1960's broadened their activities, and, in effect, became logistics managers, other traffic managers were concerned that as business logistics became the subject of growing interest, industrial traffic management as a function was either going to be replaced or at least downgraded. Although there have been some instances of downgrading traffic management, the contrary has been the more general case. In fact, some firms that attempted to downgrade traffic management when they adopted the logistics concept found that traffic management still plays a vital role in the total logistics organization and that they had made a mistake.[11] Obviously, the logistics concept does not do away with the need for effective management of the transportation function by the user. Instead, it has brought greater attention than ever before to this function and to its importance.

As we have defined the concept of logistics, conventional traffic management is a component of the logistics system—the component that is responsible for the transportation function. A good logistics system must have a well-run transportation effort. Traffic management is and always will be a functional area of logistics. In fact, in many organizations the traffic management aspect of logistics is the most important in terms of costs and also in terms of service requirements. It has also been argued that the logistics concept has increased the need for good transportation management because a system in total cannot function adequately unless the management of transportation is effectively and efficiently performed and integrated with all other logistics activities. Therefore, it appears safe to conclude that as long as logistics constitutes a major area of effort, traffic management will be a vital ingredient in the total effort of the organization.[12]

Thus, the traffic operation is part of a logistics system, regardless of whether or not there is a formal organization for logistics or whether or not the firm

[11] "Demand for Traffic Men Growing, Say Officials of Executive Placement Firm," *Traffic World*, November 12, 1973, p. 39.

[12] Donald J. Bowersox, Edward W. Smykay, and Bernard J. LaLonde, *Physical Distribution Management*, 2nd ed. (New York: The MacMillan Company, 1968), pp. 153-154.

claims to have adopted the logistics concept. Because the traffic manager is part of the system, he can contribute to making it more efficient.

But this requires that the decisions made by the traffic manager take into consideration factors outside conventional traffic management, particularly inventory control, production scheduling, and service to customers. The industrial traffic manager must think and make decisions in terms of the total logistics effort, rather than in terms of transportation alone. This is true regardless of how the firm chooses to organize to deal with logistics activities, if at all. In order to do this, the traffic manager must broaden his interests and knowledge beyond transportation and the traditional traffic functions. He must understand and appreciate the fact that his decisions are related to and have an effect on such things as inventory management, production scheduling, and order processing. He must be familiar with the objectives and methods of the total physical supply and physical distribution system. He must also be able to supply others with an accurate picture of the capabilities, limitations, and alternatives of the transportation function. And, most important, the traffic manager must be willing to *not* optimize his own position in order that he might optimize the entire logistics system. This often means making decisions in such a way that the freight bill is *not* minimized.

Thus, the need to improve the efficiency of the logistics system offers an opportunity and challenge for traffic people to broaden their interests and their responsibilities to areas or activities outside traditional traffic management.

In addition to the requirement that traffic managers undergo a change in outlook, there is the question of whether or not the traffic manager should be the person designated to lead the logistics unit should one be established. In some cases this has been done. In other cases it has not been done.[13] Whether or not the traffic manager should become the top logistics executive depends on his individual qualifications. No generalization is possible although, other things being equal, in many cases, the traffic manager is highly qualified in terms of experience with the key element in many logistics systems.

Third-Party Business Logistics Management

A developing idea in business logistics management is *third-party distribution* in which the business logistics system (usually the physical distribution side only) of an organization would be operated by a separate organization other than the shipper or receiver. The shipper or receiver would turn over the logistics functions to the third party with title to the goods remaining in the hands of the shipper or receiver. The shipper or receiver would thereby avoid the capital outlays for vehicles, warehouses, computer equipment, and so on, but would retain supervisory control over the costs and services involved. In the ideal case, the third party would handle all of the activities we have included in our discussion of logistics and could be set up as a new organization or be an extension of the usual services provided by for-hire carriers or by public warehouse companies

---

[13] Bypassing the industrial traffic manager in selecting a logistics manager is discussed in F. Clair Williams, "The New Responsibilities of Industrial Traffic Management," *Air Transportation*, October, 1964. See also Lester E. Kloss, "You, Your Future, and the Future of Physical Distribution Management," *Handling and Shipping*, May, 1976, p. 50.

(companies that sell warehouse space and, usually, some associated services, to owners of goods).

There has been only limited development of this concept in the United States, partly because of the large capital investment required by the third party, the large volume of business that would be necessary to support such an enterprise and make it economical, the lack of acceptance by shippers and receivers, and some government regulatory restrictions.

PRACTICALITY OF BUSINESS LOGISTICS MANAGEMENT

Business logistics management is a very simple concept. The difficult part of business logistics management is trying to implement the concept. Although by the early 1960's business logistics was gaining acceptance as a sound idea in business management, the implementation of the concept was and still is a difficult thing. As we have said before, it is easier to analyze the business logistics problem than it is to manage it. Organizing for and managing logistics activities are extremely difficult. Some of the early attempts were not nearly as successful as the articles praising the virtues of business logistics management that were appearing at the time. Thus, the question may well be asked: Is business logistics a mirage impossible to implement or is it a real and practical concept?

Opposition to implementation of the concept may be strong, particularly if reorganization and the establishment of a separate logistics unit are to take place, thus diluting or eliminating the control that certain individuals and departments have over logistics activities. In addition, there is the problem of coordinating widely diverse activities and decision making which, even with the availability of computers and various quantitative tools, is extremely difficult.

The result is that business logistics management has sometimes failed completely. When it is successful, it is rarely found in the real world in the pure sense as described in this chapter. It is true that many organizations have accepted the idea that the logistics approach to the movement of goods is sound and many have actually reorganized in an effort to implement the concept. However, an examination of these firms would reveal that their implementation of the concept has only been partial. They have not implemented the full systems approach covering all facets of logistics. In some cases, the logistics concept has been applied to one side of the problem only, usually the physical distribution side. In other cases, if both sides are being systemized, they are treated as two separate systems instead of one unified system that includes both physical supply and physical distribution.

In still other instances, an attempt is made to coordinate only some of the activities listed as part of the logistics problem, for example, transportation, warehouse operation, etc. There has, however, been considerable improvement along these lines. Thus, surveys of the logistics function in business firms over a ten-year period (1962-1971) have shown that the logistics activities discussed earlier have become fairly well stabilized and accepted parts of logistics units. In 1971 the firms surveyed reported that their logistics departments (usually called something else) had responsibility for transportation in 100 per cent of the cases, for warehousing in 98 per cent of the cases, for inventory management in 90 per cent of the cases, for order processing in 88 per cent of the cases, for protective packaging in 73 per cent of the cases, and for production planning in 60 per cent of the cases.[14]

Incomplete implementation of the concept also occurs when only some of the supply items or some of the outbound products have been subjected to logistics system control. Finally, some firms claim to have adopted the concept but have really done very little, if anything, to implement it and they handle the physical movement problems as they always have.

Thus, the concept of business logistics, with its possible contributions toward improvement of efficiency in the movement of goods, is generally not applied to its full potential and there is not yet complete acceptance of the idea in business firms. In fact, the majority of firms still operate with just a traffic management department.[15] However, it appears to be a real enough concept and has considerable practical applicability. As time passes, experience is gained and lessons are learned as to how to design and implement logistics systems. Business logistics management offers considerable promise and we can expect to see more complete and successful systems in the future.[16] In fact, in the future, business logistics may eventually reach beyond the confines of a single organization, whereby there will be vertical integration in which the logistics planning, methods, and schedules of an organization will be fitted to the planning, methods, and schedules of its suppliers and its customers.[17]

SELECTED REFERENCES

There is a vast amount of literature, including many articles, on the general subject of business logistics. There are several textbooks devoted to the subject, including James L. Heskett, Nicholas A. Glaskowsky, Jr., and Robert M. Ivie, *Business Logistics,* 2nd ed. (New York: The Ronald Press Company, 1973); Ronald H. Ballou, *Business Logistics Management* (Englewood Cliffs, New Jersey: Prentice-Hall, Inc., 1973); Donald J. Bowersox, *Logistical Management* (New York: MacMillan Publishing Company, Inc., 1974); and John J. Coyle and Edward J. Bardi, *The Management of Business Logistics* (St. Paul: West Publishing Company, 1976).

An early and excellent presentation of the concept of business logistics and the reasons for its development is John F. Magee, "The Logistics of Distribution," *Harvard Business Review,* July–August, 1960. The history of and reasons for the development of the business logistics concept are dealt with in Bowersox, *Logistical Management,* pp. 1–8 and "Physical Distribution in Semi-Maturity," *Air Transportation,* January, 1966 and in Heskett, Glaskowsky, and Ivie, *Business Logistics* pp. 33–39.

[14] Herbert W. Davis, "Organization and Management of the Logistics Function in Industry," p. 5.

[15] Charles A. Taff, *Management of Physical Distribution and Transportation,* 5th ed. (Homewood, Illinois: Richard D. Irwin, Inc., 1972), p. 11.

[16] Examples of firms that have adopted the business logistics concept and descriptions of how they are organized for it are frequently presented in trade magazines including *Distribution Worldwide, Handling and Shipping, Traffic Management,* and *Transportation and Distribution Management.*

[17] Kloss, "You, Your Future, and the Future of Physical Distribution Management," p. 53.

For an excellent discussion of business logistics from a marketing point of view, see Robert J. Holloway and Robert S. Hancock, *Marketing in a Changing Environment*, 2nd ed. (New York: John Wiley and Sons, Inc., 1973), Chapter 19. The chapter was written by Frederick J. Beier.

There is considerable literature on the subject of organization for business logistics management. See, for example, Herbert W. Davis, "Organization and Management of the Logistics Function in Industry," *Logistics Spectrum*, Fall, 1972 and John F. Stolle, "How to Manage Physical Distribution," *Harvard Business Review*, July–August, 1967. See also Bowersox, *Logistical Management*, pp. 426–436; Heskett, Glaskowsky, and Ivie, *Business Logistics*, Chapter 20; Ballou, *Business Logistics Management*, Chapter 12; and Coyle and Bardi, *The Management of Business Logistics*, Chapter 12.

Third-party business logistics management is discussed in Walter F. Friedman, "Physical Distribution: The Concept of Shared Ideas," *Harvard Business Review*, March–April, 1975.

6

User-Carrier Relations

The relationship between users of transportation and for-hire carriers has many of the characteristics of most buyer–seller relationships. In addition, there are aspects of the relationship that are peculiar to transportation. Major aspects of the user–carrier relationship in freight transportation are the subject of this chapter. The discussion deals with the role of the for-hire carrier in the logistics system of a user, the nature of common and contract carriage, the legal obligations for-hire carriers have when dealing with their clients, claims for loss and damage, and contractual arrangements between users and carriers.

THE FOR-HIRE CARRIER AS AN ELEMENT IN A BUSINESS LOGISTICS SYSTEM

As indicated in Chapter 5, transportation is a vital element in most business logistics systems. Consequently, the carriers that perform such transportation service are key components of a user's logistics effort.

Channels of Distribution

Most producers in both the consumer goods (goods and services purchased for personal or household consumption) and the industrial goods (goods and services, such as machinery, raw materials, electricity, etc., used in producing other goods and services) markets find that they must rely in part on middlemen or distributors and others to perform some of the marketing functions. Marketing then becomes a cooperative effort between the producer and the middlemen and others who are involved. Independent wholesale middlemen who take title to the products they deal in are referred to as *merchant middlemen.* Retailers also normally take title to the goods they handle. Wholesale middlemen who do not take title are referred to as *agent middlemen.*

The route followed by a product between the producer and the ultimate consumer or industrial buyer is known as the *channel of distribution* or the *trade channel.* A variety of definitions of a channel of distribution are available. There are, in fact, only two channels. One channel consists of the flow of ownership or the course taken in the transfer of title to a product, although some of the marketing institutions involved do not take possession of the goods. This is sometimes called the *exchange channel,* and it is the channel most commonly referred to when the term channel of distribution is used. The second channel consists of the institutions that take physical possession of the product, regardless of whether or not they also take ownership. This channel may be called the *logistics channel* and includes many of the same firms that also participate in the exchange channel. In addition to those firms, the logistics channel may also include transportation and warehouse companies to the extent that the transportation and storage functions are performed by for-hire carriers and public warehouses. Both channels include the producers and the ultimate consumers or industrial buyers as part of the channel. The channel of distribution extends from one producer to that buyer who either consumes or uses the product or significantly changes the product's form. The latter occurs when wheat becomes flour, or when iron ore becomes steel, or when a tire becomes part of a new automobile. If change of form occurs, a new channel of distribution has started.

The channel of distribution is a bridge between the producer and the consumer or industrial user, and its objective is to make it as easy as possible for the ultimate consumer or industrial user to acquire the product and to do so as efficiently as possible for the producer.

The alternative channels of distribution available to a producer are several and are shown in Figure 6-1 for both consumer goods and industrial goods. These are exchange channels in that the flow of title is represented (although agents do not take title, their function is to transfer title). These are commonly used channels and there are variations of them that are also used. Any one producer may use more than one channel for a particular product and different channels for different products in his line.

In the consumer goods market the customary or orthodox and most widely used channel is producer to merchant wholesaler to retailer to consumer.

In the industrial goods market the most common channels are direct sale from producer to industrial buyer, sale via an agent, or sale via industrial distributors (merchant wholesalers). The industrial distributor is the chief source of supply for small buyers.

Producers frequently take the initiative in establishing channels for their products. In other cases, large middlemen or industrial buyers take the initiative. Hence, the channel leader may be looking at the channel problem as a physical supply problem or as a physical distribution problem, or both. In some cases, however, the complete channel of distribution is not planned by the producer or anyone else in the channel. In other words, there is not always a channel leader or "captain" since the various institutions are not acting as part of an integrated "system." The reason for the lack of a captain may be lack of leadership or lack of understanding that members of the system are interrelated. Many businessmen, more concerned with the firms immediately above or below them, seem almost unaware that they are part of a channel. The manufacturer, for example, may little know or care what becomes of his products after they leave

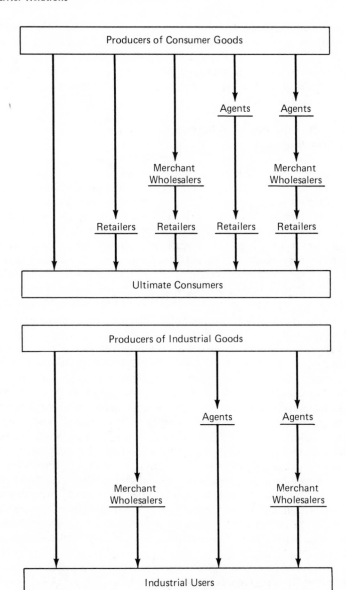

FIGURE 6-1 *Frequently Used Exchange Channels of Distribution.*

the hands of the merchant middleman who has paid him for them. A manufacturer may not even consider himself as standing at the head of a channel, but only as occupying a link in a channel that begins with his supplier(s). As one writer has said, "Some channel sequences 'just grew' like Topsy without direction or intent of known parents."[1]

---

[1] Philip McVey, "Are Channels of Distribution What the Textbooks Say?" *Journal of Marketing,* January, 1960, p. 61.

Not shown in Figure 6-1 are the various non-owning institutions or agencies that are part of a channel of distribution. These include the institutions that provide logistics services including transportation (carriers) and storage (public warehouses), as well as those that facilitate the marketing effort by performing "facilitating" functions including standardization and grading, financing, risk taking, and providing market information.

Channels of Distribution and Business Logistics Management

A channel of distribution may be longer than a single organization's physical supply or physical distribution system, as those terms were defined in Chapter 5. Thus, the channel of distribution for a consumer good may include both wholesalers and retailers, while the physical distribution system of the manufacturer of the consumer good may end with the wholesaler, who is the manufacturer's "customer" in terms of logistics. In other cases, the physical distribution system of a producer may exactly duplicate the channel, for example, when a manufacturer of industrial machinery sells machines directly to other manufacturers who use them in their manufacturing operations. The channel does not include intermediate owners; sale and physical distribution are direct from the manufacturer to the industrial buyer. Similar comments could be made concerning physical supply and the inbound channel of distribution.

One way to look at the channel of distribution is to view it as a *single system* that extends from producer to ultimate consumer or industrial user, even though title has passed and the physical distribution system of the producer is shorter than the channel of distribution. Therefore, each participant may be viewed as being dependent on every other member. Thus, if one channel member is inefficient, the entire channel may suffer. For example, as Frederick J. Beier points out, inefficient transportation at any point in a firm's channel could increase the landed cost of the goods in the market and thus put that channel system at a disadvantage when compared with the channel systems of competitors.[2] This means that in making logistics decisions it is important that the manager consider the impact of his logistics decisions on the other members of the channel, even if the manager thinks that the members are beyond the span of the logistics system itself. To be acceptable to these other members, it is probably necessary that trade offs beneficial to the user must also be beneficial to other channel members.

The For-Hire Carrier's Role in Business Logistics Management

There is no question that business logistics has presented opportunities and challenges to for-hire transportation companies. In order that a logistics sytem may operate as desired by the user, the proper transportation mode(s) and individual carrier(s) must be used. Rates charged must also be appropriate for the services obtained. One major implication of the development of the logistics

---

[2] Frederick J. Beier, "The Role of the Common Carrier in the Channel of Distribution," *Transportation Journal,* Winter, 1969, p. 13.

concept is that the logistics concept, by its very nature, is heavily service conscious when it comes to transportation and concerned about the impact of transportation on other logistics elements, and it is less concerned with the level of transportation rates as such than has been the case with traditional industrial traffic management. This forces carriers to attempt to develop user demanded services while at the same time maintaining their own profitability.

It is clear that the connecting link between the various institutions in the channel of distribution is the carrier and that coordination between carriers (whether private or for-hire) and the other institutions is required for effective management. Beier suggests that for-hire carriers should adopt a channel-wide systems view of their function and that their role should be to provide communication and physical linkages throughout the system. This involves such things as communicating routing instructions, performing tracing and expediting activities, and arranging any accessorial transportation services while keeping the receiver of goods fully informed of the status of the shipment. In effect, these carriers would be inviting users to shift the communications function, at least as it applies to physical distribution, and the transport function to them. This concept could lead to integration of the communications systems of carriers and users so that when a user makes a sale the information may be communicated directly to the carrier. The carrier can then take complete charge of the shipment, eliminating the need for the user's personnel to duplicate these activities. This means the development of carrier information systems that are custom-made for their clients. It also means that the user must be willing to delegate this responsibility to the carrier and to commit himself to a specific carrier(s) for some length of time.[3] Many user and carrier executives have recognized the need for computer-to-computer exchange of information between users and carriers in order to optimize the logistics function. Some progress has been made along these lines, usually initiated by users.

Whatever form the fitting of the carrier's services into the logistics system of a user takes, integrating for-hire carrier service into an organization's logistics system may be difficult. It may involve educating the carriers as to what is needed and asking them to adjust their services to the requirements of the logistics system.

As the logistics concept became accepted in the 1950's and 1960's and as intermodal competition intensified, some carriers became more conscious of their role in physical supply and physical distribution and what users needed in the way of transportation services and rates. They, in fact (led by the airlines), became more "marketing oriented," i.e., more oriented toward trying to satisfy the needs of users than had been true in the past. Some railroads, for example, which traditionally stressed "operations" (operating the railroad) rather than the marketing side of the business, became much more interested in marketing research and some reorganized and created marketing departments (to replace former "traffic" departments) to give a greater marketing emphasis to their efforts.

Carriers have found that it is possible to tailor their services and rates to better accommodate the logistics needs of users, i.e., they can recognize their role in the logistics function and adapt their services and rates to better perform

[3] *Ibid.*, pp. 19–20.

that role. Examples of carrier innovations that have been inspired by the quest for improved logistics management can be cited: sophisticated container systems,[4] different schedules, joint rail-truck service, terminal relocations, improved loading and unloading methods, and various rate innovations.

The sales approach of some carriers has also changed because of the logistics concept. Carriers have traditionally sold their services on a cost and service basis without special regard to the impact of those services on their customers' logistics systems. The new sales approach emphasizes the role of transportation in the overall logistics picture, including trade offs that can be made between transportation and other logistics activities. In a few cases, carriers (mainly air) offer to analyze and design total logistics systems for users using the total cost approach referred to in Chapter 5. Ultimately, for-hire carriers may operate entire business logistics systems for users in "third-party distribution," mentioned in Chapter 5.

Although these developments indicate that more carriers are recognizing that their proper role is as part of the country's total marketing effort, it appears that many carriers have still not accepted this idea and that full adaptation of for-hire carriers to the logistics needs of users is still in the future. For example, a recent comprehensive study of United States railroads concluded that railroad management must adjust its physical plant and operating procedures in a marketing-oriented manner and that railroads can tailor their services and prices in such a way that they can achieve a profit for the railroad and provide the channel of distribution with an efficient logistics system. However, the study also concluded that although top management in a few exceptional railroads has at least the beginnings of a market orientation, top rail management in general has *not* made a marketing commitment.[5]

CONCEPT OF COMMON CARRIAGE

When dealing with for-hire carriers, the user may choose between common carriers and contract carriers, with the former accounting for most for-hire carrier traffic. Common carriers have certain obligations to the user that a contract carrier does not have, obligations that are important elements in the user-carrier relationship.

The concept of common carriage developed as part of the English common law and has since been added to by common and statutory law in the United States and by lawful conditions in contracts for carriage and in freight tariffs.

Common law is a collection of principles determined from judicial decisions, learned treatises, and from common usage of people in daily life, without benefit of statutory law. Early common law recognized various occupations or activities

---

[4]Containerization is the use of a large box or "container" made of steel, fiberglass, or other durable material into which the items of a shipment (cartons or crates or bags, etc.) are loaded, usually at the shipper's door. The container is then turned over to the carrier and is delivered intact to the receiver, without being opened en route. It may have been carried by 2 or more carriers. Containers used in domestic surface transportation are often 8 feet high by 8 feet wide by 10, 20, 30, or 40 feet in length.

[5]Alan J. Stenger, *An Evaluation of the Ability of the United States Railroads to Respond to the Logistics Needs of the Shippers,* unpublished Ph.D. dissertation, University of Minnesota, 1974, pp. 394–396.

as having "common callings," including common carriers, common innkeepers, common merchants, common brokers, common schoolmasters, common surgeons, and others. These activities were considered essential to community life and were affected with the "public interest." These activities were performed only by those given specific authorization to do so. Today, the only examples that remain are the common carrier and, to some extent, the common innkeeper. Other public employments have lost both the name and their special status.[6] The concept of common carriage and the obligations of common carriers to serve the public are generally the same for carriers of passengers and for carriers of property or freight. The discussion that follows is confined to common carriage of freight only.

Common carriers of freight today are for-hire carriers who legally are *bailees for-hire*—they take possession of goods but do not own them. A *bailment* is delivery of personal property by one party to another party, without the transfer of ownership. The personal property is to be held according to the special purpose directed or implied and is to be returned or delivered over when that special purpose is accomplished.

As bailees for-hire, common carriers of property have specific obligations when dealing with their clients. The obligations to the public that were developed under the common law include the obligation to serve the public generally, to deliver the goods, to charge reasonable prices, and to avoid discrimination in prices and service. The first 2 of these 4 obligations are discussed in this chapter. The second 2, having to do with pricing and discrimination, are dealt with in later chapters dealing with government economic regulation of transportation.

OBLIGATION TO SERVE

A key characteristic of common carriage is that a common carrier has the obligation to serve the public generally. This means that a common carrier must hold himself out to serve the general public instead of restricting his service to one or a few users, but there are circumstances under which a common carrier may refuse to serve a prospective user, i.e., a common carrier is not required to serve *everyone,* to carry *everything,* or to serve *everywhere.*

What to Carry?

A common carrier may refuse to serve a particular user of freight service because of what the user is offering for carriage. Because of the vehicle and terminal facilities they have available and, in some cases, because of regulatory restrictions, or by mere choice, common carriers usually hold themselves out to carry only certain kinds of traffic. It is within this holding out that the common carrier must serve all comers without discrimination. Thus, a common carrier trucking company that operates tank trucks suitable for the carriage of liquid chemicals holds himself out to carry chemicals and may legally refuse to carry furniture,

[6] Richard R. Sigmon, *Miller's Law of Freight Loss and Damage Claims,* 4th ed. (Dubuque, Iowa: William C. Brown Company Publishers, 1974), pp. 3-4.

typewriters, petroleum, or anything else. A common carrier by air may refuse to carry cement building blocks because they are beyond the normal holding out of the carrier. He does not ordinarily carry such traffic.

The breadth of the holding out of different common carriers, even within the same mode, varies considerably. The broadest holding out is usually that of railroads which carry almost everything; there are few restrictions. Highway carriers of general commodities also have a broad holding out. A very narrow holding out is that of the highway carrier of liquid chemicals, mentioned earlier. Another is the trucking company that carries only frozen foods or confines its service to houshold goods. Oil pipelines, by their very nature, also have a limited holding out. Thus, common carriers do not serve everyone or carry everything.

In addition to refusing to carry what they do not normally hold themselves out to carry, in certain circumstances shipments may be refused even within the usual holding out of the carrier. A common carrier may refuse to carry shipments that are of extraordinary value, that are improperly packed, that are illegal, and shipments that are dangerous to carry because of riots or strikes or which might impregnate or contaminate other goods. A common carrier may also refuse to carry shipments offered to him at unreasonable times or places. A common carrier may refuse to carry either when the appropriate vehicular equipment is not available or when his capacity has been reached and there is no room on the carrier's facilities for the shipment in question.

Where to Carry?

Another major aspect of the obligation to serve the public is the geographic area in which a common carrier is expected to serve. Obviously, a common carrier cannot be expected to serve everywhere. It would be physically impossible for him to do so. In addition, regulatory restrictions in some cases prohibit carriage to any points or over any routes not specifically authorized.

Thus, the holding out to serve the public is limited to the public that wants to use the service provided over the routes and to and from the points the carrier normally serves. Any other users can be refused, but the carrier must serve without discrimination those who want to use the service normally provided. In rail transportation, however, because there is full interchanging of traffic between all railroads and because the user has the right to route traffic over two or more railroad company lines, as discussed in Chapter 4, a railroad cannot refuse to carry on a geographic basis unless there is no rail service at all to the points in question. In highway transportation, however, this is not the case, and it is not the case in other modes in which interchanging is not as prevalent as in rail transportation and in which interchanging cannot be required by government regulatory agencies.

The routes and points that are served by an individual carrier have been determined by the carriers themselves in the case of rail and oil pipeline transportation and in the case of unregulated highway, water, and air carriers. In the case of regulated highway, water, and air carriers, however, the route structure has been determined jointly by the carrier and a regulatory agency. To deviate from the route structure is a violation of the terms of the operating authority that has been awarded by the agency.

The above discussion of the obligation of common carriers to serve the public generally is in terms of the ideal situation called for by the common law obligations of common carriers. It must be recognized, however, that in actual practice the ideal situation is not always achieved and common carriers do sometimes avoid serving users and carrying traffic that are undesirable from the point of view of handling costs and profitability, even though these users and traffic fall within their normal holding out. This can be done by discouraging the submission of such traffic to them in a number of ways, including not soliciting it, giving it deliberately poor service, and refusing to interchange such traffic with other carriers. Regulatory agencies have considerable difficulty in preventing these practices.

OBLIGATION TO DELIVER

A critical issue in user–carrier relations is the common carrier's obligation to deliver property transported. This means that delivery is to be made at the right place to the right person in a reasonable length of time and in good condition.

As common law developed, not only did it develop the concept of the common carrier's obligation to serve, but it also develped the conditions under which a common carrier would be liable for loss or damage to goods carried. The rule developed was that common carriers would be liable for the full value of what they carried unless certain unusual circumstances prevailed, known as *exceptions* to liability. The original exceptions to liability found in common law were acts of God and acts of the king's enemies. These two exceptions, plus some additional ones, are now part of the common carrier liability structure in the United States. In both interstate and intrastate commerce, common and statutory law plus contractual terms agreed upon by user and carrier set forth the liability of common carriers. The federal laws, provisions of which were enacted at various times, that govern surface common carrier liability in interstate commerce are Sections 20(11), 20(12), and 219 of the Interstate Commerce Act, the Bills of Lading Act, and the Harter Act (water carriers only). In many states common law liability has also been supplemented by statute with respect to intrastate transportation. State laws and court decisions interpreting them are substantially the same as those relating to interstate traffic.

In modern United States domestic surface transportation, unless one of the exceptions to liability can be proven by the carrier to have prevailed, the carrier is liable for the loss or damage, even though no carrier negligence is involved. Even when loss or damage is the result of one of the exceptions to liability, however, the carrier is liable if he failed to use the degree of care that would have prevented or mitigated the injury resulting from the excepted cause.

The reasons that common law and modern statutory law apply strict liability conditions is that the user is in a disadvantageous position when dealing with the loss and damage problem, primarily because he is not present when the loss or damage occurs and has little ability to prove or disprove cause of loss or damage. In addition, unless common carriers are required to assume extensive liability for what they carry, the amount of damage in transportation would be much greater than it is because of careless handling by the carriers. Finally, severe loss and damage responsibility was placed on common carriers in order to avoid the problem of carriers stealing goods or conspiring with others to steal goods in their possession. Consequently, theft is *not* an exception to liability.

Liability of Railroads, Highway Carriers, and Oil Pipelines

Interstate railroads, highway carriers, and oil pipelines are liable for the full value of what they carry should loss or damage occur unless one of the several exceptions to liability is present. Rail, highway, and oil pipeline carriers generally have the same exceptions to liability. These exceptions are discussed in the following paragraphs.

Act of God. In the legal liability sense, an act of God is a natural catastrophe of some kind, for example, an earthquake or flood that has caused loss or damage to goods. Every natural catastrophe is not legally an exception to liability, however. The determining factor is usually how well in advance the carrier knew that the event was to occur and whether or not he could reasonably have been able to avoid it by moving vehicles and goods elsewhere. Thus, a flash flood would probably be considered an exception to liability but a slow rising flood probably would not. Whether or not the carrier acted to minimize the loss or damage after the goods were actually exposed to the catastrophe would also be considered.

Act of Public Enemy. An act of a public enemy in the liability sense means military action by a foreign government and has rarely been used as an exception in modern times. If it should occur, however, the carrier involved would not be held accountable for any loss or damage to goods in his possession

Act of Public Authority. When goods are legally seized from a carrier's possession by sheriffs, tax collectors, health officers, or other govenment officials, the carrier involved is not held liable for the loss to the owner of the goods. Seizure may take place for a number of reasons, including illegality of the shipment (for example, narcotics or liquor if they are prohibited by law), failure to pay taxes on the goods, and because the goods are contaminated.

Fault of the User. In many cases, particularly in rail transportation, shippers and receivers load and unload the vehicles. Here there is the possibility that the shipper or receiver may cause loss or damage by theft by his employees, by carelessness while loading or unloading, or by improperly stowing the goods into the vehicle which, among other things, could result in shifting around and damage while in transit. Whenever transgressions by the shipper or receiver can be proven, the carrier may escape liability for loss or damage. Other areas of fault by the shipper are in packing the goods for shipment, marking the goods, and in describing the goods in such a way that they are mishandled by the carrier, thus causing loss or damage.

A difficulty with all this for the carrier is establishing proof. There is also the problem of the carrier having to accuse his customers of malpractice, which does not improve user–carrier relations. The result is that many small claims for loss and damage are probably paid even though the carrier could escape them. He chooses not to do so in order to avoid detrimental effects on his relationship with his clients.

Natural Shrinkage. In those cases in which the goods in transit shrink in weight or size, via evaporation, for example, the carrier is not held liable for the difference between the origin weight or size and the destination weight or size.

Quarantine Regulation. In addition to the five exceptions to liability discussed above, the rail bill of lading[7] and often the highway carrier bill of lading include other exceptions to liability. These exceptions pertain to quarantine regulation, defect or vice in the goods, and riots and strikes. The quarantine regulation exception states that the carrier is not to be held liable if loss or damage occurs as the result of fumigation or disinfection or other acts required by quarantine regulation or loss or damage of any kind occasioned by a quarantine or enforcement thereof.

Defect or Vice in the Goods. When the carrier believes that the goods that turned up damaged at the destination point had an "inherent defect or vice" when received from the shipper, he can seek to avoid liability for damage because this is an exception to liability. Defects of this kind include fermentation, drying, decay, heating, spontaneous combustion, or rusting in transit. The most frequent situations involve damage from spoilage of perishable goods and natural death or deterioration of livestock while being transported. It also includes damage that occurred before the goods were received by the carrier. Whenever defect or vice in the goods can be established, the carrier is not liable except in the case of his own negligence.

Riots and Strikes. Loss or damage caused by riots or by labor strikes (user or carrier strikes) are grounds for exception to liability unless the carrier can be shown to be negligent.[8]

Liability of Domestic Water Carriers

The Harter Act of 1893 and the Interstate Commerce Act govern liability of domestic interstate water carriers. These carriers are liable for the full value of what is lost or damaged when a valid claim is filed against them. In addition to the act of God, act of public enemy, act of public authority, fault of the user, and defect or vice in the goods exceptions to liability, water carriers are also exempt from liability when loss or damage is caused by perils of the waters, errors in navigation, rescue efforts, and fire. This means that, in a practical sense,

---

[7] Bills of lading are discussed in a later section of this chapter.

[8] There has been some controversy over whether or not common carriers can exempt themselves from liability (through terms of the bill of lading) from loss or damage resulting from riots and strikes. It has been argued that Section 20(11) of the Interstate Commerce Act prohibits a carrier from limiting his liability in this way. A leading authority on the subject, however, has concluded that this exception does not appear to contravene any of the provisions of the Interstate Commerce Act, although the exact liability of the carrier in cases of riots and strikes is not entirely clear. See Sigmon, *Miller's Law of Freight Loss and Damage Claims*, pp. 213-218.

the water carrier has very limited liability for loss and damage; and negligence on the part of the carrier is often required before a shipper or receiver can collect.

The result is that users of domestic water transportation, if there is reasonable chance for loss or damage to occur, often avail themselves of transportation insurance to cover such risks. This insurance, of course, can also be purchased when using any other kind of transportation.

Liability of Domestic Airlines

The liability for loss and damage assumed by the domestic airline industry has varied over time and has also varied between different carriers. The situation after 1970 was that air carriers did not assume liability for the full value of what they carried (see below). Air carriers stated the usual exceptions to liability in their contracts with shippers, but they also stated that the carrier would not be liable for loss and damage resulting from reasons other than the carrier's own negligence and that the carrier must bear the burden of proving that he was not negligent. The Civil Aeronautics Board (CAB) in 1977, after a 7 year study, ordered that regulated airlines were to be liable for all goods turned over to them, subject only to the exceptions to liability that apply to railroad, highway, and oil pipeline carriers, thus eliminating the need for carrier negligence to be present before liability was assumed.[9]

It appears, then, that users of water and air transportation have been at a great disadvantage when it comes to the matter of loss and damage and that the original intent of common carrier liability as set forth in common law has not been fulfilled in these modes.

Measure of Damage

When loss or damage to freight occurs and the surface common carrier is liable, he is *fully* liable for the loss; that is, he must compensate the shipper or receiver for the entire amount of the loss, not just a part of it.[10] The amount of loss incurred is usually determined by the market value of the goods in question had they arrived in good condition at the destination point when a market value can be determined. Otherwise, the loss is usually measured by the value of the article to the claimant, determined, perhaps, by replacement cost. The market value is usually the most accurate measure of actual loss and the most convenient measure of damages suffered. For example, if a manufacturer of men's shoes in Philadelphia ships shoes to a retailer in Milwaukee, but the shoes fail to turn up at Milwaukee, the loss would probably be measured by the price that would have been paid to the manufacturer by the retailer, less any trade discounts, and not the price the retailer might have charged his customers. In some cases, however,

---

[9] *Investigation of Air Freight Liability and Claims Rules and Practices,* docket 19923.

[10] In 1969 railroads, highway carriers, and surface freight forwarders in interstate commerce established a rule that provided for limiting their liability in cases of "concealed loss and damage" generally to no more that 50 per cent of the damage when the responsibility for the damage could not be clearly established. In 1972 the Interstate Commerce Commission declared the regulation unlawful. See Lawrence M. Lesser, "New ICC Concealed Damage Liability Ruling Pleases Shippers," *Traffic Management,* May, 1972.

the claimant is awarded an amount less than the market value at destination—the actual loss is what is important. Each case is decided by the circumstances surrounding the purchase, sale, and transportation of the goods.

When loss or damage occurs in domestic transportation, the freight charges on the damaged or missing part of the shipment, if already paid, may also be claimed, if not included in the invoice price. The cost of telephone calls, tracing, inspecting the freight, and other expenses associated with filing a claim may not be claimed.

In the case of damaged goods, if any article of merchandise is only partially damaged and is repairable, the receiver may accept the damaged merchandise, have it repaired himself, and then file a claim against the carrier for 100 per cent of the actual loss. The consignee may also dispose of the damaged goods and the user may claim the full value of the actual loss from the carrier.

If goods are totally damaged, the receiver may refuse to accept delivery and a claim for 100 per cent of its value is paid by the carrier. The carrier has the right to take the goods and dispose of them in any way he sees fit. If the carrier does not take possession of the goods promptly, the receiver may dispose of them in such a manner as will serve the best interests of the carrier if the goods have any value. Any salvage value would be deducted from the payment made to the user by the carrier.

In the case of shortage, the consignee may not refuse to receive the balance of the shipment. He must accept it and then file a claim against the carrier for the missing part of the shipment.

Released Rates

As we indicated earlier, surface common carriers assume full liability for what they carry, meaning that they must compensate the claimant for the full amount of loss incurred. An exception to this occurs when a shipment is made under what is called a *released value rate*. A released rate arrangement exists when the carrier assumes less than full liability and the user pays a reduced or less-than-normal rate. In other words, the user trades full liability for a lesser transportation charge. The user relieves the carrier of liability above a certain amount.

Because of certain regulatory restrictions, however, released rates are rare in domestic surface transportation. In rail and highway interstate transportation released rates are unlawful, with the exception of passenger baggage, unless the Interstate Commerce Commission (ICC) specifically authorizes a released rate. These authorizations are given only when the commodity in question has a very high range of values, thus making claimed loss difficult to estimate, and a high susceptibility to loss and damage.

There are, however, two major areas of released rates in United States transportation. One is in household goods carriage by interstate highway carriers. Here carriers are permitted to limit their liability to only $.60 per pound per article while charging their usual base transportation rates. When damage results to an article in a shipment released to this value, the maximum carrier liability for any damaged article is $.60 times the actual weight of the article in pounds, regardless of its market value. If the shipment is completely destroyed, the carrier is liable for $.60 times the weight of the entire shipment. Instead of releasing the shipment at $.60 per pound, a user can have the carrier's liability increased to the full value by declaring a lump-sum value of the shipment. But to get this greater protection, the user must pay, in addition to the base transportation rate, a charge of $.50 for each $100 of declared lump-sum value. The maximum liability the carrier will incur is the declared value. If the user does not release a shipment at $.60 per pound or does not declare a lump-sum value, the value is automatically considered to be $1.25 per pound of the entire weight of the shipment.[11]

The other major area of less-than-full liability has been in air freight transportation where most domestic airlines limited their liability for loss and damage to freight according to the "50–50" rule, which meant they limited liability to $.50 per pound or $50 per shipment, whichever was higher. As with the case of household goods carriers, however, a user could declare a higher value and pay from $.10 to $.15 for each $100 by which the declared value exceeded the released value. The air carrier would then be liable to the full amount of that declared value. In the 1977 decision referred to earlier, the CAB, recognizing the unrealistic character of the rule, ordered that regulated airlines discontinue the "50–50" rule and assume liability at $9.07 per pound, a figure to be applied temporarily until further investigation was made by the Board. The $9.07 was the amount of liability required of international air carriers under the Warsaw Convention (also used by one all-cargo domestic carrier). Users could still declare a valuation higher than the minimum and pay from $.10 to $.15 for each $100 by which the declared value exceeded the minimum value.[12]

Coordinate Liability of Joint Carriers

When interlining or multiple-line hauls take place (2 or more connecting carriers of the same mode are involved), the question of which carrier is liable for loss and damage arises. This is a problem that occurs mainly in rail and highway transportation. Interchange arrangements are less common in the other modes of transportation. When interchange does occur, however, water and air carriers normally limit their liability to their own lines.

Under common law and the laws of some states the carrier's liability ends when the goods are turned over to a connecting carrier. After early difficulty caused by rail carriers attempting to avoid paying claims for loss and damage by shifting blame to another connecting railroad, federal legislation applying to interstate rail, highway, and oil pipeline carriers provides that when an interlined shipment carried under one bill of lading is lost or damaged, a claim for loss and damage may be filed by the user against either the originating or delivering carrier, whether or not that carrier is responsible for the loss or damage. If the claim is valid, i.e., one or more of the exceptions to liability do not apply, the claim must be paid by the carrier against whom it is filed. A claim may also be filed against an intermediate or "bridge" carrier (3 or more carriers are involved), if it can be established that the loss or damage actually occurred on

---

[11] See Edward J. Bardi, "What Every Traffic Man Should Know About Household Goods Moving," *Handling and Shipping,* May, 1973, p. 59.

[12] *Investigation of Air Freight Liability and Claims Rules and Practices.*

the lines of that intermediate carrier.[13] If the carrier who pays the claim was not himself responsible for the loss or damage, it is his responsibility to seek reimbursement from the carrier that was responsible. If responsibility cannot be determined, the carriers involved in the haul divide the cost of the claim among themselves, often according to each carrier's mileage involved in or revenue received from the haul. In any case, the user is protected because a valid claim must be honored.

One of the reasons for the lack of significant development of intermodal domestic transportation service in which carriers of different modes interchange freight with one another and establish a joint rate for the service is the uncertainty regarding liability for loss and damage. The carriers of a given mode on an intermodal move may decline claims unless there is conclusive proof that the loss or damage occurred while the shipment was in their possession. Another aspect of this is the situation in which one of the modes involved assumes less liability than the other mode, creating a problem for the user in that he may not wish to use a joint arrangement if the liability for part of the haul is limited in such a way. For example, the bulk of domestic freight moving to and from offshore states and possessions by water moves under a combination of inland and port-to-port rates. The carriers are each liable for the shipment only while the shipment is in their possession, and the rules governing the extent of their liability differ significantly. If loss or damage occurs, it is up to the user to determine which of the carriers is responsible and which set of rules governs the amount that can be recovered from the carrier.[14]

CONTRACT CARRIAGE

The discussion of carrier obligations to this point has been in terms of for-hire common carriage in which the carrier has the obligation to serve the public generally and to deliver the goods. Another for-hire carrier, referred to as a *contract carrier,* has different obligations to serve the public and to deliver goods.

A contract carrier does not have the legal obligation to serve the public generally or to deliver the goods turned over to him for transportation. Instead, he may legally pick and choose the users he wants to serve. It may be just one or a very limited number of users. He may legally refuse to serve any user, and his liability limits are worked out between him and the user instead of specified by common or statutory law.

The term "contract" carrier is derived from the fact that the carrier enters into a written contract with the shipper. He does not use a common carrier bill of lading. The contract sometimes covers a long period of time and it spells out the terms and conditions under which the transportation service is to be rendered. A highway contract carrier's agreement, for example, may cover shipments over several months and indicate what is to be carried and where, how often,

[13] The legislation which changed federal policy on this question was the Carmack amendment of the Hepburn Act of 1906 and the Cummins amendment of 1915 and the Newton amendment of 1927 to the Interstate Commerce Act.

[14] Jean V. Strickland, "Resolving the Intermodal Muddle," *Distribution Worldwide,* March, 1975, p. 31.

and what rate(s) is to be charged. It will also specify the kind of liability for loss and damage that the carrier assumes, which may be greater or less than that assumed by highway common carriers, although the majority of these contracts provide for full common carrier liability.

Contract carriage may be a feasible alternative for the user when the circumstances calling for private carriage (see Chapter 4) are present, for example, the need for specialized equipment or the need for service to out of the way points, but the user does not want to make the capital and managerial commitment to private carriage. Contract carriage may be the next best thing and is often considered a substitute for private carriage. Contract carriage is frequently found in highway transportation and also to some extent in water and air transportation.

CLAIMS

An important and sometimes difficult aspect of the user–carrier relationship has to do with loss and damage to goods while the goods are in the carrier's possession and also with overcharges or undercharges made by the carrier. If the user thinks that the common carrier is liable for loss or damage, the user files a claim against the carrier for the amount of the loss or damage. Claims for overcharge may also be filed against a common carrier. A claim against a carrier may be filed by any party entitled to recover, but it is usually filed by the party who had title to the goods when the loss or damage occurred and hence suffered the loss. Consequently, the geographic pricing practices discussed in Chapter 3 have an important bearing on this matter since the geographic pricing practice followed determines who has title to goods while they are being transported. Filing a claim for loss or damage or overcharge must usually follow specific rules and regulations laid down either by government regulation or by industry regulation or practice. Gathering evidence and filing claims are important activities in industrial traffic management.

Loss and Damage Claims

Loss and damage claims are filed by a user for payment when loss or damage to goods has occurred during transportation. The validity of the claim is determined by the circumstances, i.e., whether or not loss or damage has actually occurred and whether or not an exception to liability existed. Each claim is evaluated on its own merits, and generalizations are difficult. In the case of water and air carriers, of course, it has usually been necessary to establish carrier negligence in order for the user to collect.

In addition to claims filed when goods arrive at the destination in damaged condition or fail to arrive at all, loss and damage claims also include claims for monetary losses incurred because of delay in transportation, although the goods are actually delivered in good condition (physical damage or deterioration of the commodity being shipped can also result from delay). Such a claim may be filed when the carrier has failed to transport the shipment with "reasonable dispatch." When carriers have guaranteed a specific schedule or when a carrier has regularly over a period of time performed on a regular basis and users and carriers have come to accept these schedules and to expect that they will be met, a claim might be filed when the schedules are not met by the carrier. Compensation for the resulting losses incurred by the user can be collected from the carrier unless the carrier can successfully explain the delay by showing that it was not due to his negligence but to some other unavoidable cause that could not be anticipated, including the exceptions to liability discussed earlier. The loss that might accrue to a user is often caused by the user's receiving a lower price for his product because the shipment arrived later than he expected. This would most likely occur in those industries, such as some aspects of agricultural marketing, in which there is a daily market price that fluctuates from day to day.

Another kind of claim is a claim for misdelivery. Compensation is sought because the carrier has delivered the shipment to the wrong person, hence causing a loss for the shipper or receiver.

The loss and damage which can be seen and noted ("exception" made) at the time of delivery is referred to as *known loss and damage. Concealed loss and damage* is not visible at the time of delivery and, of course, no notation ("exception") is made at that time because the loss or damage is discovered later. Claims for concealed loss and damage require inspection by a carrier's agent for verification purposes and are far more difficult to collect on than are claims for known loss and damage. Definitely determining responsibility for the loss or damage is difficult and the possibility of fraud on the part of the claimant is great.

Rather elaborate regulations exist, either governmental or industry designated, covering the processing of claims, including the form of the claim, the supporting documents to be included, and the time periods within which claims must be filed by users and disposed of by carriers.

If a common carrier refuses to pay all or part of a claim for loss or damage, the user may take the case to court. Federal regulatory agencies do not have any role in settling these disputes. The disputes are settled by either state or federal courts. In 1975 the Transportation Arbitration Board was established by the Shippers National Freight Claim Council and the National Freight Claims Council of the American Trucking Associations to help settle disputed loss, damage, and delay claims between users and trucking companies. The agreements reached through arbitration were to be binding on the parties involved and enforceable through the courts. In 1977 an arbitration plan for settling disputed claims between railroads and users was established by the Association of American Railroads and the American Arbitration Association under which the arbitration was to be voluntary but the verdict was to be binding on both parties.[15]

Overcharge and Reparations Claims

Claims are made for overcharges. The most frequent overcharge claim is filed because the carrier has collected charges in excess of those that would result if the legally applicable rates had been applied. These claims are based on the idea that any deviation from the legally published applicable rate, regardless of the reason, is ordinarily considered unlawful. These overcharges result from an error

[15] "Truck and Shipper Claim Councils Agree to Arbitrate Cargo Claim Controversies." *Traffic World,* July 7, 1975, p. 19, "Shippers, Motor Carriers Name 20-Man Arbitration Board to Resolve Claims," *Traffic World,* December 15, 1976, p. 23, and "AAR, Arbitration Association Develop Scheme for Settling Disputed Claims," *Traffic World,* April 4, 1977, p. 75.

in the rate applied, an error in the classification applied (see Chapter 9), an error in the weight applied, an error in the description of the commodities shipped, an error in arithmetic, or duplicate payment of the same freight bill. Interest may be claimed on the amount of the overcharge if held for more than 30 days. Although there is no legal reason why interest should be paid, many railroads pay it at the annual rate of 4 per cent. Other carriers generally refuse to pay interest on overcharges. Both the ICC (surface carriers only) and the courts have jurisdiction over overcharge claims of this kind and may order that refunds be made.

A second kind of overcharge claim is filed when the shipper believes that a rate, although a legally applicable rate, is unreasonably high, or unjustly discriminatory, or unduly preferential. The shipper complains to the appropriate regulatory agency or a court instead of actually filing a claim against a carrier. If the agency or court finds the complaint to be valid, it may award reparations (refund) to the shipper. A reparations award is more like a retroactive rate adjustment than it is a payment for a claim. Interest must be paid on the money overcharged when the ICC orders a refund to be made.

Another kind of overcharge claim is a claim for misrouting. The user argues that when the carrier routed a shipment in a multiple-line haul (the user did not specify the routing himself), the carrier did not route the haul in such a way that the lowest possible rate resulted. In may also occur when the shipment has been routed differently from what the user specified, thus resulting in a higher rate. A claim for overcharge may also be filed when the carrier brought the shipment to the wrong destination and, therefore, charged an incorrect rate.

Undercharge Claims

An undercharge claim may be filed by a common carrier against a user when appropriate freight charges have not been collected—the user was undercharged and did not pay the legally applicable rate. Undercharge can occur for various reasons, including application of the wrong rate or weight in calculating the freight charges, applying the wrong classification, arithmetic errors on the freight bill, and misdescription of the shipment. Again, since any deviation from the legally applicable rate is ordinarily considered unlawful, the user is obligated to pay the applicable charges. If the carrier fails to collect the undercharge, he can proceed to file suit in the appropriate court.

Magnitude of Loss and Damage Claims

The amount of loss and damage that occurs in the American transportation system is extensive. In 1976, for example, although the percentage of railroad revenue paid out in loss and damage claims was at the lowest level in 16 years, the *claim ratio*, i.e., the percentage of gross revenue paid out in loss and damage claims by railroads was 1.36 per cent and the dollar amount paid out was approximately 237 million dollars.[16] The record high was 1.97 per cent in 1970. The net income of the 52 Class I railroads (those with annual operating revenue of

[16]"Two-Year Trend Reversed As Rail Claim Payments Dropped 15% in 1976," *Traffic World*, May 30, 1977, p. 32.

more then 10 million dollars) that account for 99 per cent of railroad traffic was $345,463,000 in 1976.[17] The claim bill, then, of the United States railroad industry was almost 69 per cent of the Class I railroads' net income.

In the highway carrier industry, the Class I (annual operating revenue of more than 3 million dollars) intercity common carriers of general freight regulated by the ICC had a freight claim ratio of 1.33 in 1974, meaning that their loss and damage claims and cargo insurance expenses amounted to 1.33 per cent of their gross revenue in that year.[18] This represented a substantial improvement over some recent years. It has been stated that for 75 Class I highway carriers, the claim ratio measured against net income, rather than gross revenue, was 27.2 per cent in both 1970 and 1971.[19]

In 1973 the nation's scheduled airlines, both domestic and international, paid out more than 10 million dollars in freight claims,[20] despite the limited liability they assumed. This represented approximately 1 per cent of the $1,038,510,000 in air freight revenue taken in by these carriers in 1973 and 4.5 per cent of the industry's net income of $222,847,000 derived from both passenger and freight traffic in that year.[21]

It can be seen from the above figures that loss and damage is a very important expense for transportation companies, particularly when calculated as a percentage of net income instead of gross revenue. The problem appears to be more acute in rail and highway transportation than in air transportation, although the figures for air transportation are somewhat misleading since the carriers assumed such limited liability in 1973, and considerable damage and loss may have occurred for which the carriers did not compensate shippers.

The true cost of loss and damage, however, far exceeds the absolute cost of claims and the percentage figures related either to gross revenue or net income because these figures account only for the amounts paid out by common carriers in claims and do not include other costs associated with loss and damage. These other costs include costs incurred by carriers and/or users and consist of the costs of investigating and processing claims, legal fees, and the ill will and lost sales created by loss and damage in transit. The American Trucking Associations has reported that for every dollar expended in paying loss and damage claims, from $2 to $5 in indirect costs are incurred by the carrier. The users say that their indirect costs are even greater, ranging from $5 to $7 for each dollar of direct cost paid out in claims by the carrier.[22] A United States Department of Transportation (DOT) study reported that for every $1 reduction in freight claims, there can be as much as a $.50 increase in net profit for the carrier.[23]

[17] Association of American Railroads, *Railroad Facts,* 1977 ed. (Washington, D.C.: Association of American Railroads, 1977), p. 22.

[18] American Trucking Associations, Inc., *American Trucking Trends, 1976 Statistical Supplement* (Washington, D.C.: American Trucking Associations, Inc., 1977), p. 9.

[19] R. Stanley Chapman, "Claim Ratio Concepts and 'Voluntary' Standards," *Traffic World,* April 1, 1974, p. 46.

[20] "Air Security Specialists Focus on Profits Flowing From Reduction in Claims," *Traffic World,* May 20, 1974, p. 35.

[21] Calculated from Air Transport Association of America, *Air Transport 1974* (Washington, D.C.: Air Transport Association of America, 1974), pp. 25 and 30.

[22] "New Variations in an Old Transport Theme," *Traffic World,* May 27, 1974, p. 5.

[23] Chapman, "Claim Ratio Concepts," p. 46.

The federal DOT reported that in 1970 an average figure for indirect cost for users and carriers was 5 times the claim dollar paid. Included in the user and carrier costs were the costs of processing claims, claim litigation, insurance premiums, and security personnel and facilities. Not included were intangible losses such as the loss of sales, loss of seasonal business, and loss of customer good will. If the estimate of 5 times the claim bill is used, the cost of loss and damage in 1970 was approximately 13 billion dollars, including $4.2 billion from theft-related losses, for rail, truck, water, and air transportation.[24]

If these estimates are accurate, the total cost of loss and damage is several times the amount paid out in claims. Obviously, it is in the interest of carriers and users to keep the loss and damage problem under control. Clearly, for the user of common carrier transportation, even if every loss and damage claim is .paid by the carrier promptly and in full, the user is much better off with no loss and damage at all.

Causes of Loss and Damage

The causes of loss and damage in common carrier transportation are many, and sometimes they are the fault of the shipper or receiver, not the carrier. Causes of loss and damage include improper packing, handling, loading, unloading, or stowing; pilferage and theft; wrecks and fires; defective vehicles or other equipment; temperature failure; delay in transit; and disappearance of freight from causes other than pilferage and theft.

A leading and increasing cause of loss in recent years has been pilferage and theft of goods while in the care of common carriers. It has been estimated that theft of goods in transit amounts to between 1 billion and 1.5 billion dollars per year.[25] According to the federal DOT, only a small share of the pilferage and theft problem is caused by hijacking and burglary; 85 per cent of the thefts occur during normal working hours and are committed by transportation employees or other persons having legitimate access to transportation facilities.[26]

The problem of theft in transportation has become so serious that in 1972 the federal government began a cooperative government-industry program to combat crime in transportation and in February, 1975 President Gerald R. Ford directed all federal and other agencies to attack the problem vigorously. The President gave specific responsibilities to the DOT and required an annual progress report on the subject from that Department.[27] In its first report in early 1976, the DOT stated that airlines had made substantial progress in reducing theft of freight, that motor trucking companies had shown slight improvement, and that railroad data were insufficient to identify any trend.[28]

Approximately 60 per cent of the stolen freight is stolen from highway

---

[24] "New 'Size-Up' of Old Transport Problem," *Traffic World,* July 10, 1972, p. 5.

[25] "Achievement in Freight Claim Prevention," *Traffic World,* April 1, 1974, p. 1.

[26] "New Variations in an Old Transport Theme," *Traffic World,* p. 5.

[27] "President Ford Orders DOT to Collect Cargo Theft Data Covering All Modes," *Traffic World,* February 3, 1975, p. 19.

[28] "With Railroad and Maritime Emphasis, DOT to Continue Cargo Security Effort," *Traffic World,* April 5, 1976, p. 9.

carriers. The most popular targets for such thieves, in order, are clothing and textiles, electrical appliances, metal and hardware, automobile parts and accessories, and food products. The vast majority of airline claims stem from theft rather than from damage. The most frequently stolen air freight items, in order, are clothing and textiles, jewelry and coins, electrical appliances, machine parts and tools, and scientific instruments. Rail shipments most frequently stolen are automobile parts and accessories, food products, chemicals, electrical appliances, and metals and hardware.[29]

The loss and damage problem is a user problem as well as a carrier problem, and shippers can help to reduce the amount of loss and damage in various ways. These include production of commodities in such a manner as to make them less liable to handling damage; proper preparation of articles for transportation, including wrapping and placing in the shipping container and proper and complete marking of the shipment; and proper loading, storing, and securing of shipments in the vehicle when the shipper does the loading. Receivers can also cooperate by exercising care in unloading.[30]

CONTRACT FOR CARRIAGE

Contract Carrier Contract

As indicated earlier, when a user makes use of a for-hire contract carrier, a written contract is entered into which specifies the terms and conditions under which the transportation is to be performed. The contract is often a fairly long-term one covering more than one shipment and covering such things as what is to be carried and where, how often, the rate(s) to be charged, and the liability for loss and damage to be assumed by the carrier. The terms and conditions of a contract carrier contract are not standardized among carriers even within the same mode, and an individual carrier may enter into different contract terms with different clients.

Common Carrier Contract

In the case of for-hire common carriers, a special kind of contract, often called a *bill of lading,* is used. Interstate rail, highway, water, and oil pipeline carriers that are regulated by the ICC must issue a bill of lading or a receipt for the goods turned over to them. Air carriers do not have such a requirement. Unlike the contract in contract carriage, the bill of lading covers one shipment only and is sometimes standardized for all carriers within a mode. For railroads, the form and contents of the bill of lading are specified by the ICC. For other modes, the carriers select their own bill of lading form and contents, but often they are very similar or identical to those used by many carriers of the same

---

[29] "Planning an Assault on Cargo Theft," *Business Week,* August 10, 1974, pp. 44–45. See also Miklos B. Korodi, "Terminal Security—It's a Systems Job," *Traffic World,* April 7, 1975, p. 47.

[30] Charles A. Taff, *Management of Physical Distribution and Transportation,* 5th ed. (Homewood, Illinois: Richard D. Irwin, Inc., 1972), pp. 458–459.

mode. There is, however, a diversity of the bills of lading used within a mode, particularly in highway transportation.[31]

Every bill of lading is a contract for carriage in that it contains the terms and conditions under which the transportation is to be rendered, including the liability for loss and damage that the carrier assumes. The bill of lading must be signed by both carrier and user. The terms and conditions are usually stated on the reverse side of the bill of lading unless the "short form" is used. In that case, although the generally accepted terms and conditions are not stated, it is understood that both parties agree that they apply to the shipment.

Every bill of lading is also a user's receipt for the goods turned over to the carrier. The signed copy of the bill of lading kept by the user is evidence that the shipment has been turned over to the possession of the carrier. This receipt is used in case loss or damage occurs and a claim against the carrier is filed.

Some bills of lading are more than a contract and a receipt. They are negotiable, meaning that they can be transferred from one party to another, and they are evidence of title, meaning that they must be produced and turned over to the delivering carrier before delivery will be made by the carrier.

Bills of lading are filled out by the shipper although they are legally issued by the carrier. Carriers furnish the bill of lading forms for shippers to use, but shippers sometimes use their own forms, which often include preprinted descriptions of items to be shipped. There are several varieties of bills of lading used by the different modes of transportation.

Uniform Straight Bill of Lading. In rail, highway, and water transportation, the most frequently used bill of lading is the uniform straight bill of lading. It is a contract and a receipt, and it is non-negotiable. A copy of a railroad uniform straight bill of lading is presented in Figure 6-2. Note that, like most bills of lading, it contains basic information about the shipment, including the place of shipment, the date of shipment, the shipper's name, the consignee's name, the place of the consignee, the routing to be followed, the delivering carrier, the car initial and number, the number of items, the description of the commodities to be carried, their weight, the applicable rate, and whether or not the shipment is to be prepaid or collect.

Uniform Order Bill of Lading. The uniform order bill of lading used by railroads, trucking companies, and water carriers is identical to the uniform straight bill, except that the surrender of the properly endorsed bill of lading is required before the carrier may deliver the goods. The bill of lading becomes evidence of title since it must be presented to the carrier before possession of the goods can be attained. It is also a negotiable instrument that can be bought and sold.

The order bill of lading is used by a shipper when he wants to be sure that payment for the goods is received before delivery to the consignee is made by the carrier. This is arranged for by the shipper consigning the shipment to himself and then, through the banking system, the properly endorsed (to the con-

---

[31] The Federal (Pomerene) Bills of Lading Act, which became effective on January 1, 1917, does not prescribe the form or contents of the bills of lading to be used by interstate carriers. Instead, it is concerned primarily with the rights of parties relating to ownership of the goods and had, as a major purpose, to expand the negotiability of order bills of lading.

Form 43

(Uniform Domestic Straight Bill of Lading, adopted by Carriers in Official, Southern, Western and Illinois Classification territories, March 15, 1922, as amended August 1, 1930 and June 15, 1941.)

Sheet 1   **UNIFORM STRAIGHT BILL OF LADING**

Shipper's No.............

ORIGINAL--Not Negotiable

Agent's No.............

SOO LINE RAILROAD COMPANY

RECEIVED, subject to the classifications and tariffs in effect on the date of the issue of this Bill of Lading,

at_____, 19____

from_____

the property described below, in apparent good order, except as noted (contents and condition of contents of packages unknown), marked, consigned, and destined as indicated below, which said company (the word company being understood throughout this contract as meaning any person or corporation in possession of the property under the contract) agrees to carry to its usual place of delivery at said destination, if on its own road or its own water line, otherwise to deliver to another carrier on the route to said destination. It is mutually agreed, as to each carrier of all or any of said property over all or any portion of said route to destination, and as to each party at any time interested in all or any of said property, that every service to be performed hereunder shall be subject to all the conditions not prohibited by law, whether printed or written, herein contained, including the conditions on back hereof, which are hereby agreed to by the shipper and accepted for himself and his assigns.

(Mail or street address of consignee—For purposes of notification only.)

Consigned to...

Destination...State of........................County of........................

Route..

Delivering Carrier...Car Initial.............Car No...............

No. Packages	DESCRIPTION OF ARTICLES, SPECIAL MARKS, AND EXCEPTIONS	*WEIGHT (Subject to Correction)	CLASS OR RATE	CHECK COLUMN	Subject to Section 7 of conditions, if this shipment is to be delivered to the consignee without recourse on the consignor, the consignor shall sign the following statement:
					The carrier shall not make delivery of this shipment without payment of freight and all other lawful charges.
					(Signature of consignor.)
					If charges are to be prepaid, write or stamp here, "To be Prepaid."
					Received $.............. to apply in prepayment of the charges on the property described hereon.
					Agent or Cashier.
					Per.............. (The signature here acknowledges only the amount prepaid.)

*If the shipment moves between two ports by a carrier by water, the law requires that the bill of lading shall state whether it is "carrier's or shipper's weight."

Note—Where the rate is dependent on value, shippers are required to state specifically in writing the agreed or declared value of the property.

The agreed or declared value of the property is hereby specifically stated by the shipper to be not exceeding

Charges advanced:

$..............

....per.....................................

....Shipper.   ....Agent.

Per....................................   Per..................................

Permanent postoffice address of shipper..................

Printed in U.S.A.

FIGURE 6-2 *Railroad Uniform Straight Bill of Lading. (Source: Soo Line Railroad Company)*

signee) bill of lading is sent to a bank in the destination city. The bank collects the invoice price for the goods from the consignee before turning the bill of lading over to the consignee. The consignee can then claim the goods from the carrier. The payment received by the bank is forwarded to the shipper's local bank and is deposited in the shippers's account.

Other Bills of Lading. In oil pipeline transportation a non-negotiable document, called a *tender of shipment*, is used as a form of bill of lading. In domestic air transportation the *air bill*, which is fairly uniform among the different carriers, is used. The air bill is non-negotiable. In addition, there is a through export bill of lading for use by surface carriers who are involved in foreign trade, an ocean bill of lading for use in domestic ocean shipping, a government bill of lading for transportation of property belonging to the federal government or when the federal government is to pay the freight bill, the uniform livestock contract which is used when railroads transport livestock and wild animals and when the carrier's liability is somewhat limited, and bills of lading or receipts issued by surface and air freight forwarders and various express and parcel companies.

SELECTED REFERENCES

There are several books available on channels of distribution, including Edwin H. Lewis, *Marketing Channels: Structure and Strategy* (New York: McGraw-Hill Book Company, 1968); Bruce E. Mallen, ed., *The Marketing Channel* (New York: John Wiley and Sons, Inc., 1967); Louis W. Stern, ed., *Distribution Channels: Behavioral Dimensions* (Boston: Houghton-Mifflin Company, 1969); and Louis E. Boone and James C. Johnson, eds., *Marketing Channels* (Morristown, New Jersey: General Learning Press, 1973). Introductory marketing texts also usually have some discussion of channels of distribution. See, for example, Theodore N. Beckman, William R. Davidson, and W. Wayne Talarzyk, *Marketing*, 9th ed. (New York: The Ronald Press Company, 1973), Chapter 9.

The role of the for-hire carrier in the channel of distribution is dealt with in Frederick J. Beier, "The Role of the Common Carrier in the Channel of Distribution," *Transportation Journal*, Winter, 1969.

Implications of the business logistics concept for carrier management are discussed in James L. Heskett, Nicholas A. Glaskowsky, Jr., and Robert M. Ivie, *Business Logistics*, 2nd ed. (New York: The Ronald Press Company, 1973), pp. 749-758.

The potential and actual adaptation of United States railroads to the logistics needs of shippers is treated in considerable detail in Alan J. Stenger, *An Evaluation of the Ability of the United States Railroads to Respond to the Logistics Needs of the Shippers*, unpublished Ph.D. dissertation, University of Minnesota, 1974. Discussion of ways in which greater user–railroad cooperation can be accomplished is Alan J. Stenger and Frederick J. Beier, "Effective Carrier Marketing Strategies: The Case of the Railroads," *Transportation Journal*, Summer, 1976.

The concept of common carriage, its origin in common law, and common carrier obligations are discussed in Martin T. Farris, "The Role of the Common Carrier," *Transportation Journal*, Summer, 1967.

The reasons for using contract highway carriage, regulatory requirements, and the specific things covered in a contract are dealt with in Blanton P. Bergen and Colin Barrett, "The Elements of Contract Carriage," *Transportation and Distribution Management*, December, 1971 and January and February, 1972.

A detailed treatment of common carrier liability, loss and damage, and the bill of lading may be found in Richard R. Sigmon, *Miller's Law of Freight Loss and Damage Claims,* 4th ed. (Dubuque, Iowa: William C. Brown Company Publishers, 1974). See also Kenneth U. Flood, *Traffic Management,* 3rd ed. (Dubuque, Iowa: William C. Brown Company Publishers, 1975), Chapters 16 and 17.

An excellent practical discussion of the freight claims procedure is George A. Gecowets, "A Distribution Manager's Guide to Handling Claims," *Handling and Shipping,* October, 1972. See also Flood, *Traffic Management,* Chapter 18.

The annual "perfect shipping" issue of *Traffic World* contains up-to-date discussions of developments in loss and damage occurrence and prevention. See, for example, the issue of April 4, 1977.

PART TWO

Providers of
Transportation Service

7

Cost Elements in a
Transportation Operation

In this chapter we begin our discussion of the providers of transportation service, i.e., the carriers, by examining some of the cost factors in a transportation operation. In Chapters 8 through 15 we shall discuss pricing in transportation, the economic and service characteristics of the carriers of the several modes, and decision making in transportation companies.

The purpose of a transportation operation is to carry goods and/or passengers from some origin point to some destination point. This should be done with minimum cost and with minimum elapsed time. In accomplishing this task, carriers should try to avoid out-of-line movements, excessive handling of freight, excessive transfer of freight or passengers, and, at the same time, they should minimize unused capacity and maximize the productivity of the capital, labor, and equipment devoted to providing transportation service.

In order to provide transportation service, any transportation operation, regardless of mode, and whether private or for-hire, must have basic physical elements that are necessary to produce transportation service and which result in costs to the transportation organization. These physical elements include ways, terminals, and vehicles.

In this chapter we attempt to review these basic elements in a transportation operation that generate costs that the carrier must cover. We also discuss the nature of those costs. It should be understood that the discussion does not attempt to include all carrier costs but, instead, only those having to do with the 3 primary kinds of physical facilities that are peculiar to transportation. These are ways, terminals, and vehicles. Each of these is defined and discussed in the paragraphs below.

KINDS OF COSTS

As with any other enterprise, the costs incurred in producing transportation service and which are associated with the 3 elements—ways, terminals, and

135

vehicles—can be described and defined in various ways and can be broken down into a very large number of cost categories. Thus, for example, the costs associated with a transportation activity can be classified as fixed, incremental, inescapable, joint, sunk, average, and so on.[1] For the purpose of discussing the costs associated with providing transportation service, however, we shall concentrate on only 4 kinds of costs—fixed, variable, joint, and common.

Fixed Costs

Fixed or overhead or constant costs are costs that do not vary with output. They are unaffected by increases or decreases in the volume of traffic carried. They include various expenses for facilities, equipment, administration, interest on investment, insurance, and taxes that are required to maintain a carrier's operation as a going concern. They are called fixed because they are incurred whether or not any traffic is carried. They can be avoided only by abandoning the entire operation or at least a considerable part of it. An example of a fixed cost in transportation companies is a local property tax levied on a piece of carrier property, a tax that does not fluctuate with the volume of business done by the carrier.

It is often difficult to assign fixed costs to any particular class or unit of traffic carried, since often no relationship exists between them and any particular kind of traffic. In such cases, they are considered to be incurred on behalf of the operation as a whole.

Variable Costs

Variable costs are costs that vary with changes in the rate of output. They are costs incurred directly as a result of the movement of traffic and which could have been avoided if the transportation service had not been rendered. They include expenses that are incurred solely as a result of producing the transportation services necessary to carry the traffic. They include not only directly measurable costs but also those arising from wear and tear on line-haul equipment used in performing the transportation service. When costs are computed for a given unit of traffic, they are sometimes referred to as *out-of-pocket costs.* Examples of variable costs in transportation are direct labor costs and fuel costs. The more traffic carried, the more labor and fuel that will be used by the carrier. Average variable cost, or unit variable cost, is determined by dividing the total variable cost by the number of units of traffic carried at a particular level of output.

In this book the term variable costs is used to designate the added costs involved in changing a carrier's volume of traffic, whether the added traffic results from adding new customers for existing services over existing routes, or from adding a new service, or from serving new routes, or some other reason. In short, the term variable costs denotes additional costs that are incurred as a

[1] Among the various costs that have been identified in economic literature are variable, fixed, out-of-pocket, incremental, opportunity, past, short-run, long-run, escapable, inescapable, traceable, untraceable, controllable, uncontrollable, replacement, alternative, direct, indirect, differential, residual, sunk, shutdown, postponable, unpostponable, replacement, original, joint, common, constant, total, average, and marginal.

result of a management decision that causes a change in the carrier's volume of traffic.

The time period being considered is very important in any discussion of costs because, as the time period increases in length, the more costs tend to become variable and, in the very long run, all costs are variable. The shorter the time period, the more likely a particular cost will be considered fixed. Consequently, what is a fixed or variable cost depends on the time period under consideration, usually referred to as either a short-run or a long-run period. The short run is a period of time too short for the carrier to alter his basic physical plant capacity, but it is long enough to permit a change in the level at which the carrier's physical plant is utilized. In other words, the carrier's plant capacity is fixed in the short run, but the volume of traffic carried can be varied (existing plant capacity can be used more or less intensively in the short run). The long run is a period of time long enough to allow a carrier to change the quantitites of all resources used to produce transportation service, including plant capacity. For a particular investment by a carrier, such as in a way, in a terminal, or in vehicles, the short run is the period in which the investment is not changed (its capacity to handle traffic remains constant). The length of time involved in the short run varies with the nature of the investment and the mode of transportation. Therefore, it is not possible to say whether a specific cost to produce a given transportation service is fixed or variable without an examination of the particular situation.

Joint Costs

Costs are said to be joint when the creation of one service unavoidably results in the creation of another service. An example in transportation is a transportation company's providing service from point A to point B and automatically providing service from B back to A in order to return the vehicles to A. Another example is a carrier's providing service from A to C, and since B is on the route from A to C, automatically providing service to B.

Common Costs

Common costs are also incurred for more than one transportation service but, unlike joint costs, the use of resources to provide one service does not automatically result in the production of another service. Thus, the costs of providing and maintaining a railroad roadbed result in the production of transportation service for grain, for steel, for bicycles, and so on. It is difficult to trace the common costs to any one of these services.

Fixed and variable costs, on the one hand, and joint and common costs, on the other, are not mutually exclusive. Fixed and variable costs may be joint or common, and joint and common costs may be either fixed or variable.

WAYS

Every transportation operation, private or for-hire, makes use of a *way* of some sort. The characteristics of the way greatly affect not only the costs of providing transportation service, but also the quality of the service relative to other modes and the geographic area a mode or a given carrier can serve. The most important factor that determines the cost structure of and distinguishes between modes of transportation is the nature of the way.

Nature of the Way

The way is the path over which the carrier operates and includes the right of way (the land area being used) plus any roadbed and tracks or other physical facilities that are needed on the right of way.

The nature of the way varies with the mode of transportation. In the case of railroads, the way consists of the right of way plus the roadbed, tracks, tunnels, and bridges that are necessary. For highway carriers, the way consists of the right of way plus the highway or street. For water carriers, the way is the lake, ocean, river, or canal. For pipelines it is the right of way plus the pipe, which may be above or below the ground. In air transportation, the way consists of the air corridor being used by the aircraft, the corridor often being part of the federal airway system.

Costs Associated with the Way

Nature of Way Costs. Whether or not any costs to the carrier are associated with the way and the kind of costs depend on who provides the way, who pays for it, and how it is paid for.

When the way is provided by the carriers with private investment and when the carriers assume responsibility for operating, maintaining, and improving the way and paying taxes on it, an important cost element is generated by the way. This is the case with railroads and oil pipelines. The heavy investment in way by those carriers results in a large required return on investment in dollars, amortization or depreciation (unrelated to the volume of traffic carried), where applicable, heavy maintenance costs, and large amounts of taxes. Since these costs to a great extent are incurred regardless of the amount of traffic carried over the way, they may be considered mostly fixed in nature as well as large in dollar amount. Unless a change in traffic volume is so great that it requires a change in the way itself, the costs associated with the way tend not to change with traffic quantity changes. The costs of the way are also to a great extent common in that the way is used to produce many different kinds of transportation services for different commodities and/or passengers.

When the carrier provides his own way, the problem of effectively utilizing the capacity of the way must be dealt with by the carrier, a problem he would not have to be concerned with if the way were provided by nature or government. The capacity of a way is the maximum amount of traffic that can be safely carried over the way without incurring excessive maintenance expense. The ideal would be to operate at full capacity, thereby spreading the costs of the way over the maximum number of traffic units and thus minimizing the way costs per unit carried.

When nature provides the way, the cost to the carrier may be zero. This would be true when nature provides the way, for example, a lake for a water carrier to use. No investment is required by the carrier and no fees are paid by the carrier for the use of the way.

When government provides the way, the costs to the carrier may again be zero if the government in question does not levy any charges for the use of the way. If, however, the government levies a charge in the form of a tax or a fee for using the way (user charge), the cost of the way is usually a variable cost because the taxes and fees paid ordinarily vary with the amount of carrier usage of the way and hence vary with the traffic volume carried.

This latter situation is complicated when government collects various taxes or fees from carriers, but the taxes or fees are not officially designated as user charges and no special fund exists to support the way in question. This was the case with airlines prior to 1970 whereby federal taxes were levied against airlines, but the revenue produced was not set aside in a special fund for airway development. In such a situation, it becomes difficult to tie the charges in with the facilities used by the carrier in terms of knowing exactly what is being paid for and exactly what the way costs are.

Joint Use of Way. In some cases, the way is jointly used by more than one carrier. For example, in highway transportation a highway is used by more than one trucking company, as well as by automobiles and other vehicles. The same is generally true in the case of the ways of water and air transportation. It is generally not true in rail and oil pipeline transportation, although some examples of it can be found in both modes. When joint use of a way exists, the cost burden per carrier is, of course, reduced below what it would be if a single carrier had to pay the entire cost of the way himself. One of the difficulties modern United States railroads have is that they are individually trying to bear the burden of the cost of their separate ways in a period of unsatisfactory earnings while most of their competitors make joint use of ways.

Cost Allocation Problem. Regardless of whether or not the way is singly or jointly used and paid for and whether or not the way costs are fixed or variable, when a carrier has costs associated with the way, the costs are to a great extent common because they are incurred in order to produce a variety of transportation services. The service provided by a transportation company should not be thought of as one homogeneous mass. Instead, it is a collection of different transportation services, such as transportation of steel beams, of men's shoes, of furniture, of passengers, and so on.

Since the same way is used to provide all of these services, the costs associated with the way are common costs and part of the costs must somehow be allocated to each different service in order to determine the true costs of transportation for each kind of service provided. This is of particular importance in pricing transportation services. Obviously, this is difficult to do in practice and is ordinarily accomplished by using arbitrary methods of one kind or another.

TERMINALS

Nature of Terminals

Terminals are places where private or for-hire carriers load and unload traffic into and from vehicles, make connections between local pickup and delivery service and line-haul service, where weighing is done, where carriers make connections between routes within their own system and with other carriers, where vehicles are routed and dispatched, and, often, where certain paper work and other administrative activities and vehicle maintenance are carried out. They are also places where passengers purchase tickets and waiting takes place and where freight shipments are stored and protected before or after line-haul transportation. Sales personnel are also often quartered in for-hire carrier terminal facilities.

Every transportation operation requires the use of terminals of some sort. The nature, size, and complexity of terminal facilities needed varies with the mode of transportation, the size of firm, and the kinds of commodities carried.

Railroad freight terminal facilities consist mainly of freight yards where freight trains are made up and broken up and where connections are made between railroads. Highway carrier freight terminals are buildings where less-than-truckload freight picked up locally is transferred to line-haul (intercity) trucks and where less-than truckload freight brought in by line-haul trucks is transferred to local delivery trucks. They are also places where freight is transferred from one highway carrier's vehicles to those of another and where truck trailers are transferred between carriers when interchanging takes place.

Water freight terminals in domestic transportation are places where goods are transferred to and from vessels and where barges are assembled into tows. In oil pipeline transportation, terminals are places where crude oil or the products of crude oil are stored prior to or subsequent to line-haul transportation. In air freight transportation, terminals are places where freight is collected after local pickup prior to line-haul air transportation and where freight is held for local delivery after line-haul air service.

In the passenger market, terminals are places where tickets are purchased, waiting space is provided, and access is made by passengers to the vehicles. These terminals are familiar to most readers.

Costs Associated with Terminals

Nature of Terminal Costs. The proportion that terminal investment and operating costs are of a carrier's total costs varies greatly between modes, but it is often a fairly large cost item. The nature of the costs associated with terminals, or whether there are any costs at all, depends on who provides the terminal, who pays for it, and how it is paid for.

When the terminal is provided by the carrier with private investment and when the carrier has the responsibility of operating and maintaining the terminal and paying taxes on it, the terminal becomes an important cost element. Private ownership and operation are usually the case in rail, highway, and oil pipeline transportation. Domestic water terminals are usually provided by government or by users. In air transportation, terminals are provided by government.

When terminals are privately owned, terminal costs are incurred by the carrier to a great extent regardless of the amount of traffic handled in the terminal. Although pickup and delivery, loading and unloading, and billing costs may vary with traffic volume, the major costs of a terminal, which include interest on the investment, taxes, maintenance, and amortization or depreciation costs (not associated with the rate of use), are not related directly to the amount of traffic carried. Terminal costs are, therefore, mostly fixed in nature and they are also common because they are incurred to produce transportation service for various kinds of traffic. Terminal costs are also largely fixed and common when the carrier leases a terminal facility from a private lessor.

When government provides a terminal facility, the costs to the carrier may be zero if no charges are levied against the carrier for the use of the terminal. If, however, government levies a charge in the form of a fee or tax of some kind, the cost of the terminal may be largely a fixed cost (for example, when airlines lease terminal space at an airport) or variable (when airlines pay a landing fee for each aircraft that uses an airport).

Joint Use of Terminals. In some instances, a terminal is used jointly by more than one carrier of a given mode, for example, several barge lines may make use of a municipally provided river terminal or several airlines may make use of the same airport facility. Such joint use of terminals may be found in any mode of transportation, but it is most often found in air transportation where it is the usual case. When joint use of terminals exists, the cost burden per carrier is less than it would be if a single carrier had to pay the entire terminal cost himself.

Cost Allocation Problem. Because of the fact that a terminal helps to produce a variety of transportation services, terminal costs are to a great extent common and part of the costs must be allocated to each different service provided in order to determine the true costs of transportation for each kind of service provided. This is, of course, difficult to do.

VEHICLES

Nature of Vehicles

Vehicles of one kind or another are used in all modes of transportation except oil pipelines. Vehicles serve as carrying units and may be power units as well. Unlike ways and terminals, vehicles are usually provided through ownership or leasing by the carrier and are not provided by government. There are also cases in which users provide the vehicles, and motive power is supplied by the for-hire carrier, as in the case of private rail cars.[2]

Costs Associated with Vehicles

Nature of Vehicle Costs. Since vehicles are usually provided and owned by the carriers themselves, all of the costs associated with vehicle owning or leasing and operation fall on the carrier, and these costs ordinarily are a major cost item. Some of these costs are fixed and some are variable.

The wear and tear on the vehicles and fuel and labor expense associated with operating vehicles may be considered variable in nature since they are incurred in relation to the volume of traffic carried.

Some other costs associated with vehicles are, however, fixed in nature. These include interest on the investment in a vehicle, maintenance cost not related to

[2] See Chapter 4 for a discussion of private rail cars.

traffic carried (related to time and/or weather instead), and amortization or depreciation expenses (not related to the rate of use).

One of the characteristics of some transportation vehicles is that there is a ready market for used vehicles and their disposal and acquisition are relatively easy. This is particularly true in highway freight transportation in which there is a well-established used tractor and trailer market that any carrier may have access to. In such a situation, carriers can fairly easily expand or contract the fleet size and change the kind of vehicles operated to conform with changes in traffic volume and in the kind of service to be provided. When disposal and acquisition of vehicles are relatively easy, the usual fixed vehicle costs—interest on investment, maintenance cost not related to traffic volume, amortization, and depreciation not related to traffic volume—may be considered variable instead of fixed expenses. Whether or not this makes any sense depends on the time period used. The longer the time period, the more likely the carrier can adjust the fleet size and character to the market.

Interchanging of Vehicles. Unlike the situation with ways and terminals, joint use of freight vehicles on a given route segment by two or more carriers (a given vehicle contains different shipments under the simultaneous control of two or more different carriers) is not generally found, but the vehicles themselves and their contents are frequently interchanged between carriers of the same mode and sometimes between carriers of different modes so that a given shipment may be transported over the lines of two or more carriers. Shipments are also sometimes interchanged between carriers without transferring the vehicle itself.

Cost Allocation Problem. A given freight-carrying vehicle is used to carry different commodities at different times or at the same time. When full-vehicle (carload, truckload, etc.) transportation is performed, the costs associated with that vehicle for that haul should be allocated to that segment of traffic. This means determining what share of the entire cost of owning (or leasing) and operating that vehicle should be allocated to that particular haul. This is, obviously, difficult.

The problem of vehicle-cost allocation is made more difficult when more than one commodity is being transported at a given time in a given vehicle. This occurs in medium-shipment and small-shipment transportation when the shipments of several shippers are carried in the same vehicle at the same time, as, for example, in less-than-truckload highway transportation and in most air freight traffic. The costs are then common, whether considered to be fixed or variable, and a share must be assigned to each commodity or shipment being carried, a very difficult task.

Back-Haul Problem. As indicated earlier, an area of joint costs in transportation is that in which a carrier moves traffic from an origin point A to a destination point B and then must return the vehicles to A in order to carry more traffic from A to B. This results in the carrier's also providing transportation service from B to A. Here a joint cost situation has arisen, i.e., the production of the service from A to B has also resulted in the production of the service from B to A.

The obvious problem in cost allocation is to determine what share of the total round-trip vehicle cost to allocate to each leg of the round-trip journey. One way would be to assign the outbound vehicle costs from A to B to that traffic, and the inbound vehicle costs from B to A to that traffic. If, however, there is insufficient or no inbound traffic, then the question arises as to whether or not to allocate the full-trip costs to the outbound traffic. Alternatively, the total vehicle costs for the entire round trip can be assigned to the combined traffic handled in both directions. These considerations have an important bearing on rate making, which is discussed in a later chapter.

Vehicle Economics

The characteristics of the vehicles used by a carrier have several important ramifications for a carrier.

Size and Weight-Carrying Capacity. The size and weight-carrying capacity of vehicles determine the size and weight of shipments or number of passengers that can be carried. The size and weight-carrying capacity of the vehicle also affect the vehicle cost per unit of traffic carried.

The greater the capacity of a vehicle, the smaller its initial cost per unit of capacity and the smaller the operating cost per ton-mile or passenger-mile carried. It generally costs less to provide a given number of ton-miles or passenger-miles of transportation service in a few large vehicles than in a large number of smaller vehicles with the same total capacity. This has led carriers of all modes of transportation to try to operate larger and larger vehicles, and, consequently, the average capacity of the vehicles used by all modes has been increasing. A major reason for the use of larger and larger railroad freight cars is that the vehicle cost per ton-mile carried falls as the size of the car increases, within limits. The economies of larger size are also clearly evident in the purchase of wide-bodied jet aircraft by airline companies.

A significant reason for the economies of large size in vehicles is the fact that the size of the crew needed to operate a vehicle is usually only slightly variable with the size of the vehicle. Consequently, the labor cost per ton-mile or passenger-mile tends to decrease as the size of the vehicle increases.

A problem associated with the trend toward larger vehicles is, of course, that the economies of larger size noted above are obtained only if a satisfactory percentage of vehicle capacity available is used. If a large vehicle is only partially loaded, it will usually have a higher operating cost per ton-mile or passenger-mile than will a fully loaded smaller vehicle because a large vehicle is more costly to operate *per vehicle mile.* It would be foolish for a carrier to replace a small freight-carrying vehicle with a large vehicle if the typical shipment size approximates the small vehicle capacity and is less than the capacity offered in the large vehicle or if the small vehicle is adequate to transport the quantity of traffic available. In addition, what might be a full vehicle load when using a small vehicle becomes a less-than-vehicle load shipment when using a large vehicle and it must be combined with the shipments of others, and thereby receive service which is often slower then vehicle-load service.

Other disadvantages associated with larger freight vehicles are (1) delay is caused because enough freight has to be accumulated to fill a large vehicle, which increases door-to-door elapsed time for the user, and (2) larger vehicles mean fewer vehicles operated and, therefore, less frequent service for the user. The latter is also a disadvantage of larger vehicles for users of passenger service.

The size of vehicles operated is limited by the physical capabilities of the way and also by governmental restrictions on size.

Combinations Versus Single Units. Whether or not vehicles move in combinations, as in railroad trains or tows of barges, affects the cost of service. The cost per unit of traffic carried falls as more vehicles are added to the combination because the power and labor needed do not rise in the same proportion as the increase in weight and cubic volume carried.

In addition to achieving the economies of multiple vehicles with one power unit, this kind of operation also has the advantage that it is highly adaptable to the demand for transportation service, meaning that a train or a barge tow can be as large or as small as it needs to be in order to meet the demand for service between the points to be served. Truck lines, except to a limited extent when double trailers are used, and airlines cannot adapt to the traffic available without adding or subtracting power units as well as vehicles, thus losing the economies resulting from combining vehicles with a single power unit.

Movement of vehicles in combinations also affects the speed and frequency of service. Delay that results from combination movements is caused by the need to accumulate traffic and the need to make up and break up the combinations. With single-unit service, a vehicle can leave for its destination when loaded, and frequent movements of this kind can be made. Obviously, when large combinations of vehicles are moved, these movements must be less frequent than single-unit moves.

Combination operations also require supporting fixed facilities, equipment, and labor, all of which add to the cost of the service.

The number of vehicles that can be combined in a single movement is limited by the physical capabilities of the way and sometimes also by legal restrictions.

Separate Power Units. Sometimes the power unit is a separate unit and sometimes it is part of the freight-carrying or passenger-carrying vehicle. An advantage to the carrier of separation of the power unit from the carrying vehicle, such as a locomotive being a separate unit from the railroad freight car or the tow boat being a separate unit from the barge, is that the carrier can retire or sell power units without having to change the fleet of vehicles, and he can retire or sell vehicles without changing the power units. Changes in the nature of demand for service, changes in operating conditions, or the availability of a new type of equipment may call for a change in either power units or vehicles when changes in the other would be costly and pointless. This flexibility is greater than that which exists when a carrier wants to replace either the power unit or the vehicle when the power unit and vehicle are one and the same. Self-propelled transport units in which the power unit and the vehicle are one and the same are a handicap to airlines, for example, when the power unit is to be replaced. The options open to the carrier are less than when a trucking company, say, needs to select new tractors to draw its old trailers.[3]

[3] See William L. Grossman, *Fundamentals of Transportation* (New York: Simmons-Boardman Publishing Corp., 1959), pp. 83–84.

Another advantage in the separation of power units from the carrying vehicles is that the carrier is able to obtain greater utilization of the power units, because the power units can be kept in service for transportation while vehicles are being loaded, unloaded, or serviced. When the power unit and vehicle are inseparable, the power unit is immobilized when loading and so on are taking place. This greater utilization of power units, in turn, reduces the number of such power units needed by the carrier—the number of power units is ordinarily less than the number of vehicles—and, therefore, keeps costs lower than they would be otherwise.[4]

Combining Vehicles of Different Modes. There are economies and service benefits associated with combining vehicles of different modes in an intermodal transportation service. Thus, when a freight carrier has 2 or more modes under his control (such as a railroad that owns trucks) or when carriers of different modes cooperate to provide intermodal service, a vehicle may be transferred from one mode to another, such as a truck trailer to a rail flatcar or a rail boxcar to a barge, for further transportation. The economies in these arrangements are in reduced transfer costs when compared with unloading and loading freight from one vehicle to another, and in the use of a lower cost mode for part of the haul than would be the case if one carrier handled the entire trip. Perhaps as important as the economies is the fact that the user may benefit from the service advantages offered by two or more modes on the same shipment.[5]

SELECTED REFERENCES

A somewhat detailed discussion of ways, transport units, and vehicles may be found in William L. Grossman, *Fundamentals of Transportation* (New York: Simmons-Boardman Publishing Corp., 1959), Chapter 4, 5, and 6. Ways, terminals, and vehicles of passenger carriers are discussed in Martin T. Farris and Forrest E. Harding, *Passenger Transportation* (Englewood Cliffs, New Jersey: Prentice-Hall, Inc., 1976), pp. 31–55.

---

[4]*Ibid.*, pp. 84–85.

[5]Intermodal transportation is discussed further in Chapter 24.

8

Theory of
Transportation Pricing

In Chapter 3 we discussed the price system in the United States, the kinds of price making that exist (market, administered or business-controlled, and government-controlled pricing), the nature of price policies, some internal and external considerations important in pricing, the relationship between costs and prices, and transportation cost as a factor in pricing decisions of users of transportation. In Chapter 7 some cost concepts were discussed along with the nature of carrier costs generated by ways, terminals, and vehicles.

In this chapter we attempt to discuss the reasoning behind pricing by for-hire transportation companies or what is often called the *theory of transportation pricing*. In this discussion we shall assume that Chapters 3 and 7 have been read.

CONTRIBUTION OF ECONOMIC THEORY TO PRICE MAKING[1]

What Is Price Theory?

A large proportion of the literature on economic theory is devoted to explaining the pricing mechanism. Price theory, or microeconomics, is concerned with the economic activities of individual economic units, such as consumers, resource owners, and business firms. It deals with the flow of products and services from business firms to consumers, the composition of the flow, and the evaluation or pricing of the component parts of the flow. Similarly, it examines the flow of productive resources (or their services) from resource owners to business firms, their evaluation, and their allocation among alternative uses.[2] In short,

[1] Major parts of this section are adapted from Donald V. Harper, *Price Policy and Procedure* (New York: Harcourt, Brace, Jovanovich, Inc., 1966).

[2] Richard H. Leftwich, *The Price System and Resource Allocation*, 4th ed. (Hinsdale, Illinois: The Dryden Press, Inc., 1970), p. 9.

one of the main objectives of price theory is to explain by means of abstract analysis how prices are determined under various kinds of market structures. A brief review of price theory and its contribution to price making may be helpful.

Cost and Demand Concepts

In order to discuss price theory it is essential that we have a clear understanding of the definitions of certain basic concepts of cost and demand, in addition to those discussed previously.

Thus, to review briefly, average total cost (ATC) is the average cost per unit and is derived by dividing total costs (which include a "normal" return on invested capital) by the number of units of product or service sold.

Marginal cost (MC), in contrast, is the change in total costs that results from producing an additional unit of product or service. In order words, it is the extra or additional cost incurred in the production of another unit.

Average revenue (AR) is the average revenue per unit sold and is derived by dividing total revenue by the number of units of product or service sold.

Marginal revenue (MR) is the change in total revenue that results from the sale of an additional unit of product or service. In other words, it is the additional revenue received from the sale of another unit.

Price elasticity of demand, you will recall, is a measure of the responsiveness of the quantity sold to price changes. Specifically, it is the ratio of the percentage response of the quantity sold to a percentage change in price. The demand for a product or service is said to be elastic if the total revenue increases as the price is reduced. Demand is inelastic if the total revenue decreases when the price is reduced. If there is no change in the total revenue when prices are changed, demand is said to display unitary elasticity. Thus, the more sensitive the quantity demanded is to price changes, the more elastic is the demand for the offering. In graphic terms, a perfectly elastic demand is illustrated by a perfectly horizontal line, and a perfectly inelastic demand is illustrated by a perfectly vertical line.

Market Structures in Price Theory

Economists have isolated several kinds of market structures in an attempt to explain how prices are determined in a free-enterprise economy. The market structure in which a firm operates is determined by 3 basic elements; the number of firms in the industry, the size of the firms in the industry, and the nature of the product or service sold, in terms of the degree of product or service differentiation. In discussing these market structures, the economist assumes that the business firm attempts to maximize profits and that the business executive knows what the firm's costs and demand characteristics are.

Pricing Under Pure Competition. In a situation of pure competition the following assumptions apply:

1. There is a large number of buyers and sellers, each of whom enjoys so small a share of the market that no single individual or firm has any influence on price.
2. There is complete freedom to enter and leave the industry.

3. The products and services sold are homogeneous (or standardized), so that the offerings of one seller of a given product or service are identical to those of all other sellers of that product or service.

4. There is full knowledge on the part of both buyers and sellers as to the terms and conditions of sale.

5. All factors of production in the economy are fully employed.

Under such circumstances, a firm has no need for a price policy; it sells at a price over which it has no control. The market itself fixes a price that equates the quantities sellers are willing to sell with the quantities buyers are willing to buy. As a consequence, the demand for the output of any particular firm is perfectly elastic; if the firm raised the price on its product or service above the established price, it would reduce demand to zero, whereas it can sell any amount of the product or service at the market-determined price. These factors produce a perfectly horizontal demand curve as shown in Figure 8-1. [Notice that in pure competition the demand curve is also the average revenue (AR) curve and the marginal revenue (MR) curve.] The only decision required of a firm under these circumstances is whether to sell at all and, if so, how much to produce. The firm would maximize its profits by producing the quantity at which marginal cost (MC) is equal to marginal revenue or price. Up to that point, an increase in output adds more to revenue than to cost; beyond that point, an increase in output adds more to cost than to revenue.

Thus, in Figure 8-1 the firm would maximize profits by producing a quantity OA, the price of which would be OB. Here the firm is earning excess profits, that is, profits in excess of a normal return on invested capital or in excess of what the capital would earn in an alternative use. These excess profits are equal to the rectangle CDEB—the difference between price and average total cost (ATC). Excess profits can exist in the short run, but, under pure competition, in the long run excess profits attract additional firms into the industry and encourage existing firms to expand, thereby causing a downward pressure on price. Therefore, in the long run, price tends to be equal to the minimum average cost of each firm. This produces equilibrium, in which there is no incentive for firms to enter or leave the industry—neither excess profits nor losses are being incurred. Figure 8-2 illustrates a typical long-run equilibrium situation for the individual firm.

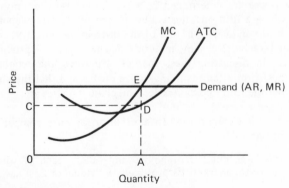

FIGURE 8-1 *Pure Competition—Short Run.*

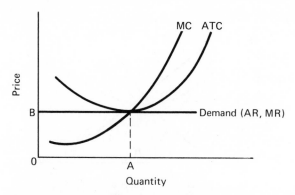

FIGURE 8-2 *Pure Competition—Long Run.*

Pricing Under Pure Monopoly. Pure monopoly is the reverse of pure competition. In a pure monopoly the seller has complete control over the output of a product or service for which there is no substitute so similar that the monopolist's sales are affected by price changes in the substitute product or service. Consequently, the demand curve for the monopolist's product or service is equivalent to the demand curve for the entire industry. This, in turn, means that as the monopolist lowers prices he will sell more units of his product or service, and that as he raises prices he will sell fewer units. The demand curve slopes downward to the right, unlike the perfectly horizontal demand curve faced by the seller under pure competition. Hence, the monopolist looks for a combination of price and output that provides him with the greatest total difference between cost and revenue, or the greatest total profit.

In both the short run and the long run the monopolist can maximize profits by equating marginal cost and marginal revenue. In Figure 8-3, for example, the firm would maximize profits at output OA and price OB, for this is the point at which marginal cost equals marginal revenue. The basic kind of adjustment that the pure monopolist needs to make to maintain the profit-maximizing position in the long run is that of changing the scale of plant.

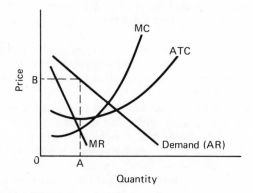

FIGURE 8-3 *Pure Monopoly.*

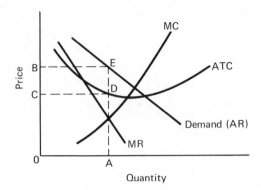

FIGURE 8-4 *Monopolistic Competition—Short Run.*

Pricing Under Monopolistic Competition. In monopolistic competition it is also assumed that there is a large number of buyers and sellers, but, unlike pure competition, there is product or service differentiation; that is, the offerings of competing firms are not identical in the eyes of the buyer. In monopolistic competition, however, as in pure competition, the actions of one seller have no perceptible effect upon the other sellers because there is a large number of competitors. Product differentiation accounts for the fact that the demand curve faced by a firm under monopolistic competition is not perfectly elastic but, instead, is somewhat inelastic and slopes downward to the right. Furthermore, because of the competition from close substitutes, the demand curve will not usually have a very steep slope. The short-run pricing situation faced by a firm under monopolistic competition is depicted in Figure 8-4.

Here we see that in the short run the firm will produce OA units and sell at price OB, thus earning a total excess profit of CDEB. With marginal cost equal to marginal revenue at this point, profits are being maximized for the firm. Notice that this does not mean that all firms in the industry will be charging identical prices if they are all maximizing profits since, by definition, firms in monopolistic competition do not produce homogeneous products or services, and each firm attempts to equate its own marginal cost and marginal revenue. However, the competition from many close substitutes may cause the prices to be relatively close together.

As in pure competition, the presence of excess profits in the short run will attract new competitiors and cause existing competitiors to expand, thereby producing a long-run tendency for excess profits to diminish. The resultant shift of the demand curve facing the firm (downward and to the left) may eliminate the excess profits, as shown in Figure 8-5. The theory of monopolistic competition recognizes that the demand curve may not be pushed to actual tangency with the average total cost curve, however, since special advantages of branding, trademarks, and patents cannot be removed completely by competition because perfect substitutes cannot be produced. Thus, it is possible that the demand curve will not be tangent to the average total cost curve in the long run. In any event, in both the short run and the long run, to maximize profits the firm under monopolistic competition attempts to equate marginal cost and marginal revenue.

Pricing Under Oligopoly. Another departure from pure competition is called oligopoly. It exists when there are so few sellers of a particular product or service that the market activities (including pricing) of one seller have an important effect on the other sellers. In such a situation, each seller is aware that the competing firms in the industry are interdependent and that in changing his prices or engaging in other market activities he must take into account the probable reactions of the other sellers. Under pure competition, pure monopoly, and monopolistic competition, the seller faces a definite predictable demand situation that can be identified by the firm, at least conceptually. This is not true in an ologopoly situation, however, as long as there is no collusion among the competing sellers. An independent price change by one seller may be expected to lead to a chain of repercussions that have no definite or predictable outcome. Thus, the oligopolist often cannot be sure what will happen if he decides to initiate a unilateral price or output change.

Because there are many different kinds of oligopolies, it is impossible to construct a general theory that will adequately explain all conceivable oligopolistic situations. Consequently, the analysis of oligopoly tends to be less specific than that of other market structures. Some of the characteristics that vary from case to case in oligopoly, and that make generalizations difficult, are the degree of product or service differentiation, the ease of entry into the industry, and the ability of the firm to predict with certainty what competing firms will do, particularly their reaction to an action that it proposes to take in the marketplace. To some extent this last characteristic is a function of the presence or lack of collusion.

In an oligopoly, as in the other competitive situations we have discussed, a firm will attempt to equate marginal cost and marginal revenue in order to maximize profits. A thorough survey of the various theories of oligopoly may be found in any text on microeconomic theory. It may be helpful, however to make a distinction between two kinds of oligopolistic situations. The first is referred to as pure or homogeneous oligopoly and the second as differentiated oligopoly.

In pure or homogeneous oligopoly there is a small number of firms in the industry, and they sell a homogeneous product or service. All sellers generally are compelled to ask the same price since the purchase decision is predominantly

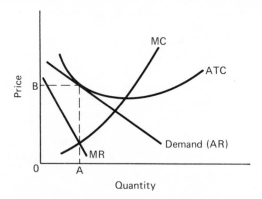

FIGURE 8-5 *Monopolistic Competition—Long Run.*

influenced by price when a homogeneous product or service is involved. Further-more, because there are only a few sellers, each seller must consider what effect his prices will have on pricing by competitiors, and each seller must expect retaliation if he reduces prices. Thus, a firm in an oligopoly will reduce prices only if it thinks it can benefit from the decrease even though competitors should match the lower price.

By way of contrast, in a differentiated oligopoly a seller is not compelled to price at the same level as his competitors since, in the eyes of the purchaser, there is some real or imagined product or service differentiation. Hence, prices vary among firms in the oligopoly, and they vary in direct proportion to the differences in the degree of product or service differentiation among the offerings of the competing firms.

Short-run price behavior in oligopolistic industries is sometimes depicted by a "kinked" demand curve, which can be used to describe either pure oligopoly or differentiated oligopoly, although it is more appropriate for pure oligopolv. Basically, the kinked demand curve is used to describe a situation in which (1) an acceptable price or cluster of prices has been well established in the industry; (2) if one firm lowers its price, other firms will follow that price or undercut the new price in order to retain their market shares, so that a unilateral price re-duction by one firm has the effect of leaving market-share distribution about where it was before or reducing it for the firm that initiated the price reduction; and (3) if one firm increases its price, competing firms will not follow the price increase, thereby causing customers of the firm to shift their patronage to other firms that offer lower prices and causing the firm that initiated the price in-crease to lose all or part of its share of the market. Such a kinked demand curve is shown in Figure 8-6.

In Figure 8-6 we assume that the established price for the firm is OB. If the firm should adjust the price downward to OD, the other firms will probably fol-low. As a result, the firm succeeds only in keeping the same share of the market that it had before (or possibly losing some of that share) while decreasing its total revenue. If the firm should increase price to OE, other firms will probably not follow the price change, and consequently, the firm will lose a considerable share of the market to other firms. For this reason the demand curve above point G is shown to be considerably more elastic than it is below point G.

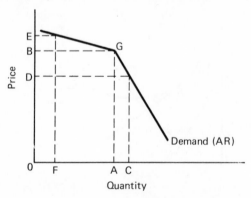

FIGURE 8-6 *Oligopoly-Kinked Demand Curve.*

Given the situation described by the kinked demand curve, the firm tends to avoid price changes in either direction since downward adjustments only decrease total revenue and upward adjustments reduce market share substantially or eliminate it entirely.

It must be kept in mind, of course, that the kinked demand curve is only one of several possible situations that can exist under oligopoly and is appropriate only when the situation in question has characteristics similar to those listed above.

Usefulness of Price Theory to the Price Maker

Bridging the gap between price theory and the practice of setting prices is difficult. The basic problem is that, to a great extent, conventional price theory does not describe the "real world" because the assumptions upon which it rests are unrealistic.

One common assumption underlying all traditional theories of price is that the entrepreneur, or businessman, carefully weighs and measures the gains and losses that accrue as a result of the price decisions that he makes. In theory, the price maker is assumed to be a rational person who is capable of analyzing the implications of his decisions and deciding accordingly. This is not a realistic assumption, however, because human beings are not as rational in their economic behavior as is supposed and because information concerning costs and demand is often not available to them in the form or to the degree that is assumed in price theory. There is, in fact, a great deal of uncertainty regarding both costs and demand in the real world.

Another assumption common to all price theories is that the firm and the price maker attempt to maximize profits. In practice, however, as we saw in Chapter 3, price makers and other business executives may be guided, at least in the short run, by motives other than, or in addition to, profit maximization.

Price theory is also limited in its usefulness because it assumes that the firm is a single-product or a single-service firm. In the real world, most firms are involved in selling several different products or services, and the fact that a firm has a multi-product or multi-service line has a great impact on its pricing decisions.

Because of these and other restrictive assumptions, theories of price are simplifications. For example, the following considerations are contrary to the special assumptions that underlie the theory of pure competition:

1. Many industries have a limited number of buyers or sellers, some of whom are very large in size.

2. Large capital requirements often make it difficult to enter an industry, and the fixed nature of some investments sometimes makes it difficult to leave an industry.

3. Products and services are rarely homogeneous. Instead, product and service differentiation is the rule, whether these differences are based solely on brand names or whether there are substantial physical differences as well in the products and services offered by competing sellers.

4. Full knowledge is generally lacking, especially on the buyers' side.

5. Furthermore, many industries often do not operate at full capacity.

Because of these considerations pure competition, as rigorously defined in theory, has never existed in practice, and it never will.

Another problem encountered in attempting to apply price theory is that in practice some market situations contain a number of rival sellers that is neither large nor small, but somewhere in between. In such cases, sellers are sometimes concerned about the actions of competitors and sometimes they are not. This means that in theoretical terms it is impossible to designate these industries as either oligopolies or as examples of monopolistic competition. They simply do not fit into a neat theoretical category.

Finally, price theory is unable to account for all of the internal and external factors, mentioned in Chapter 3, that are important considerations in pricing decisions.

Thus, it is apparent that in practice business decisions involve much more than a mechanical equating of marginal cost and marginal revenue for the purpose of determining production levels and prices, as price theory may seem to suggest. Of course, it is impossible for price theory to take into account all the economic factors and data in the real world. Abstract theory must single out what appear to be the most important or most relevant variables and from these build a general theory of how the price system operates. If this were not the case, theoretical analysis would be neither manageable nor meaningful.

Price theory has been developed primarily for use in the analysis of the effects of broad economic changes and the evaluation of social controls. It is too much to expect that the tools that are useful for social economics would also be useful in the same degree for the price maker.[3]

Nevertheless, in the analysis of how an individual firm sets its prices, price theory is helpful to the extent that it sets forth the general forces that affect pricing and offers some explanation of why these forces affect pricing. In addition, price theory permits the isolation of separate influences on prices when there are many influences operating simultaneously, and it brings to light a number of questions that the price maker should take into account.

Price theory also provides a useful standardized terminology for the discussion of cost and demand concepts. Furthermore, the several kinds of market situations described by price theory, although they are themselves somewhat unrealistic, provide a bench mark against which a "real" pricing situation may be compared. In this regard, for example, price theory points up the necessity of considering the degree of product or service differentiation and the number of sellers in an industry in any pricing decision.

Finally, price theory is relevant for price making in that it points out some broad social and economic implications of different pricing policies. These implications are important not only to government officials and others concerned with public policy matters but also to the price maker.

For these reasons, price theory is basic to an understanding of price policy and price procedure. Certainly, no business executive should attempt to assume the responsibilities of price making without first having a sound knowledge of the basic elements of price theory.

---

[3]William W. Haynes, *Managerial Economics: Analysis and Cases* (Homewood, Illinois: Dorsey Press, 1969), p. 319.

Market Structures in the Real World

As discussed earlier, traditional price theory isolates 4 basic market structures: pure competition, pure monopoly, monopolistic competition, and oligopoly. These market structures differ in number of competitors, size of competitors, and degree of product or service differentiation.

Pure Competition. We have said that pure competition in its true form has never existed in the real world. There are, however, some markets that approach the theoretical model of pure competition, thereby making it of some practical value to price makers. In some situations, the demand for the product or service approaches perfect elasticity and this, in turn, means that the price maker has very little control over price. Examples are industries in which the product or service is close to being homogeneous and in which there is a fairly large number of sellers, such as industries that produce agricultural or mineral products. Although the firm can sell virtually all that it wants to sell at the established price, it can sell practically nothing at a price that is higher than the established price, since buyers will transfer their patronage to rivals if the firm in question raises its prices unilaterally. In such a market situation, the price maker must "follow the market."

Pure Monopoly. Pure monopoly is also very rare in the real world. Those few business firms that most closely approximate pure monopoly are found in the public utility field where power companies and telephone companies are given monopoly rights by government. Even in such situations, however, a firm is not necessarily completely insulated from competition; there may be competition from substitutes, as in the case of natural gas, which faces competition from electricity and coal. Even if there is no direct competition, there are almost always other means for customers to satisfy their wants by substituting other kinds of products or services. Nonetheless, when a firm approximates a monopoly position, the price maker has an opportunity to price with little or no regard to competition. However, the price elasticity of demand is still of considerable importance since knowledge of elasticity enables the price maker to forecast the effect of a proposed price on sales volume.

Monopolistic Competition. Market situations resembling monopolistic competition are often found in the real world. Many industries are made up of a large number of sellers that offer a differentiated product or service. Examples include the retailing of hardware or bakery goods and the manufacture of women's dresses or furniture. As we have seen, in such situations the demand curve slopes downward and to the right, which means that there is room for some degree of price administration. Because of the large number of competitors in a situation resembling monopolistic competition, the price maker need not be overly concerned with the pricing decisions made by any one competing seller, unless there is practically no product nor service differentiation in the industry. If product or service differentiation is minimal, the demand curve faced by the firm is highly elastic and, as a consequence, the firm is forced to price "at the market" or very close to it. In such situations, the prices of competitors are extremely important.

As long as some substantial degree of product or service differentiation exists, however, a firm may price its products or services differently from competing products or services.

The fact that there is a large number of competitors in an industry resembling monopolistic competition and that there is some degree of product or service differentiation also means that the approach to pricing is less consistent among the firms than when the number of firms is small or when there is little or no product or service differentiation. As a result, there is a greater variety of prices available to buyers, and price is a more volatile competitive instrument.

Oligopoly. In oligopoly there is a small number of sellers, each of whom is important enough to affect the decisions of others. In other words, the sellers are interdependent. There are a number of industries in the United States that resemble oligopoly, for example, steel, automobile, cigarette, and aluminum manufacturing. In price theory a distinction is usually made between pure or homogeneous oligopoly and differentiated oligopoly. The former term is used to refer to a small number of firms that offer a homogeneous product or service, and the latter term is used to refer to a small number of firms that offer a differentiated product or service. As we mentioned earlier in this chapter, it is more difficult to generalize about oligopoly situations in price theory than it is to generalize about the other 3 basic market structures because of the interdependence of the demand curves facing each seller. Some general tendencies can be pointed out, however.

In situations that approximate pure oligopoly, the prices of different firms tend to be uniform because any attempt to set prices below those on competing products or services will lead to immediate retaliation by competitors and hence lower prices for all. Conversely, prices above those of competitors cannot produce sufficient sales volume because the product or service is very nearly homogeneous in the eyes of buyers. Consequently, under homogeneous oligopoly, the price maker usually "follows the market" in his pricing decisions.

In markets that approximate differentiated oligopoly, price uniformity is not required because there is some product or service differentiation. In such a case, the price maker need not "follow the market" but, instead, may pursue a more independent course in pricing.

The size of the competitors relative to the firm in question is a particularly important factor for pricing decisions in oligopoly-type situations. Clearly, if a firm is small relative to its competitors, its approach to pricing will probably be entirely different from what it would be if the firm were large relative to its competitors or if all firms in the industry were of approximately the same size. In short, whether or not a firm in an oligopolistic industry has much discretion or latitude in pricing is often a function of the relative size of the firm.

Freedom of Entry into the Industry

Ease of entry into the industry is an important factor that has bearing on the pricing decisions made by sellers. In some industries there are barriers to entry into the industry that insulate a firm from new competition. This, in turn, influences the nature of the demand for the output of each firm and the price policies they adopt. Generally, the demand curve faced by a firm in such a situation is more inelastic than would otherwise be the case. In other industries it is relatively easy for a new firm to begin operations. This tends to increase the elasticity of demand for the output of an individual firm and acts as a damper or limit on the discretion or control that each firm has over prices. Some of the barriers to entry that might exist, in addition to legal barriers such as licensing requirements (including entry control in transportation) or patent rights, include high capital requirements, cost advantages enjoyed by firms that are already in operation, extreme product or service differentiation, and the fact that existing firms control sources of supply of raw materials.

PRICE THEORY APPLIED TO TRANSPORTATION COMPANIES

Traditional price theory applies to pricing by for-hire transportation companies as it does to other pricing situations. The difficulties inherent in price theory are also applicable to transportation, the difficulties having to do primarily with certain assumptions upon which price theory rests. As indicated in previous paragraphs, these assumptions have to do with such things as rational behavior of the decision maker, availability of full information, the profit maximizing motive, the production of a single product or service (see further discussion of this below), and the number of firms in the industry.

Another difficulty in applying conventional price theory to transportation is that transportation itself is not a single homogeneous industry that resembles one of the market structure situations described in price theory. Instead, transportation is a collection of several modes of transportation that are different "industries," each one of which has economic characteristics, such as number of firms, size of firms, capital required to enter, and so on, peculiar to itself. Some modes have the characteristics similar to oligopoly and others similar to monopolistic competition. In addition, regardless of the general economic characteristics of a particular mode, when any one kind of traffic over a given route is to be given a fare or a rate by a for-hire carrier, the market structure situation may be different from the general industry case. For example, it may be oligopolistic while the general case for that mode is one of monopolistic competition. Consequently, a single theory of price is difficult to apply to any one mode or carrier; several theories would be more appropriate. The market structure characteristics of the several modes of transportation are described in later chapters.

In addition, price theory in the conventional sense is difficult to apply to transportation because much of the transportation system in the United States, although it is private enterprise, is under government economic regulation,[4] which becomes an important consideration in pricing not accounted for in price theory.

Also, the large amount of fixed, joint, and common costs in some transportation company operations make cost allocations and precise determination of costs extremely difficult.

Finally, an unusual feature of freight transportation pricing is that the typical transportation company has a very wide "product line" to price since each in-

---

[4] Regulation of the business of transportation, i.e., regulation of entry and exit, rates, service, mergers, etc. See Chapters 19 through 25.

dividual commodity to be carried and every combination of origin and destination points between which it could be carried is a different segment of service or "product" to be priced, resulting in dozens or hundreds or thousands of segments or "items" in the product line. In freight transportation, therefore, there is a tremendous product line to be priced and a great number of opportunities to adjust rates to encourage or discourage traffic and also to affect the traffic volume of other kinds of traffic. Price theory assumes a single product or a single service.

Because of the above limitations on the usefulness of price theory, carrier pricing cannot be categorized as pure competition, or pure monopoly, or monopolistic competition, or oligopoly. However, the following discussion of carrier pricing uses the terminology of price theory and makes reference to the traditional categories of competition.

DIFFERENTIAL PRICING IN TRANSPORTATION

Internal and External Considerations

As indicated in Chapter 3, there are several internal and external considerations important in making pricing decisions. Many of these are unaccounted for in conventional price theory. Internal considerations include the long-run and short-run objectives of the firm, who is to have responsibility for pricing, the importance of price in the marketing effort of the seller, the characteristics of the product or service being offered, and the costs associated with producing and/or distributing the product or service.

External considerations include the nature of demand for the product or service, including the elasticity of demand, the market structure or nature of competition, the nature of the organization's suppliers, the kinds of customers the seller has, economic conditions in the market, and the legal framework within which pricing decisions are made.

All of these internal and external considerations are important in pricing by for-hire carriers, with some, of course, being more important than others. However, it is not possible to discuss here each of the above internal and external factors individually as they might be dealt with in a carrier pricing decision. The variance between modes and between individual carriers of the same mode as to the importance of each of the internal and external factors, plus the different conditions affecting each mode and carrier, makes such a discussion impossible. Instead, the discussion below concentrates on 2 of the key factors—cost and the character of demand—recognizing that other factors may also be important in any carrier pricing situation. The discussion deals primarily with pricing freight transportation service, with some reference to pricing passenger service where appropriate.

Differential Pricing Defined

As indicated earlier, the principles of conventional price theory may be applied to transportation company pricing, recognizing the limitations of price theory and that the several modes of transportation have different market structure characteristics. In real-world carrier pricing, pricing freight service is dominated by *differential pricing*. Although the economic characteristics of the different modes of transportation are different, for-hire transportation companies in the United States have generally adopted the differential system of pricing, regardless of mode. Differential pricing is defined here as a system of pricing whereby the carrier charges different prices to different segments of freight traffic for essentially the same service and the differences in rates cannot be explained by differences in the cost of service or, conversely, the carrier charges the same rate for different services with different costs associated with them.[5] For example, suppose that a freight train consists of 100 boxcars of identical capacity, each car loaded to the same weight but each carrying a different commodity, and that all cars are given transportation service between A and B. It is likely that there would be 100 different rates charged per 100 pounds, that is, a different rate for each of the 100 different commodities. Some of the difference in rates is the result of differences in cost to the carrier in transporting the different commodities, but much of the difference cannot be explained by cost differences. This is the result of differential pricing. As noted below, the differences in the rates may be between commodities, as in the example above, or between places, or between times.

Cost Concepts

The cost concepts most useful in discussing carrier pricing are fixed and variable costs as those terms were defined in Chapter 7. Fixed costs, you will recall, are costs that do not vary with the volume of traffic, at least in the short run. Variable costs are those that vary with changes in the volume of traffic carried—they are additional costs that are incurred as a result of a management decision that causes a change in the carrier's volume of traffic.[6] Joint costs (the creation of one service unavoidably results in the creation of another service) and common costs (costs are incurred to provide more than one transportation service

---

[5] The terminology in transportation pricing is somewhat confusing. Various terms have been used to identify the pricing method in American transportation. These terms include differential pricing, value of service pricing, rate discrimination, charging what the traffic will bear, and the contribution method of pricing. In addition, different writers disagree on the meaning of these terms, particularly the term value of service pricing, which to some writers means only charging high rates to take advantage of monopoly situations. We have chosen to use the phrase differential pricing to describe transportation pricing.

[6] The concept of variable costs as used in transportation rate theory is somewhat different from that ordinarily used in price theory. Our concept of variable costs is that they are expenses that vary more or less in proportion with output or with traffic carried rather than the usual concept of variable costs as varying to some extent with output. In other words, our version of variable costs means that the unit variable cost is constant regardless of the volume of output. Marginal cost per unit in conventional price theory may fall as output increases and, hence, become lower than average variable cost. Since we assume that variable cost is constant per unit, however, we are also assuming that marginal cost is not falling per unit and, hence, average variable cost equals marginal cost. The approach taken here is adequate for practical purposes when we are considering rates on a particular commodity and on a particular route, which represents a small range of output. Over large ranges of output, however, the assumption that unit variable cost remains the same may be unrealistic. See D. Philip Locklin, *Economics of Transportation,* 7th ed. (Homewood, Illinois: Richard D. Irwin, Inc., 1972), footnote 30, p. 161.

but the use of resources to provide one service does not automatically result in the production of another service) are also of some importance in a discussion of carrier pricing. However, since every joint or common cost is also either a fixed or variable cost, joint and common costs are, for the most part, not discussed separately.

Kinds of Differential Pricing

Differential pricing means that the carrier charges different segments of freight traffic different prices for essentially the same service, and the differences in rates cannot be explained by differences in the cost of service or, conversely, the carrier charges the same rate for different services with different costs. The differentiation in rates between segments of traffic may be between different commodities or it may be between different places. Occasionally, it may be between different times. Differentiation between commodities is illustrated in the 100-car freight train example in which there are 100 different rates and at least part of the difference cannot be explained by cost differences.

Differentiation between places, or place discrimination, occurs when prices or rates charged by a carrier depart from the usual distance principle of rate making mentioned in Chapter 2 and the departure cannot be explained by cost differences. In other words, differences in rates over different routes cannot be explained entirely or at all by differences in costs; there is unequal treatment of 2 or more localities in the matter of rates and the inequality cannot be justified by differences in the cost of service. Thus, in Figure 8-7(1), if the rate per 100 pounds on a given commodity is $.20 from A to B and is $.40 from A to C and the distances over the two routes are equal, and the same carrier is involved on both routes, and the rate difference cannot be explained by a cost difference, this is an example of differentiation or discrimination between places, i.e., B is being discriminated in favor of or C is being discriminated against. If, as in Figure 8-7(2), the rate per 100 pounds on a certain commodity from A to B is $.30 and the rate on the same commodity from A to C is also $.30, with the same carrier involved on both routes and the distances unequal, and cost factors do not account for the identical rates on the two routes, then C is being discriminated in favor of or B is being discriminated against.

Differentiation based on time means that prices vary according to the time at which service is performed. Freight rates that vary with the season of the year are examples.

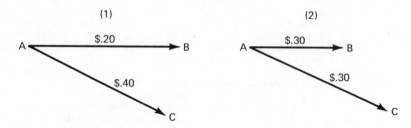

FIGURE 8-7 *Place Discrimination.*

There can also be differentiation between persons, which means that the rates per 100 pounds charged different users are different, although the commodity shipped and the carrier and route involved are the same. This is referred to as personal discrimination and is unlawful in all circumstances under federal economic regulation of transportation.

Motivation Behind Differential Pricing

Differential pricing has as its motivation the existence of fixed costs and unused or excess capacity.

When a carrier, such as a railroad or pipeline, has a large percentage of fixed costs, it is clear that the greater the volume of traffic carried, the lower will be the average or unit cost of carrying each additional unit of traffic because the fixed costs are spread over more units of traffic. Thus, the "fully distributed" or "fully allocated" cost per unit, including both the variable costs associated with the unit of traffic and a share of the fixed costs allocated to the unit of traffic, is less as more traffic is added, at least until capacity is reached.

These "increasing returns" from more complete plant utilization lead a carrier to try to increase traffic volume (it costs less and less per unit to handle each additional unit of traffic) because the possibility of greater profit exists if he is successful in doing so.

When the carrier has substantial unused or excess capacity, the incentive to add traffic is further increased because the carrier feels that it is better to use the facilities instead of having them stand idle and incur certain costs that are to be paid regardless of the volume of traffic. It is believed that some contribution to revenue is better than none at all in this stituation.

If satisfactory volume is not produced when "normal" rates are charged (a normal rate may be considered to be one that covers fully distributed costs), then the carrier has the incentive to charge lower-than-normal rates to attract the traffic desired. These lower rates may be below the fully distributed costs assignable to the traffic in question. They are in line with the "value of the service" to the shipper.

Differential pricing has also meant that carriers price above "normal" levels where the value of the service to the user is high. This might occur when the transportation alternatives available to the user are few, i.e., the carrier is in a monopolistic or semimonopolistic position.

Proper Role of Costs in Pricing

Approached in the proper manner, costs should be used to establish a floor below which a firm will not price its products or services. "The proper function of cost is to set the lower limits on the initial price charged for a product, while value to consumers sets the upper limit. The job of the pricing executive is to pick the space between these two extremes that will best serve his purposes."[7] The costs that are of crucial importance in a pricing decision are the variable costs associated with producing or distributing additional amounts of a product

---

[7]D. Maynard Phelps and J. Howard Westing, *Marketing Management,* 3rd ed. (Homewood, Illinois: Richard D. Irwin, Inc., 1968), p. 307.

or service or adding a new product or service. Unless the firm is operating at full capacity, fixed costs can usually be ignored in pricing products or services. If it has excess capacity and nothing better to do with it, the firm can sell its output profitably at any price that more than covers variable costs. Such prices make at least some contribution to fixed costs and are, therefore, profitable in the sense that if the product or service had not been sold at the low price, there would have been no contribution to fixed costs at all. However, although it is not always desirable to price products so that both fixed and variable costs are completely covered, it must be remembered that in terms of the firm's overall operations in the long run, all costs must be covered by prices.

Therefore, when a carrier decides to use differential pricing and charge a less-than-normal rate in order to attract traffic, the floor below which he should not go is the variable costs associated with the additional traffic in question. To price below that level would result in a direct loss on each unit of traffic carried.

Variable costs can be either short run or long run. Differential pricing is usually discussed as a short-run pricing practice. However, it is not necessary to distinguish between time periods, i.e., differential pricing with variable cost as the floor is a sound pricing philosophy in either the short or the long run. It is only necessary to determine the additional or directly variable costs associated with additional traffic, whether over the short or long run. Long-run variable costs include the usual wages, fuel, etc., but they also include that part of capital additions, such as introduction of a new traffic control system or construction of a new roadbed, that are directly associated with additional traffic.[8]

Value of Service Ceiling

In pricing transportation service it is recognized that there is an upper limit on how high the rate on a given segment of traffic can be. This ceiling is often referred to as the *value of service* to the user, meaning that there is a point beyond which the rate is too high in terms of what the transportation service is worth to the user. The value of service is really a measure of the elasticity of demand for the service and, usually, as the rate is increased, the volume of traffic shipped decreases. For our purposes, we define the value of service ceiling as the highest charge that can be levied without shutting off the traffic. In other words, beyond the value of service point there is no traffic of the kind in question.

The level of the value of service ceiling is determined by the nature of the demand for the transportation service in question. This, in turn, is influenced heavily by competition in the transportation industry, both intramodal and intermodal, and both for-hire and private. Thus, the value of service level for a particular kind of railroad service is affected by what other railroads are doing price-wise, what for-hire trucking companies and other for-hire competitors are doing price- and service-wise, and the costs of private carriage.

Thus, when differentiation between commodities is being practiced in rate making, the difference in rates is based on the fact that the shipper (or receiver) of typewriters has a different demand schedule for transportation than does the

---

[8]See Joseph R. Rose, "Limits on Marginal Cost Pricing," *Proceedings of Transportation Research Forum, 1963*, pp. 172-173.

shipper of gravel. The same might be said of shippers of the same commodity who ship over different routes. Although one could argue that transportation is a homogeneous service, i.e., transportation is transportation regardless of what is being carried, what is important is that the shippers or receivers of different segments of traffic have different demand schedules for transportation.

Determining a Specific Rate

Assuming that the carrier has a good idea of both the variable costs and the value of service level associated with a given kind of traffic, how can he determine where between the extremes of the variable cost floor and the value of service ceiling to set a rate per 100 pounds? At a low rate that barely covers variable costs, the contribution to fixed costs per unit carried may be small, but the volume of traffic carried at that rate may be large, thus providing a large total contribution to fixed costs. At a relatively high rate the contribution per unit carried may be large, but the number of units carried may be small, resulting in a relatively small total contribution to fixed costs. The ideal is to set the rate so that *when the volume of traffic obtained is considered,* the greatest total contribution to fixed costs is obtained. The contribution to fixed costs may be greater, equal to, or less than the traffic's share of fixed costs. This approach will result in low rates below fully distributed costs in some cases and rates above that level in others, depending on the variable cost, value of service, and fully distributed cost levels associated with the traffic. It should be kept in mind, however, that although rates below fully distributed costs are appropriate for the carrier in some cases, all or most rates charged cannot, in the long run, be below fully distributed costs because the carrier will not be able to fully cover his fixed costs. Consequently, less-than-full-cost rates are appropriate either for all or most traffic in the short run only or on some traffic only (sometimes referred to as *marginal traffic*) in the long run.

Are Low Rates Profitable?

Differential pricing means that the carrier charges some rates that are below the fully distributed costs incurred in carrying the traffic involved. The question of whether or not these rates are profitable to the carrier then arises.

In the short run for some or all traffic carried, or in the long run for some traffic carried, rates can be profitable even though they do not cover full costs. For example, in the *short run* it may be profitable to carry some or even *all* traffic at rates below full costs provided that (1) rates are high enough to cover variable costs and, preferably, that they make some contribution to the fixed expenses of the business; (2) it is *necessary* to charge such rates in order to sell the service; and (3) there is unused capacity and no better use for the facilities involved. If a service is priced so that the receipts do not cover variable costs, then every unit of traffic carried results in a loss. As to the second point above, no carrier should voluntarily charge rates below full costs unless such a policy appears to be necessary to get the traffic. In other words, unless market conditions, competition, or other factors require that less-than-full-cost rates be charged, it is unwise to do so in terms of carrier profits. Finally, only when there is no better use for the facilities involved are less-than-full-cost rates proper from the standpoint of profits.[9]

The same three considerations apply when considering whether or not to charge rates that do not cover full costs on individual segments of traffic as a *long-run* approach to pricing. The prices must ordinarily cover variable expenses, they must be required in order to get the traffic under consideration, and there should be unused capacity.

Is Cross-Subsidy Involved?

A frequently made criticism of differential pricing is that if low rates below fully distributed costs are charged some traffic, the "loss" involved (the difference between fully distributed costs and the rate charged) must be "made up" by other higher-paying traffic or, in other words, the shippers and receivers of the higher-paying traffic subsidize the shippers and receivers of the lower-paying traffic.

The fact that the rates on some traffic do not cover the full cost incurred in its carriage does not necessarily mean that the cost burden on other traffic carried is increased. The low-rate items are not subsidized by the other items *provided* that the low rates cover variable expenses and that it is necessary to charge such low prices in order to get the traffic, and, finally, there is excess capacity and no better use for the facilities. In such a case, any contribution the low-rate traffic makes toward the fixed expenses of the business actually *decreases* the fixed-cost burden on the other traffic because there would be no contribution from the carriage of the low-rate traffic without the less-than-full-cost rates. However, if the low rate does not cover variable costs, or if it is not necessary to charge the low rate in order to get the traffic, that is, if other reasons have led to the decision to adopt a low rate, or if there is no unused capacity and there is a better use for the facilities, then it is possible that the cost burden on the other traffic is increased and that, in effect, the shippers and receivers of the other items are subsidizing the low-rate item.

Market Separation as a Necessary Condition

In practice, a policy of variable-cost pricing for some portion of a carrier's total traffic and full-cost pricing for others can be used only when markets can be separated from one another, that is, when demand prices for different services produced or for the same service in different geographic areas are separate from one another. In other words, a low price for some part of the traffic carried must not make it impossible to charge higher, normal rates for other segments of traffic. Businessmen often feel that variable-cost pricing is not a sound approach to pricing because they are afraid a low variable-cost price for one segment of the firm's output will also force them to lower prices on the rest of the firm's output, with the result that there is little or no contribution toward fixed expenses. However, this will not happen if markets are separated from one another.

[9]When a firm prices its services so that prices on its *entire* offerings are not covering full costs, the firm can encounter a cash shortage, that is, it may find that it is unable to pay salaries and other fixed cash requirements out of operating revenue.

Market separation is accomplished in transportation by differentiating in the rates ("discriminating") between commodities so that a shipper (or receiver) of typewriters pays a higher rate per 100 pounds than does the shipper of gravel for the same service. The only way the shipper of typewriters can take advantage of the low rate on gravel is to ship gravel—he is separated from that market. Market separation can also be geographic in that a low rate on a given commodity on a carrier's route between A and B has no real effect on that same carrier's higher rate on that same commodity between C and D even though the distances over the two routes are approximately the same. The shipper at C can avail himself of the low A to B rate only by shipping over that route. Similar considerations apply to differentiation based on time.

Control of Competition

In order for carriers to carry out differential pricing, they must be able to charge some rates that just cover variable costs and other rates above that level. The ability to do this is made possible when markets are separated, as noted above, and it is facilitated when competition among carriers, both intramodal and intermodal, is kept under some kind of control. If competition were entirely free and carriers were able to charge whatever rates they pleased, when competition became severe the carriers would tend to lower their rates in order to be competitive. With variable cost the floor in rate making, as explained earlier, most or all rates would tend to gravitate toward variable cost and, consequently, the differentiation between rates would be reduced—they would all be at or near the variable-cost level. In effect, then, the carrier must have some degree of monopoly power.

This means that differential pricing can be carried out more successfully when competition is not so intense or when it is controlled in some way, as through government regulation of rates and/or through the rate bureau method of determining rates practices by many carriers,[10] or through differentiation in the service offered by a carrier.

Another method of control of competition is in the form of restraint on the part of each carrier, each carrier avoiding rate reductions because he knows that there will be retaliation by his competitors. This can occur when the number of competing carriers is small, i.e., an oligopolistic situation exists. In still other cases, the carrier might resort to price-fixing schemes in order to avoid what he considers destructive competition. This often occurred in railroading prior to government economic regulation.

Applicability of Differential Pricing
to Passenger Transportation

The differential approach to pricing is usually discussed in terms of freight transportation. It is, however, also applicable to transportation of passengers. Differentiation between places may, of course, be carried out. In addition, to the extent that passenger categories can be identified and separated from one another, differentiation between such categories may take place. The difficulty

---

[10]Rate bureaus are discussed in Chapter 9.

is that, unlike the large number of different commodities that might be carried and between which differential pricing might be applied, there is a limited number of categories into which passengers may be placed for pricing purposes.

Airlines have been the most successful in applying the differential concept to passenger service and have differentiated passengers by age, length of stay, family connection, military service, and so on, in addition to having first class and coach service, and have used various promotional fares to attract certain categories of traffic.

Applicability of Differential Pricing to the Several Modes of Transportation and Individual Carriers

Differential pricing as described above is followed to some degree by carriers in all modes of transportation in the United States. However, it is more applicable to some modes and carriers than to others, depending on the cost structure, existence of excess capacity, character of traffic, and size of geographic area served by each mode or carrier. Its applicability to each specific mode of transportation is discussed in Chapters 10 through 14.

Cost Structure. Carriers that have a high proportion of fixed costs are most likely to use differential pricing extensively. This is because they incur decreasing costs per unit carried as they add more traffic and thus have the incentive to encourage traffic by lowering prices below the fully distributed cost level. They also have the ability to make downward adjustments in prices because their variable costs are low and the variable costs are the floor in setting rates and fares. A carrier who has a high proportion of variable costs finds it difficult to adjust prices very far downward below fully distributed costs because the variable cost floor is high. Such carriers can more easily use the differential idea in increasing prices than in decreasing them.

Figure 8-8 shows 2 opposite kinds of short-run carrier cost structures. Carrier A has high fixed costs relative to variable costs and, thus, he is likely to find differential pricing worthwhile. Carrier B has high variable costs relative to fixed costs and, thus, he would have difficulty in using differential pricing, at least on the downward side.

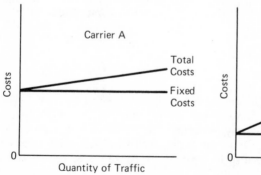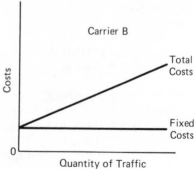

FIGURE 8-8 *Short-Run Cost Structures.*

The main determinant of the cost structure relative to fixed and variable costs is the nature of the way (discussed in Chapter 7). Carriers that provide and maintain their own ways tend to have relatively high fixed costs and low variable costs. When either nature or government provides the way, a carrier may have no way costs at all or the costs will be variable in nature. These carriers tend to have a high proportion of variable costs and a low percentage of fixed costs. Terminal costs, as discussed in Chapter 7, also affect the cost structure in the same manner as costs of way, but they are often less important than costs of way. In some cases, they are primarily a fixed-cost element; in other cases, they are primarily a variable-cost element. Vehicle costs are important in most forms of transportation and contribute both fixed and variable costs, the proportion varying with the mode of transportation and the time periods being considered.

Existence and Amount of Excess Capacity. Because the existence of unused facilities is a chief reason for a carrier to adjust prices downward in order to attract traffic that will make use of that capacity, the existence and amount of excess capacity are important factors in determining the applicability of differential pricing to a particular mode or carrier. All transportation companies have excess capacity in some form at some times and some have a chronic problem of almost continuous excess capacity. The problem varies considerably from situation to situation. The excess capacity can occur, of course, in the way, in terminals, or in vehicles. The problem of excess capacity is more acute when the carrier provides his own way and terminals than when these are provided by nature or government.

Variety of Commodities Carried. A third factor of importance in determining the degree of applicability of differential pricing to different modes of transportation and different carriers is the kind of freight traffic carried. The greater the variety of traffic carried, the more opportunities there are for differentiating between different segments of traffic. Thus, those carriers with a broad holding out to the public carry a wide variety of different commodities and can employ differential pricing to a greater extent than a carrier that carries only one or a small number of different commodities.

Size of Geographic Area Served. Because a form of differential pricing is differentiation in price between places, carriers that serve large geographic areas with many origin and destination points and routes have more opportunities to differentiate between points than do carriers serving small areas and a limited number of points and routes.

Implications of Differential Pricing for the User

Since all for-hire carriers appear to use differential pricing to some extent, it is something that most users of for-hire freight transportation service must deal with. Differential pricing means that the carrier using it has chosen to view each segment of traffic, i.e., each commodity and the combination of points between which it is to be carried, as a separate pricing problem and, therefore, a candidate for a different rate, adjusting the rate to suit the value of service (demand) and cost conditions that prevail. This alternative has been taken instead of using a more general formula-type approach to pricing that would not attempt to distinguish so finely between different segments of traffic. Such a formula-type approach might be to charge a fixed rate per 100 pounds for a given distance, regardless of the commodity, route, or other circumstance, or to quote the rates as so much per ton-mile, regardless of the commodity, route, and so on, instead of as a charge per 100 pounds or ton. One result of the individualized differential approach to pricing is that there is a tremendous number of rates quoted by the carriers because every possible combination of commodity and origin and destination points is a potential different rate. In addition, the user must recognize that all commodities, routes, and points are not treated alike and that, as we pointed out in Chapter 2, little can be assumed about the rate structure or what a particular transportation charge will be.

The result is a vast number of rates to deal with and wide variances in rates for similar services, both of which complicate the management of transportation by the user. This, in turn, makes the user's rate determination and quotation of delivered costs to buyers more difficult and decisions concerning product selection, purchasing, market selection, location, and the user's own pricing more difficult than they would be if some more standardized formula-type rate system existed. These factors, in turn, have resulted in the need for rate specialists to deal with the complications of the rate structure.

Differential Pricing Versus Prices Based on Fully Distributed Costs

Differential pricing of freight service has been subject to considerable criticism from various sources. Part of the criticism results from a misunderstanding about the meaning of differential pricing. It is understood by some critics to mean charging high rates and resulting in "monopoly" profits when the traffic is "captured" by the carrier, such as was the case in the preregulation days of railroads in the United States. Differential pricing is criticized by others on the ground that the low rates charged some traffic must, of necessity, result in higher rates for other traffic, i.e., a cross-subsidy situation exists.

Under the definition and explanation of differential pricing used here, however, neither of the objections cited above is on solid ground because, first, differential pricing in modern times does not usually result in unreasonably high rates because the combination of competition among carriers and government economic regulation prevent this from occurring. In those cases in which monopoly profits derive from differential pricing, however, it is not justified. Differential pricing should involve discrimination downward, rather than upward, and this is the general case in today's transportation environment.

Second, the subsidy argument is not valid if the conditions referred to earlier (i.e., the low rate covers variable costs, the low rate is necessary to get the traffic, and there is excess capacity) are present. Admittedly, there are cases in which the 3 conditions do not exist. Then it is true that a low rate on one segment of traffic results in higher than "normal" rates on other traffic. But if differential pricing is carried out as stated here, that result does not occur.

Another misunderstanding about differential pricing is that it means tying rates exclusively to the value of a commodity, meaning that the higher the value of a commodity, the higher the value of service and, hence, the higher the rate, and all other factors are ignored. This, of course, is not true of differential pricing as discussed here. Although the value of the commodity is one factor in determining the value of service, it is only one of several such factors, as is indicated in Chapter 9.

Another criticism of differential pricing is that it is sometimes very difficult to identify and measure the variable costs that should be assigned to a given segment of traffic. This means that somewhat artificial formulas must be used. Actually, however, the problem is no more serious than that ordinarily encountered in full-cost pricing in which, in addition to the assignment of variable costs to a specific segment of traffic, a share of fixed expenses must also be arbitrarily allocated.

Other criticisms of differential pricing are more valid. One is that it is inherently discriminatory because different segments of traffic are carried at different rates, not entirely justified by cost differences, while the service received by the users is essentially the same. There is no question that this is a result of value of service pricing. Whether or not it is justified depends on one's point of view.

Another worthy criticism of differential pricing is that it results in "wasteful" transportation in that the transportation would not occur if it were not for differential pricing and, hence, it is not needed. Therefore, it is argued, expenditures on transportation are greater than they would be otherwise. This refers to the fact that if low rates resulting from the differential approach were not charged, the traffic carried under those low rates would not move, thus eliminating that much transportation which is apparently, in an economic sense, not justified because the traffic carried cannot "pay its way"—it cannot pay fully distributed-cost rates. Full-cost rates would reflect the true economic costs of transportation and transportation service would be rendered only when the traffic could pay such rates.

It is also argued that differential pricing is wasteful because, through low rates, it enables users to stay in business who could not be in business if full-cost rates were charged because they could not pay the rates. Thus, differential pricing keeps in business inefficient firms that otherwise would be driven from the scene and thus continues investment in an activity that is neither really wanted nor needed by society.

Those who criticize differential pricing often advocate that all transportation rates cover "full costs" or that rates should cover fully distributed costs, both fixed and variable, associated with the service in question, rather than use the differential approach.[11] Full-cost rate making avoids the problems associated with differential pricing mentioned above. Actually, full-cost pricing is a popular approach to pricing in American industry and is widely practiced in the country. One reason for this is that many business managers feel that any price below full costs will result in loss to the firm. Other business managers argue that it is proper to use full-cost pricing because they are entitled to a "fair" profit. Another reason for the popularity of full-cost pricing is that prices based on full costs are easier for buyers to understand than are prices that are influenced by demand or competition.[12]

[11] There is some confusion about what is meant by full-cost pricing and the time periods being dealt with. Also, much of the controversy surrounding differential versus fully distributed-cost pricing has to do with its effect on intermodal pricing and the allocation of traffic among modes. This is discussed in Chapter 24.

[12] Harper, *Price Policy and Procedure*, pp. 52-53.

Full-cost pricing is a convenient and expeditious method of pricing and can be a proper approach if competitors follow suit. The major limitation to full-cost pricing, assuming that full costs can be accurately determined, is that such pricing often does not take account of demand considerations, such as users' needs and their ability and willingness to pay. It also tends to ignore the activities of competing carriers in the marketplace. When demand and competitive factors are neglected, only by accident would full-cost pricing produce rates that maximize profit for the carrier.[13]

Also, fully distributed-cost rate making means that all costs must be allocated to a given segment of traffic, which is exceedingly difficult in transportation because there may be considerable fixed, joint, and common costs which are difficult to assign to specific segments of traffic. Another problem associated with allocating fixed costs to individual segments of traffic with the objective of setting rates that cover fully allocated costs is that a circular effect is involved. The amount of fixed cost allocated to each unit of traffic depends on the number of units of traffic being carried and the number of units of traffic being carried depends on the rates charged.[14]

As pointed out earlier, differential pricing enables users to continue in business who would be driven out if all rates covered fully distributed costs. These are users whose locations are disadvantageous or who are dealing in low-grade products that cannot bear high transportation costs. Differential pricing enables the consuming public to have access to the products of these firms, thus increasing competition among sellers and widening the purchasing alternatives available to consumers.

Finally, differential pricing enables carriers to make use of capacity that otherwise would go unused, enabling them to be more efficient and to receive a contribution toward fixed expenses and to keep transportation costs per unit carried down. As long as unused capacity exists in the transportation system, differential pricing makes a positive contribution toward carrier efficiency.

To sum up, in differential pricing variable costs are the important costs in the carrier's pricing decision. To attempt to base all rates on full costs without regard to demand and competitive conditions is a narrow and one-sided approach to pricing, which only by accident would result in the best rates for the carrier. The needs and desires of users are neglected in such an approach. The user ordinarily does not know or care about the carrier's costs. Consequently, unless the rate that covers full costs is one that users are willing to pay, there will be no shipment via that carrier.[15]

We have tried to explain differential pricing and how it should be carried out by a carrier. We recognize that the method has been abused both at the upper end (rates too high) and at the lower end (rates too low). It is believed, however, that differential pricing, if carried out properly, is a sound pricing philosophy because it takes into account the demand for transportation service and competition in the transportation industry. Full-cost pricing does not do that. If carried out properly, differential pricing can benefit both carriers and users.

---

[13] *Ibid.*, p. 53.
[14] Locklin, *Economics of Transportation,* p. 165.
[15] Harper, *Price Policy and Procedure,* pp. 56–57.

SELECTED REFERENCES

An early explanation of railroad rate theory is A. R. Hadley, *Railroad Transportation: Its History and Its Laws* (New York: G. P. Putnam and Sons, 1885), Chapter 6 and Appendix II. See also Eliot Jones, *Principles of Railway Transportation* (New York: The Macmillan Company, 1924), Chapter 4 and D. Philip Locklin, "A Review of the Literature on Railway Rate Theory," *Quarterly Journal of Economics*, February, 1933.

An outstanding modern discussion of railway rate theory is D. Philip Locklin, *Economics of Transportation*, 7th ed. (Homewood, Illinois: Richard D. Irwin, Inc., 1972), Chapter 7. Other discussions of transportation rate theory may be found in Stuart Daggett, *Principles of Inland Transportation*, 4th ed. (New York: Harper and Brothers, 1955), Chapter 16; Dudley F. Pegrum, *Transportation Economics and Public Policy*, 3rd ed. (Homewood, Illinois: Richard D. Irwin, Inc., 1973), Chapter 8; George W. Wilson and George M. Smerk, "Rate Theory," *Physical Distribution Management* (Bloomington, Indiana: Bureau of Business Research, Indiana University, 1968); and Marvin L. Fair and Ernest W. Williams, Jr., *Economics of Transportation and Logistics* (Dallas, Texas: Business Publications, Inc., 1975), Chapter 16.

Pricing of passenger service is discussed in Martin T. Farris and Forrest E. Harding, *Passenger Transportation* (Englewood Cliffs, New Jersey: Prentice-Hall, Inc., 1976), Chapter 3.

The controversy between differential pricing and pricing based on fully distributed costs is dealt with in Thomas W. Calmus, "Full Cost Versus Incremental Cost: Again," *Transportation Journal*, Winter, 1969 and Grant M. Davis and Linda J. Combs, "Some Observations Concerning Value of Service Pricing in Transportation," *Transportation Journal*, Spring, 1975. A satirical explanation of the controversy between fully distributed-cost rates and rates below that level and the advantages of the latter may be found in Bartlett Burns, "Scientific Ratemaking: A Fable," *ICC Practitioners' Journal*, January–February, 1967.

Arguments for differential pricing are presented in Colin Barrett, "The Theory and Practice of Carrier Rate-Making," *Transportation and Distribution Management*, October, 1972; William J. Baumol et al., "The Role of Cost in the Minimum Pricing of Railroad Services," *Journal of Business*, October, 1962; John J. Coyle, "Cost of Service Pricing in Transportation: Some Reflections," *Quarterly Review of Economics and Business*, Spring, 1965 and "Dissimilar Pricing: A Logical Approach to Regulated Rates," *Public Utilities Fortnightly*, September 15, 1966; Ford K. Edwards, "The Role of Transportation Costs and Market Demand in Railroad Rate Making," *Transportation Journal*, Fall, 1969; and Merrill J. Roberts, "Transport Costs, Pricing, and Regulation," in National Bureau of Economic Research, *Transportation Economics* (New York: National Bureau of Economic Research, 1965).

Criticisms of differential pricing are presented in John R. Doyle, "National Transportation Pricing Policy," *Traffic World*, January 11, 1969, p. 74; John R. Meyer, Merton J. Peck, John Stenason, and Charles Zwick, *The Economics of Competition in the Transportation Industries* (Cambridge, Massachusetts: Harvard University Press, 1959), pp. 181–202; James C. Nelson, "Toward Rational Price Policies," in Ernest W. Williams, Jr. (ed.), *The Future of American Trans-*

portation (Englewood Cliffs, New Jersey: Prentice-Hall, Inc., 1971); Roy J. Sampson, "The Case for Full Cost Ratemaking," *ICC Practitioners' Journal,* March, 1966; and George Wilson, *Essays on Some Unsettled Questions in the Economics of Transportation* (Bloomington, Indiana: Bureau of Business Research, Indiana University, 1962), pp. 83–84.

Many writers dealing with nontransportation pricing argue that the forces in the marketplace are more important than costs in pricing. See for example, Lawrence C. Lockley, "Theories of Pricing in Marketing," *Journal of Marketing,* January, 1949, p. 366.

9

Transportation Pricing
in Practice

The typical citizen and even most businessmen have little knowledge of freight rates. Part of the problem is the mystic veil of confusion and complexity that surrounds the freight rate structure and which is, to a large extent, unnecessary. The general public is also largely uninformed concerning the pricing of for-hire passenger service. It is the purpose of this chapter to explain how and why transportation pricing is what it is, with the discussion concentrating mainly on the pricing of freight service by common carriers.

The theory of transportation pricing was discussed in Chapter 8 in which it was explained that the dominant approach to pricing in American transportation is the differential method. The subject of this chapter is transportation pricing in practice or how the differential approach to pricing is carried out by the for-hire carriers. The reader is cautioned once again that the differential method is not equally applicable or suitable to all modes or all individual carriers. This factor affects the degree to which individual modes or carriers can carry out the method in practice.

FACTORS TO CONSIDER IN PRICING FREIGHT SERVICE

As has been indicated earlier, there are many internal and external factors that might be considered in any pricing decision (see Chapters 3 and 8). All of these internal and external considerations are important in pricing freight service by for-hire carriers, some of which are more important than others. It is not possible, however, to discuss here each of the several internal and external factors individually as they might be dealt with in a transportation company rate-making decision. The variance between modes and between individual carriers of the same mode as to the importance of each of the internal and external factors, plus the different conditions affecting each mode and carrier, make such a discussion impossible. Instead, as was done in Chapter 8, the discussion that follows concentrates on 2 of the key factors—cost and demand—recognizing that other factors may also be important in any carrier-pricing decision. It should also be understood that, because of the large number of traffic segments to be priced, individual detailed analysis of the factors affecting each segment may be impossible for a large carrier and, consequently, comparisons with previously priced segments as to similarity of transportation characteristics may instead be used to determine rates.

COST

The cost of providing transportation service has traditionally been a key element in rate-making decisions. As we know, there are several different "kinds" of costs or cost categories that are found in economic theory and that fixed, variable, joint, and common costs are considered to be the more important cost concepts in transportation pricing. We also know that differential pricing emphasizes the importance of variable costs as the floor in rate making and we know that many critics of differential pricing insist that fully distributed costs should be the floor.

In pricing freight services the rate maker sets rates on individual segments of traffic or groups of similar segments of traffic. A segment of traffic is some commodity which is to be carried between two specified points. The cost factors involved (fixed, variable, joint, or common) are associated either with the nature of the commodity to be carried or with the particular route over which the commodity is to be carried.

Commodity Cost Factors

There are several cost considerations associated with the nature of the particular commodity to be carried.

Loading Characteristics. Different commodities differ as to how well they "load" into the transportation vehicle, that is, the efficiency with which they occupy the vehicle space provided. The ideal situation for the carrier is when the commodity(s) to be carried in a vehicle, such as a truck trailer, fills the space available in the vehicle and at the same time the maximum weight that can be carried in that vehicle is reached. Consequently, the weight density, i.e., weight per cubic foot, of the commodity is an important factor to take into account in rate making. A commodity that has low weight density occupies more space per unit of weight than a commodity that has a high weight density. Therefore, the commodity that has the low weight density would normally be charged a higher rate per 100 pounds than would the commodity that has a high weight density.

In addition to the basic weight density of the commodity to be carried, factors that influence space occupied are the shape of the commodity (i.e., odd-shaped commodities lead to a lot of empty space) and stowability (the ability to load multiple layers of the commodity without causing damage).

Susceptibility to Loss and Damage. An obvious factor to consider in rate making is the degree to which a given commodity is susceptible to loss and damage. The greater the susceptibility, the greater will be the cost of claims for loss and damage. Therefore, the rate charged should ordinarily reflect this. It is a primary reason why manufactured goods are usually charged higher rates than the raw materials from which they are made.

Volume of Traffic. The volume of movement of the commodity in question can affect rate making. If a commodity, such as a certain kind of grain, moves in heavy volume over a period of time, the carrier can more efficiently schedule equipment and personnel and thus reduce costs per unit of traffic handled.

Regularity of Movement. Closely allied with the economics of large volume are the economies associated with regular movement of a commodity. If traffic of a given commodity moves at regular times over a carrier's system, the carrier can more efficiently schedule equipment and personnel than he can when traffic is highly sporadic and uncertain.

Type of Equipment Required. Many commodities can be transported in ordinary boxcars, ordinary van-type truck trailers, or other general-purpose vehicles. Other commodities require special equipment, for example, some may need temperature control. Whatever the reason, different kinds of equipment result in different costs for the carrier and these cost differences may be reflected in the rate charged.

Route Cost Factors

In addition to the cost factors related to the particular commodity to be transported, costs may differ because of the route the commodity is to be carried over.

Distance. Since the costs of providing transportation service usually increase with the length of the haul, rates for longer hauls are normally higher than for shorter hauls, although, as we saw in Chapter 2, rates do not usually increase in direct proportion to increases in distance.

Operating Conditions. Since the operating conditions that prevail on different routes, such as rainfall, snowfall, temperature, grades, and curves, may vary, even within the route system of the same carrier, the cost associated with providing transportation service over different routes also varies and may be reflected in the rates charged to move a given commodity a given distance.

Traffic Density. Certain routes are normally more heavily used, in terms of the total traffic carried over them, than are other routes. The result is that, from a cost standpoint, the carrier's cost per unit carried are lower on the higher-density routes because there are more units of traffic over which to spread the fixed costs than is the case on lightly used routes. This, in turn, means that rates can be lower on the high-density routes.

DEMAND

The demand or "value of service" aspect is a very important part of the pricing process in transportation. In the theory of transportation pricing discussed in Chapter 8 we learned that the value of the service to the user sets a ceiling on how high a freight rate can be set. The factors that determine the character of demand or the value of service level are associated with the commodity to be carried or with the route over which it is to be carried.

Commodity Demand Factors

Demand factors associated with the particular commodity to be carried are several in number. These factors influence the value of service ceiling on a rate.

Value of the Commodity. The most well-known demand factor in differential pricing is the value of the commodity. High-value commodities are usually charged higher rates than are low-value commodities because the value of the transportation service is greater to the shipper (or receiver) of the high-value commodity and the shipper has a greater ability to pay a higher rate. In modern times, because of competition in transportation, the emphasis in differential rate making is on low rates on low-value commodities that cannot stand a higher rate, rather than on high rates on high-value commodities.

Economic Conditions in the User Industry. In situations of depressed economic conditions in a user industry, carriers may lower rates for such commodities, recognizing the industry's decreased ability to pay normal rates and the need to help preserve the existence of the industry as a source of traffic. The reverse may be true when the using industry is enjoying a high level of prosperity and, hence, a greater ability to pay a high rate.

Rates on Competing Commodities. It was pointed out in Chapter 8 that differential pricing can be practiced successfully only when different market segments can be kept separate from one another so that a low rate on one segment of traffic does not interfere with the ability of the carrier to charge a higher rate on other segments of traffic. As to differentiation between commodities, the market separation is accomplished by the fact that a shipper (or receiver) of typewriters can avail himself of a low rate on gravel only by shipping gravel, which he is in no position to do. Actually, the fact that gravel has a low rate is of little or no interest to him.

There are, however, situations in which commodities are close or direct substitutes for one another and the market segments are not separated, i.e., a low rate on one commodity does affect the rate that can be charged on competing substitute commodities. Examples are steel beams and aluminum beams, wool and cotton, or coal and oil.

In such situations, the carrier finds that if he attempts to charge greatly different rates per 100 pounds for one commodity than for another for similar services, the shippers and receivers of the higher-rate commodity may complain that they are unable to compete because of the rate difference. They are unable to pay the rate asked, i.e., the value of service to them is below the rate being charged. Consequently, the rates on the two commodities tend to be equalized by the carrier in order to enable both commodities to compete, the carrier hoping that the total traffic generated will maximize the contribution toward fixed expenses.

Route Demand Factors

Demand factors associated with the route in question also affect the willingness and ability of shippers to pay a rate.

Competition with other Carriers. The amount and quality of competition faced by a carrier can vary greatly between different routes. Competition may be between carriers of the same mode (intramodal) or it may be between carriers of different modes (intermodal). In either case, the competition may come from for-hire carriers or from private carriers, or from both.

Carrier competition is one of the more important rate-making considerations in modern times, unlike the case prior to 1920, and it has had substantial influence on the upper end of the rate-making scale, i.e., the value of service ceiling. For railroads, in particular, carrier competition has had a depressing effect on the ceiling on their rates.

Competition with other carriers may be a reason for establishing rates below normal levels and below fully distributed costs, as is called for in differential pricing.

Production-Point Competition. Another form of competition that must be recognized by carriers when setting rates is the competition that exists between the points served. Production-point competition exists when a commodity is produced at 2 or more different points and the producers compete in the same market area(s). Thus, in Figure 9-1 points A and B are production points of a given commodity and C is a market in which the commodity is sold, and both routes are served by the same carrier. The normal situation, if it is assumed that everything else is equal, would be for the freight rate on the commodity to be higher from A to C than it would be from B to C because of the difference in distance traveled. Shippers at A, however, may claim that they cannot sell at C with the normal rate because the landed cost to buyers at C would be too high relative to what the landed cost would be if they were to buy from producers at B. The shippers at A cannot pay the normal rate. The products involved would have to be close to homogeneous to make this argument valid. The carrier may respond by lowering the rate from A to C to a level close to or exactly equal to the rate from B to C. If 2 different carriers are involved on the 2 routes, the same result may occur. In either case, the carrier lowering the rate from A to C believes he is better off in terms of total contribution to fixed costs after the rate reduction than before.

Market Competition. A similar situation occurs when 2 or more markets (often agricultural) compete for the output of a producing area. In Figure 9-2, if A is a producing area for a certain kind of grain and B and C are market centers

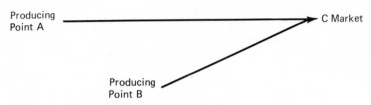

FIGURE 9-1 *Production-Point Competition.*

where grain is bought and sold, then B and C will try to encourage shippers to ship the grain to their market centers for sale.

If all other factors are assumed to be equal, including the prices paid at the 2 markets, since C is farther from A than is B, the normal situation is that the rate from A to C will be higher than from A to B, thus providing the market at B the advantage in attracting the grain since the shipper ordinarily receives the price at the market less the transportation costs involved in getting the grain to the market.

However, representatives of market center C may pressure the carrier to lower the rate from A to C so that C may compete for A's grain. The carrier may, as in production-point competition, respond by lowering the rate from A to C to a point at or near the rate from A to B, whether the same carrier or different carriers serve the two routes.[1]

A rate executive of one of the country's largest railroads, in referring to the various competitive forces that a rate maker must deal with, made the following statement:

> On a day-to-day basis the rate officer works with all of these competitive forces in a state of perpetual crisis which can be compared with an automobile traveling at a high rate of speed down a very narrow road. On the one side of the road is a ditch labeled "Too little, too late," which means that the rate officer has failed in his obligation to meet the competitive conditions . . . and the business has been lost. On the other side of this narrow road is an equally deep and dangerous ditch called "Too much, too soon," and the rate officer, by unnecessary reductions, has reduced the gross and consequently the net revenue of his railroad imprudently.[2]

Traffic Density. The fact that certain routes are normally more heavily used, in terms of total traffic carried, than are other routes was discussed earlier in this chapter as a route cost factor affecting rate making. Traffic density can also be a route demand factor if the carrier treats the situation as a demand problem instead of a cost problem. If viewed as a demand problem, rates will be set so that they are lower on low-density routes than on high-density routes in order to encourage or promote greater utilization of the low-density routes by users.

---

[1] For a discussion of production-point and market competition see D. Philip Locklin, *Economics of Transportation,* 7th ed. (Homewood, Illinois: Richard D. Irwin, Inc., 1972), pp. 200–201.

[2] Vincent P. Brown, *Meeting the Shippers' Needs,* presented at the 19th annual session, Railroad Management Institute, The American University, January 20, 1965, p. 2.

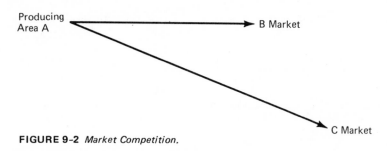

FIGURE 9-2 *Market Competition.*

RATES AND DISTANCE

A general rule followed in transportation pricing is that freight rates increase with distance but not in proportion to the increase in distance. The rates taper with distance, as was pointed out in Chapter 2. One might expect then that, in general, differences in rates on the same commodity carried over different routes would reflect differences in distances over those routes. It is clear, however, from our discussion of the various cost and demand factors to be considered in setting rates on different routes that it is possible that the rates on a given commodity carried over 2 or more different routes of equal distance may be unequal or, if carried over 2 or more different routes of unequal distance, may be equal. These departures from the distance principle of rate making can be caused by differences in the volume and/or regularity of movement of a commodity over different routes, differences in operating conditions, differences in traffic density, differences in competition faced by the carrier, and production-point competition and market competition.

Figure 9-3 illustrates situations in which the rates on a given commodity are unequal for equal distances or equal for unequal distances. The reader can readily see which of the factors listed in the preceding paragraph could be the cause of the departure from the idea that rates over different routes should reflect differences in distance.

In addition to the above reasons for rates not related to distance, there are several other circumstances that bring about departures from the distance principle.

Back-Haul Rates

A frequently occurring rate-making problem has to do with unbalanced traffic movements. Most carriers have some degree of unbalance (traffic in one direction on a carrier's route system is not equal in volume to traffic in the opposite direction). It is often referred to as the back-haul problem because it often arises when a carrier has substantial traffic on a route from, say, A to B, but light traffic from B back to A, and the carrier needs to move the vehicles back to A in order to carry traffic from A to C. This was discussed in Chapters 4 and 7.

When the back-haul problem occurs, the for-hire carrier can approach the pricing problem in several ways, and what he can do is determined by the value of service circumstances that prevail.

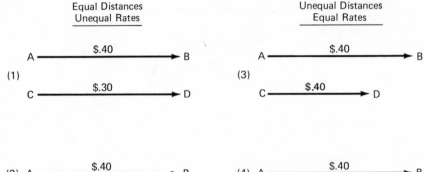

FIGURE 9-3 *Exceptions to the Distance Principle of Rate Making.*

One alternative is to charge normal rates in both directions, recognizing that the unbalanced situation is likely to continue. This may mean having higher rates on the back haul than on the front haul because cost per unit carried is greater on the back haul.

A second possibility is to charge rates on the outbound traffic that will cover the full round-trip costs incurred. Then the carrier need not be so concerned about generating traffic on the return haul. Such rates can be charged, however, only if the users involved are willing to pay those rates.

A third possibility is to charge normal rates on the outbound haul and less-than-normal rates on the return haul. Any contribution above the extra costs involved in taking on additional back-haul traffic may be considered better than not carrying it and receiving no contribution at all. Promotional back-haul rates are frequently found. One must remember, however, that there may be regulatory difficulties associated with these rates because what to one carrier is a back haul may to a competing carrier be a front haul for which normal rates are being charged.

In addition to the problem of unbalanced traffic, rates may be different in opposite directions because of cost or competitive differences.

Rates Higher Than to a More Distant Point

One of the early criticisms of railroad pricing was that there were instances of rates on the same commodity that were higher over a shorter distance than over a longer distance on the same route and in the same direction. This is shown in Figure 9–4 in which the rate on a given commodity is $.40 from A to B but only $.30 from A to C, a longer distance on the same route. This is referred to legally as long-and-short-haul discrimination and, although there are regulatory restrictions on it in railroad, water, and oil pipeline transportation, it can be found in rail and other modes.

The justification for long-and-short-haul discrimination can be found in some of the various cost and demand factors discussed earlier in this chapter. The most frequently given reason is, however, carrier competition that has depressed the rate to the longer distance point (the rate from A to C in Figure 9-4) while leaving the rate to the shorter distance point (the rate from A to B in Figure 9-4) at the normal level.

Aggregate of Intermediates

Another departure from distance rate making is that of a through rate exceeding the aggregate of the intermediate rates, as shown in Figure 9-5. The through rate from A to C is $.80, which is greater than the sum or the aggregate of the two intermediate rates on the commodity of $.40 from A to B and $.25 from B to C. Under the usual tapering principle of rate making, the through rate should be less than, not greater than, the aggregate of intermediate rates.

Again, the justification for this rate pattern may be found in some of the rate-making factors mentioned earlier. One of these may be carrier competition which may have forced the rate down between A and B while leaving all other rates at a normal level. In other words, the aggregate of intermediates was higher than the through rate prior to the rate reduction caused by competitive conditions. As with long-and-short-haul discrimination, higher through rates than the sum of intermediate rates is subject to limitation by the regulatory system in rail, water, and oil pipeline transportation.

Group Rates

A group rate exists when all points in a geographic area (group) are given the same rate on a given commodity that is shipped from (if an origin group) or shipped to (if a destination group) that geographic area to or from some point outside the group. This violates the distance principle of rate making because the same rate is paid from or to all points in a group regardless of the distance involved. Distance is accounted for, however, when there is a series of groups, each one with a different rate that reflects distance to or from the destination or origin point.

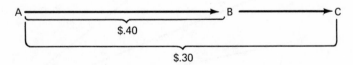

FIGURE 9-4 *Long- and Short-Haul Discrimination.*

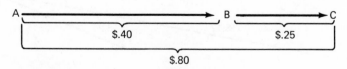

FIGURE 9-5 *Aggregate of Intermediates.*

Although group rates offer the carrier the advantage of reducing the number of individual rates to be published and quoted, a more important reason for their existence is competition between the points involved—either production-point or market competition. All production points in a group are equalized transportation costwise when an origin group is created and all market points in a group are equalized when a destination group is created. From the carrier's point of view, equalization has the potential advantage of maximizing the total traffic and contribution to the fixed costs that he will receive.

Base Rates

Some transportation charges are based on a base rate which is a departure point for other rates. A frequent approach is to make certain rates fixed differentials or percentage differentials above or under the base rate which may not be in direct relation to differences in distance. These are sometimes called *differential rate systems* (not to be confused with differential pricing as described in Chapter 8). The differential rate may be used with specific points or with groups.

Thus, in Figure 9-6 the rate of $1.10 on a specific commodity from A to B is the base rate and the rates to B from C, D, E, F, and G are expressed as fixed differentials from the A to B rate, either plus or minus (in cents) the A to B rate. The differentials are determined by competitive and other factors and may result in a rate pattern that is not in relation to differences in distance.

The differentials used do not result in equal rates for all shipping points, but they may tend toward providing equalization and permit long-distance points to compete, i.e., they are not penalized for the full distance disadvantage that they have.

Another kind of differential rate is used most often for routes that are circuitous or of inferior service compared with more direct and/or faster routes. This rate is usually lower than the standard rate from which it is derived.

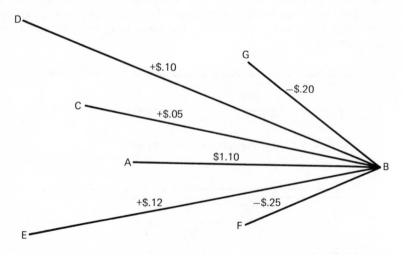

FIGURE 9-6 *Base Rates.*

KINDS OF RATES

Our previous discussion in this chapter has focused on various cost and demand factors that might be considered in pricing freight services, recognizing that other internal and external considerations might also be of some importance.

The result of price making in freight transportation is a number of different kinds of rates, all of which are based on the factors discussed previously and, in many cases, the differential approach to pricing described in Chapter 8.

Class Rates

A major kind of rate is a class rate. Early in its history railroad management realized that the large number of different segments of traffic to be priced and that the use of the differential pricing system it had adopted were resulting in a staggering number of different rates because each commodity and every pair of origin and destination points between which it could be shipped created another rate situation.

To alleviate the problem of dealing with and quoting so many different rates, the railroads, as did their predecessors, began to "classify" freight by grouping commodities with similar transportation characteristics, such as weight density, value, and so on, into a limited number of classes or groups. They then quoted the rates between 2 points on the groups rather than on each individual commodity. Thus, if there were 10 groups, there could be no more than 10 different rates between any 2 points, instead of hundreds or thousands of different rates. Subsequently, railroads began to classify freight collectively and, eventually, in 1952, the Uniform Freight Classification was adopted to apply to railroad traffic throughout the United States. In the same year the National Motor Freight Classification was adopted to apply on most highway carrier traffic.

A classification, then, is an alphabetical listing of commodities along with the class or group to which the particular commodity has been assigned, or its class "rating." The classification does not contain any rates. The class rates that are used with a classification are found in class rate tariffs, which are published separately from the classification itself. Pages from the Uniform Freight Classification and the National Motor Freight Classification showing class ratings are in Figures 9-7 and 9-8.

The class rates that are used with a classification are usually on a tapering mileage scale, and the scale is uniform throughout the area covered by the classification. This, for example, means in the Uniform Freight Classification that a rate per 100 pounds for a certain class for a 500-mile haul is the same whether the haul is in New England or in the midwest. The mileage scale used is uniform throughout the area in which the classification and class rates apply.

The class rates used with a classification system are established through the joint efforts of carriers and government regulatory agencies. The decision on how to classify individual commodities, i.e., which class each commodity should be placed in, is made by the classification committee representing the carriers of the mode involved.[3] The committee, which is permanent, has procedures for

---

[3] For the rail Uniform Freight Classification it is the Uniform Classification Committee. For the highway carrier National Motor Freight Classification it is the National Classification Board.

UNIFORM FREIGHT CLASSIFICATION 12

ITEM	ARTICLES	Less Carload Ratings	Carload Minimum (Pounds)	Carload Ratings
	TOOLS,OR PARTS NAMED (Subject to Item 89950)-Concluded:			
91890	Wedges,noibn,iron,in barrels or boxes	60	36,000	40
91900	Wedges,noibn,wooden,in packages; also CL,loose.	50	36,000	25
91910	Whetstones,noibn,sandstone,in barrels or boxes.	55	36,000	37½
91920	Whetstones,noibn,other than sandstone,in barrels or boxes	70	30,000	45
91930	Wrench sets,socket,in barrels or boxes.	70	30,000	40
91940	Wrenches,monkey or screw,loose or in packages	70	30,000	40
91950	Wrenches,noibn,with attachments,in containers in cloth bags,or in barrels or boxes	70	30,000	40
91960	Wrenches,noibn,without attachments,loose or in packages	70	30,000	40
91970	Yard sticks,in packages	70	30,000	40
91985	Toothpicks,quill,in barrels or boxes.	100	20,000R	70
91990	Tops,bottle stopper,composition,fibre,wood,or wood and metal combined, in bags,barrels or boxes	70	30,000	40
92003	Towbars or towbar assemblies,aircraft ground towing or towing and steering combined,not self-propelled,with or without wheels,in boxes or crates,having a density of:			
	9 pounds or greater per cubic foot.	100	14,000R	70
	Less than 9 pounds per cubic foot	200	10,000R	100
92005	Towers,aerial or antenna,radio or television receiving:			
	Aluminum,other than telescoped,loose or in packages	200	10,000R	100
	Aluminum,telescoped,or steel,not nested nor telescoped,loose or in packages	100	20,000R	55
	Steel,sections nested or telescoped,loose or in packages.	65	40,000	35
92010	Towers,broadcasting,radar,radio or television,SU in sections,loose or in packages.	100	20,000R	55
92015	Towers,KD,aluminum or aluminum and steel combined,loose or in packages.	85	30,000	55
92020	Towers,noibn,steel or wood,separate or combined:			
	SU,in sections or SU sections thereof	200	10,000R	150
	KD,loose or in packages	55	40,000	35
92023	Towers,water cooling,air conditioner,synthetic plastic,with or without blowers or fans,with or without metal fittings or connections,loose or in packages	200	10,000R	85
92025	Towers,water cooling,air conditioner,with or without blowers or fans, aluminum or aluminum and steel combined:			
	SU,in boxes or crates	150	10,000R	100
	KD,or parts,noibn,loose or in packages.	85	30,000	55
92030	Towers,water cooling,air conditioner,with or without blowers or fans:			
	Sheet steel,20 gauge or thinner:			
	SU,in boxes or crates	150	10,000R	100
	KD,in packages.	85	24,000R	45
	Sheet steel,thicker than 20 gauge,or steel and wood combined:			
	SU,loose or on skids.	100	16,000R	60
	KD,in packages.	70	24,000R	45
92050	Transformers,electric,old,used,having value only for reconditioning or for reclamation of parts,loose or in packages.	65	30,000	37½
92060	Traps,animal or bird,noibn,in bags or bundles,in barrels,boxes or crates,or in shipping baskets or hampers	77½	30,000	50
92070	Traps,bird,mouse or rat,wire,in barrels,boxes or crates,or in shipping baskets or hampers	150	20,000R	70
92080	Traps,fly:			
	SU,in barrels,boxes or crates	200	10,000R	100
	KD,or taken apart and parts nested or flat,in barrels,boxes or crates	100	20,000R	70
92090	Traps,Japanese beetle,in boxes (suspension rods may be in bundles). . .	70	30,000	40
92095	Traps,lobster or crab,plastic and iron combined,tops and bases separated,tops nested,in boxes.	70	30,000	45
92100	TRAYS:			
92110	Battery shipping,wooden,loose or in packages.	100	30,000	35
92120	Cabinet,counter or window display,wooden,noibn,with or without lining or trimming,in boxes or crates	100	20,000R	70
92130	Desk,wooden,in boxes or crates.	100	16,000R	70
92160	Foot bath or toilet,rubber or rubber compound,in barrels,boxes or crates	85	30,000	55
92170	Mineral wool (rock,slag or glass wool) and plastic combined,with or without steel reinforcement:			
	Not nested,in packages; also CL,loose	200	10,000R	85
	One or more completely or partially enclosed within two others. . .	150	10,000R	85
	Nested,other than solid,in packages; also CL,loose.	100	16,000R	70
	Flat or nested solid,see Note,Item 92171,in packages.	70	36,000	40
92171	NOTE.-Rule 21 will govern,except the words "½ inch" may be substituted for "¼ inch".			
92180	Serving,not silver plated,not wheeled,noibn:			
	Not nested,in boxes	100	20,000R	70
	Nested,in boxes	85	24,000R	55
92190	Shipping,wooden bottom with flaring sheet steel rims,in packages; also CL,loose:			
	Not nested.	100	30,000	45
	Nested.	70	30,000	45

For explanation of abbreviations,numbers and reference marks,see last page of this Classification; for packages,see pages following rating section.

FIGURE 9-7 *Page From Uniform Freight Classification Showing Class Ratings. (Source: Uniform Freight Classification Committee, Agent, Uniform Freight Classification 12, effective October 31, 1975, p. 866)*

NATIONAL MOTOR FREIGHT CLASSIFICATION 100-C

Item	ARTICLES	CLASSES LTL	CLASSES TL	MW
	BUILDING MATERIALS, MISCELLANEOUS, GROUP: subject to item 33570			
33940	**Cement Mixing Compound,** in bulk in barrels	60	35	40.2
33950	**Concrete Anti-spall Coating Compound,** liquid, in barrels	55	35	36.2
33960	**Concrete Bonding Compound,** liquid or paste, in barrels or boxes	70	37½	36.2
33980	**Concrete Surface Curing Compound,** in barrels	55	35	36.2
34000	**Concrete Surface Hardener,** powered iron, in bags, barrels or boxes	60	37½	40.2
34010	**Concrete Surface Hardener,** dry, NOI, in bags, barrels or boxes	70	40	36.2
34020	**Concrete Surface Hardener,** liquid or paste:			
Sub 1	In glass in barrels or boxes	85	50	30.2
Sub 2	In metal cans in barrels or boxes or in bulk in barrels, kits or pails	70	40	36.2
34040	**Concrete or Masonry Plasticizer and Water Reducing Compound,** in bags, barrels or boxes	50	35	36.2
34060	**Cores,** flush door, molded pulp, nested, in packages	200	125	10.2
34070	**Covers** or **Lids,** water meter box, vault or manhole, reinforced plastic mortar, see Note, item 34071, banded to pallets, platforms or skids, or in paperboard tubes or pallets	60	35	36.2
34071	NOTE—Applies only on covers or lids manufactured from sand and not to exceed 30 percent plastic binder, reinforced with glass fibre.			
34080	**Cribbing,** steel, **Including Fillers, Caps, Clevis Pins, Bolts and Nuts**	70	35	30.2
34090	**Culvert End Sections,** flared, aluminum, without collars, rods or bands attached, see Note, item 34092:			
Sub 1	SU, nested, in nests of 6 or more, smallest inside cross-sectional dimension when assembled:			
Sub 2	24 inches or less	125	70	16.2
Sub 3	Over 24 inches	150	100	10.2
Sub 4	NOI, smallest inside cross-sectional dimension when assembled:			
Sub 5	24 inches or less	250	100	10.2
Sub 6	Over 24 inches	300	300	AQ
Sub 7	Taken apart, sections nested	125	70	16.2
34092	NOTE—Also applies on accompanying connecting rods, lugs, nuts, toe or corner plates, providing the weight does not exceed 15 percent of the weight upon which charges are assessed.			
34095	**Culvert End Sections,** flared, aluminum, with collars, rods or bands attached, SU:			
Sub 1	Nested, in nests of 6 or more, smallest inside cross-sectional dimension when assembled:			
Sub 2	24 inches or less	150	100	10.2
Sub 3	Over 24 inches	200	100	10.2
Sub 4	Not nested or nested in nests of less than 6 smallest inside cross-sectional dimension when assembled:			
Sub 5	24 inches or less	250	100	10.2
Sub 6	Over 24 inches	300	300	AQ
34100	**Culvert End Sections,** flared, plate or sheet steel, without collars rods or bands attached, see Note, item 34102:			
Sub 1	SU, nested, in nest of 6 or more, smallest inside cross-sectional dimension when assembled:			
Sub 2	24 inches or less	85	55	24.2
Sub 3	Over 24 inches	92½	60	20.2
Sub 4	NOI, smallest inside cross-secitonal dimension when assembled:			
Sub 5	24 inches or less	150	100	10.2
Sub 6	Over 24 inches	200	100	10.2
Sub 7	Taken apart, sections nested	92½	60	20.2
34102	NOTE—Also applies on accompanying connecting rods, lugs, nuts, toe or corner plates, providing the weight does not exceed 15 percent of the weight upon which charges are assessed.			
34120	**Culvert End Sections,** flared, plate or sheet steel, with collars, rods or bands attached, SU:			
Sub 1	Nested, in nests of 6 or more, smallest inside cross-sectional dimension when assembled:			
Sub 2	24 inches or less	85	55	24.2
Sub 3	Over 24 inches	125	70	16.2
Sub 4	Not nested or nested in nests of less than 6, smallest inside cross-sectional dimension when assembled:			
Sub 5	24 inches or less	150	100	10.2
Sub 6	Over 24 inches	250	100	10.2
34140	**Culvert Headwalls or Headwall Aprons,** steel, 16 gauge or thicker:			
Sub 1	Not nested, or other than in panels	125	45	24.2
Sub 2	Nested, or in panels	85	45	24.2
34240	**Dividing Strips,** terrazzo or cement flooring, in boxes	65	45	30.2
34260	**Doors,** airplane hangar, steel, not glazed	70	40	30.2
34270	**Doors or Door Sections,** garage or industrial building, overhead, plastic and aluminum, KD flat, with door track packed in same box	92½	60	18.2
34280	**Doors or Door Sections or Grilles,** garage or industrial building, overhead, sliding, rolling or curtain type. iron or steel, see Note, item 34282, in packages; also TL, loose	70	37½	36.2
34282	NOTE—Also applies on accompanying hardware, angles, bars, castings, chain, cable, guides, hoods, pipe, rollers, springs, motors, sprockets, track, hinges, sheaves, brackets, handles, locks, hangers, rails, hooks, pulleys, rods or other fittings when in same package with the doors, door sections, grilles, partitions or shutters, LTL; or TL, in same or separate packages. or in packages when doors are loose			

For explanation of abbreviations and reference marks, see last page of this tariff.

FIGURE 9–8 *Page From National Motor Freight Classification Showing Class Ratings. (Source: National Motor Freight Traffic Association, Inc., Agent, National Motor Freight Classification 100-C, effective April 23, 1976, p. 374)*

classifying new commodities and dealing with requests for changes in existing ratings.

Freight classification systems have been adopted by the railroad and highway carrier industries, as noted above. Domestic water carriers generally use the rail classification, but sometimes they use the highway carrier classification. Airlines practice a limited form of freight classification of their own. Oil pipelines do not use the classification device.[4]

Exceptions to the Classification

An exception to the classification is a substitution of a different class rating for that contained in a classification. Exceptions are brought about by competitive or other conditions affecting a particular carrier and his users that cause him to find the class rating provided for in the classification unacceptable, usually because it results in too high a rate. The exception changes the rating to a lower one and may apply to all traffic of that commodity in the entire area covered by the classification or only to traffic between a small number of points. By using an exception rating the carrier avoids the long, involved process of trying to get the classification committee to change the classification rating for the commodity. The exception rating supersedes the rating found in the classification, unless the appropriate tariff specifically provides for alternation between the two. The large number of classes contained in the Uniform Freight Classification and the National Motor Freight Classification are designed to reduce the need for exception ratings.

Commodity Rates

Commodity rates are rates published by a carrier or carriers on a commodity or segment of traffic directly without reference to the freight classification device. Carriers use commodity rates instead of class rates because they feel that class rates are unsuitable for their particular needs. Commodity rates take precedence over class rates, unless the appropriate tariff provides for alternation between the two. Since class rates are normally based on distance, the various exceptions to the distance principle of rate making, such as back-haul rates and rates based on production-point competition, discussed previously in this chapter, are usually examples of commodity rates.

In any particular situation, then, it is possible that there exist 3 different rates—the normal class rate, a class rate based on an exception to the classification, and a commodity rate. Ordinarily, unless the applicable tariff provides for alternation, the commodity rate takes precedence over the regular class rate and the rate derived by using an exception to the classification, and the latter takes precedence over a regularly determined class rate. In addition, there is only one legal rate that can be used by regulated interstate surface carriers, and that rate is the lowest rate available, which usually is the commodity rate, if one exists, or the class rate tied to an exception rating, if no commodity rate exists.

---

[4]The use of the classification device by each mode of transportation is dealt with further in Chapters 10 through 14.

Inherent Difficulties With Freight Classification

An analysis of traffic carried would reveal that most rail traffic and much highway carrier and water carrier traffic is carried under commodity rates. It has been estimated that at least 85 per cent of all rail ton-miles is carried under commodity rates.

The reason that so much traffic is not carried under class rates is that the classification system cannot satisfy all carriers and all users in its area of applicability. The various commodities are classified or rated by a committee, as indicated earlier, and the committee decides on one classification for a given commodity— that classification to apply everywhere in the classification territory, which, in the case of the Uniform Freight Classification and the National Motor Freight Classification, is the entire United States. The class rates that are used with the classification also apply over large geographic areas and are usually tied to distance, as noted previously.

This all means that the classification committee and those who establish the class rates must deal in rather general terms with the various factors, such as loading characteristics, regularity of movement, type of equipment required, operating conditions, and competition, that are considered in classifying commodities and determining rates. They cannot take into account local conditions having to do with these factors. For example, railroads that parallel important waterways such as the Mississippi River may find that the rates provided by the class rate system are too high in view of the competition they face from water carriers. Therefore, the railroads must then establish commodity rates. Another example might be railroads in the eastern part of the country that rely heavily on coal traffic. The heavy volume of coal traffic and its regularity of movement may call for rates lower than the class rates and, therefore, a commodity rate is used.

The result is that freight classification, although its purpose was a worthwhile one (to reduce the number of rates) has to a considerable extent failed because of the classification system's inability to account for local conditions.

Rate Tariffs

Although, as a general rule, rates are published as so many dollars and cents per 100 pounds to carry a commodity between two specified points, some commodities are quoted rates per net ton (2,000 pounds) or gross ton (2,240 pounds). Some lumber rates are expressed in cents per 1,000 board feet and pulpwood rates are sometimes quoted in cents per cord. Bulk liquids are sometimes quoted rates in cents per gallon and oil pipelines quote their rates per barrel. Per car and per trailer rates are sometimes used in trailer-on-flatcar service.

Many for-hire carrier rates are not regulated, as we shall see later, and many of these unregulated rates are either not published at all or are given no more publication than would be found in any other industry. They are not required to be made available to the public. Regulated for-hire carriers, however, are usually required to publish their rates and make them available to the public. Such rates are published in rate tariffs.

Rate tariffs are complex price lists that contain either class or commodity rates. Tariffs are usually published by rate bureaus (see below), but sometimes they are published by individual carriers. In addition to the regular line-haul or point-to-point tariffs, there are also tariffs that contain charges for special services such as in-transit privileges or reconsignment and diversion or switching or storage. In addition to rates, tariffs may also contain the applicable rules and regulations governing the services to be performed plus additional information relative to special service charges and other matters. Class tariffs contain the rates on the various classes included in the corresponding classification. Commodity tariffs contain commodity rates. Pages from a class rate tariff and a commodity rate tariff showing rates charged are shown in Figures 9-9 and 9-10. The complexity of rate tariffs is apparent from these examples.

Tariffs vary considerably in size and coverage, ranging from a single page containing a single rate on a single commodity between only two points to hundreds of pages containing rates on many commodities covering many routes and points.

All tariffs of regulated interstate carriers are published subject to the requirements of the Interstate Commerce Commission (ICC) and the Civil Aeronautics Board (CAB) as to form and content and they are kept up to date by the issuance of supplements.

Specific Kinds of Class and Commodity Rates

There are dozens of different class and commodity rates, but it is not necessary for us to try to describe them all. Nevertheless, we shall describe a few of them with the understanding that those mentioned only illustrate the many different rates that exist.

Vehicle-Load Rate. A vehicle-load rate requires that a certain minimum weight be tendered (or paid for) in order to qualify for a vehicle-load rate which is lower than the rate on a smaller shipment: Examples are carload and truckload rates.

Less-Than-Vehicle-Load Rate. This rate applies to shipments that are too small to qualify for the vehicle-load rate. Examples are less-than-carload and less-than-truckload rates, which are higher per 100 pounds than the corresponding carload and truckload rates.

Any-Quantity Rate. On some commodities the rates are the same regardless of the size of the shipment. These rates are called any-quantity rates and are used for commodities that, as a rule, do not move in vehicle-load lots. Only a few large users could qualify for the vehicle-load rate. This, of course, would result in discrimination against smaller users. In some cases, any-quantity rates are used because there is no significant difference between the cost of handling the commodities as vehicle loads or as less-than-vehicle-load shipments and because a vehicle-load rate could not be justified.

Volume Minimim Rate. This rate is used by highway carriers for shipments that are greater than what can be accommodated in a single truck. The volume rate per 100 pounds is ordinarily lower than the truckload rate.

Tariff MWB 502-B

SECTION 3
TABLE OF CLASS RATES AND CHARGES
(See Items 100 and 130)

RATE BASIS NUMBER	MINIMUM CHARGE / MINIMUM TRUCKLOAD CHARGE	LINE	600	500	400	300	250	200	175	150	125	110	100	92½
			RATES IN CENTS PER 100 POUNDS											
361 TO 380	MC= 1255	LTL	4346	3445	2806	2164	1841	1516	1357	1197	1038	935	870	825
		500 #	4243	3345	2700	2062	1740	1413	1254	1091	935	831	772	721
		1000 #	3838	2999	2416	1833	1547	1250	1100	960	812	718	660	622
		2000 #	3668	2962	2373	1789	1494	1206	1059	915	772	681	623	580
		5000 #	3037	2448	1962	1477	1236	993	869	749	628	556	506	474
	MTC= 362	VT	2528	2106	1688	1268	1060	849	741	640	533	474	432	399
361A TO 380A	MC= 1265	LTL	4417	3509	2852	2199	1869	1547	1377	1212	1051	950	884	836
		500 #	4318	3404	2749	2097	1766	1440	1275	1110	948	849	780	734
		1000 #	3912	3058	2464	1868	1574	1277	1121	975	827	736	678	630
		2000 #	3752	3019	2420	1827	1527	1232	1080	937	780	691	636	593
		5000 #	3106	2498	2001	1505	1259	1012	886	766	640	564	518	480
	MTC= 362	VT	2579	2148	1723	1296	1079	864	759	649	546	481	438	404
381 TO 400	MC= 1275	LTL	4435	3524	2865	2207	1877	1549	1383	1221	1053	958	885	839
		500 #	4330	3423	2760	2103	1777	1444	1282	1116	949	856	782	735
		1000 #	3924	3073	2478	1877	1580	1282	1130	979	828	738	680	634
		2000 #	3762	3038	2434	1834	1537	1235	1090	941	783	699	637	593
		5000 #	3119	2512	2012	1514	1267	1017	895	769	641	568	519	480
	MTC= 372	VT	2588	2163	1731	1302	1087	869	763	653	548	482	440	405
381A TO 400A	MC= 1290	LTL	4519	3587	2916	2246	1913	1574	1404	1235	1068	969	901	856
		500 #	4413	3486	2812	2141	1807	1470	1299	1135	965	866	797	750
		1000 #	4008	3136	2525	1915	1611	1300	1150	996	844	753	691	649
		2000 #	3836	3094	2484	1870	1567	1264	1110	960	802	713	651	605
		5000 #	3178	2564	2055	1545	1294	1040	911	784	653	582	530	488
	MTC= 372	VT	2650	2203	1765	1326	1108	887	777	672	558	491	450	414
401 TO 420	MC= 1290	LTL	4531	3599	2923	2254	1916	1576	1407	1239	1074	969	904	856
		500 #	4426	3498	2819	2147	1817	1474	1302	1137	969	866	800	750
		1000 #	4018	3151	2536	1918	1617	1306	1152	1002	849	753	693	649
		2000 #	3858	3110	2497	1884	1575	1271	1112	962	806	713	653	609
		5000 #	3198	2573	2065	1555	1299	1043	912	787	656	582	533	493
	MTC= 387	VT	2658	2216	1775	1334	1113	891	781	676	561	494	451	420
401A TO 420A	MC= 1300	LTL	4603	3667	2976	2289	1947	1602	1431	1260	1091	984	915	865
		500 #	4496	3563	2874	2185	1843	1494	1328	1153	989	882	811	765
		1000 #	4092	3214	2585	1958	1649	1331	1177	1023	868	773	708	657
		2000 #	3944	3172	2547	1917	1608	1294	1136	979	824	732	671	620
		5000 #	3266	2624	2103	1583	1326	1066	932	804	676	596	546	503
	MTC= 387	VT	2710	2258	1809	1361	1133	912	798	688	573	502	459	428
421 TO 440	MC= 1300	LTL	4603	3667	2977	2289	1945	1602	1431	1257	1089	986	915	864
		500 #	4496	3563	2875	2185	1841	1494	1328	1151	984	883	811	757
		1000 #	4092	3214	2588	1958	1645	1331	1177	1020	864	774	708	655
		2000 #	3921	3175	2547	1917	1608	1293	1137	979	823	732	667	620
		5000 #	3246	2630	2103	1583	1326	1062	934	804	675	596	541	503
	MTC= 402	VT	2710	2259	1809	1362	1132	913	798	686	574	503	459	425
421A TO 440A	MC= 1305	LTL	4674	3728	3032	2328	1978	1632	1454	1277	1106	1001	927	873
		500 #	4572	3624	2925	2224	1873	1524	1352	1175	1001	899	824	773
		1000 #	4167	3277	2638	2000	1680	1351	1200	1038	880	783	717	672
		2000 #	4006	3240	2599	1956	1640	1322	1155	1000	839	739	680	630
		5000 #	3315	2679	2147	1617	1351	1083	953	819	686	606	555	514
	MTC= 402	VT	2761	2305	1848	1388	1159	929	813	698	583	517	470	434
441 TO 460	MC= 1310	LTL	4685	3742	3040	2334	1981	1635	1460	1282	1109	1000	928	878
		500 #	4578	3631	2937	2230	1881	1530	1359	1177	1004	898	825	776
		1000 #	4177	3291	2650	2008	1685	1366	1206	1043	883	782	718	676
		2000 #	4016	3248	2611	1966	1643	1325	1164	1001	841	739	681	630
		5000 #	3328	2692	2157	1621	1357	1087	955	820	691	606	556	514
	MTC= 418	VT	2782	2315	1854	1394	1162	931	819	700	588	518	474	436

For explanation of MC, MTC and Lines LTL, 500#, 1000#, 2000#, 5000# and VT, see Item 5000.
For explanation of abbreviations and reference marks see last page(s) of this tariff.

FIGURE 9-9 *Page From Motor Carrier Class Rate Tariff Showing Rates Charged. (Source: Middlewest Motor Freight Bureau, Agent, Tariff MWB 502-B, effective February 6, 1976, p. 344)*

2440			WTL TARIFF 5-X		2540

SECTION 1 - SPECIFIC COMMODITY RATES IN DOLLARS PER 100 LB (EXCEPT AS NOTED)

ITEM 2440 CONT'D

TO:

IL

STATION	CODE	STATION	CODE
Chicago	T1	IA West Burlington	T4
Ottawa	T3	MN Minneapolis	T7
Roscoe	T4	Minnesota Transfer	T7
Tamms	T6	St Paul	T7
IA Clinton	T2	MO St Louis	T5

FROM	TO	REF	Col 1	Col 2	Col 3	Col 4	Col 5
F1	T1	. .	1.33				
F1	T2	. .	1.10				
F1	T3	. .	1.26				
F1	T4	. .	1.14				
F1	T5	. .	1.55				
F1	T6	. .	1.69				
F2	T7	. .	1.45				

ITEM 2450

2655116.04 Drums, fibreboard, straight sided, set-up, not nested.
Col 1. Min wt 14,000 lb.

FROM:

WI

STATION	CODE	STATION	CODE
Owen	F1		

TO:

IA

STATION	CODE	STATION	CODE
Clinton	T1		

FROM	TO	REF	Col 1	Col 2	Col 3	Col 4	Col 5
F1	T1	. .	1.69				

ITEM 2460

(NOTE 1)
2655116.04 Drums, fibreboard or pulpboard, or fibreboard, pulpboard and metal or wood combined.
a. Min wt 24,000 lb . . . . Col 1
3491235.67 Drums, iron or steel.
a. Min wt 18,000 lb . . . . Col 2

FROM:

IL

STATION	CODE	STATION	CODE
Addison	F1		

TO:

MI
MN

STATION	CODE	STATION	CODE
Marquette	T2	MN Minnesota Transfer	T3
Chemolite Siding	T1	St Paul	T3
Minneapolis	T3		

FROM	TO	REF	Col 1	Col 2	Col 3	Col 4	Col 5
F1	T1	. .		1.86			
F1	T2	. .	1.38	1.79			
F1	T3	. .	1.38	1.86			

EXPLANATION OF NOTES
1. Not subject to Items 80 nor 85. Provisions of Item 320 apply.

ITEM 2470

2655116. Drums, Pails or Tubs, shipping fibreboard or pulpboard, or fibreboard, pulpboard and metal or wood combined.
Col 1. Min wt 24,000 lb.

FROM:

IL

STATION	CODE	STATION	CODE
Kankakee	F1	WI Owen	F2

TO:

	STATION	CODE	STATION	CODE
IL	Ottawa	T5	MN St Paul I	T2
	Tamms	T7	MO St Louis	T8
IA	Clinton	T4	WI Bayfield I	T1
	West Burlington	T8	Port Washington I	T3
MN	Minneapolis I	T2		
	Minnesota Transfer			
	I	T2		

CONT'D IN NEXT COLUMN

SECTION 1 - SPECIFIC COMMODITY RATES IN DOLLARS PER 100 LB (EXCEPT AS NOTED)

ITEM 2470 CONT'D

FROM	TO	REF	Col 1	Col 2	Col 3	Col 4	Col 5
F1	T1	. .	1.52				
F1	T2	. .	1.44				
F1	T3	. .	.80				
F2	T4	. .	1.04				
F2	T5	. .	1.14				
F2	T6	. .	1.44				
F2	T7	. .	1.61				
F2	T8	. .	1.24				

EXPLANATION OF REFERENCE MARKS
I Not subject to Item 80 nor 85 except via ICG (Chicago, IL) CNW.

ITEM 2480

2655116. Drums, Pails or Tubs, shipping, fibreboard or pulpboard, or fibreboard, pulpboard and metal and wood combined.
Col 1. Min wt 24,000 lb.

FROM:

MO

STATION	CODE	STATION	CODE
St Louis	F1		

TO:

WI

STATION	CODE	STATION	CODE
Merrimac (Badger Army Ammunition Plant)	T1		

FROM	TO	REF	Col 1	Col 2	Col 3	Col 4	Col 5
F1	T1	. .	1.21				

ITEM 2530

(Note 1)
0152990.15 Eggs.
Col 1. Min wt 20,000 lb.

FROM:

	STATION	CODE	STATION	CODE
MN	Winona I	F2	WI Reedsburg	F1
WI	Black River Falls	F2	Waupaca	F2
	Blair 3	F2	Whitehall 3	F1
	La Crosse	F1		

TO:

IL

STATION	CODE	STATION	CODE
Chicago	T1		

FROM	TO	REF	Col 1	Col 2	Col 3	Col 4	Col 5
F1	T1	. .	.99				
F2	T1	. .	1.01				

EXPLANATION OF NOTES
1. EXCEPTION. - Rates will not apply in connection with the SOO. For rates see SOO Tariff 360-series.

EXPLANATION OF REFERENCE MARKS
I Will also apply via GBW, Merrillan, WI thence CNW.
2 Applies only via CNW.
3 Will also apply via:
A. GBW (Merrillan, WI) thence CNW or MILW.
B. GBW (Wisconsin Rapids, WI) MILW or
C. GBW (Green Bay, WI) MILW.

ITEM 2540

3624130. Electrodes, graphite, furnace or eletroylitic bath, NOIBN.
Col 1. Min wt 50,000 lb, not subject to Rule 24 of UFC or exceptions thereto.
Col 2. Min wt 100,000 lb, not subject to Rule 24 of UFC or exceptions thereto.

FROM:

STATION	CODE	STATION	CODE
WI Milwaukee	F1		

TO:

STATION	CODE	STATION	CODE
MN Minneapolis	T1	MN St Paul	T1
Minnesota Transfer	T1		

CONT'D IN NEXT COLUMN

FIGURE 9-10 *Page From Railroad Commodity Rate Tariff Showing Rates Charged. (Source: Western Trunk Lines, Freight Tariff 5-X, effective January 10, 1975, p. 93)*

Multiple-Car, Multiple-Trailer, and Trainload Rates. Special rates may apply to multiple-car or multiple-trailer or trainload shipments. The rate per 100 pounds is, of course, less than the carload or truckload rate.

All-Commodity Rate. An all-commodity or freight-all-kinds rate is quoted on a shipment made up of more than one commodity or a "mixed" commodity shipment. These rates may be subject to a requirement that limits any one article to no more than a certain percentage of the total weight of the shipment or they may apply only when a certain number of different articles are included in the shipment. Freight forwarders are frequent users of these rates because they deal primarily in mixed shipments.

Local Rate. Local rates apply between points on a single carrier.

Joint Rate. Joint rates are used when a shipment moves over the lines or two or more carriers of the same or different modes.

Through Rate. A through rate is a single rate from origin to destination, as opposed to adding up the intermediate rates to determine a rate. A single carrier or 2 or more carriers may be involved.

Combination Rate. A combination rate is derived by adding one rate to another. If the rate on a given commodity is $.40 from A to B and $.60 from B to C, the combination rate from A to C is $1.00. A combination rate would be used if there were no through rate available from A to C.

Section 22 Rate. Section 22 of the Interstate Commerce Act permits federal, state, and local government agencies to negotiate with ICC-regulated carriers for rates less than the usual rates charged. These rates are sometimes referred to as Section 22 rates.

TOFC Rate. Trailer-on-flatcar (TOFC) rates apply to traffic that moves in truck trailers or trailer bodies carried on rail flatcars. There are several versions of this kind of traffic as categorized by the ICC (see Chapter 24).

Container Rate. Container rates are used in connection with containerized freight. Containerization is the use of a large box or "container" made of steel, fiberglass, or other durable material into which the items of a shipment (cartons, crates, or bags, etc.) are loaded, usually at the shipper's door. The container is then turned over to the carrier and is delivered intact to the receiver, without being opened en route. Sometimes the container is carried by two or more carriers. Containers used in domestic surface transportation are often 8 feet high by 8 feet wide by 10, 20, 30, or 40 feet in length.

Unit-Train Rate. A unit train is a train permanently coupled together that moves in a continuous cycle from an origin to a destination point and back to the origin. It carries a single commodity, such as coal from a mine to a power plant, and returns empty to the origin point. The rate charged is lower than the normal carload rate, reflecting lower carrier costs.

Rent-a-Train Rate. A rent-a-train rate is an offshoot of the unit train idea and was first used by the Illinois Central Gulf railroad in 1968. The user pays a certain charge per year if the carrier furnishes the cars and a lower charge per year if the user furnishes the cars. The carrier provides locomotives and the crew and the user pays so much per mile or train mile. The user can do what he will with the train between two designated points.

Incentive Rates. Railroads and highway carriers offer incentive rates to attract traffic and to increase user utilization of cars and trailers. Incentive rates include a sliding scale of rates (the rate decreases as the weight loaded in one vehicle increases above the minimum weight required) or alternative-minimum-weight rates (a specific minimum weight is required to obtain a vehicle-load rate, but there is a higher minimum weight which provides a lower rate if the larger quantity is shipped).

Space-Available or Deferred Rate. When users are not particularly concerned with door-to-door elapsed time, they may take advantage of lower-than-normal space-available or deferred rates under which the shipment will be moved when higher priority freight is not available but will move not later than a specified date. This rate is used most often in air and water transportation.

SIMPLIFYING THE PRICING SYSTEM

The freight transportation pricing system is very complex and difficult to work with for two reasons: (1) the complexity of the tariffs themselves and (2) the tremendous number of rates in the various tariffs published by the different modes of transportation.

Rate tariffs are very complicated because of the large number of commodities, origins, and destinations involved. In addition, since the rules and regulations included are stated in more or less general terms, they are open to a variety of interpretations when applied to specific situations. Some of these rules and regulations have to do with restrictions on routing, limitations on the application of rates specified in a tariff, and alternation with other rates published in the same or different tariffs. Tariffs also often lack uniformity in format and methods of stating information. Tariff complexity is also caused by the increasing use of commodity rates, the failure to cancel tariffs no longer being used, the issuance of a long series of tariff supplements to make changes, and failure to revise tariffs completely. Difficulties in working with freight tariffs are also caused by the following:

1. Origin and destination groupings of areas served differ from tariff to tariff for the same basic transportation service.
2. Tariffs frequently contain more than one rate for the same article moving between the same two points by the same carrier.
3. There is a lack of precision in commodity definitions.
4. There are numerous exceptions that have confusing definitions.
5. Nonstandard rules for shipment, packaging, handling, etc., are used. These

may alter the meaning from tariff to tariff and, within an individual tariff, from item to item.[5]

The result is an overwhelmingly complex pricing system that is a formidable obstacle for anyone trying to acquaint himself with it and make use of it.

It is, therefore, fairly widely recognized that a simplification of the system is needed. One major step in this direction would be to simplify tariffs under the leadership of regulatory agencies. This has not been done. Although the regulatory agencies have outlined in their tariff circulars general principles concerning the composition of tariffs, there has not been one specific prescription for a single procedure. The result has been differing approaches by publishing agents and individual carriers.

The vast number of rates and the fact that more than one rate may be available to use on a given shipment is a more difficult problem to deal with. One source has said, "The transportation pricing structure of this country probably is the most comprehensive system of user costs ever devised. It has developed to embrace every known article of commerce, . . . moving from any given point to any of upward of 50,000 other points in the country. *According to estimates, some forty trillion prices are involved.*"[6] During a one-year period over 300,000 freight and passenger tariffs and supplements (approximately 800,000 pages) are filed with the ICC by carriers it regulates.[7]

If differential pricing were scrapped and replaced by a fully distributed cost rate system, or if there were some formula system based on weight density, or if a system in which a flat charge per ton-mile were levied, regardless of commodity, route, or other factors, the rate structure could be simplified. Since none of these things is likely to happen in the foreseeable future, a way to simplify dealing with the rate structure is to computerize the rate quotation system. Until now the rate clerk or rate analyst has been relied upon by both users and carriers to find rates, make rate analyses, and gather and maintain tariffs and their supplements. Computerization would mean that carriers and/or users would have all rates kept on file in a computer from which the appropriate rate could be retrieved when needed. Major cost reductions could be achieved if the determination of the applicable rate were mechanized in this way.

Ultimately, computers can play the following role in the rate process:

1. Economically store, retrieve, and disseminate rate information.

2. Seek out and calculate the applicable rate or charge between any 2 points far more accurately than can be accomplished today.

3. Mechanically integrate rate information with other computerized user and carrier systems already in use, providing faster and lower cost accounting, including billing and auditing.

4. Permit economical exchange between carrier and user of data to be used for freight rate analysis and distribution planning.

[5]Herbert O. Whitten, "Updating Freight Pricing and Costing," *Distribution Worldwide,* November, 1970, p. 40.

[6]Richard C. Colton, Edmund S. Ward, and Charles H. Wager, *Industrial Traffic Management,* 5th ed. (Washington, D.C.: The Traffic Service Corporation, 1973), p. 81.

[7]Charles A. Taff, *Management of Physical Distribution and Transportation,* 5th ed. (Homewood, Illinois: Richard D. Irwin, Inc., 1972), p. 365.

5. Reduce tariff publication cost.
6. Reduce claims caused by improper rating and computation.
7. Improve statistical data for use by carrier, user, and regulatory agencies.[8]

Although there have been several attempts at computer rate retrieval, although there are some computerized railroad tariffs, although some large highway carrier rate bureaus have made use of the computer in preparing class rate tariffs, and although a few large users maintain their commonly used rates in a computer file,[9] progress has been slow. Few users or carriers have been able to make significant use of computers. According to one writer, "The computer was no more able to capture the rate structure than you are able to capture mosquitoes on a hot and sticky night. The trillions of data were just too numerous."[10] Some users using only a limited number of rates have been able to computerize the tariffs in which they have an interest. Some carriers have been able to computerize some tariff information such as minimum charges. In the main, however, the trillions of individual rates have defied computerization.[11] Nevertheless, it is hoped that general computerization of freight tariffs will eventually be accomplished. This will, however, require standardization of commodity descriptions and simplification of the tariffs themselves, including the various rules and regulations contained therein. More uniformity of format and methods of stating information between tariffs will also be required.

RATE-MAKING PROCEDURE

Initiation of Rate Proposals by Carriers

Proposals for rates on new commodities or proposals to change existing rates usually are initiated by the carrier or carriers concerned. Sometimes the carrier's proposal for a new rate or a rate change is the result of negotiation between the user and the carrier, but the proposal is really at the request of the user. When users are unable to convince a carrier or carriers of the need for a new rate or a rate adjustment, they may appeal directly to the appropriate rate bureau and/or regulatory agency for relief. Regulatory agencies may themselves, of course, initiate action to have rates changed, either on their own initiative or as the result of user or other complaints.

Role of the Rate Bureau

Usually, it is the carrier (or several carriers) who proposes a new rate or a rate change. In rail, highway, and water transportation the proposal is made to the appropriate rate bureau (unless the carrier is not a bureau member). In the case

[8] Joseph S. Coyle, "Closing Traffic's Computer Gap," *Traffic Management,* February, 1969, p. 54.

[9] For an example, see Jack W. Farrell, "Broad-Scale Rate Computerization—Now," *Traffic Management,* December, 1974, p. 36.

[10] Arthur W. Todd, "A Modern Freight Rate Structure—If We Want One, How Do We Get It?" *HANDLING AND SHIPPING MAGAZINE,* October, 1973, p. 46.

[11] Statement of A. W. Wharton, "TDCC Forum Speakers Say Computerization Is Growing But Still Has Long Way to Go," *Traffic World,* December 10, 1973, p. 29.

of oil pipeline and air transportation, where no rate bureaus exist, if the rate is subject to regulation, the proposal is made directly to the appropriate regulatory agency.

A rate bureau is an organization that represents the carriers of a given mode in a given geographic area such as the Middle Atlantic States or the Pacific Coast. The main functions of a rate bureau relative to pricing are to publish freight rate tariffs for carrier members, although carriers may publish their own tariffs, and to receive rate proposals from the carriers (or users) in the area and review them to determine whether or not the bureau is to support the proposal. Figure 9-11 is a map showing the leading rail rate bureaus. The bureau investigates the proposal and may hold public hearings at which carriers (of that mode) and users may testify. The role of railroad rate bureaus in pricing was altered somewhat by the Railroad Revitalization and Regulatory Reform (4R) Act of 1976 in which Congress prohibited railroad rate bureaus from agreeing on or voting on local or single-line rates (rates that apply between points on a single railroad) and provided that only those railroads that can practicably participate in the movement may agree on or vote on joint rates (rates charged for moving traffic over the lines of 2 or more railroads).

If the bureau supports the proposal, the proposal is filed with the appropriate regulatory agency (if necessary) with bureau support. If the bureau does not support the rate proposal, the carrier or carriers proposing it may file it with the regulatory agency anyway. This is the "right to independent action" provided for in the Reed-Bulwinkle Act of 1948 which legalized rate bureaus. Under the Interstate Commerce Act, however, the nonrailroad bureaus are permitted to protest against the proposal.

FIGURE 9-11 *Major Railroad Rate Bureau Territories. (Source: Traffic Service Corporation)*

Role of the Regulatory Agency

Since many rates charged by for-hire carriers are subject to government economic regulation at the federal and/or state level, the regulatory agencies play a large role in the rate-making process. Since regulation is dealt with in later chapters, it is not discussed in detail here. The one aspect of it that should be mentioned at this point is that when a rate proposal is being filed, at least 30 days usually must elapse before the rate can be made effective and within that period the regulatory agency has the right to "suspend" the rate or postpone its effective date while its merits are being investigated. This could delay the effective date by several months or, in extreme cases, several years. The vast majority of rate proposals, however, are not suspended and go into effect after the 30-day notice period expires. A rate proposal is not likely to be suspended unless an unusual amount of protest against it from other carriers and/or from users is received or the rate proposal is a highly innovative one not dealt with previously by the regulatory agency.

Role of the User

The user has an opportunity to play an important role in the rate-making process. To begin with, he has the right to negotiate and to bargain with carriers over rates, just as any buyers may negotiate or bargain with a seller.

Second, the user may either by letter or in person support or protest against a rate proposal being considered by a rate bureau. All rate bureaus are required by law to issue advisory bulletins of proposed new rates and rate changes. Dockets giving a brief description of each proposal scheduled for consideration by the bureau are published, usually weekly, and circulated among member carriers and such users as may request them. In addition, some bureaus use commercial publications, for example, the weekly *Traffic Bulletin*. A tabulation indicating disposition of proposals previously docketed usually is published with each docket.

Third, the user may support or protest against a rate proposal being considered by a regulatory agency.

Fourth, the user may make proposals of his own to carriers, to rate bureaus, and to regulatory agencies.

The effectiveness of user participation in the rate-making process varies with the situation, of course. Some users are better at it than others. The validity of the user's case varies also from situation to situation. The size of the user has some effect on the impact made on the carriers, the rate bureaus, and the regulators, with the larger user carrying more weight. Also, associations of users, such as industry trade associations, the National Industrial Traffic League, regional and state traffic leagues, and others, tend to carry more weight in rate-making procedures than do individual shippers. Finally, because of the time and expense involved or lack of interest, some users do not participate in the process as much as they should, and, of course, this weakens the user's role in the process. It has been estimated that probably no more than a few hundred of the tens of thousands of users of transportation in the country take any kind of active role in the transportation rate-making process. Many users are not even aware that they have an option to participate.[12] Many users apparently overestimate the expertise required and the cost involved. The expertise problem can be solved through advice from trade and other associations or from transportation consultants or attorneys.

IMPORTANCE OF KNOWLEDGE OF RATES

The reader should now be aware that the pricing system in transportation is highly compléx and difficult to deal with. There is no question that rate making and the rate structure are a highly technical and complicated part of the transportation field and it is important that people who work in carrier management, logistics management, and industrial traffic management have some knowledge and appreciation of the rate system. But it is not necessary that a person in these fields be an expert on rates or have a great deal of familiarity with rates or know how to use rate tariffs and classifications. This is a task for specialists. The relationship between carrier management, logistics management, and traffic management, on the one hand, and rates, on the other, is like the marketing research manager and statistics. The manager has to know something of the nature of statistics, but he relies on a specialist to really work with the specialty. In other words, for people to work successfully in carrier management, logistics management, and traffic management, an intimate knowledge of or even a liking for rates is not required.

CONTRACT CARRIER RATES

The preceding discussion of rate making has concentrated on common-carrier rate making. Many of the cost and demand factors discussed there might also be considered by a contract carrier in determining his prices. A major difference in pricing for the contract carrier is the fact that the entire matter of freight classification, tariff publication, different kinds of rates, and problems of the rate structure, are, for the most part, not relevant to the contract carrier. This is because he is free to negotiate rates individually with users and whatever is agreed upon is written into the user–carrier contract for carriage. There is, therefore, no "rate structure" as that term is ordinarily used.

PASSENGER FARES

Although the same general considerations must be taken into account, including both cost and demand or value of service factors, pricing passenger transportation service is much less complicated than pricing freight transportation service because of the relative homogeneity of passengers when compared with the variety of different characteristics that different commodities may have.

Some differentiation between passenger categories has been accomplished in terms of age, length of stay before return, military status, family status, and so

[12]Colin Barrett, "The Theory and Practice of Carrier Rate-Making, III, Rate-Making and the Shipper," *Transportation and Distribution Management,* December, 1972, p. 28.

on, and the differential approach has been applied to these different categories. In addition, a distinction is often made between first class and coach or tourist service, with a fairly substantial difference in fares between the two based primarily on cost and quality of service differences. Although some identification of different passenger categories is made, it is impossible to deal with commodity-oriented factors, such as loading characteristics, susceptibility to loss and damage, and value of the commodity, when dealing with the passenger market.

Route factors, however, can be considered. These include distance, operating conditions, traffic density, and competition with other carriers (both intra-modal and intermodal), as well as some aspects of production-point and market competition.

Intercity passenger fares have traditionally been tied closely to distance, and some tapering is involved. Adherence to the distance idea is modified by the need to adjust fares to account for differences in operating conditions, traffic density, and competition, and to deal also with unbalanced traffic in opposite directions on the same route.

SELECTED REFERENCES

The railroad rate structure is discussed in some detail in D. Philip Locklin, *Economics of Transportation,* 7th ed. (Homewood, Illinois: Richard D. Irwin, Inc., 1972) Chapter 8.

A detailed discussion of freight classification may be found in Richard S. Colton, Edmund S. Ward, and Charles H. Wager, *Industrial Traffic Management,* 5th ed. (Washington, D.C.: The Traffic Service Corporation, 1973), Chapter 3. See also Charles A. Taff, *Management of Physical Distribution and Transportation,* 5th ed. (Homewood, Illinois: Richard D. Irwin, Inc., 1972), Chapter 14.

For a detailed treatment of kinds of rate tariffs and their construction, freight classification, and different kinds of freight rates, see Kenneth U. Flood, *Traffic Management,* 3rd ed. (Dubuque, Iowa: William C. Brown Company Publishers, 1975), Chapters 4, 5, and 6.

Several new railroad rates designed to stimulate traffic and their effect on railroad efficiency are discussed in James P. Rakowski, "Innovative Ratemaking and Railway Efficiency," *The Logistics and Transportation Review,* Volume 9, Number 3, 1973. The development of volume railroad rates is reviewed in Thomas C. Campbell and Sidney Katell, "Railroad Volume Freight Rates: Evaluation and Analysis," *ICC Practitioners' Journal,* January–February, 1977.

The operations of rate bureaus are discussed in Taff, *Management of Physical Distribution and Transportation,* pp. 373-382.

The complexities found by the user in dealing with freight rates are discussed in Colton, Ward, and Wager, *Industrial Traffic Management,* pp. 109-113.

The need for computerization of freight rates is treated in Herbert O. Whitten, "Why Freight Rates Must Be Computerized," *Distribution Age,* March, 1966.

Basing rates on weight density rather than on the traditional rate-making factors, thus simplifying tariffs and making computerization easier, is discussed by Ronald G. Ray in "We Must Scrap Our Present Freight Pricing Program," *Traffic and Distribution Management,* November, 1962 and by Herbert O. Whitten in "Why Not Density Rates?" *ICC Practitioners' Journal,* November–December, 1968.

A mileage-based rail rate system to replace the current system is proposed by Arthur C. Roy, "Here's a Possible Route to Simpler, More Sensible Rail Rate Structure," *Traffic World,* January 24, 1972, p. 70. The advantages of and methods to use in basing rates on standard formulas are set forth in Elmer A. Mattox and Edward J. Marien, "Formula Rates: An Idea Whose Time Has Returned?" *Traffic World,* October 18, 1976, p. 76.

Pricing passenger service is discussed in Martin T. Farris and Forrest E. Harding, *Passenger Transportation* (Englewood Cliffs, New Jersey: Prentice-Hall, Inc., 1976), Chapter 3.

10

Railroad Transportation

In this and the following four chapters we shall discuss the basic economic and service characteristics of the several modes of transportation. We are concerned with the kind of ownership; number and size of firms; cost structure; market structure; pricing practices; investment, traffic, and revenue trends; and service characteristics of each mode. In this chapter we begin with a discussion of the oldest continuous form of mechanized transportation and, in some respects, our most important mode—railroads.

DEVELOPMENT OF RAILROAD TRANSPORTATION

Railroads are mainly for-hire common carriers although there are a few private carrier railroads. For many years railroads dominated the transportation scene in the United States. Beginning in the 1830's railroads were constructed in the eastern states, particularly in New York, Pennsylvania, and in New England. In the 1840's and 1850's a number of important lines were started and a through connection between the east coast and Chicago was established in 1853. Approximately 30,000 miles of railroad line were constructed in the eastern part of the country prior to the Civil War.

During the Civil War railroad building in the South virtually stopped and only a limited amount took place in the North. In the post-Civil War period many thousands of miles of railroad were built, much of them west of the Mississippi River. The peak building period was the decade of the 1880's when more than 70,000 miles were constructed. The first transcontinental railroad service was opened in 1869 (Union Pacific and Central Pacific) and was followed by several others prior to 1900. The railroad construction period was virtually over by 1910. The peak railroad mileage in the United States was 254,037 in 1916.[1]

[1] Statistics from Interstate Commerce Commission.

Railroad construction in the United States was bitterly opposed by canal and turnpike interests, innkeepers, and others associated with the older forms of transportation. However, despite some legislative attempts to discourage railroad development, government generally aided the railroads by granting the railroads the power of eminent domain (the right to take private property for railroad use without the owner's consent), there were general railway incorporation laws under which railroad companies could organize without special permission from a state legislature, and the railroads received various kinds of financial aid from local, state, and federal governments.

Since 1916 there has been very little railroad construction and there has been considerable abandonment of rail line. The total mileage in 1975 was 199,411 miles.[2] The share of freight and passenger traffic carried by rail has also substantially declined. A primary reason for the reduction in railroad mileage and share of traffic has been the competition faced by railroads, competition that was virtually non-existent prior to the 1920's. Figure 10-1 is a map showing the railroad system of the United States.

OWNERSHIP

Unlike the situation in other countries, railroads in the United States have generally been privately instead of government owned. Railroads began operating in the United States in a period (1830's) when the political situation precluded federal government ownership—the development of railroads and other "internal improvements" were thought to be best left to the states and not to the federal government. State governments engaged in railroad building in a number of instances prior to the Civil War as part of their attempts to create internal improvements. In a few cases, states acquired ownership of railroads through the failure of private companies that had received state subsidies. In most cases, because of financial difficulties, the states eventually disposed of their railroad properties to private corporations. Finally, there were a few instances of municipal ownership, but these were not of any significance and proved to be temporary in most cases.

Today the federal government owns and operates the Alaska Railroad and the Panama Railroad. Several states still own railroads acquired in the nineteenth century which are leased out to private operating companies. In recent years the failing Long Island Railroad and part of the failing Rutland Railroad were taken over by the states of New York and Vermont, respectively, in order to preserve service to the public. Michigan purchased the bankrupt Ann Arbor Railroad in 1976. Municipalities are not involved in intercity railroads, with the exception of the city of Cincinnati, owner of the Cincinnati Southern, now leased to a private operating company.

In the United States, then, we have relied primarily on private ownership through the corporation device to provide our railroad system. This is even more true today than it was in the last century. However, as we will see in Chapter 16, the role of government in providing financial aid to railroads is

[2] Association of American Railroads, *Railroad Facts*, 1977 ed. (Washington, D.C.: Association of American Railroads, 1977), p. 46. Mileage of yard tracks and sidings is not included.

FIGURE 10-1 *The Railroad System of the United States, 1976. (Source: Association of American Railroads)*

growing and could eventually lead to greater government participation as an owner of railroad facilities. Such assistance to railroads has included aid to rail commuter lines, the federal attempt to develop high-speed ground transportation, assistance to railroad intercity passenger service via the National Railroad Passenger Corporation (Amtrak), and the massive aid to railroads under the Regional Rail Reorganization Act of 1973 and the Railroad Revitalization and Regulatory Reform (4R) Act of 1976.

NUMBER AND SIZE OF FIRMS

Although there have been several thousand intercity line-haul railroads in the United States over the years since 1830, today there are only approximately 330, or a relatively small number of carriers. In addition, the industry makeup is such that, of the 330 or so intercity railroads, a fairly small number account for most of the investment, traffic, and earnings of the industry. Thus, in 1976 the 52 Class I railroads—those having annual operating revenues (total sales) in excess of 10 million dollars—accounted for approximately 99 per cent of the freight traffic carried by the industry, 96 per cent of the mileage, and 94 per cent of the employees.[3] Moreover, of the 52 Class I lines, approximately 25 accounted for the bulk of the investment, traffic, and revenues. The top 25 in 1976 included such companies as the Southern Pacific, Burlington Northern, Seaboard Coast Line, Union Pacific, Santa Fe, Chessie System, Norfolk and Western, Southern, Missouri Pacific, and Illinois Central Gulf.

There is a wide diversity in size of railroads and there are some very small companies, even in the Class I category. As noted above, however, the vast majority of the investment, traffic, and revenues is in the hands of a few carriers and these firms tend to be large in size, i.e., the industry is dominated by a few large firms. Thus, the rail and nonrail operating revenues in 1976 of the 10 carriers listed above ranged from over 2 billion dollars for the Union Pacific to approximately 626 million dollars for the Illinois Central Gulf, the tenth largest rail carrier (not including Conrail).

The tendency toward domination by a small number of large carriers in the railroad industry indicates that there are economies or large size in railroad operation. These economies of large size are caused by the nature of the railroad investment and the cost structure of the industry.

COST STRUCTURE

In Chapters 7, 8, and 9 various kinds of transportation company costs were discussed, particularly fixed, variable, common, and joint costs. It was pointed out that these 4 kinds of costs are associated with the three primary kinds of physical facilities that are peculiar to transportation: ways, terminals, and vehicles. The proportion of total costs that are fixed, variable, common, or joint varies considerably among the different modes of transportation.

[3]*Ibid.*, p. 2. In addition to the line-haul railroads, there were 154 switching and terminal companies in 1976. Interstate Commerce Commission, *Annual Report, 1976* (Washington, D.C.: U.S. Government Printing Office, 1976), p. 141.

Way

The characteristic feature of railroad costs is that a large proportion of costs are fixed and a significant amount are common costs. This stems largely from the fact that railroads provide their own way (roadbed and tracks and associated structures) with private investment and assume responsibility for operating, maintaining, and improving the way and paying taxes on it. This results in a very large capital investment requirement upon which a large dollar return must be paid, and because of which large amortization or depreciation (that unrelated to volume of traffic carried) is incurred. It also results in large maintenance costs and large amounts of property taxes. Since these costs to a great extent are incurred regardless of the amount of traffic carried over the roadbed, they may be considered mostly fixed in nature as well as large in dollar amount. Unless a change in traffic volume is so great that it requires a change in the way itself, the costs associated with the railroad way tend not to change with traffic quantity changes.

The costs of the railroad way are also to a great extent common because the way is used to produce many different kinds of transportation services for different commodities and/or passengers. Therefore, cost allocation to individual segments of traffic becomes very difficult.

Terminals

A second major contributor to high fixed and common costs in the railroad industry is the rather extensive capital investment in terminal facilities. These terminal facilities consist mainly of freight yards where freight trains are assembled and disassembled and connections are made between railroads and where maintenance of equipment takes place. They also include trackage in "terminal areas" leading from or to freight yards and from or to local shippers and receivers of freight. Sometimes the latter are owned and operated by "terminal" or "switching" railroad companies. Terminals also include the limited number of railroad passenger stations still being operated by United States railroads, most of which are now part of the Amtrak system (see Chapter 16).

Railroad terminal facilities are provided by the carrier with private investment and the carrier has the responsibility of operating and maintaining terminal facilities and paying taxes on them. Although terminal labor costs are at least partly variable, terminal costs are incurred to a great extent regardless of the amount of traffic handled in the terminals. These major fixed costs are interest on the investment, amortization or depreciation (that unrelated to traffic volume), property taxes, and maintenance costs.

Terminal costs are also to a great extent common because they are incurred to produce transportation service for various kinds of traffic. Cost allocation to different individual segments of traffic is, therefore, difficult.

Vehicles

The vehicles used by railroads—locomotives and rail cars—are usually provided by the carriers through ownership or leasing, although a large number of freight cars are supplied by users for which the railroads pay the users a fee based on mileage traveled (a variable cost). Class I railroads had 27,573 locomotives and 1,331,705 freight cars in service in 1976. In addition, there were 34,452 freight cars operated by other railroads and 332,870 owned or leased by car companies and users for a grand total of 1,699,027.[4]

When carriers provide their own vehicles through ownership, the investment can be substantial and the costs involved are both fixed and variable. The wear and tear on the vehicles and the fuel and labor expenses associated with their operation may be considered generally variable in nature because they are incurred in relation to the volume of traffic carried. Some other costs are fixed in nature, however. These include interest on the considerable investment in a vehicle, property taxes on vehicles, maintenance cost not related to traffic carried (related to time and/or weather instead), and amortization or depreciation expenses (that unrelated to rate of use). Leased vehicles result in vehicle leasing costs being fixed for the period of the lease, but labor and fuel expenses associated with operating trains tend to be variable in nature.

In addition to freight vehicle costs being both fixed and variable, they are also to a large degree common because a given locomotive or freight car is used to carry different commodities at different times or at the same time. This leads to cost allocation difficulties.

As in other forms of transportation, railroads incur joint costs in round-trip situations such as discussed in Chapter 7.

Other Expenses

In addition to way, terminal, and vehicle costs, there are general expenses of a railroad company which include the expenses of operating and maintaining office space and paying the salaries of managers and other administrative personnel not involved in the direct operation of trains or roadbed and terminal operation and maintenance. These expenses are largely fixed and common. Payroll and income taxes tend to vary with the volume of traffic. However, as indicated earlier, property taxes, which are considerable in view of the vast amount of physical property owned by railroads, are considered fixed because they have no relation to traffic volume.

Large Fixed Costs

From the above discussion, it is safe to conclude that railroads have a high proportion of costs that are fixed in the short run—the period of time in which the physical plant is not changed and its capacity to handle traffic remains constant. There has, however, been some disagreement on the proportion of fixed versus variable costs. Early writers on the subject considered fixed costs to be from one-third to two-thirds of the total railroad costs. Recent studies have questioned the claim that a large part of railroad expenses are fixed and, instead, have stated that variable costs are as much as 70 per cent to 80 per cent of total costs. A major reason for the differences in cost estimates is that the different writers have used different time periods, sometimes long enough to permit changes in the physical plant.[5] The longer the time period used, the larger

[4] Association of American Railroads, *Railroad Facts*, 1977 ed., pp. 48–49.

[5] D. Philip Locklin, *Economics of Transportation,* 7th ed. (Homewood, Illinois: Richard D. Irwin, Inc., 1972), pp. 145 and 167–168.

will be the proportion of variable costs. In addition, the proportion of fixed and variable costs varies over different railroads and different routes of the same railroad because different carriers and different routes have different traffic volumes. It should be obvious to the reader that companies or routes that have large traffic volume will have a higher variable cost proportion than companies or routes that have very little traffic.

It appears that early writers probably overestimated the importance of fixed costs in railroad operation. However, in the short run, fixed costs are a very large part of costs and, in the long run, they are an important part of costs, although only approximately from 20 per cent to 30 per cent of all costs.

To the extent that railroads have a larger than usual percentage of fixed costs, they are also subject to decreasing costs or increasing returns because the greater the volume of traffic carried, the lower will be the average or unit cost of carrying each additional unit of traffic since the fixed costs are spread over more units of traffic. Thus, the fully distributed cost per unit, including both the variable costs associated with a unit of traffic and a share of the fixed costs allocated to the unit of traffic, is less as more traffic is added, at least until capacity is reached.

Excess Capacity

In Chapter 8 it was pointed out that the existence of excess capacity is a chief motivating factor in differential pricing. The nature of railroad operation is such that there is almost generally an excess capacity situation in the way and terminal aspects of their operations. This is caused by the fact that railroads in the United States were overbuilt to begin with, that is, more railroad facilities were constructed than were needed. This was compounded by the emergence of competing forms of transportation and regulatory restraints on abandonment of little used lines. In addition, railroads generally do not jointly use the way (unlike highway carriers) resulting in much less use of a way than would be the case if the same way were used by 2 or more railroad companies. Even when rail traffic is substantial and the facilities are strained, the railroad can fairly easily expand its facilities and capacity as traffic increases. Comparatively small capital expenditures will enable the railroad to carry additional traffic. Additional passing tracks or yard tracks may be provided where traffic is heavy and capacity is being reached. Thus, a more or less perpetual condition is maintained which permits additional traffic to be carried without proportional increases in costs.[6]

Vehicle capacity, however, is a different matter. Freight car shortages are frequent, particularly in the grain business. Car shortages are caused by a combination of lack of new investment in cars by the carriers, poor car utilization, and poor distribution of cars (cars are not in the places where they are needed). Car shortages indicate shortage of vehicle capacity at times, but they do not indicate that the assumption that railroads generally have unused capacity is untrue.

[6] *Ibid.*, p. 166.

MARKET STRUCTURE

Although over a particular route and/or for a specific kind of freight traffic, an individual railroad may have no competition from other railroads and, thus, may approximate monopoly, the more usual case is, as the above discussion indicates, that the economic structure of the railroad freight industry approximates what is referred to as *oligopoly* in Chapter 8. This means that there is usually a small number of large sellers and the market activities of one seller have an important effect on the other sellers in the industry. Each carrier is aware that the competing firms in the railroad industry are interdependent and that in changing his prices or engaging in other market activities he must take into account the probable reaction of the other railroads.

Whether or not the railroad freight industry is an example of homogeneous or differentiated oligopoly, as those terms are defined in Chapter 8, depends on the attitudes of users toward railroad service. It is probably true that some users regard all railroads as being alike and think that their services are undifferentiated. In those cases, the industry may be considered in their eyes to be an example of homogeneous oligopoly. Other users believe that there are differences in the services provided by different competing railroads or that differentiated oligopoly exists. Knowledgeable users would look upon it this way because, in actual fact, perfect homogeneity of service between different railroads is impossible and it is safe to conclude that differentiated oligopoly is the true situation, although the amount of differentiation in many cases may be minimal. However, the rate bureau system of pricing (discussed in Chapter 9) and the economic regulatory system tend to result in competing railroads charging identical rates, which is what would occur under homogeneous oligopoly.

The kinked demand situation referred to in Chapter 8 often applies to the railroad freight industry, which means that railroad price makers are hesitant to go it alone with price reductions or price increases. This tends to lead to uniformity of prices between different railroads. The rate bureau system of pricing and the economic regulatory system also tend to lead competing railroads to charge identical prices.

The uncertainties regarding the reaction of competitors to price changes made by one or more railroads are reduced by the rate bureau method of pricing by permitting the railroads in a region to review the rate proposals of other railroads before the new rates go into effect. The proposing railroad(s) may in this way determine in advance what the reaction of competing railroads is to be and may withdraw or amend the proposal if appropriate. In addition, the economic regulatory system reduces the amount of uncertainty regarding the reactions of competitors to rate changes by requiring that notice be given in advance of rate changes to be made. Competitors are given the opportunity to react to the proposal before it becomes effective and the railroad(s) making the proposal may amend or withdraw the proposal before it becomes effective, if that is appropriate.

In intercity railroad passenger service the situation approximates monopoly, for example, Amtrak trains and the limited number of passenger trains operated by railroads not part of Amtrak do not have any competition on their routes from other railroads.

The reader should be aware that railroads in many cases compete against other forms of freight and passenger transportation as well as against each other. The overall market structure situation in the case of intermodal competition can vary considerably in character and exhibits various shades of approximation of oligopoly and monopolistic competition.

PRICING

Differential Pricing

Differential pricing in transportation was dealt with in some depth in Chapters 8 and 9. Differential pricing exists when a carrier charges different prices to different segments of traffic for essentially the same service and the differences in prices cannot be explained by differences in the cost of service or, conversely, when a carrier charges the same price to carry different segments of traffic that have different costs associated with them.

Railroads are the prime users of differential pricing because of the large proportion of fixed costs and associated decreasing costs per unit carried as volume increases and because of the substantial excess capacity, particularly in the way and terminals. In addition, railroads carry a very wide variety of different commodities with many opportunities for differentiation between different segments of freight traffic. Finally, railroads often serve very large geographic areas with many origin and destination points and numerous opportunities to differentiate between points. In fact, railroads are the most ideally suited mode for using differential pricing and have carried it out to a greater extent than any other mode.

Freight Classification

For many years railroads made use of 3 classifications: the Official Classification in the East, the Southern Classification in the South, and the Western Classification in the West. The number of classes in each classification differed and the largest number was 12 in the Western Classification. Beginning in 1919 the 3 classifications were published sporadically in one volume called the Consolidated Freight Classification.

In 1952 railroads adopted the Uniform Freight Classification which applies on railroad traffic throughout the United States when class rates are used. The Uniform Freight Classification contains 31 classes, that are designated by 31 different numbers ranging from class 400 down to class 13. The numbers of the classes are relative to class 100 meaning that if one were to look up a class rate that applies on class 400 traffic between any two points, the rate would be 4 times the rate that applies on class 100 traffic. The rate on class 13 traffic would be only 13 per cent of the class 100 rate. This is how differential pricing is carried out in the class rate system.

Because there were exceptions to the classification (see Chapter 9), the Consolidated Freight Classification was not completely replaced by the adoption of the Uniform Freight Classification in 1952. When the Uniform Freight Classification was adopted the carriers sought to include the exception ratings in the new classification in order to eliminate the exceptions previously in effect. Some exceptions remained, however, but they were eventually eliminated and the Consolidated Freight Classification is no longer being used.

Because of the problems of freight classification in dealing with local conditions, most rail freight traffic is carried under commodity rates instead of class rates.

INVESTMENT TRENDS

Railroading is a capital intensive industry meaning that it requires large amounts of capital. According to the Association of American Railroad (AAR), in 1973 carrier investment required per dollar of revenues was $2.17 for railroads, $.80 for barge lines, and $.22 for highway freight carriers.[7] The total investment in railroads in the United States is substantial. In 1976 the AAR reported a net investment of 27.5 billion dollars in roadbed and equipment (including cash, materials, and supplies after deducting depreciation and amortization) by Class I railroads. The average investment per each of the 52 Class I railroads in 1976 was 529 million dollars. The operating revenues of these Class I railroads were 18.6 billion dollars in 1976, or 67 per cent of the investment of 27.5 billion dollars, i.e., the "capital turnover" was .67, meaning that each dollar of investment produced approximately $.67 in revenue.[8] At today's replacement prices, however, the railroad investment is probably greatly undervalued, particularly the fixed plant part of the investment.[9] These same Class I railroads in 1976 invested 1.74 billion dollars for capital improvements for roadway, structures, and equipment. The Class I railroads made capital expenditures of 14.4 billion dollars in the period 1967-1976, inclusive.[10]

Although railroad management has spent a considerable sum for capital improvements in recent years, the railroad plant is not being kept up to high standards because of the weak financial condition of many rail carriers. In other words, the industry should be investing more than it has in recent years. Some carriers are not only unable to make capital improvements, they are also sometimes unable to properly maintain the existing facilities. The result is deterioration in facilities and numerous derailments, "slow" orders for trains, and poor service to the user.[11] One source says that 10 billion dollars is a conservative

---

[7]Association of American Railroads, *Railroads in the Cost Spiral* (Washington, D.C.: Association of American Railroads, 1973), p. 5.

[8]Calculated from data provided in Association of American Railroads, *Railroad Facts*, 1977 ed., pp. 12 and 55.

[9]According to the AAR, the cost of reproducing United States railroads in 1974 would have been 70 billion dollars. A prominent railroad executive said it would amount to 100 billion dollars. See "How to Lose Money in a Rising Market," *Business Week*, September 14, 1974, p. 162.

[10]Association of American Railroads, *Railroad Facts*, 1977 ed., p. 56.

[11]As of March 31, 1976, reporting Class I railroads (4 did not report) claimed 2.4 billion dollars in deferred maintenance on roadway, 271.5 million dollars on equipment, and a total of 3.6 billion dollars in delayed capital improvements. "'76 First Quarter Data On Deferred Maintenance Funds Under X-305 Issued," *Traffic World*, January 24, 1977, p. 73.

estimate of the cost to restore the nation's railroad network to good standards.[12]

An additional negative factor in railroad investment is the trend in recent years of railroad management to invest in business activities other than railroading in which the return on investment is better. In some cases, this has resulted in less new investment in railroad facilities than otherwise would be the case.

TRAFFIC TRENDS

Freight Traffic

Freight traffic volume trends in the railroad industry may be examined in various ways, including carloadings, tonnage originated, and ton-miles carried. Table 10-1 contains a summary of those traffic measurements for Class I railroads for the years 1929 through 1976.

Table 10-1 clearly shows that the number of rail freight carloadings has dropped significantly since the 1920's, although the actual tonnage carried was somewhat greater in 1973 and in 1976 than in 1929 and the number of freight ton-miles carried was considerably greater in 1973 (90.4 per cent greater) and in 1976 (76.9 per cent greater in a recession year) than in 1929. Thus, it is easily seen that a different impression of the condition of the railroad industry can be gained, depending on which of the 3 columns in Table 10-1 is examined.

The explanation for the disparity between the columns is easy. Carloadings are much smaller in number in the 1970's, despite a small increase in tonnage originated and a substantial increase in ton-miles carried because (1) the average car size is much greater in the 1970's so that a given amount of tonnage can be carried in fewer cars (the average freight car capacity was 73.5 tons in 1976 as against only 46.3 tons in 1929)[13] and (2) the average length of haul is greater,[14]

TABLE 10-1 *Class I Railroad Freight Traffic, 1929-1976*

Year	Revenue Carloadings	Originated Tonnage (000)	Revenue Ton-Miles (000,000)
1929	52,827,925	1,339,091	447,322
1939	33,911,498	901,669	333,438
1949	35,911,261	1,226,503	526,500
1959	31,014,549	1,232,201	575,529
1969	28,237,407	1,473,457	767,841
1973	27,338,474	1,532,165	851,809
1976	23,638,376	1,406,748	791,413

Sources: Association of American Railroads, *Railroad Facts,* 1974 ed. (Washington, D.C.: Association of American Railroads, 1974), pp. 25, 28, and 29; 1977 ed., pp. 25, 28, and 29; Association of Western Railways, *Railroad Facts,* 1959 ed. (Chicago: Association of Western Railways, 1959), pp. 24, 26, and 29.

[12] John R. Meyer and Alexander L. Morton, "A Better Way to Run the Railroads," *Harvard Business Review* July–August, 1974, p. 141.

[13] Association of American Railroads, *Railroad Facts,* 1977 ed., p. 51.

[14] 535 miles in 1976 versus 317 miles in 1929. Association of American Railroads, *Railroad Facts,* 1977 ed., p. 35.

resulting in the smaller number of cars and the similar tonnage amount being carried longer distances than in the 1920's.

Because ton-miles reflect both weight and distance, they are normally considered the better indicator of actual service performed by a transportation mode when compared with the number of vehicle loadings (carloadings) or tonnage carried. In Table 10-2 it is shown that total railroad freight ton-miles represented 36.7 per cent of the total intercity ton-mileage carried by the several modes of transportation in the recession year 1976. The 1973 ton-mileage was the largest number of ton-miles ever carried by United States railroads in one year. However, as Table 10-2 shows, the 1973 ton-mileage represented a much smaller share of all ton-miles carried than in the past, the share dropping from over 62 per cent in 1939. Thus, although railroads have increased their ton-mileage carried since 1939, they have not increased it as fast as the total freight transportation market has grown and their proportion of the total has, therefore, fallen.

Nevertheless, railroads carry a substantial amount of freight traffic as measured in ton-miles. However, there is a problem associated with the composition of the traffic that is being carried. Since the 1920's there has been a gradual erosion of higher-value and higher-rate rail traffic, particularly over shorter hauls, as highway carriers took more and more of that kind of traffic. At the same time airlines took some longer-haul traffic in high-value goods, and water carriers and oil pipelines diverted some bulk traffic over both short and long hauls. The result has been that railroads have been forced to shift from a wide range of commodities and to rely more and more on (1) lower-grade, often bulk (extractive and agricultural commodities) traffic and (2) longer-haul traffic which pays lower rates under the differential pricing system and the tapering principle and produces less revenue per ton-mile than higher-value and/or shorter-haul traffic. A United States Senate Commerce Committee report stated that in the 1960's the 3 commodity classes that constituted approximately one-half of all railroad tonnage—coal, stone and minerals, and metallic ores—contributed only 20 per cent of total rail revenues. In the same decade, of the 24 commodity groupings in manufactured products, the railroads lost ground to their competition in 16 categories.[15] Thus, as Table 10-3 shows, the average revenue per ton-mile (total freight revenue divided by total number of ton-miles carried) did not increase very much between 1929 and 1976, even though there has been considerable inflation since 1929. However, railroad operating costs have increased greatly in that period of time. The result is that although railroads in the 1970's carried more ton-miles of freight than ever before, the revenue produced by the traffic carried was inadequate. In other words, railroads in the 1970's relied too heavily on low-rate commodities and hauls in a period of rising operating costs.

Passenger Traffic

Intercity passenger travel by rail was a vital part of the American transportation scene for many years and reached its peak during World War II when, in 1944, 31.4 per cent of *all* intercity passenger-miles, private and for-hire, were

---

[15]The report is entitled *The American Railroads: Posture, Problems, and Prospects.* Cited in "An X-Ray Examination of U.S. Railroads," *Traffic World,* September 11, 1972, p. 7. See also "Senate Analysts Probe Rates and Services in Examining Rail Problems and Potential," *Traffic World,* September 4, 1972, p. 23.

TABLE 10-2 Intercity Private and For-Hire Freight Traffic by Modes, 1939-1976*

Mode of Transportation	1939		1949		1959		1969		1973		1976	
	Ton-Miles	Per Cent	Ton-Miles	Per Cent	Ton-Miles	Per Cent	Ton-Miles	Per Cent	Ton-Miles	Per Cent	Ton-Miles	Per Cent
Railroad	339	62.3	535	58.3	582	45.3	774	40.8	858	38.5	796	36.7
Highway	53	9.7	127	13.8	279	21.7	404	21.3	505	22.6	490	22.6
Water–Great Lakes	76	14.0	98	10.7	80	6.2	115	6.1	126	5.6	102	4.7
Water–Rivers and Canals	20	3.7	42	4.6	117	9.1	188	9.9	232	10.4	250	11.6
Oil Pipeline	56	10.3	115	12.6	227	17.7	411	21.7	507	22.7	525	24.2
Air	†	‡	†	‡	1	‡	3	.2	4	.2	4	.2
Total	544	100.0	917	100.0	1,286	100.0	1,895	100.0	2,232	100.0	2,167	100.0

*Ton-miles in billions. Does not include deep-sea water traffic. Includes mail and express traffic.

†Less than 300 million ton-miles.

‡Less than one-tenth of 1 per cent.

Sources: Transportation Association of America, *Transportation Facts and Trends*, 13th ed. (Washington, D.C.: Transportation Association of America, July, 1977), p. 8 and Association of American Railroads, *Railroad Facts*, 1977 ed. (Washington, D.C.: Association of American Railroads, 1977), p. 36.

TABLE 10-3   *Class I Railroad Average Revenue per Ton-Mile,**
1929-1976 (cents)

Year	Revenue per Ton-Mile
1929	1.1
1939	1.0
1949	1.3
1959	1.4
1969	1.3
1976	2.2

*Average revenue per freight ton-mile = $\dfrac{\text{total freight revenue}}{\text{total number of freight ton-miles carried}}$.

Sources: Association of American Railroads, *Railroad Facts,* 1974 ed. (Washington, D.C.: Association of American Railroads, 1974), p. 33; 1977 ed., p. 33; Association of Western Railways, *Railroad Facts,* 1959 ed. (Chicago: Association of Western Railways, 1959), p. 38.

carried by railroad, and 75.1 per cent of for-hire intercity passenger–miles were carried by railroad.[16] Since World War II, however, there has been an almost continuous decline in the number of intercity rail passenger–miles and in the rail share of all passenger traffic. As seen in Table 10-4, the 1970 rail total intercity passenger–miles were only 10.9 billion and the rail share of all for-hire intercity passenger–miles was only 7.3 per cent.

In 1971 most intercity railroad passenger service was turned over to Amtrak, as will be discussed in Chapter 16, relieving most American railroads of any further responsibility to provide intercity service except as they might under contract with Amtrak. In 1976 railroads, including Amtrak, carried fewer passenger–miles than in 1970 and the percentage of all for-hire intercity passenger–miles dropped to 5.3.

One bright spot in the intercity rail passenger picture is a new rail service called Auto-Train which began in December, 1971 when Auto-Train began to carry passengers and their automobiles between Washington, D.C. and Sanford, Florida. The Auto-Train company owns the locomotives and rail cars. The trains are operated by and over the lines of the Seaboard Coastline and the Richmond, Fredericksburg, and Potomac railroad companies under a long-term contract with Auto-Train. Terminal facilities are provided by Auto-Train.[17] To date the service has been highly successful and has been expanded to serve between Louisville, Kentucky and Sanford in cooperation with Amtrak. Plans to serve other routes are also underway.

The collapse of intercity railroad passenger service in the United States has been caused by a number of factors: the large geographic area of the country that favors travel by air, an extensive highway system and the availability of private automobiles to most people, government promotion of air and highway

[16] Transportation Association of America, *Transportation Facts and Trends,* 13th ed. (Washington, D.C.: Transportation Association of America, July, 1977), p. 18.

[17] Warren Walker, "Auto-Train: A New Transportation Hybrid," *Transportation and Distribution Management,* June, 1972. See also C. Garry Collins, "Auto-Train: An Intermodal Breakthrough," *Proceedings of Transportation Research Forum, 1973.*

TABLE 10-4 *Intercity For-Hire Passenger Traffic by Modes, 1939–1976**

Mode of Transportation	1939 Passenger–Miles	1939 Per Cent	1949 Passenger–Miles	1949 Per Cent	1959 Passenger–Miles	1959 Per Cent	1970 Passenger–Miles	1970 Per Cent	1976 Passenger–Miles	1976 Per Cent
Railroad	23.7	66.7	36.0	52.0	22.4	29.7	10.9	7.3	10.2	5.3
Highway	9.5	26.8	24.0	34.7	20.4	27.1	25.3	16.9	25.1	13.1
Water	1.5	4.2	1.4	2.0	2.0	2.7	4.0	2.7	4.0	2.1
Air	.8	2.3	7.8	11.3	30.5	40.5	109.5	73.1	152.3	79.5
Total	35.5	100.0	69.2	100.0	75.3	100.0	149.7	100.0	191.6	100.0

*Passenger–Miles in billions.

Source: Based on Transportation Association of America, *Transportation Facts and Trends*, 13th ed. (Washington, D.C.: Transportation Association of America, July, 1977), p. 18.

transportation, poor service, deteriorating equipment, lack of capital to improve rail service and unwillingness of management to make the improvements, heavy deficits for railroads in providing the service, disinterest in rail passenger service on the part of railroad management, and lack of a forceful quality oriented service policy on the part of the Interstate Commerce Commission (ICC). The possibilities for improvement under Amtrak are discussed in Chapter 16.

REVENUE TRENDS

As might be expected from the previous discussion of traffic trends and freight revenue per ton-mile, revenue trends in the railroad industry have been less than satisfactory. Table 10-5 provides information on operating revenues, operating expenses, operating ratio, net railway operating income, net income, and rate of return on investment for Class I railroads for the period 1929-1976. The total revenues received by Class I railroads amounted to 18.6 billion dollars in 1976, or 357 million dollars per each of the 52 carriers.

Table 10-5 indicates that the operating ratio, which relates operating revenues to operating expenses, is much higher in the 1970's than it was in 1929 and 1939. This means that operating expenses have risen faster than have operating

TABLE 10-5 *Class I Railroad Revenue Trends, 1929-1976 (000,000)*

Year	Operating Revenues*	Operating Expenses†	Operating Ratio‡	Net Railway Operating Income§	Net Income‖	Rate of Return on Investment (Per Cent)¶
1929	$6,279.5	$4,506.1	71.8	$1,251.7	$896.8	5.3
1939	3,995.0	2,918.2	73.0	588.8	93.2	2.6
1949	8,850.1	6,891.8	77.9	686.5	438.2	2.9
1959	9,825.1	7,704.8	78.4	747.7	577.7	2.7
1969	11,450.3	9,066.5	79.2	654.7	514.2	2.4
1973	14,795.8	11,558.6	78.1	858.7	555.2	3.1
1976	18,559.7	14,947.8	80.5	503.4	345.5	1.3

*Includes freight and passenger revenues.

†Includes freight and passenger expenses.

‡Operating ratio = $\dfrac{\text{operating expenses}}{\text{operating revenues}}$ (calculated from columns 2 and 3). Income taxes and rents for equipment and joint facilities and fixed charges are not included in operating expenses.

§Operating revenues less operating expenses, taxes, and rents for equipment and joint facilities, but before adding non-operating (nonrailroad) income and deducting fixed charges, such as interest on debt and rents for leased lines.

‖Net railway operating income plus non-operating income and less payments for fixed rentals and interest on debt.

¶The relationship of net railway operating income to net investment in transportation property, including cash and materials inventories. Net investment represents original cost less accrued depreciation and amortization.

Sources: Association of American Railroads, *Railroads Facts,* 1974 ed. (Washington, D.C.: Association of American Railroads, 1974), pp. 12, 15, 19, 20, and 22; 1977 ed. pp. 12, 15, 19, 20, and 22; Association of Western Railways, *Railroad Facts,* 1959 ed. (Chicago: Association of Western Railroads, 1959), pp. 50, 51, 62, 63, and 66.

revenues. Our previous discussion of the change in the character of traffic carried by railroads helps to explain this change.

It is clear from Table 10-5 that growth in revenues and net income over the years has been unsatisfactory, especially when one takes into account the tremendous inflation that has occurred in the period. For example, the net income of 1973 was actually less than it was in 1959 in current dollars and much less than 1959 in "real" dollars (adjusted for changes in the price level). The low net income of the recession year 1976 represents an even darker picture when compared with the past.

As to rate of return on investment, Class I railroads managed a return of only 3.1 per cent in 1973 and have had a very low rate of return for many years, often less than 3 per cent. The rate of return in the recession year of 1976 was only 1.3 per cent.

Although industry-wide figures can be misleading because they hide the fact that some carriers do better or worse than the average and that there are some relatively profitable railroads in the United States, it is a fact that the railroad industry is now in serious financial trouble, as evidenced by the figures in Table 10-5. Further evidence of this is found in the bankruptcy of several major railroads, including the Penn Central and the Rock Island, inadequate maintenance of railroad facilities, complaints about poor service, the interest of railroad management in investing outside the railroad business where the rate of return on investment is greater, and government programs to help the railroad industry (to be discussed in Chapter 16). Among the multitude of reasons for the problems of the railroads are poor railroad management in some instances, including a tendency to pay high dividends when profits are low or non-existing, and a tendency in some cases to be concerned more about operating the railroad than with marketing their services; labor rules and regulations resulting in inefficiency and payment for work not actually being performed; excessive and unfair government economic regulation (see Chapters 21 and 25); the rise of competing modes of transportation since 1920, resulting in a decline in the share of freight traffic carried by rail; government promotion of nonrail modes while not promoting railroads (see Chapters 16, 17, and 18); deficits incurred in intercity passenger service for many years; excess fixed capacity and inability to quickly abandon unprofitable lines because of regulation; regional shifts in industry locations away from railroad served areas; and the decline in the amount of rail oriented freight traffic as heavy industry, agriculture, and bulk commodities in general gave way to a service oriented, high technology economy. Actually, as noted in Chapter 1, the amount of freight transported in total by all modes has lagged behind the growth in gross national product. Between 1947 and 1972 intercity freight traffic grew at an average annual rate of 2.8 per cent, compared to an average annual growth rate of 3.8 per cent in gross national product. If oil pipeline traffic were not counted, the growth in freight traffic would be only 2.2 per cent per year.[18] The composition of freight that has grown is less suitable to rail service and is more adaptable to trucking. Finally, general inflation in the late 1960's and in the 1970's, along with high fuel prices, has had a tremendous adverse impact on the railroad industry because their costs of materials, supplies,

[18]United States Railway Association, *Preliminary System Plan*, volume I (Washington, D.C.: U.S. Government Printing Office, 1975), p. 5.

and labor increased much faster than their ability to raise their rates under a regulated pricing system. The recession of 1974–1976 also contributed to railroad difficulties, as the data for 1976 presented in this chapter clearly indicate.

The decline of railroads in the United States is to some degree a normal result of forces outside the industry itself. The problems of railroads are to a great extent problems of adjustment to competition from other modes of transportation. As the economy develops and progresses over time, entire industries decline and even disappear. The railroads themselves destroyed other forms of transportation when they entered the transportation scene in the nineteenth century. However, although one might say that the decline of an industry should be of no particular concern if it is caused by normal economic forces, there is considerable public and private concern about the railroad problem because many people believe that the decline is partly caused by non-economic forces and that railroads provide an essential public service not available from other modes of transportation. Government policy on the decline of railroads as evidenced in government economic regulation and government promotion policies is dealt with in later chapters.

SERVICE CHARACTERISTICS

Despite the great problems faced by railroads since World War II, railroads are still our most important freight carrier in terms of intercity ton–miles carried and many users rely heavily on the railroad system. Consequently, it would appear that railroads still offer a needed service to the public and that their disappearance as an industry from the freight transportation scene is not imminent. What do railroads offer to the public that has kept them in business during these troubled times?

Completeness of Service

When the shipper and the receiver each has a railroad siding, railroads perform a complete or door-to-door service. This means that railroad service begins at the door of the shipper and ends at the door of the receiver or consignee. No extra charge is levied for pickup and delivery of the freight. This is an advantage to users because they need not concern themselves with arranging for moving goods to and from railroad terminals or paying extra charges for pickup and delivery. However, if the shipper and/or the receiver does not have a rail siding, door-to-door service is not possible. This is increasingly the case as industry locates away from railroad lines and as railroads abandon light-traffic lines.

In the past, when railroads were actively in the less-than-carload freight business, they did not pick up and deliver such shipments, even when users had sidings. The service was station-to-station instead of door-to-door unless the user paid an extra charge for pickup and delivery. The fact that from the beginning of their industry highway carriers offered a complete door-to-door service on all size shipments carried and without extra charge for pickup and delivery was a serious disadvantage to the railroad industry. As a result, the railroads eventually for all practical purposes withdrew from the less-than-carload business.

Cost

Railroad freight service is cheaper on some lengths of haul (longer hauls) than some other modes because of the cost structure of railroads, but for the same reason, railroad rates are often higher on shorter hauls than the rates of their competitors. Rail rates can also be lower on some commodities (usually lower-grade commodities) than the rates of some other modes, again because of the cost structure of the railroad industry and the use of differential pricing. The cost advantage of railroads is most likely to occur on large shipments since rail-roads are at a disadvantage cost-wise in dealing with shipments of small size. The cost advantages of railroads are most evident in multiple-car and trainload shipments.

Time

Railroad freight service can be faster than that of other surface modes in some situations. Railroads do much better time-wise on longer hauls (say, over 500 miles) than they do on short hauls, when competing with other modes, because they lose a lot of time in making up and breaking up trains in terminals. The average speed of freight trains, including stops for switching and pickup and delivery of cars, is approximately 20 miles per hour. Delays in the very complex railroad terminal operations in freight yards reduce the door-to-door or overall speed considerably and it is overall speed that the user is concerned with. This means that on short hauls the railroads are at a time disadvantage, but on long hauls, where the terminal delay is a smaller part of total time elapsed, a railroad may do better time-wise than its surface competitors. However, one writer has said that although railroads have the potential ability to perform faster long-haul service than most highway carriers, obsolete work rules, terminal congestion, obsolete equipment, and lack of effective coordination between traffic (sales) and operations means that railroads usually cannot compete favorably on a service basis.[19] Another source reports that the movement of truckload traffic is generally faster than the movement of rail carloads over all lengths of haul.[20]

Flexibility

Railroads offer a very flexible service to the public in terms of what they can carry. Because they do not have as serious limitations on what they can carry, in terms of size and weight, as are often imposed by law or physical characteristics on other modes, railroads can carry almost everything, regardless of size or weight, within reason. If necessary, special routing can be arranged for unusual size shipments in order to avoid unsuitable roadbed conditions, tunnel size, or other problems. Also, rail service is available at most shipping and receiving loca-tions in the country. However, in recent years more and more industrial firms have been locating their facilities away from rail service. In addition, railroads

---

[19] Kenneth U. Flood, *Traffic Management,* 3rd ed. (Dubuque, Iowa: William C. Brown Company Publishers, 1975), p. 15.

[20] Marvin L. Fair and Ernest L. Williams, Jr., *Economics of Transportation and Logistics* (Dallas, Texas: Business Publications, Inc., 1975), p. 166.

provide a fairly large variety of equipment for the shipper to use, although railroads have had difficulty in providing the capital necessary to obtain sufficient freight cars, a factor (plus poor car utilization) which has caused car shortages at times.

Interchanging of Freight and Equipment

An important reason for the continued use of rail freight service by users is that, unlike other modes, the railroad industry offers to the public a truly nationwide service because railroads automatically interchange freight with one another by accepting each other's loaded freight cars for transportation. For example, a shipper at Milwaukee, Wisconsin may want to ship to Atlanta, Georgia, but Atlanta is not served by any railroad that serves Milwaukee. The shipper merely turns the loaded freight car over to the originating carrier at Milwaukee and, according to routing provided by the user or by the carrier (see Chapter 4), the car will be hauled to Atlanta by whatever carriers are selected when the routing is being arranged. This may involve 2, 3, or more railroads. The point is that the interchanging between the several railroads is automatic. The user will be issued only one bill of lading and one freight bill and, as indicated in Chapter 6, provision is also made for the user to file only one claim for loss and damage, when necessary. Automatic, nationwide interchanging of freight is not available from other modes. The importance of this factor is demonstrated by the fact that 75 per cent of rail tonnage is interchange traffic.[21]

Dependability

Because railroads are not affected by weather as much as other modes are, particularly highway and air carriers, they have the opportunity to provide more dependable service. Unfortunately, this dependability is often offset by derailments and other breakdowns caused by undermaintenance of railroad facilities, obsolete equipment, and congestion at terminals. As a result, highway carrier truckload service tends to be more reliable than rail service.

As to loss and damage, railroads assume liability for the full loss if loss or damage should occur. No extra charges are made for assuming this liability. Railroads are liable unless one of the exceptions to liability, discussed in Chapter 6, is present. The incidence of railroad loss and damage is fairly high, despite both carriers' and users' efforts to bring it under better control. In general, rail freight is subject to greater risk from rough handling, vibration, and shocks than is freight carried by highway carriers.

In a United States Department of Transportation (DOT) study conducted among manufacturer-users of transportation it was concluded that, overall, there was a much higher level of satisfaction with the service provided by highway and air carriers than that provided by railroads. Water carrier service was also deemed superior to railroad service. The 4 performance measures used were on-time pickup, on-time delivery, loss and damage, and equipment avail-

[21] Charles A. Taff, *Management of Physical Distribution and Transportation*, 5th ed. (Homewood, Illinois: Richard D. Irwin, Inc., 1972), p. 92.

ability.[22] A recent ICC investigation into railroad service was also critical of the undependability of the service provided.[23]

Service and Rate Innovations

In order to improve their competitive position and attract more traffic and more desirable traffic, railroads have instituted several service and rate improvements in the post-World War II years. These include expanded trailer-on-flatcar and container-on-flatcar service, the use of run-through trains that bypass most intermediate terminals and are interchanged between railroads as a whole (including locomotives), multi-level rack cars for carrying new automobiles, pooling of boxcars by some railroads via the American Boxcar Company (Railbox) with the possibility of a nationwide pooling system in the future, more multiple-car and trainload service and rates, the development of unit trains and corresponding rates, and various incentive rates mentioned in Chapter 9.

In addition, since 1945, railroads have undergone substantial technological change that has sometimes resulted in greater productivity and better service to the public, along with a substantial decline in the number of railroad employees. The railroad locomotive fleet now uses diesel fuel instead of steam, and turbine power and new versions of electric power are being explored. New kinds of freight cars were developed for specific commodities and/or greater carrying capacity. Roadbed maintenance became more mechanized and new kinds of materials were introduced, including welded or "ribbon" rail. Freight-yard operation where freight trains are made up and broken up has been computerized in many cases and traffic control on some lines (operations) has also been mechanized. Finally, the use of computers has been of great importance to railroad management. Computers have been of considerable assistance in handling the tremendous amount of paper work in railroading relative to inventories, payroll, and other such matters, and they are more recently being used to keep track of freight cars (both company-wide and industry-wide) and to classify cars in freight yards, as noted above.

ENVIRONMENT AND ENERGY

Environment

The environmental problems associated with railroads have mainly to do with unsightliness, noise, and to some extent air pollution. No particular governmental action has been taken on visual pollution, but there are government regulations dealing with noise and air pollution. Economic regulatory difficulties associated with the environment are discussed in Chapter 21.

Energy

The energy shortage of the 1970's has led to considerable discussion about diverting freight and passenger traffic to railroads and away from highway and

---

[22] J. Richard Jones, *Industrial Shipper Survey (Plant Level)* (Washington, D.C.: Office of Transportation Planning Analysis, U.S. Department of Transportation, 1975), Chapter 5.

[23] *Investigation of Railroad Freight Service,* Ex Parte 270, Sub. 2, 345 ICC 1223 (1976).

air carriers because railroads are said to use energy more efficiently, at least on longer hauls and for large movements. Studies made on energy consumption have turned up somewhat conflicting results, particularly when comparisons between rail and highway carrier energy consumption were made, because different methods of measurement were used. However, studies on energy consumption *per ton–mile* have shown that the amount of fuel used per freight ton–mile moved is substantially lower for railroads than for trucks. Inland waterways and pipeline energy consumption per ton–mile is slightly better than for railroads, however, except when railroads are operating heavy unit trains.[24] Although railroads are generally more efficient than highway carriers on a per ton–mile basis, rail transportation becomes less efficient when short trains are used. A federal DOT study concluded that for small movements up to 220 tons (approximately 5 carloads) over hauls of 10 miles or less, fuel consumption by rail is greater than fuel consumption by heavy trucks. For distances greater than 10 miles and for movements in excess of 176 tons (approximately 4 carloads), rail service uses less fuel than do trucks.[25] However, because most rail line-haul traffic is for hauls longer than 10 miles, even when picked up or delivered on a short branch line, and is carried in trains exceeding 4 or 5 cars, it can be concluded that most of the time rail service is more energy efficient than highway carrier service when efficiency is measured in terms of consumption per ton–mile.[26]

The amount of energy consumed in providing rail transportation of freight is a relatively small part of the total petroleum-based energy consumption in the United States. One source stated that in 1975 transportation used 54.0 per cent of the total domestic demand for petroleum and that railroads accounted for 2.9 per cent of the transportation demand,[27] which was approximately 1.6 per cent of the total domestic demand.

There has been some positive effect of the energy shortage on the amount of passenger traffic carried by Amtrak, but no noticeable change has taken place in the distribution of freight traffic, although such a change could occur if the shortage worsens and if the federal government wishes to encourage, through regulatory or other policy, the carriage of freight traffic by rail. Electrification of lines now powered by diesel locomotives may also occur.

Finally, as more electric power plants shift from burning oil to burning coal, railroads should benefit from hauling increased amounts of coal, one of the more important rail commodities.

Table 10-6 indicates in a general way the impact of the several modes of transportation on the environment and on the use of energy. These issues are discussed further for nonrail modes in Chapters 11 through 14.

[24] United States Railway Association, *Preliminary System Plan,* Volume I, pp. 147–148.

[25] U.S. Department of Transportation, *The Environmental Impact Statement on "The Transportation Improvement Act of 1973"* (Washington, D.C.: U.S. Department of Transportation, 1974), p. 25.

[26] The trucking industry is critical of studies that measure energy efficiency in terms of consumption per ton–mile because they do not take into account the density of the freight carried, the size of shipments carried, the circuity of routes, the quality of service provided, and other factors, i.e., like transportation services are not being compared.

[27] Transportation Association of America, *Transportation Facts and Trends,* p. 32.

TABLE 10-6 *Environmental Impact and Energy Use Efficiency of Intercity Modes of Transportation**

Mode	Air Pollution	Noise Pollution	Visual Pollution	Water Pollution	Energy Consumption per Unit of Traffic Carried
Railroad	Low	Medium	Medium	Low	Low
Highway	High	Medium to High	High	Low	High
Domestic Water	Low	Low	Medium	Medium	Low
Oil Pipeline	Low	Very Low	Low	Low	Low
Domestic Air	High	High	Low	Low	Very High

*Includes private and for-hire carriers of freight and passengers.

SELECTED REFERENCES

The railroad construction period in the United States is dealt with in some detail in D. Philip Locklin, *Economics of Transportation*, 7th ed. (Homewood, Illinois: Richard D. Irwin., 1972), Chapter 6.

The cost structure of railroads is discussed in Locklin, *Economics of Transportation*, pp. 143–147 and 167–169 and in John R. Meyer, Merton J. Peck, John Stenason, and Charles Zwick, *The Economics of Competition in the Transportation Industries* (Cambridge, Massachusetts: Harvard University Press, 1959), Chapter 3. The latter also deals with the market structure of railroads (see pp. 205–211).

The economic and operating characteristics of railroads are dealt with in Roy J. Sampson and Martin T. Farris, *Domestic Transportation: Practice, Theory, and Policy*, 3rd ed. (Boston: Houghton-Mifflin Company, 1975), pp. 53–61 and in Marvin L. Fair and Ernest W. Williams, Jr., *Economics of Transportation and Logistics* (Dallas, Texas: Business Publications, Inc., 1975), Chapter 10.

The potential sources of additional railroad freight traffic are discussed in James P. Rakowski, "Potential Sources of Railway Freight Traffic," *ICC Practitioners' Journal*, July–August, 1973. An analysis of the competitive performance of railroads versus motor carriers of freight by commodity, size of shipment, and distance is Rakowski, "Competition Between Railroads and Trucks," *Traffic Quarterly*, April, 1976. Obstacles faced by smaller users in locating facilities on railroad lines are dealt with in Frederick J. Beier, "Investment Barriers for Small and Moderate Shippers from Locating on Rail: A Need to Adjust National Policy," *ICC Practitioners' Journal*, September–October, 1976.

There is considerable literature available on the problems of railroads in modern times, much of it related to government policy which is discussed in later chapters. Some general references on railroad problems are Gilbert Burck, "The Railroads Are Running Scared," *Fortune*, June, 1969; "The Railroad Paradox: A Profitless Boom," *Business Week*, September 8, 1973; Robert S. Reebie, "Needed: Reorganization, Leadership," *Distribution Worldwide*, April, 1974;

John R. Meyer and Alexander L. Morton, "A Better Way to Run the Railroads," *Harvard Business Review,* July–August, 1974; "How to Lose Money in a Rising Market," *Business Week,* September 14, 1974; United States Railway Association, *Preliminary System Plan,* Volume I (Washington, D.C.: U.S. Government Printing Office, 1975), pp. 1–9; and D. Daryl Wyckoff, *Railroad Management* (Lexington, Massachusetts: Heath-Lexington Books, 1976).

Methods that railroads could use to improve the reliability of their service are suggested in John F. Battel, "Rail Service Reliability: A Blueprint for Improvement," *Proceedings of Transportation Research Forum, 1975.* A study of railroad and highway transportation delivery time reliability is reported on in Walter Miklius and Kenneth L. Casavant, "Estimated and Perceived Variability of Transit Time," *Transportation Journal,* Fall, 1975.

There are numerous publications dealing with the energy efficiency of the several modes of transportation. The point of view of the railroad and motor trucking industries on the relative energy efficiency of rail and highway carriers is dealt with in Association of American Railroads, *Railroads in the Energy Crisis* (Washington, D.C.: Association of American Railroads, 1974) and American Trucking Associations, Inc., *Debunking the Rail Energy Efficiency Myth* (Washington, D.C.: American Trucking Associations, Inc., 1974).

11

Highway Transportation

The highway transportation industry in the United States is complex in that, unlike railroads, there are several different kinds of carriers. A large segment of the motor trucking industry is made up of private carriers who provide their own transportation by owning or leasing trucks. The for-hire segment consists of both common carriers and contract carriers, plus many other for-hire carriers who are difficult to categorize as either common or contract carriers. These include for-hire carriers exempt from economic regulation, occasional for-hire carriers, and illegal for-hire carriers (operating without required authorization from a regulatory agency). There is also considerable diversity in the motor trucking industry as to size of firm, kinds of traffic carried, size of shipments carried, and lengths of haul. There are, in effect, a series of sub-industries within the motor trucking field that make generalizations about the industry difficult.

There is also considerable diversity in highway transportation of passengers in as much as there are private carriers (private automobiles), for-hire common and contract carriers, and other miscellaneous for-hire carriers.

In this chapter we shall discuss the basic economic and service characteristics of highway freight and passenger transportation with the emphasis on freight transportation, which we deal with first.

DEVELOPMENT OF HIGHWAY
FREIGHT TRANSPORTATION

Carriage of freight by highway on an intercity basis is a relatively new form of transportation. The freight-carrying motor truck did not make its appearance until about 1900, and it was not until after World War I that it became important as a means of intercity transport. Although trucks registered in the United States numbered slightly more than 250,000 in 1916, most of them were small trucks engaged in local delivery service.

World War I was responsible for spurring the growth of the intercity trucking industry when the practical value of the truck was demonstrated in both civilian and military use. After 1920 intercity trucking grew rapidly as a result of improvements in vehicles and roads and the growing demand for the kind of service the motor truck could offer.

The growth of intercity truck transportation was aided by technological improvements, such as the pneumatic tire, the expanding intercity use of the automobile which led to a demand for better roads, and the fact that motor trucks offered shippers a service which they needed. Inadequacies in railroad service also helped. The decade of the 1920's saw for-hire trucking established as a typical small business operation and these carriers built up an appreciable amount of traffic with hauls ranging up to 50 or 60 miles. The number of vehicles registered and intercity ton–miles carried grew rapidly.

The growth of the trucking industry continued through the depressed 1930's, aided by the limited production activities, the small inventories, and the preference for the most restricted business operations possible, which favored shipment by truck instead of by rail.

The relative position of the motor truck in intercity traffic declined during World War II mainly because of the difficulties in obtaining critical items, such as vehicles, gasoline, and tires, and government programs to conserve and maximize utilization of motor truck equipment.

Since World War II both intercity and local motor truck transportation resumed the steady growth it enjoyed before the war. The number of nongovernment owned trucks registered in the country grew from approximately 4,600,000 in 1940 to almost 25 million in 1975[1] and the total intercity ton–mileage carried grew from 62 billion to 505 billion in 1973 before declining to 490 billion in the recession year of 1976.[2] All communities depend to some degree on intercity motor truck transportation and over one-half of the communities in the country depend exclusively on truck transportation to supply them with their needs. This proportion is increasing as railroads abandon lightly used lines.

The motor trucking industry makes use of an extensive road and street system (to be discussed in a later chapter). There are approximately 3.8 million miles of roads and streets in the United States, including the National System of Interstate and Defense Highways shown in Figure 11-1.

OWNERSHIP OF FOR-HIRE TRUCKING FIRMS

For-hire trucking has always been left to private enterprise in the United States. With a tradition of private ownership in the railroad, oil pipeline, and water transportation industries, it was natural for government to also exclude itself from providing for-hire trucking service. Although there is considerable ownership of trucking facilities at all levels of government, these vehicles are not in for-hire service.

[1] American Trucking Associations, Inc., *American Trucking Trends, 1976 Statistical Supplement* (Washington, D.C.: American Trucking Associations, Inc. 1977), p 17.

[2] Transportation Association of America, *Transportation Facts and Trends,* 13th ed. (Washington, D.C.: Transportation Association of America, July, 1977), p. 8 and Association of American Railroads, *Railroad Facts,* 1977 ed. (Washington, D.C.: Association of American Railroads, 1977), p. 36.

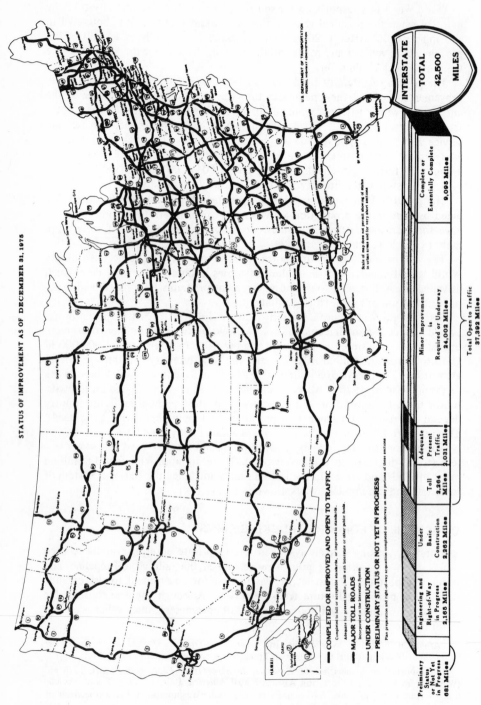

STATUS OF IMPROVEMENT AS OF DECEMBER 31, 1975

FIGURE 11-1 National System of Interstate and Defense Highways. (Source: Federal Highway Administration, U.S. Department of

The trucking industry has historically been dominated by the single-proprietorship form of organization, but there are some partnerships. The corporation device has been used increasingly in recent years, however, and most large trucking companies, accounting for a substantial share of the traffic carried, are incorporated. Many trucking corporations are, however, family controlled and do not have any publicly owned stock outstanding.

Although we have not had government ownership of trucking companies, government in the United States has contributed greatly to the growth of highway transportation by providing the extensive road and street system used by trucking companies.

NUMBER AND SIZE OF FOR-HIRE TRUCKING FIRMS

For-hire highway freight transportation is characterized by a large number of firms that are generally small in size. The limited capital required to enter the industry is a leading reason why the number of firms in the industry is large. In addition, it is usually assumed that there are no important economies of scale in the industry[3] and this precludes a strong tendency for a small number of large firms to dominate the industry.

The actual number of for-hire trucking operators in the country is unknown because many carriers are not subject to or are avoiding economic regulation and are, therefore, not reporting their activities to any government agency. It is known, however, that there are about 16,000 interstate for-hire trucking companies regulated by the Interstate Commerce Commission (ICC). Perhaps there are as many as 150,000 to 200,000 other for-hire carriers that are not regulated at all.

There has been a long-term trend downward in the number of carriers regulated by the ICC and for the size of the average carrier to increase. Thus, there were 20,872 carriers under regulation by the Commission in 1945 versus only 16,005 in 1975.[4] These trends are caused mainly by the large number of mergers between for-hire trucking companies since World War II. These mergers have had as their objective to improve service to the public and hence attract more traffic rather than to take advantage of cost savings. The better service takes the form of being able to offer single-carrier instead of multiple-carrier service over a longer haul by linking together the route systems of 2 or more carriers.

Consequently, although the industry is characterized by a large number of small firms, there are some fairly large firms in the industry, including such companies as Consolidated Freightways, which had a 1976 motor carrier sales volume of 548.7 million dollars, and operated in over 40 states and Canada.[5]

[3] See Merrill J. Roberts, "Some Aspects of Motor Carrier Costs: Firm Size, Efficiency, and Financial Health," *Land Economics,* August, 1956. Some writers disagree with this view and claim that there are significant economies of scale in the trucking industry. See, for example, Paul W. Emery, "An Empirical Approach to the Motor Carrier Scale Economies Controversy," *Land Economics,* August, 1965. Because the motor trucking industry is made up of many different kinds and sizes of carriers, the existence of economies of scale probably varies somewhat within the industry.

[4] American Trucking Associations, Inc., *American Trucking Trends, 1976 Statistical Supplement* p. 16. The number of carriers was stable between 1968 and 1974 but increased in 1975.

[5] Consolidated Freightways, *Annual Report, 1976,* p. 5.

Other large trucking companies are Roadway Express, Yellow Freight, McLean, Ryder, Spector, and Pacific Intermountain.

The above discussion has dealt with for-hire trucking operations. Private trucking operations are found in virtually all industries and in all sizes of firms and the fleets range from one-truck operations to large fleets of hundreds of tractors and trailers.

COST STRUCTURE OF FOR-HIRE TRUCKING FIRMS

Way

The for-hire trucking industry has a cost structure that is dominated by variable costs. The large proportion of variable costs is caused primarily by the fact that trucking companies do not need to invest in a way of any kind. Instead, government provides the way in the form of publicly provided roads and streets. The trucking company thus avoids the large investment needed to provide a way, the payment of the large fixed return on that investment, amortization or depreciation of that investment, and the large maintenance costs and property taxes that would be associated with ownership of the way. Although trucking companies are required to pay various user charges for the use of the road and street system, these charges generally fluctuate with the amount of traffic carried and they tend to be variable costs. Thus, fuel taxes vary with the number of miles traveled and somewhat with the weight of the load carried. When ton–mileage or mileage taxes are imposed, they vary directly with the amount of traffic carried. Vehicle registration fees are also variable to some degree since they depend on the number and size of vehicles used.

Therefore, the costs of the way, unlike in the railroad industry, tend to be variable. They also tend to be common in nature in that the way is used to produce many different kinds of transportation services for different commodities. This makes cost allocation somewhat difficult, particularly when the same vehicle carries more than one commodity (mixed less-than-truckload shipments) at the same time.

Terminals

The major fixed-cost element in for-hire trucking is in the investment in and operation of terminals, but terminal costs are ordinarily a small proportion of total costs, although the costs associated with terminals are increasing as terminals become more elaborate. Terminals consist of buildings and yards where less-than-truckload freight picked up locally is transferred to line-haul intercity trucks and where less-than-truckload freight brought in by line-haul intercity trucks is transferred to local delivery trucks. They are also places where freight is transferred from one highway carrier's vehicles to those of another carrier or where trailers are interchanged between carriers. Vehicle maintenance, paper work, and other administrative activities are also carried out at terminals.

Trucking company terminal facilities are usually provided by the carrier with private investment and the carrier has the responsibility of operating and maintaining the terminal facilities and paying taxes on them. Although labor costs associated with terminal operations tend to be at least partly variable, terminal costs are incurred to a great extent regardless of the amount of traffic handled at a terminal. Major costs involved are interest on the investment, amortization or depreciation (that unrelated to traffic volume), property taxes, and maintenance costs.

Terminal costs are also to a great extent common because they are incurred to produce transportation service for various kinds of traffic. Cost allocation to different individual segments of traffic is, therefore, difficult.

Vehicles

Single-unit trucks, truck tractors, and trailers—the vehicles used in for-hire trucking operations—are provided by the carriers through ownership or leasing. Of the 24.6 million nongovernment owned trucks in the country in 1975, 959,700, or 3.9 per cent, were in for-hire service; the rest were in private service. However, 56 per cent of the for-hire trucks were combination tractor-trailer units while only 2.6 per cent of the trucks in private carrier service were combinations, indicating that for-hire carriers operate larger vehicles than do private carriers.[6]

The investment in vehicles is the principal investment factor for trucking companies and this investment can be substantial. Trucks may be purchased outright or purchased under a credit arrangement with a vendor or by borrowing from private lenders. Trucks may be purchased new or used. There is a ready market available in which used trucks may be bought and sold. In some cases, for-hire trucking companies lease vehicles from a leasing company.

When carriers provide their vehicles through ownership, the costs involved are both fixed and variable. Wear and tear on the vehicles and the fuel and labor expense associated with operating the vehicles may be considered variable because they are incurred in relation to the volume of traffic carried. Some costs may be considered fixed, however; these costs include interest on the investment in a vehicle, maintenance cost not related to traffic carried, amortization, and depreciation expenses not related to extent of use. Leased vehicles result in fixed vehicle leasing costs for the period of the lease, but fuel and labor expense associated with operating the vehicles tend to be variable.

Since the motor truck is of small capacity and has a relatively short life, investment in vehicles can be adjusted to the volume of traffic handled by regulating the number and also the capacity of vehicles according to the demand for transportation service. This is aided by the existence of a well-established used tractor and trailer market. Thus, carriers can fairly easily expand or contract the fleet size and change the kind of vehicles operated to conform with changes in traffic volume and in the kind of service to be provided. In the very short run, it may be difficult to make these adjustments, but over a longer period of time the outlay for vehicles (the major portion of total motor trucking investment expense) can be varied with the volume of traffic handled. Thus, given a suitable time period, the fixed vehicle costs—interest on investment, maintenance cost not related to traffic volume, amortization, and depreciation not related to traffic volume—may be considered variable instead of fixed expenses.

[6] American Trucking Associations, *American Trucking Trends, 1976 Statistical Supplement* p. 20.

Vehicle costs are to a great extent common because a given vehicle is often used to carry different commodities at different times or at the same time, and trucking companies incur joint costs in round-trip situations.

Other Expenses

In addition to expenses associated with way, terminals, and vehicles, the general expenses of a for-hire trucking company include the expenses of operating and maintaining office space, paying the salaries of managers and other administrative personnel not involved in the direct operation of trucks and terminals and maintenance. These expenses are largely fixed and common. Payroll and income taxes tend to vary with the volume of traffic, but property taxes (incurred principally on terminal facilities) are considered fixed because they have no relation to traffic volume.

Large Variable Costs

Because highway carriers avoid the large fixed costs associated with investment in way, their costs tend to be highly variable. The ICC has studied motor trucking company costs many times and has concluded that, over an extended period of time (12 months), the typical for-hire interstate common carrier has costs that are at least 90 per cent variable. This conclusion is based on the fact that the vehicles and other facilities used by trucking companies can be readily adjusted to the volume of business done.[7] In other words, a fairly long-run period is being considered. The long run for trucking companies is a shorter period of time than it is for railroads, their principal competitors, whose investments are more permanent in nature and are more difficult to adjust to changes in the volume of traffic. Therefore, except for very short periods of time and for operations with just one vehicle,[8] even in what is the short run for railroads, trucking companies have a greater proportion of variable costs than do railroads.

Because trucking companies have a large percentage of variable costs, they do not enjoy the benefits of decreasing costs or increasing returns to the degree that railroads do because the greater the volume of traffic carried, the greater will be the variable costs incurred. The small amount of fixed costs when spread over

[7]For example, see Interstate Commerce Commission, Bureau of Transport Economics and Statistics, Statement Number 4616, *The Meaning and Significance of Out-of-Pocket, Constant, and Joint Costs in Motor Carrier Operations,* mimeographed (Washington, D.C.: U.S. Government Printing Office, 1946), p. 12.

[8]The operator of one truck finds that although repairs and fuel are largely proportional to miles operated, his expenses for interest on investment, maintenance cost not related to traffic volume, depreciation expense not related to traffic volume, registration fees, and insurance are of a fixed character. They are unaffected by whether he hauls half a load or a full load. However, when his business grows to the point where he adds a second truck, those same expenses become variable in part. When 5, 10, or more trucks are operated, with some lag, the amount of equipment owned and maintained becomes adjusted to the volume of traffic handled. Interest, maintenance, depreciation, registration fees, and insurance on equipment now vary almost directly with the traffic moved. The capacity he maintains will, over a period of time, be adjusted to the amount of service rendered. See Interstate Commerce Commission, Bureau of Accounts, Cost Finding, and Valuation, *Explanation of the Development of Motor Carrier Costs with Statement as to Their Meaning and Significance,* mimeographed (Washington, D.C.: U.S. Government Printing Office, 1959), pp. 7–8.

the added traffic carried will not result in a substantial reduction in average cost per unit of traffic carried. The fully distributed cost per unit carried declines only slightly as the volume of traffic increases.

Excess Capacity

Unlike the railroad industry, the for-hire trucking industry would ordinarily not be expected to suffer from a perennial condition of substantial excess capacity because the capacity of trucking companies is much more flexible and can be adjusted fairly easily to the traffic volume available. This is caused, to a great extent, by the fact that carriers have no investment in way and a relatively small investment in terminals and, as indicated earlier, the number and kind of vehicles used can be fairly easily adjusted to the amount and kinds of traffic available. Therefore, substantial excess capacity would not be expected to be a problem for trucking companies.

Nevertheless, some excess vehicle capacity does exist and studies have shown that the load factor (proportion of truck capacity actually utilized) of regulated trucking companies is sometimes as low as 50 or 60 per cent.[9] This is caused by unbalanced traffic patterns, i.e., traffic and capacity utilized may be great in one direction but small on the return haul, and also by government economic regulation. The latter results in restrictions on pricing, which prevent deep price cutting and elimination of inefficient firms, and entry control restrictions, which protect carriers from competition and artificially restrict what can be carried and where, thus creating movements with partially filled or empty trucks. These matters will be discussed further in Chapters 22 and 25.

Partially loaded trucks can also result from erroneous management decisions on investment, such as overinvestment that occurs when entry is unregulated (see Chapters 19 and 22) or failure to reduce capacity when necessary. Management inefficiency may cause overcapacity also through incorrect decisions on route selection, commodities to carry, scheduling, and other operating procedures.

MARKET STRUCTURE IN FOR-HIRE TRUCKING

The large number of small carriers in the industry and the fact that their services are differentiated (even though some users may not admit this) leads one to conclude that the motor trucking industry in general approximates monopolistic competition. Although there is service differentiation, it is often small and, because of the competition of close substitutes, the demand curve for an individual trucking company usually does not have a very steep slope and prices of different sellers are relatively close together. When differentiation is minimal, the firm is forced to price "at the market" or very close to it and the prices of competitors are very important to any one seller. When there is substantial service differentiation, a firm may price its services differently from competing carriers.

In the segment of motor trucking that is subject to government economic

---

[9]See James C. Johnson, *Trucking Mergers* (Lexington, Massachusetts: Lexington Books, 1973), p. 20.

regulation, the number of carriers is determined by the entry control policy of the regulatory agencies (see Chapter 22). Actually, the degree of competition in regulated motor trucking varies by the kind of commodity carried. In some kinds of specialized common carrier transportation, there is a very small number of carriers.

With any kind of carriers, regulated or not, and regardless of commodities carried, it is possible that over a particular route and/or for a specific kind of traffic a motor trucking company could be without motor carrier competition and would approach a monopoly position. The usual case is, however, that more than one trucking company seeks a given segment of traffic. In some cases the number is very small, but in other cases it is large. When the number is small, one cannot say that the situation is one approaching oligopoly because the firms are usually not large. Hence, the situation is a mixture of oligopoly and monopolistic competition and illustrates the difficulty in applying traditional price theory to individual transportation situations.

Regardless of the overall market structure in the trucking industry and the market structure situation surrounding any specific segment of traffic, the rates charged by competing motor trucking companies tend to be identical. This is caused in some cases by the large number of competing carriers and/or the small differences in the services offered by them. Contributing factors to rate uniformity in all cases are the rate bureau method of pricing and the economic regulatory system, as indicated earlier in our discussion of railroads in Chapter 10.

The reader is reminded that motor trucking companies sometimes compete against other forms of transportation as well as against each other. The market structure they operate in is influenced by that fact and varies with the circumstances.

PRICING IN FOR-HIRE TRUCKING

Differential Pricing

In Chapter 8 it was pointed out that the motivations for differential pricing are a large proportion of fixed costs and substantial continuing excess capacity. Trucking companies have neither of these characteristics.

Another important factor in determining the degree of suitability of differential pricing is the variety of traffic carried—the wider the variety, the more opportunities there are for differentiating between different segments of traffic. Some trucking companies, called *general commodity carriers,* carry a wide variety of commodities, but many of them confine their operations to one or a limited number of different commodities.

Finally, carriers that serve large geographic areas with many origin and destination points and routes have opportunities to differentiate between points. Some trucking companies serve large areas, but many do not.

In terms of cost structure and excess capacity, then, differential pricing does not appear to be suitable to for-hire trucking companies. As to the variety of commodities carried and the size of the geographic area served, these factors vary from carrier to carrier, so that differential pricing is more suitable to some than to others.

Despite these considerations, however, trucking companies in the United States have generally adopted the differential pricing approach. The two main reasons for this are: (1) when interstate trucking companies were first brought under economic regulation they were required to file rate tariffs and, since the chaotic conditions under which they previously operated meant that they had no organized rate structure, they merely copied the rates and tariffs then being used by railroads and filed them as their own; (2) for-hire trucking companies have always considered railroads their principal competitor and have geared their pricing to what railroads do and, since railroads are heavy users of differential pricing, the trucking company rates have tended to follow a differential pricing pattern. Since the 1930's trucking companies have to some degree modified the rate structure borrowed from the railroad industry so that the rate structure is more suitable to their own characteristics.

Because motor trucking companies have a large proportion of variable costs, one difficulty the companies encounter in using differential pricing is that they cannot lower rates very much below fully distributed costs in order to attract traffic because there is not much margin between fully distributed costs and variable costs, i.e., the variable cost floor is very high. Consequently, trucking companies find it difficult to price low enough to attract low-grade traffic or for other reasons to charge low rates. Highway carriers find that fully distributed costs tend to be an important factor in pricing and that weight density is given considerable consideration in establishing rates because of the limited space available in the vehicle.

The motor trucking common carrier competes with other modes of transportation, with other motor trucking common carriers, with contract motor carriers, and with private motor carriers. As to the latter, the cost of private carriage is an important factor in marking the upper level of rates that can be charged by common carrier trucking companies since the for-hire carrier rates usually should not be higher than the cost to users of operating their own vehicles.

Truck rates for intercity service are frequently based on rail rates and may be slightly above or below competing rail rates. Sometimes they are identical with them. Truck rates are more closely related to distance than are rail rates because motor carrier costs are largely variable and depend primarily on the length of the haul, and terminal expenses, although less variable than other motor carrier costs, are relatively unimportant.

The rates charged by contract carrier truckers are largely a matter of bargaining between users and carriers. Because the use of contract carriage is often an alternative to private trucking, the rates charged by contract carriers must be related to the cost of providing private carrier service.

Freight Classification

In 1952 trucking companies in the United States adopted a uniform system of freight classification called the National Motor Freight Classification and in 1962 this system completely replaced the previous system under which there were different ratings used in the East, South, and West. The new uniform classification applies on interstate traffic throughout the United States when class rates are used and in that sense compares to the railroads' Uniform Freight Classification. The National Motor Freight Classification has 24 classes.

In addition to the National Motor Freight Classification, there is a classification called the Coordinated Motor Freight Classification, which is used by many carriers in the New England states. The ratings in this classification are based primarily on the weight density of the commodities rated. Some trucking companies use the railroad freight classification.

Because the bulk of trucking company traffic is less-than-truckload and is less subject to special commodity rates and because most trucking company costs are variable and discrimination downward is difficult, the class rate system works better with trucking companies than with railroads and a substantial amount of truck traffic moves under class rates. No exact figure is known as to the share of truck traffic carried under class rates or commodity rates. However, in 1974 in one of the motor carrier rate bureau territories approximately 65 per cent of the tonnage moved under class rates.[10]

As indicated earlier, trucking companies originally copied the rail rate structure, including its classifications, and they have modified the system somewhat since that time to fit their needs. It soon became clear that trucking companies could not carry the lower-rated commodities profitably, especially over longer hauls, if they used the rail classification and rates. As a result, minimum rate *stops* were introduced which made the rates on low-rated commodities the same as on some higher class of freight. Thus, the fifth highest class rate might be the lowest rate a carrier would charge, even though the commodity in question might be rated at or below the sixth highest class.[11]

INVESTMENT TRENDS IN FOR-HIRE TRUCKING

Motor trucking is not a capital intensive industry, meaning that it does not require large amounts of capital. As noted in Chapter 10, according to the Association of American Railroads (AAR), in 1973 carrier investment required per dollar of revenues was only $.22 for highway carriers while it was $2.17 for railroads.[12] This is caused primarily by the lack of an investment in way on the part of highway carriers.

The total investment in for-hire trucking facilities in the United States is growing every year, but the exact figure is unknown since many carriers are not required to report this information because they are not subject to economic regulation. However, the total investment in terminals and vehicles is substantial because of the extremely large number of carriers.

The American Trucking Associations reported that in 1975 the 1,000 Class I and Class II regulated interstate trucking companies (those having annual operating revenues of over $500,000) studied had total assets of 5.4 billion dollars. These assets averaged 5.4 million dollars per carrier.[13] The 842 Class I (annual

---

[10] Charles A. Taff, *Commercial Motor Transportation,* 5th ed. (Cambridge, Maryland: Cornell Maritime Press, Inc., 1975), p. 356.

[11] D. Philip Locklin, *Economics of Transportation,* 7th ed. (Homewood, Illinois: Richard D. Irwin, Inc., 1972), p. 659.

[12] Association of American Railroads, *Railroads in the Cost Spiral* (Washington, D.C.: Association of American Railroads, 1973), p. 5.

[13] American Trucking Associations, Inc., *American Trucking Trends, 1976 Statistical Supplement* p. 4.

operating revenues of more than 3 million dollars) regulated interstate trucking companies in 1974 had operating revenues of approximately 15.9 billion dollars. Their investment in operating property was approximately 3.5 billion dollars, which meant that their capital turnover (ratio between investment and revenues) was 4.6.[14] Thus, a dollar of investment produced 4.6 dollars in operating revenue, confirming the AAR estimate reported above. The average investment in operating property per carrier was approximately 4.1 million dollars.

On the other hand, motor trucking operations are highly labor intensive meaning that they require large amounts of labor. In 1974 the total cost of wages of Class I interstate regulated common carriers of general freight was 60.7 per cent of total operating revenues. Almost 69 per cent of the wage dollar was paid to operating employees involved in terminal and transportation operations, not including managers and supervisors.[15]

TRAFFIC TRENDS IN MOTOR TRUCKING

Table 10-2 in Chapter 10 contains information on the total annual intercity ton-miles carried by trucks, both private and for-hire, since 1939. It can be seen that the rate of growth has been substantial, increasing from 53 billion ton-miles in 1939 to 505 billion in 1973, an increase of 853 per cent, before declining to 490 billion in the recession year of 1976. The share of all intercity ton-miles of freight carried by truck increased from 9.7 per cent in 1939 to 22.6 per cent in 1976. It should be noted, however, that the share of traffic carried by truck has been somewhat stable since 1958.

The figures in Table 10-2 do not give a complete picture of the importance of motor truck transportation because ton-mile figures tend to conceal the large share of total tons shipped by truck. This is true because most truck trips are short as compared with trips by rail and other modes of transportation. In addition, the data are limited to intercity traffic alone. If data were available for local or intracity ton-mileage, they would add considerably to the ton-mileage carried by truck, since most local transportation of property is conducted by motor vehicle.

The data in Table 10-2 include operations of both private and for-hire truck operators. It is difficult to say exactly what share of the total traffic carried by truck is in for-hire vehicles. Some evidence of the share is found in statistics which show that regulated interstate for-hire motor carriers carried 215 billion ton-miles of intercity freight in 1975, which was 44 per cent of all intercity freight carried by truck in that year.[16]

The success of the highway carrier in the freight market has been largely in the short-haul and higher-value commodity traffic and in less-than-truckload shipments and, to a great extent, at the expense of the railroad industry. As a result, the traffic carried by motor truck tends to provide a higher revenue per ton-mile than that produced by rail traffic. Thus, Table 11-1 shows that the average revenue per ton-mile for Class I trucking companies is considerably higher than for railroads. It also shows that highway carrier average revenue per ton-mile has increased substantially since 1945 in line with inflationary trends.

[14] *Ibid.*, p. 2.

[15] *Ibid.*, p. 9.

[16] Transportation Association of America, *Transportation Facts and Trends*, pp. 8–9.

TABLE 11-1 *Class I* Intercity Truck Common Carrier Average
Revenue per Ton-Mile,[†] 1945-1974 (cents)*

Year	Revenue per Ton-Mile
1945	4.1
1950	5.0
1955	5.8
1960	6.4
1965	6.6
1970	7.6
1974	9.3

*Carriers having annual operating revenues of over 3 million dollars (1974 definition). The definition has changed several times over the years covered in the table.

[†]Average revenue per freight ton–mile = $\dfrac{\text{total freight revenue}}{\text{total number of freight ton–miles carried}}$.

Sources: American Trucking Associations, Inc., *American Trucking Trends*, 1975 ed. (Washington, D.C.: American Trucking Associations, Inc., 1975), p. 23 and American Trucking Associations, Inc., *American Trucking Trends, 1976 Statistical Supplement* (Washington, D.C.: American Trucking Associations, Inc., 1977), p. 5.

REVENUE TRENDS IN FOR-HIRE TRUCKING

Because of the great increase in traffic carried in the post-World War II years, operating revenues of intercity highway carriers have increased greatly and the industry has generally done well in terms of profitability. Table 11-2 contains information on operating revenues, operating expenses, and the operating ratio of most Class I and II regulated interstate trucking companies. Although these figures represent only a segment of the total for-hire trucking industry in the country, they do indicate the general condition of the most important part of for-hire highway transportation.

Table 11-2 shows that total revenues have grown considerably in the period. A calculation of the average revenue per carrier reveals that it was $488,173 in 1945, $1,926,608 in 1960, and $7,129,725 in 1975, indicating a substantial growth in revenues per carrier.

Operating expenses have also risen over the period and are consistently a large percentage of total revenues. Instead of the rate of return on investment, the operating ratio, which relates operating revenues to operating expenses (but not including interest payments and income taxes) is usually used as an indicator of the financial condition of trucking companies. The ratio is consistently in the middle nineties for the years shown in Table 11-2, indicating a small return on sales for the industry, particularly when it is recalled that interest payments and income taxes are not included in operating expenses when the ratio is calculated. However, because of the small investment relative to revenues generated, an operating ratio of 95 may produce a satisfactory rate of return. Thus, 798 of the Class I trucking companies under regulation by the ICC had an operating ratio of 95.0 in 1975, with a rate of return on net investment of 13.3 per cent.[17]

[17]Interstate Commerce Commission, *Annual Report, 1976* (Washington, D.C.: U.S. Government Printing Office, 1976), p. 146.

T A B L E 11-2 *Class I and Class II* Intercity Truck Common Carrier Revenue Trends, 1945–1975*

Year	Number of Carriers	Operating Revenues (000,000)	Operating Expenses (000,000)	Operating Ratio[†]
1945	1,894	$924.6	$916.7	99.1
1950	1,934	2,503.5	2,335.6	93.2
1955	2,765	4,404.2	4,226.6	96.0
1960	3,202	6,169.0	6,014.9	97.5
1965	3,673	9,034.8	8,582.9	95.0
1970	3,413	12,837.1	12,384.4	96.5
1975	2,688	19,164.7	18,342.4	95.7

*In 1975 this included carriers having annual operating revenues of more than $500,000. A Class I carrier had annual operating revenues of more than $5,000,000 and a Class II carrier had revenues of more than $500,000 in 1975. The definitions have changed several times over the years included in the table.

†Operating ratio = $\dfrac{\text{operating expenses}}{\text{operating revenues}}$. Calculated from columns 2 and 3. Interest payments and income taxes are not included in operating expenses.

Source: American Trucking Associations, Inc., *American Trucking Trends,* 1976 Statistical *Supplement* (Washington, D.C.: American Trucking Associations, Inc., 1977), p. 6.

Industry figures such as those found in Table 11-2 hide the fact that some carriers are highly profitable, with operating ratios in the low eighties, while some are unprofitable, with ratios over 100. The fact remains that the net income of the regulated interstate trucking industry has been satisfactory, as indicated by the rate of return figure cited above, although the recession of 1974–1976 did adversely affect carrier operating revenues and net income.

SERVICE CHARACTERISTICS OF FOR-HIRE TRUCKING

Highway transportation has become a very important part of our transportation system since 1920 and it accounts for almost one-quarter of our intercity ton–mileage and most of the local transportation of property.

The phenomenal growth of the industry since the 1920's has been because it offers to the using public various service advantages that cannot be duplicated by its competitors, the railroads in particular.

Completeness of Service

A major reason for the success of trucking in competing with railroads has always been the complete door-to-door service trucking provides. Trucking companies ordinarily include pickup at the door of the shipper and delivery to the door of the receiver as part of their service. They do not ask the shipper and receiver to provide pickup and delivery and they do not levy an extra charge for pickup and delivery. This was of particular importance when railroads were still seeking less-than-carload traffic and their less-than-carload service was station-to-station instead of door-to-door, meaning that shipments either had to be brought to and from the railroad terminal by the shipper and receiver or the shipper and receiver had to pay the railroads an extra charge for doing so. By the 1970's motor trucking had captured most intercity freight shipments of less than 10,000 pounds, with the exception of small package goods. Now that railroads are virtually out of the less-than-carload business, the door-to-door advantage of trucking is not so important, but in the truckload traffic market the door-to-door advantage still exists where shippers who might wish to use rail carload service do not have rail sidings at their doors. This is becoming increasingly the case as industry locates away from railroad service and as railroads abandon lightly used lines.

✓ Cost

Highway carrier freight service can be cheaper on some lengths of haul (shorter hauls) than that of some other modes because of their law fixed costs compared with their competition, particularly railroads. Alternatively, highway carriers are often at a price disadvantage on longer hauls because their costs increase approximately in proportion to increases in distance.

Motor trucking rates can be lower than those of competitors on smaller shipments, regardless of distance, because their operations are geared primarily to less-than-truckload traffic and not movement of large quantities of freight. In addition, as noted below, on both less-than-truckload and truckload shipments highway carrier service is often faster and more frequent than that of its competitors. This is also a cost factor for it permits shippers and receivers to maintain smaller inventories and reduce the costs of carrying inventories. Motor trucking service also offers cost advantages in terms of less loss and damage and packaging costs, free pickup and delivery service, and lower labor costs associated with loading and unloading vehicles since the carriers normally provide this as part of their service without extra charge.

Highway carriers are at a disadvantage price-wise in competing for lower-grade and bulk commodities because of their high variable costs. They cannot charge the low rates required to get that traffic because these rates would likely be below their variable costs.

Despite the general tendencies noted above, the reader is cautioned that each movement of freight must be analyzed separately because exceptions to these general tendencies are frequently found.

Time

The speed advantage of highway carriers has been a major reason for the success of the industry. Highway carrier service is often faster than that of other modes, particularly over short hauls. This is partly because trucking companies have a fairly high running speed. It can be as high as 60 miles per hour which can result in an overall speed of 35 miles per hour after allowance for fuel stops, meals, traffic congestion, and so on is made. In addition, highway carriers often avoid the terminal delays of other carriers (particularly railroads) because they usually operate relatively small single units that can be quickly loaded and they do not have to make up and break up trains or tows. In fact, truckload movements may operate without any terminal delay at all by moving from the shipper's door directly to the receiver's door. This advantage is less important on longer hauls but, even there highway carriers are often able to beat the time of railroads. The speed of highway carrier service on long hauls is improved by continuous 24-hour operation of sleeper cab trucks (one driver is driving while a second driver is asleep in the cab) or by relays of drivers at spaced intervals along the route.

Another time advantage of trucking companies is found in the fact that they often offer more frequent service than their competition. This again is possible because they operate single and fairly small vehicle units.

Flexibility

An important advantage of highway carrier service is its flexibility. Trucks can go anywhere there are roads and streets, a wide variety of equipment is available from for-hire trucking companies, and the small vehicle size means it can be loaded and unloaded quickly.

On the other hand, trucking companies are handicapped because they cannot carry as wide a variety of commodities as can railroads because of the regulatory restrictions on what commodities they are permitted to carry and because of state size and weight laws limiting the size and weight of vehicles and, therefore, the shipments they can carry.

Interchanging of Freight and Equipment

Unlike the railroad industry, highway carriers are unable to provide automatic interchanging of freight and equipment among all common carriers. Although interchange agreements exist, especially among larger trucking companies, the large number of carriers in the country plus their independent attitude, lack of cooperation in some cases, and lack of standardization of equipment have made it impossible to establish a nationwide interchanging system. This may cause difficulties for a user and force him to use other modes of transportation or provide his own service via private carriage.

Dependability

Since highway carriers are more affected by weather conditions than are some other modes, they cannot always provide dependable service to the public. Trucking companies also suffer from congestion on city streets and on metropolitan area roads. However, as noted in Chapter 10, the deficiencies in railroad service dependability have to a great extent offset this disadvantage of trucking companies. A study cited in Chapter 10 indicated that manufacturers were much more satisfied with the service provided by highway carriers than with that received from railroads.

Trucking companies do somewhat better than railroads in terms of amount of loss and damage and, unless an exception to liability is present, they assume liability for the full value of what is carried[18] without making an extra charge for assuming that liability.

[18]With the exception of household goods carriers who limit the amount of liability.

Service and Rate Innovations

There has been less pressure on motor trucking companies to seek new ways of doing things than there has been on the railroad industry in recent years. Nevertheless, the trucking industry has sought new kinds of services and rates and has undergone considerable technological change since World War II. Trucking companies have participated in trailer-on-flatcar service and containerized service, developed coordinated services with airlines, increased the amount of interchanging of freight and vehicles among themselves, introduced some incentive rates, built and rebuilt many terminals, increasingly mechanized terminal operations, increased the power and efficiency of power units, launched programs to conserve fuel, increased the size of trailers, introduced new lighter-weight materials for trailer construction, developed specialized trailers for specific commodities, and increased the use of double trailers when permitted by law. In addition, larger trucking companies have computerized many activities.

TRANSPORTATION OF PASSENGERS

The intercity for-hire bus industry has long been an important part of the nation's passenger transportation system. Intercity buses provide the only means of for-hire intercity transportation for approximately 40,000 communities in the United States. In 1974 intercity bus service accounted for 27.7 billion passenger-miles. This declined to 25.1 billion in the recession year of 1976. Although the passenger-miles carried in the 1970's were less than in the peak traffic years of World War II, after which the number of passenger-miles carried declined, there has been a steady growth since 1960, with the exception of 1975 and 1976. The passenger-miles by bus were 13.1 per cent of the total for-hire intercity passenger-miles in 1976.[19] However, intercity buses carried 350 million passengers in 1976, which was 54.9 per cent of all for-hire intercity passengers carried, reflecting the shorter-haul nature of bus transportation compared with intercity rail and air.[20] The average passenger journey via Class I motor bus carriers (annual operating revenues in excess of 1 million dollars) regulated by the ICC in 1973 was 116.9 miles.[21]

Intercity for-hire bus transportation is provided by private companies, of which there are approximately 1,300, 1,141 of which were regulated by the federal government in 1976. They are generally fairly small companies. In 1976, 121 of the 1,141 carriers regulated by the ICC were Class I carriers having annual operating revenues of over 1 million dollars.[22] However, there are some large organizations. The largest is the Greyhound Corporation, a highly diversified organization involved in several activities other than bus operation, which accounts for approximately 50 per cent of the total intercity bus traffic. In 1976

[19]Transportation Association of America, *Transportation Facts and Trends*, p. 18.
[20]*Ibid.*, p. 19.
[21]Interstate Commerce Commission, Bureau of Economics, *Transport Economics*, Volume II, Number 1, 1975 (Washington, D.C.: Interstate Commerce Commission, 1975), p. 18.
[22]Interstate Commerce Commission, *Annual Report, 1976*, p. 141.

Greyhound operated approximately 4,700 buses in the United States and Canada over a total of 122,000 route miles, it owned or leased 225 bus terminals, and it was represented in smaller communities by approximately 3,200 commission agents.[23] This heavy concentration of the highway passenger business in one company is in sharp contrast to the situation in the motor trucking industry.

The cost structure of intercity bus companies is similar to that of trucking companies—a high percentage of costs are variable mainly because of the lack of an investment in way. Labor cost accounts for approximately one-half of operating expenses, with drivers' wages accounting for approximately 55 per cent of the wage bill. The operating ratio of larger intercity bus companies regulated by the federal government is usually approximately 90.[24]

Because there is no way investment, intercity bus companies do not have an excess capacity problem associated with the way. However, like all passenger carriers, there are wide seasonal, weekly, daily, and hourly variations in the demand for service, plus unbalanced traffic movements on many routes. This means that bus companies must maintain a fleet capable of handling peak traffic demand periods, resulting in unused capacity for part of the time. The load factor of larger carriers regulated by the ICC is usually approximately 50 per cent.[25]

Intercity buses compete primarily against the private automobile and are at a definite disadvantage service-wise in doing so. Intercity buses also compete against railroads, air service, and other bus companies. This competition places considerable pressure on common carrier bus companies to keep their fares at a reasonable level. The fares produced an average revenue per passenger–mile for Class I interstate regulated carriers of 5.1 cents in 1976, less than both Class I rail (6.5) and air coach (7.5) average revenue per passenger–mile.[26] The fares charged by intercity bus companies generally taper with distance.

The market structure in intercity bus transportation approximates monopolistic competition in general because it consists of a fairly large number of small firms (with a few exceptions) and some product differentiation. However, over a particular route a motor bus company could be faced with competition from only 1 or 2 other bus companies or none at all. In such cases, the market structure is close to oligopoly or monopoly, although, with the exception of a few firms in the industry, the competitors are often small in size and, hence, the true conditions of oligopoly would not be present. This and the dominance of Greyhound in an industry of large numbers and small firms illustrate the difficulty in applying traditional price theory to an individual transportation situation.

Like the trucking industry, intercity motor bus operation is not a highly capital intensive activity because there is no investment in way, although it is more capital intensive than trucking companies. The total investment in the industry is, however, substantial. In 1975 80 Class I intercity bus companies regulated by the ICC had a total net investment of approximately 429 million

---

[23] Greyhound Corporation, *Annual Report, 1976*, p. 5.

[24] Interstate Commerce Commission, *Annual Report, 1976*, p. 147.

[25] It was 44 per cent for Class I carriers in 1976. Transportation Association of America, *Transportation Facts and Trends*, p. 15.

[26] *Ibid.*, p. 7.

dollars. The average investment of the 80 firms was approximately 5.4 million dollars.[27] The capital turnover of the 80 Class I carriers in 1975 was 2.1, considerably less than that of Class I motor trucking companies.

Revenues of all federally regulated bus companies from all sources, including intercity, local, suburban, and charter passenger service and package express service, increased from 534 million dollars in 1947 to 1.42 billion dollars in 1975.[28] Class I carriers receive approximately 90 per cent of the interstate regulated carrier revenue. Despite the increase in total revenues of the federally regulated bus companies, the industry was in financial difficulty in 1977 caused by the loss of traffic to the private automobile, rising costs of operation, the adverse effects of inflation and recession on lower income people who make up much of the market for the bus industry, and competition from the National Railroad Passenger Corporation (Amtrak).

The advantages that intercity bus service offers to the public include convenience in that buses pick up and discharge passengers at almost any point the passengers desire. Buses can also go almost anywhere and can serve many points not served by other for-hire modes. Buses also offer a frequently scheduled service and can be faster than the competition on shorter hauls. Finally, as noted earlier, bus service is often less expensive than other for-hire modes.

Generally, the disadvantages of intercity bus service increase with distance when compared with air or rail travel because of the low speed of buses. However, there has been improvement in long-distance bus service because there have been many highway improvements, and coast-to-coast service without changing buses is available.

ENVIRONMENT AND ENERGY

Environment

The serious environmental problems associated with highway transportation have to do primarily with the air and noise pollution created by vehicles. There is also the environmental and social impact of highway construction. Government programs to curb air pollution are now well-established. In addition, the federal government and some state and local governments have developed a system of regulation of noise emitted by motor vehicles. Noise barriers have also been constructed along some urban freeways.

Energy

The energy shortage of the 1970's has led to numerous studies of the relative energy efficiency of different modes of transportation. As noted in Chapter 10, highway freight carriers are usually shown to be less energy efficient per ton-mile carried overall than rail or water carriers.[29] However, on very short

[27] Interstate Commerce Commission, *Annual Report, 1976*, p. 147.

[28] Transportation Association of America, *Transportation Facts and Trends*, p. 6.

[29] The trucking industry is critical of studies that measure energy efficiency in terms of consumption per ton-mile because they do not take into account the density of the freight carried, the size of shipments carried, the circuity of routes, the quality of service provided, and other factors, i.e., like transportation services are not being compared.

hauls and for small movements, highway carriers are more energy efficient than are railroads. Highway freight carriers are more energy efficient than air carriers. On the passenger side, the motor bus is more energy efficient per passenger–mile than the private automobile, the railroad passenger train, and the airplane.[30]

One source stated that highway transportation of freight and passengers accounted for approximately 85 per cent of the total transportation demand for petroleum in the United States in 1975,[31] or approximately 46 per cent of total domestic demand for petroleum. In 1974 the total consumption of motor fuel by all passenger and freight motor vehicles in the country was 106,301 million gallons, and trucks of all kinds accounted for 31,199 million gallons, or 29.3 per cent of the consumption by motor vehicles. Buses of all kinds consumed 858 million gallons, or .8 per cent.[32]

Despite the large amount of energy consumed by motor vehicles, the amount used in for-hire intercity transportation is fairly small. The bulk—68 per cent—of the truck use of petroleum is by single-unit trucks[33] that are used mainly in local service. According to one source, in 1971 trucks of all kinds used 13.2 per cent of the total domestic consumption of petroleum. Truck use of diesel fuel amounted to only 3.3 per cent of the total domestic consumption of petroleum,[34] and diesel fuel is the principal source of energy used by intercity trucks. Commercial buses used only 61.2 per cent of total bus use which, in turn, was only .8 per cent of the fuel consumed by all motor vehicles in 1974.[35] Many commercial buses are in local rather than intercity service. Consequently, any programs to conserve energy in motor transportation would have to rely on the operators of the passenger automobile and on local trucking for any major reduction in consumption.

SELECTED REFERENCES

The history of the for-hire motor trucking industry is summarized in Donald V. Harper, *Economic Regulation of the Motor Trucking Industry by the States* (Urbana, Illinois: University of Illinois Press, 1959), pp. 1–8.

A book-length general treatment of motor truck transportation is Charles A. Taff, *Commercial Motor Transportation,* 5th ed. (Cambridge, Maryland: Cornell Maritime Press, Inc., 1975). The economic and operating characteristics of the trucking industry are discussed in D. Philip Locklin, *Economics of Transportation,* 7th ed. (Homewood, Illinois: Richard D. Irwin, Inc., 1972), Chapter 28.

Economies of scale in the for-hire trucking industry are dealt with in several writings including James C. Johnson, *Trucking Mergers* (Lexington, Massachusetts: Lexington Books, 1973), pp. 19–22. See also Merrill J. Roberts, "Some Aspects of Motor Carrier Costs: Firm Size, Efficiency, and Financial Health," *Land*

[30] See John H. Jennrich, "Comparison of Efficiencies," *Highway User Quarterly,* Summer, 1974, p. 18.

[31] Transportation Association of America, *Transportation Facts and Trends,* p. 32.

[32] U.S. Department of Transportation, *Highway Statistics, 1974* (Washington, D.C.: U.S. Government Printing Office, 1976), Table VM-1, p. 67.

[33] *Ibid.*

[34] American Trucking Associations, Inc., *American Trucking and the Energy Crisis* (Washington, D.C.: American Trucking Associations, Inc., 1973), p. 1.

[35] U.S. Department of Transportation, *Highway Statistics, 1974,* Table VM-1, p. 67.

Economics, August 1956; Paul W. Emery, "An Empirical Approach to the Motor Carrier Scale Economies Controversy," *Land Economics,* August, 1965; Robert A. Nelson, "The Economic Structure of the Highway Carrier Industry in New England," in New England Governors' Conference on Public Transportation, *Motor Freight Transport for New England* (Boston: 1957); Gary N. Dicer, "Economies of Scale and Motor Carrier Optimum Size," *Quarterly Review of Economics and Business,* Spring, 1971, and James P. Rakowski, "Motor Carrier Size and Profitability," *Transportation Journal,* Summer, 1977.

The cost structure of trucking companies and the market structure of the industry are discussed in John R. Meyer, Merton J. Peck, John Stenason, and Charles Zwick, *The Economics of Competition in the Transportation Industries* (Cambridge, Massachusetts: Harvard University Press, 1959), Chapter 4 and pp. 211–224. The cost structures of for-hire and private motor carriage are analyzed in Dwight Stuessy, "Cost Structure of Private and For-Hire Motor Carriage," *Transportation Journal,* Spring, 1976. A study that examined the effects of various methods of allocating the indirect costs of common carrier truck operations on the costs of different traffic segments is David L. Shrock, *Allocating the Indirect Costs of Motor Common Carrier Operation,* unpublished Ph.D. dissertation, Indiana University, 1974.

A study of railroad and highway transportation delivery time reliability is reported on in Walter Miklius and Kenneth L. Casavant, "Estimated and Perceived Availability of Transit Time," *Transportation Journal,* Fall, 1975.

An analysis of the competitive performance of railroads versus motor carriers of freight by commodity, size of shipment, and distance is James P. Rakowski, "Competition Between Railroads and Trucks," *Traffic Quarterly,* April, 1976.

An excellent description of the intercity bus industry is Taff, *Commercial Motor Transportation,* Chapter 20.

There are numerous publications dealing with the energy efficiency of the several modes of transportation. The point of view of the railroad and motor trucking industries on the relative energy efficiency of rail and highway carriers is dealt with in Association of American Railroads, *Railroads in the Energy Crisis* (Washington, D.C.: Association of American Railroads, 1974) and American Trucking Associations, Inc., *Debunking the Rail Energy Efficiency Myth* (Washington, D.C.: American Trucking Associations, Inc., 1974).

12

Water Transportation

In this chapter we shall discuss the basic economic and service characteristics of domestic water transportation. Domestic water transportation consists of water transportation along the ocean coasts (coastal) and between coasts (intercoastal), on the Great Lakes, on rivers and canals, and also between the mainland United States and off shore states and possessions such as Hawaii and Puerto Rico. The diverse nature of the operations and vessels used in these various water trades makes generalizations about their economic and service characteristics somewhat difficult. Nevertheless, there are basic characteristics that are similar between trades and they will be discussed here. Because of the relative unimportance of passenger transportation by water, our discussion will be confined mostly to freight transportation.

Domestic water transportation is conducted by both private and for-hire carriers. A large segment of freight traffic is carried in vessels operated by users. The for-hire segment consists of both common and contract, or "charter," carriers.

DEVELOPMENT OF DOMESTIC
WATER TRANSPORTATION

Rivers and Canals

Colonial America relied heavily upon water transportation making use of the ocean and navigable rivers. Transportation by river became more important as the population moved westward and vessels of various kinds and descriptions, including the well-known river flatboat, were used.

Robert Fulton's invention of the steamboat in 1807 provided a great stimulus for the growth of water transportation on the Mississippi and Ohio rivers. Steamboat traffic on these rivers grew until railroads began to take traffic away from the rivers after about 1850. After 1880 steamboats practically disappeared.

During the same period the "canal era" came and went. Beginning with the opening of the Erie Canal in 1825, which connected the Hudson River at Albany, New York with Lake Erie at Buffalo, New York and made possible cheap water transportation between the northeast and the midwest, a number of canals were built in other states, including Virginia, Maryland, Massachusetts, Pennsylvania, Ohio, Michigan, Indiana, and Illinois. Most of these canals were state enterprises; a few were privately owned. Many were uneconomic. Like the steamboat, canals became victims of railroad competition. Although the main era of canal building ended with the financial crisis of 1937, some canal construction continued into the 1850's, and the better canals continued operating for a number of years after that.

With the decline of both steamboat and canal transportation, water transportation by river and canal was practically dormant for a number of years, but it began to revive in the World War I period and was assisted by federal government programs to improve the waterway system and the federal government's operation of a barge line to demonstrate what could be done. The tow boat-barge (tow boats actually push the barges) method of transportation came to be the common practice and eventually diesel power, rather than steam, took over.

In the 1970's river transportation is an important part of our intercity freight transportation system and it accounts for a large share of the bulk commodities transported in intercity commerce. It is unimportant in the transportation of passengers.

Federal aid to inland waterways has always played an important role in the development of the waterways used in domestic transportation and will be discussed in Chapter 17. A map depicting the waterways of the United States is shown in Figure 12-1. Excluding seacoasts and the Great Lakes, the country has approximately 25,500 miles of navigable waterways with almost 16,000 miles having a depth of 9 feet or more carrying the bulk of the internal water traffic.

Great Lakes

The Great Lakes consist of 95,000 square miles of natural waterways. Efforts to build connecting locks and canals between the lakes began in the 1820's. A major development was the opening of the locks at Sault Ste. Marie connecting Lake Huron and Lake Superior in 1855. Although domestic Great Lakes traffic was a fairly important part of the total domestic freight and passenger movement in the past, in recent years the rate of growth has been slow. A substantial amount of freight traffic moves via the Great Lakes, but much of it is international traffic carried through the St. Lawrence Seaway which was rebuilt in the 1950's.

Coastal and Intercoastal Water Transportation

Coastal water transportation predated railroads and other forms of domestic transportation. It consists of deep-water transportation along the coasts. It also includes transportation via the various coastal rivers, bays, inlets, canals, and protected channels along the coastlines which are often included as part of the "inland waterways" system. Intercoastal water transportation also developed and was greatly assisted by the opening of the Panama Railroad in 1854 and then the Panama Canal in 1914, which considerably reduced the time required to ship and travel between the Pacific Coast and the Gulf and Atlantic coasts. The submarine threat and federal government acquisition of many vessels during World War II had a serious negative effect on intercoastal and deep-water coastal transportation, and neither form of transportation has regained the position it had in the pre-war era. The difficulties since the war have been high loading and unloading costs at ocean ports, high labor costs at sea, high vessel ownership costs, slow speed, and low rates offered by competing railroads and the unwillingness of shippers and receivers to switch back to water transportation after having changed to fast and more frequent rail service during the war.[1]

OWNERSHIP

The carriage of traffic between ports in the United States is restricted by federal law to vessels that have been built in the United States, are registered under the American flag, and are owned and operated by American citizens. With minor exceptions, the for-hire carriers providing domestic water carrier service have been and are privately owned rather than government owned. Beginning during World War I and ending in 1953, the federal government owned and operated a barge line on the Mississippi, Illinois, Missouri, and Warrior rivers. The purpose was to demonstrate the feasibility of barge operations and to encourage the revival of domestic water transportation. During World War II the federal government operated some vessels in the coastal and intercoastal trades.

Although there generally has not been government ownership of for-hire water carriers, government has greatly assisted the water carrier industry through various programs to improve waterways and to provide port and habor facilities.

NUMBER AND SIZE OF FIRMS

It is difficult to determine the number and size of and other characteristics of the carriers that operate in domestic water transportation because most of them are not subject to economic regulation by government. According to the American Waterway Operators, Inc., there are approximately 1,700 private and for-hire carriers operating tow boats and barges on the river and canal system, on the Great Lakes, and in the coastal trades of the United States. These carriers operate approximately 4,200 tow boats, approximately 16,000 dry cargo barges, and approximately 3,200 tank barges and they employ approximately 80,000 persons on these vessels (not including shore personnel). Approximately 400 of these carriers are private; the rest are for-hire. The total investment in equipment by for-hire carriers (not including those on the Great Lakes) was estimated at more than 2 billion dollars in 1971.[2]

[1] See John L. Hazard, *Crisis in Coastal Shipping* (Austin, Texas: Bureau of Business Research, University of Texas, 1955), pp. 13–14.

[2] American Waterways Operators, Inc., *Big Load Afloat* (Washington, D.C.: American Waterways Operators, Inc., 1965), p. 3 and American Waterways Operators, Inc., *United for Action* (Washington, D.C.: American Waterways Operators, Inc., 1972), p. 3.

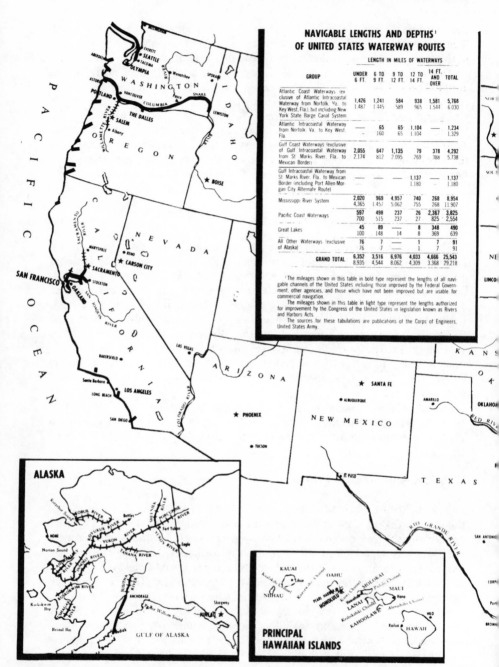

NAVIGABLE LENGTHS AND DEPTHS[1] OF UNITED STATES WATERWAY ROUTES

LENGTH IN MILES OF WATERWAYS

GROUP	UNDER 6 FT.	6 TO 9 FT.	9 TO 12 FT.	12 TO 14 FT.	14 FT. AND OVER	TOTAL
Atlantic Coast Waterways (exclusive of Atlantic Intracoastal Waterway from Norfolk, Va., to Key West, Fla.), but including New York State Barge Canal System	**1,426** 1,487	**1,241** 1,445	**584** 589	**938** 965	**1,581** 1,544	**5,768** 6,030
Atlantic Intracoastal Waterway from Norfolk, Va. to Key West, Fla.	— —	**65** 160	**65** 65	**1,104** 1,104		**1,234** 1,329
Gulf Coast Waterways (exclusive of Gulf Intracoastal Waterway from St. Marks River, Fla. to Mexican Border)	**2,055** 2,174	**647** 812	**1,135** 2,095	**79** 269	**378** 388	**4,292** 5,738
Gulf Intracoastal Waterway from St. Marks River, Fla. to Mexican Border (including Port Allen-Morgan City Alternate Route)	— —	— —	**1,137** 1,180	— —		**1,137** 1,180
Mississippi River System	**2,020** 4,365	**969** 1,457	**4,957** 5,062	**740** 755	**268** 268	**8,954** 11,907
Pacific Coast Waterways	**597** 700	**498** 515	**237** 237	**26** 27	**2,367** 825	**3,825** 2,554
Great Lakes	**45** 100	**89** 148	— 14	**8** 8	**348** 369	**490** 639
All Other Waterways (exclusive of Alaska)	**76** 76	**7** 7	— —	**1** 1	**7** 7	**91** 91
GRAND TOTAL	**6,352** 8,935	**3,516** 4,544	**6,976** 8,062	**4,033** 4,309	**4,666** 3,368	**25,543** 29,218

[1] The mileages shown in this table in bold type represent the lengths of all navigable channels of the United States including those improved by the Federal Government, other agencies, and those which have not been improved but are usable for commercial navigation.

The mileages shown in this table in light type represent the lengths authorized for improvement by the Congress of the United States in legislation known as Rivers and Harbors Acts.

The sources for these tabulations are publications of the Corps of Engineers, United States Army.

FIGURE 12-1 Waterways of the United States. (Source: American Waterways Operators, Inc. Published i... from data supplied by U.S. Army Corps of Engineers)

WATERWAYS OF THE UNITED STATES

COMMERCIALLY NAVIGABLE
WATERWAYS
OF THE
UNITED STATES

CONTROLLING DEPTHS

9 FEET OR MORE
UNDER 9 FEET
AUTHORIZED EXTENSIONS

PUBLISHED 1976 BY
THE AMERICAN WATERWAYS OPERATORS, INC.
1600 WILSON BOULEVARD • SUITE 1101
ARLINGTON, VA. 22209

Compiled from Information Supplied by
CORPS OF ENGINEERS, U.S. ARMY

These for-hire barge operators are generally small in size. The carriers on the Mississippi River all have annual revenues of less than 25 million dollars. Of 185 domestic water carriers regulated by the Interstate Commerce Commission (ICC) in 1976, 104 had annual operating revenues of less than $100,000.[3] Carriers in Great Lakes, coastal, and intercoastal nonbarge service tend to be larger than barge operators, however. The investment and revenue figures discussed below also indicate a relatively small average-size domestic water carrier.

COST STRUCTURE

Way

The waterway used by water carriers is furnished either by nature or by nature with the assistance of government paid-for improvements. On the river system, for example, these improvements include straightening and deepening rivers and construction and operation of dams and locks, as well as harbor improvements such as channel dredging and building of breakwaters. The water carrier thus avoids the large investment needed to provide a way, the payment of a large fixed return on that investment, amortization or depreciation of that investment, and the large maintenance costs and property taxes associated with ownership of a way. In addition, with the exception of vessels using the Panama Canal and the St. Lawrence Seaway, where tolls are collected and are a variable cost to the carrier, carriers are not required to pay any charges for the use of the way and hence have no way expense at all. Water carriers pay certain taxes to government, but they are taxes that any business is expected to pay, such as corporate income taxes and property taxes, and are not unique to water carriers. The proceeds from these taxes are not dedicated to a specific purpose, such as providing waterway improvements.

Terminals

Water freight terminals are places where goods are transferred to and from barges or other vessels and where barges are assembled into tows (a collection of barges moving together with one tow boat). In the river trade, line-haul tow boats often deliver to or pick up barges from a local operator of a smaller tow boat who does the actual pickup and delivery of barges at the place of the shipper or receiver. This allows the larger line-haul tow boat to operate between terminals only where it is most efficient.

Domestic water carrier terminals may be operated by carriers, but they are usually provided by government (usually local) or by users ("private" terminals). For example, some terminals are owned by municipal governments and other terminals are owned by large users such as grain firms and power companies that have sufficient water carrier traffic to justify having their own river terminals. Carriers sometimes have office and/or maintenance facilities of their own in some of the ports that they serve.

---

[3] Interstate Commerce Commission, *Annual Report, 1976* (Washington, D.C.: U.S. Government Printing Office, 1975), p. 141.

At inland public terminals the carrier must usually pay for loading and unloading and for other services provided by the terminal and, of course, must pay the operating costs of the vessel while in port. At ocean ports there are loading and unloading costs and charges for various services rendered by the terminal. In addition, there may be various charges for entering a harbor, for example, pilotage, mooring, dockage, and harbor master fees. Because loading and unloading costs in water transportation can be very high for nonbulk freight, domestic water carriers are at a cost disadvantage when competing for that kind of traffic, and it is an important reason for the predominance of bulk traffic, which can be loaded and unloaded more efficiently and cheaply, in all domestic water carrier trades. Loading and unloading charges and other terminal costs tend to vary with the amount of traffic carried and are largely a variable cost.

Terminal costs, whether fixed or variable, are to a great extent common because they are incurred to provide transportation service for various kinds of traffic.

Vehicles

Vehicles used in domestic for-hire water transportation—ships, barges, tow boats, and other boats—are provided by the carriers through ownership or leasing. The equipment used varies with the trade. On the Great Lakes large vessels are used that are designed to handle the major bulk traffic moved there, such as grain, iron ore, taconite pellets, and coal. In deep-water coastal and intercoastal transportation large ocean-going vessels are used, along with some barges and tow boats. On the rivers and the intracoastal protected waterways the shallow draft tow boat-barge method is used. Several barges are tied together into a "tow" and are pushed by a tow boat. On the lower Mississippi, for example, 30 or 40 barges or more may make up a single tow. River traffic moves mainly in barge-load lots which range from 500-ton minimums to 1,500-ton maximums. A 40-barge tow at 1,500 tons per barge amounts to 60,000 tons or the capacity of approximately 1,200 rail boxcars.

When carriers provide vehicles through ownership, the investment in vehicles is their main item of investment. The costs associated with the vehicles are both fixed and variable. The wear and tear on the vehicles and the fuel and labor expense associated with operating vehicles may be considered variable because they are incurred in relation to the volume of traffic carried. Some vehicle costs are fixed, however, unless the number, size, and kind of vehicles can fairly easily be adjusted to meet changes in demand for service. These fixed costs include interest on the investment in a vehicle, maintenance cost not related to traffic carried, and amortization or depreciation expenses (those not related to use). Leased vehicles result in fixed leasing costs for the period of the lease. However, fuel and labor expense associated with operating the vehicles tend to be variable.

The ability of the carrier to adjust the number, size, and kind of vehicles, and hence vehicle cost, to traffic volume varies with the kind of water carrier. The barge line operator can adjust the number, size, and kind of barges operated much more easily than the intercoastal deep-water carrier can adjust his fleet of ocean-going ships.

Vehicle costs are to a great extent common because a given vehicle is often used to carry different commodities at different times or at the same time. And, as in the other modes of transportation, water carriers incur joint costs in round-trip situations.

Other Expenses

In addition to the expenses associated with way, terminals, and vehicles, water carriers incur the usual general expenses of a for-hire transportation company. These include the expenses associated with operating and maintaining office space and the salaries of managers and other administrative people not directly involved in operation or maintenance of vehicles and terminals. These expenses are largely fixed and common. And, as with other for-hire carriers, payroll and income taxes tend to vary with the amount of business done, but property taxes on terminals and other fixed location facilities are fixed because their levels have no relation to traffic volume. If state and/or local taxes are levied on vehicles, these taxes tend to be fixed or variable, depending on how easy it is to adjust the vehicle number and size to the demand of service.

Large Variable Costs

Although it is difficult to generalize about water carrier costs because of the several different kinds of carriers and vessels involved in the various trades in the industry, the costs incurred by for-hire domestic water carriers tend to be highly variable, although less variable percentagewise in the short run than is true of highway carriers. The high variable costs are due to the lack of large fixed costs associated with the way and to the fact that water carrier terminal costs are largely variable. A large porportion of variable costs is particularly true of those water carriers that can adjust the fleet size and character to meet the changes in demand for their services. As with trucking companies, then, water carriers have a large proportion of costs that are variable (though not as large percentagewise as trucking companies), except for very short periods of time and one-vehicle operators, even in what is the short run for railroads. This, in turn, means that as a water carrier adds traffic, his costs also increase since variable costs are high and he does not have the railroads' advantage of sharply declining average costs per unit of traffic carried as traffic volume increases. However, water carriers enjoy decreasing fully distributed costs per unit of traffic carried as volume increases more than motor trucking companies do.

Excess Capacity

Water carriers in general have a less difficult time with excess capacity than do railroads because water carriers have no investment in way and, should excess capacity develop in the way, its burden does not fall on the water carrier. They also have a minimum terminal investment. The problem of excess vehicle capacity in water transportation varies among the different water carrier trades, depending on how easily vehicle capacity can be adjusted to changes in the demand for service. Operators of large ocean-going and Great Lakes vessels have a more difficult time adjusting to changes in demand than do barge line operators on the river system.

In addition, all water carriers must deal with the problem of unbalanced traffic patterns and some must deal with government economic regulation, both of which can cause overcapacity, although overcapacity caused by regulation is not a general problem because most domestic for-hire water carrier traffic is unregulated.

MARKET STRUCTURE

Because of the different characteristics that prevail in the different water carrier trades, and the lack of information about many carriers, it is not possible to generalize on the market structure of domestic water transportation. Barge operators in all trades are fairly large in number and are generally small in size and there is some service differentiation between them. Thus, they have the general characteristics of monopolistic competition. Nonbarge carriers in the coastal, intercoastal, and Great Lakes trades tend to be smaller in number and larger in size than barge operators and there is some service differentiation. Therefore, they can be considered to approximate oligopoly. Any individual market segment situation could, of course, have the characteristics of either monopolistic competition or oligopoly, or both, or even monopoly in any of the water carrier trades.

In any case, rates charged by competing water carriers tend to be identical because of the large number of carriers and/or the lack of substantial service differentiation, the influence of the "conference" method of pricing in the coastal and intercoastal trades whereby groups of carriers set rates collectively, the rate bureau method of pricing elsewhere, and economic regulation, where regulation exists.

As with other modes of transportation, the market structure characteristics of the water carrier industry are influenced by intermodal competition if such competition prevails.

PRICING

Differential Pricing

It has been indicated previously that the motivations for differential pricing are large proportion of fixed costs and substantial continuing excess capacity. Water carriers have neither of these characteristics. As to other characteristics that lead to differential pricing, some water carriers carry a fairly wide variety of commodities, but most domestic water carriers carry a limited number of bulk commodities. Lastly, some larger domestic water carriers serve large geographic areas with many routes and origin and destination points and have opportunities to differentiate between points. Many water carriers do not serve large areas.

Thus, in terms of cost structure and excess capacity, differential pricing does not appear to be suitable to for-hire water carriers. As to variety of commodities carried and size of geographic area served, these factors vary from carrier to carrier so that differential pricing is more suitable to some than to others.

Nevertheless, water carriers in the United States have generally adopted the differential pricing approach. The principal reason for this is that water carriers consider railroads to be their chief intermodal competitor, with the the exception of water carriers of petroleum and its products, a major competitor of theirs being the oil pipelines. Therefore, water carriers have usually geared their pricing to what railroads do—water carriers often charge a rate lower than the competing rail rate—and, since railroads use differential pricing, water carrier rates tend also to follow a differential pattern. Because a large proportion of water carrier costs are variable, water carriers find it difficult to charge rates much below fully distributed costs and still stay above variable costs. Nevertheless, this has not been a serious handicap because water carrier costs are low in general, and even a rate that covers their fully distributed costs may be below the competing rail rate which may, in turn, be below the railroad's fully distributed costs.

Domestic common water carriers compete with other modes of transportation, particularly railroads, with other water common carriers, with water contract carriers, and with private water carriers. Because of the service disadvantages associated with water transportation, for-hire water carriers ordinarily must charge rates lower than other modes. Because of the lack of economic regulation of most water carrier traffic, water carrier rates fluctuate widely in response to competition, the demand for service, and the supply of vehicular equipment.

The rates charged by contract or "charter" domestic water carriers are the result of negotiation between carrier and shipper and normally involve the use of the entire vessel. The rates are sometimes greatly influenced by the cost of private water carriage because contract carriage is often a substitute for private carriage. For both common and contract carriers by water, the tendency for many larger shippers to enter into private water carriage has meant that the ceiling on for-hire water carrier rates is sometimes the cost of private carriage to the user.

Freight Classification

Domestic water carriers do not have a freight classification system of their own. However, water carriers generally make use of the rail freight classification and sometimes the highway carrier classification when class rates are to be used. Most water carrier traffic, however, moves on commodity rates.

INVESTMENT TRENDS

Domestic water transportation is a less capital intensive industry than is railroad transportation, although it is more so than highway transportation. The lack of need of large amounts of capital is because water carriers need not invest in a way and the terminal investment is minimal. However, the investment in vehicles can be substantial. A modern river tow boat can cost several million dollars. The cost of a barge varies with size and kind—dry cargo, tank, open hopper, and so on—but can be over $150,000. The cost of an ocean-going ship or a vessel to operate on the Great Lakes can be very high. The fact remains, however, that the avoidance of an investment in a way makes the industry much less capital intensive than the railroad industry. As noted earlier, the Association of

American Railroads (AAR) has stated that the investment required per dollar of revenues in 1973 was only $.80 for barge lines while it was $2.17 for railroads.[4]

The total carrier investment in for-hire domestic water carrier facilities in the United States is small relative to rail and highway transportation. However, the exact amount of investment is unknown because many domestic water carriers are not subject to economic regulation and, therefore, are not required to report investment information. Various estimates have been made. The Transportation Association of America has estimated that in 1968 the investment of both regulated and unregulated water carriers on the river and canal system was 755 million dollars and of Great Lakes operators 270 million dollars.[5] The American Waterways Operators, Inc. has estimated that in 1971 the investment in equipment of all domestic for-hire barge operators (excluding those on the Great Lakes) was over 2 billion dollars.[6]

The ICC reported that 66 Classes A and B (annual revenues over $100,000) inland and coastal waterways carriers under its jurisdiction had a total net investment in transportation property and working capital of 579.9 million dollars in 1975 with an average investment of approximately 8.8 million dollars per carrier. Their capital turnover was 1.24.[7]

TRAFFIC TRENDS

Freight Traffic

In Table 10-2 it was shown that the rate of growth in intercity ton-miles carried by water carriers operating on the rivers and canals of the United States (including coastal protected waterways) has been substantial since 1939, increasing from 3.7 per cent of the total intercity ton-miles carried in 1939 to 10.4 per cent in 1973 and 11.6 per cent in the recession year of 1976. The actual ton-miles carried increased from 20 billion in 1939 to 232 billion in 1973 and 250 billion in 1976.

Domestic traffic moved on the Great Lakes, however, increased only slightly in the period since 1939, from 76 billion ton-miles in 1939 to 126 billion in 1973 and down to 102 billion in 1976, and the Great Lakes share of all intercity ton-miles carried actually declined from 14 per cent in 1939 to 4.7 percent in 1976. The reasons for the lack of growth in domestic Great Lakes traffic include the decline in the volume of iron-ore traffic from the Lake Superior region to the steel mills on the lower Great Lakes, the disappearance of nonbulk or "packaged" freight traffic, and the fact that some traffic that was once counted as domestic traffic is now counted as international traffic because it moves directly out of or into the country via the St. Lawrence Seaway instead of being handled partly by lake boats before or after the international part of the journey.

---

[4] Association of American Railroads, *Railroads in the Cost Spiral* (Washington, D.C.: Association of American Railroads, 1973), p. 5.

[5] Transportation Association of America, *Transportation Facts and Trends*, 13th ed. (Washington, D.C.: Transportation Association of America, July, 1977), p. 28.

[6] American Waterways Operators, Inc., *United for Action*, p. 3.

[7] Based on data in Interstate Commerce Commission, *Annual Report, 1976*, p. 148.

The difficulties of intercoastal and deep-water coastal water carriers in the post-World War II period were referred to earlier. These carriers have continued to be unable to recapture the place they occupied in domestic transportation prior to 1940. Domestic deep-sea traffic, not shown in Table 10-2, decreased from 242 billion ton-miles in 1939 to 223 billion ton-miles in 1975.[8]

Table 12-1 contains a summary of traffic carried in tons by larger domestic water carriers regulated by the ICC. The table shows that these carriers increased the total tonnage carried from 103.9 million tons to 150.4 million tons in the period 1957 to the recession year of 1975, a gain of 44.8 per cent. However, the traffic in the several different trades changed quite differently, with all except the Great Lakes and Mississippi River trades showing declines in tonnage. The most serious decline was in the Atlantic and Gulf Coast trade—62.7 per cent. The Mississippi River system, however, enjoyed a substantial increase in tonnage carried of 119.9 per cent, while the Great Lakes had a minor increase of 6.3 per cent.

The share of 1975 traffic carried in the different trades also shows the dominance of river traffic. Thus, the Mississippi River and tributaries accounted for 71.7 per cent of the tonnage and 74.1 per cent of the ton-miles carried by A and B carriers in that year.

The data in Table 10-2 include the traffic of both private and for-hire intercity water carriers operations. The data in Table 12-1 cover regulated for-hire operations of larger interstate carriers only. It is difficult to say exactly what share of domestic water carrier traffic is carried by for-hire carriers, although private or "proprietary" or "industrial" transportation is fairly extensive, particularly on the Great Lakes. It is estimated that, measured in ton-miles, only .4 per cent of Great Lakes traffic, 16.5 per cent of river and canal traffic, and 6.3 per cent of domestic deep-sea traffic in 1974 was subject to federal economic regulation.[9] The overall percentage in 1974 was only 8.7 per cent.[10] Much of the remaining traffic was private. As noted previously, approximately 400 of the 1,700 water carriers operating barge service in the river and canal, Great Lakes, and coastal trades are private carriers.

Because of the service and rate characteristics of domestic water transportation, and the high loading and unloading costs associated with nonbulk traffic, the kind of traffic carried tends to be large shipments of heavy medium-value and lower-value bulk commodities that can be loaded and unloaded mechanically and which move over fairly long hauls. These commodities include petroleum products, chemicals, grain and other agricultural products, coal and other products of mines, sand, gravel, stone, forest products, and some semifinished and finished products. The result is that the average revenue per ton-mile received by for-hire domestic water carriers is low relative to that of other modes. Table 12-2 shows that the average revenue per ton-mile of the larger carriers regulated by the ICC was approximately two-thirds of one cent in 1974. The revenue per ton-mile varies somewhat from trade to trade. In 1970, for example, the average (in cents) for all A and B carriers was $.43 but was $.89 for Atlantic and Gulf Coast carriers, $1.34 for Pacific Coast carriers, $.90 for

[8]Transportation Association of America, *Transportation Facts and Trends*, p. 8.
[9]*Ibid.*, p. 9.
[10]Interstate Commerce Commission, *Annual Report, 1976*, p. 143.

TABLE 12-1 Classes A and B* Water Carrier Traffic 1957–1975 (1,000 tons)

Year	Number of Carriers	Atlantic and Gulf Coasts	Pacific Coast	Intercoastal	Great Lakes	Mississippi River and Tributaries	Total
1957	116	13,782	19,442	4,244	17,354	48,992	103,814
1962	100	10,367	17,536	1,977	19,274	58,965	108,119
1967	89	7,254	18,375	1,507	22,598	81,436	131,171
1972	78	3,525	17,664	2,486	17,564	121,019	162,254
1973	76	4,348	17,832	3,350	18,452	115,667	159,649
1974	73	3,616	17,606	3,239	18,523	116,785	159,769
1975	71	5,141	15,827	3,224	18,452	107,720	150,364
Percentage Change 1957–1975		-62.7	-18.6	-24.0	6.3	119.9	44.8
Ton-miles Carried 1975 (000)		1,441,767	2,048,919	8,946,578	8,391,835	59,523,966	80,353,065
Percentage Share of Tons Carried 1975		3.4	10.5	2.1	12.3	71.7	100.0
Percentage Share of Ton-Miles Carried 1975		1.8	2.6	11.1	10.4	74.1	100.0

*Those with annual revenue of over $100,000.

Source: Adapted and calculated from Interstate Commerce Commission, Bureau of Economics, *Transport Economics*, various issues (Washington, D.C.: Interstate Commerce Commission).

TABLE 12-2 *Classes A and B* Water Carrier Average Revenue per Ton-Mile[†] 1964-1974 (cents)*

Year	Revenue per Ton-Mile
1964	.45
1966	.43
1968	.40
1970	.43
1972	.47
1974	.68

*Those with annual revenue of over $100,000.

[†]Average revenue per freight ton-mile = $\dfrac{\text{total freight revenue}}{\text{total number of freight ton-miles carried}}$.

Source: Interstate Commerce Commission, Bureau of Economics, *Transport Economics,* Volume III, Number 2, 1976 (Washington, D.C.: Interstate Commerce Commission, 1976), p. 4.

Intercoastal carriers, $.37 on the Great Lakes, and $.30 on the Mississippi River and tributaries.[11]

Passenger Traffic

Domestic passenger transportation by water is an unimportant element in the total domestic passenger transportation picture. In 1976 it amounted to 4 billion intercity passenger-miles, which was only .3 per cent of all intercity passenger-miles carried and 2.1 per cent of all for-hire intercity passenger miles carried.[12] This traffic consists mainly of excursion and ferry boat traffic.

REVENUE TRENDS

The increasing volume of freight traffic carried in some domestic water transportation trades has resulted in increased revenue. Annual revenues of all domestic water carriers (including some passenger revenue) regulated by the ICC increased from 131 million dollars in 1947 to 850 million dollars in 1975.[13] In 1975 the freight revenues of 71 larger regulated carriers totaled 615 million dollars and were distributed among the different trades as shown in Table 12-3.

The table indicates that the revenues received increased approximately 88 per cent for all carriers but declined after 1957 in the Atlantic and Gulf trade until 1975. Revenues were stable in the Great Lakes trade until 1974 and 1975 when they increased. Revenues in the period increased moderately in the erratic intercoastal trade. The Pacific Coast trade showed an overall increase of over 23 per cent after declining in 1974 and 1975, while revenues on the Mississippi River

[11] Interstate Commerce Commission, Bureau of Economics, *Transport Economics,* February–March, 1971 (Washington, D.C.: Interstate Commerce Commission, 1971), p. 13.

[12] Transportation Association of America, *Transportation Facts and Trends,* p. 18.

[13] *Ibid.,* p. 6.

TABLE 12-3 Classes A and B* Water Carrier Revenue Trends, 1957–1975 (000)

Year	Number of Carriers	Atlantic and Gulf Coasts	Pacific Coast	Intercoastal	Great Lakes	Mississippi River and Tributaries	Total
1957	116	$52,577	$31,730	$107,676	$30,077	$104,508	$326,568
1962	100	49,177	30,451	48,051	26,894	99,755	254,328
1967	89	35,175	29,737	39,552	25,989	119,436	249,889
1972	78	17,168	58,579	95,188	26,571	222,634	420,140
1973	76	19,870	60,054	129,898	30,052	229,618	469,492
1974	73	22,993	44,415	167,044	39,444	322,588	596,484
1975	71	42,858	39,170	174,070	45,030	314,360	615,488
Percentage Change 1957–1975		–18.5	23.4	61.7	49.7	200.8	88.5
Percentage Share of Revenue 1975		6.9	6.4	28.3	7.3	51.1	100.0

*Those with annual revenue of over $100,000.

Source: Adapted and calculated from Interstate Commerce Commission, Bureau of Economics, *Transport Economics*, various issues (Washington, D.C.: Interstate Commerce Commission).

system increased almost 221 per cent. The reader will note that the revenue changes are not always in the same proportion or direction as the traffic changes shown in Table 12-1 and that the distribution of revenue among trades is not the same as the distribution of traffic. Thus, in 1975 the Mississippi River system accounted for approximately 51 per cent of the revenues earned by the carriers covered in Table 12-3. This is considerably less than the share of freight traffic carried there, the difference being a result of the low revenue per ton-mile on the river system.

A calculation of the average revenue received per A and B carrier in Table 12-3 in all trades shows that it was 2.8 million dollars in 1957 and 8.7 million dollars in 1975.

The operating ratio of larger domestic water carriers operating on the inland and coastal waterways is usually approximately 88, somewhat less than for motor trucking companies where it is normally approximately 95. In 1975 the return on net investment of 66 large carriers regulated by the ICC operating in the inland and coastal waterways was almost 16 per cent.[14]

SERVICE CHARACTERISTICS

Domestic water transportation, particularly on the rivers, has become a very important part of our transportation system, with Great Lakes and river traffic together accounting for 17 per cent of all domestic intercity ton-miles of freight carried in 1975. As with other modes of transportation, water transportation offers various rate and service advantages and disadvantages.

Completeness of Service

Unless a user is located on a waterway, complete or door-to-door service is ordinarily not possible, because the water carrier usually does not provide pickup and delivery service to and from the waterway terminal. This must be arranged for by the user. This adds to the cost of water transportation because the cost of moving freight to and from the waterway is borne by the user. It also adds to the inconvenience of using water transportation. The lack of a complete door-to-door service limits the attractiveness of water transportation to the user not located on a waterway.

Cost

The principal advantage water transportation offers to the user is low cost. As indicated in Table 12-2, the average revenue per ton-mile received by domestic water carriers is very low in comparison with rail and highway transportation. The low revenue per ton-mile results from the fact that domestic water carriers carry mainly bulk commodities in large quantities which pay only relatively low rates. At the same time, the water carrier can charge these low rates because, first, the carrier has no way expense. Second, the tractive effort required to move weight by water at slow speeds is less than by rail or highway and hence

[14] Interstate Commerce Commission, *Annual Report, 1976*, p. 148.

requires less horsepower and energy. Third, because of the large tonnages that can be handled with a single tow boat or other power unit, the manpower and other costs required per ton or ton-mile carried is less than it is for railroads and trucking companies. Finally, terminal costs may be high for some water carriers, but they are offset by low line-haul operating costs, which means that ton-mile costs drop significantly with distance and with shipment size for such carriers.

In addition to low rates, water transportation can save a shipper or receiver money by providing cheap storage. This idea is based on the fact that because water transportation is slow and the goods are in transit a long time, the service may provide users with what is in a sense a free form of storage. This can be taken advantage of successfully by a user if it is properly integrated into the user's overall logistics system.

Slow transportation may be considered by some users as a negative cost factor because it requires larger inventories at shipping and receiving points and, in addition, the costs of carrying inventory, including the interest on the investment involved, continue while the goods are in transit and the longer the time in transit prior to delivery the higher the inventory costs will be. Also, since water transportation is a less frequent service than other forms of transportation, it necessitates larger inventories for users.

In addition, as noted above, water transportation is geographically inflexible because it can serve only where there is a waterway, and if a user is located away from a waterway, then it is necessary to bring freight to and from the waterway. The cost of doing so is borne by the user and is not covered in the low water carrier rate.

Terminal costs incurred at public terminals for storage or other services or the cost of operating a private terminal must also be taken into account by the user.

Also, since many river and coastal water routes are winding instead of direct and since the intercoastal routes are very long, there are more miles between origin and destination points than is true with more direct forms of transportation; hence, although ton-mile cost is low by water, more ton-miles are frequently required.

Finally, because water carriers assume very little liability for loss and damage to commodities while in transit, as noted in Chapter 6, when a user is concerned about the possibility of loss or damage, it is well for him to purchase insurance to cover that risk. This cost must be borne by the user.

The result is that although water carrier rates are low, there are other costs that must be taken into account in measuring the true cost of water carriage. Despite these considerations, water transportation is a low-cost form of transportation and attracts users interested in low costs.

Time

It was mentioned above that water is a slow form of transportation. Although under the right circumstances, particularly when lockages are not required, water transportation can compare favorably time-wise with rail service, water transportation is slow. On the river system, for example, because the normal slow speed of water transportation in transit is slowed further by the need to make up and break up tows of barges and by delays at locks, the origin to destination speed averages 6 miles per hour (the barge operators achieving higher speeds when running with the current and lower speeds when running against the current). Overall speed is further reduced because rivers are circuitous. Slow speed presents problems for many users of transportation in terms of cost, customer needs, and so on, and it is a leading reason why water transportation is not used. In addition, water transportation service is generally less frequent than that of other modes.

Flexibility

An important disadvantage of water transportation is its geographic inflexibility. It can operate only where there is a waterway of some sort. Therefore, its ability to serve is usually limited to users located on or near a waterway. It is also inflexible in that it operates very large-capacity vehicles that take considerable time to load and unload and the variety of equipment available to users is more limited than in rail and motor truck transportation.

However, water transportation is flexible in the sense that it can carry larger size shipments than other modes and has a broader capability than any other mode in what it can carry.

Interchanging of Freight and Equipment

Interchanging of freight and equipment between domestic water carriers often takes place where line-haul carriers interchange with local tow boat operators who perform local pickup and delivery of barges. Interchanging between two or more water carriers in the line-haul, however, is rare. This is caused in part by the fact that most water carrier traffic is not under government economic regulation and, therefore, not subject to restrictions as to where an individual carrier can serve, i.e., since an unregulated carrier can serve anywhere there is a waterway, there is no need for him to interchange freight with other water carriers. At the same time, because of the lack of economic regulation of most water carrier traffic, there is no way in which government can force most water carriers to interchange, although the ICC has the power to do so for regulated common water carriers.

Dependability and Seasonality

Water transportation is much more affected by weather conditions than are railroads. In addition to storms and high winds, water carrier weather problems include droughts and floods that may interrupt service. A principal disadvantage of water transportation is its seasonality. In the northern part of the country water routes are unusable 3 to 4 months during the winter. Although there are experiments with and discussion of de-icing the waterways in the north so that year-round water transportation would be possible (there has been some success in doing so in the upper Great Lakes), the seasonal factor remains an important disadvantage of water transportation. For the user, a 3- to 4-month shutdown means that he must use a different and, perhaps, less suitable and/or more costly form of transportation during those months, or he may concentrate all of his transportation in the months when the waterways are open, but this results in accumulating and holding extensive inventories (such as taconite pellets or iron ore in Minnesota and at the steel mills on the Great Lakes) during the cold months at considerable expense.

Water carriers assume very little liability for loss of or damage to what is carried. However, because of the bulk nature of what is carried, its lack of fragility, and the fact that much of it is impervious to action by the elements (coal, iron ore, sand, etc.), the loss and damage problem is not serious in domestic water transportation. However, when nonbulk traffic is involved, especially at ocean ports, loss and damage can be serious, particularly the problem of theft.

The federal Department of Transportation (DOT) study among manufacturers referred to in Chapters 10 and 11 found a higher level of satisfaction among respondents for water carrier service than for railroad service, although the level of satisfaction was at a lower level than for highway and air transportation. The performance measures used were on-time delivery and loss and damage.

Because of the several service characteristics discussed in the preceding paragraphs, domestic water transportation is a realistic alternative mainly for shippers and receivers of lower- or medium-value bulk commodities moving in large volume and that are not very susceptible to loss and damage and for users located on waterways who are not too concerned about speed of service.

Service and Rate Innovations

There has been a fair amount of technological change in domestic water transportation in the post-World War II period. This includes completion of the dieselization of tow boats on the rivers (in place of steam) with its greater productivity, greater horsepower for tow boats and other power units, and larger vehicle carrying capacity. Tow boats of over 10,000 horsepower are now in use on the river system. The size of barges has also increased, but barge size is limited by the size of the locks on the river and canal system. The ore boats on the Great Lakes and the vessels used in coastal and intercoastal service are also much larger than they were in the past.

Water carriers have also made use of various electronic and power devices to improve steering and navigation efficiency, have added better communications systems, have improved hull design, have introduced lighter and stronger steel, have improved loading and unloading equipment, have developed containerization, and have added more specialized vehicles to their fleets.

Other developments include the use of "LASH" (lighter aboard ship) and "Seabee" ships in ocean commerce that carry barges used in harbor areas and on the rivers (the barges are transferred to and from the larger ships for the ocean part of the journey). Another innovation is the miniship (self-propelled vessel of approximately 3,000 ton capacity), which is being tried on the lower Mississippi River. Containerships built specifically to carry truck trailers and/or containers have been developed in the deep-water domestic trade. There have also been improvements in the waterways themselves, for example, in extending navigation to new areas, constructing larger locks, and ice breaking and de-icing waterways in the northern part of the country. In addition, there has been port development for container and bulk commodity handling.

ENVIRONMENT AND ENERGY

Environment

The environmental problems associated with domestic water transportation have to do with disruption of wild life habitats and natural water flows caused by lock and port construction and dredging of channels, water pollution caused by waste disposal from vessels, and water pollution caused by cargoes contaminating waterways as a result of leakages and collisions and other accidents involving vessels. The United States Army Corps of Engineers and other government agencies have been giving greater attention to these problems than in the past and some legislation has been enacted to reflect this concern.

Energy

Studies of the efficiency of use of energy in transportation have shown that the inland waterways are more energy efficient per ton-mile at slow speeds than are railroads and highway carriers, except when railroads are operating heavy unit trains.[15] However, the circuity of the rivers and the coastal routes means that there are more miles between origin and destination points than in more direct forms of transportation. Therefore, although energy consumption per ton-mile is low by water, more ton-miles are frequently required. A basic reason for the greater energy efficiency per ton-mile of water transportation over other modes is that the tractive effort required to move a given amount of weight by water at slow speeds is less than by either rail or highway. Thus, the American Waterways Operators, Inc. has claimed that a 6,000-horsepower tow boat can move from 40,000 to 50,000 tons of freight while a rail 6,000-horsepower diesel locomotive can move only 6,000 tons.[16] Hence the use of petroleum and its products by domestic water carriers accounts for a relatively small part of the total transportation demand for petroleum. The Transportation Association of America estimated it at 3.8 per cent in 1975,[17] or approximately 2.1 per cent of total domestic consumption of petroleum-based energy.

Since water carriers carry vast amounts of both petroleum and its products and coal, they will be seriously affected by any major reduction in total energy consumed or any shift to or from either petroleum or coal as an energy source.

SELECTED REFERENCES

The history of domestic water transportation in the United States is discussed in D. Philip Locklin, *Economics of Transportation,* 7th ed. (Homewood, Illinois: Richard D. Irwin, Inc., 1972), pp. 91–102 and in Roy J. Sampson and Martin T. Farris, *Domestic Transportation: Practice, Theory, and Policy,* 3rd ed. (Boston: Houghton-Mifflin Company, 1975), pp. 18–21, 23–25, and 34–36.

[15] United States Railway Association, *Preliminary System Plan,* Volume I (Washington, D.C.: U.S. Government Printing Office, 1975), p. 147.

[16] American Waterways Operators, Inc., *Big Load Afloat,* p. 13.

[17] Transportation Association of America, *Transportation Facts and Trends,* p. 32.

The decline of coastal water transportation in the early post-World War II period is analyzed in John L. Hazard, *Crisis in Coastal Shipping* (Austin, Texas: Bureau of Business Research, University of Texas, 1955).

The economic characteristics of domestic water transportation are dealt with in Locklin, *Economics of Transportation,* Chapter 31. Water carrier costs and the market structure in water transportation are discussed in John R. Meyer, Merton J. Peck, John Stenason, and Charles Zwick, *The Economics of Competition in the Transportation Industries* (Cambridge, Massachusetts: Harvard University Press, 1959), pp. 111–126 and 235–238.

The domestic tow boat–barge industry is described in some detail in American Waterways Operators, Inc., *Big Load Afloat* (Washington, D.C.: American Water-Ways Operators, Inc., 1965).

13

Oil Pipeline Transportation

Transportation by pipeline is the most specialized form of freight transportation because it is limited to a few commodities and, although the overall impact of pipeline transportation on the nation's economy is considerable, only a small number of users are involved. The emphasis in this chapter is on the transportation by pipeline of crude oil and its refined products. Brief reference is also made to pipeline transportation of other commodities.

Transportation of crude oil and its products by pipeline is conducted mainly by for-hire carriers although there are a few private carriers in the industry. The for-hire carriers are common carriers and are regulated as such by the federal and some state governments. As to kind of traffic carried, oil pipelines are of two kinds: those that carry crude oil and those that carry the products of crude oil, including gasoline, jet fuel, kerosene, fuel oil, and natural gas liquids.

DEVELOPMENT OF OIL
PIPELINE TRANSPORTATION

Transportation of oil by pipeline is about as old as the oil industry itself. Oil was first discovered near Titusville, Pennsylvania in 1859. In 1865 the first successful crude oil pipeline, a 6-mile long, 2-inch diameter wrought-iron pipe, used to carry oil from the Pithole, Pennsylvania field to a railroad terminal, was placed in operation. This was followed by other lines built to connect wells with railroads or with refineries. As new oil discoveries were made, pipeline construction followed. The first major long-distance oil pipeline was completed in 1879 and by 1900 there were some 6,800 miles of interstate crude oil pipelines in the country and approximately 90 per cent of the investment made in them was by the Standard Oil Company (New Jersey) group of companies.[1] The principal product produced from crude oil in 1900 was kerosene.

Pipelines at the turn of the century were made of wrought iron. The typical diameter of the gathering lines was 2 inches. The long-distance or trunk lines were usually 5 or 6 inches in diameter. These pipelines were usually under the ownership of refineries.

After 1900 the Appalachian field declined in terms of the amount of oil produced and other oil fields in Ohio, Indiana, Kansas, Oklahoma, California, and along the Gulf Coast were developed. New pipelines were constructed in those areas to gather crude oil and to transport it to rail or water transportation connections or to carry it long distances to refineries. At the same time, the market for oil was shifting from illuminants (kerosene) to motor fuels and fuel oil. The dominance of Standard Oil disappeared (particularly after a court decision in 1911) and new oil companies entered the industry. Total pipeline mileage in the United States almost tripled between 1915 and 1931, amounting to 115,710 miles in 1931. Of this, 53,640 miles were gathering lines and 58,571 miles were crude oil trunk lines. Pipelines used to carry gasoline and other refined products of crude oil totaled 3,499 miles in 1931.

Transportation of gasoline prior to 1930 was limited because refiners had chosen to locate their refineries at the large consuming markets, bringing in crude oil from the producing areas. In addition, there were technical problems associated with pipeline transportation of gasoline. One was the fear that various grades of gasoline could not be transported simultaneously in the same pipe without considerable mixing. This problem was eventually solved and "batching" of different grades and brands of gasoline and different refined products in the same pipeline is common practice. Another problem was that of leakage and the resulting economic loss and danger of fire. Improved seamless and welded pipe and electric welding of pipe joints solved this problem.

World War II greatly accelerated the growth of and changes in the oil pipeline industry. Because of the heavy demand for petroleum and the critical role oil played in the war and because of the problems of ocean tanker vulnerability to submarine attack, Congress gave oil pipeline builders the right of eminent domain under certain circumstances, which meant that the builders had the power to take land for pipeline construction. The federal government also financed several pipeline projects, including 2 major lines, a 24-inch crude oil line from Longview, Texas to the New York-Philadelphia area (the "Big Inch" line) and a 20-inch products line which connected the Gulf Coast refining area with the New York area (the "Little Big Inch" line). Both lines were subsequently sold by the government and converted to use as natural gas lines. Other government built lines were also disposed of, either by sale or salvage. There was also an increase in pipeline mileage and capacity aside from government-sponsored construction during the war. Larger diameter pipe was used and products lines received increasing attention.

[1] A good discussion of the history of oil pipelines is in Arthur M. Johnson, *Petroleum Pipelines and Public Policy, 1906-1959* (Cambridge, Massachusetts: Harvard University Press, 1967). Unless otherwise stated, the statistics presented in this section on the development of oil pipelines are from that source.

The years immediately after World War II brought continued expansion of pipeline mileage as the demand for petroleum and its products accelerated. By 1950 there were 61,000 miles of gathering lines and 71,000 miles of crude oil trunk lines. Mileage of products lines totaled 21,000. At the same time, the shift toward large-diameter pipe continued, joint ownership of pipelines became more frequent, and improvements were made in scheduling, pumping, and remote control of pipeline movements.

Since 1950 the trend toward automated operation has accelerated and new producing areas have been added. The Rocky Mountain area, North Dakota, Montana, Utah, Arizona, Colorado, New Mexico, off-shore areas, and Alaska became involved in crude oil production. Oil from Canada became an important part of the oil pipeline development. Products lines were used for a greater variety of products, including liquified products of natural gas processing and aviation jet fuel. The addition of products pipeline mileage has been substantial. This has had important effects on the location of petroleum refining facilities. Prior to World War II the low cost of transporting crude oil and the comparatively high cost of transporting gasoline favored the location of refineries near large consuming markets. The rapid development of products lines with low transportation costs has tended to reduce the disadvantage of refineries located at the source of the crude oil.[2]

Today the United States is served by an extensive system of crude oil gathering and trunk lines and a large network of products lines. As of 1974, there were 69,266 miles of crude oil gathering lines, 76,250 miles of crude oil trunk lines, and 76,839 miles of products lines in the country.[3] Most of the gathering line mileage is 6 inches or less in diameter. Crude oil trunk lines and products lines range from 3 inches to 48 inches in diameter. Maps showing the general route patterns of crude oil trunk lines and products lines are in Figures 13-1 and 13-2.

In 1976 pipelines transported 525 billion ton-miles of crude oil and its products compared with 306 billion in 1965 and 127 billion in 1945.[4]

OWNERSHIP

With the exception of the federal government's participation in oil pipeline construction and operation during World War II, oil pipeline transportation in the United States has been left to private enterprise. Oil pipelines were started in a period (1865) when free enterprise and non participation by government were the rule. The federal government had adopted a policy of nonparticipation in "internal improvements" (although considerable federal aid was given to the first transcontinental railroad), and the states, following their unhappy experiences with ownership of railroads and canals, were not interested in further

[2]D. Philip Locklin, *Economics of Transportation*, 7th ed. (Homewood, Illinois: Richard D. Irwin, Inc., 1972), p. 609.

[3]William F. Gay, *Energy Statistics: A Supplement to the Survey of National Transportation Statistics*, prepared for U.S. Department of Transportation (Washington, D.C.: U.S. Government Printing Office, August, 1975), p. 11, Table 1-4.

[4]Transportation Association of America, *Transportation Facts and Trends*, 13th ed. (Washington, D.C.: Transportation Association of America, July, 1977), p. 8 and Association of American Railroads, *Railroad Facts*, 1977 ed. (Washington, D.C.: Association of American Railroads, 1977), p. 36.

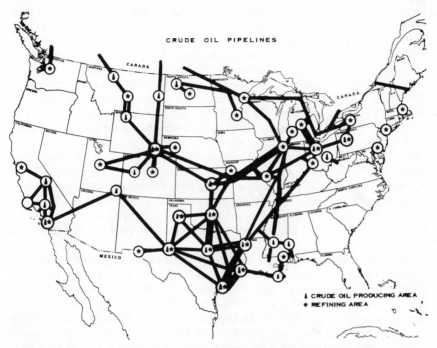

FIGURE 13-1 *Crude Oil Trunk Pipelines, 1976. (Source: Amoco Oil Company)*

FIGURE 13-2 *Products Pipelines, 1976. (Source: Amoco Oil Company)*

involvement in transportation activities. In addition, since oil pipeline transportation did not have the broad public interest nature that other modes of transportation had, government was less likely to feel reponsible for developing it.

Ownership of oil pipelines has almost always been primarily by oil refining companies. Crude oil pipelines started out as independent enterprises whose only objective was profit from transportation, but most of these were eventually taken over by the refiners who made use of them. Crude oil lines were controlled by refiners because the investment in a pipeline was large, the recovery of which depended on adequate supplies of crude oil to keep the line full and a market demand large enough to ensure a constant flow through the line. In addition, only by assuming the investment and risk of ownership of pipelines could refiners be assured of a steady, uniform quality, low-cost supply of crude oil. Finally, control of pipelines gave refiners an opportunity to control access to markets.[5] The development of ownership of products lines was similar because refiners were reluctant to develop marketing outlets without an assured low-cost, efficient products pipeline between their refinery and the marketing area.[6]

An oil producer, however, is usually not interested in providing capital for a pipeline. He prefers to convert his oil to cash and then to additional producing facilities as soon as possible. He seldom has sufficient production of his own to justify the high investment required for a pipeline and has no long-term assurance of a continuing market at the final terminal. Thus, it has become necessary for the refiner to provide the capital to construct extensions to new producing areas.[7] In modern times some oil companies are fully integrated, participating in both production and refining of crude oil and also in transportation of both crude oil and its products. There are approximately 10,000 different producers of crude oil and natural gas in the United States, but there are only approximately 130 oil refining firms.

Thus, crude oil and products lines are usually controlled by oil companies. A few lines are owned by non-oil companies; some are owned by railroad companies. It appears then that oil pipelines are more closely linked with the oil industry than with the transportation industry. Most oil pipelines are for-hire common carriers, even though many are owned by oil companies. Those owned by oil companies carry traffic for others on a for-hire basis, as well as their own traffic. A few oil pipelines owned by oil companies carry only the owning company's traffic and, therefore, are classified as private carriers. Problems associated with the ownership arrangement and arguments for divorcing for-hire oil pipelines from oil companies are discussed in Chapter 23.

Another unique characteristic of oil pipeline ownership is joint ownership, either through a corporation owned by two or more oil companies or through "undivided interest." The heavy investment required in large-diameter pipe and the fact that unit cost per barrel is less in a large-diameter pipe are the principal attractions of joint ownership. In joint ownership owners enjoy the economies of large-diameter pipe that they could not justify building just for their own traffic. The corporation form of joint ownership merely means that 2 or more

---

[5] Johnson, *Petroleum Pipelines and Public Policy*, p. 4.

[6] J. L. Burke, "Oil Pipelines' Place in the Transportation Industry," *ICC Practitioners' Journal*, April, 1964, p. 788.

[7] *Ibid.*

more oil companies establish a corporation to own and operate an oil pipeline. Undivided interest also means that 2 or more oil companies share in the ownership of a single pipeline, but each company owns a fractional undivided interest in the line. Each owner exercises full control over the traffic and rates charged on his share of the line and each owner is entitled to use the line in proportion to his ownership percentage. Allocation of costs is also based on this percentage.

NUMBER AND SIZE OF FIRMS

Oil pipeline transportation in the United States is provided by a relatively small number of fairly large firms. The large amount of capital required to enter the industry is a chief reason why the number of firms in the industry is small, plus the fact that the nature of pipelining is such that it would be highly uneconomic to have a large number of parallel lines competing for the available traffic. There are important economies of large-diameter pipe that preclude parallel pipelines because, with a full load, and other factors being equal, capacity rises more than proportionately to a given increase in diameter, while investment per mile per unit of capacity decreases, as do operating costs per barrel.[8] In other words, pipeline capacity rises rapidly with an increase in the diameter of the pipe while the required investment increases more slowly. Thus, although initial investment in a large-diameter line is larger, unit cost per barrel is lower than in a small-diameter line over the same distance. According to one writer, a 12-inch pipe can, when operating at its most economic throughput, transport 3 times as much oil as an 8-inch line, and the per barrel operating costs, not counting capital charges, for moving oil through the 12-inch line is only one-third of that of moving the same barrel through the 8-inch line.[9]

Additional factors that lead to there being a small number of firms are that oil companies are the most likely owners of oil pipelines and that the oil companies have excellent information on what traffic potentials are. This leads to the building of pipelines only when traffic volume can justify them and it keeps down the number of lines. Joint ownership arrangements, referred to earlier, also hold down the number of separate pipeline companies.

In 1976' there were 107 interstate for-hire oil pipeline companies regulated by the Interstate Commerce Commission (ICC).[10] The interstate regulated carriers account for approximately 85 per cent of the intercity ton–miles of oil pipeline traffic.[11] The balance is carried by private oil pipelines (approximately a dozen), by for-hire carriers regulated by the states, or by for-hire carriers not regulated at all.

COST STRUCTURE

The cost structure of oil pipelines is one in which fixed costs are a large proportion of the total costs.

[8] Johnson, *Petroleum Pipelines and Public Policy,* p. 3.

[9] Burke, "Oil Pipelines' Place in the Transportation Industry," p. 783.

[10] Interstate Commerce Commission, *Annual Report, 1976* (Washington, D.C.: U.S. Government Printing Office, 1976), p. 141.

[11] *Ibid.,* p. 143.

Way

The large proportion of fixed costs results from the fact that pipeline companies provide their own way by buying or leasing land and constructing pipelines and pumping stations with their own funds. This results in a large dollar investment in the way which, in turn, requires a large dollar return to investors—a fixed cost, amortization or depreciation (unrelated to the volume of traffic carried), large maintenance costs, and large amounts of property taxes. These costs are incurred to a great extent regardless of the amount of traffic carried and hence are largely fixed in nature. Unless a change in traffic volume is so great that a change in the way itself is required, the costs associated with the way tend to not change with traffic quantity changes.

The way costs of a pipeline are also to a great extent common because the way is used to produce transportation of different grades of crude oil or different refined products and different grades and brands thereof. Cost allocation to different segments of traffic is, therefore, difficult.

Terminals

Oil pipeline terminals are places where oil and its products are stored prior to or after shipment by the pipeline and where transfer from gathering line to trunk line, from refining facility to pipeline, and from pipeline to receiver takes place. These storage facilities may be provided by oil producers, refiners, or products customers. When such an investment is made by a pipeline company, the costs associated with the relatively small investment in and operation of terminals are largely fixed. These include the return necessary on the investment, amortization or depreciation (not related to the degree of use), maintenance costs, and property taxes.

Terminal costs are also to a great degree common in that a pipeline terminal is used to produce transportation service for different grades of and kinds of oil and its products. Cost allocation to different segments of traffic is, therefore, difficult.

Vehicles

Oil pipelines do not have vehicles in the usual sense of the word because the carrying unit in a pipeline operation is the pipe itself and associated pumps, which are ordinarily considered part of the way, and not as a vehicle. The fact that there is no vehicle element contributes to the high fixed costs of pipeline operation because vehicles can be a chief source of variable costs.

A significant variable cost that is avoided is that of labor cost associated with operating vehicles. This factor, plus the extreme automation that has taken place in oil pipeline operation, has resulted in a relatively small labor force compared with other modes. Automation has meant that oil pipelines of today employ a smaller number of workers than formerly to man the pumping stations on the line. Instead, electronic controls turn the motors on and off and open and close valves and fewer pumping stations are used. This change occurred as pipelines changed from steam to diesel power for pumping and finally to remote-controlled electrically powered centrifugal pumps. Oil pipelines employed only 17,000 workers in 1976, compared with 30,000 in 1947.[12]

Other Expenses

In addition to way and terminal costs, oil pipelines incur other general expenses, which include the cost of operating and maintaining office space and the salaries of managers and other administrators not involved in the direct operation and maintenance of the pipeline or its terminals. These expenses are largely fixed and common. Payroll and income taxes vary somewhat with the amount of traffic, but property taxes are fixed in nature.

Large Fixed Costs

We have indicated previously that oil pipelines have a high proportion of fixed costs. In fact, they have the largest proportion of fixed costs of all modes of transportation. The above discussion indicates that the large fixed costs stem from the need to invest in and maintain and pay taxes on a way and terminals, the lack of vehicles as such, and the relatively small amount of labor needed to operate a modern pipeline. The variable costs are mainly for the power used to move the product and the costs associated with the operation of pumping stations.

Because pipelines have a large proportion of fixed costs, they enjoy decreasing costs or increasing returns as traffic volume increases, as do railroads, because the large amount of fixed costs is spread over more units of traffic. In addition, the nature of pipeline operations is such that there are important operating economies of large-diameter pipe, as indicated earlier, that accrue when the pipe is kept full. This, plus the large fixed costs, encourages pipeline operators to seek traffic that will lower the cost per unit carried.

Excess Capacity

Oil pipelines do not have an excess capacity problem related to vehicles and they have a minimal terminal investment. However, because oil pipelines have a way in which they bear the risks of ownership, excess capacity is a problem they must deal with. Pipelines operate most efficiently when the pipe is kept full and there are diseconomies in operating at less than full capacity. The tendency in recent years toward large-diameter pipe increases the risk of having excess capacity.

The ownership arrangement in the oil pipeline industry (most for-hire oil pipelines are owned by oil refining companies) tends to reduce the risk of excess capacity because the refiner–owner can "guarantee" traffic before the line is even built, and no line is built if traffic projections do not warrant it, whereas the independent for-hire pipeline must rely on the whims of others for its traffic. In addition, the corporate and undivided interest methods of joint ownership prevent the building of duplicate lines by different oil companies and resulting overcapacity. Also, because of their one-way nature, oil pipelines do not need to face the unbalanced traffic or empty back-haul problem.

[12] Transportation Association of America, *Transportation Facts and Trends,* 12th ed., p. 23 and 13th ed., p. 23.

Nevertheless, oil pipelines do have a capacity problem to some degree. Whenever excess capacity does exist, additional traffic can be carried at very low additional cost to the carrier.

MARKET STRUCTURE

The relatively small number of fairly large carriers in the for-hire oil pipeline industry and the fact that their services are somewhat differentiated leads to the conclusion that the oil pipeline industry is one that approximates differentiated oligopoly. This situation leads to uniformity of prices charged by different oil pipeline companies, which is also encouraged by the economic regulatory system. The latter also reduces the amount of uncertainty as to the repercussions of a rate change made by an individual pipeline because of the notice period required. In addition, the small number of users and carriers, the close-knit nature of the oil industry, and the fact that users and carriers are often one and the same means that uncertainties in general are reduced.

Although the oil pipeline industry in general may be described as approaching differentiated oligopoly, the economies of operating one pipeline over a route rather than more than one (they are "natural" monopolies) result in many route situations in which a for-hire oil pipeline has no competition from other pipelines. Thus, a monopoly position is approximated. In other cases, 2 or more oil pipelines of the same kind parallel one another. In any event, the amount of oil pipeline competition faced by an oil pipeline over any particular route is usually small in terms of the number of competing oil pipeline companies.

However, oil pipelines compete against other forms of transportation in addition to their intramodal competition, and the overall intermodal market structure can vary from an approximation of differentiated oligopoly to one resembling monopolistic competition.

PRICING

Differential Pricing

The motivations for differential pricing in transportation are a large proportion of fixed costs and substantial continuing excess capacity. Since oil pipelines have a significant amount of fixed costs and have some problem with excess capacity, differential pricing appears to be suitable for them.

However, a wide variety of different commodities carried and a large geographic area served with many origin and destination points are also conditions conducive to differential pricing. Oil pipelines limit their carriage to crude oil or its products with the number of different grades and kinds relatively small, certainly less than the number of different commodities railroads or large general commodity trucking companies carry. This leads to less opportunity to differentiate between commodities than is true of railroads and some trucking companies. A given oil pipeline may serve several geographical points, but it does not usually have the extensive route system with numerous points served that a larger railroad or trucking company has and, therefore, has less ability to differentiate between places in pricing. Also, there is no opportunity to differentiate between direction of hauls because of the one-way nature of the operation.

Therefore, oil pipelines have the cost structure and to some degree the excess capacity characteristics that lead to the use of differential pricing, but the kind of traffic carried and the geographic scope of the carriers are less conducive to differential pricing. Despite the latter qualifications, however, oil pipelines make use of differential pricing, as do the other modes of transportation. In fact, according to one writer, differentiation or discrimination in the monopoly sense is more likely to be practiced by the oil pipeline industry than other modes because of the lack of competition among pipelines on many routes and the unfeasibility of using other forms of transportation.[13] This is especially true for the transportation of crude oil.

Oil pipelines quote rates on a per barrel basis (42 gallons equal 1 barrel) from point to point or zone to zone. The rates are usually on a distance basis. Minimum tender requirements are usually imposed on the shipper, meaning that shipments less than a given size (anywhere from 500 to many thousands of barrels) will not be accepted.

The major competitors of intercity oil pipelines are water carriers and railroads. A significant characteristic of oil pipeline rates is their low level, which reflect this competition, the economies of the pipeline method of transportation, and the advances in efficient operation that have been made since World War II. Because of the variety of circumstances under which transportation is performed, including different pipe diameters, different size tank cars or barges, different size tows, the circuity of some modes, different lengths of haul, and so on, it is difficult to make general comparisons between pipeline rates and rates charged by competing modes since each mode offers a range of rates depending on individual circumstances. However, recognizing these factors, oil pipelines often can carry crude oil and its products at a cost to the user per ton-mile several times less than that of railroads but at a cost often slightly higher than that of water carriers, particularly ocean tankers. A 20-inch or larger diameter pipe is said to be needed to compete price-wise with barge lines and a 24-inch or larger diameter pipe is needed to compete price-wise with ocean tankers.

Freight Classification

Oil pipelines do not make use of the freight classification device.

INVESTMENT TRENDS

Oil pipeline transportation is a fairly capital intensive industry in that fairly large amounts of capital are needed in order to provide the way and, to a minor extent, to provide terminals. On the other hand, unlike railroads that must rely heavily on rolling stock in addition to their investment in a way and in terminals, oil pipelines have no investment in vehicular equipment. The Transportation Association of America estimated that in 1968 the net investment in oil pipeline equip-

---

[13] Dudley F. Pegrum, *Transportation Economics and Public Policy,* 3rd ed. (Homewood, Illinois: Richard D. Irwin, Inc., 1973), p. 180.

ment and facilities were 3.8 billion dollars,[14] which is small relative to the total investment in railroads and in trucking companies. The ICC reported that in 1975 104 oil pipelines under its jurisdiction had a net investment in carrier property and working capital of 7.7 billion dollars, with an average investment per carrier of 73.8 million dollars.[15] This compared with the average investment per carrier of approximately 529 million dollars for Class I railroads, approximately 4.1 million dollars for larger interstate regulated trucking companies, and 8.8 million dollars per carrier for larger regulated interstate inland and coastal water carriers. These same 104 oil pipelines had a gross revenue in 1975 of 1.9 billion dollars, which means that they had a capital turnover of .41—the revenues were only 41 per cent of the investment in the industry,[16] i.e., a dollar of investment produced $.41 in revenue. This is a lower capital turnover rate than that in other modes, including railroads.

TRAFFIC TRENDS

Table 10-2 indicates that the total number of intercity ton-miles carried by private and for-hire oil pipelines has increased from 56 billion in 1939 to 507 billion in 1973 and 525 billion in 1976. In 1976 oil pipelines accounted for 24.2 per cent of the nation's intercity freight ton-mileage, compared with only 10.3 per cent in 1939. As noted previously, 85 per cent of the intercity ton-miles carried by oil pipelines are by interstate regulated for-hire carriers; the rest are by private carriers and for-hire carriers regulated by the states or not regulated at all.

The Transportation Association of America reported that in 1975 oil pipelines carried 47.9 per cent of the total petroleum tonnage (crude oil and products), while water carriers carried 22.0 per cent and motor trucks 28.4 per cent. Railroads handled only 1.7 per cent.[17] Pipelines carry approximately three-quarters of the crude oil tonnage but only one-third of the petroleum products tonnage. The local delivery of refined products is done mainly by truck which reduces the relative importance of pipelines in total tonnage transported.

The nature of oil pipeline transportation and the kind of traffic carried are such that the rates charged produce a low revenue per ton-mile. Table 13-1 shows that the average revenue received per ton-mile carried by large interstate oil pipelines was only $.32 in 1974, reflecting the efficiencies of oil pipeline operation in the face of severe inflation. The average revenue received per barrel of oil or its products carried by large interstate oil pipelines in 1975 was $.19.[18]

The stable average revenue per ton-mile in the face of steadily rising costs of construction and in operating materials, supplies, and labor has been an unusual attainment. One authority says this is attributable primarily to 3 factors:

[14]Transportation Association of America, *Transportation Facts and Trends*, 13th ed., p. 28.

[15]Interstate Commerce Commission, *Annual Report, 1976*, p. 151.

[16]Calculated from data in Interstate Commerce Commission, *Annual Report, 1976*, p. 151.

[17]Transportation Association of America, *Transportation Facts and Trends*, 13th ed., p. 32.

[18]Interstate Commerce Commission, Bureau of Economics, *Transport Economics*, Volume III, Number 2 (Washington, D.C.: Interstate Commerce Commission, 1976), p. 2.

(1) the industry's altertness to and adoption of cost reducing technical and operating improvements, (2) the steadily increasing volume of traffic, and (3) the partial isolation of pipeline costs from inflation. As to the latter point, the pipe and right-of-way represent from 80 to 90 per cent of a pipeline company's total investment. Approximately 70 per cent of operating revenue is needed to cover capital charges. Only 30 per cent of a pipeline's revenue is needed for labor, material, and other operating items. Thus, 70 per cent of a pipeline's rate is isolated from the effect of inflation. New construction is, of course, subject to cost increases.

However, the industry has, by using larger and higher strength pipe, reduced the quantity of steel needed per unit of capacity. This, combined with improved construction and operating practices, has enabled the industry to hold down cost for new capacity.[19]

Oil pipeline transportation is mainly a moderate length of haul mode with the average length of haul for federally regulated crude oil pipelines approximately 300 miles and approximately 345 miles for products lines.

REVENUE TRENDS

As the oil pipeline network has expanded and as the total traffic carried has grown, the revenues earned by oil pipeline companies have also increased. Annual revenue of oil pipelines regulated by the ICC has increased from 616 million dollars in 1955 to 1,874 million dollars in 1975, an increase of 204 per cent. Table 13-2 shows the annual revenues, expenses, operating ratio, net income, and rate of return on investment of oil pipelines regulated by the ICC in the period 1955 through 1975.

A calculation of the average revenue received per carrier included in Table 13-2 indicates that it was 8.3 million dollars in 1955 and 18.0 million dollars in

T A B L E 13-1 *Average Revenue per Ton-Mile* of Large[†] Oil Pipelines, 1947-1974 (cents)*

Year	Revenue per Ton-Mile
1947	.29
1950	.32
1955	.32
1960	.32
1965	.28
1970	.27
1974	.32

*Average revenue per ton-mile = $\dfrac{\text{total revenue}}{\text{total number of ton-miles carried}}$.

[†]Interstate regulated carriers having annual revenue of more than $500,000.

Source: Interstate Commerce Commission, Bureau of Economics, *Transport Economics,* January, 1970, p. 9 and Volume III, Number 2, 1976, p. 4 (Washington, D.C.: Interstate Commerce Commission, 1970 and 1976).

[19]Burke, "Oil Pipelines' Place in the Transportation Industry," p. 787.

1975. The operating ratio of oil pipelines is very low—in the fifties—the lowest of all modes of transportation. Net income of the industry has been growing over the years since 1955. Net income per carrier was approximately 1.8 million dollars in 1955 and approximately 4.4 million dollars in 1975.

The rate of return on investment of oil pipelines regulated by the ICC has consistently been high in comparison with that of other modes of transportation. Oil pipelines are, in fact, the most consistently profitable mode of interstate transportation, earning an adequate rate of return on investment every year. In 1975, the net operating income of 104 oil pipelines regulated by the ICC amounted to a return on net investment of 10.9 per cent. This was low compared with other recent years, as shown in Table 13-2, reflecting the economic problems of the country in the 1970's. In terms of rate of return on the value of the pipeline property (the value is determined by the ICC), which is a different kind of calculation using a base different from that used in Table 13-2, the ICC limits crude oil pipelines to a rate of return of 8 per cent and products lines to 10 per cent.

In addition to reasons discussed previously in this chapter, the financial success of oil pipelines is also due to the fact that oil pipelines are protected from much of the technological obsolescence that has plagued other industries. The technology of pipelining, i.e., the moving of liquid through a pipe, is so basic that it has not been appreciably affected by major changes in technology[20] and their resulting high costs. In addition, since the reserves in a proven oil field can be calculated reasonably well, and since refineries and population centers do not make major shifts or disappear, pipeline projects tend to be long-term, safe, and stable investments.[21]

T A B L E 13-2 *Oil Pipeline* Revenue Trends, 1955–1975*

Year	Number of Companies	Operating Revenues (000)	Operating Expenses (000)	Operating Ratio (per cent)[t]	Net Operating Income (000)[‡]	Net Income (000)	Rate of Return on Investment (per cent)[§]
1955	74	$616,154	$310,602	50.4	$305,552	$136,608	18.0
1960	82	756,331	405,466	53.6	350,865	171,684	17.0
1965	84	879,593	497,351	56.5	382,242	215,462	15.4
1970	101	1,188,254	672,336	56.6	515,918	311,852	14.2
1975	104	1,873,507	1,037,786	55.4	835,721	455,147	10.9

*Oil pipelines regulated by the Interstate Commerce Commission.

[t]Operating ratio = $\dfrac{\text{operating expenses}}{\text{operating revenues}}$. Income taxes and fixed charges are not included in operating expenses.

[‡]Operating revenues less operating expenses.

[§]Net operating income as a percentage of net investment in carrier property plus working capital. Calculated by author for 1970 and 1975.

Source: Interstate Commerce Commission, *Annual Reports,* various years (Washington, D.C.: U.S. Government Printing Office).

[20]*Ibid.*
[21]*Ibid.*

SERVICE CHARACTERISTICS

Transportation by pipeline has several unique service characteristics that are both advantageous and disadvantageous to the user. The rapid growth in oil pipeline traffic indicates that the positive aspects of oil pipeline service generally outweigh the negative aspects for users able to use pipeline service.

Completeness of Service

The nature of pipelines is such that they offer a relatively fixed route system that cannot be expected to provide a complete door-to-door service to all users. At the origin point, the shipper is usually located adjacent to the trunk pipeline or has access to it in the form of a gathering line for crude oil or a refiner-owned pipeline in the case of a refiner–shipper. At the destination point, delivery may be made directly from the trunk pipeline when the receiver is located on the line, but delivery is often made by rail or motor carrier transportation at the user's expense when the receiver is located away from the pipeline. The latter is frequently the case in the transportation of gasoline where receivers arrange to pick up gasoline at pipeline terminals in tank trunks. The inability of pipelines to provide complete door-to-door service adds to the inconvenience and cost of pipeline transportation.

Cost

A primary advantage that oil pipelines offer to the user is low cost. The cost structure of the industry, the ability to avoid substantial excess capacity, including empty back hauls, the insulation of the bulk of pipeline costs from inflation and dramatic technological obsolescence, and the application of various construction and operating advances have led to a very low cost per ton–mile carried and correspondingly low rates for the user. The low average revenue received per ton–mile is shown in Table 13-1. As indicated earlier, relative to the rates charged by its principal long-haul competitors, water carriers and railroads, oil pipeline rates are generally much lower than rail rates and are comparable to water carrier rates.

In addition to low rates, oil pipelines have a good loss and damage record, which is a cost factor. Loss and damage is low because bulk liquids are not subject to damage to the same degree that many other products are and because of the low possibility of mishap in a pipeline operation.

Another positive cost factor is that pipeline transportation may provide a cheap form of storage to the user because of the slow speed involved. However, the slow speed of pipeline transportation leads to larger inventories and associated higher cost than would be the case with a faster mode of transportation. The regular user must be willing and able to have a substantial amount of inventory constantly in the pipe.

A cost advantage in using oil pipeline transportation is the avoidance of the costs associated with providing loading and unloading facilities and demurrage and detention charges resulting from using rail and truck transportation. However, there also may be demurrage charges per barrel per day involved with pipeline transportation if a consignee does not accept delivery in accordance with the time limits provided in the pipeline tariff.

Other user costs associated with pipeline transportation may include special terminal services for which additional charges are made, including storage and blending.

Time

As indicated above, oil pipelines provide a relatively slow service, averaging from 3 miles to 5 miles per hour, somewhat slower than water and rail transportation. However, the slow speed in miles per hour is offset in part by the continuous nature of the service. Pipelines operate 24 hours a day and 7 days a week. In addition, pipeline routes are more direct than are many competing water and rail routes. Also, since a pipeline is almost always in operation, it offers the user greater frequency of service than is offered by other modes. To the extent that oil pipeline service is slow, however, shippers and receivers must carry larger inventories than if the service were faster.

Flexibility

Oil pipeline transportation by its very nature is somewhat inflexible because it does not serve as large a geographic area or as wide a number of points as do some other modes, and it is locked into a given, very inflexible route structure because of the need to construct a way and the high cost of adding mileage to the system (although it is more flexible in adding mileage than is water transportation). Pipeline transportation is also unable to carry many commodities (by restricting service to oil and its products, only a small number of users are involved), it is limited to one-way service only, and its economies are present primarily with large shipments, leading to large minimum-size shipment requirements.

Interchanging of Freight

Although interchanging of traffic between oil pipelines is more limited than in railroad transportation, it does take place. Thus, crude oil may move through the lines of several pipeline companies before it is delivered to its final destination. A measurement of quantity and a test of quality are made at each pipeline junction where custody is transferred. To the extent that interchanging is limited, the service capability of the industry is also limited and makes complete pipeline service unavailable to some users.

Dependability

Oil pipeline transportation is the most dependable of the 5 modes because pipelines are virtually unaffected by weather and mechanical failures are infrequent—they are not subject to the delays that affect other modes.

As to loss and damage, oil pipelines have an excellent record in this regard, as noted previously. When loss or damage occurs, the carriers assume liability for the full loss and no extra charges are levied for assuming this liability. They are liable unless one of the exceptions to liability, discussed in Chapter 6, is present.

Service and Rate Innovations

Oil pipelines, as noted previously, have been very progressive in applying new technology to their operations, although the basic technology of moving liquid through a pipe remains unchanged. The technical advances made include the adoption of larger diameter pipe and new kinds of steel for pipe; improved communications, scheduling, pumping, and remote control of pipeline movements; improved construction methods; better storage tanks, valves, fittings, gauges, and meters; and various welding and anticorrosion techniques. These improvements have been accompanied by a long-run downward trend in the revenue received per ton-mile carried in real terms, i.e., when changes in price levels are taken into account. It may be concluded that oil pipelines have been able to accomplish greater productivity and provide better service to the public as time passed.

In addition to continuous technical improvements such as those listed above, more revolutionary technological developments now taking place have to do with expanding the use of long-distance pipeline transportation to liquid or solid commodities other than oil and its products, natural gas, and water. For example, pipelines are used to carry anhydrous ammonia liquid fertilizer between origin points in Louisiana and Texas and destination points in several midwest states. Although the carriage of solid commodities by pipeline has been experimented with since the 1850's, there have not been any significant developments until recently. Great progress has been made with the slurry method which has been used for some solid commodities. The best example is the transportation of coal via the slurry method whereby coal is pulverized and mixed with water. The slurry is then pumped through the pipeline. A successful, 108-mile, 10-inch coal-carrying pipeline operated in Ohio between 1957 and 1963 and in 1971 an 18-inch line began operation in Arizona and Nevada over a distance of 273 miles. In both cases, the idea was to connect a coal mining area with an electric power plant where the coal is dried out sufficiently to burn. The objective has been to secure transportation costs less than the prevailing rail charges. Other similar coal-carrying lines are being planned. In addition to the long-distance coal lines, short-distance slurry lines have been used successfully to carry gilsonite and limestone in the United States and other commodities in other countries.

In addition to the slurry method of pipeline transportation of solid commodities, experimentation has been done with carrying solid commodities in capsules or with the product itself cast into spheres or cylinders, or slugs (the commodity is compressed to form a slug—no container or capsule is needed). The capsule, sphere, cylinder, or slug is propelled through the pipe by water or some other liquid commodity or by air (using a wheeled capsule). Possible candidates for carriage by pipeline via the slurry or other methods are iron concentrate, phosphate rock, various mineral tailings, copper concentrate, potash, nickel, ore, coke, wood chips, solid waste, iron ore, grain, fertilizer, sulphur, potassium chloride, mail, packages, gypsum, asbestos, aluminum, and lead/zinc concentrate.

Although the technological problems associated with expanding long-distance pipeline transportation to new commodities are probably solvable, it does not mean that pipelines will one day take over most intercity traffic because, despite the efficiency of pipeline operation, the economics are such that pipeline transportation is not appropriate in most situations because pipeline operation requires that a very large volume of traffic be consistently shipped between two points. In other words, the line must connect a large supply with a large demand. Otherwise, the economies of pipeline operation cannot be attained. In addition, the traffic must be in one direction only. Most commodities do not meet these requirements. However, to whatever extent long-distance pipeline transportation of additional commodities develops, the losers will be railroads and water carriers, because, most certainly, bulk commodities will be involved. The concern of railroads in this matter is evidenced by their opposition to the growth of solid pipelines, particularly in connection with granting them right of way through railroad property. For example, the railroad industry is strongly opposed to the proposal that Congress grant the right of eminent domain to coal slurry pipelines that would carry western coal to eastern and other markets. Such opposition will have to be overcome if solid pipelines are to develop to any substantial degree.

ENVIRONMENT AND ENERGY

Environment

The environmental problems associated with oil pipelines have to do mainly with the effect of pipeline construction on wild life, noise levels, water tables, and vegetation. In addition, there is concern about potential breaks in an operating oil pipeline that can cause land and water pollution. There are neither air nor noise pollution, little visual pollution, and no social problems because pipelines are underground in populated areas.

Some important environmental issues surrounding oil pipelines were raised in connection with the construction of a new crude oil pipeline across Alaska. Intended to tap the large crude oil reserves on the north slope of Alaska, the 48-inch line is approximately 800 miles long and connects the north slope with the port of Valdez on the southern coast of Alaska. At Valdez the oil is transferred to tanker ships for carriage to the west coast of the United States and elsewhere. First proposed in 1969 as a joint undertaking by 8 oil companies, the pipeline was opposed by environmentalists on several grounds. These included the possible negative effect of the above ground portions on the migration of caribou and other wild animals, the rather high frequency of earthquakes in the area which could cause breaks in the line, disruption of the permafrost (land that is less than 32°F for two or more years) and consequent erosion, the unstable condition of the permafrost causing below ground portions of the line to break as warm oil warms up the ground immediately surrounding the pipe, possible oil spills as oil is tranferred to ships at Valdez, and possible collision between ships in the harbor that could result in pollution of the water.

After several years of delay and certain environmental protection guaranties made by the builders of the line, in November, 1973 Congress, by statute, made it possible for the line to be built after it had been held up in federal courts. Construction began in 1974 and the first section of pipe was set in place in early 1975. The line was completed in 1977. The 1973-1974 energy shortage helped to get Congressional approval.

Similar environmental issues are associated with slurry and solid product pipelines with the additional problem of the large use of water as a propellant in water-scarce areas.

Energy

The energy shortage that became apparent with the Arab embargo in 1973-1974 will have major impact on the United States oil pipeline industry. Oil pipelines themselves are efficient users of energy and their energy consumption per ton-mile is slightly better than that of railroads, except when railroads are operating heavy unit trains.[22] The amount of energy consumed by oil pipelines is a very small part of the total transportation consumption.

Because oil pipelines are a major energy carrier, however, they will be very much affected by changes in energy sources and consumption. Declining oil production in some parts of the country, increased or decreased reliance on imported oil and petroleum products, Canada's refusal to ship oil to the United States in the future, and new Alaskan and outer continental shelf production will all work to alter the oil pipeline system. Coal slurry pipelines may grow as coal is increasingly used as an energy source instead of petroleum. This and any other substitution of other energy sources for oil will have the effect of reducing oil pipeline traffic, as will government measures (tax and/or price increases and/or allocation and rationing programs) designed to discourage the consumption of oil and its products.

SELECTED REFERENCES

The most complete discussion of the history, organization, and government policy toward oil pipelines is Arthur M. Johnson, *The Development of American Petroleum Pipelines: A Study in Private Enterprise and Public Policy, 1862-1906* (Ithaca, New York: Cornell University Press, 1956) and Johnson, *Petroleum Pipelines and Public Policy, 1906-1959* (Cambridge, Massachusetts: Harvard University Press, 1967).

The economic characteristics of oil pipelines are dealt with in D. Philip Locklin, *Economics of Transportation,* 7th ed. (Homewood, Illinois: Richard D. Irwin, Inc., 1972), Chapter 26. The cost characteristics and market structure of the industry are discussed in John R. Meyer, Merton J. Peck, John Stenason, and Charles Zwick, *The Economics of Competition in the Transportation Industries* (Cambridge, Massachusetts: Harvard University Press, 1959), pp. 126-133 and 225-227.

The economic and operating characteristics of oil pipelines are given detailed treatment in J. L. Burke, "Oil Pipelines' Place in the Transportation Industry,"

[22] United States Railway Association, *Preliminary System Plan,* Volume 1 (Washington, D.C.: U.S. Government Printing Office, 1975), pp. 147-148.

ICC Practitioners' Journal, April, 1964. Operations of oil pipelines are discussed in Fred F. Steingraber, "Pipe Line Transportation of Petroleum and Its Prodcuts," in Stanley J. Hille and Richard F. Poist, Jr., eds., *Transportation Principles and Perspectives* (Danville, Illinois: Interstate Printers and Publishers, Inc., 1974).

Transportation of solid commodities by pipelines is reviewed in Erik J. Jensen, "Capsule Pipelining—Potential Applications," *Proceedings of Transportation Research Form, 1973.* Slurry pipelines are dealt with in G. M. McLaughlin, "Applications, Technology, and Economics of Slurry Pipelines," *The Logistics and Transportation Review,* Volume 8, Number 3, 1972. The Black Mesa coal slurry line in Arizona and Nevada is described in Richard Bickerton, "Black Mesa: Issues and Answers," *Transportation and Distribution Management,* November, 1972.

14

Air Transportation

Air transportation is the newest form of for-hire transportation and dates from the middle 1920's. Primarily a carrier of passengers instead of freight, air transportation today dominates the intercity for-hire passenger transportation market.

Air transportation is conducted by both private and for-hire carriers. The private sector is usually referred to as *general aviation* and is devoted almost entirely to passenger service. There is very little private transportation of freight. General aviation consists primarily of pleasure flying, although a number of business firms also operate airplanes. It also includes commercial (such as crop dusting and survey work) and instructional flying.

Most for-hire air transportation is common carriage, although there is a fair amount of contract carriage as well.

DEVELOPMENT OF AIR TRANSPORTATION

Although the airplane dates from the early 1900's and played a part in World War I, for-hire air transportation of any consequence did not really begin until the 1920's. The war produced thousands of flyers and considerable technological change. The early post-war period was the era of stunt flying, aerial shows, sightseeing flights, and the beginning of aerial photography. Air mail service was started by the federal government in military aircraft and later in aircraft owned by the Post Office Department, but for-hire air transportation of passengers and freight on a regular and reliable basis was not developing. Instead, a very disorganized and somewhat unsafe situation existed. The Kelly Act, passed in 1925, provided that the United States Post Office Department would contract with private companies to carry mail by air and that the carriers would be required to provide facilities for the transportation of passengers. The federal government stopped operating its own planes in 1927, except for a brief period in 1934. The contract system with private companies had the effect of stimulating the development of for-hire air transportation of passengers and freight.

Progress, however, was rather slow, and on the eve of World War II the for-hire air transportation system of the country was still relatively undeveloped with technological and safety problems a serious drawback.

World War II provided a great boost to the development of the industry. Airline traffic increased substantially because of the war. Air power was a major factor in the war, and many Americans flew as either military personnel or as civilians and others worked in aircraft manufacturing plants. The result was a much greater awareness of and familiarity with airplanes and greater acceptance of them by the general public after the war than before the war. In addition, the war brought about many technological advances in airplanes that were adapted for civilian aircraft after the war, thus making a significant leap forward in the performance and safety of for-hire airline aircraft and the quality of service provided to the public.

Since World War II, for-hire air transportation of passengers has had a tremendous rate of growth. The period has seen the introduction of several new aircraft, including the advanced piston engine aircraft of the late 1940's and the 1950's, the first turbo-propeller aircraft of the 1950's, the first pure jets of the late 1950's and early 1960's, and the wide-bodied or jumbo jets of 1969 and afterward. The route mileage served by for-hire airlines expanded greatly in the period and new kinds of scheduled air carriers entered the market, including all-cargo carriers, local service airlines, and third-level (air taxi and commuter) airlines. Airlines came to dominate the for-hire intercity transportation of passengers, and air freight service expanded. In 1939 for-hire air transportation carried .8 billion passenger–miles which was only 2.3 per cent of all for-hire intercity passenger miles carried. As seen in Table 10-4, in 1970 air carriers carried 109.5 billion for-hire passenger–miles, which was 73.1 per cent of the total, and by 1976 the figures were 152.3 billion and 79.5 per cent. On the freight side, although air cargo traffic has grown rapidly over the years, it is still a small percentage of all private and for-hire intercity freight traffic carried. Table 10-2 indicates that air carriers handled only .2 per cent of all intercity freight ton-mileage in 1976.

The number of general aviation aircraft grew from 70,600 in 1959 to 181,600 in 1976 and the number of airline aircraft from 1,900 to 2,260.[1] The route structure of domestic trunk and local service airlines is shown in Figures 14-1 and 14-2. In 1976, 631 airports in the United States received scheduled airline service.[2]

OWNERSHIP

Unlike many other countries, the United States has relied exclusively upon private ownership of its for-hire airline service. Although the involvement of federal, state, and local governments in air transportation via airway, airport, and

---

[1] Air Transport Association, *Facts and Figures About Air Transportation, 1960*, p. 12 and *Air Transport 1977*, p. 28 (Washington, D.C.: Air Transport Association, 1960 and 1977).

[2] Air Transport Association, *Air Transport 1977*, p. 28.

other promotional programs is heavy, as is its involvement in the form of government regulation, the operation of aircraft in for-hire service is accomplished by private citizens. By the time air transportation arrived (after 1900), the tradition of nongovernment ownership of for-hire carriers was well-established in the United States and, also, air transportation did not appear to be of vital concern to the nation's welfare at the time and, apparently, no serious consideration was given to government ownership.

NUMBER AND SIZE OF FIRMS

Most for-hire air transportation is conducted by a small number of firms of a wide variety of sizes. The Civil Aeronautics Board (CAB) categorizes the for-hire air carriers that it regulates as shown in Table 14-1. The two major categories are domestic trunk lines that serve between major traffic centers and over major traffic routes and local service airlines that serve primarily between small cities and between small cities and larger cities with some long-haul major traffic routes as well. The nature of the other categories is obvious from the designations given in the table.

The total number of carriers in Table 14-1 is only 51 and, since there is double counting between the domestic trunk and international categories, the actual number of different companies listed is only 41. In addition to the kinds of carriers listed in Table 14-1, in 1976 there were approximately 4,100 air taxi (third-level) operators registered with the CAB restricted to the use of light aircraft (aircraft with up to 30 seats and a payload capacity of up to 7,500 pounds) of which there were 200 commuter airlines that provided mail and/or scheduled passenger or cargo service. The others provided nonscheduled passenger or cargo service.[3] Commuter airlines operate mainly between small cities and between small cities and larger cities. They serve over 500 points in the country. Finally, there are approximately a dozen scheduled intrastate air carriers not regulated by the Board. The bulk of the for-hire air traffic is carried, however, by the carriers in Table 14-1, with the domestic trunk lines making up the backbone of the United States domestic airline system.

The small number of regulated air carriers is caused, in great part, by the entry control system administered by the CAB (to be discussed in Chapter 23). There also are higher entry costs than in, say, motor trucking. These include high cost of aircraft and the need for maintenance and other ground facilities.

The size of the for-hire air carriers varies considerably. Of the trunk lines in 1976, the size in terms of total annual operating revenue from all airline operations, including domestic and international operations, ranged from 2.6 billion dollars for United to 439 million dollars for National. Allegheny, the largest local service airline, also had revenue of 439 million dollars, while Air New England, the smallest, had revenue of 15 million dollars.[4]

Of the 15.2 billion dollars in operating revenue of the 11 domestic trunk lines (including international revenue) in 1976, almost 12 billion dollars, or 78.7 per

[3] Civil Aeronautics Board, *Annual Report, 1976* (Washington, D.C.: U.S. Government Printing Office, 1976), p. 16.

[4] Air Transport Association, *Air Transport 1977*, p. 24.

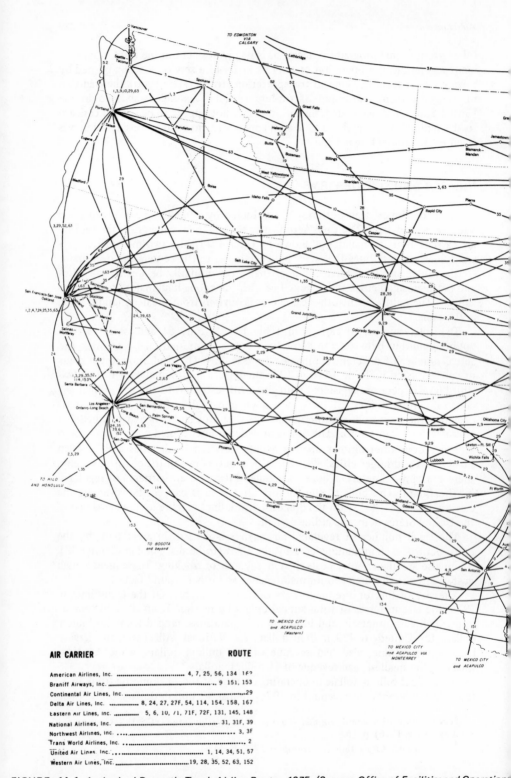

FIGURE 14-1 *Authorized Domestic Trunk Airline Routes, 1975. (Source: Office of Facilities and Operations Aeronautics Board)*

288

UNITED STATES AIR TRANSPORTATION SYSTEM
ROUTES CERTIFICATED TO TRUNKLINE CARRIERS
AUGUST 31, 1975

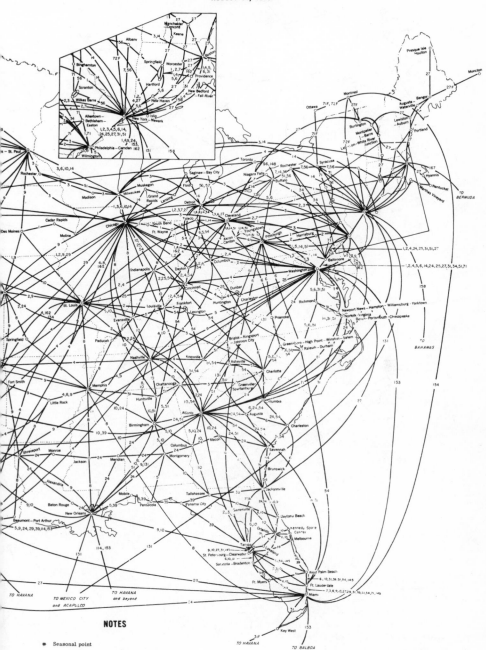

NOTES

※ Seasonal point

Route descriptions are based on certificate
as issued and do not purport to represent
flights permissible by non-stop operations.

All points to which the holder's authority has
been suspended under Section 401 (g) of the
Act, have been deleted from the Carrier's
route description.

CIVIL AERONAUTICS BOARD
OFFICE OF FACILITIES AND OPERATIONS

289

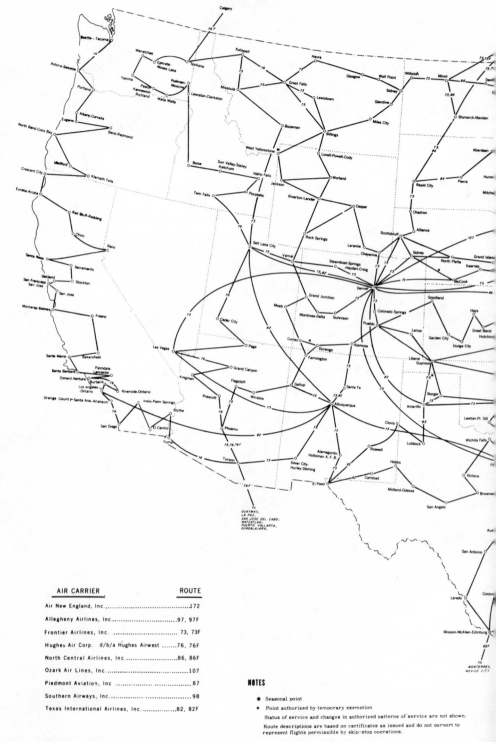

FIGURE 14-2 *Authorized Local Service Airline Routes, 1975. (Source: Office of Facilities and Operation Aeronautics Board)*

UNITED STATES AIR TRANSPORTATION SYSTEM
ROUTES CERTIFICATED TO LOCAL SERVICE CARRIERS
AUGUST 31, 1975

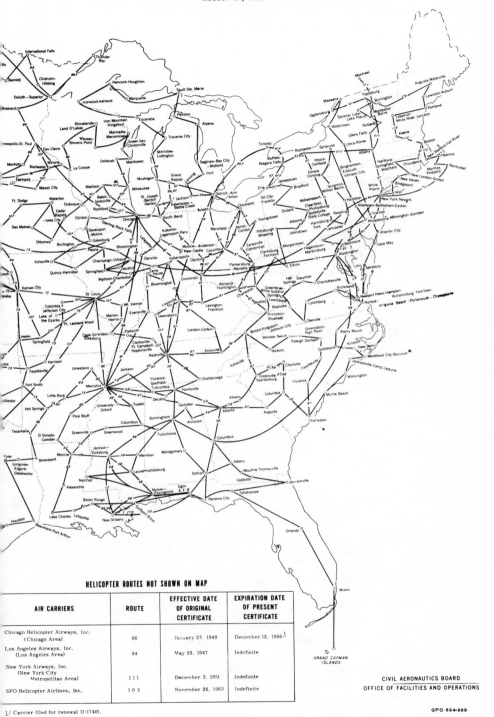

HELICOPTER ROUTES NOT SHOWN ON MAP

AIR CARRIERS	ROUTE	EFFECTIVE DATE OF ORIGINAL CERTIFICATE	EXPIRATION DATE OF PRESENT CERTIFICATE
Chicago Helicopter Airways, Inc. (Chicago Area)	96	January 23, 1949	December 12, 1966 [1]
Los Angeles Airways, Inc. (Los Angeles Area)	84	May 20, 1947	Indefinite
New York Airways, Inc. (New York City Metropolitan Area)	111	December 3, 1951	Indefinite
SFO Helicopter Airlines, Inc.	103	November 26, 1963	Indefinite

1/ Carrier filed for renewal D-17401.

To
GRAND CAYMAN
ISLANDS

CIVIL AERONAUTICS BOARD
OFFICE OF FACILITIES AND OPERATIONS

GPO 894-989

T A B L E 14–1 *United States Airlines Regulated by the Civil Aeronautics Board, 1976*

Scheduled		Nonscheduled
Domestic Trunk	Helicopter	Supplemental (charter)
American	Chicago Helicopter Airways	Capitol International
Braniff International	New York Airways	Evergreen International
Continental	San Francisco and Oakland	McCulloch International
Delta	Helicopter Airlines	Modern
Eastern	All-Cargo	Overseas National
National	Airlift International	Saturn*
Northwest	Flying Tiger	Trans International*
Pan American	Seaboard World	World
Trans World	International and Territorial	
United	American	
Western	Braniff International	
Local Service	Continental	
Air New England	Delta	
Allegheny	Eastern	
Frontier	National	
Hughes Airwest	Northwest	
North Central	Pan American	
Ozark	Trans World	
Piedmont	Western	
Southern		
Texas International		
Intra-Hawaiian		
Aloha		
Hawaiian		
Intra-Alaskan		
Alaska		
Kodiak-Western Alaska		
Munz Northern		
Reeve Aleutian		
Wien Air Alaska		

*Trans International purchased Saturn in 1976.

Source: Civil Aeronautics Board.

cent, was earned by the 6 largest carriers. Put another way, the total revenue of all the scheduled carriers listed in Table 14–1 in 1976 was 17.5 billion dollars, of which almost 12 billion dollars or 68.3 per cent, was earned by the 6 largest carriers.[5] The total domestic revenue of the 11 trunk lines in 1976 was more than 7 times that of the local service airlines. Similar statements can be made about traffic carried, investment, and other factors. The conclusion to be drawn is that the bulk of for-hire air transportation traffic is carried by a relatively small number of firms, and within that small number a still smaller number dominates.

General aviation operations by business firms (private carriage) are usually

[5] Calculated from *Air Transport 1977*, pp. 13 and 24.

confined to larger firms. It is estimated that general aviation accounts for 7.1 per cent of intercity air passenger miles.[6]

Air carriers have been heavily dependent on *indirect* carriers for freight and express traffic. These indirect air carriers have been air freight forwarders (defined later in this chapter) who provide considerable freight traffic to the airlines and REA Express which, until recently, provided pickup and delivery and other ground services for air express (very small shipments requiring expedited service) for all scheduled airlines. When REA Express went out of business in 1976, the status of air express service became uncertain.[7]

COST STRUCTURE

Way

Unlike surface carriers, air transportation does not have a way in the sense of a fixed physical roadbed or right of way. However, aircraft do make use of traffic control facilities designed to prevent accidents, and part of the system involves assigning air space to aircraft over a designated route, as well as control of traffic into and out of airports. This *airway system,* as it is called, is used by all kinds of aircraft (for-hire, general aviation, and military) and is provided and operated by the federal government through the Federal Aviation Administration (FAA). As will be seen later, aircraft operators contribute toward paying for the airway system through a system of user charges.

Because of the lack of an investment in a way, and the avoidance of the associated necessary return to investors and amortization or depreciation, maintenance costs, and property taxes, airlines and other aircraft operators avoid the large fixed costs usually associated with ownership of a way. Instead, the user charges paid by aircraft operators to help pay for the airway system are in the nature of a variable cost because they tend to increase and decrease with the volume of traffic carried.

The way costs incurred by airlines are common in the sense that they are incurred in order to provide transportation of different passengers and/or different kinds of cargo traffic. Cost allocation to different segments is, therefore, difficult, particularly when the same aircraft carries both passenger and cargo traffic simultaneously.

Terminals

Airline passenger terminal facilities are places where passengers purchase tickets, transfer between aircraft and airlines, and board and depart from aircraft and where waiting is done by passengers and visitors. Air cargo terminals are places where cargo is collected after local pickup and prior to line-haul by air, where transfer of cargo between airlines takes place, where cargo is held for local

---

[6]Transportation Association of America, *Transportation Facts and Trends,* 13th ed. (Washington, D.C.: Transportation Association of America, July, 1977), p. 18.

[7]See Chapter 23 for further discussion of this.

delivery after line-haul air service, and where cargo is picked up by local delivery trucks. Terminals may also include aircraft maintenance facilities.

Airports used by commercial airlines are provided by government. Charges are levied against airlines in the form of landing fees and rental and lease fees of various kinds for their use of the landing field, terminal building, and other physical facilities. In some cases, such as a long-term lease, the costs to the airline tend to be fixed. In other cases, such as landing fees and short-term rental agreements, the costs tend to be variable with traffic volume. In addition, some airlines operate cargo terminal facilities off airport property. The expenses associated with them tend to be incurred regardless of the volume of traffic handled, at least for short periods of time. In both passenger and freight terminal operations, labor costs tend to be at least partly variable.

Consequently, airline terminal costs are a blend of fixed and variable costs, the proportions varying with the nature of the particular airline's operation and the length of the lease or rental agreements and the amount of actual investment an airline makes.

Terminal costs are common, of course, because they are incurred to provide transportation service to different kinds of passengers and cargo. Cost allocation to different segments of traffic is, therefore, difficult.

Vehicles

Because of their great expense, their susceptibility to technological change, and their influence on service capability and on competition between airlines, the vehicles used by commercial airlines are a critical area of decision making, more so than for other modes of transportation. An incorrect aircraft choice can be devastating to an air carrier.

Aircraft expense is a large cost item for an airline company; a wide-bodied jet aircraft can cost well over 20 million dollars, including spare parts. Conventional jet aircraft, such as the Boeing 727, can cost approximately 7 million dollars, including spare parts. However, the number of aircraft needed is relatively small because of the large carrying capacity and high speed of modern jet aircraft. As noted earlier, there are only approximately 2,300 aircraft in use by scheduled United States airlines, compared with approximately 182,000 general aviation aircraft. Nevertheless, the single most important cost element for an airline is vehicles.

Aircraft are provided by the carriers through ownership or leasing (sometimes joint between 2 or more carriers). The aircraft used vary with the category of carrier. Thus, domestic trunk lines mainly use standard size (such as Boeing 707's and 727's) and wide-bodied (such as the McDonell–Douglas DC-10 and Boeing 747) aircraft; local service airlines use smaller jets (such as the DC-9) plus some turbo-propeller and piston engine airplanes. Aircraft may be purchased new or used. They may be purchased outright or under a credit arrangement with the manufacturer. Airlines frequently borrow from banks and insurance companies in order to buy aircraft.

The costs involved in ownership and operation of aircraft are both fixed and variable. The wear and tear on the aircraft and the fuel and labor expense associated with their operation may be considered variable because they are incurred in relation to the volume of traffic carried, to the extent that traffic volume dictates the number of flights made. For a given number of flights, however, the costs associated with operating the aircraft may be considered fixed, as long as the number of flights do not change. Some aircraft costs are fixed regardless of changes in the number of flights, unless the number, size, and kind of vehicles used can fairly easily be adjusted to correspond to changes in the volume of traffic. These fixed costs include interest on the investment in a vehicle, maintenance costs not related to degree of use, amortization or depreciation expense (not related to amount of traffic carried), and property taxes when the levy is not related to degree of use. There are limits as to how easily airlines can add to or subtract vehicles. Over a long period of time these adjustments can probably be made, thus resulting in vehicle costs that are largely variable. Leased aircraft results in fixed leasing cost for the period of the lease. However, fuel and labor costs associated with operating leased aircraft tend to be variable—they vary with the number of flights.

Vehicle costs are to a great extent common because a given aircraft is often used to carry different passengers and/or cargo at different times or at the same time. Airlines also incur joint costs in round-trip situations.

Other Expenses

General expenses incurred by an airline include the costs of operating and maintaining office space and paying the salaries of administrative personnel not involved in the operation of aircraft and terminal operation and maintenance. These general expenses are largely fixed and common. Payroll and income taxes are generally variable, but real estate property taxes are fixed in nature. Taxes on aircraft may be considered fixed or variable, depending on how they are levied and to what extent the vehicle fleet is adjustable.

Large Variable Costs

As with other modes of transportation in which there is no investment in way (highway and water carriers), airlines have a large proportion of variable costs, although less variable as the investment in ground facilities, such as aircraft maintenance bases, increases over time. The degree of variability is affected by the ability of the carrier to adjust the aircraft fleet to meet changes in demand for airline services. While airline costs can be reduced or increased as service is reduced or increased, for a *given level of service* costs do not vary much with traffic changes because the cost of operating an aircraft between two points depends only to a limited degree on whether the aircraft is full or empty. The same terminal facilities must be provided, the crew will be the same, and the fuel expense will be nearly the same, regardless of whether the plane carries one passenger or a planeload.[8] However, except for very short-run situations in which the level of service is fixed and for one-aircraft operators, airlines have a large proportion of variable costs, but a smaller proportion than for motor trucking companies. A major contributor to the large variable costs is the large amount of and high price of labor used in airline operations, a cost that tends to be variable.

[8]John B. Lansing, *Transportation and Economic Policy* (New York: The Free Press, 1966), p. 314.

Except in the very short run, then, as an airline adds traffic, it also adds cost and the carrier does not enjoy the benefits of sharply decreasing fully distributed costs per unit of traffic as more traffic is carried.

Excess Capacity

Airlines in modern times have been very much concerned about the excess capacity problem. It is impossible for any carrier of passengers to sell every seat offered for sale to the public because it is impossible to expand and contract the number of seat-miles available to conform with variations in the demand for seat-miles. Carriers of passengers in all modes usually are plagued with serious problems of peaks and valleys in traffic during a 24-hour period, within a week, and within a year, more so than are carriers of freight, and these peculiarities lead to an excess capacity problem. Airlines are no exception to this. Although airlines have no excess capacity problem connected with the way, they do have it in connection with vehicles and terminals. Demand for air transportation of passengers varies at different hours of the day, during different days of the week, and during different weeks and months of the year. During a typical nonholiday week, for example, the peak traffic periods are Sunday afternoon and evening, Monday morning, and Friday afternoon and evening, periods that correspond with the needs of businessmen for air transportation. During the other periods of the week airlines are faced with an off-peak situation in which there are often more seats than can be sold. But the carriers must provide the capacity necessary to carry the peak-load traffic, and it is not feasible to expand and contract the number of flights to correspond with these changes in traffic volume in the very very short run. The result is overcapacity in the off-peak periods. There is also the usual unbalanced traffic problem of traffic in one direction being greater or less than traffic in the opposite direction on the same route. There is also excess capacity caused by the need to move airplanes to where the traffic is so that a route that has little traffic may be served with an excess number of flights and seats in order to get airplanes to the destination point where there is substantial traffic to be carried to some other point.

These usual problems of passenger carriers have been accentuated in the airline business in recent years by the addition of new aircraft that has greater seating capacity and speed, federal government policy that has led to too many carriers on some routes, the tendency for airlines competing between a given set of points to schedule too many flights, the leveling off of growth in demand for air passenger service, and government economic regulation that prevents deep price cutting that would eliminate competition. Thus, United States domestic airlines have an excess capacity problem. It is normal for them to sell only approximately one-half of the seat-miles offered to the public. In 1976, for example, domestic trunk lines had a passenger load factor (number of seat-miles sold/number of seat-miles available) of 55.8 per cent for domestic service, while local service lines had a passenger load factor of 52.9 per cent.[9] The excess capacity problem of United States domestic airlines is a leading reason for the preponderance of promotional fares in the recent past designed to stimulate traffic during off-peak periods.

[9] Air Transport Association, *Air Transport 1977*, p. 9.

On the air freight side, a general overcapacity situation exists for both passenger-freight "combination" carriers and for all-cargo carriers. In the 12 months ending June 30, 1973, trunk lines had an air freight load factor of 52.7 per cent and all-cargo airlines had an air freight load factor of 60.1 per cent, both in domestic service only. All other air carriers had a load factor of only 47.9 in domestic service.[10]

MARKET STRUCTURE

There are several thousand for-hire air carriers in the country, including air taxi and commuter airlines. However, the relatively small number of carriers in the for-hire regulated scheduled airline sector, which carries the bulk of domestic airline passenger and cargo traffic, the fact that a very large part of scheduled airline traffic is carried by only 6 large carriers, and the fact that the services offered by different airline companies are somewhat different indicate that the domestic airline industry is mainly one approaching differentiated oligopoly. The strict entry control carried out by the federal government has a lot to do with this situation. The oligopolistic character of the industry, plus government economic regulation of rates and fares, leads to uniformity of prices charged by competing airlines. Government regulation also reduces the amount of uncertainity in pricing by requiring a notice period before a fare or rate change can go into effect.

Although an approximation of differentiated oligopoly appears to be the general market structure characteristic of domestic airlines, there are some routes where only one scheduled regulated air carrier serves, thus having a monopoly of scheduled air transportation service on that route. Such routes are still common among local service airlines where traffic to and from small cities is too light to justify having more than one carrier; 52 per cent of the routes served were monopoly routes in 1972. Monopoly routes are becoming relatively small in number among trunk lines; monopoly traffic was only 23 per cent in 1972.[11] There are, however, many trunk line routes where only 2 air carriers compete. The proportion was approximately 48 per cent in 1972.[12] In any event, the amount of scheduled airline competition faced by a particular scheduled airline over a particular route is usually small in terms of the number of carriers involved.

It should also be mentioned that scheduled regulated airlines sometimes compete against supplemental (charter) airlines and commuter airlines, against the private automobile, and against other modes of for-hire transportation, although the collapse of rail passenger service and the limited service provided by the National Railroad Passenger Corporation (Amtrak) has reduced considerably the amount of intermodal competition in the for-hire passenger market. The over-

---

[10] Civil Aeronautics Board, *Annual Report, 1973*, p. 96.

[11] Civil Aeronautics Board, Bureau of Operating Rights, *The Domestic Route System: Analysis and Policy Recommendations* (Washington, D.C.: Civil Aeronautics Board, 1974), Appendix A, Tables 10 and 11. See also George W. Douglas and James C. Miller, III, *Economic Regulation of Domestic Air Transport* (Washington, D.C.: The Brookings Institution, 1974), p. 113.

[12] Civil Aeronautics Board, *The Domestic Route System*, Appendix A, Table 10.

all intermodal market structure varies from an approximation of differentiated oligopoly to one similar to monopolistic competition.

PRICING

Differential Pricing

Although airlines are not a high fixed-cost industry, they do have a substantial problem of excess capacity that leads to differential pricing. However, there are definite limits to the number of categories into which passengers can be placed for pricing purposes and the number of different commodities carried in air freight service is somewhat limited, thereby limiting the opportunity to differentiate between different segments of traffic. Some airlines do, however, serve large geographic areas and a large number of origin and destination points between which differentiation may be practiced. In any event, United States domestic airlines make use of differential pricing in both the passenger and freight markets, although to a more limited extent than is found in railroad freight and in motor trucking pricing. Illustrations of differential pricing in the passenger market are found in the various promotional fares in effect at off-peak times and differences in fares over different routes of equal distances.

In the case of combination passenger–freight airlines in which both kinds of traffic are carried in the same aircraft simultaneously, the freight traffic is often considered a byproduct of the passenger service, i.e., the airline is mainly a carrier of passengers and invests in aircraft and other facilities for that purpose and, by doing so, also creates carrying capacity for freight in the "belly" of the aircraft. Because the aircraft will be flown with or without the freight traffic, carriers sometimes believe that only those costs specifically attributable to carrying freight should be assigned to freight traffic for pricing purposes, rather than assigning to freight traffic a share of all the costs incurred. Such byproduct pricing can lead to much lower freight rates than would be the case if another approach to pricing were taken.

Both passenger fares and freight rates are closely related to distance with some tapering. Passenger fares are quoted as a flat amount from airport to airport for the journey. Freight rates are quoted from airport to airport in cents per 100 pounds. Freight rates vary at different weight breaks (levels at which the rate per 100 pounds decreases as the weight of the shipment increases—such as 100, 500, 1,000, 3,000, 5,000, and 10,000 pounds) and minimum charges are usually applied on small shipments. The air freight rate structure also includes general commodity rates, specific commodity rates, charter rates, density requirements, and mixed shipment rules. Air freight rates are usually initiated by individual carriers; there are no rate bureaus in domestic air transportation, although the majority of domestic air freight tariffs are published by a single tariff publishing organization. Air express or priority service rates are both door-to-door and airport-to-airport in cents per 100 pounds.

Because of the wide separation in service characteristics between air and surface transportation and the high costs per unit of traffic incurred by airlines, airline pricing has usually been practiced without much reference to the costs of surface transportation, private or for-hire. There has usually been no way, for example, that an airline could try to charge the same rates per 100 pounds as a competing truck line because airline costs are so high. The best that can be done is to try to keep air fares and rates as low as possible.

Fares and rates charged on charter flights are generally lower per seat–mile or per ton–mile than for scheduled service. Charter service is the sale of the capacity of an entire aircraft to a single user for the movement of passengers or freight, often for one trip or one round trip only. Charter service may be provided by a scheduled airline or by a supplemental, nonscheduled airline.

Freight Classification

Different United States airlines have tried various versions of freight classification on a limited basis in the period since 1938. Currently there are two basic air freight rates. The first is a general commodity rate that most traffic is carried under. The second is a specific commodity rate that is a lower rate set up for special circumstances and is used only to a limited extent. There are also rates that are higher than general commodity rates, called *exception ratings,* for certain hard-to-handle commodities, such as certain live animals and human remains. Therefore, the freight classification idea whereby a number of different classes of freight are involved is not currently being used by United States airlines.

INVESTMENT TRENDS

Since for-hire air transportation does not have to invest in a way or in airport facilities, although some ground investment may be needed, it avoids the capital requirements associated with those investments, but the investment in vehicles is substantial.

In 1976 all United States scheduled airlines had total assets of 15.5 billion dollars. The trunk lines' share of this was 13.6 billion dollars (including both domestic and international operations) and that of the local service lines was approximately 1.2 billion dollars.[13] Thus, the average assets for the 11 trunk lines was approximately 1.2 billion dollars and for the 9 local service airlines approximately 132 million dollars. The total investment in airlines has, of course, grown considerably in the post-World War II period. Trunk line assets in 1955 were only approximately 1 billion dollars and the assets of local service lines were approximately 28 million dollars.[14]

The investment in operating property and equipment of domestic trunk airlines (domestic service only) in 1975 was approximately 9 billion dollars or 817 million dollars per carrier, and their capital turnover using this base was 1.15. The investment in operating property and equipment of local service airlines was approximately 580 million dollars, or 64 million dollars per carrier, and their capital turnover was 2.36.[15]

---

[13] Air Transport Association, *Air Transport 1977,* p. 20.

[14] Air Transport Association, *Air Transport Facts and Figures, 1959* (Washington, D.C.: Air Transport Association, 1959), p. 24.

[15] Calculated from data given in Civil Aeronautics Board, *Annual Report, 1976,* p. 142 and Air Transport Association, *Air Transport 1977,* p. 18.

TRAFFIC TRENDS

Passenger Traffic

Eighty-six per cent of the domestic revenue taken in by trunk lines in 1976 was from passenger service. Passenger service accounted for 85 per cent of the revenue of local service lines.[16] Table 10-4 contains information on intercity for-hire passenger traffic by mode of transportation, both private and for-hire, since 1939. The rate of airline traffic growth has been outstanding, the traffic increasing from only .8 billion passenger-miles in 1939, or 2.3 per cent of all intercity for-hire passenger-miles, to 152.3 billion passenger-miles in the recession year 1976, or 79.5 per cent of all intercity for-hire passenger miles carried in the country. The passenger-miles carried by air increased 1,894 per cent between 1939 and 1976, while that of all intercity for-hire carriers together increased by only 440 per cent. In the recession year of 1976 trunk lines carried 131.4 billion passenger-miles of traffic in domestic service, while local service lines accounted for 12.1 billion.[17] In addition to the intercity passenger traffic carried by for-hire air carriers, another 12 billion passenger-miles were carried in general aviation or private air carriage in 1976.[18] If all intercity passenger travel is taken into account, both private and for-hire, then the share carried by air is considerably less because of the importance of the private automobile. Thus, the 163.9 billion intercity air passenger-miles (152.3 billion for-hire plus 11.6 billion private) was only 12 per cent of the total in 1976.[19]

The success of airlines in capturing most of the for-hire intercity passenger traffic has been partly at the expense of other for-hire carriers, particularly railroads, but to a great extent it has been the result of the airlines' creating their own traffic, i.e., many of the passengers carried by air would not travel to the same destination points if fast and frequent air service did not exist—the trips would not be made at all.

Airlines have traditionally relied heavily upon the business sector to purchase the bulk of the airline tickets sold. In recent years, however, a shift toward greater reliance on the pleasure travel market has taken place.

The average revenue produced per airline passenger-mile is higher than for rail and bus companies, averaging 11.5 cents per passenger-mile for domestic scheduled first-class service, 7.5 cents per passenger-mile for coach service, and 8.2 cents per domestic passenger-mile overall in 1976. Railroad fares averaged 6.5 cents per passenger-mile and Class I motor bus revenue was 5.1 cents per passenger-mile in 1976.[20]

Air transportation is a long-haul form of transportation. The average length of haul in domestic passenger service of trunk lines was 819 miles in 1976. It was much shorter for local service lines, however, at only 320 miles.[21] A large part of airline passenger traffic involves a few larger cities.

---

[16]Calculated from Air Transport Association, *Air Transport 1977*, p. 14.

[17]*Ibid.*, p. 9.

[18]Transportation Association of America, *Transportation Facts and Trends*, p. 18.

[19]*Ibid.*

[20]*Ibid.*, p. 7.

[21]Air Transport Association, *Air Transport 1977*, p. 9.

Freight Traffic

Air cargo is defined by the airline industry to include freight, express, and mail traffic. Approximately 78 per cent of trunk line domestic cargo traffic and approximately 66 per cent of local service airline cargo traffic is freight.

Table 10–2 shows the rapid growth in air cargo traffic since 1939. The growth was from .01 billion ton-miles in 1939 to 4 billion ton-miles in 1976, but air cargo in 1976 accounted for only .2 per cent of all domestic intercity private and for-hire ton-miles carried in the country. It did, however, account for approximately 2.5 per cent of the value of the traffic carried. In the recession year of 1976 trunk lines carried 3 billion ton-miles of domestic freight, express, and mail traffic and local service airlines carried 109 million such ton-miles. All-cargo carriers carried 445 million ton-miles.[22] Very little air cargo traffic is carried by private carriers. The air freight segment of air cargo is made up predominantly of small shipments. According to one source, over 90 per cent of domestic air freight traffic is comprised of shipments weighing less than 500 pounds, 59 per cent is less than 100 pounds, 40 per cent is less than 50 pounds, and 25 per cent is less than 25 pounds.[23]

Most air freight is transported by combination (both passenger and cargo) carriers either in the belly of scheduled passenger aircraft or in aircraft used exclusively for cargo. All-cargo airlines, of course, use their aircraft exclusively for cargo.

Although the growth in air freight traffic has been rapid, air freight is still a minor part of the country's total transportation picture and produces a relatively small part of domestic passenger carriers' revenues. In 1976, for example, freight revenue was only 6.1 per cent of total domestic operating revenue of trunk lines while air express revenue was only .1 per cent.[24] Combination carriers usually find air freight service to be unprofitable and the all-cargo airlines have usually found it very difficult to be profitable as common carriers of freight. Although some progress has been made toward encouraging users to make use of air freight transportation on a regular basis for middle- and high-value commodities, most air freight traffic still is either very high-value commodities or emergency shipments, or both. The top commodities moving by air freight are wearing apparel, electronic and electrical equipment and parts, printed matter, machinery and parts, cut flowers and nursery stock, auto parts and accessories, phonograph records, tapes, television sets, radios, fruits and vegetables, metal products, photographic equipment and parts, and film. One result is that the average revenue per ton-mile for domestic airlines is much higher than for any other mode of transportation. This is shown in Table 14–2. The table indicates a very high revenue per ton-mile and that airlines, until the 1970's, held the line despite inflationary pressures, and, in effect, there was a "real" reduction in the revenue per ton-mile in that it stayed approximately the same while other prices rose. In the 1970's, however, the airline revenue per ton-mile has increased substantially.

[22] *Ibid.,* pp. 9 and 11.

[23] "Capsules," *Cargo Airlift,* May, 1975, p. 40.

[24] Calculated from data given in Air Transport Association, *Air Transport 1977,* p. 14.

TABLE 14-2 *Domestic Scheduled Airline Average Revenue per*
Ton-Mile, *1949-1976 (cents)*

Year	Revenue per Ton–Mile
1950	18.1
1955	21.2
1960	22.8
1965	20.5
1970	21.9
1975	28.2
1976	31.8

*Freight only. Express not included.

Average revenue per ton–mile = $\dfrac{\text{total freight revenue}}{\text{total number of ton–miles carried}}$

Source: Transportation Association of America, *Transportation Facts and Trends,* 13th
ed. (Washington, D.C.: Transportation Association of America, July, 1977), p. 7.

The length of freight haul is larger for airlines than for other modes. In 1976, for example, the average length of freight haul in domestic service of airlines regulated by the CAB was 1,075 miles.[25]

REVENUE TRENDS

Annual operating revenues of domestic airlines have increased substantially in the post-World War II period as traffic carried has grown, as shown in Table 14-3. The growth in operating revenue is clear from the table, totaling 11.9 billion dollars in 1976 for trunk line domestic service compared with only 524.1 million dollars in 1950, an increase of 2,265 per cent. The growth in local service airline revenue has been even faster, rising from 27.9 million dollars in 1950 to 1.6 billion dollars in 1976, an increase of 5,828 per cent. The average annual operating revenue of trunk lines was 1.1 billion dollars in 1976. It was 181 million dollars for local service lines.

The erratic nature of airline profitability is also clear from the table. The operating ratio has fluctuated considerably for both kinds of carriers, as has net profit and rate of return on investment. The operating ratio has fluctuated between 88 per cent and 99.7 per cent for trunk lines and between 91.7 per cent and 101.2 per cent for local service airlines in the years shown in the table. Net profit or loss ranged between a loss of 100.4 million dollars and a profit of 323.6 million dollars for trunk lines and between a loss of 61.4 million dollars and a profit of 51.2 million dollars for local service lines. The rate of return on investment ranged from 1.4 per cent to 11.9 per cent for trunk lines and between -3.9 per cent and 10.9 per cent for local service carriers. The CAB currently has a rate-of-return goal of 12 per cent for trunk lines and 12.35 per cent for local service lines.

During the period covered by Table 14-3 three significant dips in the eco-

[25]Transportation Association of America, *Transportation Facts and Trends,* p. 14.

TABLE 14-3 *Domestic Airline Revenue Trends, 1950-1976*

YEAR	Number of Carriers	Operating Revenue (000,000)	Operating Expenses (000,000)	Operating Ratio (per cent)[†]	Net Operating Income (000,000)[‡]	Net Profit or Loss (000)	Rate of Return on Investment (per cent)[§]
*Domestic Trunk Lines**							
1950	16	$524.1	$461.3	88.0	$62.6	$30.4	N.A.
1955	13	1,132.2	1,009.6	89.1	122.6	63.0	11.9
1960	12	1,942.6	1,907.8	97.6	34.9	.7	2.6
1965	11	3,263.2	2,847.3	87.3	416.2	221.9	11.2
1970	12	6,272.8	6,256.0	99.7	16.7	-100.4	1.4
1974	11	9,942.8	9,262.8	93.2	679.4	323.6	7.8
1975	11	10,311.4	10.227.6	99.2	83.8	-66.6	2.2
1976	11	11,872.0	11,401.0	96.0	471.0	275.8	7.4
Local Service Lines							
1950	16	27.9	27.2	97.5	$.7	$-.6	N.A.
1955	13	58.6	57.8	98.6	.7	.8	7.5
1960	13	146.5	144.3	92.2	2.2	1.9	8.2
1965	13	291.4	267.3	91.7	24.1	12.7	10.4
1970	9	736.8	745.6	101.2	-8.8	-61.4	-3.9
1974	8	1,299.7	1,199.3	93.3	100.4	51.2	10.9
1975	9	1,368.3	1,338.1	97.8	30.3	.3	3.5
1976	9	1,626.1	1,535.6	94.4	90.5	51.0	9.8

*Domestic service only.

[†]Operating ratio = $\dfrac{\text{operating expenses}}{\text{operating revenues}}$.
Calculated by author. Operating expenses do not include income taxes and interest on long-term debt.

[‡]Operating revenues less operating expenses.

[§]Rate of return on investment reflects net profit plus interest paid on the noncurrent portion of long-term debt as a per cent of total investment. Total investment is a 5-quarter average of total net worth (stockholders' equity) plus long-term debt.

N.A. Not available.

Source: Air Transport Association of America, *Air Transport* (formerly *Air Transport Facts and Figures*), various editions (Washington, D.C.: Air Transport Association).

nomic condition of domestic airlines took place—in 1960 (followed by heavy losses for trunk lines in 1961), 1970, and 1975. The causes of the decline in profitability in the first 2 periods were very similar. Certain circumstances combined to cause a serious overcapacity problem and high costs simultaneously which led to reduced profitability. These circumstances were: (1) the policy of the CAB to add additional air carriers to some routes, thus increasing the amount of service available; (2) the purchase of new greater capacity aircraft (first-generation jets in the late 1950's and wide-bodied jets in the late 1960's); (3) the added costs caused by re-equipping; (4) excessive flights scheduled by the carriers; (5) economic recession in the country and the leveling off of growth in airline traffic; (6) higher costs caused by inflation; and (7) government regulation of rates and fares that prevented carriers from raising prices to recover higher costs. The low passenger-load factors and the high costs of operating led to the losses of the 2 periods. The passenger-load factor for domestic trunk lines in 1960 was 59.5 and it was 56.2 in 1961[26] (much lower than in previous years). In 1970 it was only 49.3[27] (lower than in most of the 1960's). After 1970 there was improvement in the financial condition of the airlines, but the recession and high fuel prices and general inflation combined to produce a lower passenger-load factor and rising costs and consequent financial problems in 1975. There was considerable improvement in 1976, however.

Unlike the railroad industry, the basic trends in the economy and in technology are not against further growth in the airline industry, and it is probably true that airlines will recover satisfactorily from the problems of the 1970's. A large part of the passenger market, mainly the pleasure travel part, is still untapped by air transportation. Many Americans have never been inside an airplane of any kind. It is unlikely, however, that the rapid passenger traffic growth of the 1960's will be repeated. Instead, it appears that the industry will have small but steady growth year by year in the next decade. The industry is now in a mature stage on the passenger side of its operations and, because it now dominates the intercity for-hire passenger market, the room for growth is less than in the past. In addition, as noted earlier, the industry now relies somewhat and will rely more on the pleasure travel market than before, a market that is less dependable and predictable and that is based to a great extent on the availability of discretionary buying power and is thus more sensitive to general economic trends than the business sector market. Finally, the great technological advances made in the 1950's and 1960's will not be repeated in the coming decade. Instead of struggling to keep up with rapidly advancing technology and traffic growth, airline management will be concerned with cost cutting, a gradually rising market, and problems created by the energy shortage.

On the freight side, the market has been virtually untouched by air transportation. More rapid growth can be expected than on the passenger side, and it will be stimulated by the business logistics and total cost approach to freight movement and by aircraft and terminal developments.[28] The growth in air freight traffic will, of course, be heavily influenced by the level of air freight rates in the future; they must be reduced considerably compared with surface carrier rates in order for air freight to grow substantially.

It is generally assumed that there will be moderate annual growth in both passenger and freight traffic (perhaps 5 to 8 per cent per year) in the latter 1970's and in the 1980's. This growth will mean that a considerable amount of capital will be needed to purchase new aircraft to replace and add to the aging fleet of aircraft. A problem the airline industry faces is lack of capital to make such purchases because many airlines are unable to generate enough cash internally and lenders are reluctant to lend money to the airline industry because of its financial difficulties in the 1970's and also because of the possibility that the airline industry will be deregulated (see Chapter 25).

---

[26] Air Transport Association, *Facts and Figures About Air Transportation, 1962*, p. 22.

[27] Air Transport Association, *Air Transport 1971*, p. 26.

[28] Some experts predict that eventually airlines will rely more on freight traffic for revenue than they will on passenger traffic.

SERVICE CHARACTERISTICS

Air transportation has become a very important part of the nation's passenger transportation system, accounting for over three-quarters of the for-hire intercity passenger–mileage. It has also had some success in the freight market. The industry has grown rapidly since World War II because it offers the public various service advantages that cannot be duplicated by its competitors. Nevertheless, air transportation also has some disadvantages from the point of view of the using public.

Completeness of Service

One disadvantage of air freight transportation is that it is an airport-to-airport instead of a door-to-door service in that the line-haul rate charged usually does not include pickup and delivery. Pickup and delivery service is available at an extra charge through Air Cargo, Inc., a ground service organization established and jointly owned by the United States scheduled airlines. Its major function is to negotiate and supervise the performance of a nationwide series of contracts under which independent trucking companies provide pickup and delivery service at airport cities. Normally, it is limited to a 25-mile radius of an airport. The user may, of course, provide his own pickup and delivery service if he wishes. As noted previously, scheduled airlines rely heavily on air freight forwarders to provide air freight traffic. The service performed for users by air freight forwarders often includes pickup and delivery and air forwarder line-haul rates may include this service. Consequently, a true door-to-door service is provided in these situations. In the case of air express or priority service, the line-haul rates charged include pickup and delivery; lower airport-to-airport rates are also offered.

Cost

A major disadvantage of air transportation has always been its high cost relative to other modes. This has been true in both the passenger and freight markets, but in recent years it has been more so in the latter. The revenue per passenger-mile and per ton-mile figures referred to earlier indicate the high cost of air transportation. Until the inflation increase of the 1970's the gap between air and surface intercity passenger fares was actually narrowing, but the reverse has been true in recent years. However, the difference is not so great that the speed advantage and the more direct nature of air transportation, and its frequency, cannot cancel out the cost disadvantage. In addition, one must take into account the fact that there are expenses of traveling by rail or bus, such as tipping and meals, that are avoided when traveling by air.

Prior to the 1970's the wide difference between air freight and surface revenue per ton-mile was being reduced, but since 1970 the reverse is true. The average domestic airline freight revenue per ton–mile of almost $.32[29] in 1976 was almost 4 times that of the next highest mode—highway transportation—which had an

---

[29]The rates of all-cargo carriers are somewhat lower than those of trunk lines.

average revenue per ton–mile of slightly more than $.08 and was almost 15 times that of railroads. The tremendous speed and other advantages of air freight service to tne user have not been enough to overcome the pricing disadvantage. The result has been that air freight has not grown to the extent that it had been hoped for by its promoters and probably will not until the wide gap in rates is reduced considerably below what it was in 1976. Although air transportation is traditionally a small shipment mode and has tended to attract high-value traffic, both factors leading to high rates per 100 pounds, the average revenue per ton–mile still must be lower in order for air freight transportation to become a major part of the transportation system. Although new aircraft in recent years are more efficient and can be operated at a lower cost per ton–mile than their predecessors (when fully utilized), inflation and the problems of excess capacity have made it impossible for airlines to enjoy the fruits of the improved efficiency and thereby lower air freight rates. In addition, there are the costs to the user of pickup and delivery.

On the positive side, however, since air transportation is fast and often frequent, users of air freight service can maintain lower inventories and reduce associated costs. Air transportation also has a better loss and damage record (with associated lower packaging costs) than have railroads and trucking companies, although the amount of liability prior to the 1977 order of the CAB (see Chapter 6) has been more limited unless the user paid an extra charge. In addition, negligence had to be shown before an air carrier was liable. Because air service is more direct than surface transportation, wasted ton–miles are not incurred.

Time

The obvious major advantages of air transportation are high speed and low door-to-door elapsed time. Modern jet aircraft have a cruising speed approaching 600 miles per hour. Airlines also operate single units and, therefore, avoid the delays associated with making up and breaking up trains or tows. Since time has value in both the passenger and freight markets, the speed advantage can offset the cost disadvantages referred to earlier. In addition, air transportation can be a very frequent service, at least at large cities, which adds to its speed capability. The speed advantage is most evident in long-haul situations which helps to account for the long average length of haul in both passenger and freight service for airlines.

Nevertheless, the airlines' natural speed advantage is offset in part by delays on the ground. The difficulties passengers have in getting to and from airports, the need for passengers to check in somewhat in advance of flight departure time, delays for security checks before boarding, and delays in retrieving baggage are all part of the problem. On the freight side, time consumed in getting freight to and from airports, delays in assembly and disassembly of freight at air freight terminals, and delays in loading and unloading aircraft are problems that increase door-to-door time. An efficient truck or rail carrier can sometimes provide as fast a door-to-door service as airlines. These difficulties are most apparent and are of most consequence on short hauls and they contribute to the long-haul nature of air transportation where ground delays are a small part of the total time involved.

Flexibility

Because air transportation is not tied to a physical fixed way, it is more flexible than some other modes because it can go wherever there are adequate airports, that is, air transportation serves a wide geographic area and many origin and destination points, with air freight service available at fewer points than air passenger service. The area and points served can be easily adjusted and can be expanded as new airports are opened. Air transportation also provides a relatively small vehicle that can be loaded and unloaded quickly.

Air transportation cannot directly provide door-to-door service, which reduces its availability. An aspect of this is the fact that the distance from airports within which pickup and delivery of air freight is available is usually limited, often to 25 miles from the airport. Another limiting factor in the freight market is that air transportation does not provide a wide variety of equipment that is adaptable to different commodities. Still another disadvantage of air transportation is that it cannot carry a wide variety of commodities because there are weight and size limitations that must be observed. In fact, there are many commodities that cannot be carried at all by air.

Interchanging of Passengers, Freight, and Equipment

Because no airline serves all possible commercial airports, the necessity for interchanging or interlining of both passengers and freight is obvious. The small number of airlines would appear to make cooperation on this score easier than with some other modes. Although interchanging of passengers is frequently done, it is more limited in air freight. In most cases in which interchanging does take place, in either the passenger or freight markets, the passengers or freight are interchanged, not the aircraft. This means that there are delays and inconvenience for users at connecting points, which, of course, reduce the capability of air carriers. Liability for loss and damage to freight is limited to each carrier's own line.

Dependability

One of the major handicaps of air transportation has been its undependability. In the early period of for-hire aviation, delays and unkept schedules were frequent and were caused primarily by weather interference and mechanical failures. In modern times these two general problems have been to a great degree reduced, particularly weather problems, but the problems still do exist. In addition, congestion at major airports has been a serious matter leading to inability to keep schedules. Also, there are the difficulties that occur at connecting points, where 2 flights connect and passengers and freight are transferred from one flight to another. If baggage is lost at the connecting point, it will delay the outgoing connecting flight. If an incoming flight is late, it delays the outgoing flight and a chain reaction with other flights may set in. On-time performance (within 15 minutes of scheduled time) is achieved in approximately 80 per cent of domestic trunk line nonstop flights between major traffic points 200 miles or more apart, but there is a fairly wide variation between individual carriers.

Another aspect of the undependability problem is the safety question associated mainly with passenger service. From the beginning airlines have been handicapped by the hazard of flying and the publicity associated with airline accidents. Although the public's attitude on this matter has changed substantially since World War II and although air transportation safety has greatly improved and compares well with other for-hire modes of transportation, the hazard problem still exists to some degree.

As noted earlier, airlines have a better loss and damage record than do railroads and motor trucking companies, but the airlines' liability is less unless an extra charge is paid by the user. In addition, prior to 1977 carrier negligence had to be established in order for the air carrier to be liable.

In the federal Department of Transportation (DOT) study referred to in Chapters 10, 11, and 12 in which the performance factors of on-time delivery and loss and damage were compared for rail, highway, water, and air transportation, manufacturer–users indicated a higher level of satisfaction with air transportation than with the other 3 modes.

Service and Pricing Innovations

Of the 5 modes, air transportation has had the most frequent and dramatic changes in technology and in service to the public since World War II. Changes in aircraft size, speed, passenger comfort, and reliability are well-known to most Americans. Three of the dominant for-hire carrier aircraft of the late 1940's were the Douglas DC-3 that had a capacity of 28 passengers and a cruising speed of 180 miles per hour, the Douglas DC-6 that had a passenger capacity of 56 and a cruising speed of 310 miles per hour, and the Lockheed Constellation that had a capacity of 54 and a cruising speed of 310 miles per hour. The variety of aircraft equipment available was very limited. Today, the most numerous commercial aircraft flown by trunk lines are the various versions of the Boeing 727 that have a capacity of from 93 to 189 passengers and a cruising speed close to 600 miles per hour. Other modern aircraft include Boeing's 707, 737, and 747; McDonnell Douglas's DC-8, DC-9, and DC-10; the BAC-III; the Lockheed L-1011; and the Convair 880. Their capacities range from 65 to 495 passengers. Local service airlines operate the smaller jet aircraft and some turbo-propeller and piston engine aircraft. The freight-carrying capacity of airline aircraft has also increased substantially. The capacity (payload) of the belly compartment of a Boeing 707 or DC-8 is from 14,000 pounds to 18,000 pounds, while it is up to 70,000 pounds in the case of the Boeing 747. The capacity of the all-cargo version of the 707 and DC-8 is approximately 90,000 pounds, while the carrying capacity of a Boeing 747F all-cargo aircraft is as much as 250,000 pounds. In 1976 United States scheduled airlines operated 2,260 fixed-wing aircraft, of which 2,043 were jet, 180 were turbo-propeller, and 37 were piston engine aircraft.[30]

In the future there will be supersonic air transportation. The United States ended its formal program to develop an 1,800-mile-per-hour aircraft in 1971 when Congress refused to provide further funds because of environmental and economic reasons. The British–French 1,350-mile-per-hour Concorde program produced an operational aircraft that went into regular service in 1976. Because of its high initial cost, high fuel consumption, and relatively small seating capa-

[30] Air Transport Association, *Air Transport 1977*, p. 29.

city (approximately 100), it is not likely that more than a handful of the Concorde aircraft will be sold. Nevertheless, it is very possible that supersonic air transportation will be commonplace in the latter part of the century.

Along with larger and faster aircraft, airlines have introduced innovations in food service, various amenities while in flight, computerized reservation systems, mechanized baggage handling, and other changes in passenger service.

On the freight side, various improvements in handling freight on the ground, such as computerized ground handling and information systems, have been made, as well as adoption of better methods of loading and unloading aircraft. Pickup and delivery service via Air Cargo, Inc. has been established, along with some coordinated air-truck service beyond pickup and delivery areas. One of the most promising newer developments has been the introduction of containerization which has helped to increase the amount of air freight traffic, much of it from air freight forwarders. Lack of standardization of container sizes and types used by different airlines and different aircraft used, however, has been a handicap in developing interline container service. The wide-bodied jet aircraft promise to enable airlines to handle a wider variety of commodities and to lower freight rates, provided that capacity is sufficiently utilized. Wide-bodied jets also increase the possibility of greater coordination with surface carriers, particularly through containerization.[31] To date, however, even with containerization, the airlines have not strongly encouraged intermodal cooperation with surface carriers.[32]

There have also been improvements in and additions to the airport and airway systems (to be discussed in Chapter 17), and scheduled for-hire air service is now available at 631 cities in the country.[33]

Passenger fares have gone through various phases since the late 1940's. The emphasis has been on promotional or discount fares since the air coach fare was inaugurated in 1948. Various kinds of promotional fares have been tried over the years, including family fares, youth fares, military fares, excursion fares, and "no-frill" fares, all of which have been attempts to encourage traffic during off-peak days and times. Government economic regulation has heavily influenced this practice, as will be seen in Chapter 23.

Various innovations have been tried in the pricing of air freight service, including space-available or deferred rates (see Chapter 9), container rates, reserved space rates, and certain promotional rates.

ENVIRONMENT AND ENERGY

Environment

The principal environmental problems associated with air transportation operations are aircraft noise and air pollution. Expansion of existing airports and construction of new airports also lead to additional environmental issues related to water supplies, water pollution, the effects on wild life, and the effect on open space.

---

[31] The Boeing 747 is the only aircraft that can handle 8 foot by 8 foot by 10, 20, 30, or 40-foot surface carrier containers.

[32] See "Airline Approach to Intermodal Operations Called Reactionary," *Aviation Week and Space Technology*, November 11, 1974.

[33] Air Transport Association, *Air Transport 1977*, p. 28.

Aircraft noise emitted from aircraft has been a perplexing problem for many years and was made worse by the introduction of jet aircraft and the increased frequency of flights. Complaints about aircraft noise are usually directed at the large jet aircraft operated by for-hire airlines, although business-owned jets and turbo-propeller aircraft have also drawn some criticism.

Solutions to the aircraft noise problem are difficult to reach. They include noise-reduction technology, better control of land use around airports to prevent residential or other noise-sensitive uses, moving airports to new locations, and following noise-abatement flight procedures. The latter include use of runways that lead to flights over the least populated areas when wind conditions permit, turns away from noise-sensitive neighborhoods after takeoff and/or sharp cutbacks in thrust during climb, steeper landing glide slopes to increase the altitude of aircraft over a given location, use of less power at low altitudes, removal of airline flight training from noise-problem airports, and prohibition of flight operations at night.

Of the above possible solutions, improved technology appears to be the best long-run solution, and some progress has been made in that direction. It means that aircraft still to be built would be built with quieter engines and that aircraft now in use would be retrofitted by acoustic treatment of the engine nacelles or by nacelle redesign. In 1969 the FAA issued regulations to control aircraft noise to be effective December 1, 1969. The regulations were moderate in their effect on noise reduction and applied to the new wide-bodied jets (about 14 per cent of the airline jet fleet in 1976), but they did not apply to aircraft already in service. Consequently, there was no immediate noise reduction. In October, 1973 the regulations were made applicable to older design airplanes (such as the Boeing 727) to be manufactured after that date. In November, 1976, Secretary of Transportation William T. Coleman, Jr. ordered that airline aircraft used by United States carriers in domestic service gradually meet the 1969 FAA standards within 8 years either through replacement of the aircraft or through retrofitting engine nacelles. The questions of whether or not the program would actually be implemented and how the program was to be financed were not answered at the time of this writing. The order also required the FAA to promulgate more stringent noise requirements for aircraft not yet produced and noise-abatement aircraft operations rules.[34] The rules had not been set forth at the time of this writing.

The wide-bodied jets are considerably quieter than their predecessors, and as their number increase, as older aircraft are retired or retrofitted, and as noise-abatement flight procedures are used, the noise problem will gradually be reduced. Eventually, short takeoff and landing (STOL) and vertical takeoff and landing (VTOL) aircraft may also become important and will do much to eliminate the noise problem. At the present time, however, aircraft noise is still a serious problem at most major airports.

Energy

A major problem of air transportation is its tremendous energy consumption during a period when energy is in short supply and its cost is high. The Air

[34] See Rosalind K. Ellingsworth, "Administration Sets Noise Policy," *Aviation Week and Space Technology*, November 22, 1976.

Transport Association reported that the average price per gallon of fuel for United States scheduled airlines in 1973 was approximately $.12. In 1975 it was $.32. The cost of fuel accounted for approximately 20 per cent of total airline operating costs in 1975 as against 12 per cent in 1973.[35]

The Transportation Association of America reported that in 1975 transportation used 54.0 per cent of the total domestic demand for petroleum and that air transportation (excluding military) accounted for 7.7 per cent of the transportation demand, which was approximately 4.2 per cent of the total domestic demand.[36] Air transport is our least efficient mode in terms of energy consumed per passenger–mile or ton–mile, including the private automobile. For example, in 1975 the United States Railway Association reported that a study had shown that air freight consumed 312.5 gallons of fuel to produce 1,000 ton–miles of freight service while intercity trucks consumed only 13.7 gallons.[37] Other studies have shown similar results. The wide-bodied Boeing 747 consumes approximately 4,000 gallons of jet fuel per hour.

Spurred by the high cost of fuel and the threat of restrictive government energy policies, the scheduled airline industry has undertaken steps to use fuel more efficiently. These steps include reducing the number of flights flown, reducing the number of training flights by substituting visual simulators, reducing cruising speeds, and various operating techniques such as engine shutdown while taxiing. These steps resulted in consumption of 800 million gallons less fuel by United States domestic and international carriers in 1976 than in 1973 while the industry carried 21 million more passengers and more cargo. Passengers carried increased 10.4 per cent while fuel consumption decreased 7.5 per cent.[38]

Despite the fact that air transportation is more direct and hence requires fewer passenger–miles or ton–miles than its competitors in order to serve a given set of points, there is no question that air transportation is a high energy consumer. Consequently, although air carriers have and probably will benefit from divergence of passenger traffic from private automobiles to air transportation as the energy problem gets worse, airlines can be seriously adversely affected by the high cost of energy and any government measures designed to discourage the consumption of oil and its products, including allocation and rationing programs, as well as government inspired high energy prices and higher taxes on energy.

OTHER TRANSPORTATION AGENCIES

We are now familiar with the economic and service characteristics of the 5 modes of transportation discussed in Chapters 10 through 14. These characteristics are summarized in Table 14-4. In addition to these carriers, there are several other agencies of transportation that are not carriers or users in the true sense of those terms.

---

[35] Air Transport Association, *Air Transport 1976*, p. 6.

[36] Transportation Association of America, *Transportation Facts and Trends*, p. 32.

[37] United States Railway Association, *Preliminary System Plan*, Part II, Volume 1 (Washington, D.C.: United States Railway Association, February 26, 1975), pp. 147-148.

[38] See "Airlines Fly More People on Less Fuel," *Aviation Week and Space Technology*, March 7, 1977 and Air Transport Association, *Air Transport 1977*, pp. 5-6.

TABLE 14-4 Economic and Service Characteristics of the Several Intercity For-Hire Modes of Domestic Transportation

Economic Characteristics	Railroad Freight	Railroad Passenger*	Highway Freight	Highway Passenger	Water	Oil Pipeline	Air Passenger	Air Freight
					Mode			
Ownership of for-hire carriers	Mainly private	†	Private	Private	Private	Private	Private	Private
Number of Firms	Fairly small	One	Large	Varies	Varies with Trade	Small	Very Small	Very Small
Size of Firms	Varies	Large	Small	Varies	Varies with Trade	Fairly Large	Varies	Varies
Cost Structure	High Fixed	High Variable	High Variable	High Variable	High Variable	High Fixed	High Variable	High Variable
Excess Capacity	Considerable	Considerable	Some	Considerable	Some	Some	Considerable	Considerable
Approximate Market Structure	Differentiated Oligopoly	Monopoly	Monopolistic Competition	Monopolistic Competition	Varies with Trade	Differentiated Oligopoly	Differentiated Oligopoly	Differentiated Oligopoly
Differential Pricing	Considerable	Some	Considerable	Some	Considerable	Some	Some	Some
Investment	Large	Large	Small	Fairly Small	Varies with Trade	Large	Large	Large
Capital Turn-over Rate	Low	Low	High	Fairly High	Varies with Trade	Low	Fairly High	Fairly High

Operating Ratio	Moderately Low	High	High	High	High	Low	High	High
Traffic Trend	Marginally Positive	Marginally Positive	Positive	Positive	Varies with Trade	Very Positive	Positive	Positive
Revenue and Profitability Trend	Generally Negative	Generally Negative	Generally Positive	Generally Positive	Varies with Trade	Generally Positive	Generally Positive	Generally Negative
Service Characteristics								
Door-to-Door	Sometimes	No	Yes	No	Sometimes	Sometimes	No	No
Cost	Low	Moderately Low	Moderately High	Low	Low	Low	High	Very High
Time	Moderately Slow	Moderately Slow	Moderately Fast	Slow	Slow	Slow	Very Fast	Very Fast
Flexibility	Medium	Low	High	High	Low	Low	Medium	Medium
Interchange of Traffic	Yes	Yes	Some	Some	Some	Some	Yes	Some
Dependability	Medium	Low	Medium	Medium	Medium	High	Medium	Medium
Loss and Damage	High	—	Moderately High	—	Moderately Low	Low	—	Medium
Service and Pricing Innovations	Considerable	Some	Some	Some	Some	Some	Considerable	Considerable

Continued

TABLE 14-4 (Continued)

Other Characteristics	Mode							
	Railroad Freight	Railroad Passenger*	Highway Freight	Highway Passenger	Water	Oil Pipeline	Air Passenger	Air Freight
Environmental Impact of Carrier	Low to Medium	Low to Medium	High	High	Low to Medium	Low	Medium	Medium
Energy Consumption per Unit of Traffic Carried	Low	Low to Medium	High	Low	Low	Low	Very High	Very High

*Data in this column are for Amtrak only which since 1971 has operated most intercity railroad passenger service. The organization and operations of Amtrak are discussed in Chapter 16.
†Amtrak is a semi-government operation and cannot be categorized as either privately or government owned.

314

Freight Forwarders

Sometimes classified as an indirect carrier, a freight forwarder is a middleman in transportation who collects small shipments from shippers and consolidates the shipments into larger shipments and then buys line-haul transportation service from a for-hire carrier. Freight forwarders may also provide pickup and delivery service for customers. They usually charge the normal small-shipment rate and buy service from the for-hire carriers at the large-shipment rate, the difference being their gross profit. The benefit to the user is the faster service he receives, not a lower rate. Using a freight forwarder also solves the problem that is created when carriers attempt to avoid carrying a user's small shipments directly because the traffic is unprofitable. Freight forwarders are important to railroads, motor trucking companies, and airlines. There are approximately 165 surface and 275 domestic air freight forwarders authorized to operate under federal economic regulation.

Shippers' Associations

A shippers' association is a group of shippers and/or receivers who get together to form an association. The purpose of the association is to pool shipments and/or receipts and to buy transportation from for-hire carriers at the large-shipment rate and receive the better service accorded to large shipments. They are usually nonprofit associations because any transportation savings made are distributed to the shipper members. There are at least 150 shippers' associations in the United States.

Transportation Brokers

Brokers in any industry bring buyers and sellers together. In transportation they are found mainly in the motor trucking industry where they act as the sales representatives of small trucking companies. They are paid a commission on the business they bring in.

Express Service

Until 1969 REA Express was owned by railroad companies, but in 1969 non-railroad owners took over. Its purpose was to pick up and deliver very small shipments. Line-haul service was performed by rail or air for-hire carriers under contract with REA Express. Express traffic received priority treatment over other traffic and paid higher rates. As rail passenger service declined, REA was able to use fewer and fewer passenger trains for the line-haul and performed much of the line-haul service itself in its own trucks. In the 1970's its contract with the airlines was threatened to be discontinued by action of the CAB (see Chapter 23) and some trunk airlines stopped using REA Express. These and other problems caused REA Express to go bankrupt and out of business in 1976. As a result, the status of express service became uncertain. Many airlines now offer express ("priority") service directly as a replacement for REA air express service.

Other for-hire agencies of transportation dealing with small packages are

United Parcel Service, a motor carrier specializing in small packages and serving the entire country; bus package service; Amtrak; Federal Express, which provides a small shipment air service in part of the country; and the United States parcel post service. Most scheduled airlines also offer a small package airport-to-airport service (generally limited to 50 pounds or less) at their ticket counters.

SELECTED REFERENCES

The early development of air transportation in the United States is discussed in E. P. Warner, *The Early History of Air Transportation* (Northfield, Vermont: Norwich University, 1938). The history of for-hire air transportation is also dealt with in John H. Frederick, *Commercial Air Transportation*, 5th ed. (Homewood, Illinois: Richard D. Irwin, Inc., 1961), Chapter 3 and in D. Philip Locklin, *Economics of Transportation*, 7th ed. (Homewood, Illinois: Richard D. Irwin, Inc., 1972), pp. 770–772.

The basic characteristics of for-hire air transportation are discussed in Frederick, *Commercial Air Transportation*. The economic characteristics of air transportation are treated in Locklin, *Economics of Transportation*, Chapter 33. Airline costs and the market structure in the airline industry are dealt with in John R. Meyer, Merton J. Peck, John Stenason, and Charles Zwick, *The Economics of Competition in the Transportation Industries* (Cambridge, Massachusetts: Harvard University Press, 1959), pp. 133–144 and 227–234.

Among the many writings on the general condition of the airline industry are Michael B. Rothfield, "New Downdrafts for the Airlines," *Fortune*, January, 1974; William H. Gregory, "U.S. Carriers Mired in Varied Challenges," *Aviation Week and Space Technology*, March 17, 1975; and "Airlines' Prospects Keyed to Holding Costs," *Aviation Week and Space Technology*, March 15, 1976.

Several studies of the nature of the demand for airline passenger service are described in Randall L. Schultz, "Studies of Airline Passenger Demand: A Review," *Transportation Journal*, Summer, 1972.

The numerous writings dealing with the development and current status of air freight transportation include Howard T. Lewis, James W. Culliton, and Jack D. Steele, *The Role of Air Freight in Physical Distribution* (Boston: Division of Research, Graduate School of Business Administration, Harvard University, 1956); Lewis M. Schneider, *The Future of the U.S. Domestic Air Freight Industry: An Analysis of Management Strategies* (Cambridge, Massachusetts: Graduate School of Business Administration, Harvard University, 1973); "Air Cargo's Future Promising, If . . .," *Traffic Management*, June, 1973; "Making Money with Air Freight," *Business Week*, November 2, 1974; "Air Freight," *Distribution Worldwide*, January, 1976; and Patrick Gallagher, "Airfreight's Flight to Realism," *Handling and Shipping*, March, 1977.

The problem of aircraft noise at major airports is discussed in Donald V. Harper "The Dilemma of Aircraft Noise at Major Airports," *Transportation Journal*, Spring, 1971.

15

Decision-Making in
Transportation Companies *

We have now become familiar with the economic and service characteristics of the 5 modes of transportation. It is our purpose in this chapter to examine the management or decision-making process in transportation companies. Although the management problems in operating a transportation service are similar whether the carrier is private or for-hire and whether common or contract, in order to simplify our discussion we shall concentrate on the management of for-hire common carriers.

The objectives of a firm that provides for-hire transportation services are probably no different from most other firms in the economy. A carrier's objective is to make a sufficient return on his investment so that he will be able to survive and continue serving the public in the long run, in addition to being responsible to the community and the environment. If the objectives are the same as for other kinds of firms, why should we take the time to study carrier decision making as a special situation? The answer is that carrier managers must operate within a much more confining set of constraints than other businesses. The purpose of this chapter is to explain why transportation companies are unique and the implications this has for management in terms of organization, operations, and decision making and how carriers deal with various specific problems such as equipment selection and pricing.

WHY MANAGEMENT OF TRANSPORTATION
COMPANIES IS UNIQUE

Government Relationships and the Public Interest

One of the most distinguishing characteristics of for-hire transportation firms is that these firms are subject to a wide variety of government regulations. Al-

*This chapter was written by Frederick J. Beier, Associate Professor of Transportation and Business Logistics, College and Graduate School of Business Administration, University of Minnesota.

though some government regulation is not peculiar to transportation, some is designed specifically for transportation. These include, among others, regulation of safety in transportation and economic regulation of transportation. The latter includes regulation of the business of transportation, including control over entry into the business of for-hire transportation, control over exit from the business, regulation of rates and fares, and other matters. Economic regulation is discussed in Chapters 19 through 25.

One of the objectives of economic regulation is to limit possible abuses of economic power that one mode of transportation may enjoy vis-a-vis other modes and/or the public. The situation is complicated because carriers of some modes and some carriers within the same mode are regulated more strictly than others. This may have a significant impact on a carrier's competitive environment. That is, one carrier may be prevented from taking an action which is perfectly legal for its competitor of a different mode or the same mode.

Another unique feature of transportation firms has been that government has promoted and subsidized some modes more than others, as is discussed in Chapters 16 through 18. This has an impact on the cost structure of the competing forms of for-hire carriage.

The end result of government economic regulation and promotion is that a carrier may face competitors in another mode or the same mode with entirely different cost or service characteristics. All of these factors must be taken into consideration by the carrier decision maker.

Government Regulation—Common Carriers. Certainly the most complete economic regulation is placed on the common carrier. Common carriers are found in various degrees in all modes of transportation. As we have seen, railroads and oil pipelines are predominantly common carriers. The remaining modes have large numbers of contract, exempt, and/or private carriers. As noted in Chapter 6, the common carrier has 4 basic obligations: to serve, to deliver, to charge reasonable prices, and to avoid discrimination. Chapter 6 provided some insight into what these obligations mean to the public. The following paragraphs look at the implications for carrier managers.

As indicated in Chapter 6, the geographic scope of a regulated highway, water, and air carrier's service is defined by the operating authority issued by a regulatory agency. The operating authority may specify which routes are to be followed in serving specific points. The geographic scope of operations for common carrier railroads and oil pipelines and unregulated for-hire highway, water, and air carriers has been determined by the carriers themselves. The operating authority of regulated freight carriers may be restricted as to the type of commodity the firm is authorized to carry, as noted in Chapter 6. A motor carrier, for example, may be permitted to transport only bulk chemicals, or household goods, or a variety of other commodity descriptions. Other regulated and unregulated carriers may also restrict their holding out to certain commodities only. The point is that the public that a common carrier is obligated to serve is often limited by the terms and conditions of his operating authority and/or his own choice.

The duty to serve requires a carrier to be responsive to his public and provide it with transportation services. In general, this means that a regulated common carrier does not have the option of abandoning specific routes or communities that may be unprofitable in favor of those that are. A railroad, for example, must first gain permission from the Interstate Commerce Commission (ICC) before it can abandon a branch line. A common carrier airline must make a similar application to the Civil Aeronautics Board (CAB). Motor carriers and domestic water carriers may go entirely out of business and cease all operations without governmental authorization, but they must get permission to abandon a portion of their route structure. There is no regulation of exit of oil pipelines. It should be noted that application must also be made if a regulated common carrier (except oil pipelines) wishes to expand his operating territory.

The obligation to deliver has been well detailed in Chapter 6 in the discussion of common carrier liability. The point to be noted here is that some freight common carriers are charged with extraordinary liability in the care and handling of goods. It is not sufficient for such a carrier to say he was not negligent or that he had taken "reasonable" care of the cargo and therefore should not be liable for a user's loss. The implications of this obligation in terms of equipment design, material handling equipment, and other claim prevention programs should be obvious. These will be discussed in more detail later in this chapter.

The obligation to charge reasonable rates and fares means that the regulated common carrier's prices are subject to approval by the appropriate regulatory body. The power to initiate rates and fares rests with the carrier. However, they are subject to examination and review by the regulatory agency. If regulated interstate common carriers, either individually or collectively, wish to change rates or fares on interstate traffic, they must notify the ICC or the CAB. If the agency decides that the proposed change is not in the public interest, for any number of reasons, it will not permit the change to take place. The practical consequence of such a system for the carrier is that long delays must be endured in adjusting prices to changing market conditions. Further, if the rate or fare is controversial, substantial funds and man–hours must be invested in preparing testimony and arguments before the regulators. It is not surprising that the legal department is often one of the most important staff departments within a regulated carrier's organization.

Closely related to charging reasonable prices is the obligation to avoid discrimination in pricing. A freight carrier must price his services so that a commodity or group of commodities, or geographic location is not subject to unreasonable discrimination vis-a-vis other commodities or locations. Again, the burden falls on the carrier to defend himself before the ICC or similar agency. Further, the concept of unreasonable discrimination is an elusive one subject to much debate and interpretation. To a certain extent a carrier may be reluctant to innovate for fear that he will become involved in claims of discrimination and a long litigative process.

A carrier must guard against engaging in discriminatory services as well as prices. For example, during the initial "Russian Wheat Deal" in 1973, railroads devoted many of their special grain cars to large firms that were shipping from 50 to 100 carloads at a time.[1] While this arrangement may have been beneficial to the large user, it was discriminatory against the small user who was not able to secure rail equipment to ship his grain, perhaps only one carload at a time. The ICC issued orders limiting the number of cars that carriers could place in

---

[1] Such volumes are handled by moving all the cars as a single unit, known as a *unit train*.

unit train service in an attempt to increase the supply of this equipment to the small user.[2] Service issues also occur in other modes. Small users of motor truck service continually point out that they are not given the same kind of service as larger users. This is particularly true in terms of how long it takes a carrier to pick up a small shipment and the transit time needed to move it from origin to destination.

Government Regulation—Contract and Exempt Carriers. There are other forms of for-hire carriage besides the common carrier. Chapter 6 identified the contract carrier who picks and chooses his customers and usually offers a specialized service and escapes the above noted obligations of the common carrier. There are also for-hire highway, water, and air carriers who operate without economic regulation. These so-called exempt freight carriers are able to avoid regulation usually because of the commodities they haul, although there are other minor reasons for exemption. In general, a water carrier transporting bulk commodities and a motor carrier hauling unprocessed agricultural products, ordinary livestock, and products of the sea are exempt from regulation. The significance of this is that competition between carriers, both intermodal and intramodal, can be very intense when these exempt commodities are involved. Since the various exemptions do not apply to all modes (e.g., no specific commodities are exempt when moved by rail, oil pipeline, or air), carriers in one mode may have a distinct advantage in terms of being able to rapidly change prices or services in response to changing needs of users. For example, many of the commodities suited for rail transportation, e.g., grain, coal, bulk fertilizers, and chemicals, fall under one of the above exemptions for either water or highway transportation. It has been suggested that such uneven regulation has placed the railroads at a competitive disadvantage in certain markets.

Derived Demand

Another reason why the management of transportation companies is unique vis-a-vis other firms relates to the type of demand for transport services. As indicated in Chapter 3, the demand for freight transport services is "derived" in the sense that there must be a demand for the product before it needs to be moved. The same obviously applies to the movement of passengers, i.e., there must be a reason for traveling between any two points. Although it may be possible for a passenger carrier to stimulate demand to a particular destination, it is virtually impossible for a freight carrier to do so.[3] Expressed another way, it may be out of the carrier's control to increase the total amount of freight moving between any city pair in the short run. The implication for carrier managers is that the most direct means of increasing volume is to take it away from some other carrier—either in the same mode or a different mode. All carriers recognize this and are alert for opportunities to divert traffic from

---

[2] The ICC ordered that no more than 25 per cent of a railroad's fleet of grain cars could be placed in unit train service.

[3] Note the joint promotions between Eastern Airlines and Walt Disney World in Orlando, Florida. The point of these promotions is to encourage people to go to Orlando via Eastern Airlines.

other carriers and are sensitive to having their own traffic taken away. The susceptibility of certain commodities being shifted from carrier to carrier is increased when no special transport services are required. Carriers in such cases are, therefore, not able to create any loyalty on the part of the user. The carrier's inability to increase the total market and to differentiate his service results in intense levels of competition between carriers, particularly between carriers of different modes.

Another significant implication of derived demand is that freight carriers must always be aware of the economic needs and condition of their client industries. This is demonstrated by the trend whereby carriers have employed marketing specialists who are responsible for a certain group of customers or commodities, e.g., grain, canned goods, machinery, paper products, and so on. The purpose of these "market managers" is to learn all there is to know about the client industry and design specific transportation programs for them. Why should carriers assume this responsibility? Because the well-being of the using firm is very important to the carrier. As suggested in Chapters 8 and 9, there is a ceiling on rate increases, and indiscriminate increases may cause the client to become noncompetitive with his competition. If the user can no longer compete, then the total amount of traffic available to the carrier declines. The challenge to the carrier's marketing staff is to be aware of each user's ability to compete with other sellers and commodities. As long as the carrier can keep his clients competitive, he may continue to get the business. Thus, carrier marketing may require more knowledge about specific industries than about transportation. In the view of some, this is what makes working for a carrier such a challenge.

Geographic Scope of Operations

Many for-hire carriers operate over a wide geographic area. This is significant because it complicates a carrier's ability to control his operations. That is, operators and vehicles may be away from the terminal or "home base" for substantial periods of time and beyond immediate supervision. For those carriers who have a way to maintain, maintenance employees are widely scattered and difficult to supervise. The same is true of carriers who have many terminals. For-hire carriers are expected to provide reliable and continuous service. In the case of freight carriers, a smooth flow of materials must be maintained between shipper and receiver. Thus, if the carrier fails to adequately control his operation, the consequences may be immediate and widespread for the carrier's customers. These factors contribute to the uniqueness of managing transportation companies.

The need to control the operation of vehicles while away from home base has led transportation companies to rely heavily on an extensive set of operating rules. These rules may be very specific and are designed to control the operator's activity regardless of the situation. The railroads have probably developed such rule making to the greatest extent. For example, there are rules that dictate how a train is to be operated in the face of an infinite variety of signal combinations, over grade crossings, over specific segments of track, and so on. Very little is left to the individual discretion of the crew. If a mishap occurs, an investigation is made to determine if a rule violation has occurred. If it has, the employees are disciplined, e.g., temporary furlough or dismissal.

While a desire to control operations encourages rules, so also does a concern for safety in operations. Transportation firms, unions, and public agencies place a great deal of emphasis on safety procedures. Many rules relating to number of continuous hours of work, number of work hours per month, and the need for periodic physical examinations are all mandated by government agencies such as the Federal Highway Administration (FHWA) and Federal Aviation Administration (FAA). These agencies wish to protect the public against unsafe operations by all carriers. Carrier managements and unions are also concerned with safety and they sometimes impose company rules over and above those required by government.[4] Obviously, the carriers wish to control their exposure to public liability claims, in addition to avoiding the adverse publicity and loss of use of a vehicle(s).

One aspect of rule making goes beyond that of safety. This relates to rules regarding job protection and security for union members. This will be discussed in more detail later in this chapter. It is sufficient to note here that the existence of these rules substantially reduces the freedom with which management can schedule the work force.

The combination of the various rules noted above imposed by 3 different interest groups (management, unions, and government) may significantly reduce the flexibility of the decision maker. Other industries, e.g., manufacturing, may not be exposed to such union rules and only recently have been exposed to extensive safety requirements laid down by the Occupational Safety and Health Administration.

Need for Continuous Operations

The importance of freight and passenger transportation to society and the economy was described in Chapter 1. The impact of interrupted transportation service is quickly felt by many parts of society and of the economy and over a wide geographic area. For example, note the effects of a work stoppage by a small group of independent truck owner–operators in January 1974 to protest rising fuel prices: ". . . the impact of this brief (about two weeks) interruption in only a small proportion of the nation's transportation service was sufficient to cause major disruptions in our economy. In some instances, the National Guard had to be called out to haul foodstuffs and other essentials of life to outlying communities faced with deprivation of bare subsistence."[5] In a similar vein, it is estimated that in 1970 a 12-week Teamsters strike in Chicago caused a loss of 1.5 billion dollars to businesses and individuals. A 1-week nationwide railroad shutdown would cut the annual gross national product by 12 billion dollars to 15 billion dollars.[6]

Not all interruptions of transportation services occur on a national or regional basis. Local strikes against a carrier, mechanical breakdowns, or unfavorable weather can cause serious disruptions in schedules. To the manufacturer waiting

---

[4]One of the reasons that the impact of the Occupational Safety and Health Administration is unclear is that the carriers are already regulated as to safety.

[5]Transportation Association of America, *Transportation—A Call for Action,* (Washington, D.C.: Transportation Association of America, March, 1976), p. 7.

[6]*Ibid.*

for some critical inventory or to the retailer waiting to replace out-of-stock merchandise, the delays may be critical. The same may be true of a business executive traveling in order to attend an important meeting or to see a customer. This all points to the fact that the economy is heavily dependent on the freight and passenger transportation system, i.e., interruptions cannot be tolerated.

The flow of goods is analogous to a pipeline. The transportation system must keep products moving or else serious backups and delays will occur. In order to perform this task, many transportation firms operate 24 hours per day and 7 days per week. Material shipped on Friday may be expected to arrive on Monday, and users may insist on overnight delivery within a range of 400 miles. Thus, the operations of a transportation company must be complementary to the needs of its clients, e.g., schedules are designed to deliver goods in the morning so that they are available that day. Much of the traffic is, therefore, moved between cities at night. The daylight activities consist primarily of delivering shipments, dispatching equipment to accumulate shipments, preparing documents, and otherwise making ready for the coming night's movements.

Role of Labor

Reference has already been made to the impact of unions on the operation of for-hire transportation companies. Certainly many of the improvements in working conditions can be attributed to union efforts, as can many of the labor-management problems. There are 2 reasons why specific mention is made of the relationship between transport management and unions: (1) Unions have enormous indirect power over the economy because of their capability to strike and shut down many carriers at once. (2) There are specific labor laws and procedures that apply to transportation and not to other industries.

Railroads. Railroads are a heavily unionized industry. There are 2 major unions for operating employees: The Brotherhood of Locomotive Engineers and the United Transportation Union (UTU). The UTU is a consolidation of formerly separate brotherhoods representing firemen, conductors, trainmen, and switchmen and also represents some engineers. Nonoperating employees may be represented by as many as 28 different unions. Perhaps the most familiar of these are the Brotherhood of Railway and Airline Clerks (BRAC) and the International Association of Machinists (IAM). Other non-operating unions include specific crafts, e.g., the Brotherhood of Railroad Signalmen (BRS) or the Brotherhood of Sleeping Car Porters (SCP), as well as more general unions such as the United Steel Workers (USW) and the Transport Workers of American (TWU). Finally, some railroads operate marine service, e.g., ferryboats. In this case, there are as many as 11 unions that represent marine related employees in railroading. In general, the operating unions are organized according to craft. The craft type organization is common for the nonoperating groups but does not always hold true, e.g., the TWU.

The Railway Labor Act (RLA) was passed in 1926 to provide a clear series of steps to the settlement of transport labor disputes.[7] It was passed precisely because of the serious economic implications of widespread strikes against the

---

[7] See Herbert R. Northrup, "The Railway Labor Act: A Critical Reappraisal," *Industrial and Labor Relations Review,* October, 1971, pp. 3–31.

railroads. Figure 15-1 identifies the steps involved in settling grievances and major disputes between union and management. Notice that in the case of grievances, special machinery has been created, i.e., the National Railroad Adjustment Board (NRAB). In the case of major disputes, there are many steps in the procedure which eventually lead to the White House. The steps do not automatically lead to resolution of the issue, however. The Presidential Emergency Board can only recommend and the disputing parties are not required to follow the President's suggested solution. Thus, a strike may still occur.[8]

Two reasons why railroad disputes seem to take so long to settle and why they occur so regularly are (1) the Railway Labor Act provides many intermediate steps to a nonbinding conclusion (why shouldn't union or management keep moving to the next step in order to gain a favorable settlement?) and (2) the grievance procedure. This procedure, through the NRAB, is supported primarily by public funds. This has a tendency to increase the number of cases and magnify their apparent significance. Thus, so-called minor issues may grow into major disputes.

Steps Involved Under the Railway Labor Act

	Disputes Over Interpretation of Agreements and Grievances	Major Disputes Over New Agreements
Step 1	Collective Bargaining Between Parties.	Collective Bargaining.
Step 2	National Railroad Adjustment Board (NRAB) (17 members from carriers — 17 members from National Unions — organized into 4 divisions).	National Mediation Board (NMB) (3 members appointed by President) Attempts to bring parties to agreement.
Step 3	NRAB Awards are final and binding. If no agreement, the issue will be mediated by mutually agreeable referees.	If no agreement, NMB requests both parties to voluntarily submit to binding arbitration.
Step 4	Decisions are subject to judicial review.	If parties not willing to arbitrate, then Presidential Emergency Board is called.
Step 5		Emergency Board makes recommendation to the President.
Step 6		If Emergency Board recommendation not followed by carrier or union, union may strike after 30-day cooling off period.

FIGURE 15-1 *Steps Involved Under the Railway Labor Act.*

[8]It was anticipated that the prestige of the presidency would encourage settlement. However, when this has not worked, Congress has passed special legislation in order to avert strikes.

Another reason for our chronic railroad labor problems relates to the mobility of employees to other industries. Railroad employees are usually categorized as either operating or nonoperating. The latter group has skills ranging from clerical to certain crafts such as carpentry and metalworking. This group has some mobility in terms of moving to nontransportation industries. The operating people have no such freedom. There are limited opportunities for a locomotive engineer, switchman, brakeman, and conductor outside the rail industry. Hence, the operating unions may take rigid positions over job protection issues, and this has spilled over to the nonoperating unions as well.

Airlines. As in the railroad industry, there are a few unions in the airline industry that represent most of the operating personnel and a larger number of unions that represent the remaining employees. The Airline Pilots Association (ALPA) and the Transport Workers Union (TWU) represent most of the pilots, engineers, navigators, and cabin attendants. Among the other unions representing airline employees are the IAM, BRAC, Communications Workers of America (CWA), and even the International Brotherhood of Teamsters (IBT). In all there are approximately 15 unions that represent employees of airlines. As in the case of railroads, the craft distinction is much stronger for operating employees.

The RLA also applies to the airline industry although there is some question as to whether or not the labor problems of the 2 industries are similar.[9] Since the railroad industry is highly integrated, i.e., a large proportion of freight is interchanged between the carriers, a strike against one or a few carriers can bring the whole system to a halt.[10] A strike against a few major air carriers may not have national emergency implications. Further, much of the RLA machinery is oriented toward rail and may not be responsive to airline needs.

A unique feature of the management–labor relationship in the airline industry is the so-called *Mutual Aid Pact* which began in 1958. This is an agreement between specific carriers to "pay over to the party suffering a strike an amount equal to its increased revenues attributable to the strike during the term thereof, less applicable added direct expense."[11] The payments are limited to a certain percentage of the struck carrier's normal operating expenses. The agreement has been amended several times since 1958 and the number of carriers participating in it have also changed. The agreement applies only to those carriers who have signed it. The Mutual Aid Pact is intended to enable airlines to cope with unreasonable demands from labor unions and to prevent unions from whipsawing one carrier against another, i.e., striking against one carrier, gaining a generous settlement, and then forcing it on the rest of the industry. It also recognizes that nonstruck airlines benefit from a strike against their competitors. On the other side of the coin, carriers cannot rely on the pact unless (1) the union's demands exceed the recommendations of a Presidential Emergency Board, or (2) a strike is called before the provisions of the RLA are exhausted, or (3) a strike is other-

[9] Title 2 of the RLA applies to airline employees and was passed in 1936.

[10] See Eli L. Oliver, "Labor Problems of the Transportation Industry," and Arthur M. Wisehart, "The Airlines' Recent Experiences Under the Railway Labor Act," *Law and Contemporary Problems,* Winter, 1960 and Jacob G. Kilgour, "Alternatives to the Railway Labor Act: An Appraisal," *Industrial and Labor Relations Review,* October, 1971, pp. 82–84.

[11] *Six Carrier Mutual Aid Pact,* 29 CAB 168 (1959).

wise illegal. Thus, the carriers cannot use the agreement to discourage collective bargaining, and both sides develop greater respect for the recommendations of Presidential Emergency Boards.

Highway Carriers. Labor relations for the remaining modes of transportation are governed by the same legal framework that affects labor relations in general. However, it is important to be aware of the unions involved because of their ability to affect both carriers and industrial firms.

The International Brotherhood of Teamsters normally represents the drivers, helpers, and warehousemen who work in the motor trucking industry. Originally, Teamsters' ability to call a nationwide strike, the Teamsters' influence is still a particular market. Since the 1960's, however, the trend has been toward regional and then nationwide bargaining. National, or so-called *master agreements,* are negotiated between employer groups, e.g., intercity or local truckers, and the union.[12] These master agreements are then supplemented by local agreements reflecting local differences. The supplemental agreements contain specific information affecting the employee, such as wages, hours of work, and benefits. The master agreement contains more general provisions relative to the creation of union shops, seniority, rules pertaining to trailer-on-flatcar service, and the protection of the employees' rights, including the right not to cross picket lines and to avoid handling struck goods. These latter provisions give the Teamsters a substantial amount of power, and the existence of a national agreement suggests that there could be a nationwide strike against trucking companies.

It should be noted that every truck driver or trucking employee does not necessarily belong to the Teamsters. There are many independent truck owners or owner-operators who are their own bosses. Belonging to the union has no benefit for this group of truckers. Further, not every trucking firm may be covered by the master agreement. Although this may somewhat temper the Teamsters' ability to call a nationwide strike, the Teamsters' influence is still awesome.

Intercity bus drivers, as well as local transit workers, may be represented by the Amalgamated Transit Union (ATU). Employer–union bargaining is carried out at the local community level or at best at the regional level. Even in the case of a nationwide bus company there may be 4 or 5 separate agreements, each agreement representing workers in a particular part of the country.

Water Carriers. Water carriers face a much more fragmented labor situation than do the truckers. Instead of having a nationwide industrial union like the Teamsters, these employees are represented by a combination of craft and industrial unions. There are as many as 16 maritime unions that represent workers on the inland waterways, the Great Lakes, and in the coastal and intercoastal trades.[13] The most familiar unions are the Seafarers International Union (SIU) and the National Maritime Union (NMU). In addition, other industrial nonmaritime

---

[12]Trucking Employers Inc. is the bargaining unit for approximately 10,000 motor freight carriers. The first master agreement was signed in 1964. See Dudley F. Pegrum, *Transportation Economics and Public Policy,* 3rd ed. (Homewood, Illinois: Richard D. Irwin, Inc., 1973), Chapter 20.

[13]Edward B. Shils, "Union Fragmentation: A Major Cause of Transportation Labor Crises," *Industrial and Labor Relations Review,* October 1971, pp. 45–46.

unions have been successful in organizing workers on the Great Lakes and the inland waterways where there has been a close relationship between the industry and the commodity transported. Thus, The United Mine Workers and the United Steel Workers represent workers on various coal and iron ore vessels. In some cases even the Teamsters are involved. One interesting point is that only approximately one-third of the workers on the inland waterways are organized. The balance work for small and/or family-owned barge companies and choose not to be unionized. This is in stark contrast to the other water trades that are heavily unionized.

Oil Pipelines. Oil pipelines companies probably face the most concentrated union bargaining in all of transportation. A single union may represent all operating and nonoperating employees. The Oil, Chemical and Atomic Workers International Union represents most of the people in this industry. The same union also represents many refinery workers.

Labor and Technology. For both maritime workers and workers employed in the motor trucking industry, a major issue has been the treatment of workers who may be replaced by advancing technology. Containerization of coastal and intercoastal shipments threatens longshoremen just as trailer-on-flatcar service threatens over-the-road truck drivers. In particular, the East Coast has been plagued with labor disputes over application of containerization. As these disputes arise, the compromise solution has normally involved creation of a "technological development fund." These funds require the carrier to pay so much per container or piggyback trailer into the union's retirement fund. As workers are displaced by technology, the pool of resources for worker benefits will not necessarily decline.

The above discussion can also be extended to other modes. Previous mention was made of union work rules designed to protect the jobs of union members. The state of this art is probably most advanced in the railroad industry. Rules may apply to minimum crew size, length of workday, and the strict maintenance of seniority lists within certain crafts or skills. For example, a brakeman is not allowed to perform the duties of a freight conductor even though he is qualified to do so. In the airline industry some carriers have agreed with the pilots' union to maintain lists of pilots by aircraft type and not switch pilots between aircraft type in the short run. Motor carriers may assign routes to drivers on the basis of seniority. Compensation for a particular truck run may be the result of a compromise agreement rather than actual hours or time spent. Such motor trucking agreements tend to be inflexible while technology continues to advance. Super highways have reduced the transit time between cities, but the compensation agreements may remain unchanged.

Relationship Between Labor and Capital

Before leaving the topic of labor it is worth discussing the relationship between capital and labor in the different modes. The above discussion, as well as the previous chapters, should convince the reader that each mode faces varying degrees of labor and capital intensiveness. Pipelines are highly capital intensive while motor carriers are labor intensive. Water carriers and airlines are more capital intensive than motor carriers while railroads depend heavily on both labor and capital. Two critical questions face the manager: (1) At what rate can capital be substituted for labor and (2) can the needed capital be obtained?

Expansion of vehicle capacity is one way of substituting capital for labor. A larger airplane, vessel, or more powerful locomotive will improve productivity, given a constant crew size. This is one of the obvious advantages to a motor carrier who uses double or triple trailers per power unit instead of a single trailer. The ability of a mode to use larger vehicles may depend on outside factors, such as highway length limits, dimensions of locks and river channels, and existing airport runways. Since many of these constraints are controlled by various levels of government, carriers devote much effort either individually or through trade associations to lobbying.

Another way to reduce labor is through increased mechanization. This option holds different opportunities for the various modes. Pipelines are already so heavily mechanized that labor savings in the future are not likely to be dramatic. The opportunities for motor carriers also appear to be limited, e.g., applying computers to accounting and other control systems. Airlines are attempting to mechanize baggage and freight movements through containerization. Containerization of international and domestic water cargoes is making significant reductions in stevedoring or longshoreman costs. Railroads still have opportunities to mechanize. Labor-saving machinery is being applied to the mechanical and maintenance functions as quickly as capital sources and union rules will allow. The eventual development of management information systems will also permit labor cuts in the clerical staff now employed by accounting and other departments.

Two constraints to a wholesale substitution of capital for labor are union opposition and the supply of capital. The details of union–management negotiations over job protection is beyond the scope of this book. However, the opportunity to eliminate jobs is generally the result of granting concessions to the union in some other area. Thus, one must be ready to compromise, as has been done in the case of containerization noted above.

Compromise may not be possible relative to the supply of capital. Certain modes, e.g., oil pipelines, that have a high return on investment (ROI) may have no problem in attracting capital. But a railroad that has an ROI of around 3 per cent may have difficulty. What do carriers do when their ROI does not attract investors? They try to generate needed capital internally or they go to the bond (loan) market. In periods of a soft economy the former method may be impractical and the latter is expensive. Thus, some projects, e.g., new equipment or machines, may have to be deferred. The problem is somewhat aggravated by advancing technology, especially as far as equipment is concerned. The cost of equipment is escalating rapidly and it may become outmoded by future technological developments. Thus, investors may associate substantial risks with large acquisitions.

ORGANIZATION AND OPERATIONS

There are many similarities between the organization of transportation companies and other business firms. However, because of some of the unique features of carrier management noted above, as well as the geographic territory to be covered, there are some differences in both terminology and emphasis. This section will identify some of the general organizational principles and operational practices of the carriers.

Organization and Operational Authority

Railroads. It is very characteristic of railroads to delegate much of their operating decision making to local levels. Railroads are usually divided into geographic units called *divisions* that are controlled by superintendents. Each of these superintendents is responsible for all train operations within his division. In a sense, a division is nothing more than a small railroad that is part of a larger system. The superintendents usually belong to the transportation department.

Working very closely with the transportation department are the mechanical department, which maintains the rolling stock (freight cars) and locomotives, and the maintenance of way department, which keeps the track, roadbed, and bridges in good repair. If a division is very large, a superintendent may have control over some local maintenance of way or mechanical functions, but the trend is for these 2 functions to be centralized. The left side of Figure 15-2 is a fairly typical railroad organization pattern for operations.

Figure 15-2 also shows how the traffic or marketing department may be organized. The marketing and operating departments are the two most critical departments in a railroad, and they are normally led by positions of equal rank, e.g., vice-president. The activities of the marketing department will be discussed later in this chapter. At this point it is useful to note that the marketing department is generally more centralized than the operations department is. There are other departments not shown in Figure 15-2 which will be discussed later. These include legal, accounting, and industrial development. These activities are normally headed by a vice-president or a general manager and they report to the president or executive vice-president.

Highway Carriers. Motor trucking companies also have a decentralized organizational approach to operations, perhaps even more so than railroads do. The heart of any motor carrier's operation is at the terminal level. Typical activities performed by a motor truck terminal include local pickup and delivery, loading and

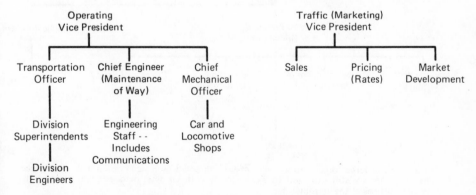

FIGURE 15-2 *Typical Railroad Organization of Operating and Traffic Departments.*

unloading at the terminal dock, sorting freight by destination, transferring freight from one highway carrier's vehicles to those of another or interchanging trailers between carriers when interchanging of freight takes place, preparing documents such as freight bills, vehicle maintenance, certain administrative activities, and, often, sales. The trucking industry tends to decentralize a little more than the railroads by putting sales at the local level. Large trucking firms may group a number of terminals under a district manager. This move is designed to coordinate activities between terminals and to reduce the absolute number of terminals reporting to a single executive. Figure 15–3 depicts a large motor carrier's organization. Note that the terminal and district managers have a direct line to the vice-president of operations. It is difficult to generalize where certain staff activities will be placed in a motor carrier's organization. Such activities as finance, law, and personnel will be close to the president, e.g., headed by vice-presidents. Accounting may be under a general manager and report to one of the other vice-presidents, e.g., finance.

Each terminal may be considered its own profit center. To emphasize the interdependence between terminals, it is not unusual that a terminal is credited with one-half the inbound and outbound revenue. Similarly, one-half of the inbound and outbound costs is charged to the terminal. The recognition of so-called *traffic lanes* between specific terminals encourages terminal managers to increase volume. Thus, when a terminal's inbound traffic exceeds its outbound traffic, the terminal must absorb some of the cost of returning those trucks empty to the originating terminals. The cost of returning empty is virtually the same as when the truck is loaded. Since the manager cannot control the amount of inbound freight, i.e., these are sales made by another terminal, all he can do is try to find some freight to eliminate the empty back haul. The costs may remain approximately the same, but at least there is some revenue to offset these costs. To accomplish this, the terminal sales force may be encouraged to find business that is going in a particular direction, or the rate department may be encouraged to establish a lower rate on certain commodities to encourage more business in the back-haul direction.

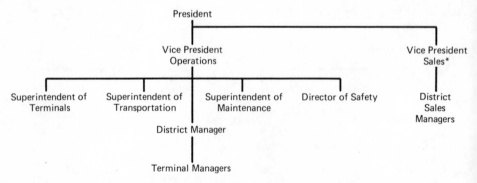

*In the case of larger organizations sales may be directed by a vice president. In such cases sales personnel are still expected to work closely with terminal managers and in fact will have their offices at the terminal.

FIGURE 15-3 *Typical Motor Trucking Company Organization (Not Including Staff Departments).*

Large bus companies also have a decentralized organization. Terminal managers report to area general managers who are primarily concerned with operating the bus company. If the company is large enough, these area managers report to regional vice-presidents who in turn report to national executives. Ticketing is considered part of operations. Sales development work, e.g., developing promotions for tours and charters, is a staff activity under the regional vice-president. In other words, all aspects of the day-to-day operations are organized by area.

Water Carriers. The following discussion pertains primarily to barge operators. There are many contract operators on the river and canal system who contract their tow boat services out to a specific shipper or barge company. These entrepreneurs are analogous to the owner–operator in the highway carrier industry. Their organization centers around the owner himself. The amount of activity depends on the demands of the market. In contrast, of the several hundred barge lines, there are only from 20 to 30 large common carriers that enjoy the majority of business on the river system. This group has a more formal organizational structure.

Operations and sales are the 2 most important departments. Both units may be led by vice-presidents or the units report directly to an executive vice-president or even the president. The departments are at an equal level and depend on much coordination. The sales department will be discussed in the following section.

The operating department is often divided into 3 units: traffic, maintenance, and personnel. Traffic is responsible for dispatching the power (tow boats) and the barges. The traffic unit of barge lines that operate on both the upper and lower river systems may be divisionalized on that geographic basis. This is primarily due to the different operating conditions below St. Louis. Even with divisional traffic offices, most of the control over long-haul barge movements is centralized. The division offices are designed to handle local operations, e.g., spotting barges for loading and unloading.

The maintenance group is concerned with keeping the fleet in good repair. It is also charged with safety programs and procedures. The third element of operations, personnel, staffs the tow boats. These units are just like ships at sea in the sense that crews spend extended time periods aboard, e.g., 30 days on followed by 30 days off. So many deckmates, cooks, and officers must be scheduled to board at various points along the river(s). Replacements must also be supplied when illness occurs on board.

The actual operations of carriers in all 3 of the above freight modes—railroad, highway, and water—are very similar. Through movements between major terminals are separated from the pickups and deliveries which may be required to gather and distribute individual shipments at origin and destination points. For example, trains are scheduled to move between major yards. Within a metropolitan area served by such a yard, switch engines are used to pick up and deliver loaded and empty rail cars. Outside these areas local trains are used. Such locals cover all the stops between 2 yards. Once the local reaches the yard, it turns around and performs the same function in the opposite direction. In the trucking industry, over-the-road trucks go only from terminal to terminal. Local trucks make the pickups and deliveries. Barge lines have a similar pattern of through movements supplemented by separate vessels performing pickup and delivery.

Oil Pipelines. Oil pipelines are a specialized form of carrier that have close ties to petroleum companies. Although some pipeline companies are independent for-hire carriers, most are controlled by a major petroleum company, e.g., Standard Oil, Exxon, and Phillips, to name a few. Because of the specialized nature of the products being transported and the captive market many pipelines enjoy, the sales or marketing function is not a dominant part of a pipeline organization. Instead, it is the dispatching or scheduling that is of critical importance.

Although it is possible to put 2 different grades of crude next to each other or 2 different refined products in a products pipeline, there is some mixing or contamination at the interface of the 2 commodities. The amount of contamination, ranging from 50 to 2,000 barrels, can be minimized by careful scheduling based on each product's specific gravity, sediment and water content, and viscosity. Attempts to minimize the number of interfaces between different grades of oil or different products encourage moving oil or products in as large a batch as possible. However, the size of the batch is also a function of the amount of storage space, i.e., tanks, which are available at origin or destination terminals. Storage must also be considered when shipments are interchanged between one pipeline company and another. Thus, the ultimate schedule may be a function of the number of products, their physical characteristics, and storage space at origin and destination as well as intermediate points. These schedules are made several days in advance, and when a carrier deals in only a limited number of products, the schedule may form a regular cycle, e.g., a specific grade of oil is shipped the same day each week.

One other aspect of pipelining deserves mention. Carriers spend much capital and effort on monitoring the flow of commodities. In addition to providing information on how many barrels have been delivered to a particular destination, constant monitoring provides indications of malfunctions or leaks. In such cases, a portion of the line is shut down and a "line-walker" determines the precise location of the leak. The importance of preventing leaks has encouraged carriers to invest heavily in electronic control systems.

Airlines. Not surprisingly, operations and sales are very significant in an airline organization. Operations may be divided into 3 departments: flight operations, ground operations, and maintenance.[14] The flight operations group is responsible for piloting, dispatching, and controlling in-flight aircraft. Ground operations controls the personnel and operation at each of the carrier's stations. Although some servicing and maintenance take place at the stations, carriers also have a specific maintenance base for major work and periodic inspections. The control over operations may be characterized as centralized.

There are two aspects that make airline organization different from the organization of the other modes. One is that there may be a separate communications and computer services department at the vice-presidential level. This reflects the airlines' heavy dependence on passenger reservation systems. Other carriers have computer departments, but they are often concerned mainly with accumulating and accessing historical data. The reservation system for airlines, however, is an important operational and selling tool that affects a carrier's service and sales

---

[14] John H. Frederick, *Commercial Air Transportation* (Homewood, Illinois: Richard D. Irwin, Inc., 1961), pp. 351–358.

volume. Thus, many resources are devoted to improving the reliability and scope of the carrier's information system. The second aspect of airline organization relates to the formal liaison established between passenger sales and operations. This often takes the form of a scheduling committee which consists of representatives of both groups plus other top executives. The purpose of these committees is to work out natural and inevitable conflicts that occur between operations and sales. For example, the desire of sales may be to maximize the number of flights, but operation's interest may be to routinize and simplify schedules. Thus, the objectives of the 2 groups may be in conflict.

Selling Function

Freight Service. Although there is great similarity in how freight carriers of different modes approach the selling function, there are some differences in the organization of the sales force. Railroads may be highly centralized, i.e., the central office takes an active hand in controlling the activities of regional and local salespeople. Water carriers either have a small, highly centralized force or they rely on brokers. As noted, trucking companies typically delegate much of the selling activity to the terminal level. In any case, in all modes, salespeople are not restricted to a particular division or part of the system as is the case for operating employees. Salespeople are expected to be familiar with the entire system regardless of mode.

Being a freight carrier's representative is both challenging and frustrating. A carrier's product is a service which the client (user) can best evaluate only after the service has been tried. In the case of new business, a user may experiment with modes and carriers until he settles on a particular pattern. Thus, a carrier has the opportunity to demonstrate the quality of his service. In the case of existing traffic carried by another carrier, however, the salesperson must assure comparable service plus some added reason to encourage the user to switch carriers. In many cases, the carrier's representative must simply ask for some business so that he may demonstrate his carrier's service. This approach is so widespread that the carrier's salespeople are usually referred to as *solicitors*.

Much of the solicitor's time is also spent in visiting existing clients and taking care of customer service problems that may develop. Obviously, the objective is to make sure that an existing user is not lured away by another carrier. Consequently, the field sales force becomes the liaison between the customer and other carrier activities such as dispatching, equipment supply, pricing, and claims. The sales staff must be able to understand the nature of these activities and have a good working relationship with the various departments within the carrier organization.

Sales representatives face another kind of challenge. It has been noted that freight transportation companies transport many different kinds of commodities and the solicitors are expected to be knowledgeable about all of them. This is not an overpowering challenge for water, oil pipeline, or airline companies because their range of commodities carried is relatively narrow. Other carriers of freight may carry a wide range of commodities—from abacuses to zirconium. In fact, the range of commodities is so great that salespeople cannot be expected to have any more than a superficial knowledge of each commodity. Yet, it is important for the carrier to be an expert in the user's products, especially those products that generate a high percentage of revenue.

As noted previously, some carriers have established market specialists or managers who are supposed to be knowledgeable about their commodity specialties. These are positions within the marketing or traffic department whose purpose is market development.[15] The market managers may be responsible for a range of tasks from developing revenue and equipment forecasts to establishing sales tools for the field sales force. The market manager's mission is to develop programs to attract new business and/or retain existing business. The interface between sales and market managers is that salespeople provide information on current user problems and new opportunities to the market manager. The manager develops a price/service package for the client and then the salesperson services the account as a regular call. The market manager is, therefore, the source of expertise for the sales force.

Passenger Service. One might suspect that selling intercity passenger transportation would be considerably more straightforward than selling freight service. The wide range of commodities is lacking and the type of travel may simply be classified into business or pleasure. Unfortunately, such perceptions are oversimplifications. The selling function in an airline, motor bus company, or the National Railroad Passenger Corporation (Amtrak) may be somewhat different from selling freight service, but it is no less complex.

There are many aspects to selling passenger service. Direct advertising, usually focusing on convenient schedules or comfortable equipment, is an important part of a carrier's total marketing effort. It is surprising how much the average consumer is bombarded by promotional messages ranging from musical Amtrak jingles to information on the benefits of one kind of bus over another. Also, one can hardly live in a metropolitan area and not be aware of which airline flies directly to other major cities or which airline has more "wide-bodies." All of this reflects 2 critical dimensions of competition between carriers, i.e., schedules and equipment. It also recognizes that the objective is to keep a carrier's name in front of the consumer.

Carriers do not consider passengers as a homogeneous group. The emergence of various promotional fares recognizes different market segments and these promotional fares are all aimed at these particular segments. Schedules are designed not only for the early morning and evening needs of the businessman, but also for the peak Friday and Sunday periods for pleasure and business travelers.[16]

Motor bus companies, airlines, and Amtrak sell both freight and passenger transportation. In the case of terminal-to-terminal package service offered by bus companies and Amtrak, the customer takes the package to the terminal and gives the agent the proper instructions. The consignee must pick up the shipment from the destination terminal. Consequently, much of the selling is done on an impersonal basis, i.e., advertising which builds customer awareness. In contrast,

---

[15] See Alan J. Stenger and Frederick J. Beier, "Effective Carrier Marketing Strategies: The Case of the Railroads," *Transportation Journal,* Summer 1976, pp. 63–72.

[16] Martin T. Farris and Forrest E. Harding, *Passenger Transportation* (Englewood Cliffs, N.J.: Prentice-Hall, Inc., 1976), p. 171.

the airlines generally have a separate sales force for air freight. This group has much the same function as other freight-oriented salespeople.

There may be 3 distinct parts to a carrier's selling organization for passenger service. First, there are the various sales offices located throughout the system and sometimes beyond the system. The purpose of the off-line sales offices is to service clients who need to travel over the system but are domiciled in some off-line location. For example, Trans World Airlines (TWA) does not serve Minneapolis–St. Paul, but it does maintain a sales office there for those people who will be connecting with TWA in their travels.[17] The offices are all connected to the airline's reservation system and can provide complete information and ticketing needs. These sales offices are very important because they represent a visible means for the public to respond to a carrier's advertisement.

Second, of great significance is the volume of business (tickets) written by the nation's travel agencies.[18] In a sense, each travel agency is another sales office for the carrier. When the travel agency sells a ticket, it gets a commission from the carrier. These commissions tend to be standardized, but travel agencies are often capable of influencing a traveler to choose one carrier over another. Thus, the carriers expend substantial effort in providing all forms of promotional material, e.g., flight bags, coasters, buttons, and other premiums, to keep the travel agencies happy.

The third part of a carrier's selling effort is the national account executive who concentrates on the travel needs of major companies who have many employees who travel. Often these executives also call on major travel agencies.

Evaluating the Selling Effort. In most cases, freight and passenger sales efforts are evaluated by the amount of traffic they generate. Traffic is most often measured in terms of the gross revenue it produces, simply because it may be the easiest measure to use. A sales representative may be assigned a specific geographic territory and is credited with the corresponding revenue. This is not to suggest that the sales force is solely responsible for all sales, but it is a commonly used barometer of its effectiveness. Many other factors may be taken into consideration in order to get a more precise measure of effectiveness. Such considerations include the state of the economy, major industrial strikes, equipment shortages, and innumerable other qualitative factors.

It is important to realize that it is a long step between maximizing revenue and maximizing contribution to profit. If the sales force is rewarded for maximizing sales revenue, it may encourage marginally profitable or unprofitable business. This phenomenon occurs very frequently in the railroad industry, perhaps because of the many low freight rates published by the carriers. Some railroads have experienced the ironic situation of suffering losses in the face of record freight revenues. Again, the sales force is not totally responsible, but when business is slow, the carrier's representatives may seek any kind of business in order to look good.

---

[17] An airline receives a portion of the revenue for booking the passenger on another carrier's flight. Thus, TWA would be willing to write the ticket even if other carriers were involved.

[18] It has been estimated that 35 per cent of United States domestic airline ticket sales and 90 per cent of international airline sales are made by travel agents. See Terry J. Hooper and Everett E. Johnston, "Marketing High-Speed Ground Transportation," *High-Speed Ground Transportation Journal*, Fall, 1974.

In order to avoid such a trap, freight carriers are devoting many dollars and man-hours to improve their information systems. The goal is to identify which commodities are the most profitable and to concentrate the marketing effort on those commodities. Commodity movements are analyzed according to a number of factors, including product type, volume, origin/destination, claim experience, and others. The results of this analysis are passed on to the sales representatives in the hope that the more profitable commodities and markets can be exploited. This is another example of the transportation industries' increasing use of computers. It appears that in the future there will be continued development and sophistication of computer applications in transportation company management.

One of the most important aspects of any carrier's selling effort is the price he charges. Pricing is such a specialized and complex activity that it is dealt with specifically later in this chapter.

Staff Functions

Finance. One of the most important staff functions in any carrier organization is finance. Providing adequate working capital, analyzing lease or buy decisions for fleet and terminal expansions, and securing long-term financing are all regular activities of the finance department. These activities are also common among most industrial finance departments. However, there are some special aspects of carrier finance that should be pointed out.

As far as some modes of transportation are concerned, and especially motor carriers, a basic measurement of health is the operating ratio. You will recall that this ratio relates the operating cost of performing the service with the operating revenue. The industry-wide operating ratios of the several modes of transportation were discussed in Chapters 10 through 14. Thus, we know that the operating ratio of Class I railroads is usually in the seventies; for larger regulated interstate motor trucking companies it is in the middle nineties; for larger regulated inter-city bus companies it is approximately 90; for larger domestic water carriers operating on the inland and coastal waterways it is usually in the high eighties; for interstate oil pipelines it is in the fifties; and for domestic trunk airlines it has been erratic, ranging from the high eighties to the high nineties in recent years.

The character of a carrier's operating ratio has great bearing on a carrier's attitude toward cost changes. Because of their high operating ratio, motor trucking companies may face immediate negative economic consequences of an increase in costs, e.g., fuel or wages, but a railroad or oil pipeline may be able to absorb these increases, if only in the short run.[19]

Operating ratios should be interpreted with some caution. Sometimes substantial operating expense is devoted to leasing vehicular equipment and facilities such as terminals. Leasing is an effective way of eliminating cash down payments and tying up capital, but it may be more expensive in the long run. Some carriers have established subsidiary leasing companies from whom they lease their equipment. The carrier charges off the entire lease expense, increasing the operating ratio, while the payments are going to another part of the same company. In

---

[19] Although the airline industry may also have a high operating ratio, a more conventional method of quickly evaluating the health of an airline is to look at the ratio of passenger-miles to available seat-miles, i.e., the load factor. A load factor over 50 per cent is usually considered acceptable.

addition to making a return on its subsidiary leasing business, motor carriers may want to inflate operating ratios to use as evidence when they request that they be permitted to raise their rates.[20]

It should be noted that there are at least 2 other ways to finance equipment: conditional sales agreements and equipment trust certificates. Both of these methods generally require cash down payments and extend up to a 15-year repayment period. Title to the asset remains with the lender under a conditional sales agreement. Trust certificates give the holder a lien against the equipment. Since both arrangements are classified as long-term debt on the carrier's financial statement, they do not affect the operating ratio.

Other Staff Functions. Although it is not usually one of the largest departments in a carrier's organization, the legal department is one of the most influential. This is a reflection of the double set of regulations to which the regulated carrier is exposed. That is, in addition to the battery of other legal specialists that any corporation needs, there are lawyers who specialize in transportation regulation. People who are working in the marketing and operating departments find themselves in regular contact with the legal department, particularly to review the legalities of proposed changes in services and prices.

The accounting department is also a critical group. The activities of this department range from billing shippers for services rendered to filing reports with the ICC or other regulatory agencies. Virtually all of the data which a carrier eventually needs, e.g., traffic flows, revenue generation, and profitability, are furnished by the accounting department. It is not uncommon for the accounting department to control the computer or management information system for the carrier.

SPECIFIC CARRIER DECISIONS

The last section of this chapter discusses some basic decisions that carriers must make in managing their enterprises. These are problems that in varying degrees confront carriers in all modes. The discussion is not meant to include an exhaustive list of decisions but only to highlight some of the more important areas of decision making.

Equipment Selection and Utilization

A carrier must analyze the demand for the use of vehicular equipment very carefully. If he overestimates demand, he will have a great deal of working capital tied up in idle equipment. If he underestimates demand, he may lose business to a competitor. The most recent example of this problem occurred in the airline industry in connection with the purchase of wide-bodied jets. Many carriers overestimated the future demand for air passenger service and found themselves with Boeing 747s, DC-10s, and L-1011s being stored or up for sale.[21] Cost of the wide-bodied aircraft is well over 20 million dollars per airplane.

---

[20] Gayton E. Germane, Nicholas A. Glaskowsky, Jr., and James L. Heskett, *Highway Transportation Management* (New York: McGraw-Hill Book Company, Inc., 1963), p. 245.

[21] Richard J. Harris, "Early Revival Unlikely as Jumbo-Plane Sales Continue to Languish," *The Wall Street Journal,* August 10, 1976, p. 1.

Equipment selection is made complex for all modes because of the increase in specialization. Freight transportation equipment is sometimes designed to fit the needs of a specific group of users. The benefits to the affected user may be decreased handling, packaging, claim, or some other cost. The carrier, however, experiences a decline in the variety of commodities for which a piece of equipment can be used. Special railroad cars have sometimes replaced the general-purpose boxcar in transporting grain, canned goods, automobiles and automobile parts, and many other commodities. Although the trend is less pronounced in trucking, there are many motor carriers who face the same problem. Many airlines debate over the advantages of all-cargo aircraft versus combined passenger and cargo configurations, and barge lines must use different equipment for different liquid and dry bulk cargoes. Oil pipelines, of course, do not face these problems.

In freight transportation some users attempt to assure themselves of a supply of special equipment through purchase or lease. For-hire carrier equipment is used in peak demand periods only. Thus, the for-hire carrier is exposed to cyclical variations in demand for his equipment. The combination of all these factors encourages the carrier to be conservative in the acquisition of specialized equipment.

All modes experience difficulties in their attempts to maximize equipment utilization. However, the problems faced by the railroad industry may be the most notorious. Delays in railroad freight yards, as well as in loading and unloading by shippers and consignees, contribute to long transit times. It is common for a freight car to take 30 days to complete a round trip between Chicago and California. Considering that there may be no load on the return trip, that means that the freight car may make only 12 revenue trips per year—if it is demanded throughout the year. Such utilization makes it very difficult to achieve a satisfactory return on investment on an asset which costs anywhere between $20,000 and $50,000 per car.

Collectively, the railroads are in the process of trying to improve utilization of equipment. Carriers are working at improving yard performance and the efficiency of equipment interchanges. Beyond that, the Association of American Railroads (AAR) is developing a massive information system designed to monitor the movements of freight cars throughout the country.[22] It is hoped that such a system will identify where delays occur and will suggest corrective action.

Similar problems exist for barge lines that are experiencing more delays on the rivers. One barge costing anywhere from $150,000 to $700,000 may make only 6 round trips per shipping season between Minneapolis and New Orleans.

The low load factors of airlines were discussed in Chapter 14. In addition to the reasons for underutilization mentioned there, airlines find that equipment may accumulate at one part of the system and has to be repositioned for the coming day. The reason that there are many night flights, even with a low load factor, is simply that the aircraft have to return anyway. Many of these flights are also used for freight.

The issue of utilization and return loads is also complicated by specialized equipment. Because specific commodities tend to flow in one direction only, it

---

[22]See William H. VanSlyke, "TRAIN II—Advanced Computerized Freight Car Control," *Traffic World*, June 23, 1975.

is difficult to find return loads, particularly if the vehicle is only suited for one commodity. Truckers cope with this problem better than other modes do. In fact, the difference between success and failure for a special-commodity motor trucking company is the company's ability to find back hauls.

Pricing

The job of setting rates and fares is one of the more difficult areas of carrier management. Chapters 8 and 9 described the theory behind various price-making strategies, price-making factors to consider in transportation, the different kinds of rates, and the price-making procedure. The following discussion will describe the practical aspects of pricing from the carrier's perspective. Pipelines are not discussed because of their specialized nature.

It is obvious that freight rates can be both raised and lowered by a carrier and, as noted in Chapter 3, rates may be increased by either a percentage amount or a fixed dollar and cents amount. Rate changes may also apply to one, a small number, or all commodities carried and/or routes served by a carrier. What is not so obvious is that it is very difficult for a carrier to individually increase the rates for a specific group of users or a geographic region or route. The affected users may claim that they are being discriminated against and switch their business to another carrier of the same or different mode if at all possible. Thus, price increases do not generally occur unless all or most of the competing carriers within the same mode wish to act together. The regulated surface carriers then petition the ICC and/or a state regulatory agency for permission to raise their rates. The request must be justified in terms of the revenue needs of the carriers to cover increased cost. It may happen that carriers of one mode, e.g., railroads, will refrain from asking for an increase, not from a lack of agreement on their part, but because of a conviction that the competing mode(s) will not react by increasing their rates, thereby encouraging the traffic to shift to a competing mode(s).

The ICC and/or state agency will examine such requests and will rule on the appropriateness of the proposed increase. It may decide that an intended general increase is not in the public interest for certain products[23] or that a smaller increase should be granted. When the regulatory agency grants permission, then all affected rate tariffs, i.e., price lists, are amended. The need for carriers to act in unison and the frequent delays while the regulatory agency ponders the case have the effect of increasing rates sporadically in a step-like manner.

While rate increases often take place in steps and are the result of collective proposals by carriers, rates can and do move down as the result of action by individual carriers and without any particular pattern. Industrial firms (users) spend many hours studying and proposing rate reductions to carriers. The proposals may be documented with arguments based on price-making factors such as those discussed in Chapter 9. In addition to looking at the validity of the user's arguments, the carrier will assess the proposal's impact on his own revenue. If he reduces a rate for one user, he may have to reduce the rates for many users who give the carrier similar business. For example, if a carrier reduces a rate on

---

[23] For example, the ICC has been reluctant to permit carriers to raise their rates on fresh fruit and vegetables and other commodities. Regulation of transportation pricing is discussed in Chapters 21 through 25.

paint at the urging of one manufacturer, all other manufacturers may make a similar request. The secondary effect is that the rate reduction may spread to other related products. Thus, varnish or resin producers may argue that they also should be granted the lower rate. One of the first considerations for a carrier is to evaluate how much his total revenue is likely to be reduced if a rate reduction is made.

Hopefully, a potential revenue loss may be offset by a gain in revenue, either in terms of new business that will move because of the lower rates or traffic that will not be lost to competing carriers or markets, and the contribution to fixed expenses may actually be greater than it otherwise might have been. This can be a very subjective analysis and the carrier may have to rely on data provided by interested users. Also, any commodity expertise on the part of carrier sales and/or pricing personnel will be made use of to evaluate the benefits of the reduction. The potential gains are then weighed against the costs.

Carriers will also look at the likely reaction of their peers, i.e., other carriers within the same mode, as well as those in competing modes of transportation. Some users will make the same proposal to a number of carriers who may disagree on whether or not the reduction should be granted. Carriers are very sensitive to the interests of their peers not only because of possible pricing retaliation on their part but also because there is a great deal of traffic that is interchanged between them. Therefore, they may not want to jeopardize their relationship with interchanging carriers who may be in a position to divert substantial traffic to other connecting lines. Further, carriers recognize that there is a need for them to cooperate on a long-term basis. Hence, a carrier may be reluctant to ignore the objections of his peers unless the prospects of revenue and profit are substantial.

The carrier will take a position on the user's proposal after he has looked at the above factors. If he is opposed, he will indicate so to the user-proponent. If there is room for compromise, the carrier may suggest changes that could make the proposal acceptable. If the carrier favors the reduction, he will then generally try to get agreement from the appropriate rate bureau. The normal practice is that a simple majority of those rate bureau members voting will carry the issue. If the bureau turns the proposal down, the individual carrier still has the right to establish the rate through "independent action." In this case, the rate will apply only to the one carrier unless other carriers establish the same rate later in an attempt to remain competitive.

The above scenario about freight rate increases and decreases applies mainly to railroads and motor carriers. These are the modes that have the most formalized common carrier pricing procedures and the modes that must make their pricing activities most public. For example, each rate proposal considered by a rate bureau, whether proposed by a user or a carrier, is summarized and distributed to every conceivable interested party. Thus, the traffic manager of a manufacturing firm knows what rate proposals are being made for all firms with whom his firm competes. If his firm will be adversely affected, he will notify the carrier(s) involved and register his feelings. Such user response not only helps the carrier decide what position to take on any issue, but it also makes the pricing department feel it lives in a fishbowl. It is clear that there will be no rate secrets between users and regulated common carriers.

The situation is a little different for domestic water carriers. Later in this book[24] it will be pointed out that many of the commodities handled by water carriers are exempt from rate regulation. These exemptions apply to bulk materials, and although motor carriers also enjoy an exemption for nonmanufactured agricultural commodities, the exemption does not have the same impact as the water carrier exemption. In fact, the vast majority of commodities transported by domestic water carriers is not subject to rate regulation. The significance of this is that most water carrier rates are negotiated with individual users; this reflects the circumstances of supply and demand without the need to file the proposed rates with a regulatory agency. Although there are water carrier rate bureaus, the rate bureau procedure is much less important in this industry. It is also difficult to determine what other firms are charging since rates may not be published because most traffic is unregulated. Under these circumstances, there is generally a great deal of informal communication among competitors on the rates being charged.

Pricing in the airline industry involves both cooperative and individual efforts. The carriers are prohibited by the CAB from formally consulting with each other on rates and fares. Although the rate bureau mechanism is not available to air carriers and rate and fare changes are proposed by carriers individually, there is substantial uniformity in rates and fares. This reflects the need for any carrier to remain competitive. Since freight carriers have been permitted to agree on rules, regulations, and classifications, a single tariff format is used by all carriers. A single publishing organization publishes most domestic air freight tariffs. The purpose of this uniformity is to encourage the development of through movements of freight, i.e., involving more than one carrier.

Bus companies and Amtrak are exposed to a great deal of price competition and must ensure that their fares are not too high. In addition to competing with Amtrak at many points, bus companies face a great deal of intramodal competition. Although the Greyhound Corporation may enjoy the lion's share of the intercity bus market, it still must compete with many small competitors throughout the country. A rate bureau, the National Bus Traffic Association (NBTA), has been set up to provide a forum for discussing fare proposals among bus operators. The NBTA also publishes the tariffs and represents the industry before the ICC. The Association has between 400 and 500 members.

Risk Management

There are two noteworthy aspects of risk management for carriers. First, most railroads and large motor freight and passenger carriers are self-insured to cover liability for damage to third parties, loss of or damage to property carried, and loss of or damage to equipment. If regulated motor carriers do not have sufficient capital to satisfy the regulatory agency's requirements to act as a self-insurer as to third party liability and cargo, they must purchase insurance protection. There usually are no regulatory agency requirements on third-party liability or cargo insurance for the other modes, but insurance is usually purchased by nonrail carriers. Such insurance is of particular importance in air

[24] See Chapter 23.

transportation in which a single accident can result in hundreds of millions of dollars in claims against a carrier, in addition to the loss of an expensive vehicle.

Second, freight carriers devote a great deal of attention to freight loss and damage control and prevention. Whether the carrier is self-insured or is carrying cargo insurance (insurance rates depend on the carrier's loss and damage record), claim prevention can result in cutting carrier costs. Carriers conduct test shipments, at no cost to users, which evaluate various methods of packaging or loading within a vehicle. Similar assistance may be provided to users in the design of packages and other protective containers. As indicated in Chapter 6, the amount of liability for loss and damage to freight carried varies somewhat by mode and, in some cases in which only limited liability is assumed, the user, in order to protect his interests, often purchases cargo insurance. This is especially true in the case of water transportation in which very little liability is assumed by the carriers.

Carrier-User Coordination Activities

Industry's widespread adoption of the business logistics concept has forced freight carriers to view their services in broader terms than just providing transportation from one point to another. Transportation is properly conceived as a critical link between consignor and consignee, not an end in itself. All 3 parties, shipper, carrier, and receiver, define an interdependent system. Thus, low freight rates may be a false economy if greater costs for inventory, claims, or packaging are incurred by other members of the system. Carriers are becoming more sensitive to what is termed the *total cost of transportation* and some carriers have attempted to coordinate their operations with the operations of shippers and receivers, as noted in Chapter 6.

Equipment design is an example of this type of coordination. Changes are occurring that encourage rapid loading and discharge of commodities, thereby minimizing the costs of handling. Carriers also participate in the design of pallet systems that facilitate handling unitized loads (see Chapter 24) on and off the vehicle. Carriers also assist in returning reusable pallets or setting up cooperative pools of pallet users.

The development of trailer-on-flatcar or piggyback service and other forms of intermodal coordination are examples of a more systematic approach to transportation that are of benefit to users. Trailer-on-flatcar and container-on-flatcar service involves voluntary agreements between railroads and motor carriers which attempt to combine rail economy with the door-to-door through service of the trucker. These services are also available to individual industrial firms and freight forwarders who wish to have their trailers, trailer bodies, or containers carried by rail. Other forms of coordinated service are also emerging between the several modes. One unusual example is found in the case of bulk commodities in which material handlers transfer, store, or process products from rail cars into trucks. This service appeals to many small users of chemicals and related commodities who either cannot order in carload quantities or are located off-rail. These material handlers not only extend rail economy to the smaller firms but also maintain door-to-door service. The ability to get low rail carload rates often offsets the cost of transfer from rail to truck. These material handlers may either be independent or be part of a carrier's organization. They may also have very mobile equipment that permits operation at almost any location.

Another area of coordination between user and carrier occurs in the area of information systems. Programs are being developed that permit direct communication between user and carrier computers. For example, many large users have established their own computer systems to monitor shipment movements on a daily basis. These programs are designed to determine if delays will occur and then advise the consignee accordingly. Thus, the receiver may be able to avoid having a crew of warehousemen standing around waiting for a shipment that does not arrive on time or at all.

MANAGEMENT OF PRIVATE TRANSPORTATION

There are a number of parallels between how a for-hire carrier manages his enterprise and how a user operates his own freight transportation fleet. For example, high levels of service are often required. Special or emergency shipments may become common if everyone wants his shipment yesterday. Counteracting the demands for service is the fact that, in large firms, such fleets are operated as profit centers that charge other divisions or departments rates for services rendered. These rates are normally based on and are competitive with rates of for-hire carriers. Failure to be competitive causes the other profit centers in the company to be reluctant to use the private system. If the managers of the private fleet fail to achieve a reasonable level of income, the system may be short lived.

Labor problems and difficulties of equipment selection and utilization are all faced by the private carrier. For example, dealing with truck drivers who are represented by the IBT may add a new dimension to a firm's labor picture. Manufacturing firms, no matter how large, rarely have a balanced flow of raw materials and finished products. Hence, their vehicles will face empty back hauls and be underutilized. As requests for emergency shipments increase, empty mileage will increase. Costs will also increase and revenue will decline. When a firm buys equipment, it must be careful not to invest in equipment that will be quickly outmoded. Special equipment may require a long-term commitment to current methods of handling commodities. In the final analysis, a user wishing to employ private transportation is entering a new business. The relevant question is whether he can do a better job of satisfying his needs than the people who are transportation specialists, i.e., the for-hire carriers.

SELECTED REFERENCES

There is a dearth of published information on carrier management. A view of current problems can be gained by examining some of the following periodicals which are aimed at carrier managers: *Aviation Week and Space Technology; Modern Railroads; Railway Age; Transport Topics* (motor trucking); and *Waterways Journal*.

Martin T. Farris and Paul T. McElhiney (eds.), *Modern Transportation: Selected Readings,* 2nd ed. (Boston: Houghton Mifflin Company, 1973) contains selections from the current literature on carrier problems in all modes. Of particular interest are the sections devoted to railroads, motor carriers, and airlines. Although somewhat dated, a great deal of background information is found in George P. Baker and Gayton E. Germane, *Case Problems in Transportation Management* (New York: McGraw-Hill Book Company, Inc., 1957). Cases apply to all modes; the pricing and scheduling cases are particularly useful. A general overview of carrier management problems is contained in Grant M. Davis, Martin T. Farris, and Jack J. Holder, *Management of Transportation Carriers,* (New York: Praeger Publishers, 1975).

Association of American Railroads, "How a Railroad Is Organized and Operated," *Transportation in America,* (Washington, D.C.: Association of American Railroads, 1947) contains good background on the practical aspects of railroading. One of the most detailed analyses of railroad management problems is Committee of Commerce, U.S. Senate, *The Penn Central and Other Railroads* (Washington, D.C.: U.S. Government Printing Office, December, 1972). A good overall description of railroad problems is also contained in D. Daryl Wyckoff, *Railroad Management* (Lexington, Massachusetts: D. C. Heath and Company, 1976).

Gayton E. Germane, Nicholas A. Glaskowsky, Jr., and James L. Heskett, *Highway Transportation Management,* (New York: McGraw-Hill Book Company, Inc., 1963) contains a general discussion of highway carrier problems and sample case problems. Among the topics included are organization, operation, traffic, and finance. A book that describes how 9 trucking companies dealt with a specific management problem is D. Daryl Wyckoff and David H. Maister, *The Motor Carrier Industry* (Lexington, Massachusetts: D. C. Heath and Company, 1977). The most complete description of highway transportation is Charles A. Taff, *Commercial Motor Transportation,* 5th ed. (Cambridge, Maryland: Cornell Maritime Press, Inc., 1975).

Nawal K. Taneja, *The Commercial Airline Industry* (Lexington, Massachusetts: D. C. Heath and Company, 1976) provides a good overview of the airline industry.

PART THREE

Government

16

Rationale of Government Promotion of Transportation; Government Promotion of Railroad and Highway Transportation

In this chapter we begin our discussion of the role of government in transportation, a role that has always been of considerable importance even though we have relied primarily on private enterprise to operate our transportation system. The role of government in transportation is extensive and the 2 most important governmental activities are promotion of transportation and economic regulation of transportation. In Chapters 16, 17, and 18 we shall deal with government promotion. In Chapters 19 through 25 we shall discuss government economic regulation of transportation.

WHAT IS GOVERNMENT PROMOTION OF TRANSPORTATION?

Government in the United States at all levels has considerable influence over the operation of private business firms in many ways. One way is through various forms of promotion of or assistance to business firms. These include such things as tax advantages including tax credits, low interest or no interest loans of money, guaranteeing of loans of money made by private lenders, provision of factory buildings and other physical facilities at low or no cost, benefits accruing to business firms from government paid-for research programs, and direct cash subsidies.

Government Promotion of Transportation Defined

The terms promotion and subsidy mean different things to different people. For our purposes, we define government *promotion* of transportation as any kind of financial or other governmental assistance to a carrier, including tax reduction programs, low cost or no cost loans and guaranteed loans, provision of facilities used by a carrier, the fallout from government paid-for research and development programs that benefits carriers, and direct cash payments to carriers by government.

Government Subsidy of Transportation Defined

We define government *subsidy* of transportation as existing whenever any part of a carrier's costs are borne by taxpayers and not by the carrier who benefits from the government promotion. In other words, subsidy exists when carriers do not repay government at all or in full for the benefits received from government promotion. Consequently, government assistance to transportation is considered to be promotion of transportation, but it may or may not be considered subsidy to transportation, depending on whether or not any or all of the expenditures made by government are repaid to government by the carriers who benefit. In the words of William L. Grossman, repayment may take any of various forms, including special taxes, fees for government services or for the use of government supplied facilities, the rendering of a service to the government or to the public without charge or at an abnormally low price, and simple "recapture" by government of part of all of the money granted.[1]

Extent of Government Promotion of Transportation

The role of government as a promoter of transportation has been an important and growing one. According to figures provided by the Association of American Railroads (AAR), federal expenditures in the aggregate to assist domestic transportation by air, highway, and water have increased over 11 times since 1952, from 970.2 million dollars in 1952 to 10.7 billion dollars in 1976. Spending by state and local governments has also increased substantially, from approximately 5 billion dollars in 1952 to 23.5 billion dollars in 1976. The total spent to assist transportation by all levels of government increased almost 6 times in the period. In 1977 the expenditures were expected to be 11.8 billion dollars by the federal government and 24.2 billion dollars by the state and local governments, for a total of approximately 36 billion.[2] These figures do not include government expenditures to support the National Railroad Passenger Corporation (Amtrak) or expenditures to support the northeast railroads or other government aid that has been given to the railroad industry. Such aid is discussed later in this chapter.

WHY IS TRANSPORTATION PROMOTED
BY GOVERNMENT?

As the reader may have gathered from previous chapters in this book, transportation is treated as unique among business activities. For example, many for-hire transportation companies have common carrier status and are required to assume the obligations of common carriers to the public, and many for-hire

---

[1] William L. Grossman, *Fundamentals of Transportation* (New York: Simmons-Boardman Publishing Corporation, 1959), p. 260.

[2] Association of American Railroads, *Government and Private Expenditures for Highway, Waterway, Railroad and Air Rights-of-Way* (Washington, D.C.: Association of American Railroads, September, 1977), Table 1 (unpublished).

carriers are subject to government economic regulation. Transportation also benefits from various government promotional programs that other industries do not benefit from. The specific reasons for this special promotional treatment of transportation are several.

Importance of Transportation

A major reason for government in the United States (and most other countries) to promote transportation is the importance of transportation to the economy and to society in general or its "public interest" nature. The various reasons why transportation is considered to be of great importance were discussed in Chapter 1 and include such things as its contribution to geographic specialization, large-scale production, economic development, national defense, time and place utility, and so on. These factors lead government to take a special interest in transportation and to promote it and, in some cases, to subsidize it or even take ownership of it.

Large Capital Requirements

The large amounts of capital required in transportation, not only for ways, but also for terminals and vehicles in some cases, sometimes make private investment difficult. This is particularly true if a satisfactory return on the large investment is doubtful or impossible. In some cases, therefore, public investment in a transportation facility is virtually unavoidable. In addition, there is sometimes the additional factor that transportation investment often results in non-economic and social benefits and, although no dollar return at all is involved for the investor, there are benefits to the public at large.

Way Factors

All modes of transportation make use of a way of some kind. In some modes the way requires vast amounts of land that can more easily be acquired by government than by private companies. There is also the fact that there is multi-company use of the way in some modes, which means that there would be complications concerning who should be the owner if several different companies are to use the way. Added to this is the further complicating fact that in some modes both private and for-hire carriers use the same way. Finally, there is the obvious need to avoid unnecessary duplication of way, as has happened in the case of railroad roadbeds where, in many cases, parallel lines exist when only one line would be sufficient to carry the available traffic. Government provision of a way avoids many of these problems.

To Develop the Country

A significant factor in government promotion of transportation in the early history of the United States was the desire of government to develop the country economically and socially and to unite it politically. The vast government aid given to early railroads is a major example of this reason for government promotion.

To Provide More Rapid Development
of Transportation

In some cases, government has promoted transportation in order to accelerate the development of a new mode of transportation, for example, federal promotion of air transportation.

To Provide Competition in Transportation

In some situations the federal government has promoted a form of transportation in order to provide competition with other modes, presumably for the benefit of the public. Public aid to domestic water transportation has been partly justified by its backers because it helps to provide competition with railroads.

Joint Effort with Other Government Programs

Occasionally, government promotion of transportation is a byproduct of some other government program or is a joint effort with other programs. For example, conservation programs designed to control floods sometimes also lead to navigable waterways. Transportation improvements paid for by government occasionally have joint transportation and defense objectives, such as is sometimes the case in highway transportation.

JUSTIFICATION FOR GOVERNMENT SUBSIDIES
TO TRANSPORTATION

Earlier in this chapter we attempted to distinguish between government promotion and government subsidy of transportation.

Subsidy, as distinguished from promotion, creates serious problems because it interferes with the normal competitive forces in transportation since government bears part of the costs of some carriers. It also makes economic regulation of transportation more difficult than it otherwise would be, particularly in connection with regulation of rates and fares. Finally, misallocation of the nation's resources can result from subsidy programs because they may encourage the growth of modes that are not the most efficient. Consequently, it is a highly controversial subject in transportation and is subject to more criticism than that directed toward promotion as such. It is, therefore, worthwhile to examine the arguments that are given for subsidy, i.e., when the direct beneficiaries of the benefits of government promotion of transportation do not reimburse government in full or at all for the benefits received.

Need to Support a New Industry

Subsidy to transportation is sometimes said to be necessary because the subsidized mode promises to provide a valuable transportation service in the future but it cannot be expected to be self-supporting in the early period of its development. The airline industry is one of our best examples. Early railroads were also subsidized at least partly for this reason.

Indirect Economic Benefits

In some instances, subsidy to transportation is justified on the ground that there are indirect economic gains (other than direct transportation benefits) that derive from the transportation facility (such as an airport) that outweigh the cost to government in subsidizing the carrier(s) involved. All modes of transportation probably contribute economic benefit to the communities and regions they serve and, in particular, the business firms located there, whether or not a particular mode or carrier receives financial or other help from government. When a mode or carrier is subsidized, however, these indirect gains are often cited as justification for the subsidy, even though the gains accrue also from modes or carriers that are not subsidized.

Non-Economic Benefits

In addition to direct transportation benefits and indirect economic benefits, there are social, political, defense, and, perhaps other non-economic benefits that are derived from transportation that may be used to justify subsidization of transportation. Local roads and streets, for example, provide for social mobility that would be difficult without them and which may be justification for their subsidization by government.[3]

METHODS OF GOVERNMENT PROMOTION OF TRANSPORTATION

Government promotion of transportation takes various forms, but they can be categorized into a limited number of general methods of promotion, some of which include an element of subsidy, depending on the government, the mode, and the method involved.

Financing the Way

Probably the earliest and most frequently found form of government promotion of transportation is for government to help finance the way used by privately owned carriers. The need for such assistance stems largely from the large capital investment required and the various complications associated with ways mentioned earlier in this chapter. In the case of early railroads, for example, much of the government aid was intended to help railroad constructors to pay for the roadbed or way.

Operating the Way

Closely associated with financing the way is actual government ownership and operation of the way, as is the case with highways and with the federal airway system. In these and other cases, the ownership and operation of a way by a single agency is far superior to some other arrangement. Carriers are permitted to use the way, but they do not have the responsibility of ownership and operation.

---

[3]Justification for subsidy to transportation is discussed in D. Philip Locklin, *Economics of Transportation,* 7th ed. (Homewood, Illinois: Richard D. Irwin, Inc., 1972), pp. 859–860.

Financing and Operating Terminals

Because of the large amount of capital required and the fact that terminals are sometimes used by many different carriers of a given mode, government has sometimes financed terminals used by privately owned carriers. This has usually taken the form of government ownership and operation of public terminals. This is done generally in air transportation (airports) and also in ocean and inland water transportation, although in the latter case, large shippers and receivers sometimes provide terminals. Occasionally, government has provided motor truck "union" terminals for motor trucking companies to use. In all cases, the carriers make use of the terminal, usually for a fee of some kind, but they do not have the responsibility of ownership and operation.

Financing Operating Costs

One of the more controversial forms of promotion of transportation is the financing of operating expenses by government, which often also means that it is a subsidy program. Operating costs for local service airlines are partly paid by the federal government. Some rail commuter passenger carriers receive government aid to help pay their operating expenses.

Providing Research and Development

A form of rather indirect government promotion of transportation is in the benefits or "fallout" received by private enterprise carriers from government paid-for research and development programs, particularly those in the federal Department of Defense and space programs. The leading example of this is the development of military aircraft by the Department of Defense and their later adaptation to for-hire airline civilian use.[4]

Complete Ownership and Operation by Government

The ultimate in government promotion of transportation is when government not only owns and operates the way but also owns and operates the carriers. We have only a few examples of this in intercity transportation in the United States, as noted in earlier chapters. Nevertheless, many urban mass transportation systems are falling under complete government ownership and operation, and intercity rail passenger service and railroads in the northeastern part of the country are potential candidates for full government ownership and operation, as we shall see later in this chapter.

Other Forms of Government Promotion of Transportation

In addition to the various kinds of government promotion of transportation discussed in the preceding paragraphs, other kinds of promotion that have been

[4]Methods of providing public aid to transportation are discussed in Roy J. Sampson and Martin T. Farris, *Domestic Transportation: Practice, Theory, and Policy*, 3rd ed. (Boston: Houghton-Mifflin Company, 1975), pp. 443–450.

used at one time or another include investment tax credits and other tax exemptions for carriers, low interest or no interest loans to carriers, and government guarantee of loans made by private lenders to transportation companies. In addition, transportation companies have often benefited from various government assistance programs that are available to any business, including accelerated depreciation for income tax purposes, the usual deduction allowed for income tax purposes, government informational and educational programs, provision of various services by local government, and so on.

GOVERNMENT PROMOTION OF RAILROAD TRANSPORTATION

Government Ownership of Early Railroads

When railroads entered the United States transportation picture in the 1830's, the political climate was such that federal ownership of railroads was rejected as part of the philosophy of the administration of President Andrew Jackson. "States' rights" and the notion that the federal government should not participate in internal improvements prevailed. Although the federal government did eventually aid private railroad construction and eventually became the owner of the Alaska Railroad and the Panama Railroad, national government ownership of railroads has not been the rule in this country.

Contrary to federal policy, however, in the first half of the nineteenth century the states engaged in railroad building in a number of instances because they were interested in internal improvements and, in particular, because they were eager to obtain improved transportation. In some cases, states acquired ownership because private companies that had received state aid had failed. In other cases, the railroad was actually built by the state. In many cases, state ownership led to financial problems, and there were also problems of corruption and incompetence in management. State-owned railroads were for the most part disposed of by turning them over to private companies at a loss.

In a few cases, municipal government ownership of early railroads took place, but this was rare.

Government Promotion of Early Railroads

Although direct ownership of railroads was the exception, government at all levels provided considerable promotional assistance to early railroads.

State and Local Promotion. The power of eminent domain, meaning the power to take property for railroad purposes without the owner's consent, with just compensation being paid, was granted by state governments. Also, general railroad incorporation laws were eventually passed by the states beginning in the 1850's. These laws enabled railroads to incorporate without special individual action by the state legislature. They contributed to the eventual overbuilding of railroads because they did not attempt to control the number of miles of railroad line constructed.

State, county, and city governments aided early railroads by purchasing railroad stock, lending money, guaranteeing loans made to railroads by private lenders, grants of cash, donating land for right-of-way purposes, donating land beyond what was needed for the right of way that the carriers could then sell or keep as they wished, donating government securities, donating various building materials, equipment, and even labor, and exempting the railroads from various kinds of taxation.

The eagerness of these various governments to aid early railroads was based on their need for transportation facilities and the economic advantages they expected from railroad service. Many of these governments went heavily into debt to aid railroads and, in many cases, they were disappointed with the results of railroad construction for their communities. The result was that constitutional provisions were added in some states prohibiting further state aid and/or local aid to railroads.

Federal Promotion. At the federal government level, aid was very limited prior to the 1850's, consisting mainly of providing the right of eminent domain and granting rights of way through federal land and the right to use timber, stone, and other materials from land along the right of way for construction purposes. In the 1860's loans to several transcontinental railroads were also made. Of the 64 million dollars loaned, all but 3.7 million dollars was eventually repaid.[5]

The most important form of early federal aid to railroads was, of course, the land grants given between 1850 and 1871, which had as their major purpose the opening of the area west of the Mississippi River. The usual procedure was to grant so many sections (one section equals 640 acres or 1 square mile) of land adjacent to the railroad for each mile of railroad built. Seventy-two separate grants were actually finalized and the total amount of land given was approximately 130 million acres. The railroads were free to sell or retain the land given. In many cases, the land was sold in order to pay for the construction of the railroad. In other cases, the land is still held by the railroad company.

Both sides benefited greatly from the federal land grant program, but it is not within the scope of this text to attempt to determine who benefited the most. However, a feature of the federal land grant program that is often forgotten is that every land grant made had conditions attached to it whereby the recipient railroad had to carry United States mail at 80 per cent of normal rates and United States personnel and property at 50 per cent of normal fares and rates. These conditions were removed partially in 1940 and entirely in 1946. Since railroads that competed with the land grant railroads also reduced their charges on government traffic in order to be competitive, the total benefit to the federal government was much greater than that received from the low charges made by the land grant railroads alone. Consequently, if one is willing to assume that the railroads paid to the federal government enough in reduced charges over many years to compensate the government for the value of the land received, subsidy, as we have defined it in this book, was not involved.[6]

---

[5] Locklin, *Economics of Transportation,* p. 133.

[6] The land-grant program and the question of subsidy and benefit are dealt with in detail in Robert S. Henry, "The Railroad Land Grant Legend in American History Texts," *Mississippi Valley Historical Review,* September, 1945. See also Paul W. Gates, "The Railroad Land Grant Legend," *Journal of Economic History,* Spring, 1954.

Government Promotion of Railroads in Modern Times

World War I. After the major railroad building era ended around the turn of the century, government promotion of railroads was virtually non-existent. Then, during World War I the federal government took over operation of most United States railroads in December, 1917. Operation was placed under the United States Railroad Administration, which was created for that purpose. The objective was to straighten out a congested and uncoordinated system that had failed to adequately move wartime traffic.

Under government control, many competitive trains and conflicting practices were discontinued, rate increases were discouraged, some wage increases were granted and other costs rose rapidly, and a deficit of approximately 1.5 billion dollars was incurred. The railroads were returned to their private owners in March, 1920, with some transitional financial aid provided, including "rehabilitation" loans made to the carriers by the federal government in the amount of approximately 351 million dollars, which was repaid with interest.[7]

The Depression of the 1930's. Railroads were generally prosperous during the 1920's, but in the early 1930's railroads, being a derived demand industry, were hit very hard by the severe economic depression. Declining traffic caused by the depression was accompanied by the emergence of new competition from other modes which reduced railroad earnings. Several carriers went into reorganization or bankruptcy proceedings.

The Reconstruction Finance Corporation, a federal government agency organized to make low-cost loans to distressed industries, helped some railroads to avoid receivership. These loans were eventually repaid, as were other loans made by the federal government. According to the AAR, total loans made to railroads during the depression were 1.1 billion dollars.[8] Also, during the depression the Railroad Credit Corporation was organized by railroads themselves to extend loans to failing carriers out of funds received from emergency increases in freight rates granted by the Interstate Commerce Commission (ICC) in 1931.

Obviously, government aid to railroads in this period was not substantial.

Guaranteed Loans. The heavy traffic of World War II, the early post-World War II period, and the Korean War brought recovery to the country and to the railroads from the depressed 1930's. However, after the end of the Korean War in 1953 and more "normal" times returned to the country, certain railroad problems began to become evident, problems that still exist today.

The share of all intercity freight traffic carried by railroad was falling while at the same time the carriers were incurring a huge deficit (calculated on a fully distributed cost basis) from their passenger service. Their rate of return on investment was low and they were having difficulty in attracting capital. These problems were made still more serious by the economic recession of 1958.

The federal Transportation Act of 1958 was an attempt by Congress to alleviate some of the problems of the railroad industry. It included certain

---

[7]The transitional aid to railroads is discussed in Locklin, *Economics of Transportation*, 3rd ed., 1949, pp. 249-251.

[8]Association of American Railroads, *Government and Private Expenditures*, Appendix A.

regulatory changes that we will discuss later. As to promotion, the law provided that the ICC could guarantee public or private loans to railroads for the purpose of financing capital expenditures for road and equipment or for maintenance work. A total amount of no more than 500 million dollars in loans could be outstanding at any one time, and the loans could be for no longer than 15 years. In addition, there had to be reasonable assurance that the loan would be repaid. The loan provisions of the law expired in June, 1963 because of lack of industry demand after a total of only approximately 243 million dollars in loans to 15 railroads (mostly in the east) had been guaranteed by the Commission. A few defaults on the guaranteed loans occurred, which meant that the federal government had to repay the lenders.

In 1971 Congress authorized certain bankrupt railroads to borrow money with the loans guaranteed by the federal government. The maximum that could be guaranteed was 125 million dollars, and 102.4 million dollars was actually borrowed.[9]

Commuter Passenger Railroads. In several of our largest cities (New York, Chicago, Philadelphia, Boston, and San Francisco) heavy reliance is made on commuter railroad passenger trains to bring workers, shoppers, and others into and out of the central city. Since World War II the decline in traffic carried by such rail carriers has been substantial. However, the decline has been mainly in the off-peak hours and days of the week while the peak rush-hour traffic, Monday through Friday, continues to be heavy. Consequently, commuter railroads are geared to operate at full capacity for approximately 20 hours per week while equipment and employees are greatly underutilized the rest of the time. Hence, a deficit condition exists. Various governments have responded to the problem in order to keep what is considered an essential service in operation. The federal government has made cash grants to some cities for use in improving commuter service, tax relief has been given to the carriers by some states and cities, cash grants and loans to commuter railroads have been given by some states, and some states and cities have purchased equipment for commuter railroads to use. New York state purchased the Long Island Railroad and the Massachusetts Bay Transportation Authority purchased the commuter lines of the Boston and Maine in order to keep commuter service in operation. The Consolidated Railroad Corporation (Conrail), to be discussed later in this chapter, went into operation on April 1, 1976 to replace bankrupt railroads in the northeast and midwest, and it operates commuter trains on its lines under contracts with state or local governments. The federal government provides money to the state and local governments to help cover Conrail's costs and 125 million dollars in federal funds was made available for that purpose.

In some metropolitan areas, including New York and Chicago, regional authorities have been established to operate and/or subsidize commuter railroad and mass transit facilities.

Federal High-Speed Ground Transportation Program. Intercity rail passenger traffic declined sharply after World War II as a result of poor service, the increase in the availability of competing transportation, the lack of railroad capital to im-

[9]*Ibid.*

prove service, and other factors. A number of passenger trains were discontinued, particularly after Congress enacted the Transportation Act of 1958 which gave final authority on such discontinuances to the ICC.

Encouraged by the success of high-speed rail passenger service in Japan, Congress in 1965 enacted legislation that provided funds for a program of research and development and demonstrations in the United States Department of Commerce. The program was designed to produce high-speed ground passenger transportation for this country. Congress added more appropriations in succeeding years and the program was transferred to the new United States Department of Transportation (DOT) in 1967. The program has had some success, particularly in connection with improving the service in the Boston–New York–Washington "northeast corridor" area, but lack of recent interest by the federal administration threatens to end the project.[10] Through 1974 approximately 100 million dollars had been spent on the program. No real technological breakthroughs have resulted from the experimenting and testing that has been done. The capital required to provide truly high-speed (150–300 miles per hour) ground passenger service on any extensive scale (probably for trips of 400 miles or less) would be tremendous because new roadbeds as well as vehicles would be necessary.

National Railroad Passenger Corporation. Some of the problems of intercity rail transportation of passengers have already been mentioned. The decline of the quality and quantity of service and the volume of traffic carried was rapid, particularly after 1958. By 1970 there were only 24 railroads operating intercity passenger trains. The number of such trains was only 547. The ICC did little to stem the tide and more or less presided over the demise of the intercity passenger train. Congress discussed the problem at length many times but did nothing until 1970 when the National Railroad Passenger Corporation was established by act of Congress, to become effective May 1, 1971. The purpose of the law was to prevent complete elimination of intercity rail passenger service and to upgrade the quality of service so that a viable rail passenger service between major population centers could be obtained and maintained.

The Act created the National Railroad Passenger Corporation, which is usually referred to as "Amtrak," which was to operate passenger trains selected by the United States Secretary of Transportation and approved by Congress. The Amtrak route system as of 1976 is shown in Figure 16-1.

The Corporation was then to contract with railroads to provide the crews and roadbeds, but the locomotives and cars were to be owned by Amtrak.[11] Contracting railroads were to be paid those costs "solely related" to operating passenger trains plus 5 per cent of that amount. In addition, they were to be paid 4 per cent of that amount for liability coverage. Contracting railroads complained that the compensation system was unfair to them because it did not provide enough revenue. This factor helped to create an attitude of indifference toward the quality of service provided. In 1974, however, contracts were entered into by Amtrak and most contracting railroads to try simultaneously to increase the

---

[10] See "High-Speed Trains Hit a Red Signal," *Business Week,* January 13, 1975.

[11] Dining car employees, porters, and reservations people have since become employees of Amtrak, not the railroads.

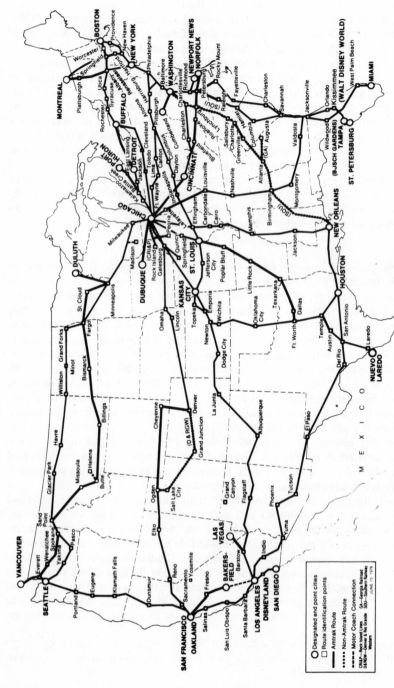

FIGURE 16-1 Amtrak Routes, 1976. (Source: Courtesy National Railroad Passenger Corporation)

compensation and improve the quality of service provided by having payments to the railroads in excess of incremental costs based on the quality of service provided (frequency of arrival time, the total magnitude of delays, the cleanliness and functioning of cars and equipment, and improvements in schedules).[12]

Railroads that joined Amtrak were relieved of all obligation to provide passenger service, excluding commuter service. Railroads that did not join Amtrak were to continue to operate their passenger trains until at least January 1, 1975, at which time they could apply to the ICC for discontinuance and go through the usual proceedings conducted by the Commission for that purpose. The railroads that joined Amtrak were also required to pay to Amtrak an amount of money based on their 1969 passenger service deficit payable to Amtrak over a 3-year period. Payment was to be in the form of cash, equipment, or future services; actually payment was made mainly in the form of equipment that the carriers would no longer have need of anyway. The total amount paid to Amtrak by the carriers was approximately 200 million dollars. In return, these railroads could receive common stock in Amtrak or they could deduct the payment made to Amtrak in calculating their federal income taxes. Most joining carriers chose the latter method.[13]

Amtrak is managed by a 17-member Board of Directors, 10 of whom are appointed by the President of the United States with the advice and consent of the Senate and the rest elected by common and preferred stockholders. Since no preferred stock was ever sold, however, the Board has never had its full complement of 17 members. In fact, only 4 railroads elected to take common stock in Amtrak rather than the tax deduction. They were the Burlington Northern; Chicago, Milwaukee, St. Paul and Pacific; Penn Central; and Grand Trunk Western. Since no one else bought any common or preferred stock, the federal government and the 4 railroads became the sole owners of Amtrak.

Congress authorized 40 million dollars as an initial start-up appropriation for Amtrak and has added a considerable amount to that since 1971. In addition, the Secretary of Transportation was authorized by Congress to guarantee lenders against loss on loans made to Amtrak originally up to the amount of 100 million dollars, but increased since, and to make loans or guarantee loans to the contracting railroads up to an aggregate amount of 200 million dollars.

The immediate effect of Amtrak was to reduce the intercity railroad passenger service route mileage from approximately 59,000 miles to approximately 23,000 miles and the number of trains from 547 to 243. Most carriers that were still operating intercity passenger trains at the time joined Amtrak. Of the 24 carriers, 20 joined, but only 14 were asked to operate trains under contract with Amtrak. The 4 that did not join were the Southern; the Chicago, Rock Island, and Pacific; the Denver and Rio Grande Western; and the Georgia railroads.

Although Amtrak has spent considerable money since 1971 to refurbish equipment and purchase new equipment, to install a modern reservations system, to add a package express service, to add service to some new points, and to delete service to some others (the Amtrak route system was 25,000 miles in

[12] For a discussion and analysis of this change, see William J. Baumol, "Payment by Performance in Rail Passenger Transportation: An Innovation in Amtrak's Operations," *Bell Journal of Economics,* Spring, 1975.

[13] An excellent description and analysis of the Act is Robert W. Harbeson, "The Rail Passenger Service Act of 1970," *ICC Practitioners' Journal,* March–April, 1971.

1976), although it has generally improved passenger service compared to what it had been, and although there has been some traffic increase,[14] the deficits have been large. Amtrak has done fairly well traffic-wise and revenue-wise on the New York-Washington, D.C. route, but it lost 147.7 million dollars overall in its first year, and it has continued to accumulate deficits since then. Congress has responded by increasing the loan guarantee ceiling to 900 million dollars and has also made direct grants to Amtrak. Total federal grants to Amtrak through December, 1976 totaled 1.1 billion dollars and loan guarantees amounted to 665.7 million dollars.[15] The total Amtrak deficit from 1971 through 1976 was almost 1.5 billion dollars. In 1976, for example, Amtrak's operating revenues were 287.2 million dollars and operating expenses were 651.7 million dollars.[16] Operating revenues were only 44.1 per cent of operating expenses.

Amtrak's basic problem is that, with a few exceptions where turbotrains and the electric metroliners are being used, it is operating an early 1950's style passenger train service in the 1970's with obsolete and poorly maintained equipment and undermaintained roadbeds that often do not permit even the speed the equipment is capable of. Amtrak has had many operating problems and cannot successfully compete on the medium and long haul against the service of the other modes. Complete government ownership is a definite possibility if the large deficits continue.[17] The energy shortage and a strong national energy policy adopted by the federal government, however, may change the situation drastically and Amtrak's traffic may grow substantially in the future. Amtrak would still, however, have the problem of trying to handle the traffic with inadequate facilities.

In the Railroad Revitalization and Regulatory Reform (4R) Act of 1976, Congress provided that Amtrak was to upgrade the Boston-New York-Washington, D.C. line (the "northeast corridor" including approximately 700 miles of line), so that the Boston-New York trip time would be 3 hours and 40 minutes and the New York-Washington trip time would be 2 hours and 40 minutes. Congress authorized 1.75 billion dollars in grants for that purpose. The Act authorized Amtrak to purchase the lines involved from Conrail before making the necessary improvements to meet the goals set forth by Congress. The purchase was made in 1976 for 87.5 million dollars.

Regional Rail Reorganization Act of 1973. Since the middle 1950's railroad financial problems have become more and more serious, as we have noted, and these problems were more serious generally in the northeastern part of the country than elsewhere because of greater intramodal and intermodal competition, excessive rail mileage, older and more obsolete facilities, a larger passenger deficit problem, greater shifts away from railroad oriented traffic, shorter hauls,

---

[14]From 3 billion passenger miles carried in 1972 to 4.1 billion in 1976, a decline from 4.3 billion in 1974 when traffic increased markedly because of the Arab oil embargo. Association of American Railroads, *Railroad Facts,* 1977 ed. (Washington, D.C.: Association of American Railroads, 1977), p. 31.

[15]Association of American Railroads, *Government and Private Expenditures,* Appendix A.

[16]Association of American Railroads, *Railroad Facts,* p. 62.

[17]Robert W. Harbeson suggested this is what should have been done to begin with. See Harbeson, "The Rail Passenger Service Act of 1970," pp. 335-337.

and so on. Although the problems were well-known for many years, nothing of any significance (with the exception of Amtrak) was done at the national government level until the Penn Central, the nation's largest railroad, which had resulted from the merger of the former New York Central and Pennsylvania railroads in 1968, went into bankruptcy in 1970 and the possibility that it would cease operations entirely became real. This, along with the bankruptcies of several other railroads in the northeast which, together with the Penn Central, comprised approximately 18 per cent of the country's railroad revenues, almost 21 per cent of the railroad employees, and approximately 13 per cent of the railroad mileage, led to considerable discussion in Congress and elsewhere because of the severe negative effects on the northeast and the rest of the country if these railroads were to cease to operate. Congress finally enacted the Regional Rail Reorganization Act in December, 1973. The Act was one version of many solutions to the problem that had been proposed.

The Reorganization Act created the United States Railway Association (USRA), a nonprofit government planning organization, which was given the authority to plan the restructuring of the northeastern railroad network in 17 states and to guarantee loans for that purpose up to an amount of 1.5 billion dollars. Grants were to be made to the bankrupt carriers to keep them in operation while the restructuring was taking place. Other grants of funds were to be provided for protecting railroad labor affected by the eventual restructuring, for upgrading rail passenger service in the northeast corridor, for subsidizing (along with the states) branch lines that would not be included in the final system plan, and for administration costs. The total amount of grants provided for in the Act was approximately 558 million dollars.

Another organization, the Consolidated Rail Corporation (Conrail), a for-profit privately managed organization, was created by the Act to operate the company that was to survive in the restructuring of the bankrupt lines.

The Board of Directors of USRA consists of 3 government members—the Secretary of Transportation, the Chairman of the ICC, and the Secretary of the Treasury—and 8 other members appointed by the President of the United States with the advice and consent of the Senate. Conrail's board of 13 members includes 6 appointed by USRA, 5 representing the estates of the bankrupt railroads, and the Chairman and President of Conrail.

In February, 1975 USRA issued its preliminary plan for restructuring the northeast railroad system and in July, 1975 it issued its final plan.[18] Congress was to have 60 working days under the Act in which to review the plan. If neither House disapproved, the plan would become effective. The legal deadline for Congress to act on the proposal (November 9, 1975) passed and no action was taken by either House. Therefore, the plan went into effect on April 1, 1976, after Congress provided the necessary funding in the 4R Act of 1976 and an appropriation measure to meet the initial cost. Meanwhile, substantial amounts of money in the form of grants, loans, and loan guarantees had been made available by the federal government to the Penn Central and other bankrupt railroads in the area.

---

[18]United States Railway Association, *Final System Plan for Restructuring the Railroads in the Northeast and Midwest Region Pursuant to the Regional Rail Reorganization Act of 1973* (Washington, D.C.: U.S. Government Printing Office, 1975).

The plan as it went into effect, although somewhat different from the final system plan of USRA, essentially carried forward the plan. Conrail took over approximately 17,000 miles of line with over 90,000 employees, 162,000 freight cars, and approximately 5,000 locomotives. The lines were drawn from the Penn Central, Erie Lackawanna, Central of New Jersey, Lehigh Valley, Lehigh and Hudson River, and Reading railroads. Some 6,000 miles were to be abandoned unless operated under a federal-state cooperative subsidy plan. The Delaware and Hudson, Norfolk and Western, Grand Trunk Western, and several other railroads purchased parts of the bankrupt lines as did 5 states and 2 regional transportation authorities. Figure 16-2 is a map of the Conrail system. Because the USRA plan to have approximately 2,000 miles of line in the area purchased by the Chessie System and the Southern Railway did not materialize because of labor difficulties, Conrail became a 17,000-mile system instead of a 15,000-mile system and is without significant railroad competition in the region served.

The cost of the restructuring plan was very high and more than originally provided for in the Reorganization Act of 1973. Conrail's early capital, rehabilitation, improvement, and equipment purchases were to be financed by Conrail's issuance of 1 billion dollars in debt securities at 7.5 per cent interest and 1.1 billion dollars in Series A preferred stock, all to be held by the federal government. Thus, the initial federal investment in Conrail was to be 2.1 billion dollars and was intended to finance the company for the first 5 years. The money borrowed was intended to be eventually repaid to the federal government and the government could eventually sell the stock to private interests some time in the future so that its participation in Conrail would eventually cease should the company become profitable and without need for federal aid. Series B preferred stock and common stock were to be issued to the estates of the bankrupt railroads, representing the value of the assets transferred to Conrail. In addition, Conrail was to engage in a 10-year capital expenditures program of approximately 7 billion dollars to take care of deferred maintenance, structural replacements, additions and improvements to track and facilities, and for new or revitalized equipment. In addition to the initial 2.1 billion dollars of federal financing, this was to be financed by a combination of private sector equipment financing, the issuance of debentures and stock (possibly to the federal government), and earnings of Conrail. USRA expected Conrail to lose money in its early years but show a profit in 1979, its fourth year.

Although the plan was approved by Congress, the necessary start-up money was appropriated, and actual operation by Conrail began on April 1, 1976, legal action against the plan proceeded on the part of the previous investors in the Penn Central and the other bankrupt railroads who disagreed with the amount and how they were to be paid.[19] Legal difficulty over the large amount of railroad line abandonment was also possible.

The federal government actually had little choice in the case of the northeast railroad crisis. The financial collapse and ending of a major part of railroad service there would be disastrous to that region and to the entire country. Whether

---

[19] In the form of preferred and common stock in Conrail and certificates of value redeemable in 12 years if the stock fails to provide fair and equitable consideration for the rail properties conveyed.

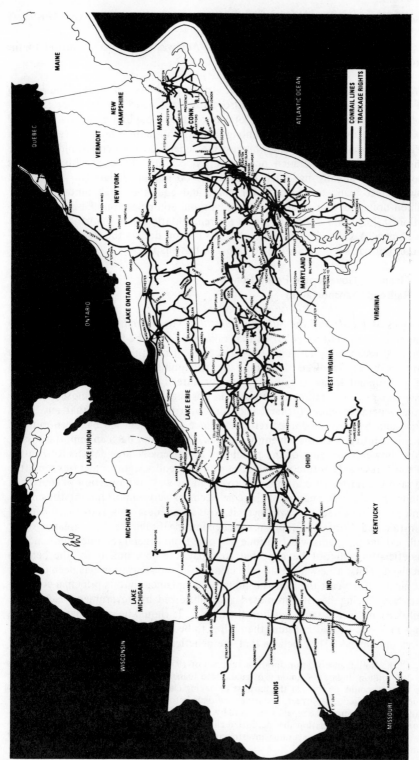

FIGURE 16-2 *Conrail System, 1976. (Source: Consolidated Rail Corporation)*

363

or not the Regional Rail Reorganization Act was the correct solution to the problem remains to be seen, however.

Other Federal Aid Provided in the 4R Act of 1976. In addition to the funding of Conrail, the 4R Act of 1976 also authorized considerable other financial aid to the railroad industry. The total amounted to 6.4 billion dollars, including that for Conrail. It included, among others, 360 million dollars over a 5-year period to finance a program whereby the federal government would subsidize uneconomic railroad branch line operation, sharing the cost with the states (some states already had such programs); 600 million dollars for government low-interest loans to railroads for plant and equipment rehabilitation and 1 billion dollars in loan guarantees for plant and equipment purchases or rehabilitation; 1.75 billion dollars in grants for rehabilitation of the northeast corridor by Amtrak, as noted previously; and 125 million dollars for assistance to commuter railroad service, mentioned earlier in this chapter.[20]

Financing Government Promotion of Railroad Transportation

Sources of Funds and the Subsidy Question. The federal land grant program in the nineteenth century required that railroads repay the federal government for the land received by reducing rates and fares; it may, therefore, be argued that no subsidy was involved, depending on one's point of view. With the exception of government loans to railroads and guaranteed loans that were repaid, other government aid to railroads discussed in this chapter has for the most part come from general revenues (general taxation) with no requirement that any funds expended by government be returned. Since government aid has been minimal in this century until the advent of Amtrak, this has not been an important issue. Now, however, because of the possibility of extremely large deficits for Amtrak in the foreseeable future and because of a tremendous government expenditure to save the northeast and other railroads under way, the question of sources of funds and ultimate bearing of the cost becomes very important. At the present time, it is expected that whatever it costs the federal government to support Amtrak and Conrail (should it not become profitable) and to finance other railroad aid programs will continue to come from general revenue funds and the beneficiaries will not be expected to repay the government for the benefits received. Thus, a new large subsidy element in transportation has been created. Ironically, for years the railroad industry complained that its principal competitors were being heavily promoted and subsidized by government. Now some railroads are in the same position themselves. It should be noted here, however, that railroads do not consider themselves to be the beneficiaries of any expenditures on Amtrak. They believe that the beneficiaries are railroad passengers and

[20]The Rail Transportation Improvement Act of 1976 increased from 230 million dollars to 350 million dollars the amount of guaranteed loans the 6 bankrupt railroads that make up Conrail could receive for the purpose of paying claims against them for debts owed to shippers, suppliers, employees, and other railroads before the railroads became part of Conrail. The loans were to be repaid to Conrail by the estates of the bankrupt railroads. In 1976 Congress enacted legislation that permitted all railroads to reduce their federal income taxes by changing the rules concerning investment tax credits and amortization of grading and tunnel bores.

that, in fact, the contracting railroads are being underpaid for performing the service.

The government's interest in promoting railroad transportation may be affected in the future by the energy shortage, as it indeed already has. Because railroad transportation of freight is relatively energy efficient per unit of traffic carried under many circumstances, there will probably be growing government interest in preserving and fostering the growth of the railroad industry. Any strong energy policy on the part of the federal government that would include allocation or rationing of energy, government-forced substantial price increases on energy, or high taxes on energy could accelerate interest in further government promotion of railroad transportation. It may also lead to more interest in government-financed electrification of railroad lines as an energy conservation move.

Nationalization of Railroads

An obvious question to ask now that the federal government has committed itself to a vast financial aid program for the nation's railroads is whether or not nationalization (government ownership) is the next logical step. Many experts believe that the aid involved in the Regional Rail Reorganization Act and the 4R Act are a giant step toward nationalization because of their belief that Conrail will never become self-sustaining under private enterprise and that the government will eventually decide to take over ownership rather than continue to spend billions to subsidize a system that will never be able to continue service without government aid. The same has been said of Amtrak.[21] Others believe that the Conrail program will have the opposite effect—that it will enable Conrail to maintain service to the public, to improve its facilities, and to eventually become profitable and without need of government aid, thus avoiding the need for nationalization.

As noted in Chapter 10, with the exception of the Alaska Railroad and a few other minor examples, the United States has avoided government ownership of railroads, although nationalization of railroads has been seriously considered by Congress several times in our history. If, however, railroads continue indefinitely to earn a very low rate of return or no rate of return on investment, and if they are unable to attract capital and, consequently, cannot maintain their facilities and serve the public adequately, disappearance of many or all railroads or ownership by government of some or all railroads or at least railroad roadbeds (which has been proposed in Congress) is inevitable, with full or partial nationalization probably preceded by a long period of loans, loan guarantees, and cash grants.

Contrary to what most Americans believe, nationalization is not all bad. In fact, it offers several important advantages over private enterprise operation. These include, among others, greater sources of capital, public need rather than profit determining whether or not a service will be provided, better planning, and elimination of considerable duplication in the railroad system. It could even result in lower costs and rates and fares if operated efficiently.

To most Americans, however, nationalization is considered to be undesirable for a number of reasons, among them the lack of a profit incentive and resulting

<hr>

[21] See "Bus Industry Leader Sees Amtrak as 'First Step' to Transport Nationalization," *Traffic World*, April 21, 1975, p. 17.

inefficiency, politics in hiring employees, the loss of tax revenue formerly paid by private owners, political pressures to provide uneconomic and unwarranted services, discriminatory policies adopted by government against nonrail modes to protect the government-owned railroad system, and the likelihood of tremendous deficits (for example, the Post Office system).[22] It is a fact that huge deficits are the general rule in countries where railroads are owned and operated by the national government although the quality of service provided is sometimes very good.[23]

One final point on nationalization is that the experience we had during World War I, when the United States government operated most of our railroad system for approximately 27 months, proves nothing one way or another as to whether or not nationalization of railroads is a good thing for the country.[24] It is true that the government ran a deficit of approximately 1.5 billion dollars in that short period, but it inherited a run-down railroad plant and incurred rising wartime costs while holding down rates. In addition, since the objective was to win the war, the usual profit-making objective was secondary. Advocates of nationalization argue that the government successfully coordinated the rail system, that the war traffic was moved, and that the war ended with a satisfactory conclusion for the country. In any event, the period was an emergency one, an abnormal one, that proves nothing one way or another about nationalization.

GOVERNMENT PROMOTION OF HIGHWAY TRANSPORTATION

Government Promotion of Early Roads and Streets

Traditionally, highways and streets in the United States have been owned and maintained by government, while the operation of for-hire and private carrier service over the highways and streets has been under private enterprise. In other words, government promotion of or aid to highway transportation has been in the form of highway and street development (financing and operating the way) rather than direct aid to carriers or other operators of vehicles who operate over the roads and streets.

In the early days of the country, however, government aid to highways and streets was minimal. In fact, some toll roads or "turnpikes" were operated by private companies, not government, although some of these were subsidized by state governments and eventually became state roads. Railroad competition beginning in the 1830's eliminated most toll roads. There also were a number of

[22] In a study of shippers' proposed solutions to the northeast railroad problem it was found that shippers overwhelmingly rejected nationalization of the northeastern railroads as a solution. See James C. Johnson and Donald V. Harper, "The Shipper Views Proposed Solutions to the Northeast Railroad Problem," *Transportation Journal,* Summer, 1974, p. 9.

[23] The financial results of nationalized railroads in other countries are discussed in Transportation Association of America, "Transport Nationalization Dangers Cited; Foreign 'Experiences' Highlighted," *Report* (Washington, D.C.: Transportation Association of America, November 19, 1973).

[24] The federal government took over operation of United States railroads 4 other times for brief periods in the years between 1943 and 1951 because of labor difficulties.

"plank" roads in the period just before the Civil War. These roads were made of wooden boards laid across wooden stringers and were usually operated by private companies that charged for their use. They were sometimes subsidized by state governments. They had high maintenance costs and were often unprofitable.

The first major federal government promotion of highways was the Cumberland Road or "National Pike" begun in 1806 at Cumberland, Maryland and extended to Wheeling, West Virginia and eventually to Vandalia, Illinois in 1838, at a cost of approximately 6.8 million dollars. No tolls were collected while this crude road was under federal ownership, but tolls were collected after the road was turned over to the states in the 1830's. Twelve other great national highways were also laid out in the early 1800's with some work being actually done on them. From 1806 to 1838 a total of 1.6 million dollars was appropriated by Congress for these roads.[25] The end of federal road building came with the administration of President Andrew Jackson who was against federal participation in internal improvements. This meant that road and street development was left largely to the states and to local government.

Government Promotion of Highway Transportation in Modern Times

Because of the dominance of railroads in intercity transportation in the nineteenth century, other forms of intercity transportation were pushed into the background. In the 1890's, however, farmers, bicyclists, automobile owners, and railroads themselves (interested in better feeder roads to railroad terminals) began to push for better roads. In the 1890's some states established highway aid systems and the first state highway departments were formed. By 1915, 45 states had enacted state aid laws and 40 states had state highway departments.

Development of the Federal Aid Highway Program. In 1912 the federal government authorized $500,000 for the improvement of roads used to carry the United States mail. It was in 1916, however, when the federal aid highway program really began. In that year Congress authorized 75 million dollars to be spent over a 5-year period to be allocated to the states for highway improvement based on area, population, and mileage. Each state receiving federal aid was required to set up a highway department along with management and construction standards acceptable to the controlling federal agency. The growth in the use of the automobile encouraged further interest in highways. Between 1921 and 1932 federal highway aid expenditures averaged 100 million dollars per year, and specific kinds of highways were designated as being eligible for federal aid. Various other changes in the program were made over the years, including the designation of an interstate system of federal aid highways and the addition of urban roads to the program in 1944. All federal aid stopped between 1941 and 1945 which, along with general neglect by the states during the war, led to the need for vast highway expenditures in the post-war period.

The current federal highway program began when Congress enacted the

[25]William J. Hudson and James A. Constantine, *Motor Transportation* (New York: The Ronald Press Company, 1958), p. 23.

Federal Highway Act of 1956, which was in large part based on a special governmental committee's report (the Clay Committee). The Act provided for the first major expenditures on a 41,000-mile interstate highway system to be called the National System of Interstate and Defense Highways. The Act also drastically changed the method of financing the federal aid program by placing all federal aid on a user charge system basis (see below), with the federal share of the Interstate program to be 90 per cent and the federal share of all other federal highway programs to be generally 50 per cent, with the states providing the balance of the money.

Since 1956 other changes have been made, including the addition of relocation assistance to persons affected by federally aided highway construction (1962), the institution of a beautification and billboard control program (1965), greater attention to urban roads and an addition of 1,500 miles to the Interstate system (1968), and giving flexibility to the states and local governments in using some federal aid highway funds for mass transit projects and the raising of the federal share of non-Interstate system projects to 70 per cent (1973).

The Federal Aid Highway Program Today. Although the federal government contributes substantially to road and street construction and improvement, it owns few roads and streets itself, and those it owns are mainly in national parks and military installations. State and local governments own most of our roads and streets and there are approximately 34,000 governmental units in all that have some roads and/or streets under their jurisdiction. Table 16-1 indicates that most roads and streets are not supported by federal aid. However, those that are in the federal aid program carry the bulk of the traffic because they are the more important arteries in the highway and street network.

Of the systems of federal aid highways shown in Table 16-1, the Interstate system is probably the most familiar to most Americans. It will eventually consist of 42,500 miles of limited-access freeway mileage, as indicated in Figure 11-1. Approximately 90 per cent of the Interstate system was open to traffic as of

T A B L E   16-1 *Total Road and Street Mileage in the United States, 1974*

System	Mileage
Federal Aid Interstate System	42,500
Federal Aid Primary System	214,259
Federal Aid Secondary System	636,574
Federal Aid Urban System	33,941
Federal Aid Urban Type II System*	26,411
Total Federal Aid Systems	953,685
Not in Federal Aid Systems	2,862,122
Total Mileage in United States	3,815,807

*The Federal Aid Highway Act of 1973 eliminated the Urban Type II System as a separate funding category.

Source: U.S. Department of Transportation, Federal Highway Administration, *Highway Statistics,* 1974 (Washington, D.C.: U.S. Government Printing Office, 1976), Table M-21, p. 210.

March 31, 1977. Its total cost, originally estimated at 27 billion dollars in 1956, will probably reach at least 100 billion when it is finally finished (hopefully in the 1980's—the original completion date was 1972), with the federal government bearing 90 per cent of the cost. Once the Interstate highways are constructed they are owned by the states.

The federal aid Primary system includes the major state highways in the country, including both their rural and urban elements. The Secondary system includes less important state highways, including both rural and urban parts thereof. The federal aid Urban and Urban Type II systems are urban roads designated for special federal aid because they serve major centers of activity and/or are high-volume roads and streets.

The federal aid highway program is administered by the Federal Highway Administration (FHWA) which is part of the federal Department of Transportation (DOT). Any state or local roads receiving federal support must meet the specifications of the FHWA. The funds are allocated to states on the basis of formulas established by Congress.

State and Local Promotion of Highways. State and local governments were ir the business of promoting highways and streets long before the modern federal aid program started and they are still the most important government agencies in terms of mileage under their control and the amount of money spent.

Most highway mileage is, in fact, under the control of the states and some form of highway organization exists in every state government for the purpose of administering highway programs. In most states the state delegates some responsibility for county and local roads to the county and local governments.

An important issue in highway development that has arisen since the middle 1960's has been the social and environmental consequences of highway construction programs. Up until the 1960's negative social and environmental effects of highway construction, particularly urban highways, were largely disregarded. These had to do with destruction of neighborhoods, parks, and schools, the creation of noise pollution and air pollution, the effect of highway construction and operation on wild life, as well as the billboard problem along both urban and intercity roads. Since the late 1960's, however, consideration of the social and environmental consequences of highway construction is an integral part of highway planning, and both federal and state laws now require such consideration.[26]

Financing Highways

Expenditures on highways and streets include construction costs, maintenance expenditures, highway and street administration (including their planning and collection of taxes and fees), police protection, and interest payments on money borrowed for highway and street purposes.

Sources of Funds. There are several possible sources of funds that a government could use for highway and street purposes. The original basic source was general

[26] See Alan A. Precup, "The Evolution of Social, Economic, and Environmental Awareness in the Federal Aid Highway Program," *Proceedings of the Transportation Research Forum, 1973.*

taxation whereby property owners and other taxpayers were expected to pay for state and local roads and streets. General taxation as the sole source of funds began to break down as long-distance roads were built that were not used much or at all by local taxpayers and as competition with nonhighway long-distance forms of transportation arose and questions of unfairness to the other modes arose. In addition, there was a limit to the ability of the local taxpayer to pay the taxes that were needed.

A second major source of highway and street financing is the user tax or charge which began in 1919 when the state of Oregon levied the first tax on gasoline. User charges are levied on the users of highways and streets and include taxes of fuel, vehicle registration fees, taxes on tires, taxes on lubricants, taxes on vehicles when purchased, taxes on parts and accessories for motor vehicles, and, sometimes, special taxes levied against for-hire carriers and/or against larger vehicles.

Of the above, fuel taxes produce the most revenue at both the federal and state levels. At the federal level, for example, in the fiscal year 1976 the fuel tax produced 4.2 billion dollars of the total user charge collection of 5.4 billion dollars that went into the Highway Trust Fund (see Table 16-2).

User charges have become the dominant source of highway money for several reasons. First, as intercity long-distance roads became more necessary, it was logical to have the direct beneficiaries instead of the local taxpayers assume the burden of the cost. Second, user charges made possible highway improvements that general taxation could not have supported. Third, user charges put highway users and railroads on a more equal competitive basis by not having the general taxpayer pay for highways. Fourth, user taxes produce a tremendous amount of revenue and are easy to collect. Finally, since the user pays the bill, he will, perhaps, insist that the highway programs be economically justifiable.

T A B L E 16-2 *Federal Highway User Taxes and Proceeds,* * *1976*[†]
(000,000)

Tax	Proceeds
Gasoline and diesel fuel (4¢ per gallon)	$4,219
Tires, tubes, and tread rubber (tires and tubes 10¢ per pound; tread rubber 5¢ per pound)	594
New trucks and buses (10% of manufacturer's wholesale price)	219
Truck-use tax ($3.00 per 1,000 pounds on vehicles with gross vehicle weight of 26,000 pounds or more)	209
Parts and accessories for trucks and buses (8% of manufacturer's wholesale price)	116
Lubricating oil (6¢ per gallon)	56
Total	5,413

*To Highway Trust Fund.
[†] Fiscal year.

Source: U.S. Department of Transportation, Federal Highway Administration.

The third source of funds for highway assistance is tolls that are collected while a road is being used. Tolls are usually in addition to whatever user charges the vehicle operator pays. As noted earlier, tolls were commonly used in early America, but they were not used to any degree for a long period after the Civil War. In the 1930's the first part of the Pennsylvania Turnpike was constructed as a toll facility. (It was partly a public works project to create jobs.) In the early post-World War II period when highways were in poor condition because of the neglect during the war, there was a flurry of toll road construction, mainly in the eastern part of the country. Among other reasons, toll roads were a method of improving highways quickly without obligating state funds. The roads were financed by selling revenue bonds that would be repaid from the earnings of the toll road. After 1956 the Interstate highway program discouraged further interest in toll roads because the same quality roads were now to be built with the federal government's paying 90 per cent of the cost.[27]

Financing Highways at the Federal Level. The share of highway money provided by the federal government has been increasing in recent years. Prior to 1956 the federal aid highway program was paid for from general revenue funds, which included the federal tax on fuel (but which was not specifically dedicated for highway purposes). The Federal Highway Act of 1956 established a new system of federal highway program financing whereby a special fund, called the *Highway Trust Fund,* was set up from which federal highway expenditures were to be made. No other sources of money were to be used. At the same time, Congress enacted some new taxes to go along with some previous taxes, the proceeds from which were to go into the Fund. These taxes, as of 1976, and the revenue produced are shown in Table 16-2.

Finally, the Act of 1956 provided that the federal government would pay 90 per cent of the cost of the Interstate program and generally 50 per cent of the cost of other federal aid programs, with the balance being paid by the states. In 1973 the share was raised to 70 per cent for the non-Interstate highways and streets.

Possible changes in the use of federal highway user tax revenue and the elimination of dedication of funds to highways or any other mode of transportation were being discussed in the federal government at the time of this writing (see Chapter 18).

The federal government currently has approximately 5.5 billion dollars annually in tax revenue to spend on highways, although some of the money in the Highway Trust Fund is now being used to improve urban mass transportation systems. Since 1967 the presidents of the United States have refused to spend all of the money available in the Fund in order to help curb inflation. As of early 1975, some 11 billion dollars had been "impounded" this way. President Gerald R. Ford, however, released 2 billion dollars of it in 1975 to help create employment. Although impounding of Trust Fund money is no longer practiced, at the end of the 1976 fiscal year there was an unspent balance of 9 billion dollars in the Fund. The entire federal program, as noted above, is on a user

---

[27] Arguments for and against the use of tolls to finance highways are discussed in Hudson and Constantine, *Motor Transportation,* pp. 127-132; Locklin, *Economics of Transportation,* pp. 633-640; and Charles A. Taff, *Commercial Motor Transportation,* 5th ed. (Cambridge, Maryland: Cornell Maritime Press, Inc., 1975), pp. 73-75.

charge basis. The total amount of money spent by the federal government between 1921 and 1976 is estimated to be approximately 104 billion dollars.[28]

The expiration date of the Highway Trust Fund has been postponed by Congress several times. It is scheduled to expire October 1, 1979, but it probably will be extended beyond that date but with some further modification as to what the funds can be used for, possibly transferring some to general revenue or combining the highway Fund with other federal transportation user taxes.[29]

Financing Highways at the State and Local Levels. At the state and local levels of government, there is more variety in the sources of highway support money than at the federal level. The actual sources used are influenced greatly by political considerations as well as by economic and transportation considerations. The ability to raise large amounts of money rather easily through user charges and the inadequacy of the general property tax are also important. The result is that the states usually rely heavily on user charges, including the large amounts received from the federal government. In many states, user charges collected are specifically dedicated to highway use only, but in other states highway user taxes are diverted to nonhighway uses, such as school construction or other purposes.

Counties and municipalities rely heavily on state funds which are mainly from user charges, but they also receive a great deal of general tax revenue for support of local roads and streets.

The degree of reliance on user charges versus general taxation at the various levels of government roughly reflects the fact that long-distance state highways mainly serve an intercommunity function and should probably be paid for mainly by those who make direct use of such roads. Since local roads and streets are primarily for the purpose of access to land and to permit intracommunity economic and social transportation, they should, therefore, be paid for in large part by local property owners who are the principal beneficiaries of these roads and streets.

The AAR estimated that state and local governments spent 21.3 billion dollars on highways and streets in 1976 and a total of 355.6 billion dollars in the period 1921 through 1976.[30]

The Subsidy Question in Highway Finance. One of the most difficult aspects of highway finance is deciding what share of highway and street costs should be paid for by users through user charges and what share should be paid for through general taxation. There is also the question of what share of the user tax burden should be borne by operators of vehicles of different sizes and kinds. The ideal situation would be for the amount paid in user taxes by a vehicle operator to reflect the use made of the highways, or the quantity of service obtained from highways, or the extra highway construction costs caused by the use of that particular vehicle. A common issue in all this is the question of how much heavy trucks should pay in comparison with other vehicles. The theories of highway

[28] Association of American Railroads, *Government and Private Expenditures,* Table 5.

[29] See "President Asks Congress for Indefinite Extension of Highway Trust Fund," *Traffic World,* July 14, 1975, p. 33 for a plan to change the fund.

[30] Association of American Railroads, *Government and Private Expenditures,* Table 5.

cost allocation and the studies that have been made on highway cost allocation are beyond the scope of this book and will not be discussed further here. In practice, however, it can be stated that wide variation exists among the various governments as to what they do and political considerations are very important in the decisions made.

Because of the problems inherent in determining what purposes individual roads and streets are intended to and actually do serve and what share of the cost of roads and streets should be allocated to property owners and other general taxpayers and to vehicle operators and, among vehicle operators, what share of user charges should be borne by owners of vehicles of different sizes and kinds, the entire question of whether or not or to what extent there is a subsidy element, as we have defined that term, in highway transportation is difficult to answer. There is also the question of what should be included in highway costs. Annual operating, administrative, and maintenance costs must be identified and measured, along with the capital investment itself. Police protection may or may not be included as a highway cost chargeable to users and/or property owners. Interest on the investment in the road or street might be included as a cost, as might depreciation or amortization charges. There is also the question of whether or not the property taxes on the property used for highways and streets that are not being collected should be included as a cost.

Consequently, there are many differences of opinion on the subsidy question in highway transportation. We do know, however, that the federal program, which is a capital investment program, is entirely on a user-charge basis and that most states rely heavily on user charges for investment and maintenance costs. If these are the only costs to be concerned with, then one might conclude that major highways are generally paid for by users (recognizing that there is variation among the states) and, therefore, there is little or no subsidy. However, there remains the question of whether or not there is a cross-subsidy factor among the users themselves, i.e., are automobile owners and owners of other small vehicles paying more than their share of the user charges while heavy trucks are paying less than their share? This claim is often made, but as yet there is no available scientific way to prove or disprove the charge. The trucking industry, meanwhile, points out that the industry pays a large amount in user taxes (see Table 16-3). User charges paid by trucks amount to approximately 38 percent of all state and federal highway user taxes collected in the United States.[31] The industry also claims that user taxes graduate sharply upward in relation to the size of the truck so that in 1973 the owner of a diesel-powered, 5-axle tractor-trailer combination with a gross vehicle weight of 72,000 pounds paid approximately 3,500 dollars in federal and state user taxes while the owner of a gasoline-powered, 3-axle tractor-trailer combination with a gross vehicle weight of 40,000 pounds paid approximately 1,800 dollars.[32]

In the future, the whole question of the amount of highway construction there will be and the amount of user-tax revenue that will be available will be muddled by the energy crisis. The uncertainty about future federal energy policy

[31] American Trucking Associations, Inc., *Truck Taxes by States*, 25th ed. (Washington, D.C.: American Trucking Associations, Inc., 1977), p. 3.

[32] American Trucking Associations, Inc., *American Trucking Trends*, 1975 ed. (Washington, D.C.: American Trucking Associations, Inc., 1976), p. 21.

TABLE 16-3 *Federal and State User Taxes Paid by Private and
For-Hire Trucking, 1940-1974 (000,000)*

Year	Amount of Taxes
1940	$463.9
1945	598.7
1950	1,127.3
1955	1,865.7
1960	2,830.7
1965	3,843.7
1970	5,632.3
1974	7,147.7

Source: American Trucking Associations, Inc., *American Trucking Trends, 1976 Statistical Supplement* (Washington, D.C.: American Trucking Associations, Inc., 1977), p. 11.

at the time of this writing makes any predictions meaningless. However, the 55 mile per hour national speed limit, the higher price of gasoline, and the more cautious use of gasoline have curtailed the amount of gasoline consumed and the amount of user-tax revenues produced. Any allocation or rationing system or further substantial rises in the price of gasoline will have the same effect. At the same time, not only may there be less money available for highway purposes, but the need for more highways and improvements to existing highways will also be open to serious question in a period of extreme energy shortage.

Government Promotion of Urban Transportation

This book is mainly concerned with the intercity movement of freight and passengers. However, because urban transportation involves highways and streets and because local movement of property and persons affects intercity transportation, it is appropriate to discuss briefly the government's role in the current attempt to improve the urban transportation systems of the country.

The Urban Transportation Problem. The urban transportation problem is familiar to most urban Americans. It consists of urban congestion, traffic tieups, wasted energy, air pollution, inadequate public mass transportation sytems, rising transit fares, and declining public ridership. The movement of both freight and people are involved in the problem, although the movement of people has received most of the attention.

Federal Programs. Urban transportation problems were for the most part neglected by government until recent years, although since 1944 there has been federal aid to urban highways and streets. At the state and local levels there were some local government-owned public mass transit systems prior to 1960, but there was no federal or state promotion of transit systems.

The federal Housing Act of 1961 provided for federal grants for experimentation with public transit systems and loans for new equipment. The major step forward, however, was the federal Urban Mass Transportation Act of 1964 which provided federal grants to public agencies for up to two-thirds of the cost of new transit equipment, buildings, and rights of way (but no operating expenses). Low-interest loans were also to be made. The program was originally administered by the Housing and Home Finance Agency, but it was transferred to the new Department of Housing and Urban Development in 1965 and finally to the new DOT in 1968, which established the Urban Mass Transportation Administration (UMTA) for that purpose.

The federal program has continued since 1964 and Congress has periodically provided increasing amounts of money. The Urban Transportation Assistance Act of 1970 gave the DOT the authority to obligate 10 billion dollars over 12 years for capital facilities, relocations, and general studies. In addition, grants for research, development, demonstrations, and managerial training were to be funded by separate appropriations. The 1973 Federal Air Highway Act provided that the federal share for capital programs would be increased from 66 $\frac{2}{3}$ per cent to 80 per cent. The Act also permitted some funds in the Highway Trust Fund to be used to improve urban mass transit systems. The National Mass Transportation Assistance Act of 1974 provided for 11.8 billion dollars to be spent over a 6-year period, with 11.3 billion dollars to be spent for urban systems and 500 million dollars to be spent for rural systems. Of the 11.8 billion dollars, 7.9 billion dollars was to be used for capital outlays and 3.9 billion dollars was to be used at local option for either capital needs or operating subsidies. The capital grant aid was to be on an 80 per cent federal and 20 per cent local basis, but the operating subsidies were to be on a 50-50 basis. The Act marked the first time that the federal government provided aid to cover operating expenses of urban mass transportation systems.

State and Local Programs. Until the last few years state governments generally ignored the urban mass transportation problem, but in the 1970's some states now provide financial support to local systems. Approximately one-half of the states in 1973 provided some form of subsidy to mass transit.[33]

Cities have long been involved with the problem and in many cases have taken over ownership of all or part of the local mass transit service. By 1975 there were 333 publicly owned urban transit systems or 35 per cent of the total.[34] In some cases, a metropolitan approach has been taken to promoting and/or owning transit systems, such as in Minneapolis and St. Paul where a commission representing a 7-county area operates the major portion of the transit system. The amount of money available, however, at both the state and local levels to improve mass transit systems is limited. Great reliance on the federal government is expected to be the case in the future, particularly since Highway Trust Fund money can now be used, operating subsidies are now available, and the federal government will assume 80 per cent of the cost of capital improvements.

The Subsidy Question. Urban mass transit systems offer little prospect of paying their own way, but they cannot be abandoned without serious consequences, particularly in view of the energy shortage problem. Public subsidy appears to be unavoidable. It is clear that the federal government, at least, has committed

[33] John W. Fuller, "Financing State Transit Subsidies," *Proceedings of Transportation Research Forum, 1973*, p. 361.

[34] American Transit Association, *Transit Fact Book, 1975-1976* (Washington, D.C.: American Transit Association, 1976), p. 25.

itself to a program of subsidy to urban mass transportation with no attempt being made to recover its costs from users. In some other areas of transportation, the federal government has been trying to reduce the subsidy element. At the state and local levels there is also a growing acceptance of the fact that the fare box will not support mass transit. The real question is what will be the source of the public funds to be used. Should it be general taxation levied against local residents, general taxation levied against all residents in a metropolitan area or an entire state, or federal general taxes? Should the funds come from taxes levied on other modes of transportation, such as highway transportation?

To date, general taxation at the local level, at the state level, and at the federal level has been the primary source of government funds used to support urban mass transportation. The Federal Aid Highway Act of 1973, however, was a major change in this philosophy in that it permitted some federal highway user taxes to be used to support mass transportation systems.[35] The question of diverting user taxes away from use only to support the mode of transportation taxed is discussed in Chapter 18.

The energy shortage of the future promises to accelerate interest in improving urban public passenger transportation systems because of their favorable energy-consumption characteristics compared with the private automobile. This will be accentuated if stern measures are taken at the federal level to control the use of energy. The result will probably be greater government efforts in promoting public passenger transportation systems. Government programs designed to reduce the amount of wasteful motor truck use of energy in urban areas, such as government-sponsored joint terminals, may also arise.

SELECTED REFERENCES

Public aid to transportation is discussed in Roy J. Sampson and Martin T. Farris, *Domestic Transportation: Practice, Theory and Policy,* 3rd ed. (Boston: Houghton-Mifflin Company, 1975), Chapter 27.

Public aid to early railroads is dealt with in some detail in D. Philip Locklin, *Economics of Transportation,* 7th ed. (Homewood, Illinois: Richard D. Irwin, Inc., 1972), Chapter 6. The federal land grant program is discussed and evaluated in Robert S. Henry, "The Railroad Land Grant Legend in American History Textbooks," *Mississippi Valley Historical Review,* September, 1945 and in Paul W. Gates, "The Railroad Land Grant Legend," *Journal of Economic History,* Spring, 1954. See also Association of American Railroads. *A Sharp Deal for Uncle Sam* (Washington, D.C.: Association of American Railroads) for the railroad view of the matter.

A good summary of the railroad passenger commuter problem is "The Story Behind the Commuter Crisis," *Business Week,* March 14, 1972.

The declining interest of the federal government in the High-Speed Ground Transportation program is discussed in "High-Speed Trains Hit a Red Signal," *Business Week,* January 13, 1975.

[35]For discussions of sources of funds for mass transit subsidy, see John C. Spychalski, "Diversion of Motor Vehicle-Related Tax Revenues to Urban Mass Transport: A Critique of its Economic Tenability," *Transportation Journal,* Spring, 1970 and Fuller, "Financing State Transit Subsidies."

The decline of intercity passenger train service is analyzed in Theodore E. Keller, "The Economics of Passenger Trains," *Journal of Business*, April, 1971. An excellent description and analysis of the bill that created Amtrak is Robert W. Harbeson, "The Rail Passenger Service Act of 1970," *ICC Practitioners' Journal*, March–April, 1971. The problems of Amtrak are dealt with in some detail in Edwin S. Patton, "Amtrak in Perspective: Where Goest the Pointless Arrow?" *Proceedings, American Economic Association*, May, 1974 and Rush Loving, Jr., "Amtrak Is About to Miss the Train," *Fortune*, May, 1974. The contracts between Amtrak and operating railroads are evaluated in William J. Baumol, "Payment by Performance in Rail Passenger Transportation: An Innovation in Amtrak's Operations," *Bell Journal of Economics*, Spring, 1975. The accomplishments of Conrail in its first year are summarized in "Conrail's First Year: A Good Track Record," *Business Week*, April 11, 1977.

The general causes of the problems of railroads in the northeast and elsewhere are dealt with in Robert W. Harbeson, "Some Policy Implications of Northeastern Railroad Problems," *Transportation Journal*, Fall, 1974. A critical review of the Regional Rail Reorganization Act of 1973 is Rush Loving, Jr., "A Costly Rescue for the Northeast Railroads," *Fortune*, February, 1974. Criticisms of the final system plan of the United States Railway Association include "Bank Official Tells Commerce Group That USRA System Plan Won't Work," *Traffic World*, September 29, 1975, p. 17 and Michael Conant, "Structural Reorganization of the Northeast Railroads, *ICC Practitioners' Journal*, January–February, 1976.

The pros and cons of a nationalized railroad system are set forth in Locklin, *Economics of Transportation*, 6th ed., 1966, Chapter 27. Arguments against nationalization of railroads in the United States are presented in Association of American Railroads, *U.S. Railroads Vs. Nationalized Operations* (Washington, D.C.: Association of American Railroads, 1973) and Paul J. Tierney, "Nationalization: A Shadow on the Future," *Traffic World*, July 1, 1974. A critical discussion of government-owned rail service in other countries is Kenneth Marshall, "They Know How to Run Them In . . . Or Do They?" *Transportation and Distribution Management*, May, 1971. An interesting discussion of government ownership of railroad roadbeds with private operation by the railroad companies over the roadbeds as an alternative to complete nationalization is in D. Daryl Wyckoff, "Public Tracks, Private Users," *Transportation and Distribution Management*, April, 1973. See also James H. Foggin, "Aspects of Railroad Right-of-Way Nationalization," *Proceedings of Transportation Research Forum, 1973*.

Early development of highways in the United States is treated in William J. Hudson and James C. Constantine, *Motor Transportation*, (New York: The Ronald Press Company, 1958), Chapter 2.

The federal role in highway aid in the period through 1956 is discussed in Hudson and Constantine, *Motor Transportation*, pp. 64–83. The federal program is described in Charles A. Taff, *Commerical Motor Transportation*, 5th ed. (Cambridge, Maryland: Cornell Maritime Press, Inc., 1975), pp. 12–35.

Financing of highways by government is discussed in Taff, *Commercial Motor Transportation*, Chapter 3. See also Hudson and Constantine, *Motor Transportation*, Chapters 5 and 6 and Locklin, *Economics of Transportation*, 7th ed., Chapter 27.

An article that describes the effects of the Interstate highway program on the

United States is Juan Cameron, "How the Interstate Changed the Face of the Nation," *Fortune,* July, 1971.

Alan A. Precup, "The Evolution of Social, Economic, and Environmental Awareness in the Federal Aid Highway Process," *Proceedings of Transportation Research Forum, 1973* discusses social and environmental issues in highway programs. See also David Solomon, U.S. Department of Transportation, Federal Highway Administration, "Environmental Research and Highways," *Public Roads* (Washington, D.C.: U.S. Government Printing Office, March, 1974), p. 297 for a discussion of environmental problems associated with highways and federal research programs on the matter.

An excellent earlier source dealing with the urban transportation problem is Wilfred Owen, *The Metropolitan Transportation Problem* (Washington, D.C.: The Brookings Institution, 1966). The urban transportation problem is also discussed in Dudley F. Pegrum, *Transportation Economics and Public Policy,* 3rd ed. (Homewood, Illinois: Richard D. Irwin, Inc., 1973), Chapter 23. The problems of urban freight movement by truck are discussed in Richard A. Staley, *Trucks and Our Changing Cities* (Washington, D.C.: Local and Short Haul Carriers Conference, 1973). See also James E. Morehouse, "Local Delivery Is Urban Transportation Too," *Transportation and Distribution Management,* April, 1973 and Bob Redding, "Urban Goods Distribution: The Lifeblood of Our Cities," *Handling and Shipping,* February, 1977. The problems of urban goods movement and possible solutions are discussed in Dennis R. McDermott, "An Alternative Framework for Urban Goods Movement: Consolidation," *Transportation Journal,* Fall, 1975.

An evaluation of the federal mass transportation program through 1971 is George M. Smerk, "An Evaluation of Ten Years of Federal Policy in Urban Mass Transportation," *Transportation Journal,* Winter, 1971. A good summary of the progress made in mass transit and alternatives for the future is John F. Due, "Urban Mass Transit: A Review Article," *Quarterly Review of Economics and Business,* Spring, 1976. See also Smerk, "Public Policy and Urban Transportation," *University of Tennessee Survey of Business,* November–December, 1976 and Owen, *Transportation for Cities: The Role of Federal Policy* (Washington, D.C.: The Brookings Institution, 1976). The urban transportation problem is discussed in Martin T. Farris and Forrest E. Harding, *Passenger Transportation* (Englewood Cliffs, New Jersey: Prentice-Hall, Inc., 1976), Chapter 6.

State subsidy to mass transit is discussed in John W. Fuller, "Financing State Transit Subsidies," *Proceedings of Transportation Research Forum, 1973.* Criticisms of diverting highway user tax funds to aid mass transit systems are presented in John C. Spychalski, "Diversion of Motor Vehicle-Related Tax Revenues to Urban Mass Transport: A Critique of its Economic Tenability," *Transportation Journal,* Spring, 1970.

17

Government Promotion of
Water, Oil Pipeline,
and Air Transportation

In this chapter our study of government promotion of transportation continues with a discussion of promotion of water, oil pipeline, and air transportation.

GOVERNMENT PROMOTION OF DOMESTIC
WATER TRANSPORTATION

We confine our discussion of water transportation in this chapter to domestic water transportation only, recognizing, however, that there is an extremely important role played by water carriers in international trade as well.

The reader will recall from Chapter 12 that domestic water transportation consists of water transportation along the seacoasts (coastal) and between coasts (intercoastal), on the Great Lakes, and on rivers and canals and also water transportation between the mainland United States and offshore states and possessions. The government promotional policies that have been followed have varied greatly among these various water carrier trades. Included in our discussion in this chapter is what is called the *inland waterways system,* which includes the Great Lakes, the internal river and canal system, the coastal rivers, and the intracoastal waterways (bays, inlets, canals, and protected channels along the coastlines). We shall also discuss deep-water coastal transportation, intercoastal water transportation (including the Panama Canal), and the St. Lawrence Seaway.

Government Promotion of Early Water Transportation

State Promotion. A large amount of canal building took place in the first half of the nineteenth century. The era of canal building began with the successful Erie Canal, which was contructed by the state of New York. It connected the Hudson River at Albany, New York with Buffalo on Lake Erie—a distance of 364 miles—at a cost of approximately 7 million dollars. The Canal opened for traffic in

1825, and although tolls were charged, it substantially reduced transportation costs between the "west" (area west of the Appalachian Mountains) and the eastern seaboard (the alternative was overland transportation with animal power). Thus, for example, farmers in Ohio could now ship their produce via Lake Erie, the Canal, and the Hudson River to New York City at a cost far less than before.

The success of the Erie Canal led to a wave of canal building in several other states. Although some of the canals were private enterprises, most were state government projects. Some of the private projects were assisted by federal land grants amounting to approximately 6.3 million acres in the period 1827 to 1866, in addition to right-of-way land grants. The federal government also provided some cash grants and loans and purchased stock in canal companies.[1]

Many of the canal projects were unwise, and little traffic was carried on some of them. Where the states had built the canals, substantial financial debts were incurred, as were also being incurred in the states' promotion of railroads and other internal improvements.

Approximately 4,400 miles of canal were constructed. The canal building era ended for the most part with the "panic" of 1837, but it continued on a small scale up until approximately 1860. The combination of lack of sufficient traffic, heavy state debts, and the development of the railroad system served to end interest in either private or government promotion of canals.

Few of the canals built in that period survive. One is the Erie Canal, which is now a toll-free canal called the New York State Barge Canal. Another is the Illinois–Michigan Canal, which is an important waterway that connects Lake Michigan with the Illinois River. Both have been improved substantially since their construction.

Federal Promotion. The federal government has always had a keen interest in developing the country's inland waterways system. Federal aid to the system began in 1789 when federal aid for improvements of harbors began. In 1823 a Rivers and Harbors Act was passed by Congress for the purpose of improving the country's inland waterways system. Since 1866 Congress has made regular appropriations to improve the system, either annually or every 2 or 3 years. In 1878, for example, Congress authorized a 4½-foot channel to be made in the upper Mississippi River. The federal government began improving connecting channels and building canals and locks in the Great Lakes as early as 1829. The "Soo" locks at Sault Ste. Marie, Michigan connecting Lake Huron and Lake Superior were opened to traffic in 1855 and were an important step toward increasing the amount of interlake traffic.

Government Promotion of Water Transportation in Modern Times

With the decline of the steamboat and domestic water transportation in general in the second half of the nineteenth century, domestic water transportation was relatively inactive for a long time as railroads dominated the intercity transportation system. This was particularly true of the river and canal system.

---

[1]"Few Segments of U.S. Economy Unaffected by Subsidies, Congressional Aides Conclude," *Traffic World*, December 24, 1960, p. 31.

However, a movement toward revival of domestic water transportation began in the 1890's. The movement was caused in part by rising interest in flood control and other conservation measures. However, a major reason then and now has been the desire for low-cost transportation by water.

The Erie Canal was modernized starting in 1903. Congress has been making regular appropriations to improve water transportation on other waterways since 1866, but construction was piecemeal and no plan for development of the system had been set up. Then, in 1902 the federal Rivers and Harbors Act, whereby a formal program of review of proposed waterway improvements was established and which is still being followed, was enacted. In 1907 a federal Inland Waterways Commission was appointed by the president of the United States to prepare a plan for improving waterways. The Commission was succeeded by the National Waterways Commission in 1909 which in 1912 recommended further federal aid to water transportation.

The federal system provides that the Army Corps of Engineers builds, operates, and maintains water improvements with money provided by Congress. Included in the program are improvements made to coastal, Great Lakes, and river harbors, and to the waterways themselves. Federal expenditures on harbor improvements are for deepening channels, continuous dredging, building breakwaters and navigational aids, and other harbor improvements and their maintenance. Federal money is, however, ordinarily not used for terminal construction and operation.

Not including the Great Lakes, the inland waterways system today consists of over 25,000 miles of improved waterways, approximately 16,000 miles of which are at least 9 feet in depth.

Statistics on total annual government expenditures on domestic waterways and ports are not available. The Association of American Railroads (AAR), however, estimated that in 1976 the federal government spent approximately 626 million dollars on domestic waterways projects related to navigation, including those in the coastal, intercoastal, Great Lakes, and river trades.[2] The total federal expenditures for these purposes through 1976 were estimated to be approximately 11.8 billion dollars.[3] The AAR estimated that approximately one-half the federal money has been spent on the inland rivers and intracoastal waterways, not including harbor improvements.[4]

In addition to federal programs, the state and local governments have spent considerable sums for port development, including provision of terminal facilities. This amounted to approximately 750 million dollars in 1976, according to the AAR.[5] The ports receiving such aid are coastal, Great Lakes, and river ports.

Panama Canal. The Panama Canal, which connects the Atlantic with the Pacific across the Isthmus of Panama, is a vital link in the intercoastal water transportation system. In 1854 the Panama Railroad opened and was a major step forward

---

[2] Excludes expenditures made by the Tennessee Valley Authority on the Tennessee River for navigation purposes. Association of American Railroads, *Government and Private Expenditures for Highway, Waterway, Railroad, and Air Rights-of-Way* (Washington, D.C.: Association of American Railroads, September, 1977), Table 6 (unpublished).

[3] *Ibid.*

[4] *Ibid.*, Table 7.

[5] *Ibid.*, Table 6.

in reducing the time involved in water carriage between the Pacific Coast and the Gulf or Atlantic coasts. In 1914 the United States government-constructed 50-mile long Panama Canal, which cuts through the country of Panama, opened. It was built at a cost of approximately 375 million dollars over a 10-year period and, by eliminating the delay in transferring from ship to rail to ship, substantially boosted the amount of intercoastal commerce. It is operated by the Panama Canal Company, a corporation owned by the United States government, under the direction of the United States Army.

Seventy per cent of the tonnage that moves through the Canal is destined to or comes from the United States. However, because of the falling off of intercoastal domestic trade after World War II, intercoastal traffic is today a small part of the total Canal traffic. For many years, until 1961, the United States government operated a ship line that carried intercoastal traffic through the Canal.

Approximately 14,000 ship "transits" are made through the Canal each year. A toll system has been in effect from the beginning, and all ships (including United States ships) except Panama and Columbia government vessels in ballast or carrying government cargoes pay to go through the Canal.

The Canal has 6 locks and a 37-foot to 40-foot depth. Because the size of merchant and military vessels has increased in recent years, many ships cannot use the Canal. There is also the problem of almost continuous friction between the government of Panama and the government of the United States over the treaty between the 2 countries which gives to the United States operating and defense control of the Canal and the 500-square mile Canal Zone "in perpetuity." In late 1977 an agreement between the United States and Panama to turn control of the Canal over to Panama in the year 2000 with the United States to retain the right to defend the Canal indefinitely was awaiting approval by the United States Senate. The building of a new, deeper and wider sea-level canal, possibly in some other country, has also been discussed and studied by the federal government.

The tolls charged to use the Canal were originally not expected to return the investment cost to the government. The total investment in the Canal is today considerably more than the original 375 million dollars since many improvements have been made since 1914. Since 1950, however, the objective has been to have the tolls cover the cost of operating and maintaining the waterway and related facilities plus interest and depreciation charges. In 1974 an increase of 20 per cent was made in the toll structure (the first adjustment made since 1914) because of projected deficits which were partly to be the result of an attempt to account for depreciation on the original investment in the Canal. Other reasons were declining traffic due to the worldwide recession, the reduction in military traffic caused by the end of the Viet Nam war, and the fact that many new ships were too large to use the Canal. At the same time, operating costs were rising. Because deficits occurred anyway, 2 additional toll increases have been made since 1974, including a 20 per cent increase in late 1976.

Coastal and Intercoastal Vessels. During World War II the submarine threat and government acquisition of many of the vessels for use elsewhere ended most coastal and intercoastal shipping. To revive such trade, the federal War Shipping Administration operated vessels in 1945 and 1946, and the United States Maritime Commission did so in 1946 and 1947. Private operation resumed in 1947.

As indicated in Chapter 12, neither the coastal nor the intercoastal trades have regained their pre-war importance and there have been no specific government promotional programs for these trades, although the carriage of goods in the nation's domestic water commerce is restricted to vessels built and registered in the United States and owned by American citizens, as required under the Jones Act of 1920. There are also federal income tax benefits that accrue to United States citizens who own or lease vessels built and registered in the United States and operating in United States commerce.

Coastal Ports. Ocean ports are mainly the responsibility of state and local governments, sometimes under the jurisdiction of port "authorities." Considerable state and local money has been spent to provide terminal facilities at ocean ports. In addition, the federal government has spent huge sums to build breakwaters, dredge channels, and provide navigational aids. The construction of 2 off shore deep water ports in the Gulf of Mexico to handle oil super tankers was approved by Secretary of Transportation William T. Coleman Jr. in late 1976. The ports were to be built by groups of oil companies.

Great Lakes and the St. Lawrence Seaway. A substantial amount of traffic is carried on the Great Lakes and much of it is also carried through the St. Lawrence Seaway. A large part of the St. Lawrence Seaway traffic is in international trade. However, because some of the Seaway traffic is in domestic commerce, the Seaway is included in our discussion here.

The connecting channels between the Great Lakes have been improved steadily over the years by the federal government and by the Canadian government, as have harbor and port and terminal facilities by state, local, and federal governments.

The St. Lawrence River provides a waterway between Lake Ontario and the Atlantic Ocean. The Montreal–Lake Ontario segment was improved several times by Canada in the nineteenth century in order to make the river navigable. By 1903 there was a 14-foot channel, but it was not deep enough for ocean-going vessels. After many years of discussion and considerable opposition by railroads, ocean ports, and other interests in the United States, in 1954 Congress passed the Wiley–Dondero Act that committed the United States government to a joint program with Canada to provide a depth of 27 feet by constructing 7 new locks. The total cost of the project was 442 million dollars, of which 70 per cent was paid by Canada and 30 per cent was paid by the United States. There were also considerable federal expenditures on interlake connections—approximately 279 million dollars, plus port development expenditures by all levels of government. Canada spent approximately 30 million dollars to improve the Welland Canal, which connects Lake Erie with Lake Ontario.

The new St. Lawrence Seaway opened in 1959. It consists of 7 locks in a distance of 189 miles between Montreal and Lake Ontario. The tolls to be collected were to pay the principal and interest costs and operating expenses for navigation facilities in the Seaway (there also are power projects involved) to the 2 countries in 50 years. The tolls were to be shared by the two countries according to the amount of money each had invested (Canada also collects a lockage fee on the Welland Canal). The United States' part of the Seaway opera-

GOVERNMENT

tion is administered by the St. Lawrence Seaway Development Corporation, which is in the federal Department of Transportation (DOT).

The Seaway has carried a tremendous amount of traffic since 1959, most of it bulk cargo in international trade, with approximately 6,000 ship transits a year. However, the tolls have not provided sufficient money to keep up with the debt retirement program, and in 1970 the Seaway was released by Congress of the obligation to pay the interest charges part of the cost. The deficits have been caused partly by a miscalculation of the amount of traffic that would move through the Seaway in its early years, a resulting error in setting the tolls, and rising costs. Other difficulties of the Seaway have been a limited navigation season, strong competition from the railroads that serve Great Lakes and ocean ports, the fact that the Seaway is too small for many newer ocean ships, and the greater time required to export through the Seaway as against land transportation to the Atlantic or Gulf and then carriage by water.

Although Seaway traffic has, in general, been heavy, it declined sharply in 1974 to 44.1 million tons from the record tonnage of 57.6 million tons set in 1973. Much of the decline was caused by labor stoppages involving the Seaway, the worldwide recession, and an accident that closed the Welland Canal for 12 days. There was improvement in the recession years of 1975 and 1976; traffic in the latter year amounted to 54.4 million tons.[6] Seaway capacity is 75 million tons annually.

Meanwhile, there is considerable discussion of raising the tolls and there are programs intended to provide year-around navigation in the Great Lakes and the Seaway by de-icing the water. There also has been some discussion of rebuilding the Seaway to make it wider and deeper to accommodate today's larger ocean-going vessels and of the United States' building a new canal to bypass Niagara Falls (where Lake Ontario and Lake Erie connect) to supplement the current 8-lock Welland Canal owned and operated by Canada or rebuilding the Welland Canal, which has been a bottleneck in the system.

The growth in domestic Great Lakes traffic that does not involve the Seaway has been disappointing, but considerable public money is invested in the ports and interconnecting channels that serve lake-bound as well as Seaway traffic.

Rivers. A major part of the federal inland waterways development program has to do with improvement of the vast river system that exists mainly in the eastern half of the country. Much of the river system was not navigable for commercial purposes in its natural state because of flooding, shallow water, rapids and falls, narrow channels, and sharp curves. To improve rivers, such as the Ohio and Mississippi, the Army Corps or Engineers spent millions of dollars in constructing locks and dams to control river flow and depth and to bypass rapids and falls, in widening channels, in straightening rivers, in providing navigational aids, and in continuous dredging operations to keep channels at a minimum depth (usually 9 feet). In addition to improved navigation, river improvements sometimes result in benefits that may be incidental byproducts of the navigation program or may be a major part of the overall program. These benefits include flood control, pro-

---

[6]U.S. Department of Transportation, St. Lawrence Seaway Development Corporation, *Annual Report 1976* (Washington, D.C.: St. Lawrence Seaway Development Corporation, 1976), inside front cover.

duction of hydroelectric power at dams, irrigation for farmland, and recreational use of the controlled rivers. Once constructed, river improvements are operated and maintained by the Army Corps of Engineers.

Among the major improvements in the river system have been the continuous improvement of the Ohio River and the development since 1930 of a 9-foot channel in the Mississippi between Cairo, Illinois and Minneapolis–St. Paul via construction of 29 locks and dams and continuous dredging. A recent major example of a federally supported waterway project is the Arkansas-Verdrigis Canal project, which made the Arkansas River into a 9-foot channel (along with some flood control and power purposes) through Arkansas and Oklahoma from the Mississippi River to Catoosa (near Tulsa), Oklahoma, a distance of 450 miles. Seventeen locks were constructed and the total cost of the project was approximately 1.2 billion dollars. It opened to traffic in 1970.

In recent years environmentally based opposition to further proposed major projects, such as making the Mississippi River channel 12 feet deep instead of 9 feet from St. Louis to Minneapolis–St. Paul and the replacing and expansion of the capacity of the deteriorating locks and dam at Alton, Illinois (environmentalists believe that this is the first step toward expanding the size of all the locks on the Mississippi system and constructing a deeper channel), has led to a slow down in further development of the domestic waterways system.[7] The construction of a new cross-Florida canal was stopped in 1971 because of environmental opposition.[8] In addition, there is considerable environmentally based opposition to the dredging operations of the Army Corps of Engineers that are required to keep river channels at the desired depth. The opposition mainly has to do with the disposal of the dredged materials along the shore of the river. There has also been an attempt by the federal government to help curb inflation by cutting back on waterway improvement projects.

Harbor improvements at ports located on rivers and canals are often jointly sponsored by federal, state, and local governments. Terminals are ordinarily provided and operated by local government, although large shippers and receivers sometimes provide their own terminal facilities.

Federal Barge Line Experiment. As noted briefly in Chapter 12, the federal government owned and operated a barge line appropriately called the Federal Barge Lines on the Mississippi, Illinois, Missouri, and Warrior rivers in the period between World War I and 1953. The purpose of the barge line was to demonstrate the feasibility of barge operations and to encourage revival of domestic water transportation. The line was operated by the United States Railroad Administration at first, then by the War Department and, still later, beginning in 1924, by the Inland Waterways Corporation whose entire stock was owned by the federal government.

The line was sold to a private buyer in 1953 for 9 million dollars. The financial success of the line varied while the government had control, with deficits

---

[7]There is also environmental opposition to a study by the Corps of Engineers of the possibility of expanding the size of the locks at Sault Ste. Marie on the Great Lakes.

[8]See "Nixon Halts Construction of Florida Barge Canal: $50 Million Already Spent," *Traffic World,* January 25, 1971, p. 19 and "Engineers Recommend End to Further Construction of Florida Barge Canal," *Traffic World,* March 7, 1977, p. 20.

being incurred in 17 of the 29 years.[9] However, the line probably did have the effect of helping to revive interest in water transportation.

Financing Government Promotion of
Water Transportation

Sources of Funds. As in the case of other modes of transportation, the possible sources of government funds to be used by government to promote water transportation are general taxation, user taxes, and tolls. All of these methods are used in water transportation. In the case of the Panama Canal and the St. Lawrence Seaway, tolls are collected according to the size of the ship and the weight carried. In the case of all other federal aid to domestic water transportation, however, general taxes are relied upon for the money spent, i.e., no user charges or tolls are collected.

At the state and local levels of government, charges are usually made for use of port facilities on the Great Lakes, the ocean coasts, and the river system. The carrier must usually pay for loading and unloading and other services that are provided at publicly owned inland terminals. At ocean ports there are also loading and unloading costs and charges for various services rendered at the port. In addition, there may be various charges for entering a harbor, such as pilotage, mooring, dockage, and harbor master fees. Shippers and receivers also must usually pay for whatever services are rendered for them at inland and ocean ports.

The Subsidy Question. As with highway transportation, in any attempt to examine the subsidy question there is disagreement over what should be included in government costs in promoting water transportation. The capital investment costs and the operating, administration, and maintenance costs must be identified and measured. Interest on the investment in the facility and depreciation or amortization charges might also be included. There is also the question of whether or not the property taxes on the property used for the facility that are not being collected should be included as a cost.

On the other side of the question is the amount paid by carriers for the use of government provided facilities. The tolls collected on the Panama Canal apparently have not been sufficient to cover all costs charged to the Canal in recent years. The tolls collected on the St. Lawrence Seaway have been insufficient to cover all capital and interest costs and operating and maintenance expenses. Thus, an element of subsidy, as we have defined that term here, exists on the Panama Canal and the Seaway. In both the Panama Canal and Seaway cases, however, the reader should keep in mind that much of their use is for international trade and that only part of their cost is assignable to domestic water commerce.

In the federal inland waterways program, which assists the river system, intra-coastal waterways, and Great Lakes and coastal harbors, no charges of any kind

---

[9] D. Philip Locklin, *Economics of Transportation,* 5th ed. (Homewood, Illinois: Richard D. Irwin, Inc., 1960), pp. 716-717.

are collected by the government and, therefore, these federal expenditures for navigation purposes are considered subsidy under our definition.

At terminals and harbor facilities provided by state and local governments, charges are often made. Whether or not the charges levied are adequate to cover the governmental costs is impossible to say and varies between ports, but it appears that a large subsidy element generally exists at the state and local levels, in addition to that at the federal level, particularly in connection with the general cargo facilities, as opposed to the bulk handling facilities of a port.[10]

To the extent that subsidy exists in domestic water transportation, the general taxpayers bear part of the cost of water transportation and the rates charged by water carriers need not reflect the entire costs of the transportation being provided. This, along with other factors noted in Chapter 12, helps water carriers to charge relatively low rates and gives the impression that it is cheaper than other forms of transportation. This, in turn, leads to further demands for expansion of waterway facilities, some of which can be economically justified and some of which cannot.

Other forms of transportation, particularly railroads, object strongly to the subsidy element in domestic water transportation and urge that user charges be imposed or increased. In addition to eliminating the unfairness to other modes, user charges of some kind serve to encourage more careful scrutiny of the projects if the carriers must help pay for them.

Many proposals have been made by the president of the United States, the federal DOT, various study commissions, and others to put the inland waterways system on a user charge basis of some kind. The various methods proposed usually include lockage fees (or tolls) or fuel taxes. A recent proposal to enact federal user charges was made in 1973 by the National Water Commission, appointed by President Lyndon B. Johnson under an act of Congress.[11] An attempt to recover all of the past and current expenditures made by the federal government on the inland waterways system would result in user charges so high as to kill off most or all water traffic. Consequently, the proposals usually are for user charges that would compensate the government only for current operating and maintenance expenses.

Efforts to impose federal user charges on the inland waterways system have, however, all failed although in late 1977 it appeared that there was some chance that Congress would enact a waterway user charge of some kind along with its approval of the building a new lock and dam facility at Alton, Illinois. (The intermodal consequences are discussed in Chapter 18.) The reader should recall, however, that there are arguments for subsidized transportation (see Chapter 16) that might justify the subsidy to water transportation, at least in the minds of those who support continuance of these subsidies.

The fact that water transportation is more energy efficient than some other modes in terms of fuel consumption per unit of traffic carried is a factor in its favor in future decisions on waterway programs. However, its nearest competi-

---

[10] See Robert C. Waters, "Role Crisis in America's Ports?" *Transportation Journal,* Winter, 1974.

[11] See Walter B. Wright and William J. Hull, "The National Water Commission Report," *Transportation and Distribution Management,* June 25, 1973 and "Waterway User Charges, Lockage Fees Retained in Final Report of NWC," *Traffic World,* June 25, 1973, p. 138.

tors—railroads and oil pipelines—are also energy efficient and it is difficult to conceive that the energy problem would significantly influence domestic government waterway policy.

GOVERNMENT PROMOTION OF OIL PIPELINE TRANSPORTATION

As indicated in Chapter 13, government has played a very minor role in the development of oil pipeline transportation in the United States. The state aid that has been given has been primarily in the form of some states granting the right of eminent domain for oil pipeline construction. At the federal level, the Cole Act was passed by Congress in 1941 in an effort to accelerate building oil pipelines as part of the national defense buildup prior to World War II. The Act was designed to prevent the obstruction of oil pipeline expansion caused by problems in securing rights of way. It provided that whenever the president of the United States found that the construction of an interstate crude oil or products pipeline was necessary for national defense purposes, the pipeline company could acquire the necessary right of way by exercising the right of eminent domain.

The Cole Act also authorized the federal government to construct oil pipelines. As indicated in Chapter 13, several such lines were constructed by the government, including two important lines, a 24-inch crude oil line (the "Big Inch" line) and a 20-inch products line (the "Little Big Inch" line). These and other government-built lines were disposed of by the government after the war by sale to private companies or by salvage. The Cole Act expired in 1946 and there currently is no national eminent domain law for oil pipelines, although, at the time of this writing, such a law for coal slurry pipelines was being considered by Congress. There have been no government-owned oil pipelines since World War II.

Finally, government has aided oil pipelines by permitting their construction on federal state, or local government-owned land. Government land used for pipeline construction is sometimes sold to the pipeline company. In other cases, a fee is charged for the use of the land.

GOVERNMENT PROMOTION OF AIR TRANSPORTATION

Of the five modes of transportation, air transportation is the most closely linked with government by virtue of the heavy involvement of government in both promoting and regulating transportation by air. In fact, to some degree, it can be said that for-hire air transportation in the United States is a creature of the federal government because the government undertook a deliberate program to develop the industry in the 1920's and 1930's through promotion and through safety and economic regulation. Today, for-hire air transportation is still heavily dependent on government to provide certain physical facilities and other aid, in addition to being heavily regulated by government, both in the form of safety and economic regulation.

Early Government Promotion of Air Transportation

Because air transportation is a relatively new form of transportation, there is no nineteenth-century government promotion to discuss. The first airplane flight was not until 1903, and government involvement did not begin until air mail service was flown in military aircraft in 1918 and then later in aircraft owned by the Post Office Department. In 1925 Congress passed the Kelly Act, which authorized the Post Office Department to contract with private air transport companies to carry mail by air and which provided that the contracting carriers be required to provide facilities for the transportation of passengers. The federal government stopped operating its own airplanes for carrying mail in 1927, except for a brief period in 1934.

The federal Air Commerce Act of 1926 authorized the Secretary of Commerce to designate and establish a system of federal airways and to establish, operate, and maintain along those airways all necessary aids to air navigation, except airports. It also provided for air safety regulation by the Department of Commerce. Eventually, under the Civil Aeronautics Act of 1938, administration of the airway system and safety regulation were placed under the Civil Aeronautics Authority and then under the Civil Aeronautics Administration. Later these functions were taken over by the Federal Aviation Agency and still later by the Federal Aviation Administration (FAA). The federal government undertook the task of providing an air traffic control system and air safety regulation because there was no suitable alternative to it—no other agency, either governmental or private, could do it.

Government Promotion of Air Transportation in Modern Times

In modern times, there have been 4 major methods of government promotion of for-hire air transportation. These programs involve the federal airway system, government promotion of airports, federal cash subsidies to airlines, and government research and development programs that benefit airlines.

The Federal Airway System. The federal airway system is a complicated, highly technical, air traffic control system designed to provide safety in the air. It includes airport traffic control towers, various radar facilities, approach lighting systems, instrument landing facilities, regional control centers, and direct voice communication between pilots and air traffic controllers. The objective is to guide the course of aircraft in flight and to control their movements in the interest of safety. In reality, the airway system is a system of highways in the sky in which air space is literally assigned to different aircraft. Aircraft operations (takeoffs and landings) in 1976 at the 423 airports that had federal control towers numbered almost 64 million, including for-hire carrier, general aviation, and military aircraft.[12] The system is owned and operated by the federal government and is administered by the FAA, an agency in the United States DOT. The FAA operates, maintains, and improves the system with funds supplied by Congress. The total amount of money spent to construct, operate, and maintain the

---

[12] Air Transport Association, *Air Transport 1977* (Washington, D.C.: Air Transport Association, 1977), p. 28.

airway system between 1925 and 1976 is estimated by the AAR to have been approximately 19.9 billion dollars, with the 1976 cost approximately 1.8 billion dollars.[13] Expenditures have been increasing since 1970 when a new financing program was enacted by Congress via the Airport and Airway Development Act, which provided that no less than 250 million dollars per year was to be spent by the federal government for new planning, development, and construction of the airway system in the 1970's. The Act was in response to the rapid growth in air traffic in the 1960's and the fact that since the federal airway and airport development programs had failed to keep pace, there was a severe strain on the air traffic control system and airports and there were considerable congestion and schedule delays. The total amount appropriated in the first 5 years of the new program was 1.3 billion dollars for air traffic control system improvements plus additional funds for research and engineering.[14]

The basic objective of the federal airway system is to achieve the maximum degree of safety in the air for all aircraft—for-hire, general aviation, and military. In addition to operating and developing the airway system, the FAA sets forth the various safety standards that are to be followed by aircraft operators. The National Transportation Safety Board (NTSB), a 5-member agency that was formerly a part of the DOT, and now an independent agency, investigates air accidents to determine their causes and makes recommendations to the FAA, when appropriate, to take steps to prevent such accidents in the future.

Although generally successful in their efforts to achieve air safety, the FAA has been criticized at certain times for not requiring certain safety procedures and, recently, for not implementing the recommendations of the NTSB.[15]

Federal Aid to Airports. There are almost 14,000 airports in the United States. Approximately 630 of these receive scheduled airline service.[16] These 630 airports usually also serve nonscheduled for-hire air carriers and general aviation. Since it is unlikely that individual airline companies, groups of airlines, or general aviation could finance airports, it was a natural thing for government to provide the airport facilities for both for-hire and general aviation use. In addition, airports are ordinarily not profitable, and private capital cannot be expected to be attracted to airport ownership and operation. Unlike the airway system, however, the responsibility for providing airports for use by for-hire air carriers and general aviation has been borne by federal, state, and local governments, not just the federal government. In fact, the major support has been from local government at the city, county, or "metropolitan area" level. The role of the federal government has actually been very small until recently, and it still

---

[13] Association of American Railroads, *Government and Private Expenditures*, Table 2. These figures include research and development costs, including the money spent to develop a supersonic transport since 1962.

[14] Air Transport Association, *Air Transport 1975*, pp. 7–8.

[15] See, for example, "A Need to Get 'Tough As Hell'," *Time*, December 23, 1974, p. 13; "Homing in on Air Safety," *Business Week*, February 10, 1975; Albert R. Karr, "The Lagging Air Safety Program," *The Wall Street Journal*, March 12, 1975; Charles E. Schneider, "FAA Effectiveness on ATC Challenged," *Aviation Week and Space Technology*, March 24, 1975; William A. Shumann, "House Unit to Watch FAA Safety Action," *Aviation Week and Space Technology*, March 31, 1975; and Charles E. Schneider, "Extensive Changes at FAA," *Aviation Week and Space Technology*, May 5, 1975.

[16] Air Transport Association, *Air Transport 1977*, p. 28.

accounts for only a small part of the total amount of money spent on the nation's airport system.

Prior to 1933 the federal government played no part in airport development. The Air Commerce Act of 1926 actually prohibited the federal government from direct construction and operation of airports. During the depressed 1930's, however, large federal expenditures were made to assist airport construction and improvement as a job-creation device. The Civil Aeronautics Act, passed by Congress in 1938, removed the prohibition against federal aid set forth in the Air Commerce Act and specifically authorized federal participation in airport development and improvement. In 1939, after a study made under authority granted by the 1938 Act, the Civil Aeronautics Authority recommended federal aid to airports, and in the first half of the 1940's appropriations were made from time to time by Congress.

In 1946 the Federal Airport Act was passed that provided a systematic approach to federal aid to airports and authorized that 520 million dollars be spent over a 7-year period. The Act of 1946 was extended by Congress several times, but the amount of money provided was relatively small. The federal share was limited to 50 per cent of the cost of certain kinds of airport construction or improvement only. In 1970, for example, the federal government spent only approximately 65 million dollars on airports, including administration of the program and research. This did not include expenditures on the two commercial airports owned and operated by the federal government—National and Dulles in the Washington, D.C. area. In that same year, state and local governments spent 969 million dollars.[17] Results of the lack of sufficient federal participation were a lag in airport development and great congestion problems at some major airports because airport development did not keep up with traffic growth.

In 1970 the Airport and Airway Development Act, referred to earlier, was passed by Congress and it largely superseded the Act of 1946. It called for a federal airport plan to be drawn up by the Secretary of Transportation, and airports included in the plan were to be eligible for federal aid. The federal share of any project was not to exceed 50 per cent, with some exceptions, and federal aid was limited to navigational or aeronautical facilities only, thus excluding parking lots, landscaping, access highways, noise buffer zones, terminal buildings, and the like. The Act of 1970 also provided for grants to planning agencies for airport planning. The Airport Development Acceleration Act of 1973 provided that the federal share could be 75 per cent for nonhub airports and 50 per cent for hub (major) airports, with some exceptions for certain kinds of projects in which the federal share could be as high as 82 per cent. An amendment of 1976 to the 1970 Act provided that federal aid could amount to 75 per cent of the cost at hub airports, except for landing and safety aids, where it could be 82 per cent. Federal aid to non-hub airports was increased to 90 per cent until 1979, when it was to be reduced to 80 per cent.

A major change made in 1970 was that the amount of money to be spent by the federal government on airports was to be 2.5 billion dollars in the period from 1971 to 1980, an increase over the previous expenditures made. The amount was raised to 3.1 billion dollars in 1973. Thus, in 1976 the federal grants for airport development amounted to approximately 269 million dollars, and

---

[17] Association of American Railroads, *Government and Private Expenditures*, Table 3.

another 26 million dollars was spent on administration and research.[18] The total amount committed in the first 5 years of the new program for airline airports was more than 1.2 billion dollars for runways and taxiways, lighting, approach aids, emergency vehicles, and other safety-related improvements.[19] In 1976 Congress increased the amount of money to be spent on airports of all kinds to 2.7 billion dollars for the ensuing 5-year period. Congress also permitted trust fund money to be used for terminal facility development and acquisition of land adjoining airports for noise abatement purposes. Total federal expenditures on airports through 1976 (excluding National and Dulles) have been approximately 4.2 billion dollars in grants and 254 million dollars for administration and research.[20]

State and Local Aid to Airports. According to the AAR, state and local expenditures on airports totaled 16.6 billion dollars through 1976.[21] The bulk of the money invested in airports, both major and otherwise, and the money used in their operation has been provided by local government and various sources of airport income. Most airports are owned and operated by local governments. State aid is usually minimal, although state agencies often participate in airport planning and state law sometimes requires that federal aid be "channeled" through a state agency to a local government. The local governments involved are cities, counties, or metropolitan agencies that represent two or more cities and/or counties. In Minneapolis-St. Paul, for example, a commission that represents a 7-county area operates the scheduled airline airport plus 5 other smaller airports. The new airport at Dallas-Fort Worth is also a regionally supported facility.

The fact that local or metropolitan governments have borne the brunt of the responsibility for airport development is partly a result of the lack of any or much federal aid in the past, the disinterest of state government in what was once considered a "local" problem, and the desire of local communities and, in particular, business interests, to obtain the various benefits of airport development.

As has been the case with other forms of transportation, the social and environmental effects of airport expansion and new airport construction have become increasingly important since the mid-1960's. These have had to do with the effect of airport expansion or construction of new airports (particularly the latter) on water supplies, water pollution, air pollution, wild life, the availability of open space, and, of course, aircraft noise.[22] The result has been that it is very difficult today to expand a major airport or to build a new one because of the social and environmental protection requirements that must be met. These factors have become an important part of airport planning at all levels of govern-

[18] *Ibid.*
[19] Air Transport Association, *Air Transport 1975*, pp. 7-8.
[20] Association of American Railroads, *Government and Private Expenditures*, Table 3.
[21] *Ibid.*
[22] For an example of the difficulty involved in finding acceptable sites for new airports, see Donald V. Harper, "The Airport Location Problem: The Case of Minneapolis-St. Paul," *ICC Practitioners' Journal*, May-June, 1971.

ment. These factors are so important, in fact, that it is very possible that no new major airports will be built in the foreseeable future.

Cash Subsidy to Airlines. Federal government promotion of for-hire air transportation began with the Kelly Act of 1925 which authorized the Post Office Department to contract with privately owned air carriers for the transport of mail. The carriers were required to provide passenger facilities in order to qualify for the mail contracts. The policy on the amount of money paid to carry air mail varied from a policy in which the payments were not to exceed the postal revenues received by the government to one of paying the carriers enough to keep them in business regardless of the postal revenues received. Finally, after 1938 the Civil Aeronautics Board (CAB) was given jurisdiction over air mail rates and began to distinguish between "service" rates and "need" rates, depending on whether the mail payment reflected only the compensation for the service provided by the carrier or contained an additional amount representing government aid needed by the carrier to continue in operation. Thus, in effect, the federal government took on the responsibility of subsidizing operating expenses of the airlines. By this time the system of contracts was abandoned and the airlines merely notified the Post Office Department of what schedules and between what points they proposed to operate with the air mail rates to be paid fixed by the CAB.

When economic regulation of air transportation was instituted by the federal government in 1938, all 16 trunk lines that then existed were receiving such subsidy. By the mid-1940's, however, the trunk lines were on their way to making it on their own without cash subsidy and by 1959 no trunk line (there were then 12 trunk lines) received any cash subsidy. During the period from 1964 to 1968, however, Northeast Airlines (since merged into Delta) received some cash subsidy to cover losses on its New England routes.

In 1943 the CAB began investigating the feasibility of air service between small cities and between small cities and large cities. Although the investigation proved that the costs of operating such services would be high and traffic prospects were not very favorable, in 1944 the CAB decided to set up an experiment that would provide for-hire air service between small cities and between small cities and large cities.[23]

Instead of authorizing the existing trunk lines to provide the service, however, and although trunk lines did show interest in doing so, the Board decided to create a new class of carriers—*local service airlines*—that would be subsidized by the federal government. The idea behind creating a separate class of carriers was that trunk lines did not have the proper aircraft for short-haul, light-traffic routes and that they would not have the proper incentive to work to build up the local service traffic.

In a series of regional decisions, 23 carriers were given 3-year authorizations to operate as local service airlines in the continental United States. Most of these authorizations were renewed several times and in 1955 Congress authorized permanent certification of local service airlines, and they have been a permanent part of our air transportation system since that time.[24]

In 1977 there were 9 local service airlines (see Table 14-1) in the continental United States, 8 of which were receiving cash subsidy from the federal

[23]*Investigation of Local, Feeder, and Pickup Air Service,* 6 CAB 1 (1944).

[24]Civil Aeronautics Board policy on entry control and mergers in the local service airline industry are discussed in Chapter 23.

government (Allegheny Airlines in July, 1974 was the first local service carrier to go off subsidy).

There have been a number of steps taken by the federal government since the early 1960's to hold down and reduce the amount of subsidy paid to local service airlines, including a reduction in the number of flights eligible for subsidy, elimination of some operating restrictions on the carriers, elimination of air service to some small cities, approval of mergers between the carriers, and allowing local service airlines to serve longer-haul routes and larger cities. There was some success in doing this, but since 1971 the subsidy to local service airlines has increased as inflation, the high price of fuel, and other problems have affected the industry.

The method of determining the amount of subsidy to be paid has been changed several times since 1944. Subsidy is paid only to carriers that carry United States mail (which includes all local service airlines), and since 1953 the amount of money for the air mail service is paid by the Postal Service and the subsidy part by the CAB.

Since 1961 the Board has used the *class rate system* to determine the amount of subsidy to be paid. It means that the local service airlines are paid on the basis of the industry costs as a *class* so that there is incentive to operate as efficiently as possible because the amount of subsidy received by an individual carrier will be greater the more efficient the operation is. The class rate system has been revised several times since 1961. The amount of federal cash subsidy to local service airlines in fiscal year 1976 was approximately 68 million dollars.[25] In 1977 local service airlines provided scheduled service to approximately 600 cities in the continental United States.

In addition to cash subsidy to local service airlines, which is referred to as *public service revenue,* the federal government has subsidized other classes of air carriers in the past, as we know, but currently it subsidizes only carriers in Alaska (4.4 million dollars in fiscal year 1976).[26] Air carriers in Hawaii have received no cash subsidy since 1969, helicopter lines since 1966, and international carriers since 1958.[27] These carriers, and also trunk lines, are all eligible for cash subsidy. The total amount of federal cash subsidy paid to the total airline industry between 1939 and 1976 was approximately 2 billion dollars.[28]

Although the CAB has adopted a rate-of-return-on-investment goal of 12.35 per cent for local service airlines, the public service revenue program is not intended to *guarantee* a profit to the subsidized carriers but to provide them with

---

[25] Civil Aeronautics Board, *Annual Report, 1976* (Washington, D.C.: U.S. Government Printing Office, 1976), p. 30. Since 1957 some local service airlines have also benefited from federal government guaranteed loans to purchase aircraft, as have helicopter lines and carriers in Alaska and Hawaii. In 1972 the law providing for such guarantees was extended through 1977 by Congress. In 1976 Congress enacted legislation that permitted all airlines to reduce their federal income taxes by changing the rules concerning investment tax credits.

[26] *Ibid.*

[27] Civil Aeronautics Board, *Subsidy for United States Certificated Air Carriers* (Washington, D.C.: U.S. Government Printing Office, 1976), Appendix VII.

[28] Calculated from *Subsidy for United States Certificated Air Carriers,* Appendices I and VII. In late 1976 the CAB granted a certificate of public convenience and necessity and authorized subsidy to the first commuter airline, Air Midwest. The Board stated that this decision did not mean that other commuter airlines would be subsidized.

a "reasonable opportunity to do so under conditions of honest, economical, and efficient management."[29] It is also well to keep in mind that not all routes of subsidized carriers are subsidized—only those that are not profitable. In 1976 the CAB ruled that service to and from all hub airports would not be eligible for subsidy after July 1, 1976. Currently, approximately 50 per cent of the local service airline routes are eligible for subsidy. In addition, any *excess* profits earned on ineligible routes are used to offset the need for subsidy on eligible routes.

Research and Development. Although many private industries probably benefit from research and development programs of the federal government, the airlines have been particularly fortunate in this respect, although, in some cases, the federal government has had no specific intention of helping the airlines.

The airlines have, of course, benefited from government research and development activities having to do with the federal airway system and the federal airport program, and they have also benefited from these programs at the state and local levels dealing with traffic control and airports.

More indirect benefits, although highly important, received by airlines from government research and development projects have had to do with the development of new aircraft. Most post-World War II aircraft used by for-hire airlines were developed initially as military airplanes for the Department of Defense and were later adapted to airline use. Consequently, the airlines were able to largely avoid the research and development expenses that would have otherwise been included in the prices of the aircraft they purchased.

The federal space program had also produced some technological advances in aviation that have been incorporated into civilian aircraft for which the airlines were not asked to pay the research and development cost.

The aborted attempt to build a United States supersonic air transport plane was a special example of the federal government's paying most of the research and development costs with the expectation that the airlines would eventually repay the government through royalty charges. The program was scrapped in May of 1971.[30]

With the decreasing emphasis on military expenditures and the difficulty in achieving further technological progress beyond what we have now that could be feasible for domestic airline service, the government research and development factor in airline costs will probably be different in the future from what it has been in the past. The decline in the space program will have the same effect. Although a United States supersonic transport aircraft may eventually come into being, for the immediate future there will be no benefits accruing to the airlines from such a development program.

Although it is clear that the airline industry has benefited from governmental research and development expenditures of various kinds, it is difficult to measure the amount of the benefits received, their value, or their effect on the industry, particularly those having to do with the fallout from the defense and space programs.

---

[29]*Ibid.*, p. 6.

[30]Since most airline pilots received their flight training in the United States Air Force, the airline industry has been able to avoid the cost of training pilots with its own resources.

Financing Government Promotion of Air Transportation

Sources of Funds. The possible sources of funds to be used by government to promote air transportation are the usual general taxation, user taxes, and tolls. All of these methods are used to some degree, although the word "toll" is not part of air transportation terminology.

Financing at the Federal Level. As noted earlier, the federal government has promoted air transportation by means of the airway system, the federal airport program, cash subsidies, and research and development programs. Prior to 1970 the federal airway and airport programs were paid for with general revenue funds, although there was a 5-per cent tax on airline passenger tickets that went into the general revenue fund but was considered to be a user tax, and a $.02 per gallon tax on aviation gasoline (but not on jet fuel). These taxes were not dedicated for use in the airway and airport programs. In 1970 the federal Airport and Airway Development Act was passed which created a new system of financing the federal airway and airport programs. A new tax structure was established, including the taxes shown in Table 17-1. The revenues from these taxes are placed in an Airport and Airway Trust Fund created by the Act and are to be used (dedicated) only for airway and airport development. Additional appropriations to the Fund may be made if they are required to carry out the program. As Table 17-1 indicates, the taxes produced 937.9 million dollars in fiscal 1976.

The Fund was to be used for capital improvements and for research and development (not operating and maintenance costs) of the airway system and for airport development. A 1976 amendment permitted the FAA to use some

T A B L E 17-1   *Federal Air User Taxes and Proceeds,* 1976[†] (000,000)*

Tax	Proceeds
Air freight (5%)	$42.1
Passenger tickets (8%)	776.6
Overseas flights ($3.00 per passenger)	47.0
Registration fee ($25.00 on all aircraft and $.03½ per pound on all jet aircraft and $.02 per pound on all piston aircraft weighing over 2,500 pounds)	21.2
Airport fuel except that used by commercial aviation ($.07 per gallon)	52.0
Aircraft tires and tubes ($.05 per pound)	.9
Total	939.8
Less taxes refunded	1.9
Proceeds from taxes	937.9
Interest on funds invested	145.9
Total added to Airport and Airway Trust Fund	1,083.8

*To Airport and Airway Trust Fund.
[†]Fiscal year.

Source: As estimated in *Appendix to the Budget of the United States, Fiscal Year 1978* (Washington, D.C.: U.S. Government Printing Office, 1977), p. 536.

Trust Fund money for airway operation and maintenance. As noted earlier, expenditures on airport improvements were generally limited to aeronautical aspects of an airport only until 1976 when Congress permitted some money to be used for terminal facility development and acquisition of land for noise abatement purposes.

Consequently, the Act of 1970 placed the federal airway and airport programs on a user charge basis. The Fund has been running a surplus because the FAA has not spent all the money available. In fiscal year 1976 the Fund income, including interest on money invested, was approximately 1.1 billion dollars, with expenditures amounting to approximately 547 million dollars. Together with balances from previous years, the surplus of uncommitted money in the fund had reached approximately 1.6 billion dollars at the end of fiscal 1976.[31] It was mentioned in Chapter 14 that in late 1976 the Secretary of Transportation ordered that airline aircraft used by United States carriers in domestic service gradually meet the 1969 FAA noise standards within 8 years either through replacement of the aircraft or through retrofitting engine nacelles. The question of how that or an alternate program was to be financed was not answered at the time of this writing. One possibility is that the surplus in the fund be used for that purpose.

The federal cash subsidy program has always been funded from general revenue and no attempt has ever been made to collect compensation from either the airlines, their customers, or the communities that benefit from subsidized air transportation.

The federal expenditures on research and development, other than those involved in the airway and airport programs, are paid for with general revenue funds.

Financing at the State and Local Levels. State and local promotion of air transportation is in the form of construction and improvement of airports, with the local governments playing the dominant role. Some states use general revenue funds for their part. Some states tax aircraft as personal property, levy taxes on aviation fuel, and/or impose registration fees on aircraft. Some of these states have a dedicated fund arrangement similar to that at the federal level. Much state money is used to finance general aviation airports rather than scheduled airline airports, however.

The local government approach to financing airports varies from airport to airport. At major airports federal, and sometimes state, funds are available. However, major reliance is placed on user charges, airport income, and local general taxation.

User charges include landing fees that are a form of toll wherein airlines, and sometimes operators of general aviation aircraft, but not United States government aircraft, are required to pay a fee to land an aircraft at an airport (a form of toll). The amount of the fee usually depends on the gross weight of the aircraft. In addition, airlines pay rental or leasing fees for the use of terminal facilities such as office and ticket counter space and for the use of hangars or other facilities provided at an airport.

[31] As estimated in *Appendix to the Budget of the United States, Fiscal Year 1978* (Washington, D.C.: U.S. Government Printing Office, 1977), p. 556.

Airports also receive income from the sale of fuel to aircraft operators, from parking lot fees, and from various renters of space in the terminal building such as restaurants, cocktail lounges, barber shops, gift shops, automobile rental companies, newsstands, insurance booths, advertising displays, flying schools, aircraft maintenance service companies, and the Postal Service. There is also income from vending machines, baggage lockers, observation decks, the rental of land for manufacturing or other purposes, and so on. It is revenue from these non-carrier sources that really determines the financial condition of a major airport. In many cases, major airports are deficit operations in which the deficits are made up from local general taxation revenues.

The Subsidy Question. Under our definition of subsidy, subsidy exists when the beneficiaries of government promotional programs either do not repay the government at all or repay only in part for the benefits received. The question of whether or not for-hire airlines are subsidized through the various government promotional programs described in this chapter is complicated by the fact that there is use of the airway system and airports by general aviation and military and other government aircraft, in addition to use by the airline industry. Consequently, all of the costs of airway and airport construction and operation should not be charged to airlines. Under the Airport and Airway Development Act of 1970, the Secretary of Transportation was to have allocated the costs of the federal airway and airport system among the various classes of users and to have recommended what revision of the user taxes should be made in order to ensure equitable distribution of the tax burden among the various classes of users. A DOT cost allocation study concluded that in 1971 airline user charges covered 84.5 per cent of the costs allocated to them and general aviation paid only 14.5 per cent of their allocated costs.[32] In early 1975 the DOT submitted recommendations to Congress that would have altered the tax structure by increasing the fuel tax paid by general aviation from $.07 to $.15 per gallon, increasing the $3.00 tax on international tickets to $5.00, and reducing the tax on airline tickets from 8 per cent to 7 per cent.[33] Other bills to change the tax structure were also considered in 1975, 1976, and 1977 but no action had been taken by Congress at the time of this writing.

In addition to the problem of allocating costs among different kinds of users, there is the problem of what costs should be included in determining whether or not subsidy exists in the airway and airport programs. Annual operating, administration, and maintenance costs and capital investment should probably be included. Interest on the investment and depreciation or amortization charges might also be included. There is also the usual question of whether or not the property taxes on the property being used for airports that are not being collected should be included as a cost.

Therefore, there is much disagreement on the subsidy question concerning the airway and airport programs. Prior to 1970 the airlines were clearly subsidized by the federal airway and airport programs, but now these programs are on

---

[32] For a discussion of the cost allocation study, see Paul F. Dienemann and Armando M. Lago, "User Taxes and Allocations of United States Airport and Airway System Costs," *Journal of Transport Economics and Policy,* January, 1976.

[33] See William A. Shumann, "Airport, Airway Plan Hits Opposition from Congress," *Aviation Week and Space Technology,* March 24, 1975.

a user charge basis and annual expenditures for planning, development, and construction are covered by user charges. However, there is no attempt to cover current operating and maintenance costs or interest and depreciation charges or past federal capital and other expenses incurred in these programs.

At the state and local levels, since many airports rely at least partly on general taxation to support their development and operation, there is a subsidy element there. In addition, there is the question of separating the aeronautical part of the airport (runways, aprons, runway lighting, guidance systems, and so on) from the terminal building operation and other parts of the airport. In some cases, the revenues from the terminal building, parking lots, and so on, help to subsidize the landing field costs when landing fees paid by aircraft operators do not cover those costs. There is also the other question of what share of whatever charges collected by state and local governments should be paid by airlines and what share should be paid by general aviation.

At any rate, if one were to calculate the *full* costs associated with federal, state, and local programs to promote airways and airports, airlines probably are subsidized, but the amount is unknown and it varies from airport to airport. General aviation is also probably subsidized as well.[34]

Obviously, the federal cash grant public service revenue program is a subsidy program as we have defined it since the government receives no compensation at all from those who benefit from it.

Any benefits received by airlines from military and space research and development programs are received free by the airlines and are a form of unintentional subsidy to the industry.

Because air transportation is our least efficient user of energy per unit of traffic carried among the 5 modes of transportation, the future of government promotion of air transportation is uncertain. At the time of this writing there have been no plans to curtail government promotion of air transportation for energy reasons. The lack of a strong and clear-cut federal energy policy makes predictions meaningless. However, it is possible that any effective program that will be adopted in the future will make it difficult for airlines to afford and/or to get fuel, which may lessen the need for government promotional programs in the future.

SELECTED REFERENCES

For a good description of the early canal building period in the United States, see D. Philip Locklin, *Economics of Transportation*, 7th ed. (Homewood, Illinois: Richard D. Irwin, Inc., 1972), pp. 96–102.

Gerald R. Jantscher, *Bread Upon the Waters, Federal Aids to the Maritime Industries* (Washington, D.C.: The Brookings Institution, 1975) reviews and evaluates the major forms of aid to the maritime industries, including the restriction of domestic commerce to American built and operated vessels. The merchant

---

[34] Subsidy to general aviation is dealt with in some detail in Jeremy J. Warford, "Subsidies to General Aviation," in Joint Economic Committee, Congress of the United States, *The Economics of Federal Subsidy Programs* (Washington, D.C.: U.S. Government Printing Office, 1973).

marine program is also evaluated in Charles Moyer and Harold Henderson, "A Critique of the Rationales for Present U.S. Maritime Programs," *Transportation Journal,* Winter, 1974. A discussion of the Jones Act is in Edward G. Lowry, III, "Jones Act," *ICC Practitioners' Journal,* September–October, 1973.

The problems of expanding obligations and the difficulties of financing American port operations are dealt with in Robert C. Waters, "Role Crisis in America's Ports?" *Transportation Journal,* Winter, 1974.

The conflict between the United States and Panama over control of the Panama Canal is summarized in "Collision on the Canal," *Time,* July 28, 1975. The Canal's deficit problem is dealt with in "The Panama Canal: An SOS to Keep Afloat," *Business Week,* March 29, 1976 and "Is the Panama Canal Worth It?" *Business Week,* December 6, 1976.

The problems of the Great Lakes and St. Lawrence Seaway are discussed in Robert Koci, "Dilemma on the 'Fourth Seacoast,'" *Transportation and Distribution Management,* June, 1971. The current status and problems of the St. Lawrence Seaway are dealt with in "The St. Lawrence Seaway System," *Traffic World,* September 15, 1975, p. 45.

The philosophy behind not having federal user charges on the inland waterways system is discussed in John P. Doyle, "The Waterways Shall Be Forever Free," *Distribution Age,* September, 1962. The pros and cons of collecting user charges on the inland waterways system are dealt with in Walter B. Wright and William J. Hull, "The National Water Commission Report," *Transportation and Distribution Management,* March, 1973. See also Locklin, *Economics of Transportation,* pp. 739–741 and James C. Johnson and Donald L. Berger, "Waterway User Charges: An Economic and Political Dilemma," *Transportation Journal,* Summer, 1977.

Government promotion of air transportation is discussed in John H. Frederick, *Commercial Air Transportation,* 5th ed. (Homewood, Illinois: Richard D. Irwin, Inc., 1961), Chapters 2, 8, and 11.

The history of the federal role in civil aviation since 1926 is given in U.S. Department of Transportation, Federal Aviation Administration, *FAA Historical Fact Book: A Chronology, 1926-1971* (Washington, D.C.: U.S. Government Printing Office, 1973).

The effect of an airport on the economy of a community is discussed in John N. Martin, "Economic Impact of Airport Investment and Use in North Carolina," *Transportation Journal,* Spring, 1972. See also Richard de Neufville and Tabashi Yajima, "Economic Impact of Airport Development," *Proceedings of Transportation Research Forum, 1971;* Ronald W. Crowley, "A Case Study of the Effects of an Airport on Land Values," *Journal of Transport Economics and Policy,* May 1973; and Robert H. Ross and Gary L. Thompson, "Direct Economic Benefits of the Oklahoma City Airports," *Proceedings of Transportation Research Forum, 1976.*

The environmental problems associated with building new major airports are illustrated in Donald V. Harper, "The Airport Location Problem: The Case of Minneapolis–St. Paul," *ICC Practitioners' Journal,* May–June, 1971. See also Dudley F. Pegrum, *Transportation Economics and Public Policy,* 3rd ed. (Homewood, Illinois: Richard D. Irwin, Inc., 1973), pp. 523–525.

Airport financing is discussed in James H. Winchester, "The Business of Airports," reprinted from *The Christian Science Monitor* in Martin T. Farris and Paul T. McElhiney (eds.), *Modern Transportation: Selected Readings,* 2nd ed. (Boston: Houghton Mifflin Company, 1973).

The U.S. Department of Transportation airway and airport cost allocation study and suggestions for changing the air user tax structure are discussed in Paul F. Dienemann and Armando M. Lago, "User Taxes and Allocations of United States Airport and Airway System Costs," *Journal of Transport Economics and Policy,* January, 1976.

State taxation of for-hire airlines is dealt with in Donald V. Harper and Nicholas A. Glaskowsky, Jr., "Economic and Managerial Aspects of State Taxation of Commercial Airlines," *Transportation Journal,* Winter, 1965.

The problem of rising landing fees is discussed in Eugene Kozicharow, "Landing Fee Increases Punish Carriers," *Aviation Week and Space Technology,* August 2, 1976.

Subsidies to local service airlines and alternatives to the subsidy program are discussed and evaluated in detail in George C. Eads, *The Local Service Airline Experiment* (Washington, D.C.: The Brookings Institution, 1972). A critical analysis of the local service airline experiment is Robert W. Harbeson, "The Economic Status of Local Service Airlines," *Journal of Transport Economics and Policy,* September, 1970. The history of and the justification for cash subsidy to airlines are discussed in Ronald Dean Scott and Martin T. Farris, "Airline Subsidies in the United States," *Transportation Journal,* Summer, 1974.

Government subsidies to general aviation are outlined in Jeremy J. Warford, "Subsidies to General Aviation," in Joint Economic Committee, Congress of the United States, *The Economics of Federal Subsidy Programs* (Washington, D.C.: U.S. Government Printing Office, 1973). See also Warford, *Public Policy Toward General Aviation* (Washington, D.C.: The Brookings Institution, 1971).

18

The Decision-Making Process in
and Evaluation of
Government Promotion of Transportation

In the preceding 2 chapters we discussed the reasons for government promotion of transportation and the various promotional programs that have been carried out. In this chapter we shall examine the decision-making process in government promotion of transportation and attempt to evaluate the promotional efforts we have had to date.

DECISION-MAKING PROCESS IN GOVERNMENT
PROMOTION OF TRANSPORTATION

The decision-making process in government promotion of transportation involves several levels of government, different agencies within the same governments, the carriers, and the users of transportation service.

Decision-Making Process at the Federal Level

Since the federal government provides a large share of the promotional funds in transportation, as indicated in the previous 2 chapters, the decision-making process followed there is of extreme importance. The process involves both the legislative and executive branches of the federal government.

Role of Congress. Money spent by the federal government on transportation or any other activity must ultimately be provided by Congress, and many of the promotional programs in transportation originate in Congress. Within the 2 houses of Congress, various committees review transportation legislation before it reaches the floor of these 2 bodies. Figure 18-1 indicates the more important committees involved in promoting transportation in the Senate and in the House of Representatives in 1976. They were the Commerce and Public Works committees in the Senate and the Interstate and Foreign Commerce, Merchant

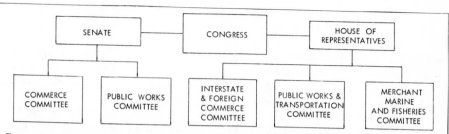

The present standing committee structure of Congress includes several committees which have both direct and indirect jurisdiction over policies affecting the transportation industry. The organizational chart above indicates the positions of these committees within the structure of the Congress. The table of functions points up the major areas of the transportation industry covered by the various committees, as well as the similarity of their respective jurisdiction.

SENATE COMMITTEE	HOUSE COMMITTEE
Commerce	**Interstate & Foreign Commerce**
Regulation of interstate railroads, buses, trucks, pipe lines, freight forwarders, domestic water carriers and domestic and international air carriers. Inland water-ways. Promotion of civil aviation, including subsidies and airport construction.	Jurisdiction over railroads and the Railway Labor Act (which also covers airline labor).
	Merchant Marine & Fisheries
International water carriers generally, including registering and licensing of vessels and small boats; navigation and the laws relating thereto; measures relating to subsidies; and the inspection and safety of vessels. Approve Maritime Administration programs.	Same basic jurisdiction over international water transport as Senate Commerce Committee, plus unregulated domestic ocean-going water transportation. Approve Maritime Administration programs.
	Public Works & Transportation
Public Works	
Projects for the benefit of water navigation and rivers and harbors. Measures relating to the construction or maintenance of highways.	Same basic jurisdiction as the Senate Public Works Committee, plus jurisdiction over interstate buses, trucks, pipelines, freight forwarders, and water carriers; and domestic and international air carriers.

Legislation affecting transportation also comes within the jurisdiction of several other Congressional committees, such as:

Appropriations	——	Actual appropriation of funds
Government Operations	——	Transportation operations of Federal agencies.
Judiciary	——	Rules and procedures for regulatory agencies.
Post Office & Civil Service	——	Parcel post service
House Ways & Means / Senate Finance	——	Financial matters, with House Committee originating all tax bills.
House Education & Labor / Senate Labor & Public Welfare	——	Transport labor generally, including mediation or arbitration of disputes. (Note House I & FC Committee's jurisdiction over rail labor.)

FIGURE 18-1 *Standing Congressional Committees Having Jurisdiction Over Transportation. (Source: Transportation Association of America,* Transportation Facts and Trends, *12th ed. (Washington, D.C.: Transportation Association of America, July, 1976), p. 33)*

Marine and Fisheries, and Public Works and Transportation committees in the House.[1] Other Congressional committees, including those dealing with such subjects as banking and currency, agriculture, armed services, aeronautics, the postal service, and government operations, are also sometimes involved in trans-

[1] In early 1977, a reorganization of the Senate committee structure took place. The Commerce Committee became the Commerce, Science, and Transportation Committee and the Public Works Committee became the Environment and Public Works Committee.

portation promotion. In addition to these committees, all tax bills must be originated in the House Ways and Means Committee and these tax bills are reviewed by the Senate Finance Committee. The actual appropriation of funds is handled by the Appropriations Committee in each of the 2 houses. An obvious difficulty in the committee structure in Congress is that jurisdiction over promotional programs is divided and coordination of the programs is made difficult.[2] There has been considerable criticism of this situation in recent years. In early 1977, the Senate reorganized its committee structure to reduce its number of committees which improved somewhat the situation in regard to transportation.

When these committees approve legislation, it is then sent to the floor of the Senate or the House where debate takes place. If a bill passes both houses, perhaps after a special conference committee works out differences between the versions passed by the 2 houses, it is sent to the president for approval. If the bill is vetoed by the president, Congress may override the veto by a two-thirds vote in both houses.

Role of the Executive Branch. In addition to the presidential approval needed for legislation enacted by Congress, the executive branch of the federal government administers most of the various promotional programs and acts in a leadership capacity in doing research, in planning transportation programs, and in recommending legislation to Congress.

Although many federal cabinet level departments and agencies are involved in transportation promotional programs, including the departments of Interior, Commerce, State, Housing and Urban Development, and Defense, the most important is the Department of Transportation (DOT) which was established by Congress in 1967, under the urging of President Lyndon B. Johnson. Its purpose was to bring together under a single department many of the agencies that previously dealt with research, planning, and promotion in transportation, and regulation of safety in transportation. A recent organization chart of the federal DOT is shown in Figure 18-2. The chart indicates that the DOT administers the airport and airway programs through the Federal Aviation Administration (FAA), the highway program through the Federal Highway Administration (FHWA), some of the federal railroad programs through the Federal Railroad Administration (FRA), the United States part of the St. Lawrence Seaway through the St. Lawrence Seaway Development Corporation, and the federal urban transportation program through the Urban Mass Transportation Administration (UMTA).

The reader may have noticed that several federal transportation promotional programs discussed earlier are not under the jurisdiction of the DOT. These include the National Railroad Passenger Corporation (Amtrak, a private corporation), the United States Railway Association (USRA, a nonprofit government planning and financing organization), the Consolidated Rail Corporation (Conrail, a private corporation), the Panama Canal Company (a government-owned corporation), domestic waterway improvements (constructed, maintained, and operated by the United States Army Corps of Engineers), and the federal cash subsidy pro-

---

[2] For a discussion of this problem, see Paul W. Schuldiner, "Institutional Constraints on Comprehensive Transportation Planning at the Federal Level," *Proceedings of Transportation Research Forum, 1974* and "Committees of Congress and Transport," *Traffic World,* November 24, 1975.

gram for air transportation [administered by the Civil Aeronautics Board (CAB)] . Finally, the federal subsidy program for ocean vessels used in international trade (not discussed previously) is administered by the Federal Maritime Administration, which is also outside the DOT's jurisdiction.

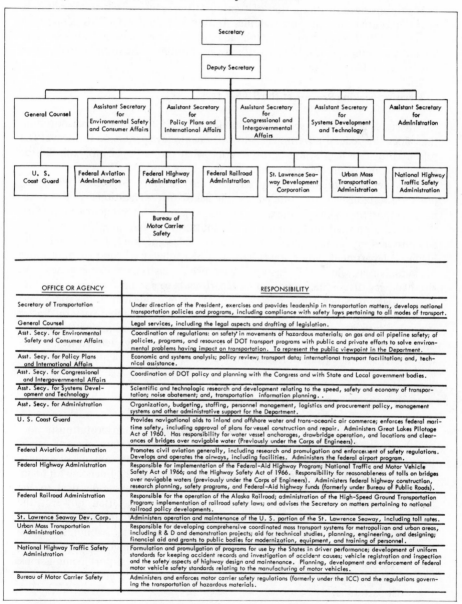

OFFICE OR AGENCY	RESPONSIBILITY
Secretary of Transportation	Under direction of the President, exercises and provides leadership in transportation matters, develops national transportation policies and programs, including compliance with safety laws pertaining to all modes of transport.
General Counsel	Legal services, including the legal aspects and drafting of legislation.
Asst. Secy. for Environmental Safety and Consumer Affairs	Coordination of regulations: on safety in movements of hazardous materials; on gas and oil pipeline safety; of policies, programs, and resources of DOT transport programs with public and private efforts to solve environmental problems having impact on transportation. To represent the public viewpoint in the Department.
Asst. Secy. for Policy Plans and International Affairs	Economic and systems analysis; policy review; transport data; international transport facilitation; and, technical assistance.
Asst. Secy. for Congressional and Intergovernmental Affairs	Coordination of DOT policy and planning with the Congress and with State and Local government bodies.
Asst. Secy. for Systems Development and Technology	Scientific and technologic research and development relating to the speed, safety and economy of transportation; noise abatement; and, transportation information planning. .
Asst. Secy. for Administration	Organization, budgeting, staffing, personnel management, logistics and procurement policy, management systems and other administrative support for the Department.
U. S. Coast Guard	Provides navigational aids to inland and offshore water and trans-oceanic air commerce; enforces federal maritime safety, including approval of plans for vessel construction and repair. Administers Great Lakes Pilotage Act of 1960. Has responsibility for water vessel anchorages, drawbridge operation, and locations and clearances of bridges over navigable water (Previously under the Corps of Engineers).
Federal Aviation Administration	Promotes civil aviation generally, including research and promulgation and enforcement of safety regulations. Develops and operates the airways, including facilities. Administers the federal airport program.
Federal Highway Administration	Responsible for implementation of the Federal-Aid Highway Program; National Traffic and Motor Vehicle Safety Act of 1966; and the Highway Safety Act of 1966. Responsibility for reasonableness of tolls on bridges over navigable waters (previously under the Corps of Engineers). Administers federal highway construction, research planning, safety programs, and Federal-Aid highway funds (formerly under Bureau of Public Roads).
Federal Railroad Administration	Responsible for the operation of the Alaska Railroad; administration of the High-Speed Ground Transportation Program; implementation of railroad safety laws; and advises the Secretary on matters pertaining to national railroad policy developments.
St. Lawrence Seaway Dev. Corp.	Administers operation and maintenance of the U. S. portion of the St. Lawrence Seaway, including toll rates.
Urban Mass Transportation Administration	Responsible for developing comprehensive coordinated mass transport systems for metropolitan and urban areas, including R & D and demonstration projects; aid for technical studies, planning, engineering, and designing; financial aid and grants to public bodies for modernization, equipment, and training of personnel.
National Highway Traffic Safety Administration	Formulation and promulgation of programs for use by the States in driver performance; development of uniform standards for keeping accident records and investigation of accident causes; vehicle registration and inspection and the safety aspects of highway design and maintenance. Planning, development and enforcement of federal motor vehicle safety standards relating to the manufacturing of motor vehicles.
Bureau of Motor Carrier Safety	Administers and enforces motor carrier safety regulations (formerly under the ICC) and the regulations governing the transportation of hazardous materials.

FIGURE 18-2 *Organization and Responsibilities of U.S. Department of Transportation.* *(Source: Transportation Association of America,* Transportation Facts and Trends, *12th ed. (Washington, D.C.: Transportation Association of America, July, 1976), p. 35)*

In addition, it should be noted that although the DOT administers several promotional programs, the decisions on the amount of money to be spent are made by Congress.

Consequently, several agencies in the federal government, in addition to the DOT, are involved in promotion of transportation, some of which are not even in the executive branch (for example, Amtrak and the CAB). This, along with the control by Congress of the actual amounts of money available, has severely limited the ability of the DOT to effectively coordinate the promotional expenditures at the federal level.

Decision-Making Process at the State Level

The states collectively spend more money annually to promote transportation than does the federal government. Most of the money spent is on highways. The role of the state legislatures is to prescribe what promotional programs will be engaged in and to provide the money for these programs.

The executive branch usually has the responsibility of administering the programs established and funded by the legislature. Traditionally, the states have supported highway construction and improvement programs more than they have supported other modes of transportation. These programs have been administered by state highway organizations of some kind, for example, the highway department. Some states have also had tollway or turnpike authorities or commissions where toll highways have been constructed. Some states have also had executive branch aeronautics departments to administer airport development programs. Since 1960, however, approximately one-half of the states have established state departments of transportation, many of them patterned after the federal DOT, with the objective of planning and coordinating the various promotional programs in transportation, including highway, aeronautics, waterway, port, and mass transportation programs. These departments have met with varying success.[3]

Decision-Making Process at the Local Level

Local governments, as we have seen, are involved in transportation promotional activities such as those concerning local roads and streets, mass transportation systems, port facilities, and airports. The local city council or county board is usually the source of these programs, as is much of the financing for them.

The executive branch of local government is sometimes identical to the legislative branch—the legislative branch plays a dual role. Often, however, the executive branch is separated from the legislative branch. In any event, local government has made use of various kinds of organizations to administer transportation promotional programs, including public works or highway departments, transit authorities or commissions, port authorities, and airport commissions. The variety of agencies used is large and it is impossible to generalize on what the usual pattern is.

---

[3]The trend toward state departments of transportation is discussed in James W. Bennett, Jr., and William J. DeWitt, III, "The Development of State Departments of Transportation— A Recent Organizational Phenomenon," *Transportation Journal*, Fall, 1972.

Role of the Carrier

The carrier is the direct beneficiary of government promotional programs and sometimes the carrier is the source of some or all of the funds expended. The carrier, however, does not make decisions on what programs there will be and how they will be financed. Instead, the carrier role is to try to influence those who do make these decisions at the governmental level. This is done through various lobbying efforts to promote or to work against specific programs being considered and includes testifying at legislative and administrative hearings and investigations, contacting individual legislators, and publicizing the carrier position on a given issue by providing information to the news media, the general public, educators, businessmen, and others.

Although individual carriers may engage in the process, they are usually represented by very vocal carrier trade associations, including major groups such as the Association of American Railroads, the National Association of Motor Bus Operators, the American Trucking Associations, Inc., the American Waterways Operators, Inc., the National Waterways Operators, the Association of Oil Pipelines, and the Air Transport Association of America.

In short, the carriers are usually well-represented in the decision-making process regarding government promotion of transportation, although in some modes and on certain issues it is difficult for a carrier association to truly reflect the diverse views of its membership.

Role of the User

The role of the user of transportation in the decision-making process relative to government promotion of transportation is less clear than the governmental role and the carrier role.

Individual users have the right to be heard from in the legislative and administrative process, but most users do not take advantage of the opportunity because of the lack of time, money, expertise, or interest in the subject at hand. The individual users that do participate tend to be large business firms. The smaller user, if interested, usually relies on a trade or other association to represent him.

The users of transportation—passengers, shippers, and receivers—are much less well-organized than are the carriers and, therefore, they are less able to present the user point of view on a particular promotion issue. Of course, there are some organizations, such as the National Industrial Traffic League and the Associated Traffic Clubs of America, that represent freight shippers and receivers in general, and there are some industry trade associations that can represent shippers and receivers in particular industries on promotion matters. There are also the Highway Users Federation for Safety and Mobility, which represents various users of roads and streets, and various chambers of commerce. However, they are far from unified in their approach to and interest in promotional programs and do not, by any means, represent all users.

The Transportation Association of America, which is a national organization that represents both carriers and users, issues policy statements and its representatives often testify in legislative and administrative hearings on transportation matters, including promotional questions. It is the only important organization that represents both carriers and users.

Individual citizens are often not much interested in transportation promotional programs. Those who may be interested (as taxpayers, passengers, or people affected by promotional programs involving the transportation of freight) have in the past been the least effectively represented in the process because of lack of organizations to represent them. In recent years, however, various citizen groups and environmental organizations have played an increasing role in the process. The issues these groups are concerned with are mainly the social and economic consequences of promotional programs rather than the economic or transportation issues as such. The termination of the United States supersonic air transport program and some recent changes in highway programs and highway financing were brought forth in part by such groups.

DIFFICULTIES IN TRANSPORTATION PLANNING

There are various problems involved in planning government promotion programs in transportation so that there is coordination between programs, a minimum of conflict and duplication, an integration with private investment in transportation facilities, and assurance that the greatest benefit possible is received from government expenditures on transportation. The several reasons for this are discussed below.

Multi-Government Participation

As indicated earlier, government promotion decisions are made at the federal, state, and local government levels. This means that because of the lack of sufficient coordination between the various governments involved, conflicting policies may exist on what programs to engage in, how the programs are to be financed, and what costs are to be borne by beneficiaries. Since the federal government exerts a stronger leadership role and requires that federal aid will not be given unless state and local governments comply with federal guidelines and regulations, the possibility of conflict between programs at different levels of government is somewhat reduced.

Lack of Coordination Between Agencies
of the Same Government

A serious problem in planning government promotion of transportation is the lack of coordination between agencies of the same government, federal, state, or local. It would be ideal if the planning and administration of all transportation programs were under one governmental agency. This would at least provide an opportunity for coordinating the programs to avoid conflict and duplication. Concentration in one agency is, however, usually not the case. Our previous discussion of the federal DOT indicated that several important transportation promotional programs are outside the jurisdiction of the DOT and the control of the funds for most programs is in Congress, thus making it difficult for the federal government to coordinate planning of its promotional programs. It is entirely possible, for example, that directly conflicting and/or duplicating highway and waterway improvements can be made simultaneously by the federal government because the planning and control of the programs is not in the same federal agency. The same problem often occurs at the state and local levels of government. For example, airport development may be handled by one agency while access highways to serve airports may be under another agency and the 2 may or may not be working together. In some cases, the formation of state departments of transportation has brought some improvement.

Lack of Uniform Standards for Investment Decisions

A problem related to the lack of coordination between different governments and between agencies of the same government is that in most cases there is a lack of uniform standards used by different governments and agencies in deciding what to spend on government promotional programs and what kinds of programs there should be. The different governments and agencies tend to use different standards.[4] Thus, at the federal level, the amount of money spent on the federal airport program is determined without any reference to the standards used to determine highway appropriations or to the overall transportation needs of the country. Cash subsidies to local service airlines are largely based on the need of the carriers without reference to other federal transportation programs. Decisions on financing Amtrak are made mainly on the basis of what is needed to keep Amtrak alive, without considering the overall federal transportation promotional program. Similar problems exist at the state and local levels.

The lack of uniform investment standards and the lack of coordination between different governments and agencies of the same government lead to unneeded programs, a misallocation of traffic among the modes, and an unbalanced development of the nation's transportation system.

Lack of Good Cost-Benefit Analysis Tools

Perhaps the most difficult problem of all in planning promotion of transportation is that of the lack of adequate methods by which the costs and benefits of a given proposed program can be measured. This problem would exist even if we had fully coordinated planning of such programs. Cost-benefit analysis seeks to measure total social costs and total social benefits or gains, the assumption being that if the gains exceed the costs, the project is worthwhile. But then the gains should be compared with the gains from other possible projects, within and outside of transportation. If the costs exceed the gains, the project should, of course, be abandoned.

The complications involved in cost-benefit analysis are beyond the scope of this book. One example, however, is that since some of the costs and gains are not measurable in monetary terms, they must in some way be converted into such terms, and considerable controversy is often the result. Environmental costs are an example, as are recreational gains. It is sufficient to say here that since it is very difficult to measure the costs and gains, considerable disagreement on

[4] See Grant M. Davis, "The Necessity for Uniform Standards in Federal Transportation Investment Decisions," *Alabama Business* (University, Alabama: Center for Business and Economic Research, Graduate School of Business, University of Alabama, May 15, 1971) for a discussion of this problem at the federal level.

what costs and benefits to include and how to measure the costs and benefits involved in a proposed promotional program often develops. Cost-benefit analysis is an inexact method of evaluating proposed programs, but better tools of cost-benefit analysis would improve the government promotional role. The result of the problem has been that the decisions are often made on a political, emotional, or military basis instead of on an economic basis. Indeed, the political factor weighs heavily on the government decision-making process.

Crisis Decision Making

Our discussion of government promotion of transportation in Chapters 16 and 17 indicated that in many instances government promotional programs in transportation have been a response to a crisis situation and have not been part of a well thought out, long-run plan. Examples are Amtrak and Conrail in railroad transportation, the federal urban transportation program, and the airport and airway program of the 1970's. In fact, just about all promotional programs have had the crisis element behind them to some degree, meaning that the decision-making process followed has not produced long-range planning that anticipates and/or attempts to avoid crisis situations.

The obvious negative results of crisis decision making are that considerable loss is incurred by users, carriers, and the general public when a crisis develops that could have been avoided by better government (and carrier) planning, that crisis decision making makes for programs that are more expensive than they would have been otherwise because considerable expensive crash "catching up" is often necessary, and that it results in programs that are not as well thought out as would be the case if the crisis element were not present. Amtrak is an excellent example of the latter.

EVALUATION OF GOVERNMENT PROMOTION OF TRANSPORTATION

The above paragraphs indicate that there are some valid criticisms of the decision-making and planning process in government promotion of transportation. In addition to the factors discussed above, other difficulties with government promotional programs exist, including the lack of enough consideration of social and environmental repercussions of promotional programs in the past, which has helped to bring about the tremendous social and environmental barriers that now must be overcome in order to develop the transportation system of the country. Certainly, consideration must be given to social and environmental factors in these programs, but these considerations cannot be permitted to stop all progress in developing the transportation system. Some compromise between the social and environmental considerations and the need for transportation must be reached.

Another difficulty with our promotional programs has been the unequal treatment of several modes of transportation that leads to misallocation of traffic among the modes, overexpansion of heavily promoted facilities, and premature obsolescence of the lesser promoted facilities. These factors are discussed further in a later section of this chapter.

Finally, the success of the different government promotional programs has varied.

Railroad Transportation

Government promotion of railroads in modern times has been mainly a reaction to crisis situations, for example, the depression of the 1930's and the collapse of the northeast railroads in the 1970's.

The World War I takeover of most railroads was generally successful, except for the large deficit incurred but which can probably be justified. Government aid to railroads in the 1930's, the late 1950's, and the early 1960's was moderately successful, but it did nothing about solving long-run problems in the railroad industry. Public aid to commuter railroads has been sporadic, has not had a national plan, and is more successful in some cities than in others. The High-Speed Ground Transportation Program has had some success, but it appears to be in the process of being downgraded at the time of this writing. Amtrak has had some successes and it has had some failures. More money will be needed in the future, and it will eventually probably become a totally government enterprise if Amtrak continues to attempt to serve medium-distance and long-distance routes, since such passenger service by rail probably cannot be made profitable. The success of Conrail is unknown at the time of this writing. However, it appears that considerable federal money will be necessary and that the federal government is running the risk of eventual nationalization of the northeast and, perhaps, other railroads as the next step in the process of government assistance.

Highway Transportation

Because promotion of highway transportation is conducted by all levels of government, it is difficult to generalize on the success or failure of individual programs—it probably varies somewhat geographically. Unlike railroad programs, however, government promotion of highway transportation at all levels of government has been more of a planned long-run program rather than a reaction to crisis, although crisis has played some part. The success of the programs has varied geographically, but these programs have generally been a great success in terms of the quantity and quality of roads and streets produced, and they have greatly spurred the development of highway transportation and have created great population mobility and other social and economic benefits that stem from highways. However, highway construction has probably been overdone in comparison with other government programs to aid transportation, such as aid to commuter railroads, airports, and urban transportation. But it is probably true that the extensive highway promotion in the 1950's and 1960's is what the public wanted at the time and the legislatures merely responded to that demand.

Urban Transportation

Federal participation in improving urban transportation was late in coming. A crisis situation finally brought it about. Although the federal program did not provide enough money until the 1970's, it did lead to some research and development efforts that did not exist before and it did help to improve some systems.

It also retarded the deterioration of local urban mass transportation systems in general.

State and local governments also neglected the problem until recently. They have not had much money to work with and are currently heavily dependent on federal aid.

Although progress has been made in improving urban mass transportation systems in some cities, there is still a long way to go and, in general, all programs have, unfortunately, neglected the problem of freight movement in urban areas.

Water Transportation

Decisions on promoting water transportation have often been based more on political considerations than on economic considerations. Deep-water coastal and intercoastal water transportation and domestic Great Lakes shipping have received only moderate governmental assistance and have not been strong in recent years. The St. Lawrence Seaway has not been successful financially, although it handles a lot of traffic and has probably benefited the geographic areas served. Although some inland waterways projects have been highly successful, some are difficult to justify on economic grounds. The lack of user charges in the federal program is another reason for criticism. These programs have, however, generally been successful in attracting industry.

Air Transportation

The federal airway program has generally been successful, although there have been problems associated with who should pay for it and the question of subsidy, difficulty in keeping up with technological change and with traffic growth, and lack of sufficient funds prior to 1970. There have also been periods when the program has been criticized for not providing sufficient safety in the air.

The federal airport program generally suffered from a lack of enough money prior to 1970, which contributed to airport congestion and other difficulties. Federal money has also been overly restricted as to what kinds of airport improvements it can be used for. State and local airport programs are difficult to evaluate without examining each one individually. Certainly, however, some state and local airport programs have been more successful than others.

The federal cash subsidy program succeeded in the sense that cash subsidy is no longer needed by domestic trunk lines and most other airlines. The program that assists local service airlines has provided service to smaller communities at a modest cost to the taxpayer. However, it has also resulted in what appears to be a permanently subsidized service and questions may be raised about the quality of service rendered and whether or not the service is worth the cost to the taxpayer.

GOVERNMENT PROMOTION OF TRANSPORTATION AND INTERMODAL RELATIONSHIPS

We know that we have 5 different modes of domestic transportation and we know that each mode has its own economic and service characteristics. We also know that carriers in each of these modes compete against carriers in other modes in intermodal competition, in addition to competing against carriers of their own mode in intramodal competition. Although carriers of different modes sometimes seek and actually carry the same kinds of traffic, the ideal situation would be that each of the 5 modes would carry only that traffic that it is best suited to carry in terms of costs and service. This would enable us to get the most efficient use of our resources devoted to transportation. This is sometimes referred to as *transport coordination*[5] or *economic coordination* of transportation. In other words, airlines would usually not carry cement blocks and barge lines would usually not carry emergency shipments of high-value computer parts. Those are obvious examples. Since other cases are not so clear, there may be difficulty in deciding which is the more appropriate mode to carry a given kind of freight or passenger traffic.

Effects of Government Promotion on Intermodal Relationships

It is clear from our discussion in Chapters 16 and 17 that government promotion is unequal among the modes. Some modes are promoted more than others and some modes are subsidized more than others. Thus, for example, water transportation is not only heavily promoted by government while oil pipeline transportation is not, thus affecting the competitive relationship between them, but water carriers are also heavily subsidized through the promotional programs while oil pipelines are not.

The result of unequal promotion and subsidy of the several modes is that there is overexpansion of the modes that are heavily promoted (highways, for example) while premature obsolescence and overcapacity occur in the lesser promoted modes (railroads, for example). In some cases, the lesser promoted modes are unable to develop rapidly enough to keep up with traffic demands (airport promotion, for example).

In addition, there is a misallocation of traffic among the modes, because the more heavily promoted facilities are able to advance in their general technological development faster than the other modes, whether or not they are the most suitable modes for the traffic they attract. There is also the fact that heavily promoted modes have their business risks reduced by government provision of a large part of their capital requirements. This, of course, gives them an advantage over modes, such as railroads (until recently) and oil pipelines, that have not benefited any or much from such government promotion. The misallocation of traffic is made more serious when subsidy is involved because a subsidized mode need not cover all its costs in its overall rate structure since some of its costs are borne by the taxpayer. This enables the subsidized mode to attract traffic through lower rates that it otherwise would not be able to get if it charged rates that collectively had to cover the costs involved. Misallocation of traffic means that the traffic is not being carried by the modes best suited for it and the whole problem of fitting the modes together into a logical coordinated system is made more difficult.

Unequal promotion also makes it difficult for government regulatory agencies

[5]See D. Philip Locklin, *Economics of Transportation,* 7th ed. (Homewood, Illinois: Richard D. Irwin, Inc., 1972), p. 844.

to determine which mode of transportation has the inherent advantage in any individual case.[6] Finally, the promotional programs have served to intensify the railroad problem because, until recently, railroads in modern times did not benefit from promotion while some of their competitors did.

Part of the problem is the lack of coordination of promotional activities between governments and between agencies of the same government, as discussed earlier in this chapter. In fact, the so-called *National Transportation Policy* statement enacted by Congress in 1940, which attempted to deal with the intermodal problem, makes no mention whatsoever of government promotion of transportation.[7] Consequently, there is no national policy on this question. There have, however, been some encouraging steps taken. In September, 1975 the Secretary of Transportation proposed to Congress a "Statement of National Transportation Policy" which generally supported a private-enterprise transportation system with as little government financial backing as possible and which advocated user charges for domestic water carriers and more equitable use of federal subsidies with minimal detrimental effect on competing modes.[8] The statement has no binding effect until it becomes the basis for legislation by Congress. The Railroad Revitalization and Regulatory Reform (4R) Act of 1976 required the federal DOT to conduct a number of planning studies, including a study to develop a national railroad plan. Finally, the highway aid authorization act of 1976 provided for the creation of a 19-member National Transportation Policy Study Commission that was to produce (by the end of 1978) a report on the nation's transportation needs through the year 2000 and to recommend policies that would most likely ensure that adequate transportation systems would be in place that would meet the needs for safe and efficient movement of goods and people. Appointments to the Committee were completed in October, 1976.

Although unequal treatment of the modes has greatly affected competition among the modes and has had some negative effects, as noted above, some unequal treatment of the modes was probably unavoidable because some modes by their very nature cannot operate without government promotional programs. The reasons for promotion were discussed in Chapter 16.

The Subsidy Question and Intermodal Relationships

Objections to the unequal treatment of the modes would be reduced if the subsidy element were removed from the promotion of transportation. The difficulties of measuring benefits and costs and of allocating costs among different beneficiaries have already been discussed in Chapters 16 and 17 and in this chapter. If these problems could be solved and if the objective were to eliminate all subsidy from government promotional programs, significant changes would take place in our transportation system, with all modes except oil pipelines having to pay new or higher user charges or tolls of some kind in different degrees.

---

[6] Inherent advantage will be discussed further in Chapter 24.

[7] This policy is discussed further in Chapter 24.

[8] *A Statement of National Transportation Policy by the Secretary of Transportation* (Washington, D.C.: U.S. Government Printing Office, 1975).

If such an improbable step were taken, then transportation rates and fares would more likely reflect actual transportation costs and each mode would more likely find its most useful place in the transportation system. Competitive conditions among the modes would, in effect, be more equalized. There would also be less of a tendency to overexpand transportation facilities and to engage in uneconomic projects if the carriers involved had to pay the costs involved. To the extent that it is politically and practically possible, subsidies probably should be removed from transportation and the modes should be made more self-supporting than they are now. In those cases in which it is impossible to put the modes on a self-supporting basis, the question of whether or not the need to help develop a mode, indirect economic benefits, and non-economic benefits are sufficient to warrant general taxpayer support should be examined.

ROLE OF SUBSIDY PROMOTIONAL PROGRAMS IN THE FUTURE

The subsidy question has been referred to several times in the preceding 2 chapters and in this chapter. Subsidy to transportation is a highly controversial subject and it is criticized by persons both within and outside transportation. Most Americans probably believe that "everybody should pay his or her own way" and that subsidy should be eliminated from all government programs whenever possible.

Trends in Subsidy

In a sense, there has been a long-term trend away from government subsidy in transportation at all levels of government. Highway programs are now largely on a user charge basis, although some question can be raised as to whether or not the user charges cover all the costs incurred and whether or not some users are paying more than they should and, therefore, are subsidizing other users who pay less than they should.

Urban transportation programs in the future are probably destined to be subsidized programs because there is no set of users who could support them. They will be deficit operations in which the deficits are to be paid for from general revenue sources or other sources, such as highway user tax money.

User charges are often collected by state and local governments from water carriers at ports. Here again we have questions of how much should be paid and how much is actually being paid. The Panama Canal and the St. Lawrence Seaway are paid for in part through user charges. The federal Congress has considered imposing user charges for the use of the domestic inland waterway system many times, but no bills have passed at the time of this writing. The pressure for some sort of user charges appears to be increasing.

The airway and airport programs at the federal level have been on a user charge basis since 1970. The same questions can be raised about these programs as with others in terms of how much should be paid and by whom. At the state and local levels, although some major airports are self-supporting, there is usually a subsidy element involved.

The general trend toward greater reliance on user charges is contradicted, however, by an opposite trend in railroad transportation. The several modern programs, including aid to commuter railroads, the federal High-Speed Ground Transportation program, and Amtrak, are all programs in which the governments involved do not expect to receive compensation and are clearly subsidy programs, some of which, particularly Amtrak, are growing. Conrail may turn out to be a long-term deficit operation in which the federal government will play a large subsidy role.

The energy shortage may affect governmental attitudes toward subsidy in the future. User charges could be used to discourage the development and use of certain high-energy consuming modes of transportation while subsidy could be used to encourage the development and use of low-energy consuming modes. No such programs have been established at this writing, although President Jimmy Carter's proposed energy program in 1977 included higher taxes on gasoline to discourage consumption.

The "Transportation Fund" Idea

Much criticism is made of the *dedicated trust fund* practice whereby user taxes are collected from the carriers of a given mode and the money is spent only for improving facilities for that particular mode. Dedicated funds have the advantage that they permit longer-range planning in that the funds for the future are assured, they link revenues to expenditures so that only what is produced in user taxes is spent, and they make certain that each mode of transportation contributes to the promotional costs incurred for that mode. The federal Highway Trust Fund and the federal Airport and Airway Trust Fund are examples, as are state highway funds. One criticism is that the funds become self-perpetuating. For example, the more highway user tax revenue received, the more roads are built; the more roads available for use, the greater are the tax revenues which enable the building of more roads which produces more tax revenue, and so on. This then is said to lead to overexpansion of the mode involved since the tendency is often to spend what is available regardless of need.

A second criticism is that the dedicated fund idea does not recognize that transportation modes are interrelated and that expenditures on one mode's facilities affect other modes. The effect is disregarded when user taxes are automatically spent on the mode from which they are collected.

Third, it is claimed that the dedicated fund idea ignores the needs of other modes that have no such funds and are being supported by general revenue sources because of their inability to produce user charge revenue.

Fourth, it is said that dedicated funds do not take into account the needs of other government programs, perhaps not in transportation at all, because the funds are automatically spent for the dedicated purpose.

Finally, dedicated funds are criticized because the application of cost-benefit analysis to proposed projects may be neglected and budgetary control and review may be more difficult because the use of the money may not be carefully scrutinized.

Therefore, some critics argue that federal and state *transportation trust funds* should be created into which all transportation user charges from all modes would be placed. The money would not be dedicated to any one mode but, instead, would be spent where needed the most according to priorities established by government. Although there are merits in the proposal, it assumes that there is a national or state transportation plan for transportation development which, as we have seen, usually does not exist. In addition, considerable resistance to the transportation fund idea comes from the modes for which dedicated funds now exist, namely, highway and air transportation. However, it appears likely that some steps will be taken in the direction of eliminating special dedicated funds in the near future and in the establishment of a general transportation fund, at least at the federal level. The energy shortage may encourage such a step because the establishment of a general transportation fund would enable the federal government to spend user charge revenue in such a way as that it would encourage the development of low-energy consuming modes and would discourage the development of high-energy consuming modes. It may also encourage the federal government to levy charges accordingly.

SELECTED REFERENCES

The United States Department of Transportation (DOT) has been the subject of numerous writings. The original organization and powers of the DOT are described in "The Department of Transportation: Organization, Powers, Functions," *Transportation and Distribution Management,* November, 1966 and in "Department of Transportation: A Summary of Its Organization, Executive Positions, Responsibilities," *ICC Practitioners' Journal,* November–December, 1967. The most complete study of the federal DOT is Grant M. Davis, *The Department of Transportation* (Lexington, Massachusetts: D. C. Heath and Company, 1970).

The trend toward state departments of transportation is discussed in James W. Bennett, Jr., and William J. DeWitt, III, "The Development of State Departments of Transportation—A Recent Organizational Phenomenon," *Transportation Journal,* Fall, 1972. See also Thomas D. Larson, "Towards a More Effective State Role in Transportation," *Proceedings of Transportation Research Forum, 1972.*

The division of authority over transportation matters in Congress and in the executive branch of the federal government is dealt with in Paul W. Schuldiner, "Institutional Constraints on Comprehensive Transportation Planning at the Federal Level," *Proceedings of Transportation Research Forum, 1974.* For a discussion of the role of the president, Congress, and the carrier associations in formulating federal national transportation policy, see Hugh S. Norton, *National Transportation Policy: Formulation and Implementation* (Berkeley, California: McCutchan Publishing Corporation, 1966), Chapters 8, 9, 12, and 13.

The problem of the lack of uniform standards in federal promotion programs is discussed in Grant M. Davis, "The Necessity for Uniform Standards in Federal Transportation Investment Decisions," *Alabama Business* (University, Alabama: Center for Business and Economic Research, Graduate School of Business, University of Alabama, May 15, 1971).

The theory of investment as applied to transportation projects is dealt with in John B. Lansing, *Transportation and Economic Policy* (New York: The Free Press, 1966), Chapter 3. The problems involved in allocating economic resources to transportation are discussed in Dudley F. Pegrum, *Transportation Economics and Public Policy,* 3rd ed. (Homewood, Illinois: Richard D. Irwin, Inc., 1973), pp. 441–444. The problems of analyzing proposed transportation projects on a cost-benefit basis are dealt with in Marvin L. Fair and Ernest W. Williams, Jr., *Economics of Transportation and Logistics* (Dallas, Texas: Business Publications, Inc., 1975), pp. 510–516.

Subsidies to transportation, user charges, and the intermodal competition problem are discussed in D. Philip Locklin, *Economics of Transportation,* 7th ed. (Homewood, Illinois: Richard D. Irwin, Inc., 1972), pp. 845–860. The advantages and disadvantages of dedicated trust funds are set forth in Clarkson H. Oglesby, "Trust Funds: Pro and Con," *Highway User Quarterly,* Winter, 1976.

19

Rationale of Government Economic Regulation of Transportation

In addition to the promotion of transportation, the other major role of government in transportation in the United States is in economic regulation. In this chapter we shall examine the rationale of or the reasons for government economic regulation of transportation. In subsequent chapters the decision-making process in economic regulation and the form that economic regulation takes for the several modes of transportation are discussed, as are the impact of regulation, its effectiveness, and suggestions for changes in regulation.

OTHER GOVERNMENT REGULATION OF TRANSPORTATION

Transportation is subject to considerable regulation by government and much of this regulation is not peculiar to transportation since it applies to many different industries. In addition to economic regulation, regulation of transportation has to do with a variety of matters, including labor legislation, such as collective bargaining laws; licensing and zoning laws that affect terminal buildings and other facilities; environmental protection regulation, such as air and noise pollution control laws; safety regulation, such as regulation imposed by the Federal Aviation Administration (FAA) on airlines; and regulation to protect the way, found in highway weight restrictions that apply to trucks.

In other words, economic regulation is only one of several kinds of government regulation that apply to transportation. Although economic regulation is usually of more significance to the carrier than are other kinds of government control, regulation having to do with environmental protection is becoming more important in transportation and may some day be of more significance to carriers than economic regulation. The same may be true of energy-use controls that may be imposed by government in the future.

WHAT IS GOVERNMENT ECONOMIC REGULATION
OF TRANSPORTATION?

Government economic regulation of transportation is regulation of the business of transportation and includes control over entry into the business of for-hire transportation, control over exit from the business, regulation of rates and fares, regulation of carrier service, regulation of accounting practices, regulation of financial matters including security issues, control of mergers and consolidations, and, of course, the filing of numerous reports covering the activities of the regulated carriers.

The specific reasons why economic regulation was instituted varied with the mode of transportation, as we shall see. However, the basic objective in all cases has been to provide the public with adequate transportation service at reasonable cost.

WHY IS TRANSPORTATION SUBJECTED TO
GOVERNMENT ECONOMIC REGULATION?

A major reason why transportation has been subjected to government economic regulation while most other industries are not placed under such control is the importance of transportation to the economy and to society in general. The several reasons why transportation is considered to be of extreme importance to the economy and to users of transportation were discussed in Chapter 1, and they need not be repeated here. It is sufficient to say that the importance attributed to transportation led to its special treatment under the common law and eventually under statutory law in the form of economic regulation, the belief being that its importance required that it be treated differently from other business activities and that it be controlled by government to ensure that it served the public as well as possible.

The second reason for bringing transportation under government economic regulation was the belief that, if left to itself without government control, transportation would not operate effectively and in the public interest because parts of it tend toward monopoly and parts of it tend toward destructive competition. The belief is that either tendency is undesirable from the point of view of the public because of the adverse effect they have on the quality of service provided and/or the level of rates and fares charged.

To sum up, the accepted reasoning behind economic regulation of transportation is that it was necessary because of the importance of transportation to the economy and society in general and the belief that it does not operate in the public interest when left unregulated. The specific reasons why each mode was subjected to economic regulation by government are discussed in the remaining sections of this chapter.

RATIONALE OF ECONOMIC REGULATION OF
RAILROAD TRANSPORTATION

As noted in Chapter 16, railroads were eagerly welcomed by the public in the early railroad construction period because the public expected economic and other benefits that improved transportation would bring. The various governmental promotional programs in the nineteenth century were evidence of that feeling.

Reasons for Economic Regulation in the Nineteenth Century

In the latter part of the nineteenth century the public's attitude toward railroads changed considerably. The railroads were accused of various malpractices and, in some cases, the economic and other advantages that railroads were supposed to bring did not actually occur or were less in magnitude than expected. Taxpayers in communities that had heavily subsidized railroad construction were especially upset. In other cases, the failure of some railroads to provide investors with satisfactory returns caused the investors to criticize the railroads.

The main criticism that led to economic regulation, however, had to do with the malpractices railroads were accused of. It was a period of laissez faire or complete non-intervention by government, and managers of railroads and other businesses took advantage of the situation and did many things that would be illegal today. The exploits of Jay Gould, Jim Fisk, and Daniel Drew in their operation of the Erie Railroad and Cornelius Vanderbilt of the New York Central Railroad are well-known in American history. The practices of these people and other railroad managers ultimately led to a demand for economic regulation of the railroad industry.

Fraudulent Practices. One of the specific malpractices complained about was the railroad construction fraud in which the purpose of building some railroads was to obtain the public aid being granted to railroads. The incentive was to build the railroad as cheaply as possible in order to make the greatest profit from the endeavor and then get out of the railroad business as soon as possible. The famous Credit Mobilier scandal of the 1860's, which involved the building of the Union Pacific Railroad, revealed that certain directors of the Union Pacific were also stockholders in the construction company that was hired to build the railroad. These directors approved highly profitable contracts with the construction company which, in turn, built the railroad as cheaply as possible. The conspiring stockholders pocketed the excess profits earned, much of it at the expense of the federal government which had heavily promoted the Union Pacific through land grants.

There were other fraudulent schemes after the railroads were built, for example, stock market manipulation, overissuing stock (stock "watering"), and appropriation of company assets for personal use. In addition, there was much foreign investment in railroads, which was considered "absentee ownership" and undesirable.

High Prices. Another practice complained about was the charging of high railroad rates and fares. Since a railroad had a monopoly position in many situations, the management was often free in the laissez-faire environment to charge whatever prices it wished, provided the elasticity of demand was such that sufficient volume of traffic would result.

Unjust Discrimination. A related problem was the excessive or unjust discrimination in pricing and in service. If a railroad had a monopoly position, it could and often did charge high prices, as noted above, and neglected the quality of service, but it charged lower prices and paid more attention to service where intramodal or intermodal competition existed.

In addition to unjust geographic discrimination of the above kind, there was the problem of excessive discrimination among commodities. Higher value commodities were charged extortionate rates. There was also personal discrimination which often was exercised through secret rebating. Shippers (or receivers) of the same commodity over the same route would all pay the same rate per 100 pounds or other unit shipped, but the user whom the carrier wished to favor would receive part of his payment back in the form of a kickback or a rebate— the net rate paid was less than that paid by his competitors. In some cases, the practice of rebating was made even more objectionable because the carrier paid to the favored user part of the revenue received from the competing users. This was known as a *drawback*.

Fluctuating Prices. Another difficulty with railroad rates and fares was that they fluctuated so much in some cases that it was difficult for the user to plan his transportation costs in advance. If the carrier enjoyed a monopoly position, fluctuating prices were not a problem, but when 2 or more railroads competed for the same traffic, which was sometimes the result of the overbuilding of railroads, competition often led to rate wars. One carrier would cut his prices and then a competing carrier(s) would retaliate by cutting his prices, after which the first carrier would make a further cut, and so on. Usually, this eventually led to some sort of an agreement between the carriers to end the war. Then the rate would remain stable (at a higher level) for awhile until the price agreement would be broken by one of the railroads and a new price war would commence.

Price Fixing. Because railroad management recognized the destructiveness of price competition between railroads, various schemes were invented that resulted in fixing of prices by competing railroads. The schemes had varying degrees of effectiveness and sometimes would not last very long. These schemes included direct price fixing between individual carriers, the formation of *traffic associations,* which were price-fixing organizations, and *pooling,* whereby the competing carriers fixed prices and then divided the traffic (traffic pool) or the revenue (money pool) among themselves on a prearranged basis. In some cases, merger or takeover of one carrier by another solved the problem of competition and placed the survivor in a monopoly situation.

Other Monopoly Practices. In addition to high prices and excessive discrimination in pricing and service, railroads of the nineteenth century were accused of other practices that stemmed from their monopoly position in transportation and their importance in the economy. The public was almost entirely dependent on railroads for long-distance transportation. These objectionable practices included manipulation of governmental officials in order to receive favored treatment from government on taxes, rights of way, public aid, and other matters; undesirable working conditions for employees; and unfair competitive advantage over nonrailroad firms in industries in which railroads had ownership, such as coal mining.

Early Regulation

Because of the malpractices referred to above, the railroads came under heavy criticism by at least some segments of the public, particularly after the Civil War ended in 1865. Assuming that the accusations made against the railroads were probably true, it is easy to see why certain people would be unhappy with them. It should be noted however, that railroad management was probably not much different from management of other kinds of business of the time. In the laissez-faire philosophy of the period the buyer and the investor had no protection, and unethical practices on the part of business managers were commonplace.

The above does not excuse the railroad managers, but it does lead to the question of why railroads were selected for control by government while other industries that were equally guilty were not. The answer probably lies in the fact that (1) railroads were the giant corporations of the period and, therefore, the most logical candidates for regulation when it came about,[1] and (2) the importance of transportation to the economy and to society in general made malpractices more difficult to put up with than in other industries. In any event, railroads were the first industry in the United States to be placed under an organized system of government economic regulation.

Prior to economic regulation of railroads by statute, the common law was relied upon, but it was not able to cope with the problems presented by railroad monopoly.

Charter Regulation. Before there were any general railway incorporation laws, early railroads were usually required to obtain charters from the states in which they operated. These charters sometimes included provisions relative to the maximum level of rates and fares that could be charged, but the provisions were generally ineffective, sometimes because the maximum rates and fares prescribed were higher than the most profitable prices.

Early Commissions. Special commissions to regulate railroads were created in a few states before the Civil War, but the commissions were primarily concerned with problems of eminent domain and railroad safety and with gathering statistics from railroads instead of with economic regulation.

The Granger Laws, 1871-1874. It was not until after the Civil War that the system of economic regulation of railroads that we know today really started. The malpractices and other problems associated with the railroad industry were given more attention as the economy of the nation deteriorated in the post-war period. Agriculture had a difficult time, suffering from overproduction brought about by the high demand of the war years which had now disappeared and farmers were in a state of discontent. The National Grange of the Patrons of Husbandry was formed in 1867 as a farmers' organization. The farmers' protest movement against various claimed injustices became known as the *Granger movement.*

---

[1] See Robert W. Harbeson, "Transportation Regulation: A Centennial Evaluation," *ICC Practitioners' Journal,* July–August, 1972, p. 630.

Among the things farmers protested against in particular were high and excessively discriminatory freight rates on agricultural products and supplies. Although the National Grange itself did not push for economic regulation of railroads, the laws that were enacted by 4 states between 1871 and 1874 to regulate railroads are called the *Granger Laws*.

The states were Illinois, Iowa, Minnesota, and Wisconsin and the laws dealt mainly with the maximum level of railroad rates, by fixing the level in the statute itself or by delegating the power to a commission to set the level of rates. The Granger Laws also tried to stop the practice of charging a higher rate for a shorter distance than for a longer distance. Finally, the Granger Laws forbade combination among competing railroads and prohibited railroads from giving free passes to government officials, a matter of extreme interest at the time.

Since the Granger Laws were not well thought out or constructed, they did not work very well in practice. Within a short time all but the Illinois law were repealed and replaced by weak regulation. The depression that followed the panic of 1873 contributed to the financial difficulties of the railroads and aided them in their attempt to discredit what they called repressive regulation. As a result, state regulation remained ineffective for the remainder of the nineteenth century.[2]

The Granger Cases, 1877. The railroads and grain warehouses that were regulated by the Granger laws opposed the legislation in the courts and their opposition resulted in the Granger Cases of 1877, a series of 6 cases heard by the United States Supreme Court. The most well-known case was *Munn v. Illinois,*[3] which involved grain warehouses.

The carriers and warehouses claimed that the states (1) had no right to regulate prices involving interstate commerce because that was a power delegated to the federal government by the federal Constitution and (2) the states could not regulate their prices because that was the same as taking their property (income) and, under the Fourteenth Amendment to the federal Constitution, a state may not deprive a person (including corporations) of property without due process of law.

On the first point the Court ruled that as long as the federal Congress had not acted to regulate rates involving interstate commerce, the states could do so. On the second point the Court agreed that the states were taking property from the carriers and warehouses but that the states could legally do so in the case of railroads and grain elevators because they were businesses "affected with a public interest"—apparently meaning that they were of public consequence and affected the community at large. Since the Middle Ages public callings and business occupations, or those affecting the public interest, had been subject to control and regulation. In the Granger cases the Court carried this practice forward to justify economic regulation of railroads and grain elevators. The monopoly character of the grain warehouses was also important in the Court's decisions and, although the monopoly factor was not mentioned in relation to

[2] Dudley F. Pegrum, *Transportation Economics and Public Policy,* 3rd ed. (Homewood, Illinois: Richard D. Irwin, Inc., 1973), p. 270.

[3] 94 U.S. 113.

railroads, it apparently was a reason for the "public interest" attribute attached to the railroads by the Court.

The result of the Granger cases was that although the Granger Laws themselves were ineffective, the validity of economic regulation of railroads by the states was upheld by the Supreme Court. This laid the groundwork for further state and federal regulation of railroads in the future.

The Wabash Case, 1886. Further refinement of the validity of economic regulation was needed, however, because the states applied their regulation to both interstate and intrastate commerce, even though the federal Constitution provides in the "commerce clause" that regulation of commerce between the states is delegated to the federal government.[4] In the Munn case the Supreme Court had ruled that state regulation of interstate prices was lawful as long as the federal government had not acted in that area. In the Wabash case of 1886,[5] however, the Court ruled that the state of Illinois could not regulate railroad rates beyond its borders because such regulation violated the commerce clause in the Constitution.

Because most railroad traffic was interstate at the time, the result of the Wabash case was that if economic regulation of railroads was to be made effective, federal action would be required; otherwise, such traffic would remain unregulated.

The Act to Regulate Commerce, 1887. Since 1874 the federal Congress had been considering regulation of railroads and, finally, possibly spurred on by the decision in the Wabash case, in 1887 it enacted the Act to Regulate Commerce, which is now Part I of the Interstate Commerce Act.

The Act brought interstate common carrier railroads under economic regulation to be administered by a 5-member agency, the Interstate Commerce Commission (ICC). This was the first federal government independent regulatory agency.

The Act contained a heavy emphasis on rates and on collective action by carriers. Basically, it was an anti-monopoly, anti-malpractices, negative law designed to stop the railroads from engaging in certain undesirable practices. Rates were to be just and reasonable, personal discrimination was to be outlawed, undue preference or prejudice of any kind was prohibited, long- and short-haul discrimination in rates (charging more for a shorter haul than for a longer haul on the same route in the same direction) was prohibited unless special exception was made by the ICC, pooling agreements among railroads were banned, all rates and fares were to be published and strictly adhered to, and rates and fares could not be raised except on 10 days' notice and no reductions made without 3 days' notice.

The Act worked fairly well at first, but because Congress had made some basic mistakes in writing the law, possibly because of its inexperience, the railroads found loopholes in the statute and began to evade regulation. They were upheld in their efforts by the courts so that by 1900 the Commission had lost much of its intended regulatory authority.

---

[4] Article I, Section 8, Clause 3.

[5] *Wabash, St. Louis, and Pacific Railway v. Illinois,* 118 U.S. 557.

Strengthening Federal Regulation

Beginning in 1903, Congress enacted a number of laws and amendments that were designed to strengthen and broaden the scope of regulation as administered by the Commission. The Elkins Act of 1903 made the personal discrimination section more effective. The Hepburn Act of 1906, among other things, gave the ICC additional powers over railroad pricing and made the enforcement of Commission decisions more effective. The Mann–Elkins Act of 1910 increased the effectiveness of the ICC's power to control long- and short-haul discrimination and gave the Commission the power to suspend (postpone) rate and fare proposals made by railroads. The Transportation Act of 1920 was an extensive piece of legislation that added to the rate regulation powers of the ICC and gave it jurisdiction over security issues and abandonments and ordered it to prepare a plan of consolidation for United States railroads. In regulation of rates, the Commission was now to take into account the railroads' need for adequate revenue. The Emergency Transportation Act of 1933 contained some temporary anti-depression measures and also a change in the rate-making authority of the ICC. The Transportation Act of 1940 eliminated the railroad consolidation plan of the Commission and added factors the ICC must consider in railroad merger cases. The rate-making power was also changed and a "National Transportation Policy" was enacted. The Railroad Modification Act of 1948 had to do with altering the terms of railroad securities and the Reed–Bulwinkle Act of the same year legalized railroad and other rate bureaus. The Transportation Act of 1958 strengthened the authority of the ICC over intrastate rates and discontinuance of passenger train service, and it modified the rate-making power once more. In 1970 the Commission was given jurisdiction over the quality of interstate railroad passenger service, including that of Amtrak.[6] The Railroad Revitalization and Regulatory Reform (4R) Act of 1976 provided for substantial relaxation in the regulation of railroad rates, a change in the regulation of railroad mergers, and a change in the regulation of railroad abandonments.

The result of all this legislation and numerous federal court decisions has been an extensive system of regulation which reaches most aspects of railroad operation and which is carried out by a commission that has broad powers and considerable strength and impact on the railroad industry. In addition, the states have improved their regulation of railroad transportation since the turn of the century and most states impose economic regulation to some extent.

RATIONALE OF ECONOMIC REGULATION OF HIGHWAY TRANSPORTATION

The circumstances surrounding the introduction of economic regulation of highway transportation were entirely different from those in railroad transportation. The economic and service characteristics of the 2 industries and the time period involved were very different. The demand for regulation was less

---

[6] See D. Philip Locklin, *Economics of Transportation*, 7th ed. (Homewood, Illinois: Richard D. Irwin, Inc., 1972), Chapters 9, 10, 11, and 12 for an excellent discussion of the development of federal regulation of railroads.

clear in the case of highway transportation and the source of the demand was also different.

Reasons for Economic Regulations in the 1920's and 1930's

As noted in Chapter 11, highway transportation is naturally a highly competitive industry that consists of many small firms. Consequently, unlike the railroad situation, the problems of monopoly power were not present, instead, the problems were associated with excessive or destructive competition.

The laws that brought highway transportation under economic regulation did not spring from the public's bitter resentment. There was, in fact, little popular demand for the regulation of highway transportation. The demand came from the transportation industries. Many truck and bus operators wanted relief from what they considered destructive competition. The railroads, already regulated themselves, insisted that their competitors be treated similarly.

Excess Competition. The starting point in economic regulation of highway transportation was the belief that there was need for restriction of excessive competition in the industry. In the early days of highway transportation, particularly transportation of property, the fact that business could be begun with only a small capital outlay, sometimes with only a down payment on a single used vehicle, attracted more carriers than the available traffic warranted. Carriers responded to the situation by cutting prices and they often were compelled to accept traffic at ridiculously low prices because of the severe competition. The situation was made worse by the fact that operations were often conducted by persons lacking in knowledge of sound business practices and adequate financial resources. In freight transportation, many users took advantage of the situation and "shopped around," playing one trucker off against another, forcing carriers to offer rates below the level they would otherwise have offered.

Under such circumstances, responsible carriers found it difficult to operate at a profit and were unable to establish standards of continuous and efficient service. At the same time, it became difficult for them to attract capital and obtain credit. Many carriers operated substandard equipment, did not pay damage claims, ignored contracts and other agreements with users, did not maintain schedules, discontinued service without notifying users, and otherwise did not fulfill the responsibilities of for-hire carriers.

Many carriers failed and left the business, but the overcapacity problem was not eliminated and an "equilibrium" or "balance" was not achieved because their places were quickly taken by new entrants. As a result, the turnover of operators was heavy and the losses were great. The unstable conditions were accelerated by the depression of the 1930's when many unemployed people who had no knowledge of or preparation for the transportation industry entered the trucking industry as a temporary source of income and added service in an industry that was already suffering from overcapacity.

These conditions led to a demand on the part of some users who wanted better service, some motor carriers who wanted to make a long-run commitment to the industry, and the railroad industry for economic regulation of the highway transportation industry. The demand for economic regulation of the trucking industry was opposed by some users who sought to benefit from the existing conditions, namely, low rates.

The primary problem, then, was believed to be the conservation of the industry in the interests of the public generally and to bring order out of the chaos of competition. Although highway transportation was not monopolistic, regulation was thought to be necessary in order to prevent competition from destroying the industry.

Railroad Arguments. The railroads played a large role in the demand for economic regulation of highway transportation because they wanted to protect themselves. A major objective of early state economic regulation was to protect the railroads from the competition of passenger and property motor carriers. This competition had resulted in the abandonment of thousands of miles of rail lines, and, of course, the investment in railroads was reduced in value. It was claimed that motor carriers in competition with railroads had to be regulated, not only to prevent competition from destroying the highway transportation industry, but also to prevent destruction of the railroads.

The railroads requested regulation of highway transportation also on the ground that they themselves were under elaborate public control. In addition, they realized that the motor carrier competition was using highways provided and maintained largely at the expense of the general taxpayer. Since the railroads were large taxpayers in many states, they resented being required to contribute to the support of a competitor without any public control over its activities.

Early Regulation

The overall objective of economic regulation of highway transportation was to provide the public with adequate motor carrier service at reasonable prices by stabilizing rates and fares and ensuring that the carriers were financially responsible and stable. This meant that entry had to be controlled. The cornerstone of effective economic regulation of highway transportation is the control over entry system under which carriers must apply to enter the industry. The regulatory agency controls both the number and quality of carriers allowed to enter.

Early State Regulation. As was the case with economic regulation of railroads, the states preceded the federal government in instituting economic regulation of highway transportation. Regulation began in 1914 and took the form either of interpreting existing public utility laws so as to make them applicable to motor carriers or of separate, specific acts designed especially for highway transportation regulation. The majority of state regulatory systems were established by the latter method.

In the years just prior to the entrance of the United States in World War I, 7 states undertook regulation. The post-World War I period witnessed activity in the enactment of state regulatory measures. By the end of 1925 there were 37 states that had begun regulation of motor transportation to some degree. In addition, several other states claimed the right of jurisdiction over motor carriers but had not as yet exercised such right.[7]

[7]Donald V. Harper, *Economic Regulation of the Motor Trucking Industry by the States* (Urbana, Illinois: University of Illinois Press, 1959), p. 34.

Interstate Carriers. As highway transportation grew in the early 1920's, motor truck and bus operations were extended beyond state boundaries and the problem of the interstate carrier arose. At first the states assumed that in the absence of any federal legislation providing for regulation of highway transportation they could regulate interstate motor carrier traffic, and the provisions of the early state regulatory laws were applied to interstate as well as to intrastate carriers.

In early 1925 the question of whether or not a motor carrier intending to operate interstate was subject to state entry control requirements reached the United States Supreme Court. There were several cases, but the two most important ones involved the regulatory laws of the states of Washington[8] and Maryland.[9] In both cases the Court held to be unconstitutional the requirement that operating authority be obtained from a state regulatory agency before interstate motor carrier operations could be started because such power was vested in the federal government by the commerce clause of the federal Constitution. Hence, as with the Wabash case earlier, the doctrine of regulation of interstate commerce by the states in the absence of federal regulation was destroyed, so far as the power of the state to deny operating authority was concerned.

Contract Carriers. A second problem arose in the late 1920's, the question of the constitutionality of economic control of contract carriers. Since the contract motor carrier confined his operations to service for a selected user or users and operated under separate and individual contractual agreements, there appeared to be a sound basis for believing that the business of the contract carrier was not one affected with a public interest in the same sense as was the business of the common carrier. The early state statutes, therefore, applied to common carriers only, but this led not only to schemes to avoid being classified as a common carrier in order to evade regulation but also to considerable growth in unregulated contract carriage at the expense of common carriage. It was recognized that regulation of common carriage was largely futile without regulation of contract carriage also.

The states encountered considerable difficulty in attempting to regulate contract carriers. Some of them made no distinction in their regulatory laws between common and contract carriers. The laws of Michigan,[10] California,[11] and Florida[12] were held to be unconstitutional by the United States Supreme Court, generally because they applied their regulation to both common and contract carriers without distinguishing between them, thus failing to recognize the different obligations of the 2 classes of carriers to the public and, in effect, treating them both as "public" carriers when, in fact, contract carriers did not have the obligation to serve the public generally.

This problem was solved when several states began to separate common and contract carriers for purposes of regulation and several of the laws were upheld by the federal courts. The most comprehensive scheme of regulation of contract carriers in the period was that of Texas, which treated common and contract

---

[8] *Buck v. Kuykendall,* 267 U.S. 307 (1925).

[9] *Bush v. Maloy,* 267 U.S. 317 (1925).

[10] *Michigan Public Utilities Commission v. Duke,* 266 U.S. 570 (1925).

[11] *Frost v. Railroad Commission of California,* 271 U.S. 583 (1926).

[12] *Smith v. Cahoon, Sheriff,* 283 U.S. 553 (1931).

carriers separately, providing a set of regulations for each, although many were common to both. The identity of the 2 classes was retained and their differences were emphasized. The law was based largely on the right of the state to protect its highways and to minimize traffic congestion in the interest of the public safety and in the interest of other highway users. The United States Supreme Court upheld the law in the case of *Stephenson v. Binford*[13] in 1932 and the decision was followed by the enactment of contract carrier regulation in many other states.

The Federal Motor Carrier Act, 1935. By 1933 there were 42 states that had instituted some form of control over common carriers of property. Contract carriers of property were under regulation in 31 states. All states except Delaware had placed motor transportation of passengers under regulation.[14] The period of the early 1930's was one in which state motor carrier laws were strengthened to deal with the tendency of the unemployed to try to enter the trucking business.

By 1935 the for-hire highway transportation industry had become subject to a large degree of regulation by the states, but the effectiveness of regulation varied widely among the states and there was little uniformity in their regulatory programs.

One of the most serious problems faced by the states was the lack of any regulation of interstate motor carrier operations. This permitted excessive competition to continue in interstate commerce. This was not only injurious to those carriers, but it also demoralized intrastate rates and fares and subjected intrastate users and communities to unfair disadvantage. At the same time, state regulation was weakened because carriers could easily convert their operations to those of interstate carriers in order to avoid regulation by extending their terminals across state lines for short distances or by making short detours over state lines. Several studies at the federal level convinced Congress that federal legislation was necessary to curb the uneconomic conditions that existed in the interstate branch of motor transportation and to save regulation at the state level. Proposals to institute federal regulation of interstate highway transportation were supported by state regulatory agencies.

Bills to regulate interstate highway transportation had been in Congress since 1925 and, finally, in 1935 Congress passed the Motor Carrier Act, which is now Part II of the Interstate Commerce Act.

The Act placed under the jurisdiction of the ICC for-hire motor carriers of passengers and property engaged in interstate and foreign commerce. The provisions required that common carriers must obtain a certificate of public convenience and necessity from the Commission before they could enter the industry, that carriers must publish their rates and fares and adhere to them, that 30 days' notice must be given before a rate or fare could be changed and such proposed changes could be suspended by the ICC, that the Commission could

[13] 287 U.S. 251.

[14] *Coordination of Motor Transportation,* 182 ICC 263, 371 (1932) and Federal Coordinator of Transportation, *Regulation of Transportation Agencies,* 73rd Congress, 2nd Session, Senate Document Number 152 (Washington D.C.: U.S. Government Printing Office, 1934), p. 173.

prescribe the maximum, minimum, or actual rates and fares to be charged, that the ICC had control over the adequacy of service, that the Commission had control over consolidations and mergers and security issues, and that personal injury, property damage, and cargo insurance must be carried.

The requirements imposed on contract carriers were generally not as severe as those imposed on common carriers. This reflects the fact that contract carriers do not have the obligations to the public that common carriers have. Some of the provisions covering common carriers also applied to contract carriers, but there were some major differences. Contract carriers were to obtain permits to enter, not certificates of public convenience and necessity, and were to have less rigorous entry conditions to meet. They were to file their minimum rates and not charge less than the minimum. The Commission could prescribe only the minimum rates. Contract carriers were not required to carry insurance to cover cargo, but they were required to have public liability and property damage coverage.

A major difference between federal regulation of motor carriers and federal regulation of railroads is that there were several categories of for-hire carriage that were exempted from highway transportation regulation. The major exemption excluded from economic regulation motor vehicles used in carrying livestock, fish, and horticultural and agricultural commodities, not including manufactured products thereof.

The passage of the federal Motor Carrier Act in 1935 not only lessened the excessive competition in interstate highway transportation but also made state regulation of the intrastate carrier more effective since it became impossible to avoid regulation by crossing state lines. In addition, the federal act became a model upon which several state statutes and amendments were based. The result was more uniformity among the states and more effective state regulation. Most states eventually enacted legislation to regulate both freight and passenger intrastate highway transportation.

RATIONALE OF ECONOMIC REGULATION OF DOMESTIC WATER TRANSPORTATION

Reasons for Economic Regulation

Because domestic water transportation consists of several different trades, each with somewhat different economic and service characteristics, it is difficult to generalize on why these different carriers were brought under government economic regulation.

None of the several trades—coastal, intercoastal, Great Lakes, and river and canal carriers—exhibited monopoly tendencies or the abuses that railroads were accused of, at least to any substantial degree. The problem appeared to be one of too many carriers and excessive competition, at least in some trades, caused mainly by the relatively small amount of capital necessary to enter the business which, in turn, was a result of the lack of an investment in a way. Excess competition apparently led to price cutting, poor financial condition of the carriers, an unstable industry, and poor service. The problem was, of course, far less severe than in highway transportation.

In addition, there was the intermodal competition factor. The railroad industry pushed strongly for the institution of economic regulation of domestic water transportation because of the adverse effect of such transportation on railroad freight traffic. The railroads hoped that regulation would protect them from entry of and/or price cutting by competing water carriers.

Early Regulation

Economic regulation of domestic water transportation has a very complex history at the federal level, dating back to 1887.

The Act to Regulate Commerce, 1887. As indicated earlier the Act to Regulate Commerce of 1887 brought interstate railroads under the jurisdiction of the ICC. In addition, the Act subjected to regulation interstate carriers partly by rail and partly by water for continuous carriage, meaning railroad-owned water carriers engaged in joint rail–water transportation and independent water carriers that interchanged freight with railroads.

The Panama Canal Act, 1912. The Panama Canal Act of 1912 contained a provision designed to prevent railroads from taking over and destroying domestic water carriers. It prohibited any railroad from owning a water carrier with which it was or might be in competition, although the Commission could make exceptions to this. In no case, however, could a railroad control a water carrier that operated through the Panama Canal.

The Shipping Act, 1916. The Shipping Act of 1916 established the United States Shipping Board and gave it regulatory jurisdiction over common carriers by water operating in interstate or foreign commerce on the high seas and Great Lakes. After several name and organizational changes over the years, in 1961 the Shipping Board became the Federal Maritime Commission (FMC).

The Intercoastal Shipping Act, 1933. The Intercoastal Shipping Act of 1933 was designed to increase the extent of regulation over both common and contract intercoastal water carriers operating through the Panama Canal. In 1938 these additional regulatory powers were extended to the common carriers in the coastal service and on the Great Lakes.

The Transportation Act, 1940. By the late 1930's there existed a somewhat confusing regulatory system regarding domestic water carriers, as the above discussion implies, with both the United States Maritime Commission (a successor to the Shipping Board) and the ICC having some jurisdiction. An important segment of domestic for-hire water transportation—river and canal traffic—was unregulated.

The Transportation Act of 1940 had several important parts, one of which established a new system of economic regulation of domestic water carriers. All economic regulation of domestic water transportation was brought under the ICC, including river and canal traffic which was brought under regulation for the first time. The United States Maritime Commission (now the Federal Maritime Commission) retained jurisdiction over water transportation in foreign commerce and commerce between the mainland United States and territories and possessions of the United States and, later, to offshore states when Alaska and Hawaii achieved statehood in the later 1950's. The provisions of the Transportation Act of 1940 relating to water transportation were added as Part III of the Interstate Commerce Act.

Some sections in Part I (railroads) of the Interstate Commerce Act were applied to water carriers, for example, Section 4 (the long- and short-haul clause). Part III applied only to water carriers and included entry control over both common and contract carriers, regulation of common carrier rates similar to that for rail and highway transportation, and less restrictive regulation of contract carrier rates—contract carriers were to publish and file with the Commission only their minimum rates and the Commission could prescribe only their minimum rates.

An unusual feature of regulation of water carriers was the large number of exemptions, the most controversial of which has been that for bulk commodities. These exemptions will be discussed further in Chapter 23.

Approximately 30 states have some degree of economic regulation of intrastate water transportation.

RATIONALE OF ECONOMIC REGULATION OF OIL PIPELINE TRANSPORTATION

Reasons for Economic Regulation in the Early Twentieth Century

The economic characteristics of oil pipelines, including large capital investment, great economies of scale, and the ruinous effect of too much capacity on a route, lead the industry toward monopoly tendencies, much as railroads are often said to be a "natural monopoly." The oil pipeline industry tends toward monopoly naturally because its economic characteristics mean that monopoly is the likely result of free enterprise. The tendency toward monopoly would probably have led to economic regulation of oil pipelines eventually, even if the peculiar ownership arrangement, discussed below, had not existed.

It was pointed out in Chapter 13 that an unusual characteristic of oil pipeline transportation is that oil pipelines since their beginning have for the most part been owned by oil refining or integrated oil companies. This arrangement eventually led to discriminatory practices on the part of the owning oil companies when offered oil for carriage by competing oil companies. The owning company was in the position of being able to refuse to carry at all for competitors, to impose unreasonably high "minimum tender" requirements (minimum size of shipment), to carry only if the oil were sold to it at prices acceptable to the buyer, or to carry only at high rates. Such practices had the potential of destroying competition in the oil industry.

The possible negative consequences of the situation were enhanced by the fact that much of the oil pipeline mileage was owned by the Standard Oil Company of New Jersey or affiliated companies, a company whose competitive practices were open to much criticism. The Standard Oil Company had come to dominate the oil industry in the early 1900's, partly because of its control over pipeline facilities and its success in receiving rebates from railroads and the resulting advantage it had over its competitors. In 1900 approximately 90 per cent of the investment in crude oil pipelines was by Standard Oil affiliated companies. The *trust busting* period of the early 1900's was in part a reaction to the practices and monopoly position of Standard Oil, as well as other companies in other industries. Economic regulation of oil pipelines was in part a result of that movement.

Early Regulation

By 1906 most of the older oil-producing states had some kind of common carrier requirement for oil pipelines, meaning that they were to assume the obligations of common carriers. The requirements were, however, generally ineffective because the carriers evaded regulation by buying the oil they carried[15] and because most pipeline traffic was interstate in nature and, therefore, beyond the jurisdiction of the state.

The Hepburn Act, 1906. A federal Congressional investigation into oil pipeline practices had reported that Standard Oil had profited from secret railroad rates and that its advantage over competitors was reinforced by the use of pipelines. It was charged that a combination of high pipeline and railroad rates denied independent oil companies access to oil transportation on terms that would allow them to compete with Standard Oil. It was also charged that the development of the pipeline system by Standard Oil was the result of special agreements with railroad companies.[16] At the same time, there was mounting pressure to strengthen the powers of the ICC dealing with railroads. The bill that eventually was enacted for this purpose was the Hepburn Act, which was amended to bring oil pipelines under the jurisdiction of the Commission.

The Hepburn Act contained many provisions designed to improve regulation of railroads, and it also included provisions that brought interstate pipeline transportation of oil and other commodities, except water and natural or artificial gas, under the regulatory jurisdiction of the ICC by extending provisions of the Interstate Commerce Act relating to railroads (Part I of the Act, discussed above) to the pipeline industry, with some exceptions. The Hepburn Act declared interstate pipelines to be common carriers.

The Pipe Line Cases, 1914. Many of the oil pipeline companies denied that they were common carriers and subject to the Hepburn Act and refused to cooperate with the Commission. Some companies avoided the appearance of interstate carriage by reorganizing so that a different pipeline company carried oil within each state and interchanged with another oil pipeline, owned by the same owners, at state borders. Some oil pipeline companies insisted on purchasing all oil offered to them for carriage by other oil companies. Then they claimed that since they were carrying their own oil, they were private, not common, carriers.

The ICC eventually ordered some 60 interstate oil pipeline companies to file

[15] Arthur M. Johnson, *Petroleum Pipelines and Public Policy, 1906-1959* (Cambridge, Massachusetts: Harvard University Press, 1967), p. 21.

[16] *Ibid.,* pp. 24-25.

tariffs, but 13 declined to do so. In June, 1912 the Commission ordered the 13 to file schedules of rates and charges by September 1, 1913. The pipeline companies appealed the order to the Commerce Court, which issued an injunction against enforcement of the Commission's order. The ICC then appealed to the United States Supreme Court.

In the *Pipe Line Cases*[17] of 1914, involving 6 oil pipeline companies, the Court upheld the ICC's attempt to regulate oil pipeline rates by ruling that the carriers involved in the cases, except one which carried only its own oil from its own wells to its own refinery, were common carriers in substance if not in form, even though the carriers compelled outsiders to sell oil to them to have it carried. They were, in fact, carrying everybody's oil to market. The Court held that the purchase of the oil was a mere subterfuge to avoid regulation. Later, however, in another case the Court clarified its position by ruling that oil pipelines whose services were unused, unsought after, and unneeded by independent oil companies were not subject to regulation by the Commission.[18]

The *Pipe Line Cases* decision did not require the oil pipelines to continue in operation, but it did require them not to continue to transport oil for others or oil purchased by themselves except as common carriers.

In 1977 Congress created a new federal Department of Energy to which responsibility for economic regulation of oil pipelines was eventually to be transferred from the ICC.

State economic regulation of oil pipelines has been insignificant. Slightly more than one-half of the states have instituted economic regulation of intrastate oil pipeline transportation to some extent.

RATIONALE OF ECONOMIC REGULATION OF AIR TRANSPORTATION

Reasons for Economic Regulation in the 1930's

There were several reasons for the institution of economic regulation of air transportation in the United States in the 1930's, some of which were peculiar to air transportation in that they were not of consequence in the decision to begin economic regulation of the other modes of transportation.

To Stabilize the Industry. The need to stabilize a mode of transportation so that it could serve the public adequately at reasonable prices was involved in the introduction of economic regulation of highway and water transportation, as noted previously. In the case of air transportation, the industry was said to be somewhat unstable in the 1930's, even though safety regulation and federal subsidies through the air mail program had been in effect since the mid-1920's. The instability argument was the chief reason for bringing air transportation under a system of economic regulation.

Air transportation was said to be characterized by fluctuating prices, unreliable service, and high turnover among carriers. Overcapacity in the industry

---

[17]234 U.S. 548.

[18]*United States v. Champlin Company*, 341 U.S. 290 (1951).

and the competitive bidding process for air mail contracts were said to have led to absurdly low bids and disastrous price wars. The fact that no investment in way was needed made entry relatively easy capital-wise, although the problem of overcapacity apparently did not approach that of the highway transportation industry in the 1920's and 1930's. Economic regulation was encouraged by the air transport industry. "Beginning in 1934, the air carriers themselves sought federal regulation, realizing that the history of transportation demonstrated that the absence of such regulation led to evils from which not only the public, but the industry itself, would suffer."[19] According to Dudley F. Pegrum, by 1938 the air transportation industry faced critical financial difficulties, many of the major lines faced the threat of bankruptcy, and much of the original investment in airlines had been dissipated. Financial difficulties were also aggravated by a series of accidents in the winter of 1936-1937 that undermined public confidence.[20] The fact that rail and highway transportation was already regulated had set a precedent for regulation that encouraged its enactment in air transportation.

To Improve Air Safety. Federal regulation of air transportation safety had been in effect since 1926, but it was recognized that safety regulation could not reach its maximum effectiveness if the industry were unstable and if the carriers were financially weak and unable to afford the safety precautions and devices necessary. Therefore, economic regulation was intended, in part, to stabilize air transportation so that the carriers would have the financial capacity to pay for whatever was needed to conform with safety regulation and to provide safe air transportation. The safety question was not of significance in the introduction of economic regulation in the other modes of transportation.

To Reduce Cash Subsidy. Another, although minor, reason for bringing air transportation under economic regulation was the fact that air carriers had been subsidized through the air mail program since the mid-1920's. It was believed that the amount of subsidy needed could be reduced by stabilizing the industry through economic regulation. A stabilized, financially strong airline industry would need less subsidy from the federal government. This was not a factor in the introduction of economic regulation in the other modes of transportation.

Early Regulation

Regulation Prior to 1938. The federal Air Mail Act of 1934, amended in 1935, gave certain regulatory powers over air transportation to the Post Office Department and to the ICC. The Post Office Department could prescribe the number and frequency of schedules, stops, and the departure times of aircraft carrying mail and it could prescribe a system of accounting to be used by air mail carriers. The Post Office Department also awarded contracts for carrying mail and, by doing so, helped determine the routes that would be served by airlines.

---

[19] John H. Frederick, *Commercial Air Transportation,* 5th ed. (Homewood, Illinois: Richard D. Irwin, Inc., 1961), p. 110.

[20] Pegrum, *Transportation Economics and Public Policy,* p. 337. See also Howard D. Westwood and Alexander E. Bennett, "A Footnote to the Legislative History of the Civil Aeronautics Act of 1938 and Afterward," *Notre Dame Lawyer,* February, 1967, p. 323.

The ICC had some authority over determining reasonable rates of compensation to be received by the airlines for transporting mail.

The Civil Aeronautics Act, 1938. In 1935 a special aviation commission reported to Congress and recommended that economic regulation be instituted in the airline industry. After considerable legislative maneuvering and discussion of the exact way in which regulation was to be carried out administratively,[21] Congress finally responded by enacting the Civil Aeronautics Act in 1938. The Act brought interstate air transportation under economic regulation by the Civil Aeronautics Authority. The ICC was to be relieved of any involvement in regulation of air transportation. A separate agency to regulate air transportation was set up because it was believed that the ICC was overloaded and to avoid analogies to other forms of transportation.[22] The Authority was a very complex organization that was to administer economic regulation and safety regulation and also handle promotional functions. The Authority was reorganized in 1940 by executive order of President Franklin D. Roosevelt. The Civil Aeronautics Board (CAB) of 5 members was established to administer economic regulation of air transportation, to prescribe safety standards, and to investigate aircraft accidents and make recommendations designed to prevent them in the future. The CAB was to be an independent agency, although for a time it was placed in the Department of Commerce.

The economic regulation imposed on airlines set up in 1938 was not altered by the reorganization of 1940. It provided basically the same kind of regulation that had previously been instituted in railroad, oil pipeline, and highway transportation. It applied to interstate common carriers and all carriers of mail. Contract carriers were exempt. Regulated domestic carriers were subjected to entry control by the Board, rates and fares were to be published and tariffs strictly adhered to, 30-days' notice was required before changing a rate or fare, rates and fares were to be just and reasonable, undue preference and prejudice in prices and service were prohibited, the CAB could prescribe the maximum, minimum, or actual rates and fares, abandonment of routes and mergers among air carriers could not be accomplished without approval of the Board, and pooling agreements among carriers had to meet the approval of the CAB. The Board was not given authority over airline security issues.

Unlike the regulatory systems in the other modes of transportation, the CAB was given the power to exempt any carrier or class of carriers from economic regulation, with certain exceptions, if it found that enforcement of these provisions would be an undue burden on the carrier or carriers.

Another unusual feature of air transportation regulation is that the CAB, in exercising its authority, was to consider the encouragement and development of civil aeronautics. In other words, the Board was expected to promote the development of air transportation and not restrict its development through restrictive regulatory policies. This has not been the case with the ICC.

In 1958, in a restructuring of air safety regulation and air promotion at the

---

[21] See Westwood and Bennett, "A Footnote to . . . and Afterward," p. 323.

[22] *Report of the Federal Aviation Commission,* 74th Congress, 1st Session, Senate Document Number 15 (1935), p. 244.

federal level, Congress passed the Federal Aviation Act which reenacted without substantial change the provisions of the Act of 1938 relating to economic regulation. The CAB was, however, taken out of the Department of Commerce and became a completely independent agency. Authority to establish air safety regulations was transferred from the Board to the new Federal Aviation Agency [now the Federal Aviation Administration (FAA)], but the CAB retained its accident-investigation function until 1967 when it was transferred to the new National Transportation Safety Board (NTSB).

Approximately 20 states have some degree of economic regulation of intrastate air transportation.

SELECTED REFERENCES

An excellent discussion of the development of economic regulation of railroads is D. Philip Locklin, *Economics of Transportation,* 7th ed. (Homewood, Illinois: Richard D. Irwin, Inc., 1972), Chapters 9, 10, 11, and 12. See also Dudley F. Pegrum, *Transportation Economics and Public Policy,* 3rd ed. (Homewood, Illinois: Richard D. Irwin, Inc., 1973), Chapters 12 and 13.

The background of federal economic regulation of railroads and the question of whether or not the railroads benefited more from such regulation than the public did are discussed in Robert W. Harbeson, "Transportation Regulation: A Centennial Evaluation," *ICC Practitioners' Journal,* July–August, 1972, pp. 628–633. See also Harbeson, "Railroads and Regulation, 1877–1916: Conspiracy or Public Interest?" *Journal of Economic History,* June, 1967. The view that the institution of economic regulation of railroads was primarily a response to the railroads themselves to give them rate and profit stability that they had not been able to achieve under free enterprise is presented in Gabriel Kolko, *Railroads and Regulation, 1877–1916* (Princeton, New Jersey: Princeton University Press, 1965) and George W. Hilton, "The Consistency of the Interstate Commerce Act," *Journal of Law and Economics,* October, 1966.

The reasons for subjecting highway transportation to economic regulation are discussed in G. Shorey Peterson, "Motor Carrier Regulation and Its Economic Bases," *Quarterly Journal of Economics,* August, 1929; Parker McCollester and Frank J. Clark, *Federal Motor Carrier Regulation* (New York: The Traffic Publishing Company, 1935), pp. 30–35; and Donald V. Harper, *Economic Regulation of the Motor Trucking Industry by the States* (Urbana, Illinois: University of Illinois Press, 1959), pp. 26–31.

The development of economic regulation of highway transportation is dealt with in John J. George, *Motor Carrier Regulation in the United States* (Spartanburg, South Carolina: Band and White, 1939); McCollester and Clark, *Federal Motor Carrier Regulation;* Harper, *Economic Regulation of the Motor Trucking Industry,* Chapter 3; William J. Hudson and James A. Constantine, *Motor Transportation* (New York: The Ronald Press Company, 1958), Chapter 19; Pegrum, *Transportation Economics and Public Policy,* pp. 310–321; and Locklin, *Economics of Transportation,* Chapter 29.

The complex history of the development of economic regulation of water transportation is summarized in Locklin, *Economic of Transportation,* pp. 745–760.

The development of early economic regulation of oil pipelines is discussed in Arthur M. Johnson, *Petroleum Pipelines and Public Policy, 1906-1959* (Cambridge, Massachusetts: Harvard University Press, 1967), Chapters 2 and 5.

The legislative background of the Civil Aeronautics Act is discussed in Howard D. Westwood and Alexander E. Bennett, "A Footnote to the Legislative History of the Civil Aeronautics Act of 1938 and Afterward," *Notre Dame Lawyer,* February, 1967. The rationale behind the institution of economic regulation of air transportation in the 1930's has been questioned by several authors. See, for example, Lucille S. Keys, *Federal Control of Entry into Air Transportation* (Cambridge, Massachusetts: Harvard University Press, 1951), Chapter 3. See Chapter 25 for additional references of this kind.

20

The Decision-Making Process
in Government Economic Regulation
of Transportation

Economic regulation of transportation is ordinarily carried out by a commission or board of some kind. However, in addition to regulatory agencies, legislatures, executive branches, courts, carriers, and users are all involved in determining regulatory policy. Therefore, economic regulation is the result of many and, sometimes, conflicting points of view. It is the purpose of this chapter to explain the role of the regulatory agencies, legislatures, executive branches, courts, carriers, and users in the regulatory decision-making process.

ROLE OF THE REGULATORY AGENCIES
IN THE DECISION-MAKING PROCESS

Reasons for the Commission Form of Regulation

From almost the very beginning, economic regulation of transportation has been set up in such a way that the legislative body (Congress or state legislature) enacts regulatory laws specifying in general terms what it wants regulated and then delegates the actual carrying out of regulation to a regulatory commission or board of some kind. This is known as the *commission* form of regulation. Reasons why the commission form is used are discussed below.

Legislatures Cannot Legislate Specifically Enough. The first is that the legislature would find it very difficult to regulate directly itself because it would require a statute(s) that would spell out specifically when a particular transportation practice, such as a rate or a merger, would be acceptable and when it would not be acceptable. It is impossible for such a law to anticipate and account for every possible circumstance that could come up that could justify or not justify a particular practice. It is more practical for the legislature to state in general terms what it wants regulated and then permit the regulatory agency to apply that to individual cases when they arise, interpreting the intent of the legislature and taking into account the particular circumstances surrounding the case. Even when legislatures have set down specific regulation in transportation, exceptions can be made by the regulatory agency.

Need for Expertise. A second reason is that transportation and its regulation are somewhat complex in nature and considerable knowledge about the industry is required to be effective in regulating it. Since the legislature and courts ordinarily do not have such knowledge, it appears logical to entrust the carrying out of regulation to a commission or board whose members are experts in the field of transportation. Consequently, the commission form of regulation appears to make sense, provided the regulatory agency members are truly experts.

Need for Independence. The commissions and boards established to regulate transportation are usually independent regulatory agencies, that is, they are intended to be independent from the legislative, executive, and judicial parts of government. Although the independence is not and cannot be complete, regulatory agencies are much more insulated from political pressures and influence in their decision making than would be the case if the legislature attempted to regulate transportation directly itself or if regulation were made the responsibility of the executive branch of government.

Court Work Load. The commission form of regulation provides a mechanism whereby only a handful of regulatory cases reach the courts, thereby preventing a flood of such cases into the court system. Without the commission form of regulation, the procedure would probably be that the legislature would enact laws to regulate and the interpretation in individual cases would be by the courts, not by a commission or board. The number of court cases would be tremendous and would probably lead to a breakdown of the judicial system.

In addition, courts cannot initiate action on their own motion. They can act only on the issues brought before them. A regulatory agency, however, can act on its own initiative or motion. Courts also lack the expertise that a regulatory agency may be able to have.

Functions of Regulatory Agencies

Regulatory agencies are responsible for interpreting and executing the statutes designed to regulate transportation. As such, the agencies exercise legislative executive, and judicial powers. When they prescribe action to be followed by carriers in the future, for example, when they prescribe rates, they are acting in a legislative capacity. When they act to enforce the law and rules of the agency, they are acting in an executive capacity. When they decide on the reasonableness of a rate or other practice or when they award damages, they are acting in a judicial capacity.

Federal Regulatory Agencies

There are 3 federal agencies that are primarily concerned with economic regulation of transportation: the Interstate Commerce Commission (ICC), the Civil Aeronautics Board (CAB), and the Federal Maritime Commission (FMC).

Each of these was mentioned briefly in our discussion of the rationale of economic regulation. The jurisdiction and major functions of the 3 are shown in Figure 20-1. In 1977 the annual salary of a regulatory agency member was $50,000, not $38,000 as indicated in Figure 20-1.

Interstate Commerce Commission. The oldest regulatory agency at the federal level, the ICC, has under its jurisdiction most of the domestic regulated transportation system, including rail, highway, water, and oil pipeline transportation, and also the surface freight forwarders. In 1977 Congress created a new federal Department of Energy to which responsibility for economic regulation of oil pipelines was eventually to be transferred from the ICC. The Federal Power Commission was abolished and its authority to regulate natural gas pipelines was transferred immediately to the new Department.

The ICC consists of 11 members who are appointed by the president. (A bill to reduce the size of the Commission to 7 members was being given serious consideration by Congress in 1977.) They serve 7-year terms and are eligible for reappointment. The chairman is designated by the president. The vice-chairman is elected annually by the members. The functions of the ICC vary somewhat with the mode of transportation regulated.

In order to speed the process of regulation, the Commission is allowed by law to organize itself into divisions, which it has. A division may act in behalf of the entire Commission. Under the 1977 arrangement, there are 3 ICC divisions and each division has 3 commissioners. One division deals with rates, tariffs, and valuations (freight rates, passenger fares, and valuation of rail and pipeline carriers' property), one division deals with operating authority (issuing certificates, permits, and licenses to carriers, brokers, and surface freight forwarders), and one division deals with finance and service matters (including the sale of carrier securities, consolidations and mergers, acquisitions of control of carriers, and regulation of service). The chairman and the vice-chairman do not serve on a division.

In the fiscal year 1976 (ending June 30, 1976) the ICC had an annual budget of approximately 52 million dollars and employed approximately 2,100 people.[1]

Informal Commission proceedings begin with a letter of complaint and are handled entirely by mail. They do not involve appearances before the ICC.

The decision-making process followed by the Commission in formal cases is shown in Figure 20-2. A formal case may first be heard by an Employee Board, a group of 3 or more ICC employees (not commissioners) who are authorized to review cases when testimony is not taken at a public hearing and when opposing parties do not submit evidence. The Board's decision may be appealed to the 3 commissioners of the appropriate division. The cases reviewed by Employee Boards are relatively minor ones, having to do with such things as discontinuance of highway carrier service, applications for temporary operating authority, and so on.

The more important formal cases involving matters of general transportation interest begin by being heard by an administrative law judge (formerly called a hearing examiner), a Commission employee, who collects written testimony and hears oral testimony in a public hearing. The judge usually does this in the geographic area where the case is of interest.

[1] Interstate Commerce Commission, *Annual Report, 1976* (Washington, D.C.: U.S. Government Printing Office, 1976), p. 139.

The Federal transportation regulatory agencies are arms of the legislative branch of the Government. They are NOT courts. They do have recourse to the courts in order to enforce their orders, although they exercise quasi-judicial powers, as well as quasi-legislative powers. Their members are appointed by the President with Senate approval at salaries of $38,000 with chairmen receiving an additional $2,000. Not more than a majority of one can be from any one political party.

INTERSTATE COMMERCE COMMISSION

The ICC was created in 1887 by the Act to Regulate Commerce. It currently consists of eleven members who serve terms of seven years. Its Chairman is appointed by the President, and its Vice Chairman is elected annually by the members. The following table indicates the types of domestic interstate carriers over which the Commission has economic jurisdiction, as well as its other major funcitions.

Modes Regulated	Major Functions
Railroads (1887), Express Companies, Sleeping Car Companies (1906) Oil Pipe Lines (1906)* – Common carriers only Motor Carriers (1935) Private carriers and carriers of agricultural commodities exclusively are exempt, as are motor vehicles used by farm co-ops. Water Carriers (1940), Water carriers operating coastwise, intercoastal, and on inland waters of the U.S. Carriers of liquid and/or dry bulk commodities are exempt. Freight Forwarders (1942) Non-profit shippers' associations exempt. *Gas Pipelines regulated by Federal Power Commission.	Regulates, in varying degrees by mode of transport, surface carrier operations, including rates, routes, operating rights, abandonment and mergers; conducts investigations and awards damages where applicable and administers railroad bankruptcy. Prescribes uniform system of accounts and records, evaluates property owned or used by carriers subject to the act; authorizes issuance of securities or assumption of obligations by carriers by railroad and certain common or contract carriers by motor vehicle. Develops preparedness programs covering rail, motor, and inland waterways utilization.

CIVIL AERONAUTICS BOARD

The CAB, as it exists today, is an outgrowth of the Civil Aeronautics Act of 1938, Presidential Reorganization Plans of 1940, and the Federal Aviation Act of 1958. There are five Board members, each serving terms of six years. The Chairman and Vice Chairman are appointed annually by the President.

Regulates	Major Functions
U. S. domestic and international air carriers	Regulates carrier operations, including rates, routes, operating rights, and mergers; determines and grants subsidies. Assists in the development of international air transport, and grants, subject to Presidential
Foreign air carrier operations to, from, and within the U. S.	approval, foreign operating certificates to U.S. carriers and U.S. operating permits to foreign carriers.

FEDERAL MARITIME COMMISSION

The present FMC was established by Presidential Reorganization Plan 7 of 1961, although most of its regulatory powers are similar to those granted its predecessor agencies by the Shipping Act of 1916 and subsequent statutes. The Commission consists of five members appointed to five-year terms by the President with Senate approval. The President designates the Chairman. The Vice Chairman is elected annually by the members.

Regulates	Major Functions
All U.S.-flag and foreign-flag vessels operating in the foreign commerce of the U. S. and common carriers by water operating in domestic trade to points beyond the continental U. S.	Regulates services, practices, and agreements of water common carriers in international trade. Regulates rates and practices of water common carriers operating in domestic trade to points beyond continental U. S.

FIGURE 20-1 *Federal Transportation Regulatory Agencies. (Source: Transportation Association of America,* Transportation Facts and Trends, *12th ed. (Washington, D.C.: Transportation Association of America, July, 1976), p. 36)*

After reviewing and digesting the evidence presented, the judge writes a report, which is actually a recommendation to the appropriate ICC division; the judge cannot make a decision. If no exceptions are filed, or if the division lets the recommended order stand, the recommended order becomes the order of

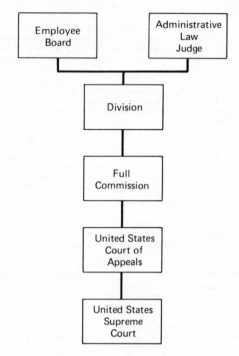

FIGURE 20-2 *Steps Involved in Interstate Commerce Commission Cases.*

the ICC. If the order is stayed, the division may or may not accept more testimony. In any event, the division makes a decision which becomes the official decision of the Commission (the division may act for the entire Commission).

If a party to a case is displeased with the decision of the division, he or she may appeal for reconsideration by the division and/or to be heard by the full Commission of 11 members. The Commission will accept a case for review if it considers the matter in question to be of "general transportation importance." If the party is denied review by the full Commission or if review is granted and the decision is unfavorable, the party involved may appeal to the federal courts for review (see below). Most cases, however, end with the decision by the division.

ICC decisions are appealable to a federal court of appeals whose decision is appealable to the United States Supreme Court.[2]

In March, 1977, a new law, the so-called Government in the Sunshine Act, went into effect which requires that some 50 federal regulatory and other agencies open most of their meetings to the public, provide transcripts of minutes of closed meetings, and announce meeting plans well in advance. The ICC, CAB, and FMC were included. The new law was the result of a growing interest in making government decision making more open to the public.

The federal transportation regulatory agencies are also subject to the require-

---

[2]Prior to 1975 most ICC decisions were appealed to federal district courts whose decisions were appealable directly to the Supreme Court.

ments of the National Environmental Policy Act of 1969 which means that they must look into the environmental consequences of their decisions. In addition, the Energy Policy and Conservation Act of 1975 requires these agencies to provide a statement of energy impact in major proceedings that describes the probable impact of such major regulatory action on energy efficiency and energy conservation.

Civil Aeronautics Board. The CAB has a much more limited jurisdiction than the ICC. It is confined to economic regulation of United States domestic and international airlines, with some jurisdiction over foreign airlines that serve the United States. In addition to regulatory functions, however, the Board is charged with promoting and developing air transportation and handles the cash subsidy program for airlines, discussed in Chapter 17.

The CAB consists of 5 members who are appointed by the president. They serve 6-year terms and are eligible for reappointment. The chairman and vice-chairman are designated by the president.

The Board had an annual budget of approximately 20 million dollars, not including money paid out by the CAB as cash subsidy to airlines, and employed approximately 750 persons in fiscal year 1976.[3]

The decision-making process in the Board is less complex than in the ICC because there are no divisions and no Employee Boards. The CAB makes more use of informal procedure than does the ICC. More than 80 per cent of its cases are informal. This means that a complaint is filed by letter and the matter is settled through correspondence. Any matter that cannot be dealt with informally may be made the subject of a formal proceeding.

Formal cases are dealt with initially by an administrative law judge, a Board employee, who recommends action by the Board. The full Board then makes its decision. The decision may be appealed to a federal court of appeals whose decision is appealable to the United States Supreme Court.

Federal Maritime Commission. The FMC is a descendant of the Shipping Board established in 1916. It deals primarily with regulation of international water commerce, but it also has regulatory jurisdiction over domestic water carriers operating between the mainland United States and offshore possessions and states.

The Commission consists of 5 members who are appointed by the president. They serve 5-year terms and may be reappointed. The president designates which member will serve as chairman; the vice-chairman is elected annually by the members.

The decision-making process of the Commission is identical to that of the CAB.

State Regulatory Agencies

Nature of State Agencies. Each state and the District of Columbia has a regulatory agency of some kind that deals with economic regulation of transportation. The names given to these agencies vary and include Public Service Commission,

---

[3]Civil Aeronautics Board, *Annual Report, 1976* (Washington, D.C.: U.S. Government Printing Office, 1976), p. 66.

Public Utilities Commission, Railroad Commission, Commerce Commission, Transportation Commission, and Corporation Commission. In many cases, the regulatory agency has under its jurisdiction nontransportation industries, such as electric power, natural gas, and public warehouses, as well as transportation. They usually regulate both railroad and highway transportation. In approximately 20 states air transportation is subject to economic regulation. State regulation of some kind applicable to water carriers and oil pipelines is found in approximately 30 states.[4]

The size of the state commissions and boards is usually from 3 to 5 members. They are appointed by the state governor in approximately two-thirds of the states and they are elected by the general public in the remaining states, with the exception of 2 states in which the state legislatures elect the members.[5]

The degree of jurisdiction over the carriers regulated varies widely from state to state. In some states regulation is very severe on such things as entry control in the highway carrier industry. In other states regulation is lax. The influence of state regulation in transportation has deteriorated over the years because Congress and the courts have granted the federal government greater authority to interfere in intrastate transportation matters.

State regulatory agencies generally operate with much smaller budgets, numbers of employees, and lower salaries than is true at the federal level. In Minnesota, for example, the Public Service Commission, which consists of 5 members appointed by the governor with the consent of the state Senate, has an annual budget of approximately 3.4 million dollars and a working force of approximately 150 people for regulatory purposes.[6] The effort and money that are expended varies widely between states.

The procedures followed in handling cases at the state level are similar to the procedures followed by federal agencies, although some state agencies do not have employee boards, administrative law judges, or hearing examiners. Instead, the commission or board itself hears every formal case from the beginning.

Federal-State Relations. Under the Interstate Commerce Act, the ICC shall appoint a joint board consisting of state regulatory agency representatives to act for the Commission in highway carrier matters involving 3 states or less. The decisions of such joint boards are appealable to the ICC. Many highway carrier cases are handled by joint boards.

Another kind of federal-state cooperation was made possible by federal legislation enacted in 1965 that provides for federal-state joint efforts to eliminate illegal motor truck transportation (unauthorized for-hire trucking service). The law permits states to require interstate truck operators to register and provides for cooperative agreements between the ICC and the states for investigation of illegal practices, facilitation of information flow between the states and the ICC, state-federal training schools for enforcement personnel, and joint road checks by the states and the ICC.

Finally, there is the question of federal or state regulatory jurisdiction over a

---

[4]Charles F. Phillips, Jr., *The Economics of Regulation,* 2nd ed. (Homewood, Illinois: Richard D. Irwin Inc., 1969), p. 91.

[5]*Ibid.* See also Roy J. Sampson and Martin T. Farris, *Domestic Transportation: Practice, Theory, and Policy,* 3rd ed. (Boston: Houghton Mifflin Company, 1975), p. 393.

[6]Minnesota Department of Public Service, *Biennial Report, 1974-1976* (St. Paul, Minnesota: Department of Public Service, 1976), p. 13.

given transportation matter. The commerce clause of the federal Constitution delegates the regulation of commerce between the states to the federal government, as noted previously. Regulation of intrastate commerce is left to the states. Several court cases were referred to in Chapter 19 that helped define the jurisdiction of the 2 levels of government. These were the Granger cases, the Wabash case, and the several cases dealing with early state regulation of entry into the highway transportation industry. When a matter is clearly interstate in nature, the federal government ordinarily has jurisdiction. When it is clearly intrastate in nature, the state government usually has the right to regulate.

However, despite the court decisions discussed earlier, there remains some problem of state regulations that apply to interstate carriers. If a state regulates carriers in interstate commerce and if the federal government has not instituted regulation of that particular subject matter, the state regulation is allowed to stand, provided the effect on interstate commerce is minor and is not discriminatory against interstate commerce. If, however, the federal government should institute interstate regulation of that matter, the federal regulation supersedes that of the state.

Specific problems in distinguishing between interstate and intrastate commerce and the jurisdiction of the federal and state regulatory agencies arise from time to time and are discussed in Chapters 21, 22, and 23. It is sufficient to state here that the role of the states in regulating intrastate transportation has diminished as the role of the federal government in intrastate matters has increased over the years.

ROLE OF THE LEGISLATURE IN THE DECISION-MAKING PROCESS

The source of economic regulation of transportation is the federal Congress or the state legislature. These bodies enact the statutes providing for regulation, they create the regulatory agencies, and they provide the money with which regulation is carried out. Regulation and the regulatory agencies are, therefore, creatures of the legislatures and can be weakened, strengthened, or abolished by legislatures either by enacting changes in regulatory laws or by adjusting the amount of money provided to carry out regulation.

The legislature often also must pass on appointments to the regulatory agencies made by the president or state governor.

The statutory relationship between the legislature and the regulatory agency at the federal level, and usually at the state level, is that the legislature enacts laws containing general statements on what regulation is to achieve and consist of and the regulatory agency applies the general statements to individual cases. The legislature does not attempt to spell out in detail what is and what is not acceptable. Thus, for example, the Interstate Commerce Act provides that an interstate highway carrier shall not be authorized as a contract carrier unless the ICC finds, among other things, that the proposed operation will be "consistent with the public interest." Railroad rates are to be "just and reasonable." In these and other instances, Congress did not attempt to spell out what was meant by "consistent with public interest" or "just and reasonable." Instead, that task was left to the body of experts, i.e., the regulatory agency. Although the Constitution provides that Congress cannot delegate its legislative power to others, the delegation of power to the regulatory agencies has been upheld by the United States Supreme Court because Congress does provide standards, such as "consistent with the public interest," for the agencies to follow, although, admittedly, they are very broad and to some persons vague.[7] In 1977, a year in which government regulatory agencies of all kinds were under severe criticism, several bills were being considered by Congress that would tighten up the control exercised by Congress over the independent regulatory agencies, including those in transportation.

As noted in Chapter 18, legislatures rely on committees to screen proposed legislation before it reaches the full body for debate and vote. In the federal Congress the important committees that deal with economic regulation of transportation are the Commerce, Science, and Transportation Committee in the Senate and the Interstate and Foreign Commerce Committee and the Public Works and Transportation Committee in the House of Representatives. New legislation dealing with economic regulation is referrred to these committees. Hearings are held, compromises are made, and a decision either to support or not to support a proposal and send it forward to the full legislative body is made. Bills for the actual appropriation of funds must be reviewed by the Appropriations Committee in each house. When these various committees approve legislation, it is sent either to the floor of the Senate or the House where the legislative process continues, as described in Chapter 18. Thus, as with promotional programs, authority over legislation dealing with economic regulation of transportation is divided among several committees, and there is a problem of lack of coordination among these committees and among them and other committees dealing with other aspects of transportation, particularly promotion of transportation.

ROLE OF THE EXECUTIVE BRANCH IN THE DECISION-MAKING PROCESS

At the federal level, and usually at the state level, the primary role of the executive branch of government is to appoint the members of the regulatory agencies, usually with the "advice and consent" of the upper house of the legislature or both houses of the legislature. Thus, appointments to the ICC, CAB, and FMC are made by the president of the United States with the advice and consent of the Senate. The president also has the authority to designate which agency member will serve as chairman.

In order to keep the regulatory agencies as independent as possible and free from political pressure, there usually are restrictions within which the appointment process may be exercised by the executive. This usually includes restrictions on how many members may be of the same political party. The members serve for fixed terms of so many years (usually longer than a single term of the executive), and they cannot be removed from office unless it can be shown that

[7]There have been many court cases on this issue. The United States Supreme Court held in *Schechter Poultry Corporation v. United States*, 295 U.S. 495 (1935) that the National Recovery Act was unconstitutional because it, among other things, constituted a delegation of legislative authority by Congress to the president of the United States, without providing legislative standards to limit the exercise of the power that was delegated.

inefficiency, neglect of duty, or malfeasance in office has taken place, which rarely happens. Finally, the terms of the members usually expire at different times (they are "staggered") so that a given executive rarely has opportunity to appoint all the members of a given agency during his or her term of office.

Another connection between the executive branch and regulatory agencies is in the budgetary process. Although the executive cannot appropriate money, he may recommend to the legislature how much money the agencies should have and may veto appropriation bills enacted by the legislature.

The executive may also take a leadership role by doing research and recommending legislation on economic regulation and may exert considerable influence over what laws are passed. In addition, he or she also has the veto power over regulatory legislation. The executive usually has more influence in the legislature than does the regulatory agency.

Finally, the enforcement of obedience to the regulatory laws is partly the responsibility of the executive branch. At the federal level, for example, the regulatory agencies usually refer violations of the regulatory statutes to the United States Attorney General for criminal prosecution. In civil matters in which the agency is trying to recover penalties (fines), to compel the filing of reports, or to stop respondents from engaging in some practice, the Attorney General is also asked to take action. The Attorney General also represents the agencies in court when an agency order or decision is in dispute. This has led to some awkward situations because the United States Department of Justice and the regulatory agencies are sometimes not in agreement on a particular issue. The ICC and CAB, as a result, have asked Congress to be permitted to represent themselves in court.

ROLE OF THE COURTS IN THE DECISION-MAKING PROCESS

The courts play an important part in economic regulation of transportation. Their function is to act as a review body (see below), hear cases and impose penalties for violations of the regulatory statutes, compel observance of orders and compliance with the law by injunction or mandamus, consider civil suits involving regulatory laws and award damages, try criminal cases, enforce the common law obligations of the carriers when they are not covered by statute, determine the constitutionality of the regulatory laws, and compel the regulatory agencies to carry out their responsibilities.

A regulatory agency usually must rely on the courts to assist in enforcing its orders and to levy penalties. Orders of regulatory agencies are usually binding upon the parties involved unless set aside by a court order stemming from an appeal. In some cases, fines begin automatically upon the effective date of an agency order. The agency has the right to seek court action to enforce compliance if a carrier continues to disobey the order. A writ of injunction (an order to stop or to do something) or a writ of mandamus (an order to do something) may be issued by a court in such cases and, under the Interstate Commerce Act, this would be automatically done if the order of the ICC is properly made and duly served. This is rarely resorted to by the Commission.

The aspect of judicial participation in the regulatory process that is of most interest here is that of judicial review. Whenever a legislature delegates significant power to a regulatory agency, there is the danger that the agency will abuse that power through arbitrary or capricious action or by acting beyond the authority given to it. Consequently, some check on what the agencies do is necessary. But checking on or reviewing every decision made by a regulatory agency would have the effect of degrading the agency and making it virtually without real authority because the "real" decisions are made elsewhere. This is actually what did happen to the ICC in its early years. Therefore, some compromise between no review at all and complete review of every decision appears to be what is needed.

The issue at the federal level was settled in 1910 and 1912 when the United States Supreme Court set forth the policy that would be followed henceforth by the federal courts in reviewing decisions of the ICC.[8] The policy is essentially the same for the other federal transportation regulatory agencies. The Supreme Court stated that the federal courts would accept for review only those cases that involved the power and right of the ICC to make the decision in question. They would not accept for review cases that involved "findings of fact" or were of a strictly "administrative" nature in which the Commission was well-qualified to make such decisions and if there were no questions of power and right involved. Thus, decisions on whether or not a rate is reasonable or discrimination is unjust are left to the agencies to determine; the courts will not substitute their judgment.

What this means is that to get a federal regulatory agency's decision reviewed by a federal court, the plaintiff must convince the court that there is reason to believe that a question of the power and right of the agency to make such a decision is involved. Such questions could be based on a number of grounds or reasons; the law itself is unconstitutional; the agency exceeded its authority under the law; the decision is not supported by the evidence in the case; the agency misinterpreted the statute; or a constitutional guarantee has been violated. Matters of law must be argued; the courts generally accept the agency's determination of facts and the agency has "primary jurisdiction" to determine what is "just and reasonable" or "unduly preferential" and to determine other such matters, as noted earlier.

The above discussion applies to cases in which the regulatory agency has ordered the respondents to do or not to do certain things. Any case in which the regulatory agency has awarded the payment of money to one party by another is reviewed by the courts, regardless of the existence of power and right issues.

The result of the policy on judicial review is that most decisions made by federal regulatory agencies are not reviewable by the courts because they do not involve questions of power and right.

ROLE OF THE CARRIER IN THE
DECISION-MAKING PROCESS

The carriers are deeply involved in the regulatory process because they are the ones being regulated. Consequently, although they themselves do not make regulatory decisions, regardless of their views on regulation and whether or not

[8]*Interstate Commerce Commission v. Illinois Central Railroad Company*, 215 U.S. 452 (1910) and *Interstate Commerce Commission v. Union Pacific Railroad Company*, 222 U.S. 541 (1912).

they want to participate, they are forced to participate and, in fact, it is in their best interest to do so to whatever extent is possible in order to protect their interests.

Legislative Decision Making

Since the source of economic regulation is the legislature, it is in the interests of the carriers to try to influence the decisions made by legislators regarding regulatory legislation. As with government promotional programs, this is done through various lobbying efforts to promote or work against specific legislation being considered and includes testifying at legislative hearings and investigations, contacting individual legislators, and publicizing the carriers' position on a given issue by providing information to the news media, the general public, educators, businessmen, and others. Although individual carriers may do this, it is usually accomplished by carrier trade associations such as the American Trucking Associations. In this way, the carriers are usually well-represented in the legislative decision-making process and probably have had considerable influence on the decisions that have been made at the federal and state levels, although their effect is difficult to measure. The official position of a carrier organization may not entirely reflect the views of all the members, particularly in the larger associations that have thousands of members.[9]

Regulatory Agency Decision Making

Because the carriers are the parties being regulated, they have no choice but to participate in the decision-making process of the regulatory agencies. Consequently, the carriers' point of view is always heard in the process.

Most of the issues dealt with by the regulatory agencies are initiated by carriers; only occasionally are the users or the agencies themselves the initiators, although the agencies, unlike courts, can initiate investigations, hearings, and rule making on their own motion. Carrier initiative takes the form of a carrier or carriers proposing a rate change, or a merger, or whatever. The regulatory agency then begins the process described earlier, often with the assignment of the case to an administrative law judge if a federal agency is involved. Other carriers, users, and other government agencies may come into the case as proponents or opponents.

The carriers, as initiators, proponents, or opponents, must prepare evidence to present to the regulatory agency and must appear at agency hearings and court proceedings. This may involve considerable time, expense, and knowledge and, as a result, some carriers participate more actively than others. It can be done through carrier associations as well as individually, of course.

In addition to these activities, carriers are required to file numerous periodic reports which are of use to regulatory agencies in making decisions and recommending legislation.

---

[9]The role of industry associations in the regulatory process is dealt with in Hugh S. Norton, *Modern Transportation Economics,* 2nd ed. (Columbus, Ohio: Charles E. Merrill Publishing Company, 1971), pp. 325–328.

ROLE OF THE USER IN THE
DECISION-MAKING PROCESS

Legislative Decision Making

The purpose of economic regulation of transportation is to provide the public with adequate transportation service at reasonable cost. Therefore, the user of transportation should be expected to play an important role in the regulatory decision-making process. The user, either of passenger or freight service, or user organization (such as those mentioned in Chapter 18), has the right to be heard from in the legislative process, although most users do not take advantage of the opportunity because they lack the time, money, knowledge, or interest. The individual users that do participate at the legislative level tend to be large business firms. Smaller users tend to rely on a trade or other association to represent them. As is the case with legislation dealing with promotion of transportation, users are less well organized than are carriers and are much less unified in their approach to and interest in regulatory legislation than are the carriers.

Individual citizens are rarely interested in regulatory questions, but they have the right to participate in and influence the legislative process. They have been the least effective of the various parties because they do not have organizations to represent them, although in recent years various citizen groups and environmental organizations have played an increasing role.

Regulatory Agency Decision Making

Users may participate in the decision making of regulatory agencies. To begin with, users of freight and passenger service may negotiate with or bargain with the carriers on prices and services provided, just as they may in most other industries. When an agreement has been reached, the carrier must then propose the new price or service (if it is a regulated matter) to the appropriate state or federal regulatory agency (perhaps through a rate bureau first), at which time the regulatory process described previously begins. Many proposals made by carriers are at the request of users. However, the larger user is more likely to be able to strike a satisfactory bargain with a carrier than is the smaller user. Group effort through trade or other associations can help to alleviate this problem for the smaller users.

In the regulatory process the freight or passenger service user has the right to participate as a proponent or opponent of what is being considered. This may require gathering and presenting evidence at agency hearings and court proceedings, which, of course, may involve considerable time and expense for the user.

Unfortunately, many users do not actively participate in the regulatory process, or they do so only infrequently because they lack the time, money, expertise, or interest. The users that participate most frequently and regularly tend to be the larger users, although representation through trade or other associations may also permit smaller users to participate. In a way, then, the decision-making process in regulation is discriminatory against smaller users because they are in a weaker bargaining position with carriers and cannot participate as fully in the regulatory process itself. In 1977 the ICC established a Small Business Assistance Office to help small carriers and to assist small shippers and receivers in using transportation service.

Finally, there are the individual citizens who may be interested in regulatory proceedings. They have been ineffective in influencing decision making directly, although in recent years various citizen groups and environmental organizations have become more active. The lack of adequate consumer or public representation in the proceedings of regulatory agencies has been criticized by consumer groups.[10] However, the ICC believes that the "public" that it should be concerned with, at least on the freight side of things, consists of the business firms and other organizations that buy freight transportation service, and not the individual citizen.[11] The Railroad Revitalization and Regulatory Reform (4R) Act of 1976 established an Office of Rail Public Counsel as an independent office affiliated with the Commission to represent the public interest, to participate in cases before the ICC, and to bring issues before the Commission. In 1974 the CAB redesignated its Office of Consumer Affairs as the Office of the Consumer Advocate and authorized it to participate as a party in proceedings before the Board. The Office can initiate proceedings before the CAB and provide expertise on topics of consumer concern, in addition to its previous function of handling complaints from consumers of air transportation service.[12]

ISSUES IN THE COMMISSION FORM OF REGULATION

The commission form of economic regulation of transportation was adopted because there did not seem to be any alternatives that were better (for the reasons given at the beginning of this chapter). The commission form of regulation is far from perfect. Some of the specific criticisms of the commission form of regulation are discussed in this section. The issue of whether or not economic regulation, per se, whether through the commission or some other form, should be continued in its present form, should be modified, or should be eliminated is dealt with in Chapter 25.

Quality of Personnel

A frequent criticism of the regulatory system is that the people who are appointed to regulatory agencies are not the most qualified people available. It is a fact that many appointments to transportation regulatory agencies at both the federal and state levels are political in nature, that is, the appointment is made to repay a political debt or to provide employment for a party worker or former office holder, regardless of whether or not the appointee has any training or experience for the job. Although many of these appointees do eventually become excellent agency members, some do not and considerable time must elapse before they become effective contributors even when that happens. The problem appears to be worse at the state level than at the federal level, although recent presidents have shown a lack of interest in appointing highly qualified

---

[10] One of the criticisms made of the ICC by a consumer-interest organization report on the Commission was the lack of public or consumer representation. See Rober Fellmeth, *The Interstate Commerce Omission* (New York: Grossman Publishers, 1970), chapter 1.

[11] See Colin Barrett, "A Difference in Philosophy," *Transportation and Distribution Management*, May, 1970.

[12] Civil Aeronautics Board, *Annual Report, 1975*, p. 68.

people to the federal agencies. The unfortunate fact is that a well-qualified regulatory body and a mediocre law provide better regulation than do a good law and a mediocre regulatory body.

Arbitrary Action

A possible danger in the commission form of regulation is that the agency will act arbitrarily, capriciously, or unfairly in dealing with the carriers under regulation. Judicial review, as discussed earlier, is designed to prevent this, but, as we have seen, judicial review has been limited by the United States Supreme Court to cases of power and right. Therefore, the regulatory agencies are to a great extent not subject to review and, as a result, have a considerable amount of freedom of action.

Independence of the Agency

Regulatory agencies have been established at the federal level, and often at the state level, as independent agencies. This means that the agencies are insulated from political interference from the legislative and executive branches of government, particularly the latter, as much as possible. The various restrictions on the executive as to the political party of the appointees, fixed terms of office, and so forth, are intended to provide for independence of the agency from the executive. However, even though in most cases the president or governor can appoint only a limited number of members from his own party, it is usually not difficult to find someone of the other political party who is in agreement with the president or governor.

Nevertheless, for the most part, the system has worked well at the federal level but not as well at the state level. It should be noted that there have been efforts in the past to place the federal regulatory agencies under the executive branch, and this has actually happened in some states. The result of such a structure is that regulation becomes an instrument of the current administration's political policy and it loses its objectivity and impartial character. The fact that the president now designates who is to be the chairman of the federal agencies to some degree makes the chairman the instrument or representative of the president and, therefore, the independence of the agencies is somewhat diminished.

Control by the Regulated

A frequently made charge is that the regulatory agencies eventually become "captured" by the carriers under regulation, that is, they regulate in the interests of the carriers instead of in the interests of the public. This is often used as an argument for eliminating economic regulation entirely. It was noted earlier that the carrier side is always well represented in the agency decision-making process but that the user side is frequently not well represented. This can lead to carrier-oriented regulation.

There have been occasional instances of unethical conduct on the part of agency members involving their relationships with regulated carriers. Carriers, however, often claim that the regulators are too hard on them. In other words, opposite arguments are made on this point and some evidence supporting both arguments can probably be found. It is beyond the scope of this book to delve into this any further. In any event, the interests of the carriers must be recognized in economic regulation because, without adequate revenue and financial strength and stability, the transportation system cannot provide adequate service to the public. Nevertheless, the public interest must be foremost and regulators must regulate primarily in the interest of the public, not the carriers. Balancing these two somewhat opposite goals is difficult for regulators to accomplish.

Inconsistent Decisions

Because the personnel and the circumstances involved change over time, as does the legislation upon which regulation is based, there is the potential problem of inconsistency in decision making by the regulatory agencies. This has been more of a problem with some federal agencies than with others.

Slowness and Inefficiency

Perhaps the most serious and valid criticism of the regulatory process is its slowness. The time required to reach a decision is often very long. For example, in June, 1976 there were 7,382 formal cases pending before the ICC.[13] It was reported in 1976 that the average length of time required by the Commission to handle formal cases of different categories ranged from 11.6 months to 25.1 months.[14]

The time problem is caused by the large volume of work handled by regulatory agencies,[15] the fact that the agencies try to hear everyone who has a legitimate interest in the matter at hand and, probably, some inefficiency on their part. The federal agencies have taken various steps to speed up their decision-making process in recent years. Several provisions of the 4R Act of 1976 had the objective of speeding up ICC decision making on railroads, but a critical and, it appears, permanent problem associated with economic regulation is the time problem.

A Single Regulatory Agency

When air transportation was brought under federal economic regulation in 1938, it was decided, after considerable debate, to place such regulation under the jurisdiction of a new and separate regulatory agency, which is now the CAB, instead of placing it under the jurisdiction of the ICC. A predecessor of the FMC already existed at that time.

Since then it has been proposed many times that all federal economic regulation of transportation be consolidated into one regulatory agency instead of

---

[13] Interstate Commerce Commission, *Annual Report, 1976*, p. 119.

[14] *Ibid.*, pp. 113–114.

[15] In fiscal year 1976, for example, the ICC handled 8,844 formal cases and 19,057 informal cases, was involved in 267 court challenges, and received 353,047 tariffs filed by regulated carriers. Interstate Commerce Commission, *Annual Report, 1976*, p. v.

3.[16] The reasons usually advanced for this are that it would be more efficient and less duplicative and it would result in coordinated regulation instead of fragmented regulation wherein the 3 agencies regulate without regard to what the other agencies are doing. It would also simplify the problem of intermodal cooperation through interchange of traffic, containerization, and ownership of carriers of one mode by carriers of another mode.

Counter agruments are that consolidation would result in even more inefficiency and delay than we already have because of the large size of the agency and its tremendous work load. Also, as far as air transportation is concerned, it is argued that the special economic and service characteristics of air transportation would not be recognized by the single regulatory agency.

To date, nothing has been done to move toward the single agency approach to economic regulation of transportation. In fact, the eventual transfer of the responsibility for economic regulation of interstate oil pipelines from the ICC to the new Department of Energy is a step in the opposite direction.

SELECTED REFERENCES

There is a large amount of literature available on the independent regulatory agencies. An excellent review of the regulatory agencies in general is Roy J. Sampson and Martin T. Farris, *Domestic Transportation: Practice, Theory, and Policy,* 3rd ed. (Boston: Houghton-Mifflin Company, 1975), Chapter 24. See also D. Philip Locklin, *Economic of Transportation,* 7th ed. (Homewood, Illinois: Richard D. Irwin, Inc., 1972), Chapter 13 and Henry J. Friendly, *The Federal Administrative Agencies* (Cambridge, Massachusetts: Harvard University Press, 1962).

A good discussion of the procedures followed by the ICC, CAB, and FMC is Charles A. Taff, *Management of Physical Distribution and Transportation,* 5th ed. (Homewood, Illinois: Richard D. Irwin, Inc., 1972), pp. 480–490. See also John Guandolo, *Transportation Law,* 2nd ed. (Dubuque, Iowa: William C. Brown Company Publishers, 1973), Chapters 55, 56, and 57 and Marvin L. Fair and John Guandolo, *Transportation Regulation,* 7th ed. (Dubuque, Iowa: William C. Brown Company Publishers, 1972), Chapter 9.

Current developments in federal regulatory agency jurisdiction, organization, and procedures are summarized in the annual reports of the Interstate Commerce Commission, Civil Aeronautics Board, and Federal Maritime Commission available from the U.S. Government Printing Office, Washington, D.C.

The organization and jurisdiction of state regulatory agencies are described in Charles F. Phillips, Jr., *The Economics of Regulation,* 2nd ed. (Homewood, Illinois: Richard D. Irwin, Inc., 1969), pp. 90–101. See also the annual reports of the National Association of Regulatory Utility Commissioners, Interstate Commerce Commission Building, Washington, D.C.

---

[16]See, for example, *National Transportation Policy,* 87th Congress, 1st Session, Senate Report Number 334 (Doyle Report) (Washington, D.C.: U.S. Government Printing Office, 1961), pp. 107–111 and the President's Council on Executive Organization, *Report on Selected Independent Regulatory Agencies* (Ash Report) (Washington, D.C.: U.S. Government Printing Office, 1971), pp. 61–85.

The question of the declining independence of federal regulatory agencies is dealt with in A. Everette MacIntyre, "Status of Regulatory Independence," *Federal Bar Journal*, Winter, 1969.

The process of judicial review of decisions of federal regulatory agencies is discussed in Herbert Burstein, "Judicial Review of ICC Orders," *ICC Practitioners' Journal* January–February, 1971 and Locklin, *Economics of Transportation*, pp. 293–299. See also Guandolo, *Transportation Law*, Chapters 58, 59, and 60 and Fair and Guandolo, *Transportation Regulation*, Chapter 10.

Criticism of the lack of a role for the public or the consumer in the regulatory process is presented in Robert J. Fellmeth, *The Interstate Commerce Omission* (New York: Grossman Publishers, 1970), Chapter 1. Charles A. Webb, "Mr. Nader: Meet the Consumers of Transportation," *ICC Practitioners' Journal*, July–August, 1970 is a response to that criticism. See also Colin Barrett, "A Difference in Philosophy," *Transportation and Distribution Management*, May, 1970.

For a discussion of the role of the president, Congress, the regulatory agencies, the courts, and carrier associations in formulating federal regulatory policy, see Hugh S. Norton, *National Transportation Policy: Formulation and Implementation* (Berkeley, California: McCutchan Publishing Corporation, 1966), Chapters 8 through 13.

General discussions of the problems associated with the commission form of regulation are Dudley F. Pegrum, *Transportation Economics and Public Policy*, 3rd ed. (Homewood, Illinois: Richard D. Irwin, Inc., 1973), pp. 491–501 and Phillips, *The Economics of Regulation*, pp. 691–712. Highly critical discussions of regulatory agencies are Fellmeth, *The Interstate Commerce Omission* and George W. Hilton, "The Basic Behavior of Regulatory Commissions," *Papers and Proceedings, American Economic Association*, May, 1972 and "The Two Things Wrong with the Interstate Commerce Commission," *Proceedings of Transportation Research Forum, 1970*. See also Grant M. Davis, "The Basic Behavior of Regulatory Commissions—A Reply," *Transporation Journal*, Fall, 1972. Recent critical Congressional reports dealing with transportation regulatory agencies are reported on in "House Subcommittee, Using ICC Data, Finds Commission 'Anti-Competitive'" *Traffic World*, October 25, 1976, p. 11 and "Senate Unit Lists 53 Recommendations After Analyzing Regulatory Agencies," *Traffic World*, February 28, 1977, p. 32. The time problem in commission regulation is dealt with in Robert H. Haskell, "Why the Regulatory Lag?" *ICC Practitioners' Journal*, July–August, 1967.

Reorganization of the federal regulatory structure has been studied several times. Recent studies include James M. Landis, *Report on Regulatory Agencies to the President-Elect* (Washington, D.C.: U.S. Government Printing Office, 1960) and the President's Advisory Council on Executive Organization, *Report on Selected Independent Regulatory Agencies* (Ash Report) (Washington, D.C.: U.S. Government Printing Office, 1971). The latter endorsed consolidation of transportation regulation into a single agency and is reviewed in Stephen Breyer, "The Ash Council's Report on the Independent Regulatory Agencies," *Bell Journal of Economics and Management Science*, Autumn, 1971. The question of a single federal transportation regulatory agency is dealt with in Grant M. Davis, "An Evaluation of the Propriety of Establishing One Consolidated Transportation Regulatory Commission," *ICC Practitioners' Journal*, July–August, 1971.

21

Government Economic Regulation
of Railroad Transportation

In this chapter our purpose is to discuss the economic regulation of railroad transportation as it exists today. The emphasis is on what is regulated and on regulatory policy rather than on the mechanisms involved in carrying out regulation.

Economic regulation of railroads by the federal government dates from 1887 and is the result today of a long series of laws and amendments and Interstate Commerce Commission (ICC) and court decisions. It is a very complex structure in terms of what is regulated, what regulatory policy is, and how such regulation is carried out. In the following paragraphs we shall attempt to review federal economic regulation of railroad transportation as it exists in the 1970's, focusing on 6 major areas of regulation: entry, exit, rates and fares, service, accounting and financial matters, and consolidations or mergers. Unless otherwise noted, the regulation discussed applies to the National Railroad Passenger Corporation (Amtrak).

REGULATION OF ENTRY

Early regulation of railroads focused heavily on the pricing function and ignored questions of entry and exit and many other aspects of railroad operation. Entry into the railroad industry was not controlled by the federal government until 1920, when the Transportation Act of that year provided that a certificate of public convenience and necessity be obtained from the ICC before new interstate railroad lines or extensions of lines could be constructed. Because the railroad building era was essentially over by 1920, this entry control provision has had little effect on the industry.

New construction does occasionally take place, but it is usually for short distances to serve new industries and, in such situations, the Commission takes into account the effect the new construction might have on other railroads and whether or not a useful public service will be provided.

EXEMPTIONS FROM REGULATION

Prior to 1976 all for-hire interstate railroad common carriers were subject to economic regulation by the ICC, i.e., there were no exemptions from regulation. The Railroad Revitalization and Regulatory Reform (4R) Act of 1976, however, provided that if the Commission determines that the application of regulation to any person, class of persons, or services is unnecessary to effectuate the National Transportation Policy, would be an undue burden on such person, class of persons, or on interstate or foreign commerce, and would serve little or no useful public purpose, it may exempt such person, class of persons, or services from the provisions of Part I of the Interstate Commerce Act. Whether or not this exemption provision will result in any significant change in the scope of ICC jurisdiction over railroads remains to be seen.

REGULATION OF EXIT

Line Abandonment

Nature of the Abandonment Problem. Since the early 1900's many thousands of miles of railroad line have been abandoned in the United States. The mileage declined from approximately 254,000 miles of line in 1916 to approximately 200,000 miles in 1975.[1]

The reasons for abandonment include competition from other modes of transportation, closing down of industry on the line, rising operating and maintenance costs, depletion of natural resources in the area, population shifts, the need for extensive rehabilitation of the line in the face of low traffic volume, and the fact that the line never should have been built. The basic problem is that the railroad feels that the traffic is insufficient to produce revenue that will cover the cost of operation and maintenance and, perhaps, rehabilitation of a deteriorated roadbed and track.

ICC Policy on Line Abandonments. Regulation of exit of railroads is intended to prevent hardship on the users of railroad service. Ever since Congress enacted legislation in 1920 the federal government has had virtually complete control over railroad abandonments, including those in intrastate commerce. The Interstate Commerce Act provides that a railroad must secure a certificate of public convenience and necessity from the ICC before it can abandon. Excluded from Commission jurisdiction is abandonment of spur, industrial, team, switching, or side tracks located in one state.

[1] Association of American Railroads, *Railroad Facts,* 1977 ed. (Washington, D.C.: Association of American Railroads, 1977), p. 46. Figures do not include yard tracks or sidings and they do not reflect the fact that a mile of railroad line may include 2 or more parallel tracks.

The policy of the ICC in handling railroad abandonment cases has varied somewhat over the years since 1920 and has been the subject of considerable controversy in recent years. The Commission has had to balance the interests of the users in retaining railroad service and the losses incurred by the railroad including, in many cases, the cost of rehabilitating a deteriorated line. The users and communities that rely on the line in question stress the costs, such as disruptions in businesses, loss of employment, declining property values, and higher rates paid to other modes of transportation. The railroads wish to eliminate an aspect of their business that is either marginally profitable or that is a contributor of losses. Each case has been handled individually on its own merits.

The Commission authorized the abandonment of 68,785 miles of railroad line from 1920 through June 30, 1976.[2] When abandonment was permitted, the Commission believed that losses to the carriers would outweigh the benefits of keeping the lines in operation. Not all of this mileage went out of service because some of it was taken over by other railroads or other operators. In a few instances the carrier decided not to abandon even though approval had been obtained.

The number of applications for abandonment received by the ICC per year has increased. They averaged approximately 80 per year in the 1950's and over 100 in the 1960's. In the early 1970's they averaged over 200 per year.[3] The majority of the applications are disposed of by the Commission without a public hearing because there is a lack of significant protest or there is no general importance attached to the case. A study of applications filed and cases decided between fiscal 1961 and fiscal 1970 showed that 25 per cent of the cases were handled by public hearing. Over 90 per cent of all applications were approved and many of the remainder were withdrawn. Even those that were denied were usually resubmitted and eventually approved. The fact that there is regulation of abandonment, however, means that railroad management assesses the chances of receiving approval, given the conditions needed for abandonment as evidenced by previous ICC decisions, and will apply for abandonment only when it is probable that it will be approved. The railroad will also compare the benefits of abandonment with the costs of submitting the application, which may be considerable.[4] Therefore, the result is that a high percentage of applications are approved because only those that have a high likelihood of approval are submitted.

In most cases there has been considerable delay. Commission abandonment cases that involved a public hearing in the 1960's took an average of 410 days from the filing date to the decision date.[5] In 1972 the ICC attempted to speed up and clarify the process of handling abandonment cases by adopting the "34 car rule," which provided that a presumption exists that public convenience and necessity do not require the maintenance and/or continued operation upon proof that, on the average, fewer than 34 carloads of freight per mile were carried over the line during the 12 months preceding filing of the application.

[2] Interstate Commerce Commission, *Annual Report, 1976* (Washington, D.C.: U.S. Government Printing Office, 1976), p. 119.

[3] W. Bruce Allen, "ICC Behavior in Rail Abandonments," *ICC Practitioners' Journal,* July–August, 1974, p. 554.

[4] *Ibid.,* pp. 554–555.

[5] *Ibid.,* p. 555.

This ruling was upheld by the United States Supreme Court in 1973.[6] Because the ICC adopted new procedural regulations covering abandonments in late 1976 to comply with the provisions of the 4R Act of 1976, the Commission decided that the 34 car rule was no longer needed and it was dropped. The new procedural regulations outline the data to be given in an application to abandon, the steps to be taken by those who wish to oppose an abandonment, and set forth standards to be used to determine the costs and revenues of the line to be abandoned.

Railroad mileage not included in the United States Railway Association (USRA) Final System Plan for restructuring the northeast railroads (see Chapter 16) was abandoned without being subjected to ICC review or proceedings. After the creation of the USRA in 1973 and prior to the formation of the Consolidated Rail Corporation (Conrail), abandonments by the bankrupt railroads in the northeast were under the jurisdiction of USRA, not the Commission, as are abandonments by Conrail during its first 2 years. After Conrail has been in operation for 2 years, abandonment of Conrail lines must receive prior approval of the ICC.

The 1976 4R Act provided that each railroad must submit to the ICC a diagram of its system identifying any lines that are potentially subject to abandonment. No line can be abandoned unless it has been on the list for at least 4 months. The Commission is to postpone abandonment if any financially responsible person (such as a state government) offers financial assistance to continue service that will cover the difference between revenue attributable to the line and the avoidable cost, along with a reasonable return on the value of the line. Federal financial aid to states was provided for the purpose of purchasing rail lines or rehabilitating or improving lines. Federal aid in the amount of 360 million dollars over 5 years was provided, with the federal share to decrease from 100 per cent in the first year to 70 per cent in the fourth and fifth years. Some state aid programs to avoid abandonment existed prior to 1976.

Railroad abandonments have had environmental and energy implications in that questions are raised concerning the air pollution and energy consequences of shifting from rail to motor truck service when rail abandonment occurs and concerning the use to which the railroad land is to be put after abandonment takes place. Under the National Environmental Policy Act of 1969, the ICC is responsible for looking into the environmental consequences of railroad abandonment.[7] Under the Energy Policy and Conservation Act of 1975, the Commission must provide a statement of energy impact in a major proceeding of any kind, including railroad abandonment cases.

Discontinuance of Passenger Service

Discontinuance of railroad passenger service is another aspect of the exit problem and is regulated under Section 13a. Discontinuance of passenger train

---

[6]*Abandonment of Railroad Lines, Commonwealth of Pennsylvania, et al. v. United States, et al.*, 414 U.S. 1017 (1973).

[7]See *Harlem Valley Transportation Associates v. Stafford*, 500 F. 2d 328 (1974) and *Aberdeen and Rockfish Railroad Company v. Students Challenging Regulatory Agency Procedures*, Number 73-1966, June 24, 1975 for discussion of how consideration of the environment in abandonment cases is to be carried out by the Commission.

service not included in the Amtrak system remained under the control of the Commission when Amtrak was created. Until October 1, 1976 (originally July 1, 1973) service provided by Amtrak that was part of its "basic" system (the original Amtrak route system laid out by the Secretary of Transportation plus additional service operated for 2 or more years) could not be discontinued. Service added after January 1, 1973 could not be discontinued until March 1, 1977. After those dates, Amtrak could discontinue or add service based on criteria developed by Amtrak and approved by Congress early in 1976. The ICC is not involved in Amtrak discontinuances. The criteria used by Amtrak are several and include the financial contribution of the service, the financial impact of a service change on other parts of Amtrak's system, the capital investment needed to maintain or change the system, the potential passenger market, the alternate modes of transportation available, and energy and environmental issues.

Federal-State Relations

Federal legislation in 1920 gave to the ICC virtually complete control over all railroad line abandonments, even those in intrastate commerce. The jurisdiction of the Commission in abandonment of intrastate railroad segments was clarified in court decisions in the 1920's. In one case the United States Supreme Court ruled that the ICC could permit abandonment in interstate commerce of purely intrastate railroads, but the states retained control of the intrastate operation. However, if the intrastate operation was a burden on interstate commerce, the Commission could permit abandonment in intrastate commerce.[8] It is doubtful that the intrastate operation would be profitable if the interstate operation were abandoned. Therefore, the federal decision to permit abandonment of the interstate operation amounts to permission to abandon completely. In another case the Court decided that the ICC was allowed to require abandonment of both interstate and intrastate operations of a line located wholly in one state because continued operation would burden interstate commerce.[9]

In effect, the role of the states has been reduced to protesting against abandonment of railroad lines in ICC cases.

Since 1958 the Commission has had final decision-making authority on railroad passenger train discontinuances, including those in intrastate commerce, with the exception of trains operated by Amtrak.

REGULATION OF RATES AND FARES

The reader will recall that the emphasis in early economic regulation of railroads was on the problems associated with railroad pricing. The result has been that from the very beginning and until the present there has been extensive regulatory activity in the pricing area. Regulation of freight rates is far more important than regulation of passenger fares because of the decline of passenger service and the lack of jurisdiction by the ICC over fares charged by Amtrak.

[8] *Texas v. Eastern Texas Railroad Company*, 258 U.S. 204 (1922).
[9] *Colorado v. United States*, 271 U.S. 153 (1926).

Regulation of rail freight rates and passenger fares is an extremely complex matter and we shall limit our discussion to several basic aspects of it.

What Is Regulated?

The Interstate Commerce Act provides that rates and fares of regulated railroads must be filed with the ICC and no changes in rates and fares may be made except upon 30 days' notice to the Commission and to the public. The ICC has the authority to suspend (postpone) such rate and fare proposals for as long as 7 months while investigation is made and a decision is reached. If a proposed rate or fare is not suspended, it goes into effect at the end of the 30-day notice period.

The ICC may fix the maximum, minimum, or actual rate or fare being charged by a regulated railroad. All rates and fares must by published in tariffs (price lists) and made available to the public. It is illegal for a carrier to charge any rate or fare other than the rate or fare in a published tariff. The Commission is empowered to investigate existing rates and fares upon receiving a complaint or on its own initiative.

As indicated above, proposals for new rates or fares or changes in existing rates or fares must be filed with the ICC which has the authority to accept or reject the proposal. The burden of proof in new price or price change proposals is on the railroad. Most railroad freight rates are determined by negotiation between users and carriers and very few of them are rejected or even suspended by the ICC. Less than 1 per cent of *all* rate and fare proposals received from *all* modes regulated are suspended. The transportation industry's knowledge of regulatory standards probably tends to eliminate proposals that would be unreasonably high or low.[10]

Certain important changes in the procedural aspect of freight rate regulation were made in the 4R Act of 1976. The suspension period could be extended from 7 months to 10 months in a particular case if the Commission reported to Congress in writing to explain the delay. For the 2 years following the effective date of the Act, the railroads were permitted to raise or lower specific rates and fares (not rates or fares in general) by as much as 7 per cent from the level in effect at the beginning of each year without suspension because of the reasonableness of the proposed rate or fare, but the Commission could suspend a proposed price because of possible violation of the unjust discrimination parts of the Interstate Commerce Act, or because there was a complaint that a rate or fare would be unfair, destructive, predatory, or otherwise undermine competition, or whenever the carrier was thought to have "market dominance." The Act also provided that the ICC was required to reach a decision within 180 days on any proposed rate or fare that involved a capital investment of 1 million dollars or more by a carrier or by a user of rail service. Once such a rate or fare went into effect, it could not be changed for 5 years unless found to be below variable costs.

---

[10]Interstate Commerce Commission, *The Regulatory Issues of Today,* January, 1975, p. 7.

Regulation of the Rate Level

A major area of regulation of pricing is regulation of the overall level of railroad freight rates. The problem for the regulatory agency is that it must protect the public against rates that are unjustifiably high and at the same time permit the carriers to receive revenues that are sufficient to enable them to provide adequate service to the public. The problem in the railroad industry emerges in what are known as *general rate-level cases* in which the entire railroad industry or carriers in a large geographic area propose to increase all of their rates and charges, usually by some percentage amount. These cases have been numerous since World War II and have increased in number in the period after 1968 when inflation and rising costs became a serious problem for railroad management.

Prior to 1920 recognition of the need of railroads for adequate revenue was not part of the federal regulatory system and emphasis in regulation was on the protection of the public against excessive rates and discrimination in rates. The courts, however, handed down important decisions relative to the rate level, including the famous *Smyth v. Ames*[11] decision in which the United States Supreme Court decided in a Nebraska railroad case that the carriers were entitled to receive a fair return on the fair value of the property being used for railroad purposes and that the public should be charged no more than the services rendered were worth. Although the *Smyth v. Ames* decision dealt with both sides of the question—what the carriers should receive and what users should be asked to pay—the decision is usually referred to as the *fair-return-on-fair-value rule,* meaning that the carriers should be able to receive a fair return on their investment. And, although the Court meant fair return on fair value to be a floor, it actually became the standard and regulatory agencies and courts adopted this standard in dealing with the level of railroad rates. It should be kept in mind that adoption of the fair-return-on-fair-value standard did not guarantee a fair return if economic conditions or other factors made it impossible.

In 1920 Congress for the first time recognized by statute the need of railroads for adequate revenue by incorporating the fair-return-on-fair-value idea into Section 15a (the "rule of rate making") of the Interstate Commerce Act. The fair-return-on-fair-value objective was eliminated by Congress in 1933, partly because of the difficulty in determining the fair value of railroad property, and was replaced by a new rule of rate making that stated that in regulating railroad rates the ICC must consider the need of the carriers for sufficient revenue but without specifying the method of determining the level. The Commission was also directed to consider the effect of rates on the movement of traffic (demand for service) and the need of the public for railroad service. In the 1940's the fair-return-on-fair-value objective as a formally required rate-making factor was further deemphasized when the United States Supreme Court, in a nonrailroad case, refused to look into the value of property question and, instead, stated that it would concern itself only with the question of whether or not the regulated companies had earnings sufficient to maintain their credit standing and attract capital.[12] This so-called *credit standard* has often been used by the federal courts in railroad and other industries' rate level cases. The

[11] 169 U.S. 466 (1898).

[12] *Federal Power Commission v. Hope Natural Gas Company,* 320 U.S. 391 (1944).

regulatory agencies themselves, however, are free to use the fair-return-on-fair-value standard, and the ICC, in fact, has done so along with other factors required to be considered in the rule of rate making.

In the 4R Act of 1976 Congress repealed the rule of rate making for railroads and replaced it with a new rule of rate making. It required the ICC, within 24 months after the effective date of the Act, to develop and promulgate reasonable standards and procedures for the establishment of revenue levels adequate to cover total operating expenses, including depreciation and obsolescence, plus a fair, reasonable, and economic profit or return (or both) on capital employed in the business. Such revenue levels were to be adequate to support prudent capital outlays, assure the repayment of a reasonable level of debt, permit raising needed equity capital, cover the effects of inflation, and ensure retention and attraction of capital. The Commission was to make an adequate and continuing effort to assist railroads in attaining such revenue levels.

This provision brought back the rate-of-return-on-investment goal and combined it with the credit standard. It also placed the ICC in the position of promoting adequate revenue levels for railroads. The provision also indicated that Congress was concerned about the need of the railroad industry for adequate earnings.

In dealing with the general level of railroad rates the ICC deals with the carriers in large groups, sometimes all United States railroads at one time. This means that the rate-of-return-on-investment calculations are for a group of railroads and not for individual railroads.

The rise in operating and other costs of railroads since World War II and the railroads' inability to generate enough cash for capital expenditures have been the chief reasons presented for asking for general rate increases in the dozens of ICC cases handled since then. The Commission usually permits some increase to take place, although it is often less than what was proposed. The increase is not allowed at all or is limited for certain kinds of traffic when the ICC believes that the full increase will have a particularly negative effect on the volume of traffic carried. Usually, there is several months' delay before the increase is granted, although occasionally a temporary or interim increase is permitted pending a final decision by the Commission. The total amount of increases granted has been substantial, even in the short period since 1968.

The Commission ordinarily has not stipulated to what use the increased revenue is to be put. In 1974, however, the ICC required in a general rate increase case that part of the increase be used for deferred maintenance and delayed capital improvements. The United States Supreme Court upheld the decision of the Commission in 1976, stating that the ICC could order railroads to use the increased revenue for the purposes specified by the carriers when they asked for the increase.[13]

Despite the frequency of the increases and their size, the railroad industry rate of return on investment remains low and a fairly large number of railroads have been in financial trouble and even bankruptcy. This is some indication that the problems of railroads probably are not solvable by rate increases

---

[13] *United States, et al. v. Chesapeake and Ohio Railroad Company, et al.*, 426 U.S.500 (1976). See "Revenue-Usage Control by ICC Ruled Legal by Supreme Court," *Traffic World*, June 21, 1976, p. 20.

alone. In fact, general rate increases may contribute to railroad problems if the ICC does not accurately forecast the effect of an increase on the amount of traffic carried.[14]

Regulation of Individual Rates and Fares

Reasonable Rates and Fares. Section 1 of the Interstate Commerce Act requires that railroad rates and fares be "just and reasonable." The ICC is given the authority to apply this requirement to existing individual rates and fares and to individual rate and fare proposals. The general level of railroad earnings is not relevant to these cases.

The rule of rate making in Section 15a, as amended by the 4R Act of 1976, applies not only to the general level of rates and fares but also to individual prices.

There are literally millions of freight rates and passenger fares under the jurisdiction of the Commission and several hundred thousand proposals for new or changed freight rates are received by the ICC each year. In fiscal year 1976 the ICC received 54,207 railroad freight rate tariffs and a total of 353,047 freight rate and passenger fare tariffs and schedules from all its regulated carriers.[15] Because of the large number of filings, the Commission cannot examine each one in detail and, as noted earlier, suspends less than 1 per cent of the rates and fares filed. Although the reasonableness of any rate or fare filed is judged on its own merits, the large number of freight rate filings and the impossibility of examining each one in detail lead the ICC to make comparisons of the characteristics of the commodity and the route involved in a rate proposal with other commodities and routes for which rates already exist, i.e., similar traffic in the same general territory. Commodities and routes that have similar transportation characteristics will, under this approach, have similar rates. In the final analysis, however, the subjective opinion of the Commission, based on the particular circumstances of each individual case, is most important.

The transportation characteristics considered and compared include those we discussed in Chapter 9 and are cost and demand (value of service) factors.

The cost factors associated with the *commodity* in question include loading characteristics, susceptibility to loss and damage, the volume of movement of the commodity over time, the regularity of movement, the kind of railroad equipment required to carry the commodity, and special services, such as heating or refrigeration, required.

Cost factors associated with the *route* in question include distance, operating conditions, traffic density, and unbalanced traffic conditions.

Demand factors considered and compared that are related to the *commodity* in question are the value of the commodity, economic conditions in the user industry, and rates on competing (substitute) commodities.

Demand characteristics associated with the *route* in question are intramodal and intermodal competition with other carriers, competition between produc-

---

[14]The Commission entered into an intensive investigation of the railroad rate structure and railroad rate base and rate of return in the early 1970's. See *Investigation of Railroad Freight Rate Structure,* Ex Parte Number 270 (1976) and *Net Investment–Railroad Rate Base and Rate of Return,* Ex Parte Number 271.

[15]Interstate Commerce Commission, *Annual Report, 1976,* p. 121.

tion points, competition between markets, traffic density, and unbalanced traffic conditions.

In regulating railroad rates and fares the ICC has recognized that each rate or fare need not cover the fully distributed costs associated with the service rendered. The Commission also usually considers a rate or fare below variable costs to be noncompensatory and, therefore, not reasonable, but it has also found rates and fares that were between variable costs and fully distributed costs to be unreasonably low. No specific general ICC prescribed ceiling has existed on railroad rates and fares, although rates are not necessarily excessive when they are higher than fully distributed costs.

The Commission has said that a "zone of reasonableness" is used within which freight rates are allowed to fluctuate, the boundaries of which have been set forth in Commission decisions.[16] This means that a rate is unreasonable if it is below variable costs or above a "maximum reasonable level," which apparently is above the level justified by what the service is worth to the user or is unreasonable when compared with rates on the same or similar commodities for comparable distances under similar conditions in the same general territory.[17]

Under the provisions of the 4R Act of 1976, railroad rates and fares that contribute to the "going concern value" of a carrier shall not be found to be unreasonable on the ground that they are too low. A rate or fare that equals or exceeds variable costs is considered to contribute to going concern value under the Act. No rate or fare is to be found to be unjust or unreasonable on the ground that it is too high unless the Commission first finds that the carrier has "market dominance" over the traffic. The ICC was to define the term "market dominance" within 240 days of the effective date of the Act. Despite the fact that the Commission claimed that it had made use of a "zone of reasonableness" (see above), Congress felt it necessary to legislate the variable cost floor and a specific maximum level into use. In addition, as noted earlier, for a 2-year period the railroads were permitted to raise or lower their rates and fares by as much as 7 per cent from the level in effect at the beginning of each year without suspension because of the reasonableness of the proposed price. The ICC retained its power to suspend any rate or fare proposal because of possible violation of the unjust discrimination provisions of the Act, because of a complaint that a rate or fare would be unfair, destructive, predatory, or otherwise undermine competition, or because a carrier is found to have market dominance.

In October, 1976, the ICC set forth its definition of market dominance. According to the definition, the situations in which a presumption of market dominance will be found to exist include: (1) when a rate or fare has been determined or approved under the antitrust immunity contained in the Interstate Commerce Act (rate bureau proceedings); or (2) when a carrier has handled 70 per cent or more of the traffic involved during the year before the new rate or fare was filed; or (3) when the price in question exceeds the variable cost of service by 60 per cent or more; or (4) when a shipper or receiver protesting against a rate can establish that he has made a substantial investment in railroad equipment that prevents or makes it impractical to use another carrier or mode. In addition to the above situations, market dominance may be found to exist also

---

[16] Interstate Commerce Commission, *The Regulatory Issues of Today*, pp. 6–7.

[17] See Marvin L. Fair and John Guandolo, *Transportation Regulation*, 7th ed. (Dubuque, Iowa: William C. Brown Company Publishers, 1972), pp. 125–126.

if a predominance of any other relevant evidence indicates that effective competition does not exist.[18] Because they thought the definition to be too restrictive, that is, market dominance would frequently be found to exist, 38 major railroads asked a United States court of appeals to set aside the market dominance definition of the Commission.

Environmental and energy considerations in regulating railroad rates and fares were not given attention until recent years. The question of the effect of a freight rate on the environment has been brought up in connection with "recyclable" commodities, such as scrap iron and steel. Environmentalists have suggested that rates on such commodities should be kept low in order to encourage recycling. The National Environmental Policy Act of 1969 requires that the Commission take into account the effect of a freight rate on the environment, although no significant changes in Commission rate regulation have as yet resulted. However, several cases involving recyclables were pending in 1976 and in that year the ICC began a study of the effect of freight rates on recyclables and recycled materials, as was required by the 4R Act of 1976. The study was completed in early 1977. The Commission concluded that rates on most recyclable commodities were reasonable (including scrap iron and steel), although reductions were ordered on some.[19] Energy considerations have not been of significance in railroad price regulation to date.

Discrimination. Discrimination in railroad rates and fares receives particular attention in the Interstate Commerce Act. Section 2 outlaws personal discrimination by railroads. Section 3 contains a blanket prohibition of all forms of undue preference or advantage and any undue prejudice or disadvantage on the part of railroads. Section 4 provides that long-and-short-haul rate discrimination by railroads is prohibited unless special permission is given by the ICC. Section 4 also prohibits railroads from charging greater compensation as a through rate than the aggregate of the intermediate rates unless special exception is made by the Commission. Section 6 requires that all railroad rates and fares be filed with the Commission and that railroads keep open to public inspection their schedules showing their rates and fares. It also requires strict adherence to the published rates and fares (as does the Elkins Act of 1903). All deviations are forbidden. Section 10 and the Elkins Act prohibit the solicitation of rebates and concessions by users or the offering of rebates or concessions by a railroad.

Unjust discrimination in railroad pricing was a major reason for the criticisms of railroads that led to the institution of economic regulation in the nineteenth century. Such unjust discrimination took place between persons, between places (geographic discrimination), and between commodities, as noted in Chapter 19. Personal discrimination in all its forms was eventually made illegal under the federal regulatory system, although instances of such discrimination still arise. Discrimination between places and between commodities is unlawful only when it is undue, unjust, or unreasonable, and the railroad freight rate structure con-

---

[18] *Special Procedures for Making Findings of Market Dominance as Required by the Railroad Revitalization and Regulatory Reform Act of 1976,* Ex Parte Number 320 (1976).

[19] *Investigation of Freight Rates for the Transportation of Recyclable or Recycled Materials,* Ex Parte Number 319 (1977).

tains many rates that are discriminatory. The ICC has the responsibility of determining when discrimination is or is not acceptable.

Personal discrimination in all its forms is illegal, as noted above, and is not a major problem in regulation today. However, the ICC is very conscious of the evils of such discrimination and, as one result, has tended to be against quantity discounts in railroad freight pricing beyond the discount for carload shipments versus less-than-carload shipments, because they favor the large user. In recent years, recognizing the cost justification involved, the Commission has approved some multiple-car rates that are lower than carload rates per unit of weight. The ICC has also approved some trainload and unit train rates that are lower than carload rates per unit of weight, and sometimes it has approved low rates based on the movement of minimum annual tonnages. Rates based on annual minimum tonnages have been permitted only when the traffic would not exist otherwise and the service provided was different from that provided at regular rates or there was an absence of competing users.[20] At the same time, efforts of United States railroads to make use of "contract" or "guaranteed" rates under which users guarantee to ship all or a minimum percentage of their traffic over a year's time via a railroad in return for a reduced rate per ton have been rejected by the Commission.[21]

Discrimination between places occurs when there is unequal treatment of 2 or more places (points) in pricing and the inequality cannot be justified by differences in distance. Discrimination between places may also consist of equality of prices when there are differences in distance that appear to justify differences in rates. Figures 8-7 and 9-1 through 9-6 illustrate various kinds of place discrimination. They represent situations in which the railroad(s) has charged equal freight rates per 100 pounds for the same service performed over unequal distances or has charged unequal rates for the same service provided over equal distances, or in some other way rates do not reflect the differences in distance traveled. They include long-and-short-haul discrimination and the situation in which the through rate exceeds the aggregate of the intermediate rates, which are given special treatment in the Interstate Commerce Act as it applies to railroads. These are all cases of differential or discriminatory pricing but may or may not be held to be unjust and, thus, unlawful by the Commission. The reasons for charging prices that result in place discrimination are discussed in Chapters 8 and 9.

Although generalizations are difficult because each case is decided on its own merits, in order for discrimination between places to be held unjust by the ICC and, therefore, unlawful, the Commission has said that certain factors must be present. The determination of legality involves a comparison of rates. A rate that is, in itself, just and reasonable may be found to be unjustly discriminatory when compared with another rate to or from some other point. The same carrier must be involved in both rates; otherwise unjust discrimination cannot exist. A competitive relationship between the places involved must exist before unjust discrimination can be held to take place, and injury to one of the commu-

---

[20] D. Philip Locklin, *Economics of Transportation,* 7th ed. (Homewood, Illinois: Richard D. Irwin, Inc., 1972), p. 478.

[21] For example, *New York Central Railroad Company v. United States and Interstate Commerce Commission,* 368 U.S. 349 (1962).

nities must be shown. If the rate relationship (differences or sameness) is justified by cost and/or demand factors, such as those discussed in Chapter 9, then
unjust discrimination would be held not to exist. Cost factors include distance,
operating conditions, traffic density, and unbalanced traffic. Demand factors are
competition with other railroads and other modes, production-point competition, market competition, traffic density, and unbalanced traffic.

Discrimination between commodities occurs when 2 or more commodities
receive essentially the same service but different freight rates and when the
differences in rates cannot be explained by differences in the cost of providing
the service. Conversely, commodity discrimination also takes place when rates
on 2 commodities are the same for the same service provided but the costs
involved in providing the service are different. The reasons why a railroad
discriminates in this way are discussed in Chapters 8 and 9. Whether or not the
Commission would find unjust discrimination to exist depends on similar considerations discussed in connection with place discrimination. Unjust discrimination cannot be found unless a rate on a commodity is compared with the
rate on another commodity that receives essentially the same service from the
carrier. A rate that is, in itself, just and reasonable may be found to be unjustly
discriminatory when compared with a rate on another commodity. The same
carrier must be involved in both rates, the commodities compared must be in
competition with one another, and actual injury caused by the rate discrimination must be shown. If the rate relationship (differences or sameness) is
justified by cost and/or demand factors, such as those discussed in Chapter 9,
then unjust discrimination would not be found to exist. Cost factors include
loading characteristics, susceptibility to loss and damage, volume of traffic,
regularity of movement, and kind of equipment required. Demand factors include value of the commodity, economic conditions in the user industry, and
rates on competing commodities.

Federal–State Relations

We have previously pointed out that the federal government has jurisdiction
over interstate commerce by virtue of the commerce clause of the federal
Constitution and that regulation of intrastate commerce is left to the states.

Because most states regulate railroad rates and fares, there is the potential
for conflict between state and federal regulation of railroad pricing. This occurs
when a state regulates the prices on intrastate traffic and these prices have an
effect on interstate commerce. If a purely intrastate railroad rate or fare has the
effect of unjustly discriminating against traffic in interstate commerce, the Interstate Commerce Act provides that the ICC may require that the low intrastate
rate or fare be changed in order to remove the unjust discrimination. This
"Shreveport" doctrine was set forth in court cases in 1913 and 1914,[22] and in
1920 Section 13 of the Interstate Commerce Act was amended to give the
Commission the power to prescribe intrastate rates when necessary in order to
remove discrimination against interstate commerce. In addition to the authority
the Commission has in cases in which intrastate rates discriminate against traffic
in interstate commerce, the amendment of 1920 has been interpreted to mean
that the Commission can raise purely intrastate rates if they do not contribute

[22] *Minnesota Rate Cases,* 230 U.S. 352 (1914) and *Shreveport Cases,* 234 U.S. 342 (1914).

a fair share of the revenue needed to maintain an adequate system of interstate transportation.

In the 4R Act of 1976 Section 13 was amended to give to the ICC exclusive jurisdiction to change intrastate rail rates and fares in order to have them conform with interstate rates and fares, provided that a state regulatory agency has not acted on a carrier's price proposal within 120 days. This provision was intended to deal with the situation in which the ICC has authorized a general interstate rate increase but a state agency has failed to act on a request for a similar general increase in intrastate rates. However, the provision limits the Commission's authority to interfere to situations where a state agency has failed to act.

REGULATION OF RAILROAD SERVICE

Regulation of railroad service has to do with regulatory efforts to provide the public with adequate service and to prevent unjust discrimination in service. Regulation of service is very difficult in any mode of transportation because, unlike rates, mergers, and some other aspects of economic regulation, quality of service and discrimination in service are somewhat subjective and difficult to measure quantitatively.

Several sections of the Interstate Commerce Act authorize the Commission to regulate specific aspects of railroad service. In addition, Section 3 of the Act contains a blanket prohibition of unjust discrimination which includes service. Finally, under the common law, railroads have the obligation to avoid discrimination in service.

Freight Service

The ICC has jurisdiction over several facets of railroad freight service. One of the most important has to do with freight car supply. The Interstate Commerce Act requires that railroads provide adequate facilities and equipment to serve the public, as does the common law governing common carriers. Freight car shortages have been a serious problem in the post-World War II period, particularly the shortage of cars used for carrying grain during harvest periods. The periodic shortages are caused by a combination of lack of railroad capital to invest in cars, thus causing the total car supply to be less than it would be otherwise, inefficient use (underutilization) of the cars the railroads do have, and poor car distribution (cars are sometimes available but they are in the wrong place). The ICC relies heavily on the Association of American Railroads (AAR) to handle car distribution, but the ICC also exercises its power to order railroads to deliver freight cars to other railroads in shortage areas, to expedite the placement, removal, and forwarding of cars, and to hasten repair work and other aspects of car utilization. The Commission also has the authority to fix the "per diem" charges (charges paid by one railroad for the use of the freight cars of another railroad) and can use this as an incentive to encourage the return of cars to owning railroads when shortages occur, but the Commission has chosen not to use this power to any substantial degree. The ICC also regulates demurrage charges [charges levied by railroads against users for detaining freight cars for loading or unloading beyond a period of "free" time of 24 hours (48 hours prior to 1975)] .

Finally, the Commission attempts to prevent unjust discrimination when freight cars are in short supply. Under such circumstances, the railroads could favor certain users over others by giving the favored users better treatment when they allocate the limited number of cars available. Rules have also been adopted by the railroads themselves for the distribution of cars during shortages.

Another important aspect of federal regulation of railroad service has to do with cooperative services provided by 2 or more railroads. The ICC has authority to require 2 or more railroads to jointly use the same terminal facilities, to establish interchange facilities with one another, and to interchange freight with one another by establishing through routes and joint rates.

Other aspects of railroad service that are regulated by the Commission are construction of switch connections with private sidings, extension of credit to users, diversion and reconsignment of freight (changing the destination and/or consignee while en route), and transit privileges (the user pays the through rate, plus a transit charge, if any, even though the shipment is stopped for processing and/or storage at some intermediate point).[23]

Passenger Service

Prior to 1970 the ICC had no authority to regulate the quality of railroad passenger service, although it had jurisdiction over railroad passenger fares, including discrimination in fares, and after 1958 it had complete jurisdiction over discontinuance of passenger train service.

The Rail Passenger Service Act of 1970, which created Amtrak (see Chapter 16), gave the Commission the power to regulate the quality of passenger train service provided by Amtrak and also the limited service not operated by Amtrak. In April, 1974 passenger service regulations prescribed by the ICC went into effect. They were amended in 1976. They cover reservation systems, seating space, on-time performance, meal service, baggage handling, temperature control, and other matters. The regulations permit exemptions for specific trains and stations when the carriers can demonstrate that compliance would be unduly burdensome or impractical. Several exemptions have been given to Amtrak trains.

The Amtrak law also gave the ICC the power to require the upgrading of tracks used in intercity railroad passenger service, but the Commission had done little to exercise that authority at the time of this writing. The Commission has no jurisdiction to establish through routes and joint fares.

REGULATION OF ACCOUNTING AND FINANCIAL MATTERS

Accounting Procedures

Regulation of rates, abandonments, mergers, and other matters requires reliance on various kinds of data, including accounting information. In addition,

---

[23] An ICC report issued in 1976 was highly critical of the quality of railroad freight service. See *Investigation of Railroad Freight Service,* Ex Parte Number 270, Sub. 2, 345 ICC 1223 (1976).

for purposes of standardization of information reported to the regulatory agency by the regulated carriers, establishment of uniform accounting systems is necessary. For these reasons, since 1887 the ICC has had the authority to prescribe the accounting systems used by regulated interstate railroads. Also, the accounts of all regulated railroads must be made available for inspection by the Commission at any time.

The accounting system used by the railroads in the 1970's was prescribed by the ICC in 1907 and only minor changes were made after that. Much criticism was directed at the Commission for not modernizing the system, and in 1973 the ICC began working on a revision. In 1976 the 4R Act required that the Commission issue new regulations and procedures prescribing a new uniform cost and revenue accounting system for railroads. In 1977, the ICC adopted a new accounting system for railroads to become effective on January 1, 1978.

Security Issues

The Transportation Act of 1920 gave the ICC the authority to regulate the issuance of securities (capital stock and bonds) by railroad companies under its jurisdiction (Section 20a). This means that a railroad may not issue any new securities, except notes maturing in less than 2 years and aggregating not more than 5 per cent of the securities of the carrier then outstanding, without the prior approval of the Commission. The ICC may attach such terms and conditions to its approval as it deems appropriate. The Interstate Commerce Act also provides that a railroad may not assume any obligation or liability of another person without ICC approval. Any security issued or obligation assumed by a railroad shall be void if issued or assumed without Commission approval having first been obtained. The ICC has proposed to expand the definition of securities to include all credit arrangements, including conditional sales and deeds of trust.

The Commission's purpose in controlling security issues is to promote a financially strong railroad system, especially by preventing overcapitalization—the liabilities of a carrier in the form of capital stock and long-term debt exceed the value of the carrier's assets—and to protect against dishonest financing.

Until 1976 the ICC's jurisdiction over railroad security issues was exclusive, that is, no other federal agency could assert authority in this area, including the Securities and Exchange Commission (SEC). The Interstate Commerce Act also specifically gave the Commission exclusive jurisdiction over interstate railroad security issues, regardless of state regulation on the subject, and a railroad could issue securities approved by the ICC without securing approval of state regulatory agencies. In 1976 the 4R Act provided that the jurisdiction of the ICC over railroad security issues was to be shared with the SEC.

Reorganization

Reorganization proceedings occur when a railroad company finds that because of inadequate earnings it cannot meet its obligations to its creditors, including bond holders who have loaned money to the company, and it seeks to change its capital structure, including capital stock and indebtedness outstanding, so that earnings can be expected to support it. In other words, the company is going through bankruptcy proceedings and is attempting to make a new start with a reduced capital structure.

Under Section 77 of the federal Bankruptcy Act of 1898, which was added in 1933 and amended in 1935,[24] the appropriate federal court appoints trustees to take charge of the railroad property. The trustees must be approved by the Commission. The company is required to file a plan of reorganization with the court and the Commission. Reorganization plans may also be filed by the trustees, creditors, stockholders, or other interested parties. After public hearings on the reorganization plan(s), the ICC must submit a report approving a plan of reorganization, which may be the same as or different from any plans filed. This approved plan is submitted to the court for its approval. If the court disagrees with the Commission's plan, it is referred back to the ICC for reconsideration. After a plan is approved by both the Commission and the court, it is submitted for approval by creditors and stockholders. If creditors and stockholders representing two-thirds of the claims or stock approve, the plan becomes effective.[25]

In carrying out its role under the Bankruptcy Act, the ICC has tried to reduce the total capitalization of the reorganized railroads to an amount that the expected earnings may support.

Many railroad reorganizations have taken place since 1933. The time involved in such cases has been extensive. Cases lasting 9 or 10 years have been common and one case lasted 20 years. The delay is caused partly by the dual role of the ICC and the courts.[26]

In 1975 there were 12 railroads seeking reorganization under Section 77, most of them in the northeast.[27] Six of these carriers became part of ConRail in 1976.

Instead of following the proceedings under the Bankruptcy Act, a railroad may voluntarily change its capital structure without going through bankruptcy proceedings by making use of the provisions of the Railroad Modification Act of 1948. This law provides that a railroad may modify its capital structure by extending the maturity date of bonds, reducing the interest rate on bonds, substituting income bonds and stock for fixed-interest bonds, and making other changes if the new capital structure is accepted by holders of at least 75 per cent of the principal amount or number of shares of each class of securities affected and by the ICC.

REGULATION OF MERGERS

Unification of 2 or more railroads through consolidation, merger, or acquisition of control, henceforth referred to as *mergers*, has been an important part of American railroading from the beginning of the industry. Since 1830 many hundreds of railroads have lost their identity through mergers. These mergers

[24] Prior to 1933 railroad reorganizations were handled under the common law and all creditors had to agree to the reorganization.

[25] Even if a plan is rejected by a group of creditors or stockholders, it can be made effective if the court believes that the plan makes adequate provision for fair treatment of their interests and that their rejection was not justified.

[26] Oscar Lasdon, "The Evolution of Railroad Reorganization," *ICC Practitioners' Journal*, May-June, 1972, pp. 549-551.

[27] Interstate Commerce Commission, *Annual Report, 1975*, p. 14.

have been either side-by-side mergers (parallel railroads serving the same general area and, perhaps, many of the same points merge) or end-to-end mergers (railroads that connect with but do not parallel one another merge). Many railroad mergers have, of course, had both side-by-side and end-to-end characteristics.

Statutory Provisions

Prior to 1920 there was no federal legislation dealing specifically with railroad mergers, although pooling was prohibited in 1887. The ICC had no jurisdiction in such cases. Instead, they were dealt with under the antitrust laws. The Transportation Act of 1920 gave the Commission authority over railroad mergers and modified the prohibition against pooling by permitting pooling when it did not unduly restrain competition and was specifically authorized by the ICC. The Act of 1920 ordered the Commission to prepare a plan of consolidating United States railroads into a limited number of systems. The ICC plan was drawn up in the 1920's, but it was ineffective because railroads would not voluntarily merge according to the plan and the plan was not complusory. The plan was discontinued by Congress in 1940. Consolidations brought about through the holding company device were brought under Commission jurisdiction in 1933.

Section 5 of the Interstate Commerce Act provides that interstate railroads may not merge without approval of the ICC, and when the Commission is deciding a merger case, it must take into account the effect of the proposed merger on adequate transportation service to the public, the effect on the public interest of the inclusion or exclusion of other railroads, the total fixed charges resulting from the merger, and the interest of the railroad employees involved. Railroad workers are not to be placed in a worse position with respect to their employment as a result of a merger for a period of not less than 4 years after the merger takes place. The ICC may require protection for a longer period than 4 years. Mergers approved by the Commission are exempt from the antitrust laws.[28] Other laws now require that environmental and energy implications of a merger be taken into account but these factors have not been of consequence in merger cases thus far.

ICC Policy

Between 1955 and 1970 a large number of railroad merger applications were filed with the ICC. In large part, the applications were a reaction to the deteriorating financial condition of railroads in that period. The major benefits sought through merger included cost reduction through elimination of duplicate facilities and effort (mainly in side-by-side mergers) and longer-haul service over the

[28]There have been several United States Supreme Court cases that have examined the role of the antitrust laws in railroad merger cases, particularly in reference to the question of reducing the amount of competition among railroads. The conclusion of the Court has been that in a railroad merger case the ICC may not ignore the policy of the antitrust laws and must consider the effects of the curtailment of competition among railroads but, if the Commission has done so, the decision of the Commission is outside the jurisdiction of the antitrust laws. See *McLean Trucking Company v. United States,* 321 U.S. 67 (1944); *Minneapolis and St. Louis Railroad Company v. United States,* 361 U.S. 73 (1959); *Seaboard Airline Railroad Company v. United States,* 382 U.S. 154 (1965); *Penn Central Merger Cases,* 389 U.S. 486 (1968); and *Northern Lines Merger Cases,* 396 U.S. 491 (1970).

lines of one carrier without interchanging freight (in end-to-end mergers primarily). Other possible benefits were a larger car supply under one management and better car distribution as a result, economies of greater purchasing and borrowing power, and more specialized management. The public interest in these mergers could be served if the above benefits resulted in improved service and/or lower rates.

Most of the applications for merger between railroads decided upon by the Commission between 1955 and 1970 were approved despite strong opposition from those who were concerned about the elimination of competition among railroads, competing and interchanging railroads that were not included in the merger, communities that feared loss of rail service and/or railroad employment, and railroad labor who feared loss of jobs. According to the AAR, from January, 1955 through February 10, 1972 there were 57 merger proposals filed with the Commission. Of those, 38 were approved by the ICC, 6 were denied, 9 were withdrawn or dismissed, and 4 were pending.[29]

The Commission apparently believed that we should strive toward a limited number of large railroad systems, although no overall plan of railroad consolidation existed and each case was decided on its own merits. The cases decided by the ICC also indicate that intramodal competition is no longer of primary concern, but that the long-run goal is the strengthening of intermodal competition by developing balanced regional railroad systems.[30] Mergers also present an opportunity for the Commission to solve the problem of chronically weak railroads by requiring that they be included in a merger, as was done when the New York, New Haven, and Hartford Railroad was made part of the Penn Central merger.

The 2 most important mergers approved by the ICC were the merger of the Pennsylvania Railroad and the New York Central Railroad which in 1968 became the Penn Central Transportation Company in the northeast quadrant of the United States and the merger of the Great Northern, the Northern Pacific, the Chicago, Burlington, and Quincy, and the Spokane, Portland, and Seattle which in 1970 became Burlington Northern, Incorporated in the northwest quadrant of the country. The Penn Central had a route system of approximately 20 thousand miles, approximately 6 billion dollars in assets, and an annual operating revenue of approximately 2 billion dollars at the time of the merger. It was the largest merger in dollar terms in any industry in United States history. Figure 21-1 is a map showing the principal routes of the Penn Central. The Burlington Northern had a line mileage of approximately 25,000 miles, approximately 3 billion dollars in assets, and an annual operating revenue of approximately 1 billion dollars at the time of the merger. Figure 21-2 is a map showing the main routes of the Burlington Northern. The Penn Central went into bankruptcy in 1970 and disappeared in April, 1976 under the reorganization of northeast railroads which created ConRail (see Chapter 16.)

A major difficulty with and criticism of ICC railroad merger policy have to do with the length of time involved in handling merger cases. Railroad merger cases

[29] Association of American Railroads, *Railroad Merger Movement Down to One* (Washington, D.C.: Association of American Railroads, February 10, 1972), p. 5.

[30] Charles F. Phillips, Jr., *The Economics of Regulation,* 2nd ed. (Homewood, Illinois: Richard D. Irwin, Inc., 1969), p. 520.

are lengthy legal and political battles. In a typical case, there are dozens of interveners including rail, highway, and water carriers, as well as counties, municipalities, shippers and receivers, civic and labor organizations, and individual states and state regulatory agencies. The United States Department of Justice has also intervened in many of these proceedings. For example, the application for the Burlington Northern merger was filed in 1961 and the final United States Supreme Court decision approving the merger did not issue until 1970. The merger of the Pennsylvania and New York Central railroads took nearly 6 years from the date of application. Excluding the court appeals, there were 120 hearing days before 2 ICC administrative law judges, involving 19,750 pages of transcript, 291 prepared statements, 352 exhibits, 463 witnesses, and appearances by 338 attorneys.[31]

The 4R Act of 1976 required that railroad merger case proceedings be concluded by the ICC within 2 years and that a decision must be made by the Commission within 180 days thereafter. An alternative merger procedure was also provided (through 1981) whereby a merger proposed by railroads or by the Secretary of Transportation could be reviewed by the Secretary and hearings could be held by him. A report would then be made by the Secretary to the ICC, which would then determine whether or not the merger was in the public interest. The ICC could hold hearings, but it was placed under tight time limits as to when a decision had to be made—no longer than 16 months after the

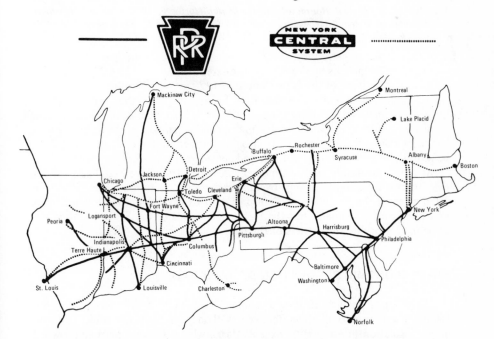

FIGURE 21-1 *Principal Routes of the Penn Central, 1968. (Source: "Penn Central Merger Approved by ICC; New Haven, Susquehanna Lines Included,"* Traffic World, *April 30, 1966, p. 48). The routes of the New York, New Haven, and Hartford Railroad, which was included in the merger, are not shown in the map.*

[31] *Ibid.,* footnote 127, p. 519.

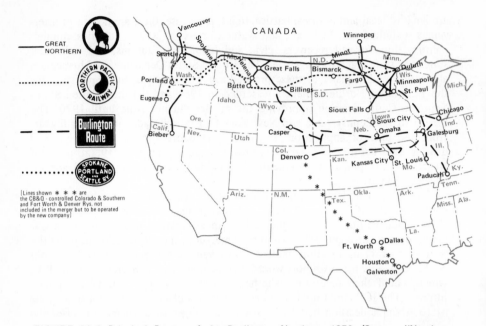

FIGURE 21-2 *Principal Routes of the Burlington Northern, 1970. (Source: "Northern Lines Parted at the Altar Again." Reprinted from the May 25, 1968 issue of* Business Week, *p. 102, by special permission.* © *1968 by McGraw-Hill, Inc.)*

application was received by the Commission—although the period could be extended to 24 months by the ICC at its discretion.

Since the collapse of the Penn Central in 1970 interest in railroad mergers has waned, although several proposals have been made since then, and more are likely to be made in the future. The northeast railroad plan is, of course, a giant merger proposal that seeks to solve the northeast railroad problem by merging bankrupt railroads into Conrail. It also involves acquisition of some parts of the bankrupt railroads by other railroads and considerable line abandonment.

As noted previously, railroad merger cases since 1940 have been handled on a case-by-case basis, without any overall master plan to follow. The 4R Act of 1976 directed the Secretary of Transportation to develop proposals for mergers of United States railroads, but the recommendations of the Secretary were not to be mandatory on the carriers or the ICC.

STATE ECONOMIC REGULATION OF RAILROADS

There was a revival of state economic regulation of railroads after 1900 following a long period of ineffectiveness. Today railroads are subject to economic regulation in every state except Alaska where the only railroad is owned by the federal government. Railroad regulation varies from state to state and a variety of aspects of railroad operation are subject to regulation. However, the fact that most railroad traffic is interstate limits the jurisdiction of the states. In addition, the federal government has taken over several major areas of regulation of intrastate railroad operation. Federal regulation of intrastate railroad abandonments is virtually complete. The ICC can also interfere in intrastate rail rate and fare matters when discrimination against interstate commerce exists and, under the 4R Act of 1976, has exclusive jurisdiction over any intrastate rate if the state regulatory agency has not acted on a carrier proposal within 120 days. The states lost control of discontinuance of intrastate passenger train service to the ICC in 1958. In addition, state regulation of interstate railroad security issues has been superseded by federal regulation. It is obvious, therefore, that state economic regulation of railroads is of minor importance and is limited to strictly local matters.

SELECTED REFERENCES

The development of federal economic regulation of railroads is discussed in some detail in D. Philip Locklin, *Economics of Transportation,* 7th ed. (Homewood, Illinois: Richard D. Irwin, Inc., 1972), Chapters 9, 10, 11, and 12. See also Dudley F. Pegrum, *Transportation Economics and Public Policy,* 3rd ed. (Homewood, Illinois: Richard D. Irwin, Inc., 1973), Chapters 12 and 13.

The current status of federal economic regulation of railroads is described in Hugh S. Norton, *Modern Transportation Economics,* 2nd ed. (Columbus, Ohio: Charles E. Merrill Publishing Company, 1971), Chapter 13. A rather detailed discussion of economic regulation of railroads with case illustrations is John Guandolo, *Transportation Law,* 2nd ed. (Dubuque, Iowa: William C. Brown Company Publishers, 1973). See especially Chapters 1, 2, 24, 26, 27, 28, 35, 36, 37, 46, and 51. Current developments in federal economic regulation of railroads are summarized in the annual reports of the Interstate Commerce Commission available from the U.S. Government Printing Office, Washington, D.C.

Elements that go into abandonment decisions of railroads and the elements regulatory agencies should consider in deciding abandonment cases and alternatives to abandonment are treated in John F. Due and Nancy D. Sidhu, "Private v. Social Decision Making for Railway Abandonments," *Quarterly Review of Economics and Business,* Winter, 1974. A theoretical model describing ICC decisions on railroad abandonments is presented in W. Bruce Allen, "ICC Behavior in Rail Abandonments," *ICC Practitioners' Journal,* July–August, 1974. A study of ICC abandonment policy in Minnesota is reported on in H. Barry Spraggins, *An Evaluation of Interstate Commerce Commission Rail Line Abandonment Policy and Procedure in Minnesota,* unpublished Ph.D. dissertation, University of Minnesota, 1976. Regulation of railroad abandonments is dealt with also in Charles Cherington, *Regulation of Railroad Abandonments* (Cambridge, Massachusetts: Harvard University Press, 1948) and Michael Conant, *Railroad Mergers and Abandonments* (Berkeley: University of California Press, 1964). A case study of the impact of railroad abandonments on communities served is Benjamin J. Allen, "The Economic Effects of Rail Abandonments on Communities: A Case Study," *Transportation Journal,* Fall, 1975. See also Spraggins, *An Evaluation of Interstate Commerce Commission Rail Line Abandonment Policy.* The problem of carriers being required to get approval to abandon while users have no commitment to the railroad to continue using railroad service is dealt with in John C. Spychalski, "Imperfections in Railway Line Abandonment Regulation and Suggestions for Their Correction," *ICC Practitioners' Journal,* May–June, 1973. The factors that determine whether or not a short line railroad will seek abandonment are discussed in John F. Due, "Factors Affecting the Abandonment and Survival of Class II Railroads," *Transportation Journal*, Spring, 1977.

Regulation of the railroad rate level is discussed in Locklin, *Economics of Transportation*, Chapter 15 and Norton, *Modern Transportation Economics*, Chapter 18. Regulation of the reasonableness of individual rates is discussed in Locklin, *Economics of Transportation*, Chapters 18 and 19. An analysis that indicates that many railroad rates are below variable costs is Robert W. Harbeson, "Toward a More Compensatory Rail Rate Structure," *ICC Practitioners' Journal*, January–February, 1973. Regulation of rates on recyclable commodities is dealt with in Philip B. Schary, "Transportation Rates and the Recycling Problem," *Transportation Journal*, Spring, 1977. Regulation of rate discrimination between places and commodities is discussed in Locklin, *Economics of Transportation*, Chapter 22 and Norton, *Modern Transportation Economics*, Chapter 19. The long-and-short-haul clause is dealt with in Locklin, *Economics of Transportation*, Chapter 21. Regulation of discrimination in railroad pricing is discussed also in Marvin L. Fair and Ernest W. Williams, Jr., *Economics of Transportation and Logistics* (Dallas, Texas: Business Publications, Inc., 1975), Chapter 22. The history and interpretation of Sections 2, 3, and 4 of the Interstate Commerce Act are presented and analyzed in Jordan J. Hillman, *Competition and Railroad Price Discrimination* (Evanston, Illinois: The Transportation Center at Northwestern University, 1968). ICC policy on volume railroad rates is reviewed in Thomas C. Campbell and Sidney Katell, "Railroad Volume Freight Rates: Evolution and Analysis," *ICC Practitioners' Journal*, January–February, 1977. Railroad rate regulation as administered by the ICC is described in detail with illustrative cases in Marvin L. Fair and John Guandolo, *Transportation Regulation*, 7th ed. (Dubuque, Iowa: William C. Brown Company Publishers, 1972), pp. 116–197.

Regulation of railroad service by the ICC is discussed in Locklin, *Economics of Transportation*, Chapter 25. The same author deals with ICC regulation of accounting practices of railroads in Chapter 23 and with ICC regulation of railroad finance in Chapter 24. The freight car shortage problem is discussed in Pat J. Calabro and Thomas W. Speh, "Historical Perspectives on the Freight Car Supply Problem: The Role of Demurrage," *ICC Practitioners' Journal*, May–June, 1976. The need for revision of the accounting system prescribed for railroads is dealt with in Herbert O. Whitten, "Functional (Managerial) Cost Accounting for Railroads," *ICC Practitioners' Journal*, March–April, 1976. An analysis of the ICC's interpretation of its authority to regulate railroad and motor carrier security issues and its attempt to broaden the definition of securities is Judith E. Minsker, "The Regulation of Carrier Securities: Section 20a of the Interstate Commerce Act," *ICC Practitioners' Journal*, May–June, 1972. The history of railroad reorganizations is presented in Oscar Lasdon, "The Evolution of Railroad Reorganizations," *ICC Practitioners' Journal*, May–June, 1972.

There is considerable literature on railroad mergers. The subject is discussed in some detail in Pegrum, *Transportation Economics and Public Policy*, pp. 420–431. The merger wave among railroads that began in the mid-1950's is dealt with in Gilbert Burck, "Mating Time for Railroads," *Fortune*, January, 1961 and in Robert W. Harbeson, "New Patterns in Railway Consolidation," *Quarterly Review of Economics and Business*, February, 1962. Michael Conant in "Railroad Consolidations and the Antitrust Laws," *Stanford Law Review*, May, 1962 argues that competition among railroads is not important and should not be a factor in merger cases. That maintenance of intramodal railroad competition is of crucial importance is argued by Carl H. Fulda, "Antitrust Aspects of Recent Transportation Mergers," *Minnesota Law Review*, March, 1964. The history of mergers among western railroads from 1920 to 1974 is discussed in William L. Bush, "Western Railroad Mergers—Then and Now," *ICC Practitioners' Journal*, January–February, 1975. Public interest considerations in railroad merger cases are discussed in Marvin L. Fair, "Railroad Mergers and the Public Interest," *Transportation Journal*, Winter, 1966. A classic discussion of the diseconomies of large size and hence mergers in the railroad industry is Kent T. Healy, *The Effects of Scale in the Railroad Industry* (New Haven, Connecticut: Committee on Transportation, 1961). The relationship between railroad mergers and the antitrust laws is discussed in Edward J. Zimmerman, "Carrier Mergers and the Relevance of Antitrust," *ICC Practitioners' Journal*, September–October, 1967 and John J. Delaney, "Rail Mergers v. Anti-Trust Laws," *Distribution Age*, May, 1967. The collapse of the Penn Central is discussed in Rush Loving, "The Penn–Central Bankruptcy Express," *Fortune*, August, 1970. The success of the Burlington Northern merger is described in Rush Loving, Jr., "A Railroad Merger That Worked," *Fortune*, August, 1972. The changes in regulation of railroad mergers brought about by the 4R Act of 1976 are discussed in some detail in T. P. Ellsworth, Jr., "The Merger Merry-Go-Round: Rail Consolidation Under the 4-R Act," *ICC Practitioners' Journal*, May–June, 1977.

The supremacy of the federal government over the states in economic regulation of railroads is described in J. J. Burchell, "Federal Supremacy in the Regulation of Commerce," *ICC Practitioners' Journal*, November–December, 1975.

22

Government Economic Regulation

of Highway Transportation

Economic regulation of highway transportation began at the state level in the World War I period and at the federal level in 1935. Although a few amendments have been made to the federal Motor Carrier Act of 1935, which is now Part II of the Interstate Commerce Act, federal regulation in the 1970's is essentially the same as it was in 1935. In this chapter we shall discuss federal economic regulation and review the same 6 major areas of regulation that we did in connection with railroad transportation in Chapter 21. They are regulation of entry, exit, rates and fares, service, accounting and financial matters, and mergers. In addition, exemptions from economic regulation and illegal transportation will be discussed.

REGULATION OF ENTRY

Because the need for economic regulation of highway transportation stemmed from the problems caused by easy entry, as noted in Chapter 19, the cornerstone of economic regulation of highway transportation has from the very beginning been government control over entry into the industry. This means that the Interstate Commerce Commission (ICC) has authority to determine how many carriers there will be, who they will be, what areas, routes, and points they can serve, and what they can carry. The purpose is to prevent excess capacity to ensure that qualified operators are in the business.

Operating authority cases involving highway carriers account for more than 75 per cent of the Commission's formal cases. During the 1976 fical year 6,800 formal cases involving applications for motor carrier operating authority were decided by the ICC. This figure does not include the thousands of applications for temporary operating authority that were handled under informal procedure.[1]

[1] Interstate Commerce Commission, *Annual Report, 1976* (Washington, D.C.: U.S. Government Printing Office, 1976), pp. 113-114.

Since 1935 the Commission has made over 90,000 permanent grants of operating authority that are still in use by motor carriers, and from 3,000 to 4,000 new ones are made each year.[2]

Common Carriers

The Interstate Commerce Act requires that anyone who seeks to serve as an interstate common carrier of passengers or property by motor vehicle or to extend routes or add additional traffic apply to the ICC for permission to serve. The law further provides that in order to be granted operating authority, the applicant must be fit, willing, and able to perform the proposed service and that the proposed service is required by the present or future public convenience and necessity.[3] "Fit, willing, and able" means that the carrier will be able to perform the proposed service and conform to the provisions of the Act and the rules and regulations of the Commission. In determining this, the ICC considers several factors, including the financial resources of the applicant, past serious violations under the Act, length of time in operation, experience and skill of personnel, ability to buy new equipment, reputation with respect to dependability and service, and adequate insurance coverage.

If permitted to enter, the applicant is given a Certificate of Public Convenience and Necessity which specifies where the carrier can serve and, in the case of a trucking company, what commodities it can carry. The certificate may contain restrictions on the route(s) served, area(s) served, points served, commodities carried, size of shipments to be carried, types of trucks that can be used, the season of operation, and the classes of users to be served. Some common carriers are authorized as *regular route* carriers, which means that they are certificated to operate on specific routes only. Others are *irregular route* carriers, which means that they are certificated to operate in a given geographic area but specific routes are not specified.[4] Approximately 31 per cent of the common carrier trucking and 7 per cent of the contract carrier trucking grants are for regular route operation.[5] Most common carriers of passengers enter a regular route service. Approximately 95 per cent of the service is of this kind.[6]

The ICC has handled thousands of applications for operating authority since 1935 and each case has been somewhat different from the others. Nevertheless, certain basic principles have been developed by the Commission that are applied in common carrier entry control cases where the applicant must meet the test of public convenience and necessity. The latter is not precisely defined in the statute and the ICC has the responsibility to determine its meaning in each case. The ICC has said that the issuance of operating rights is based on the following considerations: (1) whether or not the new operation or service will serve a

---

[2] Charles A. Taff, *Commercial Motor Transportation*, 5th ed. (Cambridge, Maryland: Cornell Maritime Press, Inc., 1975), p. 435.

[3] Carriers who were in business on June 1, 1935 were allowed to continue in business under a "grandfather" provision of the Motor Carrier Act.

[4] See Charles A. Taff and David Rodriguez, "An Analysis of Some Aspects of Operating Rights of Irregular Route Motor Common Carriers," *Transportation Journal*, Winter, 1975.

[5] Taff, *Commercial Motor Transportation*, p. 444.

[6] *Ibid.*, p. 499.

useful public purpose, responsive to a public need; (2) whether or not this need can or will be served by existing carriers; and (3) whether or not this need can be met by the applicant with the new operation or service proposed without endangering or impairing the operations of existing carriers contrary to the public interest.[7] This means that the ICC tries to determine if there is a public need for the service proposed, i.e., that it would be a useful service that the public would make use of. Whether or not there is already a highway carrier(s) on the route or in the area serving the same kind of traffic, the adequacy of the existing carrier service, and whether or not the existing carrier(s) can perform the proposed service are examined. Finally, the Commission tries to determine what the effect of a new entrant would be on the existing carrier(s).

The net effect of this policy is that if there is no public need, a certificate will not be granted. If there is a public need but an existing motor carrier(s) can provide the service, a certificate will not likely be granted. If there would be a serious negative effect on an existing carrier(s), a certificate would not likely be granted. As indicated above, the adequacy of existing highway carrier service is given careful consideration in entry control cases. There are, however, other elements considered, and a certificate may be granted even though there is no finding of inadequacy of existing service. The Commission will not consider low rates proposed by an applicant as a factor in an entry control case. The Commission believes that the rate regulation process is where that issue should be dealt with.

Considerable protection is given to already authorized carriers when applications for new operations or service are considered by the ICC, although the Commission says that it recognizes the value of competition and tries to permit as much as possible without creating destructive competition. In fact, the Commission has stated that most applications are granted in whole or in part. In fiscal year 1974 of the 4,762 applications for common and contract carrier freight and passenger service considered in formal cases by the ICC, 82.1 per cent of the applications were granted in whole or in part.[8]

Because of the need to show that the applicant is fit, willing, and able and because of the factors that the Commission considers in deciding fitness and ability to serve (see above), an existing carrier has an advantage over a newcomer to the industry in seeking operating authority to serve a given route or area and kind of traffic. Thus, in fiscal year 1973 of the 4,299 motor carrier applications for operating authority that were granted in whole or in part in formal cases, only 507 applicants were issued authorization for the first time to provide service as for-hire regulated carriers.[9]

The effect of a new motor carrier entry on other modes of transportation as a factor to consider in entry control cases is discussed in Chapter 24.

The results of federal common carrier entry control policy have been mixed relative to the amount of competition that has been allowed to occur. Some routes in the trucking industry are monopoly routes while others are highly competitive, despite entry control.

[7]*Pan American Bus Lines Operation,* 1 MCC 190, 230 (1936) and Interstate Commerce Commission, *The Regulatory Issues of Today,* January, 1975, p. 15.

[8]Interstate Commerce Commission, *The Regulatory Issues of Today,* p. 15.

[9]Interstate Commerce Commission, *Annual Report, 1973,* p. 31.

Entry control has produced a situation in which thousands of certificates are currently in effect. A single carrier may hold dozens of certificates covering different parts of his route system that have been granted or purchased over a period of time. It has also led to somewhat extreme *particularization* of certificate terms and conditions, meaning that the terms and conditions are often very detailed in the specific things they will permit a common carrier to do in respect to where he may serve and what he may carry.[10] The particular factors covered in a motor truck certificate may include geographic routes, points, and areas served, the kind of commodity(s) transported, the kind of equipment used (tank trucks, refrigerated vehicles, regular vans, etc.), the size of shipments to be carried, the classes of shippers to be served, the direction of movement, and other factors.

The ICC has recently relaxed some of these restrictions by permitting both freight and passenger carriers to use the Interstate highways instead of the previously designated highways in order to promote more direct routes and by eliminating some *gateway* restrictions, which are requirements that a carrier operate through a certain point (gateway) even though more direct service could be possible by not operating through that point. These moves by the Commission have been partly to conserve energy, to reduce air pollution, and to reduce traffic congestion and they have been partly a response to the criticism of entry control voiced by some critics of economic regulation.

The environmental impact of any single ICC decision in an entry control case is ordinarily very slight and is difficult to measure. Therefore, environmental issues have not as yet affected Commission decisions in this area.[11]

Once a common carrier certificate is granted, it is usually indefinite in term (permanent authority), but it may be suspended or revoked by the Commission for willful failure to comply with the Interstate Commerce Act or any order or rule or regulation of the Commission or any terms of the certificate. Revocation is, however, rare. It is, in fact, not a very effective punitive device because the ICC must investigate, obtain evidence, and prove at a hearing that the carrier has violated some provision of the Act. The Commission then orders the carrier to comply, and thereafter the certificate can be revoked only at a second proceeding in which the ICC must prove that the carrier thereafter *willfully* violated the first order. The certificate cannot be revoked if the carrier discontinued the violation within the 30-day period after he was ordered to discontinue.[12]

Contract Carriers

Contract carrier regulation is included in the federal regulatory structure mainly to protect the interests of common carriers who have the obligation to serve the public generally, and contract carriers are regulated only to the extent thought necessary to meet that end.

[10] See Byron Nupp, "Control of Entry as an Economic and Regulatory Problem," *ICC Practitioners' Journal,* May–June, 1968 for a critical discussion of this issue.

[11] See *Jones, Inc., Extension–Antipollution Control Commodities,* 118 MCC 253 (1973) and *Milne Truck Lines, Inc., Extension–San Francisco,* 112 MCC 149 (1975).

[12] Marvin L. Fair and John Guandolo, *Transportation Regulation,* 7th ed. (Dubuque, Iowa: William C. Brown Company Publishers, 1972), p. 235.

The Interstate Commerce Act provides that a permit must be received from the ICC before anyone can operate as a contract carrier or extend operations as a contract carrier by motor vehicle in interstate commerce. The requirements that must be met by a contract carrier applicant are less stringent than for common carrier applicants. The applicant must be fit, willing, and able to perform the proposed service but need only demonstrate, in addition, that the proposed service is "consistent with the public interest" and the national transportation policy of the Act.[13] This means that the applicant does not have to show that there is a general public need for the proposed service but must demonstrate that there is a user(s) who is willing to enter into a contract with the carrier. The adequacy of existing common and contract motor carrier service is taken into account, as is the possible effect of the authorization on existing motor carriers. However, other factors, including the special needs of the proposed user(s) and the benefits of a different kind of service, improved service, and more competition in the area, are also taken into account. Thus, the presence or absence of other common or contract carriers in the area and the adequacy of their service are not, in themselves, the determining considerations. These factors carry less weight in contract carrier entry cases than they do in common carrier entry cases.[14] The reason for not adopting a rigid policy of barring the entry of contract carriers in order to protect existing common carriers is that to do so would deprive the public of a different kind of service that common carriers do not provide, including their ability to serve the specialized needs of users.

A problem associated with control over contract carrrier entry is a definitional one. Because entry control requirements, as well as other aspects of regulation, are less restrictive for contract than for common carriers, it is important that the ICC be able to tell the difference between the two. The basic difference, as pointed out in Chapter 6, is that the common carrier holds himself out to serve the public generally, while the contract carrier limits his service to one or a small number of users and usually offers a specialized kind of service and has no obligation to serve the general public. Because the ICC had some difficulty in developing a clear distinction between the 2 classes of for-hire carriers, with the resulting danger that contract carriers would, in fact, actually operate as common carriers, the Interstate Commerce Act was amended in 1957 to provide that a contract carrier is one who serves one person or a limited number of persons either for the furnishing of transportation through the assignment of vehicles for the exclusive use of each person served or for the furnishing of transportation services designed to meet the distinct needs of each individual customer. Congress did not specify the limited number of users that was acceptable. The Commission has said that it varies with the circumstances but that con-

---

[13]Contract carriers that were in operation on July 1, 1935 were allowed to continue in business under a grandfather provision of the Act. In the case of passenger service, contract carriage is to be distinguished from charter service. Charter service entails providing transportation for a group assembled by someone other than the carrier who contracts for exclusive use of a bus for the duration of a particular trip or tour. It is an irregular call-on-demand type of service. Charter service may be provided by interstate regulated common carriers under rules and regulations prescribed by the ICC.

[14]See *Interstate Commerce Commission v. J–T Transport Company, Inc.*, 368 U.S. 81 (1961) in which the United States Supreme Court reversed an ICC decision in which the Commission attempted to bar the entry of a contract carrier because existing common motor carrier service was adequate.

tracts with more than 6 or 8 users are beyond the limited number if the service provided is not very specialized.[15] In calculating the number of users, the ICC counts each unit in a conglomerate organization as a separate unit.[16]

A contract carrier permit may be suspended or revoked, as is the case with common carrier certificates, and the procedures to be followed are the same.

Dual Operation

The Interstate Commerce Act provides that a person cannot operate as a common carrier and a contract carrier simultaneously unless good reason is shown. Because the danger in dual operation as both a common carrier and a contract carrier is that the holder of both kinds of operating authority may discriminate between competing users by serving some as a common carrier and some as a contract carrier, dual operation is permitted by the Commission usually only when the routes or territories and/or commodities carried under the two kinds of authority are different.

Federal-State Relations

The states are barred from subjecting interstate highway carriers to any economic regulation, including entry control. However, the states can and do require that an interstate carrier obtain operating authority as a formality before conducting interstate operations over state highways, provided such requirement does not burden interstate commerce. Many states have such a requirement; others require that interstate carriers register with the state regulatory agency. The purpose of these requirements is to aid in the enforcement of state police regulations to which interstate truckers are subject. The power of the states to require interstate carriers to obtain such state operating authority for their interstate operations has been recognized for a number of years.[17]

A carrier desiring to operate as a common carrier in interstate commerce but within the confines of a single state, including carriers who provide pickup and delivery motor carrier service for interstate motor carriers and railroads, where the traffic has an origin or destination outside the state, has a choice of 3 procedural alternatives under the Interstate Commerce Act as far as operating authority is concerned: (1) The carrier may submit a conventional application to the ICC for a certificate of public convenience and necessity. (2) The carrier may seek a certificate of exemption from regulation from the ICC.[18] (3) The carrier may apply for a certificate of registration if the carrier has received intrastate operating authority from the state regulatory agency.[19]

---

[15] *Umthun Trucking Company Extension—Phosphatic Feed Supplements,* 91 MCC 691 (1962).

[16] See *Keller Trucking, Inc., Extension—United States,* 121 MCC 42 (1975).

[17] Donald V. Harper, *Economic Regulation of the Motor Trucking Industry by the States* (Urbana, Illinois: University of Illinois Press, 1959), pp. 81-82.

[18] The Commission has exempted interstate motor carriers in Hawaii from federal regulation except those that are affiliated with other carriers operating outside Hawaii. *Motor Carrier Operations in the State of Hawaii,* Ex Parte MC-59, 84 MCC 5 (1960).

[19] See George H. Hart, "Single State Operation," *ICC Practitioners' Journal,* September-October, 1972.

The intrastate operations of an interstate motor carrier are subject to state regulation in the same manner as are the operations of exclusively intrastate operators. Unless state law directly interferes with or burdens the carrier's interstate business and as long as all intrastate operators must meet the same requirements, the state has the authority to control the entry of interstate motor carriers into the intrastate field.[20]

EXEMPTIONS FROM REGULATION

Several kinds of highway carriers are exempt from economic regulation at the federal level. These include private carriers and several classes of for-hire carriers.

Private Carriers

Private passenger transportation, which is conducted mainly in private automobiles, is, of course, exempt from economic regulation. Interstate private truck transportation (the shipper or receiver and the operator of the vehicle are one and the same) is also exempt from economic regulation by the ICC, although not exempt from safety regulations administered by the federal Department of Transportation (DOT).

Many definitional problems have emerged since 1935 concerning what is and what is not private carriage. In view of the exemption, the definitional question is important because the ICC seeks to ensure that unauthorized for-hire carriage is not conducted under the guise of private carriage. The policy developed by the Commission and by Congress, in a 1958 amendment to the Act, is that a private carrier can collect transportation charges from others but that the traffic carried must be in line with the "primary business" of the operator, which is manufacturing, retailing, or whatever.[21] The drivers and vehicles must be under the full control of the user and the burden of risk must be on the user.[22] Joint private carrier arrangements between 2 or more users are not considered legitimate private carriage by the Commission.

Private carriers operated by one unit in a conglomerate have generally been prevented by the Commission from hauling for other units in the same conglomerate for compensation. If they do, they can no longer retain their exempt private carrier status. This has been upheld by the United State Supreme Court.[23]

The problem of illegal transportation performed under the guise of private carriage is discussed later in this chapter.

Mixed private and for-hire service by the same carrier is usually not permitted by the ICC unless the for-hire service is not competitive with regular authorized for-hire carriers or there are no adverse effects on regular common carriers.[24]

---

[20] Harper, *Economic Regulation of the Motor Trucking Industry*, p. 82.

[21] *Woitishek Contract Carrier Application*, 42 MCC 193 (1943) and *Lenoir Chair Contract Carrier Application*, 51 MCC 65 (1949).

[22] See *H. B. Church Truck Service Company*, 27 MCC 191 (1940) and *United States v. Drum*, 368 U.S. 370 (1962).

[23] *Schenley Distillers v. United States*, 362 U.S. 432 (1946).

[24] See *Geraci Contract Carrier Application*, 7 MCC 369 (1938) and *Ralph A. Veon, Inc., Contract Carrier Application*, 92 MCC 248 (1963).

For-Hire Carriers

Certain kinds of for-hire interstate transportation of persons and property by motor vehicle were made exempt from regulation by the federal Motor Carrier Act, either because Congress intended to reduce the number of carriers to be regulated in order to make regulation practical or because of pressures from the people involved. Exemption means that these for-hire carriers are exempt from entry control and all other aspects of economic regulation but are subject to DOT safety regulation.

Kinds of Exemptions. The exemptions are either specific or conditional. Specifically exempted by the Act are school buses; motor vehicles owned or operated by hotels; trolley buses; motor vehicles incidental to air transportation; motor vehicles under the authority of the Secretary of the Interior which are used in transporting people in national parks and monument areas; motor vehicles controlled and operated by farmers to transport agricultural commodities from farms and to transport supplies to farms; motor vehicles controlled and operated by cooperative associations or federations of cooperative associations as defined in the Agricultural Marketing Act of 1929; motor vehicles used principally in carrying ordinary livestock, fish (including shellfish), and agricultural (including horticultural) commodities, not including manufactured products thereof; motor vehicles used exclusively in the transportation of newspapers; vehicles operated exclusively on rails; and motor vehicles operated by or for railroads, express companies, freight forwarders, or water carriers for transfer, pickup, or delivery service in terminal areas, since they are already subject to regulation by the Commission under other parts of the Act.

Conditional exemptions are those that the ICC may permit to the extent that it finds it necessary to carry out the National Transportation Policy in the Act. They include the interstate transportation of people or property wholly within a municipality, between contiguous municipalities, or within a zone adjacent to and a part of a municipality or municipalities; and casual, occasional, or reciprocal transportation for compensation by any person not engaged in transportation by motor vehicle as a regular occupation or business.

Agricultural Commodities. The most controversial of the exemptions has been the exemption granted to agricultural commodities. The Act provides that for-hire transportation of ordinary livestock, fish, and agricultural commodities, not including manufactured products thereof, if such vehicles are not used to carry other property or passengers for compensation, is exempt from economic regulation. The reasons for the exemption were that agricultural interests did not want transportation of agricultural commodities placed under economic regulation because they claimed that the need for truck service varied greatly throughout the year as harvest periods came and went, but that under entry control the supply of truck service would be inflexible and be unable to respond to the changing needs. In addition, there was the fact that unregulated transportation of agricultural commodities would probably result in lower rates than would regulated transportation. The Motor Carrier Act could not have been passed in 1935 had the exemption not been included.

The exemption of agricultural commodities has produced very difficult problems of definition and interpretation of what is an agricultural commodity and when is it manufactured. The ICC's attempts to limit the scope of the exemption by narrowly interpreting the word "manufactured" were defeated in the courts. In 1958 Congress by legislation froze the list of exempt commodities; nothing after that could be added to the list unless it was being proposed for the first time. For new proposals, the United States Supreme Court's doctrine that a commodity is not manufactured if it maintains its substantial identity after the processing or other operation has occurred is applied.[25]

In addition to definitional and interpretation difficulties brought about by the agricultural commodity exemption, major objection to the exemption is made by the railroads because where the same commodities are carried by rail, they are fully regulated. Common carrier truckers also object to the exemption because it aids private carriers by providing back hauls for them, and even though common carriers can carry the exempt commodities, the rates are sometimes very low, and, therefore, unattractive because of the intense competition that exists. Some agricultural commodity haulers have complained that the excess competition in their industry makes it difficult for them financially and have asked for some form of entry control.

Agricultural Cooperatives. Another exempt area that has created problems is that of transportation performed by agricultural cooperatives. An agricultural cooperative is an organization of farmers whose purpose is to market the farmers' produce and/or purchase farm supplies. Vehicles operated by these ogranizations are exempt from economic regulation if they are carrying agricultural commodities and farm supplies for their members. If they carry on a for-hire basis for nonmembers (interpreted to mean on back hauls), a 1968 amendment to the Act provides that such traffic is also exempt, but it cannot exceed 15 per cent of the cooperative's total interstate tonnage. The "15 per cent rule" has been difficult to police and enforce. In addition, there are organizations that are not agricultural cooperatives at all but claim that status and the exemption from regulation for the purpose of providing for-hire truck transportation without authorization by the ICC.

REGULATION OF EXIT

Regulation of exit is a minor aspect of economic regulation of highway transportation. The ICC has no authority to prevent the abandonment of operations by a regulated highway carrier if the carrier discontinues operations entirely. However, should a carrier wish to stop providing part of the service authorized by a certificate or permit, permission from the Commission must be obtained, since the terms of the certificate or permit would not be complied with by the carrier.

Because abandonment of a particular motor carrier service usually does not have the implications for the public that a railroad abandonment has, and because even if the public is negatively affected, a replacement service is likely to be proposed by someone else, the abandonment question has received far less public attention than have railroad abandonments.

---

[25] See *East Texas Motor Freight Lines, Inc. v. Frozen Food Express,* 351 U.S. 49 (1956) and *Home Transfer and Storage Company v. United States,* 141 Fed. Supp. 599 (1956).

REGULATION OF RATES AND FARES

Although entry control is the cornerstone of economic regulation of highway transportation, regulation of rates and fares is also of considerable importance.

What Is Regulated?

The requirements in the Interstate Commerce Act concerning ICC regulation of highway common carrier rates and fares are very similar to those of the railroads. The requirements concerning common carriers regarding filing rates and fares, proposing changes in rates and fares, and the suspension power of the Commission [prior to the Railroad Revitalization and Regulatory Reform (4R) Act of 1976] are identical, as are the powers of the ICC to investigate rates and fares and to fix rates and fares and the requirement that the carriers publish rates and fares and that carriers may not deviate from the published rates and fares. As with railroads, only a small percentage of proposed rates and fares are suspended by the ICC.

Contract carriers under regulation of the ICC are subject to less stringent price regulation than are common carriers. Contract carriers must file with the Commission and publish and make available to the public their contracts and the rates charged and must adhere to them. They must give 30 days' notice of any proposed reduction in a rate or fare or a new charge of any kind. The ICC has the authority to prescribe only the minimum rates or fares of contract carriers and not the maximum or actual prices, unless they happen to be the minimum prices charged. Consequently, unless a contract carrier files a rate or fare that is a reduction or is below the minimum prescribed, there is no possibility of suspension or investigation by the Commission.

Regulation of the Rate Level

Many highway freight carriers belong to rate bureaus or *conferences* and seek general rate increases as a group. The charges are usually increased by some percentage amount. Examples of such bureaus are the Southern Motor Carriers Rate Conference, the Rocky Mountain Motor Freight Bureau, and the Pacific Inland Tariff Bureau. General rate increase proposals are usually not made by the carriers nationwide, although the ICC may have under simultaneous consideration proposals for general rate increases from several rate bureaus. The bureaus are not necessarily requesting the same amount of increase. Often the proposals are in several parts, with a different percentage increase proposed for different size shipments, for example, under 500 pounds, 500 pounds to 1,000 pounds, and over 1,000 pounds. In addition, there are some regulated carriers that do not belong to a bureau. Such *nonconference* carriers are free to adopt the rate increases approved for the bureau in the area in which they operate, and they often do so.

General rate level increase cases have been numerous in the post-World War II period and especially after 1968 when inflation and rising costs became a serious problem for highway carriers.

Passenger carriers propose general adjustments in rates and fares on a national basis through the National Bus Traffic Association.

The rule of rate making in the Interstate Commerce Act (Section 216i) that applies to common motor carriers provides that in regulating motor carrier rates and fares the ICC shall consider the inherent advantages of highway transportation, the effect of rates or fares on the movement of traffic, the public's need for adequate transportation, and the carriers' need for revenues sufficient to enable them to provide good service. This rule of rate making is very similar to that of the railroads that was in effect prior to its repeal and replacement in 1976.

The need for adequate carrier revenue is recognized in the rule of rate making, but no specific standard for use in determining that level has been set forth. In interpreting this in general freight rate and passenger fare level cases, the Commission looks to the operating ratio instead of the rate of return on investment as a standard. The reader will recall that the operating ratio relates the operating revenues to operating expenses (but not including interest payments and income taxes). It is used as a standard because the Commission believes that in the motor carrier industry the risk is in the great amount of expense instead of in the relatively small investment. We noted in Chapter 11 that federally regulated larger motor trucking companies have a capital turnover of approximately 5, meaning that the annual gross revenue is 5 times the investment. The ICC has said that the motor carrier investment is so small in relation to the volume of business done that the margin of revenues over expenses required to pay a normal rate of return on investment would be so small that a slight miscalculation of probable revenues or expenses could leave the carrier with revenues insufficient to pay operating expenses.[26] The Commission has usually used an operating ratio of 93 as the standard in deciding motor carrier rate and fare level cases.

Although considerable criticism of the operating ratio as a standard for determining rates has been voiced, partly because it is claimed that it rewards carriers for inefficient management and high expenses, the ICC has continued to use it instead of the rate-of-return-on-investment standard. The reader should keep in mind that the operating ratio standard used is for a fairly large group of carriers and it is in an individual carrier's interest to be as efficient as possible in order to do better than the average for the group in terms of net income.

Since the mid-1960's the ICC has required motor carriers to supply several additional kinds of information to supplement the usual data needed to determine the operating ratio. More information on subsidiary or affiliate organizations and more detail concerning expense items are required than in the past. Various other kinds of financial data have also been required that help to indicate the revenue needs of the carriers. These data have included the sum of money needed to attract capital, which is similar to the credit standard referred to in our discussion of regulation of railroad rates. Also required is information on the rate of return on equity and the rate of return on investment. The Commission places great stress on the return to equity, and the operating ratio carries less weight than it did in the past.[27]

The sharp rise in operating costs since World War II has been the chief reason given by motor carriers for asking for general price increases. Trucking com-

---

[26] See *Middle West General Increases,* 48 ICC 541, 552–553 (1948).

[27] A detailed discussion of ICC policy on revenue needs of motor carriers is Harvey A. Levine, "A Historical Analysis of the Criteria to Determine the Revenue Need of Motor Common Carriers," *ICC Practitioners' Journal,* January–February, 1973.

panies are usually expected to seek a general increase in rates after signing new labor contracts with the Teamsters union. The ICC frequently grants all or part of the increases. The time delay problem is also present, as it is in railroad general rate increase cases.

General rate increase cases involve common carriers only because contract carrier rates are the result of individual bargaining between user and carrier.

Regulation of Individual Rates and Fares

Reasonable Rates and Fares. Part II of the Interstate Commerce Act requires that all charges made by regulated common carriers under the Act shall be just and reasonable, and the ICC has the authority to interpret this requirement as it applies to existing and proposed individual rates and fares. The operating ratio and the general level of earnings are not relevant in regulating individual rates and fares.

As noted earlier, the motor carrier rule of rate making in the Act requires consideration of the effect of prices on the movement of traffic, the need of the carriers for sufficient revenue, and the need of the public for motor carrier service.

The task of regulating the prices of highway carriers is a formidable one for the ICC. In the fiscal year 1976 the Commission received 216,967 common motor truck freight rate tariffs and 4,085 common motor bus passenger tariffs of the total of 353,047 tariffs and schedules received from all carriers regulated by the Commission. The ICC also received almost 16,000 motor contract carrier freight rate schedules.[28] The Commission deals with the large number of common carrier rates and fares filed much as it does with the thousands of rail freight rates filed. Most are not suspended and the comparative method is often used in judging their reasonableness. The subjective opinion of the Commission is highly important.

The cost and demand factors considered and compared by the ICC in examining a rate or fare proposal or an existing rate or fare are the same as those considered and compared in regulating railroad prices. In the case of freight rates, both commodity cost and demand (value of service) and route cost and demand factors are considered. The same standards for compensatory and noncompensatory rates and fares are used as with railroads, and the claimed "zone of reasonableness" of the ICC has also been used.

Because of the high percentage of variable costs in the motor carrier industry, the carriers and the ICC find that the noncompensatory level is reached rather quickly when rates are lowered and that motor carrier freight rates have more of a tendency to cover fully distributed costs than is true in the railroad industry. Both trucking companies and the Commission are also more concerned than are railroads about the weight density and loading characteristics of traffic carried because the capacity of the vehicles operated is smaller than that of the railroads.

Because the ICC has jurisdiction over only the minimum rates and fares of contract carriers, there has been relatively little price regulation activity. The objective of regulating contract carriers is to protect common carriers. The minimum rate power is intended to prevent contract carriers from charging unduly low rates and fares and thereby taking traffic from common carriers. However,

[28] Interstate Commerce Commission, *Annual Report, 1976*, p. 120.

the ICC has recognized that contract motor carriers often have lower costs than common carriers do, and as a general rule, the ICC does not require that contract carriers charge minimum rates and fares at least as high as competing common carrier prices.[29]

The effect of motor carrier rates and fares on the environment and energy usage has not been of any consequence thus far in ICC cases.

Discrimination. Discrimination in rates and fares was not the major issue in bringing about the institution of economic regulation of highway transportation. However, Section 216d of the Interstate Commerce Act prohibits any motor vehicle common carrier from making, giving, or causing any undue or unreasonable preference or advantage or any unjust discrimination or any undue or unreasonable prejudice or disadvantage. Section 216d is similar to Section 3 of the railroad part of the Act. There is no specific section dealing with personal discrimination (although Section 217d prohibits rebating and departure from published prices), with long-and-short-haul discrimination, or with the problem of the aggregate of intermediate prices. However, the blanket prohibition of unjust discrimination in Section 216d presumably covers these kinds of discrimination. The Act requires that every common carrier file rates and fares with the Commission, that rates and fares be published and made available to the public, and that the published rates and fares be strictly observed.

The ICC's policy in the regulation of price discrimination in common carrier highway transportation is the same as in railroad transportation. As to personal discrimination and the matter of quantity discounts, the Commission has approved some discounts in the form of *volume minimum* rates (rates on quantities greater than a truckload) and multiple-trailer rates. As to discrimination between places, comparisons of rates and fares are made. The same carrier must be involved in both prices, there must be a competitive relationship between the places involved, and injury to one of the communities must be shown before unjust discrimination can be shown to have taken place. If the discrimination is justified by cost and/or demand factors, then unjust discrimination would be held not to exist. Unjust discrimination between commodities cannot be found unless a rate on a commodity is compared with the rate on another commodity that receives essentially the same service. The same carrier must be involved in both rates, the commodities compared must be in competition with one another, and actual injury caused by the rate discrimination must be shown. If the discrimination is justified by cost and/or demand factors, then unjust discrimination would not be found to exist.

There are no specific provisions relative to rate discrimination by contract carriers. These carriers have the right to charge whatever rates and fares they can agree on with their customers as long as the rates or fares are above the prevailing minimum prices, but the carriers must adhere to the prices filed with the Commission.

Federal–State Relations

We noted that the "Shreveport" rule, which is in Section 13 of Part I of the Act, gives the ICC power to prescribe intrastate railroad rates and fares when

---

[29]The case that established this policy was *New England Motor Rate Bureau, Inc. v. Lewers and McCauley*, 30 MCC 651 (1941).

necessary to remove discrimination against interstate commerce and that the 4R Act of 1976 gives the Commission exclusive jurisdiction over intrastate rail rates if a state agency does not act on a rate proposal within 120 days. Part II of the Act, however, specifically states that the Commission has no power to interfere in intrastate rates or fares in highway transportation for the purpose of removing discrimination against interstate commerce or for any other purpose whatever.

REGULATION OF HIGHWAY
TRANSPORTATION SERVICE

The Interstate Commerce Act is not very specific about regulation of motor carrier service. The Act merely states that common carriers must provide safe and adequate service, equipment, and facilities for the transportation of persons or property. Determination of service standards or minimum levels of service by the ICC is not specifically required by the Act. The provisions of the Act concerning common carrier certificates of public convenience and necessity, however, state that the ICC is to specify in the certificate issued the services to be performed, although the Commission may not restrict the right of a carrier to add to his equipment and facilities over the routes or within the territory specified in the certificate. The Commission may specify in contract carrier permits the scope of the services to be rendered, but the carrier has the right to substitute or add to his equipment and facilities. As indicated earlier, the ICC has the authority to suspend or revoke certificates and permits for willful failure to comply with the Act or any lawful rule or regulation set forth by the Commission or any provision of a certificate or permit. The ICC may also allow the entry of additional carriers if existing carriers provide unsatisfactory service.

The Commission has no authority under the Act to require carriers of property to interchange freight and to establish through routes and joint rates with each other, but the Commission does have this power in connection with common passenger carriers. Common carriers may not interchange freight or passengers with contract carriers and contract carriers may not interchange traffic with each other.

As to discrimination in service, common carriers subject to the Act are covered by the blanket ban (in Section 216d) against undue preference or advantage, undue discrimination, and unreasonable prejudice or disadvantage of any kind.

In addition, common carriers by motor vehicle have the obligation of common carriers to serve, to deliver, and to avoid discrimination, as discussed in Chapter 6.

The ICC has set forth some regulations covering in some detail the required mode of operation of regulated carriers. These regulations deal with interchange of traffic between carriers, leases and interchange of vehicles, observance of common carrier schedules, terminal standards for passenger carriers, detention of equipment by shippers and receivers, extension of credit to users, and the use of *owner-operators* (persons who own vehicles but have no operating authority) by regulated carriers.

As in other modes of transportation, regulation of the adequacy of and discrimination in service is difficult. In fact, it is especially difficult in highway transportation because of the large number of carriers involved. A major difficulty in regulating the service of highway carriers of freight has been in connection with the attempts of some common carriers to avoid carrying "undesirable" traffic, even though they are authorized to carry it in their operating authorities. This includes unprofitable traffic of one kind or another, usually small shipments and/or traffic to or from small and/or out-of-the-way communities. Carriers may avoid such traffic by not soliciting it, by giving it poor service when they get it, charging high rates to carry it, and refusing to interchange it with other carriers. Although these tactics do not amount to absolute refusal to carry, since they discourage the shipment of such traffic, the result can be virtually the same. The common carrier obligation to serve and carry within the holding out of the carrier is not being fulfilled in such situations, and the terms of their certificates are not being complied with. Such action might also be found to be unjustly discriminatory. The ICC, however, has not been able to completely prevent avoidance of undesirable traffic because the matter is difficult to police and deliberate avoidance is difficult to prove. In addition, the Commission has no authority to force motor trucking companies to interchange undesirable or any other kind of freight with one another or with other kinds of carriers.

REGULATION OF ACCOUNTING AND FINANCIAL MATTERS

Accounting Procedures

The ICC has the authority to prescribe the accounting systems used by all regulated highway carriers, and the accounts of all regulated carriers must be made available for inspection by the Commission at any time. A new uniform system of accounts went into effect for common and contract carriers of property on January 1, 1974. Regulation of accounting practices is intended to aid the ICC in its regulation of rates, security issues, mergers, and other matters and in gathering information for statistical reporting purposes.

Security Issues

The issuance of securities—capital stock and bonds—by regulated passenger and freight motor carriers is subject to the provisions of Section 20a of Part I of the Act. The purpose of regulating security issues is to ensure the financial solvency of the carriers and to prevent dishonest financial practices. Regulation by the Commission means that a motor carrier may not issue any new securities, except notes maturing in less than 2 years and aggregating not more than 200,000 dollars, without the prior approval of the ICC. However, an exception is made for smaller carriers in that only if the securities proposed to be issued, together with those outstanding, exceed 1 million dollars is approval of the Commission necessary. The ICC may attach such terms and conditions to its approval as it deems appropriate. In addition, a motor carrier may not assume any obligation or liability of another person without Commission approval. The ICC has exclusive jurisdiction over the issuance of securities by interstate motor carriers, and no one else may exercise authority in this area, including the states.

Insurance

All passenger and freight common and contract carriers by highway regulated by the ICC must carry insurance in such amounts as the Commission may require. These requirements may include coverage for damage to third parties (liability insurance) and loss and damage to property carried. This requirement reflects the fact that many motor carriers were financially weak at the time regulation was imposed and were unable to pay claims filed against them. The ICC requires that carriers of property must have on file with the Commission evidence of insurance, surety bonds, or qualification as a self-insurer. In 1975 the minimum amounts required were 2,500 dollars on any one motor vehicle, 5,000 dollars for loss or damage at any one time and place for cargo liability (contract carriers need not file evidence of cargo liability security), 100,000 dollars for injury or death of one person and 300,000 dollars for all injuries or deaths in any one accident, and 50,000 dollars for each accident for damage to property of others (excluding cargo). Since most carriers consider these minimum requirements too low, many carriers carry liability security in excess of the minimum.

REGULATION OF MERGERS

Mergers (consolidations, mergers, or acquisitions of control of one motor carrier by another) and pooling among regulated passenger and freight motor carriers are subject to Section 5 of Part I of the Act. Regulated highway carriers may not merge without the approval of the ICC, and when the Commission is deciding a merger case, it must find the merger to be consistent with the public interest before approval can be given. The ICC must consider the effect of a proposed merger on adequate transportation service to the public, the total fixed charges resulting from the transaction, and the interests of the carrier employees affected. Mergers are exempt from this provision if the total operating revenues of the to-be-merged companies involved do not exceed 300,000 dollars. However, because the Commission has control over any transfers of certificates and permits, even mergers among smaller motor carriers can be controlled by the ICC. Mergers approved by the Commission are exempt from the antitrust laws.

There have been hundreds of merger cases heard by the ICC since the Motor Carrier Act went into effect in 1935. There has been a relatively greater degree of merger activity among motor bus companies than among motor truck companies although, because of the larger number of trucking companies, there have been more trucking mergers than there have been bus mergers.

The reasons for the large number of mergers in the trucking industry include the availability of a large number of carriers for sale because of retirement from the business, unprofitability of the company, or other reasons; the opportunity for cost savings, particularly in side-by-side mergers; the opportunity to provide better service by performing one-carrier service over longer hauls without interchange of freight in end-to-end mergers; and the desire of the buyer to acquire the right to serve the route or area and/or the commodities because it results in a more logical overall system. Related to the latter 2 points is the fact that it is often easier to purchase additional operating authority than to apply for an extension of operating authority through the entry control process. Other reasons for mergers are the desire to diversify operations into different commodities, the psychological factor of managing a larger enterprise, the purchasing power and borrowing power stemming from larger size, and the internal operating improvements and economies related to a larger organization.[30] More trucking mergers are end-to-end mergers than side-by-side mergers. Since in a merger, contract carriers cannot "tack" new routes onto the old routes and provide through service, there are very few contract carrier merger applications.

Opposition to motor carrier mergers, when it does occur, often comes from other motor carriers instead of from users, from labor, or from the general public. The fact that many are end-to-end mergers eliminates the question of reducing the amount of competition among parallel carriers, but it does raise the question of how the merged carrier might affect other motor carriers in the same general area. These are carriers that interchange with one of the merged companies or will compete against the merged company. The ICC has included the interest of competing motor carriers in determining the consistency of a proposed merger with the public interest.

Most motor carrier merger proposals have been approved by the Commission. The specific reasons for approval have included improved service to the public, revival of ailing firms, operating economies that will result, managerial advantages that will occur, reduced labor costs, lower purchasing costs, lower financing costs, and corporate simplification.[31]

It is apparent that the Commission intends to make motor carriers larger and stronger financially. The result of the ICC policy has been to help reduce the number of federally regulated trucking companies from 20,872 in 1945 to 16,005 in 1975 (see Chapter 11) and to create several giant carriers, including 9 in 1975 whose transcontinental operations were the result of mergers.[32]

Environmental and energy considerations have not been of significance in motor carrier merger cases.

ILLEGAL TRANSPORTATION

Nature of Illegal Transportation

Any for-hire highway transportation that is subject to regulation by the ICC or a state regulatory agency but is performed without having been authorized (by certificate or permit), is considered to be illegal. Such illegal transportation is primarily in the transportation of property and it take many forms, some of them highly unique, ingenious, and complex.

[30]See American Trucking Associations, Inc., *Mergers in the Trucking Industry* Current Report Number 21 (Washington, D.C.: American Trucking Associations, Inc., 1968), pp. 7–10; Colin Barrett, "The Big Company Era in the Trucking Industry," *Traffic World,* February 22, 1969, p. 81; and Taff, *Commercial Motor Transportation,* pp. 459–460.

[31]James C. Johnson, *Trucking Mergers* (Lexington, Massachusetts: D. C. Heath and Company, 1973), pp. 65–80.

[32]Taff, *Commerical Motor Transportation,* p. 455.

The various kinds of illegal interstate truck transportation include outright solicitation of regulated for-hire traffic by persons who have no operating authority with no attempt to pretend that the transportation is not for-hire; various kinds of arrangements between vehicle owners and users to provide for-hire service while making the arrangement appear to be a lease of vehicles instead of for-hire trucking service; unauthorized for-hire carriage by private carriers, often on the back haul, including "buy-and-sell" operations in which the private carrier buys commodities at a point, carries them to another point, and sells them at what he paid for them plus some charge for transporting them;[33] carriage of traffic beyond local areas by exempt for-hire local cartage carriers; carriage of regulated commodities on a for-hire basis by carriers of exempt agricultural commodities; for-hire carriage of regulated commodities by organizations pretending to be exempt agricultural cooperatives; for-hire carriage by legitimate agricultural cooperative in excess of the 15 percent limitation referred to earlier; and violation of certificate and permit provisions by regulated carriers whereby they carry commodities and/or serve points, routes, areas, or users not authorized in their operating authorities.

Although the amount of illegal trucking in the United States is difficult to measure, it is said to be substantial, particularly when one includes both interstate and intrastate traffic. It has been estimated that illegal truck transportation amounts to at least 5 per cent of the total truck ton–miles in the country, although no one really knows what the amount is.[34]

Attempts to control illegal truck transportation at both the federal and state levels have been more successful since 1965, when Congress provided by statute some enforcement improvements and provided that there could be greater federal-state cooperation. Because of the vast number of vehicles and highway miles in the country, however, it is virtually impossible to prevent all illegal truck transportation, although thousands of arrests are made each year. Enforcement is also made difficult by the fact that the enforcement staff of the ICC and the fines imposed on illegal truckers are relatively small (the average fine levied has been only about $50) and because of the failure of some states to be active in this area. In 1974, 44 reporting states made almost 35,000 arrests for some form of illegal truck transportation of the kind discussed here and they collected fines totaling 2.4 million dollars.[35]

Federal-State Relations

In 1965 Congress amended the Interstate Commerce Act and provided that in order to discourage illegal truck transportation, the states could require ICC regulated motor carriers to register with the state regulatory agency (this had been possible before 1965), that the ICC could enter into cooperative agreements with the states to enforce regulatory laws (this had been prohibited prior

---

[33] Buy-and-sell operations are not confined to private carriers. Other persons who own trucks but have no operating authority may also engage in such practices.

[34] "Gray Area Transportation: Fading, But Still Clouding Your Costs," *Handling and Shipping*, May, 1968, p. 72.

[35] "Illegal Trucking Declines for Second Year in Row; '74 Arrests Total 34,800," *Traffic World*, December 8, 1975, p. 32.

to 1965), and that the ICC and the states could exchange information relative to enforcing motor carrier regulatory laws. The ICC was also given authority to enforce the law against any carrier or user involved without regard to where the carriers or other persons reside, even though outside the state in which the violation(s) occurred.

The enactment of this amendment and the cooperative programs between the ICC and most of the states have somewhat improved the enforcement of economic regulation at both the federal and state levels.

STATE ECONOMIC REGULATION OF
HIGHWAY TRANSPORTATION

The states began economic regulation of highway transportation long before the federal government entered the picture. After 1935 the federal Act became a model upon which some state statutes and amendments were based. The federal law of 1935 also made state regulation more effective because it became impossible to avoid regulation by crossing state lines, as had been the practice prior to 1935. The result was more uniform and effective regulation at the state level. Nevertheless, there remains considerable variation among the states in the definitions used, in what is regulated, in how it is regulated, and in the overall effectivenss of regulation.

Today, intrastate motor carriers of passengers are subject to economic regulation in every state and motor common carriers of freight are under economic regulation in 48 states (Delaware and New Jersey are the exceptions). Contract carriers of freight are regulated in 48 states.[36] The fact that a great deal of motor carrier traffic is intrastate means that state regulation of highway transportation is much more important than state regulation of railroad transportation. In addition, the federal government has been less inclined to take over regulation of intrastate highway transportation than it has in the case of railroads.

State economic regulation includes requirements that operating authority be obtained before operations may begin, with exemptions for certain kinds of for-hire transportation, such as local trucking and carriage of agricultural commodities; regulation concerning dual operation as both a common and contract carrier, mixed private and for-hire service, and abandonment of service; regulation pertaining to the filing and approval of motor carrier rates and fares, fixing of rates and fares by the state regulatory agencies, and prohibition against unjust price discrimination; regulation dealing with the adequacy of service, interchange of freight and equipment, and the leasing of equipment; control of security issues and regulation of accounts and reports; and regulation of mergers, transfers of operating authority, and railroad control of motor carrier facilities. The extent to which each of these various phases of regulation is found among the states varies widely. However, some aspects of regulation are practically universal at the state level.[37]

---

[36]Charles F. Phillips, Jr., *The Economics of Regulation*, 2nd ed. (Homewood, Illinois: Richard D. Irwin, Inc., 1969), pp. 91–95.

[37]The most recent complete study of state economic regulation of motor truck transportation is Harper, *Economic Regulation of the Motor Trucking Industry*.

The entry control policy followed by the states varies considerably from state to state in terms of the amount of competition permitted, varying from a restrictive monopoly-type approach to practically no control over entry into at least some types of for-hire motor carrier transportation.

Although federal authority is exclusive in the matter of security issues, there is a specific prohibition in the Interstate Commerce Act against the ICC's interfering with intrastate rates and fares that discriminate against interstate commerce or for any other purpose.

Not only has the federal government interfered little with regulation of intrastate highway transportation, it has also relied upon the states to aid in regulation of interstate motor carrier transportation. We have already noted that in the area of illegal truck transportation the ICC and the states have often cooperated to try to reduce this problem, as authorized by the Act. The Interstate Commerce Act also provides that the ICC shall, when a case involves not more than 3 states, or may, when the operations involved are in more than 3 states, refer to a joint board to handle the case. A joint board consists of 1 member from each state within which the motor carrier operations are or are to be conducted. The state representatives are nominated by the regulatory agency in each state, if there is such an agency, from its own membership. They are nominated by the governor of the state if there is no such agency. In effect, the joint boards act as would an administrative law judge of the ICC. Recommended orders of a joint board become orders of the ICC unless they are overturned by the Commission. The purpose of the joint boards is to reduce the work load of the ICC and its staff. The use of joint boards also places responsibility for regulation on those most familiar with the area involved.

For these reasons, then, state participation in economic regulation of highway transportation is much more significant and effective than it is in regulation of railroads.

SELECTED REFERENCES

A general reveiw of economic regulation of highway transportation is Charles A. Taff, *Commercial Motor Transportation*, 5th ed. (Cambridge, Maryland: Cornell Maritime Press, 1975), Chapter 17. See also D. Philip Locklin, *Economics of Transportation*, 7th ed. (Homewood, Illinois: Richard D. Irwin, Inc., 1972), Chapter 30. A critical discussion of economic regulation of highway transportation is Dudley F. Pegrum, *Transportation Economics and Public Policy*, 3rd ed. (Homewood, Illinois: Richard D. Irwin, Inc., 1973), Chapter 14. A rather detailed discussion of economic regulation of highway carriers with case illustrations is John Guandolo, *Transportation Law*, 2nd ed. (Dubuque, Iowa: William C. Brown Company Publishers, 1973). Especially see Chapters 3, 6, 13, 14, 15, 16, 18, 19, 22, 23, 24, 26, 27, 35, 36, 37, and 46. Current developments in federal economic regulation of highway transportation are summarized in the annual reports of the Interstate Commerce Commission available from the U.S. Government Printing Office, Washington, D.C.

A general discussion of entry control in the motor carrier industry is Taff, *Commercial Motor Transportation*, pp. 435-455. A detailed study of federal entry control is Alexander Volotta, *The Impact of Federal Entry Controls on Motor*

Carrier Operations (University Park, Pennsylvania: College of Business Administration, Pennsylvania State University, 1967). A rather detailed legalistic discussion of federal regulation of entry into the highway transportation business is Marvin L. Fair and John Guandolo, *Transportation Regulation*, 7th ed. (Dubuque, Iowa: William C. Brown Company Publishers, 1972), pp. 217-246. An explanation of how a user can participate in the entry control process in regulated highway transportation is found in Herbert A. Dubin, "The Role of The Supporting Shipper," *Transportation and Distribution Management*, December, 1971. The general characteristics of the operating authority of irregular route common carriers are discussed in Charles A. Taff and David Rodriguez, "An Analysis of Some Aspects of Operating Rights of Irregular Route Motor Common Carriers," *Transportation Journal*, Winter, 1975. The nature of common carrier entry control and the certificates granted by the ICC and the problem of overparticularized restrictions in them is dealt with in Colin Barrett, "Competition and Controls," *ICC Practitioners' Journal*, July-August, 1973 and in Byron Nupp, "Control of Entry as an Economic and Regulatory Problem," *ICC Practitioners' Journal*, May-June, 1968. Court and ICC decisions upholding the concept that the effect on common carriers should not be considered in contract carrier entry control cases are discussed in Thomas H. Ploss, "Contract Carrier Applications: An Anomaly," *ICC Practitioners' Journal*, November-December, 1966. A study of grants of operating authority to interstate contract carriers is reported on in Taff, "Grants of Motor Contract Carrier Operating Authority— 1970-1975," *Transportation Journal*, Winter, 1976. The ICC's policy of eliminating gateway restrictions is discussed in Philip L. O'Neill, "The Implementation of Complex, Remedial Regulations: The ICC Gateway Elimination Policy," *ICC Practitioners' Journal*, July-August, 1976. Operating authority alternatives for carriers in interstate commerce that operate solely within 1 state are dealt with in George H. Hart, "Single State Operations," *ICC Practitioners' Journal*, September-October, 1972.

The impact of economic regulation on private carriers is discussed in Colin Barrett, "Elements of Private Carriage, Part II: A Matter of Law," *Transportation and Distribution Management*, August, 1970. See also Barrett, "Transport: What's Legal and What's Not in Private Carriage," *Transportation and Distribution Management*, May-June, 1976.

For an account of the background of the agricultural commodities exemption in the federal Act, see Charles A. Taff, *Operating Rights of Motor Carriers* (Dubuque, Iowa: William C. Brown Company Publishers, 1953) and John C. Spychalski, "Political Considerations in the Formation of Transport Policy: Products of Legislative Compromise," *ICC Practitioners' Journal*, January-February, 1967. The place of agricultural cooperatives in transportation is discussed in W. H. Thompson and R. L. Carstens, "The Role of Agricultural Cooperatives in Transportation," *Transportation Journal*, Fall, 1976.

There have been numerous writings on the operating ratio and regulation of the level of earnings in the motor carrier industry. The pros and cons of using the operating ratio as a standard in regulating motor carrier rates are dealt with in R. Nevel and W. Miklius, "The Operating Ratio as a Regulatory Standard," *Transportation Journal*, Winter, 1968. The conflicting results of the operating ratio versus rate-of-return-on-investment as a rate-making standard are discussed in George W. Wilson, "The ICC Profit Criteria—Rail v. Truck," *Transportation Journal*, Fall, 1966. Other articles on the regulation of highway carrier earnings include Harvey A. Levine and Nai Chi Wang, "Motor Carrier Financing and Earnings Regulation: The Other Side of the Coin," *ICC Practitioners' Journal,* November–December, 1974; Robert R. Nelson, "Motor Carrier Regulation and the Financing of the Industry," *ICC Practitioners' Journal,* May–June, 1974; Harvey A. Levine, "A Historical Analysis of the Criteria to Determine the Revenue Need of Motor Common Carriers," *ICC Practitioners' Journal,* January–February, 1973; and Paul Weiner, "The Use of the Operating Ratio–Revisited," *Public Utilities Fortnightly,* August 5, 1971.

An analysis of the ICC's interpretation of its authority to regulate railroad and motor carrier security issues and its attempt to broaden the definition of securities is Judith E. Minsker, "The Regulation of Carrier Securities: Section 20a of the Interstate Commerce Act," *ICC Practitioners' Journal,* May–June, 1972.

A general discussion of regulation of motor carrier mergers is Taff, *Commercial Motor Transportation,* pp. 455–465. The most complete recent study of federal policy on motor carrier mergers is James C. Johnson, *Trucking Mergers* (Lexington, Massachusetts: D. C. Heath and Company, 1973). An earlier study is John E. Altazan, *Interstate Commerce Commission Policy Concerning Consolidations and Acquisitions of Control in the Motor Carrier Industry* (New Orleans: Committee on Research, College of Business Administration, Loyola University, 1956). An early Congressional study is Walter Adams and J. G. Hendry, *Trucking Mergers, Concentration and Small Business: An Analysis of Interstate Commerce Commission Policy,* 85th Congress, 1st Session, Senate Select Committee on Small Business (Washington, D.C.: U.S. Government Printing Office, 1957). A study of recent merger activity at the federal level is Thomas M. Corsi, "The Policy of the ICC in Trucking Merger, Control, and Acquisition of Certificate Cases, 1965–1972," *ICC Practitioners' Journal,* November–December, 1975. A study of ICC decisions on mergers and their effects on competition and concentration in the motor carrier industry is Jay A. Smith, Jr., *The Interstate Commerce Commission's Policy Regarding Mergers and Acquisitions of Regulated Interstate Motor Carriers: An Industrial Organizational Analysis,* unpublished Ph.D. dissertation, University of Maryland, 1972. See also Smith, "Concentration in the Common and Contract Motor Carrier Industry–A Regulatory Dilemma," *Transportation Journal,* Summer, 1973.

The most recent comprehensive study of economic regulation by the states is Donald V. Harper, *Economic Regulation of the Motor Trucking Industry by the States* (Urbana, Illinois: University of Illinois Press, 1959).

23

Government Economic Regulation

of Water, Oil Pipeline,

and Air Transportation

Our objective in this chapter is to discuss the economic regulation of water, oil pipeline, and air transportation as it currently exists. As noted in Chapter 19, 2 of the characteristics of transportation that led to its economic regulation by government are that parts of it are thought to tend toward monopoly and parts of it are thought to tend toward destructive competition. Either characteristic is considered undesirable from the point of view of the public interest because of the adverse effect it has on the quality of service provided and/or the level of rates and fares charged.

The 2 basic regulatory approaches to the problems of monopoly and destructive competition in transportation were illustrated in some detail in our discussions in Chapters 21 and 22. We saw in Chapter 21 how an industry that is thought to tend generally toward monopoly (railroad transportation) is regulated and in Chapter 22 how an industry that is said to tend generally toward destructive competition (highway transportation) is regulated. It is obvious that there are significant differences in the regulation of the 2 modes along with many similarities.

The remaining 3 modes of domestic transportation (water, oil pipeline, and air transportation) have economic characteristics similar to either railroad or highway transportation and can be categorized as generally being thought of as exhibiting a tendency toward monopoly or a tendency toward destructive competition, although each mode has some elements of both tendencies. These modes are approached regulation-wise in a general way as either problems of monopoly (as are railroads) or problems of destructive competition (as are highway carriers). Consequently, because of the similarities that exist in either economic regulation of railroads or highway transportation, it is not necessary in our ensuing discussion of economic regulation of the 3 other modes to go into as much detail as we did in Chapters 21 and 22 because the basic form of regulation in each remaining mode is similar to what we have already described in those chapters.

ECONOMIC REGULATION OF DOMESTIC
WATER TRANSPORTATION

The current federal regulatory system as it applies to domestic water transportation was instituted in 1940 and has changed only slightly since that time. The reader will recall from Chapter 12 that domestic water transportation consists of several different "trades." These are coastal, intercoastal, Great Lakes, and river and canal transportation, as well as water transportation between the mainland United States and offshore states and possessions. All interstate traffic in these trades, except the last one listed, has been subject to economic regulation by the Interstate Commerce Commission (ICC) since 1940. The Federal Maritime Commission (FMC) has regulatory jurisdiction over water transportation between the continental United States and the states of Hawaii and Alaska, and between the United States and its various possessions, even though such transportation is technically domestic interstate commerce. Such regulation by the FMC is not included in our discussion in this chapter.

We shall discuss federal economic regulation of domestic interstate water transportation, as administered by the ICC, in terms of regulation of entry, exit, rates and fares, service, accounting and financial matters, and mergers. Exemptions are also discussed. Statutory requirements are found in Part III and in some sections of Part I of the Interstate Commerce Act. Railroad owned water carriers engaged in joint rail-water transportation are regulated under Part I of the Act. Because of the insignificance of interstate transportation of passengers by water, we shall confine our discussion mainly to the transportation of property, although the regulatory system is the same for both freight and passenger transportation.

The number of water carrier cases dealt with by the Commission each year is small because most water carrier traffic is exempt from regulation.

Regulation of Entry

Because a pre-regulation problem that existed in domestic water transportation, at least in some trades, was said to have been one of too many carriers and excessive competition, caused mainly by the relatively small amount of capital necessary to enter which, in turn, was a result of the lack of an investment in a way, entry control was included as a major part of economic regulation. As with entry control in highway transportation, the ICC has the authority to determine how many carriers there will be, who they will be, what areas, routes, and points they can serve, and what they can carry. Only a few entry control cases have been decided by the ICC. Many of these cases involved extension of service to newly improved waterways.

Common Carriers. The Interstate Commerce Act requires that those who seek to serve as a common carrier of freight or passengers by water or to extend service as a common carrier by water apply for a certificate of public convenience and necessity from the ICC. The applicant must show that he is "fit, willing, and able" and that the service proposed is required by the present or future public convenience and necessity.[1] Certificates of public convenience and necessity specify either the route or routes over which or the ports to and from which the carrier is authorized to operate.

The Commission has interpreted the entry control provision in a fashion very similar to its interpretation of the entry control provision regarding common carriers by highway (see Chapter 22) in regard to the meaning of the phrases "fit, willing, and able" and "public convenience and necessity." As to the latter, the ICC takes into account the public need for the proposed service, the adequacy of existing water carrier service and whether existing water carriers can provide the proposed service, and the effect on existing carriers of a new entrant. When service is already available from another carrier in the territory involved, the applicant must usually show that the existing service is inadequate in some material respect and must establish that existing water carriers cannot, or will not, meet the transportation requirements of the users between the points involved. Water carriers in the area are usually accorded the right to transport all the traffic that they can handle adequately, efficiently, and economically before a new operation is authorized. So long as such carriers are fit, willing, and able to handle the traffic, they are not usually subjected to competition of new service.[2]

This approach provides considerable protection to existing carriers, although the ICC says that it tries to encourage competition whenever feasible and that reasonable competition is in the public interest. In fact, new operating authority has sometimes been awarded over the objections of existing water carriers, particularly if it would result in a more efficient and economical service for the applicant and where projected growth of regulated traffic meant that there would be no appreciable effect on the operations of existing carriers.[3]

Because of the test used to determine if an applicant is fit, willing, and able to serve, carriers already in operation have an advantage over newcomers to the water carrier industry in getting operating authority.

The effect of a new water carrier entry on other modes of transportation is a factor to consider in entry control cases and is discussed in Chapter 24.

Many freight carrier certificates authorize the carrier to carry "general commodities," instead of a specified commodity or commodities, and the restrictions on routes and points to be served are less specific than in motor carrier certificates.

The environmental consequences of a new water carrier operation or an extension of an existing operation are minor and have not been of any significance in ICC entry control cases. Energy use implications have not been of any importance thus far.

Water carrier certificates may be suspended or revoked by the ICC for failure to provide service thereunder. This authority was added by Congress in 1965 in order to eliminate the problem of unused or "dormant" operating authority.

---

[1]Common carriers by water in operation on January 1, 1940 were allowed to continue in operation under a grandfather provision in the Act of 1940.

[2]John Guandolo, *Transportation Law*, 2nd ed. (Dubuque, Iowa: William C. Brown Company Publishers, 1973), p. 149.

[3]See, for example, *Sioux City and New Orleans Extension–Mississippi River*, 343 ICC 412 (1973) and *Hennepin Towing Company, Extension–Upper Mississippi River*, 343 ICC 422 (1973).

Contract Carriers. Contract carriers by water are regulated only to the extent necessary to protect common carriers. The Interstate Commerce Act provides that a permit must be obtained from the ICC before anyone can operate as a contract carrier of freight or passengers or extend operations as a contract carrier by water in interstate commerce. The requirements that must be met by an applicant are less stringent than for a common carrier applicant. The applicant must be fit, willing, and able to provide the service proposed but need only show, in addition, that the proposed service is "consistent with the public interest" and the national transportation policy declared in the Act.[4] The permit granted specifies the business of the contract carrier and the scope thereof.

The policy followed by the Commission in water contract carrier cases is similar to that followed in highway carrier cases in that no general public need must be shown, but it must be demonstrated that a user(s) is willing to enter into a contract with the carrier, and the adequacy of and effect on existing water carriers is taken into account, as are other factors. Contract carrier applications have generally been denied when existing water carriers could provide the user with the type of service required. The Commission has held that existing carriers are entitled to transport all of the traffic which they can handle adequately, efficiently, and economically without the competition of a new service in the territory. Contract carrier permits have been issued when existing carriers could not provide the necessary service. Unfavorable experiences with existing carriers must usually be shown in such cases. Occasionally, a contract carrier has been admitted even when existing common or contract water carrier service was adequate if there were a need for transportation that could not be met by existing carriers.[5]

Water carrier permits may be suspended or revoked by the ICC for failure to provide service thereunder.

The definition of a contract water carrier in the Act is much less specific than the definition of a highway contract carrier in Part II. In distinguishing between common and contract water carrier service, the major test is whether or not the carrier holds himself out to serve the public generally and whether or not some sort of specialized service is involved.

Dual Operation. Dual operation as both a common and contract carrier by water is prohibited by the Act unless the ICC makes a special exception. The Commission has done so when the services to be provided were entirely different, in terms of routes or areas or commodities carried, and were not competitive with one another.

Exemptions from Regulation

The most peculiar and controversial aspect of economic regulation of domestic water transportation is the broad exemptions that were provided by Congress in the 1940 legislation.

Private carriers are, of course, exempt from regulation. There is no provision

---

[4]Contract carriers by water in operation on January 1, 1940 were allowed to continue in operation under a grandfather provision in the Act of 1940.

[5]See Guandolo, *Transportation Law*, pp. 190–194.

in the Act that prohibits mixed private and for-hire service by the same operator. The Commission has sometimes permitted such mixed operations if the for-hire service served a public need, but the Commission normally will not do so on the ground that it would adversely affect common and contract carriers.

In addition to the exemption for private carriers, the Act of 1940 provided specific exemption from economic regulation for the for-hire carriage of liquid commodities carried in bulk, dry-bulk commodities if not more than 3 different commodities were carried in the same vessel or tow (combination of barges), contract carriage when it was not substantially competitive with common carriage of any kind regulated by the ICC, and transportation incidental to transportation by railroad, motor carrier, or express company that is in the nature of transfer, collection, or delivery service in terminal areas or has to do with floatage, car ferry, lighterage, or towage. Conditional exemptions are at the discretion of the ICC and include interstate transportation within the limits of a single harbor or between places in continuous harbors when not part of a through movement to or from places beyond; transportation by small craft of not more than 100 tons carrying capacity; and ferries and certain other operations.

The most important exemption is, of course, that for bulk commodities since bulk commodities constitute most domestic water carrier traffic. It will be recalled that railroads were strong advocates of regulation of water carriers. The exemption of bulk commodities was included, at least in part, apparently because it was thought (in 1940) that such transportation was not competitive with railroads or motor carriers because of the large size of the shipments and the low rates involved. In any event, such is not the case today and railroads are very much involved in not only the bulk commodity business but also in large shipments, and provide multiple-car, trainload, and unit-train service and rates to the bulk commodity shipper. As a result, the railroads complain bitterly about the exemption by water because when the same commodities are carried by rail they are fully regulated.

Despite the protests of railroads and their demand that the bulk commodity exemption for water carriers be repealed, an opposite trend has occurred. In interpreting the bulk commodity exemption, the ICC ruled in 1941 that dry-bulk commodities could not be carried in the same vessel or tow with non-exempt commodities. To do so would mean that all dry-bulk commodities in that vessel or tow would be under regulation. This became known as the *mixing rule*. The rule, however, was never actually enforced because of expected Congressional legislation on the subject. The 3-commodity limitation rule as it applied to dry-bulk commodities was not entirely complied with by the carriers and was never the subject of formal Commission enforcement action. Following a United States Department of Transportation (DOT) study of the matter published in 1973,[6] which recommended legislation prohibiting the Commission's mixing rule and eliminating the 3-commodity restriction on dry-bulk commodities, in late 1973 Congress passed such legislation which was signed by the president. This step was taken ostensibly to recognize that barge line technology had made it possible to move many more barges in a single tow than was the case

---

[6] A summary of the report is Wesley A. Rogers, "Inalnd Waterways," *ICC Practitioners' Journal,* July–August, 1973.

in the past and it was exceedingly difficult for a carrier to either confine the traffic in a tow to only 3 different dry-bulk commodities or to avoid mixing exempt and regulated commodities. The result was either regulation of the tow or small and less flexible and less efficient tows. Consequently, the legislation means that the exemption has been expanded in its scope instead of eliminated or contracted.

The obvious result of the broad exemptions provided for water carriers is that only a few carriers are actually under regulation by the ICC. They numbered only 185 in 1976.[7] Approximately 9 per cent of the domestic private and for-hire water carrier intercity ton-mileage in all trades is regulated by the Commission.[8]

Regulation of Exit

The Interstate Commerce Act contains no provision for abandonment of regulated domestic water carrier service. Therefore, such carriers are free to discontinue operations completely without ICC interference. However, authorized carriers may not discontinue service in part without Commission approval because they would then not be in compliance with the terms of their operating authorities.

Regulation of Rates and Fares

Common Carriers. The same Interstate Commerce Act requirements regarding just and reasonable rates and fares and unjust discrimination in pricing apply to water common carriers as apply to railroads and motor carriers. Thirty days' notice must be given before a rate or fare can be changed, the ICC may suspend such proposed rates or fares, and rates and fares must be published in tariffs and strictly adhered to. The Commission may investigate existing rates and fares on complaint or on its own initiative and it may prescribe the maximum, minimum, or actual rates and fares of water carriers. Unlike motor carriers, water carriers are subject to Section 4 of Part I of the Act that deals with long-and-short-haul discrimination. A "rule of rate making," similar to that found in Part II of the Act, is included in Part III, including the requirement that the Commission consider the revenue needs of the carriers in regulating water carrier rates and fares.

There were 6,204 water common carrier freight rate tariffs filed with the ICC in fiscal year 1976. Only 25 common carrier passenger fare tariffs were filed. No contract carrier schedules were received by the Commission.[9] These are small numbers compared with the numbers received from rail and highway carriers. The Commission has been fairly inactive in prescribing either maximum or minimum rates for water carriers.

In regulating water common carrier rates and fares, the Commission follows the same principles discussed earlier that are used in regulating rail and motor carrier rates. The ICC finds it difficult to deal with the general level of freight

---

[7]Interstate Commerce Commission, *Annual Report, 1976* (Washington, D.C.: U.S. Government Printing Office, 1976), p. 141.

[8]*Ibid.,* p. 143.

[9]*Ibid.,* p. 120.

rates and the revenue needs of the water carriers as a separate matter because water carrier rates are often tied to the competing railroad rates. In fact, water carriers often ask for and receive the same general rate increases that are given to the railroad industry because the water carriers' costs have increased in the same way as have railroad costs and because there is a need to keep a fairly constant relationship between water carrier and rail rates.[10]

As to the reasonableness of individual rates and fares and the matter of unjust discrimination in prices, the same policy is followed by the ICC as in regulating railroad and highway carrier rates and fares. There have been few complaints about the rates on particular commodities and routes.

Environmental and energy factors have not been of any significance in common carrier rate cases.

Contract Carriers. Regulated contract carriers by water are required to file with the ICC and make public only their minimum rates and fares. The minimum prices filed must be the lowest prices actually used. Thirty days' notice is required to reduce a minimum rate or fare or charge or new rate or fare, and a carrier may not charge a rate or fare lower than the minimum. The ICC may prescribe only minimum charges for contract water carriers.

Federal-State Relations. As is the case in federal regulation of highway transportation, federal interference with intrastate water carrier rates and fares to remove discrimination against interstate commerce or for any other purpose is prohibited by the Act. This permits state regulatory agencies to have greater control over water carrier rates than they do over rail rates.

Regulation of Water Transportation Service

The Act requires regulated water carriers to assume the duty of providing transportation upon reasonable request therefor. Determination of service standards or minimum levels of service by the Commission is not specifically required in the Act. However, the ICC may specify in certificates and permits the services to be performed which must be complied with. The Commission may not restrict the right of a common carrier by water to add to his equipment, facilities, or service within the scope of the certificate. The Commission may not restrict the right of a contract carrier to substitute or add contracts within the scope of his permit or to add to his equipment, facilities, or service within the scope of the permit. The ICC may authorize the entry of additional carriers if existing carriers provide unsatisfactory service.

The Commission has the authority to require regulated water common carriers to interchange traffic and establish joint rates and fares with other water common carriers.

As to discrimination in service, common carriers by water are covered by the blanket prohibition against unjust discrimination found in Part III.

Finally, common carriers by water have the obligation of common carriers to serve, deliver, and to avoid discrimination discussed in Chapter 6.

---

[10]D. Philip Locklin, *Economics of Transportation,* 7th ed. (Homewood, Illinois: Richard D. Irwin, Inc., 1972), p. 764.

Regulation of Accounting and Financial Matters

The ICC may prescribe the accounting system used by regulated water carriers, and has done so, but has no jurisdiction over the issuance of securities or insurance matters.

Regulation of Mergers

Water carriers are subject to Section 5 of Part I of the Act dealing with mergers (consolidations, mergers, or acquisitions of control of one water carrier by another) and pooling among water carriers, and to Section 312 of Part III relating to transfers of certificates and permits. As indicated in Chapters 21 and 22, Section 5 requires that a merger between regulated water carriers must receive prior approval of the ICC and the Commission must first find it to be consistent with the public interest. The ICC, in doing so, must consider the effect of a proposed merger on adequate transportation service to the public, the total fixed charges resulting from the transaction, and the interests of the carrier employees affected. Mergers approved by the ICC are exempt from the antitrust laws.

In the few merger cases decided by the Commission, the same factors were considered as in mergers among railroads or among motor carriers. Environmental and energy consideration have not been important.

State Economic Regulation of Water Transportation

According to a 1968 study, only 30 states exercised some degree of economic regulation of intrastate water transportation in that year.[11] In some states the degree of regulation is very limited and in most cases the amount of traffic under state control is small because a large amount of water carrier traffic is interstate and, thus, outside the jurisdiction of the states. However, the fact that the ICC has no authority to interfere with intrastate water carrier pricing helps to make state regulation somewhat more meaningful than it otherwise would be.

ECONOMIC REGULATION OF OIL
PIPELINE TRANSPORTATION

Interstate oil pipelines (crude oil and products lines) have been under federal economic regulation since 1906, although effective regulation did not begin until the *Pipe Line Cases*[12] were decided in 1914 (see Chapter 19). Oil pipelines are regulated under the railroad part (Part I) of the Interstate Commerce Act[13] and in 1977 were regulated by the ICC. In that year, however, Congress created a new federal Department of Energy to which responsibility for economic

[11] Charles F. Phillips, Jr., *The Economics of Regulation,* 2nd ed. (Homewood, Illinois: Richard D. Irwin, Inc., 1969), pp. 91–95.

[12] 234 U.S. 548.

[13] The Act applies to all interstate carriers by pipeline except those carrying water and natural or artificial gas. One coal slurry and one anhydrous ammonia pipeline were under regulation by the ICC in 1977.

regulation of oil pipelines under the Interstate Commerce Act was eventually to be transferred from the ICC. Consequently, many of the aspects of regulation we discussed in Chapter 21 also apply to oil pipelines. In this section we shall discuss federal economic regulation of interstate oil pipeline transportation by examining regulation of rates, service, and accounting and financial matters. There is no federal economic regulation of entry, exit, or mergers. The only exemption from economic regulation is for private carriage; all for-hire interstate oil pipelines are subject to regulation. It was pointed out in Chapter 19 that in the *Pipe Line Cases* of 1914 and in the Champlin case of 1951[14] oil pipelines that carried only their own oil or oil products and whose services were unused, unsought after, and unneeded by independent oil companies were ruled by the United States Supreme Court to be not subject to economic regulation by the ICC.

In reviewing economic regulation of oil pipelines, the reader should keep in mind the unusual ownership arrangement in the industry: most for-hire oil pipelines are owned by oil companies.

There have been only a few cases involving oil pipelines handled by the ICC since 1906. The ICC has actually been fairly inactive in oil pipeline regulation, other than in the area of valuation of pipeline property, which is required by the Act. Although the Commission has been more active in the post-World War II period than before the war, apparently none of its actions has imposed significant new constraints on managerial decision making in the oil pipeline industry.[15]

Regulation of Rates

The various provisions of Part I of the Act concerning railroad rates referred to in Chapter 21 apply to oil pipelines as well, except for the provisions added by the Railroad Revitalization and Regulatory Reform (4R) Act of 1976. All rates must be filed with the ICC and no changes can be made without 30 days' notice to the Commission and the public. Proposals are subject to suspension for as long as 7 months. The Commission may fix the maximum, minimum, or actual rates, and all rates must be published in tariffs and made available to the public. Carriers must not charge any rate other than that in a published tariff. The ICC may investigate existing rates upon receiving a complaint or on its own initiative. The railroad rule of rate making that existed prior to the enactment of the 4R Act of 1976 also applies to oil pipelines, as does the long-and-short-haul clause.

There are no rate bureaus in the oil pipeline industry and, therefore, rates are proposed by individual carriers and not collectively by a group of carriers. Only 2,726 freight tariffs were filed with the ICC by oil pipelines in fiscal year 1976,[16] a very small number when compared with other modes. There have been only a handful of oil pipeline rate cases since 1906. Rarely are suspension and investigation of a pipeline rate asked for by any party. In fact, in 1944, 30 years after the constitutionality of pipeline regulation was upheld, the ICC decided the first

---

[14] *United States v. Champlin Refining Company*, 341 U.S. 290.

[15] Arthur M. Johnson, *Petroleum Pipelines and Public Policy, 1906-1959* (Cambridge, Massachusetts: Harvard University Press, 1967), p. 407.

[16] Interstate Commerce Commission, *Annual Report, 1976*, p. 120.

pipeline rate case in its history brought by bona fide users against the defendant pipelines.[17] The lack of rate cases is possibly the result of the ownership arrangement and the close-knit character of the oil and oil pipeline industries which means that problems are worked out without resorting to the ICC. In addition, the fact that the Commission has had a long-standing rate-of-return-on-investment rate policy concerning oil pipelines may also have reduced the number of cases because the guidelines, at least on maximum rates, are well-known to carriers and users alike. In late 1975, however, the Commission began an examination of the proper rate of return for oil pipelines.[18]

Regulation of the Rate Level. The cases that have come before the Commission have dealt with the reasonableness of minimum tender requirements (minimum shipment size accepted by carriers), the reasonableness of crude oil rates in general, and the reasonableness of products rates in general, and there were a few cases in which individual oil companies protested against a specific rate or rates. The ICC uses the rate-of-return-on-investment criterion in judging the reasonableness of the level of pipeline rates and has used an objective of a 10 per cent rate of return for products lines and an 8 per cent rate of return for crude oil lines. The higher rate of return for products lines is supposedly based on the greater risk involved and the relatively high rate of return objective for pipelines in general is supposedly based on higher risk than in some other modes of transportation. The risk is in the hazards of carrying oil or its products and the supposed uncertainty of traffic quantity in the future.[19] Despite the relatively high rate of return allowed by the ICC over the years, oil pipeline rates are low in comparison with other modes.

Regulation of Individual Rates. The Commission deals with rate proposals involving individual rates by following the same policies discussed in Chapters 21 and 22 relative to the reasonableness of rates and unjust discrimination in rates. Occasionally, personal discrimination is raised as an issue in a rate case in which a user claims that favorable treatment has been given to the oil company owner of the pipeline. An important rate case pending in 1977 dealt with the rates to be charged by the Alaska pipeline in which the ICC refused to approve the rates proposed because they were too high.[20]

The Elkins Act of 1903, which prohibits rebates, concessions, and other forms of personal discrimination, has been applied to dividends paid by oil pipeline companies to stockholders who are also stockholders in an oil company. Because the United States Department of Justice claimed that such dividends amounted to personal discrimination in the form of rebating to a user and violated the Elkins Act and the Interstate Commerce Act, a consent decree[21] was

---

[17]The case was *Minneslusa Oil Corporation et al. v. Continental Pipe Line Company, et al.,* 258 ICC 41 (1944). See Johnson, *Petroleum Pipelines and Public Policy,* p. 395.

[18] *Valuation of Common Carrier Pipelines,* Ex Parte 308.

[19] See J. L. Burke, "Oil Pipelines' Place in the Transportation Industry," *ICC Practitioners' Journal,* April, 1964, pp. 797–799 for a review of regulation of oil pipeline rates.

[20] See "TAPS Pipeine" Tariffs Suspended; Revised 'Interim' Rates Allowed," *Traffic World,* July 4, 1977, p. 61.

[21] A consent decree means that the accused party does not admit guilt and is not found guilty but agrees to some conditions laid down in a court order to do or not to do something.

agreed to by the accused oil pipelines under which they agreed not to pay to any shipper-owner dividends that were in excess of such stockholders' share of 7 per cent of the value of the pipeline's property.[22] Earnings beyond this amount go into a special surplus account and may be used only for new construction or retirement of debt that was incurred for construction purposes.[23] If all the stock in a pipeline company is owned by stockholders of oil companies, then the consent decree limits all dividends to 7 per cent of the valuation of the pipeline. If there are non-oil company stockholders in a pipeline company, they may receive dividends in excess of their share of 7 per cent of the valuation, while oil company stockholders are limited to their share of 7 per cent.

There have been numerous difficulties in interpreting the consent decree, and several court cases have resulted because of the disagreement over what is the correct valuation of the pipeline property.

Environmental and energy considerations have not been important in oil pipeline rate cases to date.

Federal-State Relations. The "Shreveport rule" of Section 13 of Part I of the Act, which authorizes the ICC to prescribe intrastate rates when necessary to remove discrimination against interstate commerce, applies to oil pipelines as well as to railroads. However, there have been no cases on this issue because no complaints have been filed with the ICC concerning discrimination against interstate commerce.

Regulation of Oil Pipeline Service

As are other common carriers under the jurisdiction of the ICC, oil pipelines are expected to provide transportation upon reasonable request. Determination of service standards or minimum levels of service by the Commission is not specifically required by the Act and most of the service provisions in Part I apply only to railroads. Since there is no entry control in oil pipeline regulation, the ICC cannot regulate service by prescribing service to be performed in a certificate or permit, and it cannot penalize inadequate service by authorizing new competition to enter the industry.

Although the Commission has the authority to require regulated oil pipelines to interchange freight and establish through routes and joint rates with one another, it has never done so because no complaints have been filed concerning this question.

Oil pipelines are subject to the blanket prohibition of unjust discrimination, as stated in Section 3 of Part I.

Finally, oil pipelines have the obligations of common carriers to serve, deliver, and avoid discrimination, as discussed in Chapter 6.

---

[22]The ICC has the responsibility to determine the value of each oil pipeline under its jurisdiction.

[23]*United States v. Atlantic Refining Company et al.,* Civil Action Number 14060 in United States District Court for District of Colombia, December 23, 1941 and *United States v. Atlantic Refining Company,* 360 U.S. 19 (1959).

Regulation of Accounting and Financial Matters

Although the ICC has the authority to prescribe a uniform system of accounting for regulated oil pipelines, and has done so, it has no control over security issues of or insurance carried by such carriers.

Separation of Oil Pipelines from Oil Companies

As we have indicated previously, most oil pipelines are owned either by oil refining companies or by integrated oil companies. The possible dangers in this arrangement were discussed in Chapter 19 and were a reason for placing oil pipelines under regulation by the ICC. Despite regulation, some elements of discrimination against non-owning oil companies are said to persist, and there is also raised the question of lack of competition in the oil industry. Therefore, proposals occasionally are made to separate oil pipelines from the oil industry and bills to that effect have been introduced in Congress over the years, but no legislation has resulted. Interest in the subject has increased since the energy shortage became apparent, and legislation to break up integrated oil companies was being considered by Congress in 1977.

The primary supposed benefits of separation are that "real" competition in the oil pipeline industry and in the oil industry itself would result and discrimination against non-owning oil companies would be removed once and for all. Objections to separation include the fear that there would be difficulty in getting new pipelines laid to new oil fields because only oil companies would be willing to undertake the risk of such investment—independent oil pipeline companies would not build new lines unless a considerable flow of oil were assured. Another argument is that oil pipelines under the present ownership arrangement have relatively low rates, and, unlike other modes, they operate without the need for government financial assistance. Finally, the benefits derived from economies of scale made possible through the construction of large diameter pipelines may be impossible without joint ownership by 2 or more oil companies.

In early 1976 the ICC opened an investigation to determine if the control of pipelines by oil firms lessens competition and creates a monopoly.[24]

State Economic Regulation of Oil
Pipeline Transportation

State economic regulation of oil pipelines preceded federal regulation, but it mainly dealt with the obligations of oil pipelines as common carriers. Early regulation was largely ineffective because even then most oil pipeline traffic was interstate and carriers evaded regulation even on intrastate traffic by purchasing the oil they carried. After the enactment of federal economic regulation in 1906 and the decisions in the *Pipe Line Cases* in 1914, which made such regulation constitutionally possible, state regulation became of even lesser importance. The fact that most oil pipeline traffic is interstate contributes to this situation. The fact that the Shreveport rule applies to intrastate oil pipeline rates further

---

[24] *Investigation of Common Carrier Pipelines,* Ex Parte 308, Sub. 1.

reduces the importance of state regulation, although the rule has never been applied by the ICC. As of 1968, however, 27 states had some degree of economic regulation of oil pipeline transportation.[25]

ECONOMIC REGULATION OF AIR TRANSPORTATION

In this section we shall discuss economic regulation of domestic air transportation which began in 1938 and is administered by the Civil Aeronautics Board (CAB). The system of regulation established in 1938 is essentially the same today and is similar in many respects to regulation of the other modes described previously. The aspects of regulation to be dealt with in this section are regulation of entry, exit, rates and fares, service, accounting and financial matters, and mergers. Exemptions from regulation will also be discussed. The statutory requirements are in the Federal Aviation Act of 1958, which is a reenactment of the Civil Aeronautics Act of 1938 as far as economic regulation is concerned. The Act applies to common carriers in interstate commerce and "overseas" transportation to and from offshore states and possessions and to carriers of mail in all areas of commerce, both interstate and intrastate. Contract carriers are not regulated. As noted in Chapter 19, the CAB is to consider the encouragement and development of civil aviation when carrying out economic regulation, i.e., the Board is expected to promote the development of air transportation and not restrict its development through restrictive regulatory policies. This promotional role, which includes determination of which carriers receive cash subsidy and the amount of the subsidy, has an effect on the regulatory policy of the Board.

The reader will recall from Chapter 14 that there are several categories of air carriers under regulation by the CAB—domestic trunk, local service, intra-Hawaiian, intra-Alaskan, helicopter, all-cargo, international, and supplemental carriers. All but the latter are scheduled carriers. Unless otherwise noted, our discussion applies to all of these categories of carriers.

Regulation of Entry

The system of economic regulation established in 1938 stemmed primarily from the belief that it was necessary to stabilize the for-hire air transportation industry that was said to be characterized by excess capacity, fluctuating prices, unreliable service, and high turnover among carriers. The low capital requirements to enter the industry were said to be a principal reason for the problems of the industry. Consequently, a strong emphasis on entry control was included in the Civil Aeronautics Act of 1938 and entry control has been a major activity of the CAB since then. Entry control means that the Board has the authority to determine how many common carriers of passengers and/or freight there will be and what routes and points they will serve. The purpose is to prevent excess capacity and to ensure that qualified carriers are in the common carrier business. The primary activity of the CAB, until recently, has been entry control.

Before anyone can operate as an *air carrier* (for-hire common carrier in interstate or overseas commerce or a carrier of mail) or extend routes or serve addi-

[25]Phillips, *The Economics of Regulation*, pp. 91–95.

tional points, a certificate of public convenience and necessity must be obtained from the Board authorizing such service. The Act requires that the Board shall issue a certificate to a scheduled carrier if it finds that the applicant is "fit, willing, and able" to perform the service and that the service is required by the public convenience and necessity. Otherwise, the application is to be denied.[26] The certificate specifies the points between which the scheduled carrier is authorized to serve and the service to be rendered. The effect of a new air carrier route award on other modes of transportation is not considered by the CAB.

For many years, until approximately 1970, the main effort of the CAB was expended in entry or route award cases in which the Board handled hundreds of applications. Starting with 19 grandfather carriers in 1938, the CAB has, on a case-by-case basis, developed the scheduled route structure that exists today. In 1976, there were 631 points in the United States that received scheduled airline service,[27] most of it provided by carriers certificated by the Board.

The phrase "fit, willing, and able" has been interpreted by the Board in much the same way as the ICC interprets the phrase. The prior operating record is important, as is the financial condition of the applicant.

As with other modes of transportation, a public need must be shown in order to demonstrate that the proposed scheduled service is required by the public convenience and necessity. In fact, the entire matter of entry control is handled by the Board in a fashion similar to that of the ICC. In addition to public need, the CAB inquires whether or not the proposed service can be provided adequately by existing carriers and whether or not the service can be provided by the applicant without impairing the operations of existing carriers. When carriers involved in a case are receiving cash subsidy from the federal government, as is currently the case with domestic local service lines and Alaskan airlines, the cost of the proposed service to the government has also been taken into account and has been balanced against the benefits that would accrue to the public.

Domestic Trunk Lines. Most of the entry control cases handled by the CAB since 1938 have involved domestic trunk and local service airlines. In the case of the former, the amount of competition to allow on a given route or between a given set of points or city pair eventually became a critical issue, once the basic trunk line system had been established. In other words, cases in the past 2 decades have often involved the question of adding a second, third, fourth, or even fifth carrier to a route already served by a domestic trunk line(s), even though the existing carrier(s) may have been able to expand in order to handle the projected traffic to be carried.

The CAB's entry control policy has been fairly flexible and has not followed a preconceived plan. Instead, it has been decided case-by-case on the basis of carrier-filed applications. The Board's policy on the desirable amount of competition has varied considerably over the years, ranging from one of extreme pro-competition to a very conservative position in which the Board was reluctant to add new carrier service. The most recent period of route expansion was in the

[26] Carriers in operation on May 14, 1938 were permitted to continue in operation under a grandfather clause in the Act.

[27] Air Transport Association of America, *Air Transport 1977* (Washington, D.C.: Air Transport Association of America, 1977), p. 28.

late 1960's. The character of the membership of the Board and, more important, the economic condition of the airline industry, have had a lot to do with the policy adopted by the CAB. The Board's policy on competition has generally followed (after a lag) general economic conditions. In periods of high traffic growth and carrier profits the Board has tended to authorize a large amount of new service, particularly competitive service. In periods of poor traffic growth and unprofitability, or uncertain periods, the Board has tended to not authorize additional competition and has authorized new service primarily when there was a requirement for new or improved service and there was little or no competitive impact.[28]

The obvious dangers in not permitting sufficient competition are complacency on the part of the carriers and possible poor service and high prices. The dangers in having too much competition on a route are excess capacity, low load factors, and financial distress for the carriers and, possibly, high rates and fares and need for cash subsidy. The question of economies of scale is important in deciding on how many carriers should serve a given route because if there are no important cost advantages in having one carrier serve a route and 2 or more carriers can carry the available traffic at as low a cost per unit carried as a single carrier, there is obvious justification for authorizing competitive service in order to provide incentive to efficient operation. There is no clear evidence of the existence of substantial economies of scale in the airline industry after a moderate size has been reached, although experience on this subject has been almost impossible to accumulate because equipment changes have occurred so frequently.[29] If, in fact, there are no important economies of scale, the policy of authorizing competitive service over a route whenever traffic volume permits seems to be in order.

In any event, periods of liberal entry and encouragement of competition twice helped to bring about substantial excess capacity in the trunk airline industry in recent years. This occurred in the early 1960's and early 1970's. The problems of the early 1970's led the Board to unofficially adopt a moratorium on new route awards, meaning that between 1970 and 1975 most applications were denied or were not acted upon.[30]

The CAB's trunk line route award policy resulted in a situation in which in 1972, 23.2 per cent of the trunk line revenue passenger miles were in monopoly markets (markets served by only 1 carrier), 48.3 per cent of the trunk line markets were served by 2 carriers, 20.5 per cent were served by 3 carriers, and 8 per cent were served by 4 or more carriers.[31]

One unusual feature of the CAB's trunk line entry control policy is that all route awards made since 1938 in the continental United States have been to

---

[28]Civil Aeronautics Board, Bureau of Operating Rights, *The Domestic Route System: Analysis and Policy Recommendations* (Washington, D.C.: Civil Aeronautics Board, 1974), pp. 4 and 33-34.

[29]Hugh S. Norton, *Modern Transportation Economics*, 2nd ed. (Columbus, Ohio: Charles E. Merrill Publishing Company, 1971), p. 286 and Locklin, *Economics of Transportation*, pp. 816-817.

[30]It should be noted that because so many route applications are filed, the CAB cannot, even in an expansionary period when new awards are being made, hear every case presented, given the administrative resources available. See Civil Aeronautics Board, *The Domestic Route System*, p. 39.

[31]*Ibid.* pp. 103-104 and Appendix A, Tables 10 and 11.

carriers already in operation, i.e., they were extensions to serve new routes and/or points. No new trunk line companies have entered the industry. As a result of mergers, the 16 trunk lines that were given grandfather rights in 1938 numbered 10 in 1976, plus Pan American Airways, which is now classified as a domestic trunk line because it performs some domestic service. The CAB obviously has believed it better to develop larger and long-haul air carriers than to permit the entry of a number of new airline companies that would probably operate on a smaller scale. Another feature of the CAB entry control policy is that when the need for a new kind of air transportation service arose, the Board and Congress, instead of granting authority to provide such service to old or new trunk lines, created new classes of carriers for that purpose, including local service, all-cargo, and supplemental airlines.

Domestic Local Service Airlines. The development of the cash subsidy program for local service airlines since the mid-1940's was discussed in Chapter 17.[32] These airlines became eligible for permanent certificates by act of Congress in 1955. The CAB uses the same procedures and policies to handle route awards for the local service airlines as they do for trunk lines, with the additional factor of how much subsidy that could be involved taken into account. In several "area" cases, service to smaller cities was set up by the Board. Since 1965 a number of entry cases involving local service airlines have involved applications to serve on intermediate and long hauls between larger cities, sometimes on a nonstop basis. Because the Board has been eager to improve service and to strengthen these carriers in order to reduce the amount of subsidy needed, and because the long-haul and large city routes are not subsidized, many of these requests have been granted. The result has been that local service airlines have become junior or regional trunk lines along with their small city service, much to the dismay of the regular trunk lines. In addition, the monopoly markets served by local service carriers dropped from 68.7 per cent in 1960 to 52.2 per cent in 1972, as local service airlines competed more and more with trunk lines.[33] In granting such authority, the Board has considered the usual factors of public need, whether or not the existing carriers could provide the service, and the potential effect on existing carriers. There were 9 local service airlines in 1976. In 1977, however, Air New England, which had been regulated as a local service airline, was redesignated by the CAB as an "area air carrier," a special category separating it from local service and trunk airlines.

All-Cargo Airlines. In 1949 the CAB, in a close 3 to 2 decision, issued certificates of public convenience and necessity on a 5-year temporary basis to 4 all-cargo airlines to serve as common carriers of freight only on an area basis, with no cash subsidy to be available. They could not carry air express or mail.[34] Several all-cargo carriers had been serving since 1947 under "letters of registration" issued by the Board. The majority of the CAB thought that the potential air freight volume was great and that all-cargo carriers would develop their

---

[32] See *Investigation of Local, Feeder, and Pickup Air Service*, 6 CAB 1 (1944).

[33] Civil Aeronautics Board, *The Domestic Route System*, pp. 111–112 and Appendix A, Tables 10 and 11.

[34] *Air Freight Case*, 10 CAB 572 (1949). A vigorous dissent was written by Board member Harold A. Jones.

own freight traffic and not divert it from certificated combination passenger-freight airlines that up until then had not done much to develop air freight traffic. Since they were not to receive cash subsidy, the carriers, it was thought, would be forced to develop an efficient service. The idea of the certification was to provide evidence on which to base future decisions concerning air freight transportation.

Since the mid-1950's all-cargo airlines have been permitted to carry air express and mail, but they have not been made eligible for cash subsidy. They also hold permanent operating authority. There were 3 all-cargo carriers in operation in 1976. The financial experience of the all-cargo carriers as scheduled common carriers has been less than satisfactory and they have depended heavily on charter freight and passenger traffic in order to survive.

Energy and Environment. The energy shortage and environmental issues of the 1970's have not as yet affected the entry control process to any major degree because for several years the Board declined to act on or denied most applications for new service because of the excess capacity that existed in the trunk line industry and the general economic recession of the time. However, the Board must provide an environmental impact statement if it feels that an entry case would constitute a major action affecting environmental quality. In the 1970's several entry control proceedings were delayed for further investigation so that a record on environmental issues could be developed.

The Board must also comply with the Energy Policy and Conservation Act of 1975 and prepare a statement of energy impact in major cases.

Changes in Certificates. Once a certificate of public convenience and necessity is granted to a scheduled carrier, it is usually permanent (indefinite in term), but it may be revoked, modified, or suspended by the CAB. Revocation may be accomplished only if the carrier has intentionally failed to comply with the Act, orders of the Board, or the terms of the certificate. Suspension or modification is possible if the Board feels that such a step is required by the public convenience and necessity. Because the holder must be found to have failed to comply with an order of the Board commanding obedience to the provisions of the Act or regulations of the Board or terms of a certificate violated by the carrier, revocation has been rare, unless it was at the request of the carrier. Suspension and modification have been fairly frequent and have often taken the form of adding or subtracting the right to serve particular points.

Charter Service by Scheduled Airlines. As noted previously, air contract carriage is not subject to regulation by the CAB. Contract carriage is considered to serve a limited number of customers and includes flights over a relatively long period of time and may require exclusive use of the equipment. It often entails a specialized service. *Charter* service, however, is considered common carriage. The Act provides that any air carrier, other than a supplemental air carrier, may perform charter trips without regard to the points named in the certificate or the type of service specified therein, under regulations specified by the Board. Charter service is the sale of the capacity of an entire aircraft to a single user for the movement of freight or passengers, often for one trip or one round trip only, and does not have the narrow restrictions of contract carriage. Scheduled carriers may provide charter service on or off their certificate routes, but, as of 1976, the off-route charter service, was limited in mileage per year by CAB regulation to 2 per cent of the scheduled on-route revenue plane mileage flown in the previous calendar year. Most trunk, local service, and all-cargo airlines perform charter passenger service and some provide charter freight service.

Scheduled carriers need not secure special operating authority to provide charter service, but they must provide such service under the rules and regulations established by the Board. Such rules and regulations concerning passenger service relative to what constitutes a legal charter arrangement have been changed several times during the period of regulation. There were 9 different charter plans approved by the Board as of 1977. One of them was the *affinity charter* under which the passengers carried belonged to the same group or organization. This requirement was said to discriminate against those who were not in any affinity group, and it also led to considerable cheating through the creation of pseudo affinity groups for the purpose of buying charter service and receiving the low charter fares. Another of the 9 approved plans was adopted in 1975 and was called a *one-stop tour charter* (OTC). It provided that passengers were to be grouped by travel agencies or tour operators and had to travel together, stay at their destination a minimum of 4 days, spend at least $15 a day on ground arrangements, and return together. Fares were to be based on having a high low factor—hopefully 100 per cent—and were considerably lower than regular fares. The purpose of the various restrictions (such as the 4-day and $15 rules) was to limit the amount of diversion from regular scheduled service and fares

In late 1976, the CAB approved, on a 5-year experimental basis, the use of the *advance booking charter* (ABC). To become a member of an ABC group, a prospective passenger had to purchase round-trip transportation from an independent charter operator or travel agent 30 days in advance of departure date for domestic flights. The passenger was not required to be a member of an affinity group, to purchase ground accommodations or any other tour package, or be subjected to any time limits. Prices were not regulated by the CAB. All charter groups had to contain at least 40 people. The ABC charter plan had the fewest restrictions of any charter plans approved by the Board and was expected to draw considerable traffic away from scheduled airline service.

Supplemental Airlines. Charter service may also be provided by supplemental airlines, and the charter plans approved by the CAB are available to them. These carriers were at one time designated as nonscheduled or irregular carriers and they were exempted from regulation by the Board. There were various restrictions on what kind of service these carriers could perform. The objective was to prevent them from draining traffic away from scheduled airlines. They later became known as *supplemental airlines,* and in 1961 the Board for the first time granted them permanent certificates as regulated carriers. This was under authority from Congress, which decreed that their operations were eventually to be restricted to charter operations only, which they now are. They were also declared by Congress to be ineligible for cash subsidies.

An applicant for a certificate to engage in supplemental air transportation service may be given such authority if the applicant is fit, willing, and able to perform the proposed service and to conform with the Act and the regulations of the CAB and if the service is required by the public convenience and necessity.

The Board may include in a certificate such limitations as are necessary to ensure that the service rendered will be limited to supplemental air transportation. A supplemental airline certificate shall designate the points to be served only insofar as the Board shall deem practicable and otherwise shall designate only the geographic area or areas within or between which service may be rendered.

Supplemental carrier certificates are normally for an indefinite period of time. Permanent certificates held by supplemental carriers may be modified, suspended, or revoked in whole or in part by the CAB for the same reasons that other airline certificates may be modified, suspended, or revoked. In addition, specific grounds for modification, suspension, or revocation are included in the Act for supplemental airlines, including failure to comply with the insurance requirements of the Act, failure to provide the minimum levels of service prescribed by the CAB, failure to file necessary reports, and failure to comply with the continuing requirement that a supplemental carrier be fit, willing, and able. These special provisions for modification, suspension, and revocation reflect the fact that supplemental carriers have had less satisfactory financial and service records than have scheduled airlines. Suspension and revocation have frequently taken place, sometimes at the request of the carrier.

There were 8 certificated United States supplemental air carriers in 1976.

Federal-State Relations. The CAB has jurisdiction over the entry into interstate and overseas for-hire common carrier air transportation and all transportation of mail. The states have the authority to regulate entry into intrastate for-hire air transportation when mail is not to be carried. The CAB may, however, take control over an intrastate carrier if such carrier participates in a "substantial" way in carrying interstate traffic or if the carrier flies over a place(s) outside a state even though the origin and destination points are in the same state. However, because an intrastate carrier's operations affect interstate commerce does not itself, under the Federal Aviation Act, lead to jurisdiction by the Board.[35] In a recent case, the CAB declined to assert jurisdiction over the intrastate operations of Southwest Airlines Company, a carrier authorized by the state of Texas to operate intrastate, even though Southwest provided substantial competition against interstate carriers authorized by the Board. the CAB felt that the impact of the intrastate carrier's operations on interstate commerce did not give it jurisdiction to compel the carrier to cease its operations or to subject it to regulation by the Board. This decision was upheld by a federal court of appeals.[36]

Exemptions from Regulation

Private air transportation is exempt from economic regulation by the CAB. In the case of for-hire carriers, contract carriage is exempt. An unusual feature of

[35] See Gene R. Beaty, "Air Carriers—Intrastate Regulation—Limits on Federal Jurisdiction," *Journal of Air Law and Commerce,* Autumn, 1969, pp. 664–665 and Ben H. Sheppard, Jr., "State–Federal Economic Regulation of Commercial Aviation," *Texas Law Review,* January, 1969, pp. 285–286.

[36] *Texas International Airlines and Braniff Airways v. CAB,* 473 F. 2d 1150 (1972).

the Federal Aviation Act is that it authorizes the Board to exempt any for-hire carrier or class of carriers from any provisions of the Act if the Board finds that enforcement would be an undue burden on the carrier(s) by reason of the limited extent of or unusual circumstances affecting the operations of such air carrier or class of carriers and if enforcement is not in the public interest. This is a much broader power to exempt than the ICC has under the conditional exemption power it has in highway and water transportation, and it is a more flexible power because no specific exemptions are set forth in the Act, unlike the specific exemptions provided in the Interstate Commerce Act. The CAB's exemption power is similar to that granted to the ICC for railroads in the 4R Act of 1976.

Under the exemption authority, the Board at one time exempted nonscheduled airlines and since 1952 it has exempted small aircraft. Since July, 1972 "air taxi," "commuter," or "third-level" for-hire carriers are exempt if the aircraft operated have a capacity of no more than 30 passengers and a net takeoff weight of no more than 7,500 pounds (the weight carried, exclusive of the weight of the aircraft itself). This ruling replaced an earlier ruling that had more restrictive seat number and weight limitations. Some commuter airlines have recently asked to be certificated by the CAB and in late 1976 the CAB granted a certificate of public convenience and necessity and authorized subsidy to the first commuter airline, Air Midwest. The Board stated that this decision did not mean that other commuter airlines would be certificated and granted subsidy.

In 1976 a total of 4,100 air taxi operators were registered with the Board. Of these, 200 were commuter airlines that transported mail and/or performed scheduled passenger or cargo service. The others provided nonscheduled passenger or cargo service.[37]

Regulation of Exit

CAB Policy. The Federal Aviation Act provides that no regulated air carrier may abandon any route or part thereof unless the CAB shall find the abandonment to be in the public interest. No total abandonment by a trunk line has taken place. Carriers that have left the industry did so through merger with another trunk line. Several local service airlines have abandoned their services entirely, as have some all-cargo and supplemental carriers because the carriers were unable to continue because of financial difficulty.

Some trunk routes have been turned over to local service airlines. In addition, several routes have been abandoned by local service carriers who wished to cease serving unprofitable cities. The CAB has attempted to set up guidelines for such cases, for example, the "use it or lose it" policy adopted in 1959 under which a city was to lose its local service airline service if it did not produce a minimum of 5 enplaned passengers per day. This was affirmed in other cases later, but it has been difficult for the Board to enforce because of the pressure on the CAB to continue the service. Therefore, enforcement has been erratic. In some instances, the Board has permitted local service carriers (and some trunk lines) to discontinue service to a point if a third-level air carrier would serve the locality.

---

[37]Civil Aeronautics Board, *Annual Report, 1976* (Washington, D.C.: U.S. Government Printing Office, 1976), p. 16.

In some of these cases, the local service airline has been permitted to "subcontract" the right to serve a city to a third-level carrier, and the local service line guaranteed a minimum level of revenue to the small carrier.

Federal-State Relations. If the CAB authorizes an interstate air carrier to abandon service, a state may not force the carrier to provide service over an intrastate segment of a route. A state supreme court has ruled that Congress has preempted the regulation of all routes served by interstate carriers, that federal authority is paramount, and that a state agency has no authority to require continued service.[38]

Regulation of Rates and Fares

Because regulation of air transportation was dominated by the entry control issue until the late 1960's, regulation of airline pricing was treated as a secondary issue by the CAB. The Board was frequently criticized for not developing any principles of price making. In recent years, however, the Board has spent considerable time and effort on the pricing question.

What Is Regulated? The requirements of the Federal Aviation Act concerning regulation of air carrier rates and fares are very similar to those of the Interstate Commerce Act for surface carriers. Regulated air carriers must file all rates and fares with the Board and make them available to the public; 30 day's notice is required before a rate or fare can be changed; the Board may suspend a rate or fare proposal for a maximum of 180 days; the CAB may investigate existing rates or fares on complaint or on its own initiative; the Board may prescribe the maximum, minimum, or actual rate or fare charged (only the maximum and/or minimum for overseas service); and carriers must publish rates and fares in tariffs and may not deviate from the published rates and fares. A "rule of rate making" similar to that for other modes is included, including the requirement that the CAB, in regulating rates and fares, take into consideration, among other factors, the effect of the prices on the movement of traffic, the need of the public for adequate air transportation at the lowest cost consistent with the furnishing of such service, and the need of each carrier for revenue sufficient to enable such carrier, under honest, economical, and efficient management, to provide adequate and efficient air carrier service.

These provisions apply to all scheduled and charter service under regulation by the CAB. In fiscal year 1976, 130,000 pages of tariffs were filed with the Board.[39]

Regulation of the Rate Level. Because air carriers do not have rate bureaus and do not file rates and fares collectively (rate bureaus are prohibited by the CAB), the Board does not deal with them in groups in general rate level cases, as is done with railroads, highway carriers, and water carriers. The rule of rate making in the Federal Aviation Act requires the Board to consider the revenue needs of regulated carriers when regulating rates and fares, but no specific standard for

---

[38] *Frontier Airlines v. Nebraska Department of Aeronautics,* 122 N.W. 2d 476 (1963).
[39] Civil Aeronautics Board, *Annual Report, 1976,* p. 65.

determining this is set forth in the Act. In the late 1950's and in the early 1970's, however, the CAB conducted extensive investigations into the pricing of passenger service by domestic airlines.[40]

Although the operating ratio standard might seem to be suitable for airlines, the Board rejected the operating ratio as a rate-making guide in the 1950's investigation and adopted the rate-of-return-on-investment policy. The same conclusion was reached in the 1970's investigation, called the *Domestic Passenger Fare Investigation* (DPFI), in which the CAB decided that domestic trunk lines should have a rate of return of 12 per cent (it was 10.5 per cent in the 1950's case) and that local service airlines should have a rate of return of 12.35 per cent as a regulatory objective. However, a standard load factor of 55 for trunk lines and 44.4 for local service airlines was also adopted in computing the necessary level of revenues. This meant that the revenue needs of the carriers were to be calculated on the basis that those load factors would actually exist. The idea was to avoid having the public pay excessive fares to support overcapacity in the industry. Under this arrangement, which was intended to apply to each class of carrier as a whole, individual airlines could earn more or less than the group as a whole, depending on their management efficiency, route structures, and other factors. Because of financial difficulties of the airline industry in the 1970's, however, the rate-of-return objectives had not been attained at the time of this writing. This has raised questions about the ability of airlines to finance the purchase of new aircraft needed in the 1980's.

The CAB has been relatively inactive in regulating freight rates until recently. The Board established a minimum freight rate system in 1948 to curb extensive rate cutting, but it was canceled in 1961. A *Domestic Air Freight Rate Investigation* (DAFRI) was under way in the 1970's (begun in 1970) which was intended to lead to a formalized policy on air freight rates and the level of airline earnings.[41]

The Board also has authority to regulate rates paid to carry mail and has distinguished between "service" and "need" rates, the former intended to cover the costs of providing the service received and the latter intended to include a subsidy amount that is needed by a carrier that is not self-sufficient. The former is paid by the Post Office and the subsidy element in the latter is paid by the CAB under the class rate system discussed in Chapter 17.

After 1968 a number of passenger fare and freight rate increases were granted to domestic trunk and local service airlines, particularly after 1973 when the price of fuel escalated rapidly. Since the carriers do not apply for increases as a group, increases are granted to individual carriers, but sometimes all carriers of a given class, such as trunk lines, ask for the same percentage adjustment. In some cases, however, the increases do not apply to all carriers in a particular class. Freight rate increases granted sometimes vary with length of haul, between general commodity and specific commodity rates, and between containerized versus noncontainerized traffic. Minimum charges are also sometimes adjusted upward.

Regulation of Individual Rates and Fares. The Act requires that air carriers establish just and reasonable rates and fares. The Act also prohibits in a blanket

---

[40] The cases were *General Passenger-Fare Investigation*, 32 CAB 291 (1960) *and Domestic Passenger Fare Investigation*, 1970–1974, docket 28166.

[41] *Domestic Air Freight Rate Investigation*, docket 22859.

provision undue or unreasonable preference or advantage or prejudice or disadvantage in any way whatever. The rule of rate making requires Board consideration of the effect of prices on the movement of traffic, the need of the public for air transportation service, and the need of the carriers for sufficient revenue. The CAB has the authority to interpret these various rate regulation requirements as they apply to existing and proposed individual rates and fares of air carriers.

Similar principles are used by the CAB as by the ICC in interpreting the phrases "just and reasonable" and "unjust discrimination." Both value of service and cost factors have been recognized in the past as being important in rate and fare regulation.

As indicated previously, rate and fare proposals are filed by individual carriers instead of by groups of carriers, and the Board has handled these proposals on a case-by-case basis. In the DPFI of 1970-1974, which covered all aspects of costing and pricing of scheduled passenger service and in which standards were adopted for testing the reasonableness of fares in the future, certain policies were established by the Board regarding individual passenger fares. These included the principle that airline fares should be cost related instead of demand related and that family plan and reserved and standby youth promotional (discount) fares were unlawful and were to be eliminated by June 1, 1974. The Board decided that these fares were unjustly discriminatory against payers of regular fares and, because they were low, resulted in higher fares on regular traffic. The Board rejected the idea that promotional fares did not divert traffic away from the full-fare market, the value of service idea of pricing, and the idea that low prices may contribute to cover the fixed cost burden of the carrier. The CAB also decided that, in order to align fares with the "taper" in costs of air carriers, short-haul fares were to be raised as much as 20 per cent and long-haul fares lowered as much as 5.5 per cent. Finally, the Board changed the relationship between coach and first-class fares by raising first-class fares relative to coach fares so that first-class fares would be at least 150 per cent but not more than 163 per cent of coach fares, depending on distance. The relationship had generally been 130 per cent. The CAB also ordered all regulated airlines to offer joint (instead of combination) fares in all markets and in all classes of service in which such joint fares did not exist.

Despite the Board's decision on promotional fares, the economic difficulties of airlines in the 1970's and more liberal CAB charter rules led to a series of proposals by carriers to institute various kinds of promotional fares for scheduled service, other than the kind discarded by the Board, including the "no-frill" fare (travel on off-peak days and in off-peak months and reduced amenities in exchange for a lower fare) and various round-trip fares based on advanced reservations, travel at off-peak times and on off-peak days of the week or in off-peak months, and rules concerning the time period between departure from origin point and return to that point. Fares were usually from 20 per cent to 35 per cent less than the regular coach fares.[42] The Board approved many such plans, at least temporarily, contrary to its policy on family plan and youth fares which,

---

[42] See "Insanity Comes to Air Fares Again," *Business Week,* April 21, 1975 and "Discount Mania Hits the Airlines," *Business Week,* August 8, 1977.

of course, involved different conditions that the passenger had to meet in order to receive the discount.

Regulation of passenger fares has resulted in fare uniformity among competing airlines because competing carriers propose fares that match those that have been approved by the Board for other carriers and the Board is reluctant to permit deep price cutting. Since this is said to force carriers to compete on a service basis, there has been a tendency to overdo things on the service side to get passenger traffic. Service or nonprice competition takes the form of equipment improvements, scheduling frequency, comfort, entertainment, food, drink, and cabin service. Excessive scheduling is particularly costly because it can lead to low load factors and eventual financial difficulty for the carriers.

The usual rate-making factors have been used by the CAB in regulating air freight rates. The DAFRI of the 1970's resulted in a decision by the Board in 1977 that scheduled domestic trunk and all-cargo freight, mail, and express rates should not exceed industry average fully allocated costs, including a reasonable return on investment, and local service airline rates should not exceed industry average fully allocated costs, including a reasonable return on investment, by more than 30 per cent. Rates above those levels were held to be unjust and unreasonable but rates below those levels were not held to be unjust and unreasonable unless they were below industry average variable costs (termed noncapacity costs by the CAB). The Board decided that it was not necessary to prescribe minimum rates or to prohibit discount rates provided variable costs are covered by such rates.[43] It was not clear at the time of this writing how this decision would affect the level of rates.

Environmental and energy considerations have not been of importance in regulation of air rates and fares by the CAB.

Federal-State Relations. The states have the authority to regulate intrastate air transportation, including rates and fares. The Federal Aviation Act permits the states to regulate all rates and fares within the state whether charged by an interstate or an intrastate carrier. Because there is no provision in the Act that specifically prohibits or authorizes federal interference in intrastate rates and fares if they should discriminate against interstate commerce or for any other reason, such interference is probably possible, although it has not been tested in the courts.

Regulation of Air Transportation Service

Regulated air carriers are required by the Act to provide air transportation, as authorized by their certificates, upon reasonable request therefor. Determination of service standards or minimum levels of service by the CAB is not required by the Act. However, as with other modes, the Board may specify in certificates issued the services to be performed. These requirements must be complied with. The Board, however, may not restrict the right of scheduled air carriers to add to or change schedules, equipment, accommodations, and facilities as the development of their business and the demands of the public may require, but the

---

[43] See "CAB Approves Cost Formula For Domestic Freight Rates," *Traffic World,* August 29, 1977, p. 70.

CAB may do so for supplemental carriers in order to be sure that such service is truly supplemental air transportation. The Board may also, of course, authorize the entry of additional carriers if existing carriers provide unsatisfactory service.

The CAB has the authority to require air carriers to interchange traffic and establish through routes and joint rates or fares (but not equipment) with one another.

Unjust discrimination in service is prohibited by a blanket ban against all forms of undue or unreasonable preference or advantage or any undue or unreasonable prejudice or disadvantage in any respect whatsoever.

And, finally, common air carriers have the obligation of common carriers to serve, deliver, and avoid discrimination discussed in Chapter 6.

Regulation of service in air transportation, as in other modes, is difficult. Quality of and discrimination in service are subjective factors and are difficult to measure and control. The CAB has, in conjunction with regulation of passenger fares, issued various rules and regulations on seating configurations of aircraft and amenities (meals, drinks, in-flight motion pictures, etc.) that can be given by airlines to passengers. As noted previously, because fares of competing carriers tend to be identical, competition often takes the form of various service attractions, which must be kept under some sort of control in order to prevent the carriers from incurring unnecessary and excessive costs. The CAB has also established service regulations dealing with other matters, including overbooking (selling tickets to customers beyond the capacity of an aircraft), bumping (refusing transportation because a flight has been overbooked), the responsibility of the carriers to pay for meals and hotel accommodations when excessive flight delays occur, lost and damaged baggage, on-time performance, interchanging of equipment, and the minimum number of flights provided between city pairs.

The fact that the Board usually has no control over the number of flights scheduled by scheduled airlines holding certificates beyond a minimum number of flights has contributed to the periodic overcapacity problem of domestic airlines. As indicated in Chapter 14, carriers tend to schedule flights in such a way that an excessive number of flights and low load factors may result.

The energy shortage of the 1970's led the Board to approve some "capacity agreements" among some competing airlines under which they were permitted to agree on the number of flights they would have in order to reduce excess capacity and raise load factors in order to reduce energy consumption. This had also been done previously in the late 1960's for the purpose of reducing excess capacity and to reduce airport congestion. Some agreements between American, Trans World, and United were ruled invalid by a United States Court of Appeals in April, 1975 on the ground that the Board had failed to determine their effect and need for them.[44] In addition, most airlines have independently reduced the number of scheduled flights in order to conserve fuel.

Regulation of service has been of particular importance to local service airlines. When they were first authorized in the 1940's, the idea was that they should serve between small cities and between small cities and large cities. Several restrictions were placed on their service, such as requiring a local service carrier to serve every intermediate point on every flight and a minimum number

[44] "Capacity Pact Blocked by Court," *Aviation Week and Space Technology,* April 28, 1975.

of flights per day per city served. The purpose was to prevent local service airlines from competing directly with trunk lines and to be sure that the small cities received at least a minimum level of service. Eventually, the stop restrictions were relaxed and, as noted previously, local service airlines have been granted authority to serve between large cities on relatively long hauls, sometimes on a nonstop basis, and to discontinue service at some small cities. These moves have been made by the Board primarily to reduce the need for cash subsidy.

As indicated in Chapter 14, for many years (since 1927) scheduled airlines had a contract with REA Express or its predecessors to provide ground transportation for air express traffic which was an expedited, priority service for small shipments. In 1973, the Board ruled that the relationship should be terminated in 1974 because it gave REA Express a monopoly position, there was little need for air express service, the need that did exist could be met by the airlines themselves, REA was in financial difficulty, and there was a strained relationship between some airlines and REA Express. The decision of the CAB was stayed by a United States Court of Appeals and the Court ordered the CAB to look into the matter again. The controversy ended, however, when REA Express went into bankruptcy and out of business in February, 1976. Express service, sometimes referred to as *priority service,* has since been offered directly by most airlines as a replacement for REA air express service.

Regulation of Accounting and Financial Matters

The Federal Aviation Act provides that the CAB may prescribe the accounting system to be used by regulated air carriers, and the CAB has done so. The Board has no jurisdiction over air carrier security issues and it has no authority to require air carriers, except supplemental airlines, to carry insurance. The latter must carry insurance required by the Board to cover liability for injuries or death of any person or loss of property of others. The Board may also require a supplemental airline to file a performance bond or equivalent security arrangement to protect travelers, shippers, and receivers against failure on the part of the carrier to perform air transportation service. These provisions reflect the concern of Congress and the CAB about the reliability of supplemental airlines.

Regulation of Mergers

Mergers (consolidations, mergers, and acquisitions of control of one air carrier by another) and pooling among regulated air carriers are subject to control by the CAB. Actually, the Board is *required* by the Act to approve mergers unless the Board finds that the proposed transaction will not be consistent with the public interest. The CAB may not approve any merger that would result in creating a monopoly or monopolies and thereby restrain competition or jeopardize another air carrier. In addition, any transfer of certificates issued by the Board may not be accomplished unless approved by the CAB as being in the public interest. Mergers approved by the CAB are exempt from the antitrust laws. The president of the United States must approve air carrier mergers or other transfers of certificates if international routes are involved.

Very few merger cases have been handled by the CAB since 1938. Only 6 mergers were accomplished between trunk lines by 1977, thus reducing the number of trunk lines from 16 to 10 (plus Pan American). Several other merger applications were disapproved or withdrawn. There were 4 mergers among trunk lines in the 1950's and a major merger between Capital Airlines and United Airlines in 1961. Several mergers were proposed in the 1960's and early 1970's, but they were never consummated either because the applications were withdrawn or they were denied by the CAB or an administrative law judge. In 1972 Delta Airlines was authorized to acquire Northeast Airlines.[45]

Trunk line interest in mergers has risen and fallen with changes in economic conditions in the industry. Merger applications increase in number when conditions are bad and decrease when conditions are good. Specific reasons for merger applications have been interest in creating larger and more efficient carriers and the desire to serve longer hauls and thus avoid connections between carriers, thereby making service more attractive to the public. Merger has also sometimes been considered to be an easier way to get into a new market or route than through the entry control procedure. In some cases, the carriers sought to reduce competition by merging parallel systems (side-by-side mergers), but these have been turned down by the Board. The trunk line mergers that have been approved and taken place have been mainly end-to-end mergers and have not involved the issue of a significant reduction in competition between carriers serving the same city pair(s).

In merger cases, the CAB has considered, in determining the public interest, a number of factors, including the elimination of the acquired carrrier as a competitor, the price to be paid in the acquisition, improved service that may result, the integration of routes, savings to be realized, the effect on other carriers, the size and competitive position of the acquiring carrier, degree of control of interchange traffic, development of connecting service, financial condition of the carriers, and the effect of the transaction on employees.[46]

A primary factor considered in trunk line mergers appears to have been the effect on competition and on other air carriers. Since many proposals are end-to-end mergers, direct reduction in competition over a given route is not usually a major consideration. However, competition and other carriers are affected because of the size of the proposed merged company that will be competitive with other carriers and the effect the merger may have on interchanging or connecting airlines. The Board has shown an aversion to creating giant carriers needlessly, the domination of an area by a large carrier, and the concentration of economic power in the industry. The Board has favored building up smaller carriers through merger. It has also declined to permit merger of profitable trunk airlines and has wanted to avoid encouraging "defensive" mergers in response.

Another factor considered has been the financial condition of the applicants. The two most recently approved trunk line mergers (United–Capital and Delta–Northeast) involved the *failing business doctrine* [one of the merger partners was on the brink of bankruptcy and discontinuance of all service (Capital and Northeast) and a strong carrier purchased the company]. The mergers were approved in order to preserve the service of the failing carrier.

[45] Airline mergers are discussed in George W. Douglas and James C. Miller, III, *Economic Regulation of Domestic Air Transportation* (Washington, D.C.: The Brookings Institution, 1974), pp. 121–122.
[46] See Guandolo, *Transportation Law*, p. 848.

The CAB has been much more prone to approve mergers among local service and other subsidized carriers than among trunk lines, and several were approved in the 1960's and 1970's. The number of local service carriers was reduced from 13 to 8 (increased to 9 in 1975 with the addition of Air New England). The apparent objectives of the Board in approving local service airline mergers were to strengthen such carriers in order to improve their service and to reduce the amount of cash subsidy needed.

Environmental and energy implications have not been of importance in airline merger cases.

State Economic Regulation of Air Transportation

As noted previously, the states may impose economic regulation over intrastate for-hire air transportation, but they have no jurisdiction when mail is carried by air in intrastate commerce. The CAB has declined to force an intrastate carrier to cease operations or become subject to CAB regulation even when there has been some impact on interstate carriers and the Shreveport rule has not been applied by the Board, although it probably could be applied since it is not prohibited by the Act. State authority is secondary to federal authority in abandonment situations.

It is sometimes suggested that the federal government be given complete jurisdiction over economic regulation of intrastate air transportation. The broad interpretation given to the term "interstate commerce" by federal courts in recent years means that federal jurisdiction could probably be extended by Congressional action to virtually all aspects of air transportation.[47] No legislation has as yet been enacted by Congress for this purpose. However, the authority of the states is actually very limited because most for-hire air transportation is interstate in character instead of intrastate.

According to Charles F. Phillips, Jr., 20 states regulated air transportation to some degree in 1968.[48]

Under the Federal Aviation Act, the CAB is empowered to confer with or hold joint hearings with any state agency and to avail itself of the cooperation, services, records, and facilities of such state agencies in enforcing the Act. Joint boards made up of state representatives are, however, not authorized by the Act as they are in Part II of the Interstate Commerce Act.

SUMMARY OF ECONOMIC REGULATION OF EACH MODE

We have now completed our discussion of government economic regulation of domestic transportation as it applies to each of the several modes. It is clear that there are great differences and similarities in the form and scope of regulation applied to each of the different forms of transportation. The main features of federal economic regulation are summarized in Table 23-1.

---

[47]Beaty, "Air Carriers—Intrastate Regulation," p. 665.
[48]Phillips, *The Economics of Regulation*, pp. 91–95.

TABLE 23-1 Scope of Economic Regulation of Domestic Common Carrier Interstate Transportation by Modes, 1977

Mode	Regulatory Agency	Entry	For-Hire Carrier Exemptions	Exit	Prices	Service	Authority to Prescribe Through Routes and Joint Rates
Railroad Freight	ICC	Yes	No*	Yes	Maximum Minimum Actual	Yes, in some detail	Yes
Railroad Passenger Non-Amtrak	ICC	Yes	No*	Yes	Maximum Minimum Actual	Yes, in some detail	Yes
Railroad Passenger Amtrak	ICC	No	No	No	No	Yes, in some detail	No
Highway Freight	ICC	Yes	Agricultural commodities and others	Yes, if not complete	Maximum Minimum Actual	Yes, in general terms	No
Highway Passenger	ICC	Yes	Several minor exemptions	Yes, if not complete	Maximum Minimum Actual	Yes, in general terms	Yes
Water Freight	ICC	Yes	Bulk commodities and others	Yes, if not complete	Maximum Minimum Actual	Yes, in general terms	Yes
Water Passenger	ICC	Yes	Several minor exemptions	Yes, if not complete	Maximum Minimum Actual	Yes, in general terms	Yes
Oil Pipeline	ICC**	No	No	No	Maximum Minimum Actual	Yes, in general terms	Yes
Air Freight	CAB	Yes	Small aircraft‡	Yes	Maximum Minimum Actual§	Yes, in general terms	Yes
Air Passenger	CAB	Yes	Small aircraft‡	Yes	Maximum Minimum Actual§	Yes, in general terms	Yes

Mode	Accounts	Security Issues	Insurance	Mergers	Shreveport Rule Authority	Regulation of Contract Carriers
Railroad Freight	Yes	Yes	No	Yes	Yes	No contract carriage exits
Railroad Passenger Non-Amtrak	Yes	Yes	No	Yes	Yes	No contract carriage exits
Railroad Passenger Amtrak	Yes	Yes	No	Yes	No	No contract carriage exits
Highway Freight	Yes	Yes	Yes	Yes	Prohibited	Yes
Highway Passenger	Yes	Yes	Yes	Yes	Prohibited	Yes
Water Freight	Yes	No	No	Yes	Prohibited	Yes†
Water Passenger	Yes	No	No	Yes	Prohibited	Yes†
Oil Pipeline	Yes	No	No	No	Yes	No contract carriage exits
Air Freight	Yes	No	No‖	Yes	No	No
Air Passenger	Yes	No	No‖	Yes	No	No

* ICC may exempt any person, class of persons, or services under certain circumstances.

** Eventually to be transferred to Department of Energy.

† ICC may exempt contract carriage under certain circumstances.

‡ CAB may exempt any carrier or class of carriers under certain circumstances.

§ Maximum and/or minimum only for carriers in overseas service.

‖ Insurance is required of supplemental airlines.

SELECTED REFERENCES

A summary of federal economic regulation of domestic water transportation is
D. Philip Locklin, *Economics of Transportation,* 7th ed. (Homewood, Illinois:
Richard D. Irwin, Inc., 1972), pp. 754–765. See also Hugh S. Norton, *Modern
Transportation Economics,* 2nd ed. (Columbus, Ohio: Charles E. Merrill Publish-
ing Company, 1971), pp. 291-296 and Dudley F. Pegrum, *Transportation
Economics and Public Policy,* 3rd ed. (Homewood Illinois: Richard D. Irwin,
Inc., 1973), pp. 359-363. A discussion of economic regulation of water carriers
with case illustrations is John Guandolo, *Transportation Law,* 2nd ed. (Dubuque,
Iowa: William C. Brown Company Publishers, 1973), Chapters 4, 7, 16, 19, 26,
27, 35, 36, 37, and 46. Current developments in federal economic regulation of
water transportation are summarized in the annual reports of the Interstate
Commerce Commission available from the U.S. Government Printing Office,
Washington, D.C.

R. Bruce McGehee, "Federal Regulation of Dry-Bulk Commodities Transport by
Water and Rail," *Transportation Journal,* Spring, 1969 deals with the history of
the dry-bulk commodity exemption and the mixing and 3-commodity rules
in water transportation. Wesley A. Rogers, "Inland Waterways," *ICC Practitioners' Journal,* July–August, 1973 summarizes the U.S. Department of Transportation report on the mixing and 3-commodity rules. Paul J. Donovan, "Water
Carrier Barge Mixing Rule Legislation of 1973," *ICC Practitioners' Journal,*
March–April, 1974 describes the legislation of 1973 that removed the mixing
and 3-commodity regulations.

The development of government policy toward oil pipelines after 1906 is given
detailed treatment in Arthur M. Johnson, *Petroleum Pipelines and Public Policy,
1906-1959* (Cambridge, Massachusetts: Harvard University Press, 1967). A summary of federal economic regulation of oil pipelines is Locklin, *Economics of
Transportation,* pp. 612-620. See also Norton, *Modern Transportation Economics,* pp. 296-297 and Pegrum, *Transportation Economics and Public Policy,*
pp. 363-365. A review of the history and form of federal economic regulation of
oil pipelines is J. L. Burke, "Oil Pipelines' Place in the Transportation Industry,"
ICC Practitioners' Journal, April, 1964, pp. 796-802. Current developments in
federal economic regulation of oil pipeline transportation are summarized in the
annual reports of the Interstate Commerce Commission available from the U.S.
Government Printing Office, Washington, D.C.

Separation of oil pipeline ownership from oil companies is discussed in Johnson,
Petroleum Pipelines and Public Policy, pp. 421-422.

A general review of economic regulation of air transportation in Locklin, *Economics of Transportation,* Chapter 35. See also Norton, *Modern Transportation
Economics,* Chapter 15 and Pegrum, *Transportation Economics and Public
Policy,* pp. 336-359. Economic regulation of air transportation with case illustrations is discussed in Guandolo, *Transportation Law,* Chapters 5, 20, 30, 40,
43, 49, and 50. Current developments in economic regulation of air transportation are summarized in the annual reports of the Civil Aeronautics Board available from the U.S. Government Printing Office, Washington, D.C. Federal
economic regulation of air transportation prior to 1961 is dealt with in John H.
Frederick, *Commercial Air Transportation,* 5th ed. (Homewood, Illinois: Richard
D. Irwin, Inc., 1961), Chapters 6, 7, 8, and 9.

Economic regulation of air transportation has been the subject of criticism in many writings, some of which are listed as selected references in Chapter 25.

The regulation of entry and competition among trunk airlines is discussed in William E. Fruhan, Jr., *The Flight for Competitive Advantage* (Boston: Harvard University Graduate School of Business Administration, 1972). A description of the domestic airline route system and CAB policy on entry control is Civil Aeronautics Board, Bureau of Operating Rights, *The Domestic Route System: Analysis and Policy Recommendations* (Washington, D.C.: Civil Aeronautics Board, 1974).

CAB policy regarding local service airlines is dealt with in Robert W. Harbeson, "Economic Status of Local Service Airlines," *Journal of Transport Economics and Policy,* September, 1970. See also Craig Mathews, "Certificated Air Service at Smaller Communities: The Need for Service as a Determinant of Regulatory Policy," *Journal of Air Law and Commerce,* Winter, 1968. A critical review of CAB policy on local service airlines is George C. Eads, *The Local Service Airline Experiment* (Washington, D.C.: The Brookings Institution, 1972). The growth of third-level carriers and the regulatory issues involved in their service to small cities are discussed in Virgil D. Cover, "The Rise of Third-Level Carriers," *Transportation Journal,* Fall, 1971.

CAB policy in dealing with supplemental airlines is dealt with in F. James Kane, "Air Law—Supplemental Air Carriers," *Notre Dame Lawyer,* May, 1959.

A study of airline pricing is Paul W. Cherington, *Airline Price Policy* (Boston: Harvard University Graduate School of Business Administration, 1958). The Domestic Passenger Fare Investigation of 1970–1974 is discussed in George W. Douglas and James C. Miller, III, "The CAB's Domestic Passenger Fare Investigation," *Bell Journal of Economics and Management Science,* Spring, 1974. See also Douglas and Miller, *Economic Regulation of Domestic Air Transportation* (Washington, D.C.: The Brookings Institution, 1974), Chapter 8. Criticism of the 12 per cent rate of return objective for all trunk airlines, without regard to risk incurred, in the Domestic Passenger Fare Investigation case is expressed in Richard D. Gritta, "Risk and the Fair Rate of Return in Air Transportation," *Transportation Journal,* Summer, 1974. Pricing and regulatory policy relative to freight carried by combination airlines is dealt with in Frank M. Lewis, "Is Belly Cargo Profitable?" *Proceedings of Transportation Research Forum, 1971.*

Airline capacity agreements are evaluated in George Eads, "Airline Capacity Limitation Controls: Public Vice or Public Virtue?" *Proceedings of the American Economic Association,* May, 1974 and William A. Jordan, "Airline Capacity Agreements: Correcting a Regulatory Imperfection," *Journal of Air Law and Commerce,* Spring, 1973.

Government policy on airline mergers is discussed in Lucile S. Keyes, "Notes on the History of Federal Regulation of Airline Mergers," *Journal of Air Law and Commerce,* Number 3, 1971; Robert E. Gallamore, "Observations on the Domino Theory of Airline Mergers," *Proceedings of Transportation Research Forum, 1970;* Arthur H. Travers, Jr., "An Examination of the CAB's Merger Policy," *Kansas Law Review,* March, 1967; and Douglas and Miller, *Economic Regulation of Domestic Air Transportation,* pp. 121–122.

State economic regulation of air transportation and its relationship to federal regulation are dealt with in Ben H. Sheppard, Jr., "State-Federal Economic Regulation of Commercial Aviation," *Texas Law Review*, January, 1969 and Gene R. Beaty, "Air Carriers—Intrastate Regulation—Limits on Federal Jurisdiction," *Journal of Air Law and Commerce*, Autumn, 1969. Criticism of state economic regulation of air transportation is expressed in Frederick, *Commercial Air Transportation*, pp. 117–123.

24

Government Economic Regulation
and Intermodal Relationships

The relationships between the several modes of transportation and the economic and physical coordination of the transportation system are important aspects of the total transportation network of the country. In this chapter we shall discuss intermodal relationships and transport coordination and the effect economic regulation has on these facets of transportation in the United States.

TRANSPORT COORDINATION

The 5 modes of intercity transportation have their own economic and service characteristics, they are the beneficiaries of government promotion and subsidy to different degrees, and they are subject to somewhat different forms of government economic regulation. These modes are also to some extent in competition with one another. The ideal situation would be that each of the 5 modes would carry only that traffic that it is best suited to carry in terms of costs and/or service. This would enable us to get the most efficient use of our resources devoted to transportation. As indicated in Chapter 18, this is sometimes referred to as *economic coordination* of transportation. Of course, there is no rigid line of demarcation between modes as to what they can do, and technological changes are being made continuously so that a somewhat fluid situation exists between modes. However, there are general differences between modes that indicate what traffic each is best suited for, for example, air transportation offers great speed, water transportation offers low rates, and highway transportation offers great flexibility.

Another potential desirable feature in transportation would exist if the several modes would work together so that a user could get the cost and/or service advantages of 2 or more modes on any one transaction (shipment, trip). This may be referred to as *physical coordination* to distinguish it from *economic coordination*. It is often desirable for a freight shipper, for example, to utilize different modes of transportation for a given shipment. The principal reasons for this are the service characteristics and costs of different modes. Thus, the limits on the ability of airlines to serve beyond airports require that they coordinate with some surface carrier to pick up and deliver freight. Railroads, water carriers, and oil pipelines also must often rely on some other kind of carrier (usually motor truck) for pickup and delivery.

The result of physical coordination of this kind is the maximization of the advantages inherent in each mode and the minimization of the disadvantages, but the combined services will have both the good and bad aspects of the modes utilized. For example, the coordination of railroad and water transportation will provide a lower total cost than an all railroad movement would have, but it will have a higher cost than an all water carrier movement. Transit time will be less than by an all water carrier movement, but greater than if carried entirely by rail.[1]

LEGISLATION DEALING WITH INTERMODAL RELATIONSHIPS

Statement of National Transportation Policy

Government policy on either economic or physical coordination of the United States transportation system has been vague or absent entirely. The statement of the National Transportation Policy enacted by Congress in 1940 attempted to recognize the fact that there were several different modes of transportation and that the regulatory process as administered by the Interstate Commerce Commission (ICC) should be guided by certain standards set forth by Congress in dealing with a multi-modal system. The statement reads as follows:

> It is hereby declared to be the national transportation policy of the Congress to provide for fair and impartial regulation of all modes of transportation subject to the provisions of this Act, so administered as to recognize and preserve the inherent advantages of each; to promote safe, adequate, economical, and efficient service and foster sound economic conditions in transportation and among the several carriers; to encourage the establishment and maintenance of reasonable charges for transportation services, without unjust discriminations, undue preferences or advantages, or unfair or destructive competitive practices; to cooperate with the several States and the duly authorized officials thereof; and to encourage fair wages and equitable working conditions;— all to the end of developing, coordinating, and preserving a national transportation system by water, highway, and rail, as well as other means, adequate to meet the needs of the commerce of the United States, of the Postal Service, and of the national defense. All of the provisions of this Act shall be administered and enforced with a view of carrying out the above declaration of policy.

The reader will note, as we indicated in Chapter 18, that there is no reference to government promotional policy in the statement. In addition, since the state-

[1]John J. Coyle and Edward Bardi, *The Management of Business Logistics* (St. Paul, Minnesota: West Publishing Company, 1976), p. 168.

ment realistically applies only to regulation as administered by the ICC, air transportation is not included.

The statement of policy was the first time Congress formally recognized the multi-modal nature of the transportation system and, in that sense, was a positive step in the development of economic regulation. However, the wording of the statement has been difficult to interpret because it lists so many factors to consider and it is not sufficiently specific because it contains a series of broad objectives that almost anyone could agree with. At the same time, phrases such as "inherent advantages" and "destructive competitive practices" are left to be interpreted by the ICC and, as a result, there has been much disagreement between the Commission and others. The ICC or anyone else can probably find justification for a variety of positions on the same issue.

The law that created the federal Department of Transportation (DOT) in 1967 provided that the Secretary of Transportation was to develop a statement of national transportation policy. This was finally done by Secretary William T. Coleman, Jr., in September, 1975. The 53-page statement generally supported a healthy, private-enterprise transportation system with as little government interference and financial backing as possible. It called for a revival of the railroad industry, user charges for the waterway system, more equitable use of federal subsidies (as noted in Chapter 18), less regulation of entry and rates for all modes of transportation, and elimination of unreasonable barriers to intermodal cooperation.[2] In general, the statement contained principles that previously had been advocated by the DOT. Since the statement has no binding effect until it becomes the basis for legislation by Congress, the policy did not affect the policies followed by the ICC and the Civil Aeronautics Board (CAB), and the policy enacted in 1940 remained the official national transportation policy of Congress.

Further interest in the coordination problem is evidenced by the inclusion in the federal highway aid authorization act of 1976 of a provision that required the creation of a National Transportation Policy Study Commission which by the end of 1978 was to prepare a report on the nation's transportation needs through the year 2000. The study was to include the ability and the proper mix of the several modes of transportation to meet the projected needs; the energy requirements and energy availability to meet the needs; the federal policies and programs that affect transportation development; and whatever new policies will be required to develop national transportation systems to meet projected needs. The Commission was to recommend those policies which are most likely to ensure adequate transportation systems that will meet the needs for safe and efficient movement of goods and people. The Commission was to have 19 members, 7 appointed by the president and 6 members from each house of Congress. Appointments to the Commission were completed in October, 1976.

Other Legislation

Other than the statement of National Transportation Policy enacted in 1940, Congress has not very often specifically legislated on the matter of intermodal relationships. The Interstate Commerce Act empowers the ICC to require rail-

[2] *A Statement of National Transportation Policy by the Secretary of Transportation* (Washington, D.C.: U.S. Government Printing Office, 1975).

roads and water carriers to interchange traffic with one another and establish through routes and joint rates or fares, but no such authority has been given to the Commission (although the ICC has asked for such authority) or to the CAB to require interchange between other combinations of modes. The Federal Aviation Act authorizes the chairmen of the CAB and the ICC to designate a like number of members of each agency to act as a joint board to consider and act upon matters relating to through routes and joint rates and fares established between air carriers and carriers regulated by the ICC. These joint boards have the same authority over these matters as the Board has over air carrier rates and fares. However, no joint board has ever been convened for a formal proceeding. Arrangements between air and surface carriers are routinely approved by the CAB, and no complaints have been filed about such rates and no joint board meetings have been needed.[3]

Since no specific prohibition of interchange arrangements between different modes is included in either the Interstate Commerce Act or the Federal Aviation Act, such arrangements can be made but cannot be required by the regulatory agencies except in the case of rail-water interchange.

Congress has also provided some legislative guidance in dealing with integrated transportation and intermodal rates cases, which will be discussed later in this chapter, but, for the most part, Congress has not given either the ICC or the CAB a detailed course to follow in dealing with the questions of economic and physical coordination.

Because of the lack of much specific direction provided by Congress, the matter of economic and physical coordination between the several modes of interstate transportation has been left to the carriers and the regulatory agencies to work out. The economic and physical coordination that we have is the result of voluntary cooperation on the part of the carriers, integrated transportation, and regulated competition between the modes.

VOLUNTARY COOPERATION BETWEEN MODES

Voluntary cooperation between the modes of transportation mainly has to do with physical coordination rather than economic coordination of transportation. Because carriers of all modes typically try to secure some traffic even when they are not the best suited for it, particularly under conditions of excess capacity, it is not to be expected that they would voluntarily forego traffic for the sake of economic coordination. Voluntary cooperation to achieve physical coordination is more likely to occur because it offers some possible advantages to the modes involved.

The benefits of physical coordination to the user of transportation are obvious and were referred to previously in this chapter. Physical coordination basically provides the user with the opportunity to take advantage of the most suitable kinds of transportation on any transaction, even though more than one mode is necessary to achieve this, each mode serving where it is best suited.

However, the obstacles to physical coordination are several and they are important. The major obstacle is the unwillingness of carriers to cooperate with what they consider to be a competitor in another mode because such coopera-

---

[3] Jean V. Strickland, "Resolving the Intermodal Muddle," *Distribution Worldwide,* March, 1975, p. 32.

tion helps the competitor to exist and to grow. The carriers are willing to coordinate when the traffic normally could not be transported in its entirety by any one of the carriers involved. But when a carrier can carry the traffic the entire distance over its own lines, the carrier is hesitant to coordinate with other carriers.[4]

Another major obstacle is the lack of authority to require physical coordination by the ICC and CAB, with the exception of interchange between rail and water carriers, as indicated previously. If the regulatory agencies had such authority, they might be able to encourage more cooperation than has existed to date.

Other obstacles are lack of standardization of equipment, questions about ownership of vehicles if they are to be interchanged, uncertainty over responsibility for loss and damage, objections by labor unions, and administrative difficulties in establishing and carrying out cooperative arrangements.

A final obstacle is the lack of coordination between federal regulatory agencies when interchange involves 2 or more carriers regulated by different agencies. This has not been a problem in arrangements between air and surface carriers, but it has been of particular difficulty in joint service between continental surface carriers and water carriers serving offshore states and possessions.[5]

Interchange of Freight

Despite the obstacles to cooperation and physical coordination, some cooperation between modes has occurred. Some interchange of freight and the establishment of through routes and joint rates in domestic commerce do take place, especially between rail and water carriers and between airlines and motor truck lines.[6] In the former case, a major reason is the ICC's authority to require it. However, in spite of the Commission power, coordination of railroad and water transportation by establishment of through routes and joint rates has not become widespread because of railroad opposition and hesitancy on the part of the Commission, plus the high costs of transferring freight between a railroad and a water carrier. In addition, water carriers today are not suitable for much rail traffic because water carriers do not carry much nonbulk freight.[7] In the case of airlines working with motor trucking companies, a major reason for the development of cooperation is that airlines must rely on motor trucking companies (or freight forwarders) to provide pickup and delivery service to and from airports because airlines ordinarily provide airport-to-airport service only.

Trailer-on-Flatcar and Containerized Service

Unit load systems are a form of freight transportation that facilitates intermodal physical coordination. It consists of a pallet load, a container, a truck

[4]Coyle and Bardi, *The Management of Business Logistics*, p. 169.

[5]See Strickland, "Resolving the Intermodal Muddle."

[6]Cooperation has been more evident in international transportation where it takes place between ocean water carriers and rail or motor truck lines. An obvious reason for more willingness to cooperate is that the cooperating modes do not consider themselves competitors of one another and neither mode could carry the traffic the entire distance.

[7]Marvin L. Fair and Ernest W. Williams, Jr., *Economics of Transportation and Logistics* (Dallas, Texas: Business Publications, Inc., 1975), pp. 491–492.

trailer body, a trailer on its chassis, a rail car, or even a barge [in lighter-aboard-ship (LASH) service]. Unit loads encourage physical coordination because they permit transfer between carriers of different modes without costly and time-consuming transfer of the individual pieces in a shipment—the unit load is transferred as a single unit. The intermodal service may be provided by an integrated transportation company (see below) or through the cooperation of separate independent carriers who have established cooperative arrangements among themselves.

Trailer-on-flatcar (TOFC) or piggyback service is a unit-load example that has had a fair amount of growth since the 1950's. It consists of truck trailers, trailer bodies, or containers carried on railroad flatcars. In the recession year 1976 the number of trailers, trailer bodies, and trailer-size containers carried by railroads totaled approximately 2.4 million. The number of freight cars involved was approximately 1.4 million. This compared with approximately 250,000 cars in 1957. The carloadings in 1976 were 6 per cent of all rail carloadings in that year.[8]

The ICC has approved several categories or plans of TOFC service, and in 1977, there were 5 such basic plans. In the plans the Commission has attempted to identify with whom the TOFC arrangements can be made by a railroad (independent trucking companies, users, and freight forwarders); the ownership of the trailers, trailer bodies, or containers and the ownership of the flatcars; the kind of bill of lading used, the rates that apply and how the parties involved are compensated; and whether the service is to be door to door or station to station. The railroads may arrange TOFC service with independent trucking companies, users, and freight forwarders. Ownership of the trailers, trailer bodies, containers, and flatcars may be by these same persons or by the railroad. More than 60 railroads participate in some form of TOFC. The plans most frequently used are those under which the trailers, trailer bodies, or containers used and the flat cars are all owned by the railroad. Consequently, a great deal of intermodal cooperation does not exist, although there is a fair amount of TOFC traffic. In any event, according to one source, TOFC has served to keep the railroads in long-haul less-than-carload service as well as to render them more competitive for truckload lots of high-value traffic.[9]

As noted above, containerization is found in TOFC service when trucks are involved in bringing containers to and carrying containers from railroad team tracks or terminals. Sometimes containers do not require truck service if the shipper and receiver are both located on a rail siding.

Containerization of air freight has grown rapidly in recent years, both for shipments handled directly by airlines and shipments given to airlines by freight forwarders. Most airlines, however, use their own containers that are designed to fit their aircraft. These are usually used only between airports and not for door-to-door service between shipper and receiver. Therefore, the shipper and receiver are not really involved in the containerization process. It is used more as a means of getting freight on and off aircraft than as a device for intermodal movement of freight.[10] As noted in Chapter 14, however, the wide-bodied jet

[8] Association of American Railroads, *Railroad Facts,* 1977 ed. (Washington, D.C.: U.S. Government Printing Office, 1977), p. 27.

[9] Fair and Williams, *Economics of Transportation and Logistics,* p. 476.

[10] *Ibid.,* p. 477.

aircraft increase the possibility of greater coordination with surface carriers through containerization because they offer the possibility of the extensive use of regular 8 by 8 by 10-, 20-, 30-, or 40-foot surface carrier containers.

Truck trailers, trailer bodies, and containers are sometimes carried by domestic water carriers, principally in the coastal and intercoastal trades and between the continental United States and offshore states and possessions.

The handicaps faced by all forms of both TOFC and containerization are, in addition to the unwillingness to cooperate and the lack of regulatory authority to require cooperation, the uncertainty concerning responsibility for loss and damage, the lack of standardization of trailer and container size, the lack of standardization of flatcars and airplanes, the lack of standardization of tie-down methods, the lack of general rules covering the interchange of trailers, trailer bodies and containers, questions about ownership of trailers, trailer bodies, and containers, and the opposition from labor unions. Finally, the ICC has not aggressively promoted the concepts.

A form of railroad–highway cooperation in the passenger market is Autotrain, referred to in Chapter 10, in which passengers and their automobiles are carried in railroad cars.

Effect of Voluntary Cooperation on Physical Coordination

The various obstacles to interchange of freight, either with or without TOFC or some sort of containerization, have been such that there has been only a limited amount of physical coordination. The benefits of physical coordination are, for the most part, being denied the user of transportation. Voluntary cooperation has not resulted in substantial physical coordination of the domestic transportation system.

INTEGRATED TRANSPORTATION

Concept of Integrated Transportation

Integration of transportation means that a for-hire carrier in a given mode of transportation owns or controls a carrier(s) in another mode, for example, when a railroad owns and operates a motor truck or airline service. Integration is sometimes referred to as *common ownership* or the *transportation company* idea or the *department store* concept of transportation. The idea is that instead of for-hire carriers confining their activities to one mode, they would be able to offer to the public the services of 2 or more modes and, in the extreme case, service of all modes would be available from one "transportation company."

Among other arguments, the proponents of integrated transportation argue that it would lead to easier economic coordination of transportation because the management of the integrated company would route the traffic over the modes most suitable to it. The problem of fitting together the modes into a logical system would thus be solved. Another argument is that physical coordination would be made easier because the management of the integrated company would route traffic to gain the maximum cost and service advantages from each mode under its control, and this would avoid the problems of voluntary cooperation when the modes are not integrated.

Strong opposition has, however, been raised against the concept of integrated transportation companies. These include the arguments that there would be less competition in transportation, with possible negative effects for the public; that railroads would be the mode most likely to try to "take over" carriers in other modes and would tend to keep as much traffic as possible on the railroad part of their operations and discourage the development of the nonrailroad parts because of the desire to protect the substantial investment they have in railroad facilities; and that the railroads would eliminate independent motor and water carriers by deep price cutting on their motor and water service and then, after the competition is eliminated, the railroads would raise prices to an abnormally high level.[11]

Federal Policy on Integrated Transportation

ICC Policy. Federal government policy on integrated transportation has generally been negative. Most of the cases that have arisen have involved attempts by railroads to acquire or institute motor truck operations. The Interstate Commerce Act provides that *acquisition* of a motor carrier by a railroad must receive prior approval of the ICC and that the Commission shall not approve such control unless it finds that the transaction will be consistent with the public interest and enable such carrier to use service by motor vehicle to public advantage and will not unduly restrain competition.

Institution of motor carrier service by a railroad cannot be accomplished without a certificate or permit from the ICC, but the Act does not distinguish between railroads and others who might apply for such operating authority. The Commission, however, takes this factor into account.[12]

The issue of railroad control of motor carrier service has mainly involved the question of railroad control of truck service. Although there are thousands of motor trucks operated by United States railroads, the usual policy of the ICC in handling acquisition or institution cases has been to permit railroad controlled truck service only when such service is auxiliary to or supplemental of the rail service.[13] The idea has been to not permit operations that would compete with the railroad itself, that would compete with an established motor carrier, or that would invade to a substantial degree a territory already adequately served by a railroad.

To restrict the service to that which would be auxiliary to or supplemental of the railroad service, the ICC has set forth various conditions under which the motor vehicles may be operated. These conditions have included that the motor carrier service be substituted only for less-than-carload rail service, that only

[11] This argument apparently assumes that there would be no regulation of minimum or maximum rates.

[12] Railroad operations of motor vehicles that existed prior to the enactment of the federal Motor Carrier Act in 1935 were allowed to continue under the grandfather provision of the Act.

[13] This policy has been followed generally since 2 cases decided in the 1930's. They were *Pennsylvania Truck Lines, Inc.–Control–Barker Motor Freight*, 1 MCC 101 (1936), 5 MCC 9 (1937), 5 MCC 49 (1937) and *Kansas City Southern Transport Company, Inc., Common Carrier Application*, 10 MCC 221 (1938), 28 MCC 5 (1941).

points on the rail line be served by truck, that the traffic carried by truck have a prior or subsequent rail haul, and that only certain points (usually smaller communities) be served by truck. In a few cases, the Commission has permitted railroads to operate motor truck service without these restrictions, usually when there was a lack of independent motor carrier service or the independent motor carrier service was inadequate. In other cases, railroads operate without restriction because they did so prior to the beginning of federal regulation in 1935.

In 1974 there were 17 United States railroads that owned one or more Class I or Class II motor freight carriers. Seven of them collectively owned 12 carriers of which each had combined operating revenues of more than 10 million dollars. There are also a small number of Class III motor carriers owned by railroads. The combined revenues of all Class I and II railroad-owned motor carriers account for less than 3 per cent of the total revenues of all ICC regulated Class I and Class II general freight carriers. This percentage has not changed in over 10 years.[14]

Other integration cases that have come before the ICC have included those in which railroads sought to acquire or institute water carrier service. The Panama Canal Act of 1912 (now part of the Interstate Commerce Act) provides that a railroad cannot control a competing water carrier unless it will not prevent the water carrier from being operated in the public interest and with advantage to the convenience and commerce of the people and unless it will not exclude, prevent, or reduce competition on the route by water. In no case, however, can the Commission authorize railroad control of a water carrier that operates through the Panama Canal.

The Commission permitted railroad control of water carrier service in several early cases, and it is evident that mere interest of a railroad in a water carrier and the fact that some competition exists between the rail and water carriers do not in and of themselves warrant a denial of an application by a railroad to acquire control of a competing water carrier. Also, because some reduction in competition might result would not necessarily justify an adverse finding.[15] In 1962, however, the ICC denied 2 railroads the authority to acquire control of a competing water carrier service in an important case.[16] The ICC has allowed control when the water carrier service in question was not competitive with the railroad and this has been upheld by the United States Supreme Court.[17]

There are no specific provisions in the Interstate Commerce Act dealing with acquisition of control or institution of service of one mode of transportation by carriers of another mode, except for the provisions dealing with railroad control of motor carrier and water carrier service discussed above. Thus, the Interstate Commerce Act makes no reference to control of motor carriers by nonrailroad carriers. The number of cases involving this issue has been small. In some of the cases handled by the ICC, the ICC has permitted water carriers to control motor carriers, has permitted common control of both motor and water carrier service,

[14] Charles A. Taff, *Commercial Motor Transportation*, 5th ed. (Cambridge, Maryland: Cornell Maritime Press, 1975), p. 454.

[15] John Guandolo, *Transportation Law*, 2nd ed. (Dubuque, Iowa: William C. Brown Company Publishers, 1973), p. 786.

[16] *Illinois Central Railroad Company—Control—John I. Hay Company*, 317 ICC 39 (1962).

[17] *Water Transport Association v. United States*, case number 74-1296 and *American Waterways Operators v. United States*, case number 74-1297, 1975.

and has refused to attach conditions requiring that the motor carrier service be auxiliary to or supplemental of the water carrier service, stating that the restrictions required in railroad acquisition cases did not apply to a water carrier acquisition of a motor carrier.[18]

Because there is no regulation of acquisitions of control or entry into the oil pipeline industry, the Commission has no jurisdiction when carriers of another mode seek to acquire or institute oil pipeline operations, which railroads have done in several instances.

There are no specific provisions in the Interstate Commerce Act relative to acquisition of control of railroads by other kinds of carriers or institution of railroad service by nonrail carriers. The same is true of highway carrier control of water carriers and control of motor carriers by oil pipelines. No cases involving any of these possible combinations have been dealt with by the ICC.

The usual position taken by the ICC on the integration question, (where it has jurisdiction) has been to confine it to service that is auxiliary to or supplemental of rail service (motor carriers operated by railroads) or to deny it entirely (railroad control of competing water carriers). No change will be made in this policy unless Congress specifically directs the Commission to do so, which Congress has not done. A criticism of the policy of the Commission and Congress is that the possible benefits of economic and physical coordination that could stem from integrated transportation are being denied to the public and an opportunity to diversify into more profitable forms of transportation is being denied to the railroads, thus making the "railroad problem" more difficult to solve.

CAB Policy. The Federal Aviation Act contains no specific reference to institution of air carrier service by surface carriers. The Act does provide that if a carrier other than an air carrier seeks to acquire control of an air carrier, the applicant shall, for the purposes of the Act, be considered an air carrier, and hence be subject to the merger provisions of the Act cited in Chapter 23. The Board shall not approve the acquisition unless it finds that the proposed transaction will promote the public interest by enabling the carrier to use aircraft to public advantage and will not restrain competition.

The Board has interpreted its authority over acquisition of control of air carriers by surface carriers to mean that the controlled certificated air service must be auxiliary to or supplemental of the surface carrier's service, similar to the ICC policy on railroad control of highway transportation service, although only a few cases have been decided by the Board on this issue. The Board is likely to follow the same policy in cases involving institution of air carrier service by a surface carrier.[19] The CAB, however, has said that it sees no threat to competition in surface carriers controlling air taxi airlines whose services are extremely limited because they present no competitive threat to certificated airlines. The Board

---

[18] See *St. John's River Line Company–Purchase–H. R. Edwards et al.,* 36 MCC 338 (1941); *R. J. Acheson–Control, Black Ball Freight Service–Control, Black Ball Transport, Inc.–Purchase–Puget Sound Navigation Company,* 60 MCC 115 (1954); and *TTC Corporation–Purchase–Terminal Transport Company, Inc.,* 97 MCC 380 (1965).

[19] D. Philip Locklin, *Economics of Transportation,* 7th ed. (Homewood, Illinois: Richard D. Irwin, Inc., 1972) p. 868.

has approved some applications of trucking companies to control air taxi cargo lines by granting an exemption to the air taxi service involved.[20]

In the case of air freight forwarders, in 1969 and 1970 the CAB allowed 4 railroads and 11 trucking companies to enter the air freight forwarding business without restrictions on an experimental basis. The idea was to find out if the surface carriers would be able to expand the geographic area served by freight forwarders, which up until then had been limited. In 1977 the authority was extended for 10 more years for the 3 railroads and 8 trucking companies that were still in the air freight forwarding business.

The case of an air carrier seeking to control a surface carrier is not specifically covered in the Interstate Commerce Act, but the Federal Aviation Act provides that an air carrier may not merge or consolidate with another kind of common carrier without Board approval and the provisions covering mergers between air carriers apply. The potential conflict between the Board and the ICC in such cases is obvious but has not occurred.

REGULATED COMPETITION BETWEEN MODES

The third way in which economic and physical coordination of transportation is achieved is through competition under regulation. In other words, the competitive struggle between the several modes of transportation has an impact on whether or not the traffic carried by each mode is the kind of traffic each mode is best suited to and whether or not carriers of one mode will want to or be forced to work with a carrier of another mode.

The competitive struggle or relationship between modes is affected by a number of factors over which government has control. These include unequal government promotion and subsidy of transportation, inequality in the scope of economic regulation, entry control, and regulation of intermodal rate competition.

Unequal Government Promotion and Subsidy

As indicated in Chapter 18, government promotion and subsidy are unequal among the modes and they lead to overexpansion of modes that are heavily promoted and premature obsolescence of the lesser promoted modes. There is also a misallocation of traffic because some traffic is not being carried by the modes best suited for it. Determining the inherent advantages of each mode of transportation is clearly made more difficult, as is the fitting of the modes together into a logical coordinated system.

Inequality in the Scope of Economic Regulation

In our previous discussion of economic regulation of the 5 modes of domestic intercity transportation, we noted that federal economic regulation varies between the modes, for example, there is variation in the form of regulation, the regulatory coverage or kinds of things regulated, and the degree to which exemp-

[20] "CAB Approves Motor Carrier Control of Cargo-Only Air Taxi Operators," *Traffic World*, November 11, 1974, p. 76.

tions from regulation are permitted for for-hire carriers (see Table 23-1). Thus, oil pipelines are not subject to entry and merger regulation, but motor trucking companies are. Motor trucking companies are not subject to control of exit if abandonment is complete, but airlines are. Airlines are not subject to regulation of their security issues, but railroads are, and so on. Control of intermodal ownership also varies, depending on the modes involved. In addition, there are differences in the scope of regulation relative to common and contract carriage within the same mode. These differences in what is regulated mean that the impact of regulation, whether negative or positive, varies between modes.

The most obvious difference in federal economic regulation between modes is, of course, the matter of exemptions from economic regulation. Although there are no exempt for-hire carriers in rail and oil pipeline transportation, such exemptions do exist in the other 3 modes and are of particular importance in highway and water transportation with the result that only approximately 44 per cent and 9 per cent, respectively, of the domestic intercity ton–mileage of freight (both private and for-hire) is under federal regulation.[21]

These differences in economic regulation between modes clearly affect the competitive relationships between them and, in turn, contribute to the problems of misallocation of traffic among modes, determining the inherent advantages of each mode, and fitting the modes into their proper places in the transportation system because the "natural" competitive relationships among the modes are distorted.

Entry Control

One aspect of economic regulation that could have a direct influence on economic coordination is the entry control policies followed by the ICC and CAB. Although entry control is usually thought of as a means to prevent excessive entry and destructive competitive practices within a mode, it can also be used to prevent entry in order to protect carriers of one mode from competition of carriers of another mode. Neither the Interstate Commerce Act nor the Federal Aviation Act contains specific provisions on this question.

In most cases, the ICC has authorized motor carrier service despite the objections of railroads that claimed they would be adversely affected, principally because motor carrier service has inherent advantages that railroads cannot provide. The Commission has generally followed the principle that users are entitled to the service of both rail and motor carriers. Nevertheless, the ICC has refused to authorize motor carrier service in some cases in which inadequacy of rail service and/or superiority of motor carrier service could not be shown and/or the effects on competing railroads would be serious. In one important case a decision of this kind was reversed by the federal courts because the inherent advantages of the highway carriers would be denied if entry were barred.[22] On the whole, the ICC policy has been to not to give much protection to railroads when competing highway transportation service is proposed because it has been relatively easy to demonstrate the advantages highway transportation service has over railroad service.

---

[21] Interstate Commerce Commission, *Annual Report, 1976* (Washington, D.C.: U.S. Government Printing Office, 1976), p. 143.

[22] *Schaffer Transportation Company v. United States,* 355 U.S. 83 (1957).

The Commission has not taken into account the possible effect of a highway transportation entry on nonrailroad forms of transportation. It has also not protected railroads or other modes in considering applications of water carriers to enter. There is no entry control in oil pipeline transportation, and entry control in the railroad industry is inconsequential because of the lack of applications for new entry.

The CAB does not take into account the effect of an air carrier entry on other modes of transportation when it is handling route award cases.

The result of ICC and CAB entry control policy, then, has been to not provide much protection of one mode from competition of carriers of another mode. This seems to be the correct policy to follow because to do otherwise would prevent the public from benefiting from the cost and service characteristics of different modes and the right to choose between them.

Regulation of Intermodal Rate Competition

Intermodal rate cases arise when carriers of 2 or more modes of transportation compete for the same freight or passenger traffic and the carrier(s) of one mode proposes a price reduction. The proposal is often opposed by the carrier(s) of the other mode(s). These cases occur mainly in regulation of freight rates as administered by the ICC. They do not occur in CAB regulation of pricing because the Board regulates only air transportation and has no obligation to consider the effect of an air freight or passenger price on carriers of other modes.

Although ICC intermodal freight rate cases have actually been few in number, they are extremely important because they establish precedents for carriers to follow in making competitive rate proposals and they have a lot to do with the distribution of traffic among the modes regulated by the Commission, particularly railroad, highway, and water transportation. This is true because the rates offered by competing carriers, along with their service characteristics, are usually a very important factor that users take into account when deciding on what modes and carriers to use. Consequently, Commission decisions in such cases have the effect of helping to determine the allocation of traffic among the several modes of transportation. In other words, the matter of economic coordination—the fitting of the several modes into a logical system of transportation whereby each mode carries only that traffic it is best suited for—can be heavily influenced by the policies adopted by the ICC in intermodal rate cases.

Intermodal rate cases have been among the most important and difficult kinds of cases handled by the Commission. From the beginning the ICC, for the most part, took the conservative or "safe" position of avoiding or preventing deep rate cutting that would shift substantial amounts of traffic from one mode to another. Under this policy, the Commission believed that it was permitting all carriers of all modes an opportunity to compete for the traffic and, at the same time, that it was preventing destructive pricing.

The railroad industry, which advocated the idea that variable costs should be considered to be the floor in intermodal rates cases (this idea was rejected by the ICC), was very critical of the policy adopted by the Commission. Railroad criticism became intense in the 1950's as the railroad financial situation deteriorated. This ultimately culminated in Congress' passing the Transportation Act of 1958, which was an attempt to assist the faltering railroad industry. The Act contained several provisions designed to do this, including an amendment to

Section 15a, the railroad rule of rate making, that provided that in an intermodal rate case the rates of a carrier shall not be held up to a particular level to protect the traffic or any other mode of transportation, giving due consideration to the objectives of the National Transportation Policy declared in the Interstate Commerce Act.

The effects of the 1958 amendment were indeterminate for some time. Several major intermodal rate cases were decided by the ICC in the late 1950's and early 1960's, but they were not clearly in favor of or against a major change in Commission policy. In one case, the ICC had ruled that proposed TOFC railroad rates had to be at least 6 per cent above competing trailer-on-ship rates and railroad car-on-ship rates, even though the proposed lower rates would have been above the TOFC variable costs. The United State Supreme Court reversed the decision of the Commission in the New Haven case[23] on the ground that simple diversion of traffic from one mode to another was not destructive, as the Commission had claimed and, therefore, in violation of the National Transportation Policy.

Although the New Haven decision appeared to give the railroads greater freedom to cut rates when they were in competition with other modes of transportation, another case in the 1960's appeared to move the situation back to where it was prior to 1958. In the Ingot Molds case the Commission ruled, in a situation involving a railroad rate versus a barge–truck joint rate, that the rail rate, although it was above the railroad variable costs but below rail fully distributed costs and below the barge–truck fully distributed costs, was unlawful because it was lower than the fully distributed costs of the barge–truck service, the latter recognized by the Commission as the low cost carrier and, therefore, the rate-setting carrier. The inherent advantage and the floor in this case were determined by the costs of the carrier that had the lowest fully distributed costs. The case eventually reached the United States Supreme Court which, in 1968, upheld the ICC and said that the New Haven case did not dictate that variable costs should be the floor and that the Commission had the right to determine which measure to use as the rate floor—variable costs or fully distributed costs— and a floor of variable costs would be inconsistent with the purpose of the 1958 amendment to the rule of rate making, as evidenced by the hearings and discussions in Congress that preceded the enactment of that law and the fact that Congress had previously rejected the legislative proposals made by railroads.[24]

This decision left the Commission free to use fully distributed costs to determine which carrier is the low cost carrier in an intermodal rate case. The carrier that has the lowest fully distributed costs is often not the railroad, although the railroad may have the lowest variable costs. Although the railroads were given somewhat more freedom by the Commission in adjusting rates downward, criticism of the ICC policy by railroads and others, including some economists and the federal DOT, continued. In the meantime, the Commission undertook studies of cost standards to use.

Finally, in early 1976 Congress passed the Railroad Revitalization and Reg-

---

[23] *Interstate Commerce Commission v. New York, New Haven, and Hartford Railroad Company*, 372 U.S. 744 (1963).

[24] *American Commercial Lines et al. v. Louisville and Nashville Railroad Company et al.*, 392 U.S. 571 (1968).

ulatory Reform (4R) Act which may change the situation significantly. As noted in Chapter 21, the 4R Act provided that railroad freight rates that contribute to the "going concern value" of a carrier shall not be found to be unreasonable on the ground that they are too low. A rate that equals or exceeds variable costs is considered to contribute to going concern value. The Act also deleted the amendment of 1958 to the rule of rate making (along with the rest of the rule) as it applied to railroads and specifically provided that no rate of a railroad is to be held up to protect the traffic of another carrier or mode of transportation unless the ICC finds that the low rate would reduce the going concern value of the railroad charging the rate. As noted above, any rate equaling or exceeding variable costs is considered to contribute to going concern value. In addition, for the 2 years following the effective date of the Act, railroads were authorized to raise or lower their individual rates (not general rate changes) by as much as 7 per cent from the level in effect at the beginning of each year without suspension because of the reasonableness of the proposed rate. The ICC retained its power to suspend any rate proposal if the carrier had "market dominance," because of possible violation of the unjust discrimination provisions of the Interstate Commerce Act, or upon a complaint that the proposed rate is unfair, destructive, predatory, or otherwise undermines competition.

The effect of the 4R Act on intermodal competition is yet to be determined because before it can be implemented, the Commission must determine the meaning of such terms as "variable cost," "going concern value," "predatory," and "destructive." It is possible, however, that the long sought-after freedom to reduce competitive rates to variable costs will finally be given to the railroad industry. This may create a problem because the 4R Act applies only to railroads and leaves other regulated modes with less rate freedom than the railroads will have, thereby adding to the total problem of regulation being inconsistent and unequal between the modes and distorting the competitive relationships between them.

The preceding discussion of voluntary cooperation, integration, and regulated competition between modes leads one to conclude that, for the most part, economic regulation of transportation has contributed little to either economic or physical coordination of our transportation system. In fact, it has made such coordination more difficult.

SELECTED REFERENCES

Among the many writings on the subject of national transportation policy, including the statement on the subject enacted by Congress in 1940, are Marvin L. Fair and Ernest W. Williams, Jr., *Economics of Transportation and Logistics* (Dallas, Texas: Business Publications, Inc., 1975), Chapter 26; Roy J. Sampson and Martin T. Farris, *Domestic Transportation: Practice, Theory, and Policy,* 3rd ed. (Boston: Houghton-Mifflin Company, 1975), Chapter 29; Martin T. Farris, "National Transportation Policy—Fact or Fiction," *Quarterly Review of Economics and Business,* Summer, 1970 and "Definitional Inconsistencies in the National Transportation Policy," *ICC Practitioners' Journal,* December, 1967; Hugh S. Norton, *National Transportation Policy: Formation and Implementation* (Berkeley, California: McCutchan Publishing Corporation, 1966); John F. Weisser, Jr., "A New National Transportation Policy—The Single Improvement of the Interstate Commerce Act Which Is Most Needed," *ICC Practitioners' Journal,* February, 1966; and Howard Hosmer, "Twenty-five Years of the National Transportation Policy (NTP)," *ICC Practitioners' Journal,* February, 1966.

Transportation coordination and intermodal relationships in general have been the subject of much research and writing. They are discussed in some depth in D. Philip Locklin, *Economics of Transportation,* 7th ed. (Homewood, Illinois: Richard D. Irwin, Inc., 1972), Chapters 36 and 37. See also Hugh S. Norton, *Modern Transportation Economics,* 2nd ed. (Columbus, Ohio: Charles E. Merrill Publishing Company, 1971), Chapter 21; Marvin L. Fair and E. Grosvenor Plowman, *Coordinated Transportation: Principles and Problems* (Cambridge, Maryland: Cornell Maritime Press 1967); and Merrill J. Roberts and Associates, *Intermodal Freight Transportation Coordination: Problems and Potential* (Pittsburgh: Graduate School of Business Administration, University of Pittsburgh, 1966). An early discussion of various meanings of the term "coordination" and the concept of economic coordination is G. Shorey Peterson, "Transport Coordination: Meaning and Purpose," *Journal of Political Economy,* December, 1930.

Physical coordination of transportation is dealt with in Fair and Williams, *Economics of Transportation and Logistics,* Chapter 24. Ways to achieve physical coordination are discussed in Lynn E. Gill, "The Transportation Challenge," *Transportation Journal,* Spring, 1972. Problems associated with achieving physical coordination are treated in Rupert L. Murphy, "Is Voluntary Intermodal Transportation Possible?" *ICC Practitioners' Journal,* March–April, 1968. See also William H. Dodge, "Common Goals of Common Carriers—A Blueprint for Intermodal Coordination," *ICC Practitioners' Journal,* October, 1963. The relationship between economic regulation and physical coordination is discussed in some detail in Samuel P. Delisi, "Coordinated Freight Transportation Service: Legal and Regulatory Aspects," *ICC Practitioners' Journal,* April, 1967 and May–June, 1967. Problems associated with establishing through routes between rail and water carriers are dealt with in Joseph L. Frye, "An Analysis of Rail–Water Coordinate Service," *Transportation Journal,* Spring, 1967. The lack of coordination between the ICC and the Federal Maritime Commission in facilitating intermodal cooperation is discussed in Jean V. Strickland, "Resolving the Intermodal Muddle," *Distribution Worldwide,* March, 1975.

Integrated transportation or common ownership has been the subject of a very large number of writings. A full-length study of federal policy on integrated transportation is Robert C. Lieb, *Freight Transportation: A Study of Federal Intermodal Ownership Policy* (New York: Praeger Publishers, 1972). See also Lieb, "Intermodal Ownership: Experience and Evaluation," *ICC Practitioners' Journal,* July–August, 1971. Regulatory policy regarding integrated transportation is dealt with in Byron Nupp, "Regulatory Standards in Common Ownership in Transportation," *ICC Practitioners' Journal,* November–December, 1966. A pricing scheme that would foster an economic allocation of traffic under common ownership is set forth in Dodge, "Transportation Pricing Innovation to Promote Economic Efficiency," *ICC Practitioners' Journal,* July–August, 1970. A study that used a simulation to compare the operations of an integrated transportation company with those of separate single carriers is described in Robert S. Tripp, Normal L. Chervany, and Frederick J. Beier, "An Economic Analysis of the Multi-Modal Transportation Company: A Simulation Approach," *The Logistics and Transportation Review,* Volume 9, Number 1, 1973. Arguments for integrated transportation are presented in James E. Suelflow and Stanley J. Hille, "The Transportation Company: An Argument for Intermodal Ownership," *Land Economics,* August, 1970; Carl Helmetag, Jr., "Common Ownership of Rail and Motor Carriers: The Case for the Railroads," *Texas Law Review,* May, 1970; and George L. Buland and Frederick E. Fuhrman, "Integrated Ownership: The Case for Removing Restrictions on Common Ownership of the Several Forms of Transportation," *George Washington Law Review,* October, 1962. Opposed to integrated transportation are Peter Douglas, "The Economic Irrelevance of Common Ownership," *ICC Practitioners' Journal,* July–August, 1974; Carolyn C. Stitt, "Common Ownership of Rail and Motor Carriers: The Case Against the Railroads," *Texas Law Review,* January, 1970; and Peter T. Beardsley, "Integrated Ownership of Transportation Companies and the Public Interest," *George Washington Law Review,* October, 1962.

There is a vast amount of literature on the subject of regulation of intermodal rate competition. Some of the more recent writings include Fair and Williams, *Economics of Transportation and Logistics,* Chapter 23; John J. Coyle, "The Compatibility of the Rule of Rate Making and the National Transportation Policy," *ICC Practitioners' Journal,* March–April, 1971 and "The Ingot Molds Case and Competitive Rate Making," *ICC Practitioners' Journal,* May–June, 1969; Philip M. Carroll, "The Interstate Commerce Commission, Court Decisions, and Intermodal Rate Disputes," *Quarterly Review of Economics and Business,* Spring, 1970; Robert W. Harbeson, "The Supreme Court and Intermodal Rate Competition," *ICC Practitioners' Journal,* March–April, 1969 and "Recent Trends in the Regulation of Intermodal Rate Competition in Transportation," *Land Economics,* August, 1966; Dodge, "The Dilemma of Intermodal Rate Competition," *ICC Practitioners' Journal,* July–August, 1969; George W. Hilton, *The Transportation Act of 1958: A Decade of Experience* (Bloomington, Indiana: Indiana University Press, 1969); Bernard J. McCarney, "ICC Rate Regulation and Rail–Motor Carrier Pricing Behavior: A Reappraisal," *ICC Practitioners' Journal,* July–August, 1968; Harvey A. Levine, "The Railroad Industry's Experience Under Section 15a(3) of the Transportation Act of 1958," *ICC Practitioners' Journal,* January–February, 1968; and Joseph R. Rose, "Regulation of Rates and Intermodal Transport Competition," *ICC Practitioners' Journal,* October, 1965. A classic article that recommends that incremental cost be used as the floor in determining intermodal rate levels is William J. Baumol and others, "The Role of Costs in the Minimum Pricing of Railroad Services," *Journal of Business,* October, 1962.

25

Evaluation of
Government Economic Regulation
of Transportation

In the preceding 6 chapters we reviewed the rationale of government economic regulation of transportation, the decison-making process in economic regulation, the form of economic regulation of the 5 modes of domestic intercity transportation, and the effect of economic regulation on intermodal relationships. Government economic regulation involves a highly complex structure that has considerable impact on carriers, users, and the general public, and it has always been somewhat controversial in terms of the need for such regulation and the form it should take. In this chapter we shall attempt to examine the impact or effects of economic regulation on carriers, users, and the general public. We shall also discuss proposals to alter the system of regulation for the future.

The effects of economic regulation on regulated carriers, users of transportation, and the general public are both negative and positive. The impact varies somewhat by mode, given the inequalities in the scope of economic regulation between modes. The impact also varies by mode, depending on how active the regulatory agencies are in regulating a given mode and/or in regulating specific aspects of a mode's operations. The effects, however, are very similar for all modes and are discussed below.

IMPACT OF GOVERNMENT ECONOMIC
REGULATION ON CARRIERS

Carriers that are regulated by the Interstate Commerce Commission (ICC), the Civil Aeronautics Board (CAB), or the states are often heavily involved in regulation and this regulation has great impact on their operations and on intramodal and intermodal competition.

Negative Effects of Economic
Regulation on Carriers

Restrictiveness of Regulation. One of the important negative consequences of economic regulation is that the carriers find it very restrictive because there are certain things they would like to do that are prohibited by the regulatory system. For railroads, this includes the prevention of large-scale integration or common ownership. For highway carriers, it includes the inability to serve at will any route that appears to offer strong possibilities for profit. In general, economic regulation reduces the freedom of any regulated carrier to add or subtract services, to change prices, and to make other changes that unregulated industries make without much difficulty.

Delay in Decision Making. A second major disadvantage of economic regulation for the regulated carrier is that regulation, even when proposals made by carriers are approved, slows down the decision-making process where regulated activities, such as pricing or exit from the industry, are concerned. Decisions in regulated areas must receive approval from a regulatory agency, and the process may take days, months, or years. This makes it difficult for the regulated carriers to react to changes in the competitive environment in which they operate. This is an inefficient decision-making process because even if the decisions are approved by the regulatory agency, the time delay means that there is a lag between the need for a decision and when the decision can be made effective unless, of course, the carrier is able to anticipate in advance what changes are needed and make proposals in advance of when the decision actually must be made.

Expense. Regulated carriers find that it is expensive to be regulated. The expense takes the form partly of the aforementioned delays in decision making and is most obvious in the case of price increase proposals which, even though eventually approved by a regulatory agency, force the carriers to forego the revenues from the increase while the case is pending. It also takes the form of the inefficiencies forced on the carriers by regulation, such as those created by route, point, commodity, and other restrictions in operating authorities. These inefficiencies can also cause excessive energy consumption by creating underutilization of equipment. There is also the expense of participating in the regulatory process itself. To actively participate means a carrier must keep abreast of regulatory developments, including proposals made by competitors, prepare evidence, appear at hearings, file reports, and so on. Depending on the mode and the individual carrier, the expense can be substantial.

Quality of Management. Finally, there is the effect of regulation on the quality of management. Regulated industries sometimes find it difficult to attract management talent because of the aversion some prospective managers have to work in a regulated industry. There is also the question of to what extent regulation itself encourages bad management practices because of the fact that the rewards may go to those best able to deal with the regulatory process rather than to those who are the most effective and efficient managers.[1] There is also the matter of incentives being reduced or dampened in an atmosphere of controlled competition, which may lead to less aggressive and less innovative management.

Positive Effects of Economic Regulation on Carriers

Although there are negative consequences for regulated carriers, economic regulation also has an important positive impact on them.

Avoidance of Destructive Competition. The major positive effect on regulated carriers is, of course, that regulation prevents destructive competition on an intramodal and intermodal basis. It also provides regulated carriers with the opportunity to protest against or support proposed actions of other carriers.

Stable Environment. Economic regulation also provides a stable environment in which carriers may operate because it prevents rapid change in prices, services, and other aspects of transportation operations. Planning for the future is, therefore, somewhat easier than it would be otherwise because future conditions are easier to predict under regulation.

IMPACT OF GOVERNMENT ECONOMIC REGULATION ON USERS OF TRANSPORTATION

Unlike carriers, the users of transportation are not required to participate in the regulatory process, although it is often in their interest to do so. Whether or not they participate, however, economic regulation can have significant negative and positive impact on users.

Negative Effects of Economic Regulation on Users

Inflexibility of Transportation Service. One of the negative effects that economic regulation has on users is the inflexibility in transportation service, meaning that carriers cannot easily and quickly adapt to the needs of users because if the activity involved is regulated, the required regulatory procedures must be followed and the adaptation may be rejected by the regulatory agency. The carrier may be prevented from doing things that users would benefit from.

Delay in Decision Making. A second difficulty for users is that regulation delays decision making for users as well as for carriers. Because decisions of the regulated carriers must be approved by regulatory agencies, which may take a long time, decisions of users that are tied to the decisions of carriers are also delayed. This delay makes it somewhat difficult for users to promptly adjust to changes in their competitive environment, and there is a lag between the need for some adjustment and the time at which the adjustment can actually be made, if at all.

---

[1] See Paul H. Banner, "Regulation: Its Effect on Economic Costs of Transportation," *Proceedings of Transportation Research Forum, 1965,* p. 166.

Expense. Economic regulation creates expenses for users as it does for carriers. These expenses are caused by delays in decision making, the fact that regulated carriers may be less efficient because of economic regulation and this inefficiency finds its way into the carriers' pricing structure, and the expense of the regulatory process. The latter is a problem only for those users who actively participate in the regulatory process and must, therefore, incur expenses to keep up with what is happening in economic regulation, to gather information, and to attend and testify at regulatory proceedings. This is, of course, a reason why some users do not actively participate.

Quality of Management. Economic regulation may have an effect on the quality of management on the user side. Because users of transportation must deal with a regulated industry, they sometimes find it difficult to get top-quality people to work in the transportation-distribution area because these people dislike dealing with a regulatory system, even though they themselves are not regulated.

Reduction in Transportation Alternatives. Lastly, an important drawback for the user in economic regulation is that when entry control is part of the regulatory system, there is likely to be a reduction in the number of carriers and different services available to the user between any 2 points. This is an obvious result of effective entry control because the purpose of entry control is to limit the number of carriers in the market. Economic regulation also prevents the development of one-carrier service over long hauls in some situations and forces the user to make use of interchanged service between 2 or more carriers.

Positive Effects of Economic Regulation on Users

Avoidance of Destructive Competition. A major positive effect of economic regulation on the user of transportation service is that it prevents destructive competitive practices between carriers and the resulting poor service and high turnover in the transportation industries. Proponents of regulation argue that the control of competition in transportation has enabled the carriers to develop on a sound basis and render a satisfactory level of service to the user.

Stable Environment. Economic regulation has also produced a stable condition in transportation that benefits users as well as carriers. Users can plan ahead with some assurance that the transportation prices and services available will also be available in the near future.

Elimination of Unfair Treatment. For the most part, economic regulation has eliminated unfair and discriminatory treatment of users in the form of unjust discrimination in prices and service and exorbitant prices. Economic regulation protects the user before the damage is done rather than after the fact, as would be the case if there were no system of economic regulation and if complaints were handled by the courts.

Whether or not rates and fares in general are higher under economic regulation than they would be without economic regulation varies with the individual mode and individual carrier and the amount of competition each would face without economic regulation. Rates and fares are probably higher under economic regulation in some cases and lower in others, but they are probably higher overall, particularly in highway and air transportation. The benefits to the user in better service may, however, offset the disadvantage of higher rates and fares.

IMPACT OF GOVERNMENT ECONOMIC
REGULATION ON THE GENERAL PUBLIC

In the case of passenger transportation, the interests of the user and the interests of the general public are similar because they are generally the same people, although the large number of business people who buy passenger service from regulated for-hire carriers may be considered to have interests somewhat different from those of the general public.

On the freight side, of course, user interests may be different from those of the general public because most buyers of freight service are business and other organizations instead of individual citizens. In recognition of this fact an independent office of Rail Public Counsel to represent the public interest and to be affiliated with the ICC was required by the Railroad Revitalization and Regulatory Reform (4R) Act of 1976. The CAB has an Office of Consumer Advocate that can participate as a party in Board proceedings, handle consumer complaints, and provide information to consumers.

In any event, if inefficiency, expense, excess capacity, excessive fuel consumption, and needlessly high rates and fares accrue from economic regulation, they are ultimately paid for by the general public in the form of higher passenger fares and higher prices for the goods carried by the freight transportation system. In addition, it may be true that the ability of the carriers to pass off the "costs" of regulation to the public may reduce their incentive to strive for improvement in the regulatory system.

However, the general public is, ultimately, also the principal beneficiary of the improved service and the avoidance of the wastes of destructive competition and the high rates of monopoly that are said to result from economic regulation.

Do the actual benefits of economic regulation outweigh the actual disadvantages for the general public? That question has no answer that can be based on fact because it is impossible to measure the benefits or the costs of economic regulation to the general public. The critics of regulation and the advocates of regulation have opposite views on the subject, neither one of which is grounded in a great deal of fact. Attempts have been made, for example, to estimate the "costs" of economic regulation but because of the impossibility of doing so, they are seldom accepted as being accurate.[2]

SOME OBSERVATIONS ON THE RESULTS
OF ECONOMIC REGULATION BY MODE

The general negative and positive effects of economic regulation on carriers, users, and the general public have already been discussed in this chapter. The

[2]One such estimate is Thomas G. Moore, *Freight Transportation Regulation: Surface Freight and the Interstate Commerce Commission* (Washington, D.C.: American Enterprise Institute for Public Policy Research, 1972).

objective of economic regulation is to provide adequate transportation service to the public at reasonable cost. The extent to which this has been accomplished varies by mode, is very difficult, if not impossible, to measure, and is the subject of considerable controversy. It is beyond the scope of this book to analyze in depth the effectiveness of economic regulation in each mode of transportation. However, some brief observations are presented in the following paragraphs.

Railroad Transportation

The criticisms of economic regulation concerning restrictiveness, delay, expense, inefficiency, and the quality of management are probably most clearly evident in railroad transportation because of the long history of such regulation and the resulting buildup of procedural red tape and precedents, the cumbersome and patchwork Part I of the Interstate Commerce Act, and the completeness of economic regulation (most aspects of railroad operation are subject to economic regulation). Economic regulation of railroads is, in fact, probably too extensive and too restrictive. Nevertheless, it has prevented both destructive competition and monopoly practices, has stablilized the railroad industry, and has protected the user against unfair treatment. In any event, some reform of economic regulation of railroads, in addition to that produced by the 4R Act of 1976, is probably in order. One must, however, be careful to take into account that the problems of the American railroad industry involve much more than its regulatory problem and regulatory reform will not, in itself, solve those problems.

Highway Transportation

The disadvantages of economic regulation relative to restrictiveness, delay, expense, inefficiency, and the quality of management are present to some degree in regulated highway transportation. In fact, the terms of operating authorities given to motor carriers probably overrestrict the routes and points that can be served and the traffic that can be carried. At the same time, the exemptions provided in highway transportation regulation leave important areas unregulated and create problems in the regulated segment of highway transportation. Also, completely effective economic regulation of highway transportation is impossible because of the large number of carriers and highway mileage, the definitional problems associated with regulation, and the existence of exempt for-hire carriers. Despite these problems, economic regulation has stabilized a chaotic industry which has been beneficial to both carriers and users and to the general public.

Water Transportation

Economic regulation of domestic water transportation has the same negative and positive effects on carriers, users, and the general public as has regulation of the other modes. However, the broad exemptions mean that the impact has been relatively light overall because most for-hire traffic is not regulated. Even the regulatory authority that has been given to the ICC has not resulted in much regulatory activity. The Commission has found little reason to prescribe maximum rates and has done little with minimum rates. Regulatory activity in connection with operating authority has been of little importance.

It appears that economic regulation of water transportation should either be extended in its scope or eliminated entirely. The fact that most domestic water carrier traffic is carried successfully without regulation may indicate that such regulation serves no useful purpose and that unregulated competition is workable in the water carrier industry.[3]

Oil Pipeline Transportation

Although the usual negative and positive effects of economic regulation are present in oil pipeline transportation, the fact that several important aspects of pipeline decision making, including entry, mergers, and abandonment, are not regulated at the federal level and the fact that there have been few complaints and little activity by the ICC in oil pipeline regulation mean that the overall impact has been less than in railroad and highway transportation. The oil pipeline companies and the users appear to be satisfied with the current regulatory system. The natural tendency toward monopoly in the pipeline industry and the ownership arrangement probably mean that regulation is necessary to prevent monopoly practices, although regulation has not been as effective as it might be if the ICC were more active and if the statute covered more aspects of oil pipeline management.

Air Transportation

Air transportation regulation has the same negative and positive effects that appear in the other modes. Since air transportation is subject to fairly complete economic regulation at the federal level, the effects of regulation are very important not only for both carriers and users, but also for the general public.

The administration of economic regulation of air transportation is vulnerable to criticism, and serious questions have been raised about the CAB's entry control policy, the creation of an all-cargo category of carriers, the lack of any pricing policy until recently, and so on. However, economic regulation has stabilized a chaotic, fledgling industry and has helped it to grow on a sound basis until it is now one of the country's largest and most important industries.

Need for Economic Regulation Today

Regardless of the reasons for institution of economic regulation and whether or not the reasons were valid and regardless of the impact and results of economic regulation to date, is economic regulation of transportation needed today? The answer is that the need for regulation probably varies with the mode of transportation, the need being much more clear cut in some modes than in others. In any case, a danger in examining each mode of transportation in isolation to determine the need for economic regulation is that the intermodal implications of a major change in regulation may be forgotten. For example, one might conclude that economic regulation of highway transportation is not necessary

---

[3] See John C. Spychalski, "On the Nonutility of Domestic Water Transport Regulation," *ICC Practitioners' Journal,* November–December, 1969.

because the highway transportation industry is naturally a competitive industry and would do very well without regulation. However, the effects on the railroad industry of elimination of highway transportation regulation should also be included in the analysis. In other words, it is logical to insist that any review of the need for economic regulation must include the need for economic regulation in connection with intermodal relationships as well as its need in terms of intramodal considerations. Unfortunately, this is usually not done.

The question of the current need for economic regulation has not been explored in a factual and all-inclusive way. Instead, there has been a good deal of conjecture and speculation concerning the need for economic regulation, but the conjecture and speculation usually cover a single mode instead of all the modes simultaneously. Consequently, the need for economic regulation of transportation remains a debatable issue in the late 1970's and the lack of an overall scientific analysis of the issue does not help to clarify the situation.

SUGGESTIONS FOR CHANGES IN ECONOMIC REGULATION

From the start economic regulation of transportation has been a controversial subject, and especially since the 1930's when new competition developed and regulation was extended to nonrailroad modes. Various proposals have been made by government agencies, United States senators and representatives, academicians, some carriers, some users, consumer groups, and others for changes to be made in economic regulation of transportation. These proposals range all the way from adding to economic regulation to abolishing it and the regulatory agencies altogether.

Some of the problems associated with economic regulation are caused by the people who are doing the regulating more than by the concept of economic regulation itself. Good regulators are more important than good regulatory legislation. Since the regulatory agencies have been given only broad guidelines by the legislatures, the agencies can adopt a wide range of different policies and procedures. Therefore, it is critical that the best qualified people be appointed to these agencies. Unfortunately, the appointments made by the presidents and state governors have often been highly political in nature and without regard to the qualifications of the appointee to carry out the important responsibilities associated with the appointment.

Proposals for regulatory change include adding to economic regulation, increasing the flexibility of regulation, speeding up the regulatory process, and reducing the amount of regulation.

Adding to Economic Regulation

Recognizing that economic regulation is not complete and that it has certain gaps, some have suggested that certain aspects of transportation be brought under regulation that are not under control now or that regulation in certain areas be strengthened. These suggestions include more effective regulation of railroad car supply, elimination of certain exemptions of for-hire transportation (such as the agricultural exemption in highway transportation), strengthening of control over common carrier obligations to serve the public whether the traffic is "desirable" or not, extension of the authority of the ICC to require all carriers in all modes to interchange traffic with one another and with carriers of another mode, and greater control over financial dealings of regulated carriers, particularly when carriers are part of "conglomerates" and when carriers invest in nontransportation activities.

Increased Flexibility

It has been proposed that those areas of regulation that now exist be made more flexible, particularly the area of price regulation. It has been suggested that regulation should interfere only when needed, i.e., a proposed price or other practice should be allowed to go into effect immediately and the regulatory agency should not interfere unless the price or practice proved to be causing a problem. A suggestion directed at achieving greater flexibility is to permit regulated highway carriers to carry exempt commodities along with regulated commodities in the same vehicle. Another suggestion is to reduce the amount of restrictiveness in highway carrier operating authorities relative to commodities, routes, direction of movement, territory, and other matters. It has also been suggested that the restrictions that are now making it difficult for intermodal cooperation and, in particular, for intermodal integration could be relaxed.

Speeding up the Regulatory Process

A major criticism of economic regulation is its slowness and consequent delay in decision making for all concerned. Many proposals have been made to speed up the process, for example, by adding more employees, making more money available to the regulatory agencies, changing the procedures followed by the agencies (such as suspending rates only after they have been in effect and have presented a problem), setting time limits within which decisions must be made, and eliminating regulation of some aspects of transportation operations.

Reduction in the Amount of Regulation

The more important proposals of the 1970's have had to do with reducing the amount of regulation, including eliminating it entirely. Many studies have been made at the federal level dealing with federal regulatory policy and the regulatory agencies. Most studies have concluded that more market competition in transportation should be allowed.[4] President John F. Kennedy's transportation message to Congress in 1962 also advocated the need for less economic regulation of transportation.[5]

[4]One of the most thorough studies was Committee on Commerce, U.S. Senate, *National Transportation Policy*, 87th Congress, 1st Session, Senate Report Number 445 (Doyle Report) (Washington, D.C.: U.S. Government Printing Office, 1961) which recommended reorientation of regulation instead of substantial reduction in regulation.

[5]John F. Kennedy, *The Transportation System of Our Nation*, 87th Congress, 2nd Session, U.S. House of Representatives Document Number 384 (Washington, D.C.: U.S. Government Printing Office, 1962).

Suggestions for reduced economic regulation include more freedom of carriers to do things without government approval, including changing rates and fares within some sort of acceptable "zone" without having every proposed price go through the regulatory process, elimination of rate and fare regulation other than the regulation of maximum and minimum prices, less restriction of the formation of integrated transportation companies, permitting intramodal mergers under a certain size to take place without government interference, reducing the number and kind of restrictions that can be placed in operating authorities, and so on. Proposals for reduced regulation sometimes include deregulation of some kinds of traffic, such as agricultural commodities when carried by rail. Some proposals for reduction in regulation would eliminate major aspects of regulation, such as consideration of the effect of a new entrant on existing carriers in entry control cases, or would eliminate economic regulation entirely, at least in some modes. These proposals collectively are part of the drive to deregulate transportation in the United States, although they usually are proposals to reform regulation rather than to eliminate it entirely. The interest in regulatory reform is mainly in connection with railroad, highway, and air transportation.

Issues Involved. The issues involved in the drive toward less or no economic regulation are several and rather complex. The critics of economic regulation usually charge that entry control and rate regulation (and the use of rate bureaus) lead to less incentive to the carrier to strive for efficiency, and also lead to poor service, wasteful use of energy, and high transportation prices. It is claimed that there is less managerial initiative and interest in technological change and in improving service to the public. Instead, economic regulation protects the inefficient carrier from competition. Reformers generally want freer entry, freer exit, and more reliance on the marketplace to set prices in transportation. Proponents of substantial reduction or elimination of economic regulation charge that the reasons for bringing transportation under economic regulation do not exist in modern times and, in fact, sometimes they claim the reasons never existed at all.

The 4R Act of 1976. The movement to liberalize economic regulation of transportation has been active for a number of years and accelerated in the 1970's with the collapse of the Penn Central, the difficulties of Pan American and some other airlines, problems in transportation service to the public, the energy shortage, environmental concern, the consumer movement, the sharp rise in inflation and an associated interest in reducing costs, and general disenchantment with government regulation in all industries. The drive eventually was led by the federal Department of Transportation (DOT) which supported regulatory reform bills introduced in Congress in 1971 and 1974 but which did not pass. In November, 1974 President Gerald R. Ford began very active support of regulatory reform in all industries, including transportation, and he strongly supported the DOT bill which eventually became the 4R Act of 1976. This law was the first important result of the deregulation effort. It contained many regulatory changes, only the more important of which are summarized below. Some of these were discussed in Chapter 21 and 24.

The 4R Act brought about what may turn out to be significant changes in economic regulation of railroads, particularly in the area of price regulation.

A new rule of rate making was added and the old one was repealed. The new rule requires the Commission to develop and promulgate standards and procedures for the establishment of revenue levels adequate to provide a fair profit or return and pay debts and attract capital, among other things. The ICC is to make an effort to assist railroads in attaining such revenue levels.

The law provides that railroad rates and fares that contribute to the going concern value of the carrier cannot be found to be unreasonable on the ground that they are too low. A rate or fare that equals or exceeds variable costs is considered to contribute to going concern value. Market dominance must be found before a rate or fare can be found to be too high. No rate or fare of a railroad is to be held up to protect the traffic of another carrier or mode of transportation unless the ICC finds that the low rate or fare would reduce the going concern value of the carrier charging the rate or fare and, as noted above, any rate or fare equaling or exceeding variable costs is considered to contribute to going concern value.

For the 2 years following the effective date of the law railroads could raise or lower specific prices by as much as 7 per cent from the level in effect at the beginning of each year without suspension because of the reasonableness of the proposed rate or fare. Proposed rates or fares could be suspended, however, if there was probable violation of the unjust discrimination provisions of the Act, if there was a complaint that a rate or fare would be unfair, destructive, or predatory or would otherwise undermine competition, or if the carrier was found to have market dominance.

Railroad rate bureau procedures were also changed by the Act and a time limit of 180 days was placed on the Commission on any proposed rate or fare that involves a capital investment of 1 million dollars or more by a carrier, shipper, or receiver. Once such a rate or fare goes into effect, it cannot be changed for 5 years unless found to be below variable costs.

The ICC, for the first time, was authorized to exempt any person, class of persons, or services from railroad regulation under certain circumstances.

In some respects, the law added to regulation in that the ICC was directed to determine market dominance standards, to develop standards and procedures for the establishment of adequate revenue levels, and to make an effort to assist railroads in achieving those levels, as indicated above. The Commission was also directed to establish within one year standards and procedures for railroad rates based on seasonal, regional, or peak-period demand for railroad service. The ICC was also given exclusive jurisdiction to adjust intrastate rail rates and fares in order to have them conform with interstate rates and fares, provided the appropriate state regulatory agencies have not acted on a rate proposal within 120 days.

The railroad abandonment process was also changed by requiring each railroad to submit to the ICC a diagram of its system identifying any lines that are potentially subject to abandonment. No line can be abandoned unless it has been on the list for at least 4 months. The Commission is to postpone abandonment if any financially responsible person offers financial assistance to continue service that will cover the difference between revenue attributable to the line and the avoidable cost, along with a reasonable return on the value of the line. Federal financial aid to states was provided for the purpose of purchasing rail lines or rehabilitating or improving lines.

The Act requires that railroad merger case proceedings be concluded by the ICC within 2 years and that a decision must be made by the Commission within 180 days thereafter. This was an attempt to speed up the regulatory process in railroad merger cases. An alternative accelerated merger procedure was also made available through the year 1981 to be conducted mainly by the Secretary of Transportation with final approval required by the ICC.

Finally, the 4R Act made certain changes in Commission procedures and required the ICC to propose, within 2 years, a modernization and revision of the Interstate Commerce Act and, within one year, to propose changes in the rules of practice under which railroad cases are handled by the Commission with specific time limits to be imposed in the rules for disposition of cases.

The impact of the 4R Act on regulatory reform is not yet known at the time of this writing and may not be known for some time because it will take time for the ICC to define and test in the courts concepts such as "variable costs," "market dominance," "going concern value," and "predatory" and to test other aspects of the new law in the courts. Some critics of the Act claim that it serves largely to make regulation more cumbersome and difficult because of the ambiguous terminology and will largely be of benefit to attorneys instead of carriers, users, and the general public.

Other Legislative Proposals. In the meantime, bills to substantially deregulate the motor trucking and airline industries were being considered by Congress in 1977. The bills would reduce the amount of economic regulation by liberalizing both entry control and price regulation. President Jimmy Carter endorsed reduced regulation of the airline industry. The CAB itself proposed in 1976 that air freight and air charter operations be subject to virtually free entry and exit and that air freight rates be subject to suspension only if unjust discrimination were involved. The Board has also proposed other changes in the Federal Aviation Act that would liberalize regulation. Meanwhile, bills to increase the control of Congress over all federal regulatory agencies, to require every federal regulatory agency to justify its existence periodically, and to set a timetable for restructuring the federal regulatory machinery, among other bills, were also being considered by Congress in 1977.

Views of Carriers on Regulatory Reform

The drive for regulatory reform focused mainly on railroads until recent years, but in the 1970's it stressed modification of economic regulation in highway and air transportation as well.

For the most part, railroads have sought modification of or liberalization of the regulation of their mode in the form of greater price-making freedom, more freedom to abandon service, and fewer delays in abandonment and other cases. Railroads endorsed the 4R Act of 1976. Motor trucking companies have usually steadfastly opposed any modification of regulation of their industry, particularly any change in entry control. Most regulated scheduled airlines have taken the same stand on reform of economic regulation of air transportation, especially in connection with entry control. Organized labor in the trucking and airline industries has also usually been opposed to regulatory change. Regulated domestic water carriers have been critical of deregulation proposals and have supported the idea that water carriers carrying exempt commodities publish their rates on such traffic. Oil pipelines have not been involved in the regulatory reform question to date, although there are signs that Congress will take more interest in regulation of oil pipelines in the future than it has in the past, as a result of the energy problem. This greater interest is indicated by the fact that, in 1977, Congress provided that the responsibility for economic regulation of oil pipelines was eventually to be transferred from the ICC to the newly created federal Department of Energy. This could lead to more stringent control instead of less regulation of that mode of transportation. The different modes of transportation express their views on regulatory reform primarily through their trade associations, although executives of the larger transportation companies often testify at Congressional hearings.

Views of Users on Regulatory Reform

Unfortunately, users of transportation are not as well organized as are carriers, and no one individual, group, or organization can speak for the user side in discussions about economic regulation. When the user voice is heard on the freight side of things, it is usually the voice of the transportation, traffic, or distribution executive, not the voice of the top management of the organization. The user of passenger service, except in the case of business and other organizations, is not well represented because of lack of organization, although various consumer groups have voiced their opinion about regulation and may be considered to be representative of the purchaser of passenger service. Consumer advocates have sometimes been critical of economic regulation as causing higher rates, fares, and prices of goods carried because of stifled competition, lack of incentive, and price fixing by government.

Actually, very little has been done to determine user opinion on the need for economic regulation of transportation and the question of regulatory reform. What little that has been done seems to indicate that on the freight side of the matter many transportation, traffic, and distribution executives employed by users of transportation believe that there should be less economic regulation of transportation, although not necessarily complete elimination of regulation. There appears to be a trend among these executives toward being more critical of economic regulation and in favor of some sort of reform than has been true in the past.[6]

Views of the General Public on Regulatory Reform

The views of the general public on the question of modification of economic regulation of transportation are generally not known, and the general public is not well informed on the subject. As noted above, however, consumer groups have sometimes been highly critical of economic regulation and have, as a result,

---

[6]See Donald V. Harper and James C. Johnson, "The Shipper Views Deregulation of Transportation," *ICC Practitioners' Journal*, March–April, 1974. In early 1977, the National Industrial Traffic League, a large organization of industrial traffic and distribution executives, urged some modification of regulation but not complete deregulation or abolishment of the independent regulatory agencies. See R. Stanley Chapman, "Regulatory Reform Action Urged In NIT League's 'White Paper,'" *Traffic World*, January 10, 1977, p. 8.

sought regulatory reform. To what extent the position of these groups is representative of the attitude of the public in general is unknown. In any event, to the degree that legislators express the views of their constituents, the general public will ultimately make the decisions on regulatory reform through their elected representatives in Congress and in state legislatures.

Prospects for Regulatory Reform

Unfortunately, much of the argument on both sides of the issue of regulatory reform is not based on fact and, for the most part, represents the viewpoints of the various special interest groups directly involved. Research into the probable results of deregulation and, perhaps, some sort of experimentation with reduced or no regulation are needed.

Complete elimination of economic regulation of transportation, at least for some modes, has been advocated by some. It is not probable that this will happen in the foreseeable future for it is politically and practically impossible because of the opposition to it on the part of many carriers and users and the uncertainty as to how well free competition would work in transportation. Whether or not chaotic conditions would return with free entry into highway and air transportation in the 1970's and 1980's is not definitely known. Research on the subject is needed. If chaotic conditions should return, it would mean entry of an excessive number of carriers with resulting deterioration of service to the public, less attention to safety standards, and lack of service to "undesirable" traffic. In addition, there is some traffic that is "captured" by one mode and for which there would be no intermodal competition and no protection against excessive prices. There must also be consideration of the billions of dollars that have been invested in user facilities because of present transportation relationships. Furthermore, there is the practical problem that the public demands some transportation services that are not economic. Regulation is one way to ensure that such service is provided. Critics of deregulation insist that complete deregulation would mean that service to undesirable traffic, including service to small and out-of-the-way places, would be abandoned while intense competition would develop on the better routes and where the traffic was more desirable. Finally, an argument against complete deregulation is that the courts would be unable to handle all the cases that would fall on them if there were no independent regulatory agencies to handle transportation problems. Actually, it is unlikely that anyone on either the carrier or user side really wants complete deregulation of transportation. The arguments for such a step come mainly from people and organizations outside the transportation industry who are neither carriers nor professional users of transportation.

Thus, we shall probably get some reform of economic regulation instead of complete deregulation. The 4R Act of 1976 illustrates this tendency. The moderate approach to eliminating the deficiencies in regulation involves the least break with the traditional way of doing things, it involves the least risk, it will satisfy the reformers, at least in part, and it is politically more acceptable than complete elimination of economic regulation. It could involve both adding to and subtracting from regulation, but mainly the latter.

Actually, there need be few, if any, legislative changes for regulatory reform to be accomplished because most of the changes under serious discussion are potentially achievable within the scope of the current law. Cases can be handled more expeditiously, less restrictive interpretation of the authority already given to the regulatory agencies by legislatures can be made, and certain exemptions from regulation can be granted by the agencies under current law. Thus, it is not necessary that legislation be enacted by Congress or state legislatures for some regulatory reform to take place. Many reforms can be made by the regulatory agencies themselves without statutory action by a legislature. There has, in fact, been some indication of initiating reform on the part of both the ICC and the CAB in the form of making regulation less time-consuming and more efficient.

No matter what form further federal regulatory change takes, if it takes place at all, it should not be made on a piecemeal basis as has been the case thus far with the 4R Act of 1976. Congress should deal with the entire interstate domestic transportation system simultaneously instead of with each mode separately. The implications of any regulatory modification are intermodal as well as intramodal, and this must be recognized, along with the need for a truly coordinated transportation system, both in the economic and physical sense of that word. A complete rewriting of the Interstate Commerce Act is in order because, as we know, it is an inconsistent patchwork of legislation enacted by different people at different times to meet different particular problems, and it is not really in tune with the needs of the modern transportation system. Consideration should also be given to reviewing and revising the Federal Aviation Act and the possibility of consolidating all economic regulation of domestic interstate transportation under one regulatory agency.

SELECTED REFERENCES

That economic regulation of transportation has had a positive effect on economic growth is argued in Joel C. Harper, "The Effects of Government Regulation of Transportation on Economic Growth," *Proceedings of Transportation Research Forum, 1964*. The economic costs of economic regulation of transportation are discussed in Paul H. Banner, "Regulation: Its Effect on Economic Costs of Transportation," *Proceedings of Transportation Research Forum, 1965*. An analysis of the effect of economic regulation on the utilization (empty mileage) of private and for-hire trucks is Edward Miller, "The Effects of Regulation on Truck Utilization," *Transportation Journal*, Fall, 1973. That economic regulation results in higher motor truck rates in Canada than would otherwise be the case is argued in James Sloss, "Regulation of Motor Freight Transportation: A Quantitative Evaluation of Policy," *Bell Journal of Economics and Management Science*, Autumn, 1970 and John Palmer, "A Further Analysis of Provincial Trucking Regulation." *Bell Journal of Economics and Management Science*, Autumn, 1973. Estimates of the costs of economic regulation of transportation to the public are made in Thomas G. Moore, *Freight Transportation Regulation: Surface Freight and the Interstate Commerce Commission* (Washington, D.C.: American Enterprise Institute for Public Policy Research, 1972).

There is a tremendous amount of literature on the subject of the need for, criticisms of, and reform of economic regulation of transportation, but only a selected number of such writings is listed here. A summary of the pros and cons of deregulation as indicated in the literature on the subject is James C. Johnson and Donald V. Harper, "The Potential Consequences of Deregulation of Transportation," *Land Economics*, February, 1975. A collection of readings on the deregulation question is Grant M. Davis, ed., *Transportation Regulation: A Prag-*

matic Assessment (Danville, Illinois: The Interstate Printers and Publishers, Inc., 1976). The alternatives available in reforming economic regulation are discussed in D. Philip Locklin, *Economics of Transportation*, 7th ed. (Homewood, Illinois: Richard D. Irwin, Inc., 1972), Chapter 38. The problems associated with economic regulation are dealt with in Hugh S. Norton, *Modern Transportation Economics*, 2nd ed. (Columbus, Ohio: Charles E. Merrill Publishing Company, 1971), Chapters 23 and 24. A moderate view of the need for regulatory reform is Colin Barrett, "Regulation–The Winds of Change," *ICC Practitioners' Journal*, July–August, 1975. A popular description of the debate over regulatory reform is "Freedom from Regulation," *Business Week*, May 12, 1975.

Books critical of economic regulation of transportation include Allen R. Ferguson and Leonard L. Lane, eds., *Transportation Policy Options: The Political Economy of Regulatory Reform* (Washington, D.C.: Public Interest Economics Foundation, 1976); the first 3 essays in Almarin Phillips, ed., *Promoting Competition in Regulated Markets* (Washington, D.C.: The Brookings Institution, 1975); Dudley F. Pegrum, *Transportation Economics and Public Policy*, 3rd ed. (Homewood, Illinois: Richard D. Irwin, Inc., 1973), Chapters 8, 14, 15, 17, and 21; Alfred E. Kahn, *The Economics of Regulation: Principles and Institutions*, Volume II (New York: John Wiley and Sons, Inc., 1971), pp. 14–28, 178–193, 209–220, and 268–276; Robert Fellmeth, *The Interstate Commerce Omission*, (New York: Grossman Publishers, 1970); Charles F. Phillips, Jr., *The Economics of Regulation*, 2nd ed. (Homewood, Illinois: Richard D. Irwin, Inc., 1969), Chapter 14; Ann F. Friedlaender, *The Dilemma of Freight Transportation Regulation* (Washington, D.C.: The Brookings Institution, 1969); George W. Hilton, *The Transportation Act of 1958; A Decade of Experience* (Bloomington, Indiana: Indiana University Press 1969); Hugh S. Norton, *National Transportation Policy: Formation and Implementation* (Berkeley, California: McCutchan Publishing Corporation, 1966); and John R. Meyer, Merton J. Peck, John Stenason, and Charles Zwick, *The Economics of Competition in the Transportation Industries* (Cambridge, Massachusetts: Harvard University Press, 1959), Chapter 9.

Articles generally critical of economic regulation of transportation include James C. Nelson, "The Economic Effects of Transport Deregulation in Australia," *Transportation Journal*, Winter, 1976; George W. Wilson, "Regulation, Public Policy, and Efficient Provision of Freight Transportation," *Transportation Journal*, Fall, 1975; John W. Snow, "Exploding Myths About Transportation Regulatory Reform," *ICC Practitioners' Journal*, September–October, 1975; James C. Nelson, "Impact of Entry Control on Transport Pricing," in Marvin L. Fair and James C. Nelson, eds., *Criteria for Transport Pricing* (Cambridge, Maryland: Cornell Maritime Press, Inc., 1973) and "Toward an Efficient Role for Transportation Regulation," in *1970 Conference on Mass Transportation–National Transportation Policy* (New York: Popular Library, 1970); Byron Nupp, "A Revised Transport Regulatory System Consistent with Modern Management Performance," *ICC Practitioners' Journal*, March–April, 1972; Edward J. Donohue and Stanley J. Hille, "National Transportation Policy and the Regulatory Agencies," *MSU Business Topics*, Spring, 1971; George W. Wilson, "The Goals of Transportation Policy," Dudley F. Pegrum, "Restructuring the Transport System," and James C. Nelson, "Toward Rational Price Policies," all in Ernest W. Williams, Jr., ed., *The Future of American Transportation* (Englewood Cliffs, New Jersey: Prentice-Hall, Inc., 1971); George W. Hilton, "The Two Things Wrong with the Interstate Commerce Commission," *Proceedings of Transportation Research Forum, 1970* and "Competitive Transportation: The Law of the Jungle—Or Is It?" in *1968 Conference on Mass Transportation—The Government Role* (New York: Popular Library, 1969); Merton J. Peck, "Competitive Policy for Transportation," in Paul W. MacAvoy, ed., *The Crisis of the Regulatory Commissions* (New York: W. W. Norton and Company, 1970); and Lester S. Levy, "A Positivistic View of Commission Regulation," *ICC Practitioners' Journal*, May, 1965.

Criticism directed specifically at economic regulation of railroad transportation is in Robert M. Spann and Edward W. Erickson, "The Economics of Railroading: The Beginning of Cartelization and Regulation," *Bell Journal of Economics and Management Science*, Autumn, 1970. Among the writings critical of economic regulation of highway transportation are Byron Nupp, "Control Over Entry as an Economic and Regulatory Problem," *ICC Practitioners' Journal*, May–June, 1968; Dudley F. Pegrum, "The Economic Basis of Public Policy for Motor Transport," *Land Economics*, August, 1952; and James C. Nelson, "New Concepts in Transportation Regulation," in National Resources Planning Board, *Transportation and National Policy* (Washington, D.C.: U.S. Government Printing Office, 1942). Criticism of economic regulation of domestic water transportation is found in John C. Spychalski, "On the Nonutility of Domestic Water Transport Regulation," *ICC Practitioners' Journal*, November–December, 1969. Economic regulation of air transportation has been the subject of criticism in many writings. The most recent full-length publication of this nature is George W. Douglas and James C. Miller, III, *Economic Regulation of Domestic Air Transportation: Theory and Policy* (Washington, D.C.: The Brookings Institution, 1974). Another recent full-length treatment is William A. Jordan, *Airline Regulation in America: Effects and Imperfections* (Baltimore, Maryland: Johns Hopkins Press, 1971), which uses the intrastate experience in California to argue against federal regulation. See also Leigh B. Boske, "Cost Efficiency in the Domestic Trunk Airline Industry," *Journal of Economics and Business*, Winter, 1976; Theodore E. Keeler, "Airline Regulation and Market Performance," *Bell Journal of Economics and Management Science*, Autumn, 1972; Kahn, *The Economics of Regulation*, Volume II, pp. 209-220; Mahlon R. Straszheim, "Airline Profitability, Financing, and Public Regulation," *Transportation Journal*, Summer 1969; Michael E. Levine, "Is Regulation Necessary? California Air Transportation and National Regulatory Policy," *Yale Law Journal*, July, 1965; Richard E. Caves, *Air Transport and Its Regulation—An Industry Study* (Cambridge, Massachusetts: Harvard University Press, 1963); Samuel B. Richmond, *Regulation and Competition in Air Transportation* (New York: Columbia University Press, 1961); Hardy K. Maclay and William C. Burt, "Entry of New Carriers Into Domestic Trunkline Air Transportation," *Journal of Air Law and Commerce*, Spring, 1955; Lucile S. Keyes, "A Reconsideration of Federal Control of Entry Into Air Transportation," *Journal of Air Law and Commerce*, Spring, 1955 and *Federal Control of Entry Into Air Transportation* (Cambridge, Massachusetts: Harvard University Press, 1951).

Articles generally defending economic regulation and/or against substantial deregulation include Lee A. Melton, "The Competitive Transportation System: A Myth," *Transportation Journal*, Summer, 1975; Robert J. Corber, "Regulatory Reform—Seeking the Least Circuitous Route to the Public Interest," *ICC Practitioners' Journal*, July–August, 1975; John Heads, "Some Lessons from Transportation Deregulation in Canada," *ICC Practitioners' Journal*, March–April, 1975; Grant M. Davis and Charles S. Sherwood, "Transportation Regulation: Another Dimension," *ICC Practitioners' Journal*, January–February, 1975; John C.

Spychalski, "Criticism of Regulated Freight Transport: Do Economists' Perceptions Conform with Institutional Realities?" *Transportation Journal,* Spring, 1975, "An Evaluation of Messrs. Hilton's and Sampson's Proposed Cures for Regulatory Defects," *Transportation Journal,* Fall, 1972, and "On Transport Deregulation: Some Questions for Messrs. Houthakker, McLaren, et al," *ICC Practitioners' Journal,* November-December, 1971; Kenneth H. Tuggle, "To Regulate or Not to Regulate," *ICC Practitioners' Journal,* January-February, 1972; Robert W. Harbeson, "Transportation Regulation: A Centennial Evaluation," *ICC Practitioners' Journal,* July-August, 1972; Peter S. Douglas, "The Appalling Fallacy in the CEA's Analysis of Transportation," *ICC Practitioners' Journal,* January-February, 1972; Colin Barrett, "Deregulation: A Study in Illogic," *ICC Practitioners' Journal,* November-December, 1971; Charles A. Webb, "Mr. Nader: Meet the Consumer of Transportation," *ICC Practitioners' Journal,* July-August, 1970; John J. Doyle, "Regulation of Transportation: Too Much?–Too Little?–Is It Needed?" in *1968 Conference on Mass Transportation;* and Glenn L. Shinn, "Rate Regulation on Trial," *ICC Practitioners' Journal,* June, 1964. The ICC attempted to answer some of the criticisms of its regulatory practices and policies in Interstate Commerce Commission, *The Regulatory Issues of Today,* January,1975.

An article specifically in defense of railroad regulation is John W. Thomson, "Railroad Regulation: A Perspective," *ICC Practitioners' Journal,* July–August, 1975. Arguments in defense of economic regulation of highway transportation are presented in Cecil Hynes, "Small Business and Deregulation of the Motor Common Carriers," *Transportation Journal,* Spring, 1976; Nicholas A. Glaskowsky, Jr., Brian F. O'Neil, and Donald R. Hudson, *Motor Carrier Regulation: A Review and Evaluation of Three Major Current Regulatory Issues Relating to the Interstate Common Carrier Trucking Industry* (Washington, D.C.: American Trucking Associations Foundation, 1976); American Trucking Associations, Inc., *Transportation . . . Regulation or Disaster?* (Washington, D.C.: American Trucking Associations, Inc., 1975); and Alan C. Flott, "The Case Against the Case Against Regulation," *ICC Practitioners' Journal,* March-April, 1973. A vigorous defense of economic regulation of air transportation is Robert Hotz, "A Dangerous Fantasy," *Aviation Week and Space Technology,* April 28, 1975. Other writings in support of economic regulation of air transportation are Stephen Wheatcroft, *Air Transport Policy* (London: Michael Joseph, 1964), Chapter 3; Robert L. Clark, "Freedom of Entry in Air Transportation," *Public Utilities Fortnightly,* September 13, 1956; and Stuart G. Tipton and Stanley Gewirtz, "The Effect of Regulated Competition on the Air Transport Industry," *Journal of Air Law and Commerce,* Spring, 1955.

Studies of the views of users of transportation concerning economic regulation are reported on in Roger E. Jerman, Ronald D. Anderson, and James A. Constantin, "Shipper Views on Regulation," *Distribution Worldwide,* January, 1977; Grant M. Davis and Leon J. Rosenberg, "Physical Distribution and the Regulatory Constraint: An Analysis," *Transportation Journal,* Spring, 1976; "Survey: The Regulators: Part II," *Transportation and Distribution Management,* March–April, 1976; Grant M. Davis, L. J. Rosenberg, and Charles S. Sherwood, "An Empirical Assessment of the Traffic Executive's Perceptions Regarding Controversies in Transportation Regulation," *ICC Practitioners' Journal,* November–December, 1976; Donald V. Harper and James C. Johnson, "The Shipper Views Deregulation of Transportation," *ICC Practitioners' Journal,* March–April, 1974; Robert A. Nelson, "Interest Conflicts in Transportation," *Journal of Business,*

April, 1964; and Donald V. Harper, "The Shipper Views Economic Regulation of For-Hire Trucking," *ICC Practitioners' Journal,* December, 1963.

The need for better legislation and rehabilitation of the ICC in order to improve economic regulation is urged in Dudley F. Pegrum, "Should the ICC Be Abolished?" *Transportation Journal,* Fall, 1971.

A summary and analysis of the main regulatory reform provisions of the Railroad Revitalization and Regulatory Reform (4R) Act of 1976 are in Robert W. Harbeson, "Progress and Poverty in Transport Regulatory Reform," *Quarterly Review of Economics and Business,* Summer, 1977. See also Fritz R. Kahn, "The Reformation of Railroad Regulation," *ICC Practitioners' Journal,* May–June, 1976 and "A Milestone in Regulatory History," *Traffic World,* April 19, 1976, p. 80.

A satirical presentation of the idea that complete deregulation of transportation would bring about the need for reinstitution of regulation is George W. Wilson, "A Transportation Fable for Our Times," *Transportation Journal,* Summer, 1965.

Index